AN AMERICAN LOOKS AT BRITAIN

AN AMERICAN LOOKS AT BRITAIN

RICHARD CRITCHFIELD

ANCHOR BOOKS
Doubleday

NEW YORK LONDON TORONTO SYDNEY AUCKLAND

To the editors of *The Economist*
whose idea this was

An Anchor Book
PUBLISHED BY DOUBLEDAY
a division of Bantam Doubleday Dell Publishing Group, Inc.
666 Fifth Avenue, New York, New York 10103

ANCHOR BOOKS, DOUBLEDAY, and the portrayal of an anchor
are trademarks of Doubleday, a division of Bantam Doubleday
Dell Publishing Group, Inc.

An American Looks at Britain was originally published
in hardcover by Doubleday in 1990.
The Anchor Books edition is published by arrangement with Doubleday.

Acknowledgments for permission to quote
from copyrighted sources will be found on pages xii–xvi.

Library of Congress Cataloging-in-Publication Data
Critchfield, Richard.
   An American looks at Britain / Richard Critchfield.
     p. cm.
   Includes index.
   1. Great Britain—Civilization—20th century.
   I. Title.
DA589.4.C75 1990   90-2997
941.082—dc20   CIP
ISBN 0-385-24457-6

CONTENTS

ACKNOWLEDGMENTS

To David Owen, Norman Tebbit, and Tony Benn, my thanks for each spending a full morning to acquaint me with a center, right, and left view of contemporary British history and politics; this was indispensable. So too were George Steiner's generous insights into British articulacy and Peggy Ashcroft's gracious help with two chapters. The hospitality and kindness of so many people made this book a great pleasure to do.

This is not just an American's Britain but the view of a Midwesterner with no special expertise or credentials, not even the Anglophile tradition of our Eastern establishment. So I needed to talk to a lot of people and see a lot of places. For giving their time, advice, and ideas, I am grateful to: Sir Antony Acland, Mohammed Ajeeb, Eric Ambler, Eric Anderson, Dr. Christopher Andrew, Jeffrey Archer, the late Sir Alfred Ayer, Beryl Bainbridge, Kenneth Baker, Paul Barker, Kevin Barron, Calvin Beale, Nora Beloff, Tony Benn, Sir Isaiah Berlin, Lindy Beveridge, Baroness Blackstone, Alan Bleasdale, David Blunkett, Dr. Norman Borlaug, Ronald Bowlby (Bishop of Southwark), Jimmy Boyle, Dr. John Bradfield, Clive Bradley, Melvyn Bragg, Simon Brett, the late Kingman Brewster, Lord Briggs, Sir Paul Bryan, Archie and Lesley Burnett, Lord Callaghan, Simon Callow, Lord Carrington, Barbara Cartland, Field Marshall Lord Carver, Alison Chitty, Jeff Collinson, Henry Steele Commager, Sir Terence Conran, Sheila Cooper, Christopher Cviic, John Davidson, Clifford Davies, Dennis Duncanson, John Edmonds, Joseph Epstein, John Ermisch, Dr. Dick Flavell, Sir Denis Forman, John Forsyth, Sir Leslie Fowden, John Fowles, Lord Franks, Christopher Frayling, John Gladwin, Maria Glot, General Sir James Glover, Roy Glover, Bryan Gould, Gillian Greenwood, John Habgood (Archbishop of York), Sir Peter Hall, David Hare, Julie Harris, Sir John Harvey-Jones, Ronald Harwood, Jim Hastie, Max Hastings, Denis Healey, Sir Nicholas Henderson, Michael Heseltine, Dame Wendy

Hiller, Sir Michael Howard, Douglas Hurd, Jeremy Irons, Jeremy Isaacs, Geraldine James, Peter Jay, David Jenkins (Bishop of Durham), Lord Jenkins, Simon Jenkins, Graham Jones, Margaret Kameena, Richard Kinsey, John Lea, Mike Leithrow, Bernard Levin, Tom Lyom, Duncan Maclennan, Brenda Maddox, Neville Maxwell, Robert McCrum, William H. McNeill, Hugh Montefiore, Charles Moore, Sheridan Morley, Christopher Morahan, Sir Claus Moser, Senator Daniel P. Moynihan, Paul Mugnaioni, Tadashi Nakamoe, Derek Nightingale, Rev. William Oddie, Peter O'Keefe, Iona Opie, Sir Michael Palliser, Allan Parry, Christopher Patten, Patricia Phillips, Alan Pickford, Tim Pigott-Smith, Henry Pleasants, Enoch Powell, Lord Prior, Craig Raine, Sir Peter Ramsbotham, John Ranelagh, John Redwood, Lord Rees-Mogg, Ruth Rendell, Tony Roberts, Douglas Robertson, Richard Robinson, Allan Rogers, Lord Roll, Brigadier W. E. Rouse, Larry Rowe, Lord Sainsbury, Alex Sinclair, Mike Skidmore, Andreas Whittam Smith, Norman Stone, Vic Symonds, Ken Taylor, Paul Theroux, Joyce Thirkill, David Thomas, Howard Thomas, Sir Robert Thompson, Sir John Thomson, Donald Trelford, Alan Tuffin, William Waldegrave, Nigel Wattis, Detective Superintendent Tom Wood, Professor Harold W. Woolhouse, Susan Wooldridge, Peregrine Worsthorne, and Sir Oliver Wright. Gratitude extends to perhaps an equal number who gave me verbal views of which I kept no record.

There were, I suppose, close to three hundred interviews in all, more than half of them taped; mainly these are quoted. Very few turned down a request for an interview. One who did, actor Albert Finney (*Tom Jones*), said he would "rather devote time to my own projects, but good luck with yours." Columnist AuberonWaugh wrote that he felt anything he had to say on Britain would be "too frivolous." A reply to a request to see Prince Charles, from his private secretary, Sir John Riddell, conjured up the royal world of palaces, Yeoman of the Guard, and people wearing ermine: "His Royal Highness is not, I regret, for the time being giving interviews however benign the purpose and distinguished the interviewer." Mrs. Thatcher agreed to have her picture taken for the original *Economist* survey, but gave no interview. She posed at her kitchen stove, an apron tied around her middle, making what seemed to be soup; it was like the kitchen scene in *Alice* except that the Duchess, not the cook, was leaning over the fire, pepper pot in hand. And nobody dared to sneeze.

Amazingly, almost everybody else said yes. An "A to Z" street directory, the Underground, and British Rail make London an easy place to get around. Since most people invited you to their homes, fewer to their offices, you saw a lot of the city. ("Let's see, at 9:30 it's Lord Roll at 55 King William Street. H-m-mm, that's the District Line, get out at Monument.") Academics, writers, people in the media, politicians, what the English call the "chattering class," tend to live comfortably rather than showily—worn rugs, lumpy sofas, a view of the garden, good art, and lots of books. Not a bad way to live.

Coffee, not tea, was mainly served, except at teatime. (Tony Benn, Ruth Rendell, and Simon Brett, among others, dashed out to the kitchen to make it themselves.) Wives tended to bring in afternoon teas with cakes (Enoch Powell, Ken Taylor). Sometimes there were maids (Lord Franks, all the bishops), sometimes it was done in baronial splendor (Barbara Cartland), sometimes just sitting at the kitchen table (Susan Wooldridge). Interviews were over breakfast (Bernard Levin of *The Times* at Selfridges Hotel); lunch (many, but my favorite was at Iona Opie's big—and cold—Victorian country house in West Liss where she had me and a visiting photographer just carry in bread, cheese, and fresh vegetables from the kitchen); and dinner (another favorite: baked potato and beans at a Pakistani fast-food joint in Hammersmith with Simon Callow before he went back to play Part Two of the title role of *Faust*).

Many interviews were at clubs (the Athenaeum, Travellers', Reform, Brook's, Garrick and East India), in National Theatre dressing rooms between rehearsals and performances, in the Palace of Westminster—Denis Healey as shadow foreign secretary had just a tiny cubbyhole, but Norman Tebbit, close to Mrs. Thatcher, rated a spacious eyrie with conference table. Down the Embankment was the Norman Shaw North Building where there were even more modest parliamentary offices. The entire staff of Bryan Gould, the Labour Party's shadow trade spokesman, for example, busy on typewriter and telephone, seemed to be his pretty wife. Peers at the House of Lords have elegant little red-leather and polished-oak "interview rooms"; Oxford dons medieval paneled suites; military men historic regimental trappings, and the bishops their palaces. But the grandest monarchical style probably surrounds Britain's bankers. I interviewed the chairman or vice-chairman of five—Midland, Rothschild's, Warburg's, Morgan Grenfell and Hambros—and you'd have to go to Westminster or Buckingham Palace to outdo all the courtiers and palatial settings.

A lot of the interviews were fun, like the time at Barbara Cartland's estate of Hatfield when we'd finished tea and my taxi failed to come. I said I'd wait in the library, but she said no, come back in the drawing room and have a whiskey. So I turned off the tape recorder and we had a grand time exchanging stories of our travels. It was the same having lunch with Eric Ambler. Good company.

Once I went to see Dr. John Habgood, the Archbishop of York. His secretary said I couldn't stay long, he was convalescing from an operation. Since his beautiful palace, Bishopthorpe, was three miles from the York station and I hoped to catch an evening train to London, I asked the taxi driver to wait. I left him listening to his radio. The Archbishop, once a scientist at Cambridge and a learned man, talked much longer than expected. His operation, for a hernia, he said, was minor. He then insisted on showing me about the palace, including the portrait gallery of previous archbishops, telling me who got beheaded, and who got tried in this very room. (One forgets how much English history has been decided by the bloody crunch of an axe.)

When we came out of the palace, the Archbishop walked me to my taxi; the driver was still listening to the radio. The taxi refused to start; I had been gone nearly two hours and the battery had gone dead. There was nothing to do but push. So I went around to the back of the taxi. So did the Archbishop. Just in time I remembered. "Oh, no!" I blurted out. "Your hernia operation! . . . *Your grace.*" A gardener came running to help push. With a jolt and roar, the engine started. I jumped in, we shot off in an explosion of backfires, and I shouted back in embarrassed apology to the amused Archbishop, "This is one interview you won't easily forget!"

Another time I went to see Peter Jay, a former British ambassador to Washington and an ex-son-in-law of former Labour Prime Minister James Callaghan. What I didn't know until I got to the address was that Jay was chief aide to Robert Maxwell, the tycoon who owns everything from London's *Daily Mirror* and Macmillan to football teams. Born Jan Ludwick Hoch (he later changed his name), the son of a poor Czech peasant murdered by the Gestapo, Maxwell is said to be worth £675 million (over $1.1 billion), making him Britain's eleventh richest man. That morning he was on a rampage. As I got off the elevator to face a battery of receptionists and a lot of mirrors and flowers, Maxwell was standing in the door of a conference room down the hall, furiously shouting at its occupants. A giant of a man, built like a pro football tackle and with jet black hair, he stormed up and down, shouting at quaking underlings and giving me who-the-hell-are-you scowls (I just sat smiling politely in a huge green chair and when a uniformed maid offered me a cup of coffee on a silver tray, took it). He finally went into his office.

I got in to see Jay—about forty minutes late—and suggested maybe it was a bad day. Chain-smoking, ashen-faced, and looking shaken, he said it was. But since I was there we might as well start. We got about a half hour into what was a good interview. Suddenly the intercom crackled on. A roaring, deafening voice practically knocked us out of our chairs. Oaths, four-letter words, threats. It could only be Robert Maxwell. Jay was frantically fumbling on the desk. Then I realized he was trying to find the "off" button on my tape recorder.

So you never knew, setting out for the day, just what was in store. It was the same when I tackled this project in 1986. Eric Sevareid in Washington gave me his ideas on Britain; I owe a debt to him for providing a place to start. Sevareid told me, "They are paying the price now for their cultural and class divisions." Which, as it turned out, is the story. Timothy Dickinson also discussed what might go into the survey; we later met in Washington as I began and ended the manuscript. For his wise and witty corrections *and* improvements, all accepted, I am grateful.

I am also indebted to Rupert Pennant-Rea, editor of *The Economist*, for asking me to write about Britain in the first place, and to members of its staff: Frances Cairncross, Gordon Lee, Stephen Hugh-Jones, Avril Walker, Nick Harmon, and Jim Rohwer. I also want to thank Sir Claus Moser, Clifford Davies, and the fellows of Wadham College, Oxford, for their hospitality during my several stays in Britain. I am grateful to Luther Nichols, former West Coast editor of Doubleday, who edited my earlier books and, now retired, again went over the manuscript with me and offered his ideas; William P. Bundy, former editor, *Foreign Affairs*, who reviewed the chapters on Anglo-American affairs and made judicious comments; Lord Franks, Sir Michael Palliser, Sir Antony Acland, and Eric Anderson, who went over some chapters and made suggestions; Robert Donahue of the *International Herald Tribune* in Paris for his ideas; my brother James Critchfield, for advice on geopolitics and oil; Adriana Orr, long with the Supplement to the Oxford English Dictionary, for research at the Library of Congress; Robert W. Alvord and Peggy Ann Trimble, my longtime mainstays in Washington, for their unfailing support; my agent, Stuart Krichevsky of Sterling Lord Literistic, Inc., for arranging joint American and British publication; and Carolyn Dawnay of Peters, Fraser and Dunlop, for representing us in London.

I want to express particular thanks for their editorial help, constructive criticism, and encouragement to my two editors, Loretta A. Barrett of Doubleday in New York and Christopher Sinclair-Stevenson of Hamish Hamilton in London. I am also grateful to Peter Straus and Joanna Jellinek of Hamish Hamilton and to Susan Higginbotham of Doubleday for her skillful copy editing.

Lastly I want to thank my old English friends—Brian and Barbara Beedham, John and Kerry Parker, Brian and Mary Ritchie, and Rosanna Groarke Ismail—just for being themselves. And to mention my brother Bill, whose death in mid-1989 meant the loss of my most valued authority on mysteries, books in general, the theater, and the English language itself. Though a scientist, he loved words and I notice from the inscription in my old beat-up Oxford Dictionary, used day in and day out all these years, that he gave it to me in 1956. Thanks again, Bill.

Grateful acknowledgment is made to the following for permission to reprint previously published material.

Robert Frost, excerpts from "The Gift Outright" and "Stopping by Woods on a Snowy Evening" from *The Poetry of Robert Frost* edited by Edward Connery Lathem. Copyright © 1969 Holt, Rinehart & Winston, Inc. Copyright © 1975 Lesley Frost Ballantine. Reprinted by permission of Henry Holt & Company, Inc. and Jonathan Cape Ltd.

Hugh Kenner, from *A Sinking Island.* Copyright © 1987 Hugh Kenner. Reprinted by permission of Alfred A. Knopf, Inc. and Barrie and Jenkins Ltd.

Paul Theroux, from *The Kingdom by the Sea.* Copyright © 1983 Paul Theroux. Reprinted by permission of Hamish Hamilton and Houghton Mifflin Company.

Sir John Betjeman, excerpt from "A Subaltern's Love Song" from *Collected Poems.* Copyright © Sir John Betjeman, 1958, rev. 1970. Reprinted by permission of John Murray.

Anthony Sampson, from *The Changing Anatomy of Britain.* Copyright © 1982 Anthony Sampson. Reprinted by permission of Hodder & Stoughton, Ltd., and Random House.

Stephen Jay Gould, from *Time's Arrow, Time's Cycle: Myth and Metaphor in the Discovery of Geological Time.* Copyright © 1987 President and Fellows of Harvard College. Reprinted by permission of Harvard University Press.

F. Scott Fitzgerald, from *Tender Is the Night.* Copyright © 1933, 1934 Charles Scribner's Sons; renewed © 1961, 1962 Frances Scott Fitzgerald Lanahan.

Peter Jenkins, *Mrs. Thatcher's Revolution.* Copyright © 1987, 1988 Peter Jenkins. Reprinted by permission of Harvard University Press and Peter Jenkins.

Caryl Churchill, excerpt from song, "Five More Glorious Years" by Ian Dury and Chaz Jankel from *Serious Money.* Copyright © 1987 Caryl Churchill. Reprinted by permission of Methuen London Ltd.

Ronald Harwood, excerpt from *J. J. Farr.* Copyright © 1988 Paracier Holdings Ltd. Reprinted by permission of Amber Lane Press.

William H. McNeill, from *Mythistory and Other Essays.* Copyright © 1986 The University of Chicago. Reprinted by permission of the University of Chicago Press.

Henry Steele Commager, from *Britain Through American Eyes.* Copyright © 1974 Henry Steele Commager. Reprinted by permission of The Bodley Head, Sterling Lord Literistic Inc., and Henry Steele Commager.

Margaret Halsey, *With Malice Towards Some.* Copyright © 1938 Margaret Halsey. Reprinted by permission of Simon & Schuster.

Norman Gelb, *The British; A Portrait of an Indomitable Island People.* Copyright © 1982 Norman Gelb. Published by Everest House. Reprinted by permission of Norman Gelb.

Iona and Peter Opie, from *The Oxford Dictionary of Nursery Rhymes, 1951,* and *The Classic Fairy Tales,* 1974. Reprinted by permission of Oxford University Press and Iona Opie.

Lewis Carroll, from *Alice's Adventures in Wonderland* and *Through the Looking-Glass.* Originally published in 1895. Quotations taken from *The Annotated Alice,* Penguin Books Ltd.

Kenneth Grahame, from *The Wind in the Willows,* Copyright © 1933, 1935 Charles Scribner's Sons. Originally published in 1908. Courtesy of Charles Scribner's Sons and Penguin Books Ltd.

Daisy Ashford, from *The Young Visiters.* First published 1919. Courtesy of Estate of Daisy Ashford, Chatto & Windus and The Hogarth Press and Doubleday.

R.S. Surtees, from *Mr. Sponge's Sporting Tour.* First published 1853. Courtesy of Oxford University Press.

Rudyard Kipling, *Kim.* First published 1901. Courtesy of Macmillan.

Bernard Levin, from *Enthusiasms.* Copyright © 1983 Bernard Levin. Reprinted by permission of Bernard Levin and Jonathan Cape.

Gilly Fraser, excerpt from script, "East Enders," Episode 319, 1988. Reprinted by permission of Judy Daish Associates, Ltd. and British Broadcasting Corporation.

J. B. Priestley, from *English Journey.* Copyright © 1934 J. B. Priestley. Reprinted by permission of William Heinemann Ltd.

Danny Danziger, from *Eton Voices.* Copyright © 1988 Danny Danziger. Viking. Reprinted by permission of Penguin Books Ltd. and Toby Eady Associates Ltd. and Danny Danziger.

Margaret Drabble, from *A Writer's Britain.* Copyright © 1979 Thames & Hudson Ltd. Reprinted by permission of Thames & Hudson Ltd.

Branwell Brontë, quoted by Daphne du Maurier in *The Infernal World of Branwell Brontë.* Copyright © 1960 Daphne du Maurier. Reprinted by permission of Victor Gollancz.

Beryl Bainbridge, from *English Journey; or, The Road to Milton Keynes.* Copyright © 1984 Beryl Bainbridge. Reprinted by permission of Beryl Bainbridge and John Johnson Ltd.

Alan Bleasdale, excerpts from scripts, *Scully.* Scripts © 1984 Alan Bleasdale. Reprinted by permission of Grafton Books and Lemon, Unna and Durbridge.

Jimmy Boyle, from *A Sense of Freedom.* Copyright © 1977 Jimmy Boyle. Reprinted by permission of Canongate Publishing Ltd.

Richard Kinsey, John Lea, and Jock Young, from *Losing the Fight Against Crime,* 1986. Reprinted by permission of Basil Blackwell.

John Mortimer, from *Character Parts.* Copyright © 1986 Advanpress Ltd. First published by Viking. Reprinted by permission of Peters, Fraser and Dunlop.

Alan Bleasdale, excerpts from scripts, *Boys from the Blackstuff.* Copyright © 1985 Alan Bleasdale. Reprinted by permission of Grafton Books and Lemon, Unna and Durbridge.

Beryl Bainbridge, from *Forever England: North and South.* Copyright © 1987 Beryl Bainbridge. Reprinted by permission of Beryl Bainbridge and John Johnson Ltd.

Geoffrey Pearson, from *The New Heroin Users*. Copyright © 1987 Geoffrey Pearson. Reprinted by permission of Basil Blackwell.

W. H. Auden, excerpts from "On This Island" (1935) and "In Memory of W. B. Yeats" (1940) from *Collected Poems 1909–62*. Reprinted by permission of Faber & Faber Limited and Random House.

Philip Larkin, excerpts from "Going, Going," "Homage to a Government," "This Be the Verse," and "Annus Mirabilis" from *High Windows*. Copyright © 1974 Philip Larkin. Reprinted by permission of Farrar, Straus & Giroux, Inc., and Faber & Faber Limited. Excerpt from "Toads Revisited" from *The Whitsun Weddings*. Reprinted by permission of Faber & Faber Limited. Excerpt from "Aubade" from *The Collected Poems of Philip Larkin*. Reprinted by permission of Faber & Faber Limited.

John le Carré, from *Tinker, Tailer, Soldier, Spy*. Copyright © 1974 John le Carré. Reprinted by permission of Alfred A. Knopf, Inc., Hodder & Stoughton, Ltd. and David Higham Associates, Ltd.

Philip Larkin, excerpt from a letter of Charles Monteith of Faber & Faber Limited. Reprinted by permission of the literary executors of the Philip Larkin estate.

Craig Raine, excerpts of poem and prose from *Rich*. Copyright © 1984 Craig Raine. Reprinted by permission of Faber & Faber Ltd.

Graham Greene, from his introduction to *My Silent War* by Kim Philby. Introduction Copyright © 1968 Graham Greene. First published MacGibbon & Kee Ltd. Reprinted by permission of Grafton Books, William Collins Sons & Company, Ltd.

Graham Greene, from *The Quiet American*. Copyright © 1955 Graham Greene. First published Viking. Reprinted by permission of William Heinemann Ltd. and Laurence Pollinger Ltd.

Eric Ambler, from *The Night-Comers (State of Seige)*. Copyright © 1956 Eric Ambler. Reprinted by permission of Alfred A. Knopf, Inc. and William Heinemann Ltd.

Eric Ambler, from *Here Lies*. Copyright © 1985 Eric Ambler. Reprinted by permission of Weidenfeld & Nicolson Ltd. and Farrar, Straus & Giroux, Inc.

Agatha Christie, from *The Body in the Library*, 1942. Reprinted by permission of Aitkin & Stone, Ltd. and Harold Ober Associates, Inc. Copyright © 1941, 1942 Agatha Christie Mallowan.

Ruth Rendell, from *A Judgement in Stone*. Copyright © 1977 Ruth Rendell. Reprinted by permission of Doubleday.

Ruth Rendell, from *Put On by Cunning (Death Notes)*. Copyright © 1981 Ruth Rendell. Reprinted by permission of Peters, Fraser and Dunlop on behalf of Century Hutchinson and Random House.

Simon Brett, from *What Bloody Man Is That?* Copyright © 1987 Simon Brett. Reprinted by permission of Charles Scribner's Sons, an imprint of Macmillan Publishing Company and Victor Gollancz Ltd.

Simon Brett, from *Murder in the Title*. Copyright © 1983 Simon Brett. Reprinted by permission of Charles Scribner's Sons, an imprint of Macmillan Publishing Company and Victor Gollancz Ltd.

John Mortimer, from *In Character*. Copyright © 1983 Advanpress Ltd. Reprinted by permission of Allen Lane and Peters, Fraser and Dunlop.

Jeffrey Archer, from jacket copy, *Kane and Abel*, quoted by permission of Simon & Schuster; and from jacket copy, *What Shall We Tell the President?* Reprinted by permission of Fawcett Books.

Barbara Cartland, from *A Hazard of Hearts*. Copyright © 1949 Barbara Cartland. First published by Rich & Cowan. Reprinted by permission of Rupert Crew Ltd. and Barbara Cartland.

Gwen Robyns, from *Barbara Cartland: An Authorized Biography*. Copyright © 1984 Gwen Robyns. Reprinted by permission of Cassell PLC.

Christopher Hibbert, from *London: The Biography of a City*. Copyright © 1969 Christopher Hibbert. Reprinted by permission of Penguin Books Ltd.

Howard Brenton and David Hare, lines from *Pravda*. Copyright © 1985, 1986 Howard Brenton and David Hare. Reprinted by permission of Methuen London Ltd.

Douglas Hurd and Stephen Lamport, from *The Palace of Enchantments*. Copyright © 1985 Douglas Hurd and Stephen Lamport. Reprinted by permission of Hodder & Stoughton Ltd. and St. Martin's Press.

Simon Callow, from *Being an Actor*. Copyright © 1984 Simon Callow. Reprinted by permission of Methuen London Ltd.

David Dalton, from *James Dean: The Mutant King*. Copyright © 1974 David Dalton. Reprinted by permission of St. Martin's Press.

David Hare, lines from *Saigon: Year of the Cat* from *The Asian Plays*. Copyright Introduction © 1986 David Hare. Copyright *Saigon* © 1983 David Hare. Reprinted by permission of Faber & Faber Limited.

Anton Chekhov, from *The Seagull*. Quoted from Penguin Classics edition.

Melvyn Bragg, "The South Bank Show," from *The Modern World: Ten Great Writers*. Excerpts published with permission from London Weekend Television Limited.

Marcel Proust, from "Swann's Way," *Remembrance of Things Past (À la recherche du temps perdu)*.

T. S. Eliot, excerpts from "The Love Song of J. Alfred Prufrock" and *The Waste Land* from *Collected Poems 1909–1962*. Reprinted with permission of Faber & Faber Limited and Harcourt Brace Jovanovich Inc.

Patrick Swinden, from *Paul Scott: Images of India*. Copyright © 1980 Patrick Swinden. Reprinted by permission of Macmillan Press Ltd.

Paul Scott, from *The Jewel in the Crown* (first volume of The Raj Quartet). Copyright © 1966 Paul Scott. Reprinted by permission of William Heinemann Ltd. and William Morrow and Co. Inc.

Michael Billington, from *Peggy Ashcroft*. Copyright © 1988 Michael Billington. Reprinted by permission of John Murray (Publishers) Ltd.

Ken Taylor, excerpts from two scenes of original dialogue written for Episode Eight, "The Day of the Scorpion," from screenplay of Granada Television series, *The Jewel in the Crown*, based on Paul Scott's Raj Quartet. Copyright © 1983 Granada Television. Reprinted by permission of Sir Denis Forman, Chairman, Granada Television, and Ken Taylor.

Ken Taylor, excerpts of adapted dialogue from Episode Fourteen, "A Division of the Spoils," and Episode Nine, "The Towers of Silence," from screenplay of Granada Television series, *The Jewel in the Crown*, based on Paul Scott's Raj Quartet. Copyright © Granada Television, 1983. Reprinted by permission of Sir Denis Forman, Granada Television, William Heinemann Ltd. and William Morrow and Co. Inc.

James Cameron essay, "The Last Days of the Raj," from *The Making of* The Jewel in the Crown, Granada Publishing. Copyright © 1983 Granada Television. Reprinted by permission of Sir Denis Forman and Granada Television.

E. M. Forster, from *A Passage to India*. Copyright © 1924 Harcourt, Brace & World, Inc.; Copyright © 1952 E. M. Forster. Reprinted by permission of Harcourt Brace Jovanovich.

Paul Scott, from *Staying On*. Copyright © 1977 Paul Scott. Reprinted by permission of William Heinemann Ltd. and William Morrow & Co. Inc.

Paul Kennedy, from *The Rise and Fall of the Great Powers*. Copyright © 1988 Paul Kennedy. Reprinted by permission of Unwin Hyman Ltd.

Henry Brandon, from *Special Relationships*. Copyright © 1988 Henry Brandon. Reprinted with permission of Atheneum Publishers, an imprint of Macmillan Publishing Company.

Jan Struther, one passage of dialogue from screenplay adaptation of novel, *Mrs. Miniver* (1939). Copyright © 1949 Lowe's, Inc. Renewed 1969 Metro-Goldwyn-Mayer Pictures, Inc. Reprinted with permission of Turner Entertainment Co. All rights reserved.

John Cleese, two passages of dialogue from screenplay of *A Fish Called Wanda* from an original story by John Cleese and Charles Crichton. First published by Applause Theatre Book Publishers. Copyright © 1988 Metro-Goldwyn-Mayer Pictures, Inc. All Rights Reserved.

Charles Jencks, reproduced from *The Prince, the Architects and New Wave Monarchy* courtesy of Academy Editions, London. Copyright © 1988 Charles Jencks.

While I tried to secure every permission, in the case of John Gibbs, who wrote the lyrics of *Irish Ways and Irish Laws,* I was unable to locate the copyright holder, despite assistance from WEA Records (Ireland) Ltd. in Dublin, the cassette's distributor, which had no contact address for Gibbs in Northern Ireland. For this, or any other instance where I have missed a copyright holder, I apologize for any apparent negligence. Also, the value of the pound fluctuates; I have used the exchange rate of £1 = $1.70 throughout.

PREFACE

Margaret Thatcher challenged the Britain of the old boy network and class distinctions, rooted in Eton and the top public schools, and in Oxford and Cambridge. And in the end the "men in grey suits," the Tory old guard, did her in. But they failed to elect their man.

It was Margaret Thatcher's victory, maybe her greatest one, that at the moment of her fall she got the Conservative Party to choose as Britain's new Prime Minister a young man of the humblest origins, John Major, who embodies the "class society" they both want to bring about.

Major, says *The Economist*, is "nothing if not likeable."

He is also remarkable: the son of a trapeze artist, the boy who left school at 16, the youngster with a spell on the dole, the man making his way in a bank, the MP, junior minister, cabinet minister, foreign secretary (three months), chancellor of the exchequer (one year). It is the CV of Walter Mitty, but John Major has done it all.

Understandably, he puts education at the top of Britain's needs, as do I. He came up through the school of hard knocks, so he is convincing when he says, "No one should feel left out and no one should feel handicapped by their background." When he talks of the "frustrations" of the poor, he knows what it is like not to have a "proper" start in life.

"If we are to improve people's, and particularly young people's, chances in life," Major says, "better education is key." He supports Mrs. Thatcher's school reforms, but would go way beyond them to spend more money on teachers' pay. "We cannot guarantee better results in the classroom," he argues, "until we restore teachers' self-respect, authority, and respect in the community."

In a book with the hypothesis that Britain is failing in education, science, and industry—and the public school Oxbridge elite must take a lot of the blame—John Major's arrival on the scene is like a happy ending.

Until the past year, very few people noticed him. His succession was a very near thing. Mrs. Thatcher resigned last November after eleven-and-a-half years as Prime Minister and fifteen years as party leader after 372 Tory members of Parliament voted 204–152 in her favor, with 16 abstentions. It was 55 percent of the vote, but 4 votes short of the 15 percent lead she needed to win. A 50 percent victory would have carried the second ballot. Instead of urging her on, a cabal of Tory elders and Cabinet ministers, Oxbridge almost to a man, pushed her out.

Thatcher loyalists were furious. Norman Tebbit bitterly complained, "Are you telling me that the person who gets the most votes is the loser?" Among those who urged her to stand down were Tom Renton, the chief whip (Eton and Oxford); Cranely Onslow, chairman of a backbenchers committee (Harrow and Oxford); and Viscount Whitelaw (Eton and the Guards). Several Oxbridge members of her Cabinet told her she was finished. She asked each one how, after she had won the Tories three general elections, "in this funny old world my future as Prime Minister is being put into doubt?"

It seemed a funny old world to the rest of us too. We learned that in British politics, as in Jacobean drama, intrigues and cabals can end a political era just as surely as the normal way of a popular election. Many said Mrs. Thatcher brought on her own downfall; if her bloodymindedness to get her own way—a mixture of pride and obstinacy, iron will and courage, somehow so insular and so British —was her greatest strength, it also left plenty of enemies when the chance came to do her in.

In Saudi Arabia, where he was visiting American troops, President Bush was told by a young Marine, "I thought she'd duke it out." "So did I," Bush replied.

So did I. With faith that Mrs. Thatcher, as she said, would just "go on and on and on," *An American Looks at Britain,* which is really about British culture, is written in the present tense. This gives it, with Mrs. Thatcher gone, something of the air of a long flashback, though we come back to the present and 1991 in the conclusion. When I started this book, Rupert Pennant-Rea, editor of *The Economist,* asked, "Will it be about Britain or Thatcher's Britain?" "Britain," I said at once, since it mostly goes into long-term cultural and economic trends. Still, from May 3, 1979 until November 22, 1990, Mrs. Thatcher pretty much *was* Britain.

To put my main finding very simply, I concluded that Mrs.
Thatcher's revolution was failing because she was not prepared to
spend enough on education to break the public school Oxbridge
elite's hold on British society. She had won her crucial battles with
the left, the labor unions, and Labour militants, but her battle with
the Tory old guard was by no means over. "To me," I wrote near the
end of the book, "the fight that matters in Britain is not the fight
between socialism and free market economics, important as that is,
nor even the fight between 'a dependency culture' and 'an enterprise
culture.' It is the old, old fight over class and power: who is in control?"

In hindsight, I think we can say that once her power began to
wane, Mrs. Thatcher saw it as the old, old fight over class and power
too. The way she groomed John Major with such haste and, her own
battle lost, engineered his election as Tory leader, was a formidable
display of her instinct, will, and hardheadness.

Major, so cheerful, well-mannered, and self-deprecating (he is
"nothing if not likeable," said *The Economist*), has his tough side
too. "Belying his mild appearance," said the *Observer*, "he is Thatcherite in tooth and claw, nakedly hostile to what one of his supporters calls 'Etonianism'—the privileged class whose entrenched power
in the party Mrs. Thatcher has destroyed. Social class is the unacknowledged core issue of the contest." Not quite unacknowledged.
Foreign Secretary Douglas Hurd (Eton, Cambridge) was driven to
protest that he was running for leadership of the Conservative, not
the Marxist, Party, while Lord Whitelaw complained about discrimination against public schoolboys.

How did Mrs. Thatcher snatch Major's victory out of her own
defeat, transforming a rank outsider into Prime Minister within five
days?

It was eighteen months in coming. Major arrived in the House
of Commons in the first Thatcher wave in 1979. He first caught Mrs.
Thatcher's eye when he stood up to her during a dinner-party debate
at Downing Street. She may have seen, under his engagingly modest
manner, an iron will like her own; she began promoting him with
dizzying speed.

By mid-1989 inflation, down to 3.3 percent in 1988, had begun
its relentless rise (to just short of 11 percent when Mrs. Thatcher
fell). On top of a worsening economy were the related battles over
Britain's future in Europe and Mrs. Thatcher's style of governing. In
June 1989 Foreign Secretary Sir Geoffrey Howe and Chancellor of

the Exchequer Nigel Lawson threatened to resign. A month later
Mrs. Thatcher demoted Sir Geoffrey to be leader of Commons and
catapulted Major into the Foreign Secretary's job. When Lawson resigned in October, she made Major the Chancellor.

That December Sir Anthony Meyer, a Tory MP and baronet
(Eton, Oxford), and a "stalking horse" candidate in the first challenge to Mrs. Thatcher since 1975, got 60 Conservative MPs to either
vote for him or abstain. Major, doing a credible job as Chancellor,
was allowed to persuade Mrs. Thatcher to reverse herself and take
Britain into the European Community's Exchange Rate Mechanism
—the issue over which Lawson had resigned.

In 1989 the polls also began to show a widening Labour Party
lead. They also showed that if former Defense Secretary Michael
Heseltine, who had walked out of Mrs. Thatcher's Cabinet in 1986,
were to lead the Conservatives into a new election, the Labour Party
could probably win. Heseltine, fifty-seven, rich, patrician, and ambitious (public school, Oxford), had been campaigning for Thatcher's
job for five years.

To make it harder for leftist majorities in local governments to
raise revenues, Mrs. Thatcher had shifted property taxes to a highly
regressive poll tax. When it took effect in March 1990, there was a
bloody riot in Trafalgar Square, with angry crowds surging toward
Downing Street. The poll tax, a per-capita levy that does not distin-
guish between rich and poor, showed Mrs. Thatcher at her worst,
insensitive to social inequity and the problems of the poor. By late
1990, polls showed that as many as two thirds of Britons wanted her
to stand down. The cry "Thatcher must go" had gone up before but
never so urgently.

The last chapter of this drama began with the Rome summit of
European Community leaders last October. Mrs. Thatcher once
more opposed a single currency for Europe, claiming her opposition
reflected the views of the British people. After she was outvoted,
11–1, she intemperately accused her fellow leaders of "living in
Cloud Cuckooland," the kind of reckless rhetoric she had started using when referring to Europe. It was too much for Sir Geoffrey
Howe. When he objected, he was fired but was designated as "deputy prime minister," an empty title he soon resigned to protest Mrs.
Thatcher's rejection of a single currency.

Walter Bagehot, *The Economist*'s great Victorian editor, once
observed that a difference between the British and American governments is that a single debate in the House of Commons can

shake a government. In a devastating attack on Mrs. Thatcher, Sir Geoffrey precipitated her final crisis, though the air of plots, intrigue, and treachery afoot had been evident at Westminster for some time. In his speech, Howe bitterly attacked Mrs. Thatcher's style and stance on Europe and deplored what he called her "nightmare image . . . of a continent . . . teeming with ill-intentioned people." He declared that it was essential for Britain "not to cut ourselves off from the realities of power, not to retreat into a ghetto of sentimentality about our past." Sir Geoffrey ended by openly inviting others to challenge Mrs. Thatcher's leadership: "The time has come for others to consider their own response to the tragic conflict of loyalties with which I have myself wrestled for too long." Michael Heseltine obliged.

The London *Times* called Heseltine's challenge "monstrous cruel." It editorially decried what it called "squalid manuevering by an introverted male establishment terrified it might lose office."

William Pfaff, the astute *International Herald Tribune* columnist, wrote from Paris:

> The Heseltine challenge failed, narrowly on Tuesday, but on Thursday it produced Mrs. Thatcher's withdrawal. The deciding motive, one suspects, was hatred: to keep Mr. Heseltine from winning. The new candidates, John Major and her foreign secretary, Douglas Hurd, are thought to have better chances against him.
> It is a sad story, the vanity of politicians . . .

Hatred there was. Mrs. Thatcher accused Heseltine of near socialism—he was an exponent of "intervention, corporatism, everything that pulled us down." He was "all glamour and no substance," motivated by "personal ambitions and private rancour." A Heseltine victory, she declared, would "jeopardize all I have struggled to achieve."

But I think, once she made up her mind she had to go, the good of the Tory Party and Britain were uppermost in her mind. Her real enemy, as she was once more finding out, was the public school Oxbridge elite. This establishment had gone along with Mrs. Thatcher's free-market, sound-money economic policies, her Victorian values and Little Englander sentiments, as long as she kept its members in power. When she began to look like a loser, they were prepared to jettison her and Thatcherism too.

Heseltine defended his pro-Europe stand: "It is not about selling out, about federalism or throwing away sovereignty. It is about whether a larger, more competitive market place can enhance the

City of London as the third financial center of the world." It is not surprising that Howe, Lawson, and such arch-establishment figures as Lord Carrington, another former Foreign Secretary, as well as big money, came out for Heseltine.

But it didn't go the establishment's way. A succession of Oxbridge elders told Mrs. Thatcher the battle was lost. Twelve of nineteen Cabinet members advised her she could not win against Heseltine in the second round. Polls gave Labour a fifteen-point lead. They supported Heseltine's claim to be the Tory contender most likely to win the next election. (This proved to be totally ephemeral; once the Tories chose Major, Labour's lead evaporated overnight.)

The night before she gave up, Denis Thatcher, her husband of thirty-nine years, is said to have told her, "Margaret, it is time to go." It was, one gathers, a time of anguish and tears. Alone, with Denis, she decided. The next morning, November 22, she got up early as always, informed her staff, phoned the Queen, and met her Cabinet to read out her resignation statement:

> Having consulted widely among colleagues, I have concluded that the unity of the party and the prospect of victory in a general election would be better served if I stood down to enable Cabinet colleagues to enter the ballot for leadership.

Leaving for Buckingham Palace, she once more repeated, "It's a funny old world." Abroad it was almost unthinkable she was going. She had greatly helped to end the division of Europe, she was the first to recognize the "courage and vision" of Mikhail Gorbachev and that the "Cold War is over," and she had the guts to tell Saddam Hussein that he must either get out of Kuwait or "we and our allies will remove him by force."

She pulled out of the leadership race just in time for Major and Hurd and no once else to put in their names as candidates. Hurd, sixty, a former diplomat, the son of a baron, member of the Beefsteak Club, as Oxbridge as they come, was also a Thatcher loyalist; in a three-way race it was felt he would draw establishment votes away from Heseltine, as he in fact did.

In her last speech in the House of Commons as Prime Minister, Mrs. Thatcher gave a bravado performance, rallying the Tories against a nonconfidence motion proposed by Labour leader Neil Kinnock.

> Eleven years ago, we rescued Britain from the parlous state to which socialism had brought it. Once again Britain stands tall in the Councils

of Europe and in the world. Over the last decade, we have given power back to the people on an unprecedented scale.

As she blasted the evils of socialism and the Eurocrats' ambitions, Mrs. Thatcher drew laughter when she said with gusto in an aside, "I'm enjoying this."

By now there was pandemonium in the Commons corridors. Working hard among backbenchers for Major were some fifty loyal Thatcherites, among them a fiercely faithful Norman Tebbit. The night before the second vote, Mrs. Thatcher's Press Secretary Bernard Ingham and other close aides put out the word that Mrs. Thatcher wanted John Major to succeed her. *The New York Times* was told by an anonymous aide, probably Ingham, "She regards him as a true man of the people and has had her eye on him a long time."

When it came to the vote, Major got 185, missing a needed majority by 4. Heseltine dropped to 131 and Hurd got 56. Soon after the votes were tallied, Heseltine conceded victory. The vote suggests that after all the years of Thatcherism, the Conservative Party is still split down the middle between the old Tories of Eton and Oxbridge, the landed gentry, big money and London intellectuals, and the lower-middle and working class Thatcherites.

Major at once called for party unity, his immediate overriding concern. He asked Hurd to stay on as Foreign Secretary. And to make the punishment fit the crime, he asked Heseltine to come back into the Cabinet as Environment Secretary, which means he has to do something about the poll tax (hopefully scrap it and go back to the old property tax).

With Major's victory, Mrs. Thatcher showed just how far she had come to creating a society where merit, not class origin, matters. Just forty-seven when he became Prime Minister, a cautious, reasonable man with a pleasant, classless accent, Major's family history is as colofrul as he is not. When he was born in London in 1943, his father, then sixty-seven, had not only retired as a trapeze artist, but had been a vaudeville performer, mercenary in Brazil; he was then making the painted plaster gnomes you see in so many English gardens. He went broke ten years later, and the family moved into a two-room flat in the tough south London slum of Brixton.

Major left school at sixteen to support his parents, never went to university, worked as an office clerk and manual laborer, and spent some months on welfare. One story even has it that he was rejected as a ticket collector on a London bus because he couldn't count. At twenty-two he settled down to a career in banking, where he rose to be a senior executive with the Standard Chartered Bank. "There *is* life outside politics, you know," he says, "and I did work for an international bank for seventeen years with experience in Africa, south of the Sahara, the Americas, and the Far East." A natural Thatcherite, he joined the Young Conservatives and reached Parliament on his third try. Once he caught Mrs. Thatcher's attention, his rise was meteoric.

Interestingly, he says of her, "Apart from admiring her, I *like* her. She is a jolly nice woman. If you *know* her, you *like* her. She's a very powerful political personality; she has very strong views. But there's a whole wellspring of absolute humanity that people have never appreciated." Major's wife, Norma, an opera buff who has written a biography of Joan Sutherland, will not be taking up residence with their two teenage children in Downing Street, but will try to lead a seminormal life in their Huntingdonshire home near Cambridge. She has admitted that she has sometimes cried over the loss of normal family life which has accompanied Major's extremely sudden rise.

Sir Geoffrey Howe ("I am not an assassin") and Michael Heseltine look like the villains behind the plots and skullduggery at Westminster (though early on Heseltine expressed the fear that "he who wields the dagger seldom wears the crown"). But we have them to thank for our happy ending. For by deposing Margaret Thatcher, they have unexpectedly provided Britain, and the rest of us, with a new British Prime Minister who looks as though he can, if more quietly and calmly and cheerfully, carry on her social revolution at home and move Britain into the European sphere.

What will happen to Mrs. Thatcher herself? Duchess of Dulwich? Countess of Grantham? "Retire into silence" as her biographer Hugo Young advises? Surely not. When the Queen made Denis Thatcher a hereditary baronet—he can pass the title on to their son, Mark—his wife wanted no part of a ladyship. "I have done pretty well out of being Mrs. Thatcher," she said. "Life begins at sixty-five!" she toasted her staff in a farewell toast at No. 10. David Owen amusingly proposed she become Secretary-General at the United Nations. "The bureaucrats in the U.N. would be horrified at the prospect of being handbagged," he wrote in the *Daily Express*. "But those who want the U.N. to count in the world would be delighted."

My guess is that she will go right on, from her backbencher's Finchley seat in Parliament, doing what she has been doing, marching forward, banner held high, with her beleaguered band of radical populist subversives, rallying behind their young new leader and forever on guard against the treacherous designs of Tory toffs and the Oxbridge elite. As Mrs. Thatcher herself has said, the time comes when "you have to hand over to someone new, fresh, young, dynamic. You do not want to cling on so they have to say: 'Who is going to tell the old girl she had better go?' " And go she did. But in John Major I think she has found someone at last who can "take the banner forward with the same commitment, belief, vision, strength, and singleness of purpose."

In the Gulf War, Major proved his mettle, and, as in Mrs. Thatcher's years, Britain was again our staunchest ally, Americans and British fighting side by side as they did in World War II. Major's premiership, which is enjoying the highest approval ratings in Britain since Churchill's fifty years ago, is to be warmly welcomed. Indeed, the war once again proves British character itself in time of adversity, with all its dogged steadfastness and patriotism, as in the rush to enlist in the military or give blood. Saddam Hussein is the kind of brutal tyrant the British see themselves traditionally fighting. War also tends, while it lasts, to heal Britain's class and North-South divisions, breaking down barriers in a common cause.

Even Major seemed to be on the front line when terrorists, apparently from the IRA, in February fired three mortar rounds from a van at No. 10 Downing Street, scoring a hit in the back garden during a war cabinet meeting. After everyone dove for the floor as windows shattered, the unflappable Major said, "I think we'd better start again somewhere else." Later he told the House of Commons that it was a deliberate attempt "both to kill the cabinet and do damage to our democratic system of government." Even the Queen was moved to publicly protest the attack.

The gulf crisis raises troubling questions about Europe's future. Germany's grudging and timid political response and its failure to spontaneously join America and Britain in the war effort, like Belgium's refusal to sell Britain extra munitions for the gulf, revealed a disturbing every-man-for-himself attitude in continental Europe. While this was an ill omen for European unity, I think we can say that the special relationship between America and Britain is unexpectedly and reassuringly as important as ever.

Columnist William Safire caught the American feeling well. He
wrote:

> . . . No weaseling or waffling: 40,000 British warriors are on the Amer-
> icans' side, with British tactical air forces doing much of the most dan-
> gerous bombing and suffering the highest losses.
>
> This stalwart stand was not the personal decision of Margaret
> Thatcher; if that were so, her successor would not be so overwhelm-
> ingly supported in the war effort as he is, by British public opinion.

The British eloquently showed what they stand for, and it is what we
stand for too.

One advantage of writing a new preface to a previously-
reviewed book is that it gives an author the chance to have the last
word. I was happy, when this book came out, at the American reception and the kindness of many British reviewers. But a few of the
English were furiously indignant ("oafish ignoramus," "transatlantic
travesty," "perfectly fatuous," "incoherent").

To them I'd like to offer these lines from *Alice:*

> "Now, if you're ready, Oysters dear,
>   We can begin to feed."
> "But not on us!" the Oysters cried,
>   Turning a little blue.
> "After such kindness that would be
>   A dismal thing to do!"
> "The night is fine," the Walrus said.
>   "Do you admire the view?"

INTRODUCTION

It was the best of times, it was the worst of times, it was the age of wisdom, it was the age of foolishness, it was the epoch of belief, it was the epoch of incredulity, it was the season of Light, it was the season of Darkness, it was the spring of hope, it was the winter of despair, we had everything before us, we had nothing before us, we were all going direct to Heaven, we were all going direct the other way—in short, the period was so far like the present period, that some of its noisiest authorities insisted on its being received, for good or for evil, in the superlative degree of comparison only.

CHARLES DICKENS

TODAY THE WORDS of Dickens ring as true as they must have in the 1850s when he wrote them, even if that was the heyday of the Industrial Revolution and Britain, its birthplace, was using its steam engines and trusty muskets and all its new technology to rule the waves and a third of the world. Most British men and women have pretty good ideas about what has gone right and wrong since.

The last thing I ever expected to do was to write a book about it. My decision to do so was based on a presumption and a discovery. The presumption is to assume, unless the contrary is proved, that one can take a society about which one knows next to nothing—our common English language, Protestantism, constitutional government, soccer, the Beatles, "Masterpiece Theatre" and all the rest aside—go about it and talk to people and come up with a valid "outsider's view." The discovery was to find, once I did so, that as soon as you get past the famous reserve, the British are a remarkably open and hospitable people. And they are the world's best talkers. So I did this book.

It happened this way: I was spending the summer of 1986 in rooms at Wadham College, Oxford. I'd never been to Oxford before, or hardly at all to Britain for that matter, except for the odd two- to three-day stopover to and from Asia and Africa over the years. I had gone into reporting just as America's post-World War II imperial era, in some ways succeeding the British Empire, was in full swing. I had spent, starting in 1959, a quarter century reporting the Third World, much of the time from villages. Western science, at last, was spreading everywhere and age-old peasant societies—for good or for ill—were becoming something else. As I wrote in *The Economist* in a 1979 article headlined "A great change has started": "Times change and men, once they have the technological means and enough years to culturally adjust, change with them." Just about wherever you went English was the lingua franca. If the wise old colonial hands steadily got fewer, the legacy of the British Empire was much in evidence. Britain itself you didn't think much about; it was just there, vaguely the cultural heart of the West, possessing so much of its wisdom even as power had passed on to us.

The Oxford summer went quickly, in a haze of green foliage, pubs, baroque music, golden spires, and chiming bells. Once I got used to the baleful scowl of the Bishop of Cloyne from his gilt-framed portrait in my enormous tutorial drawing room, with its white paneling, Jacobean window seats, green velvet drapes, Chippendale chairs, ancient smells, and sagging floors, and the nightly terrors of the Senior Common Room ("Eh . . . We pass to our *left*"), Wadham was pleasant. I escaped to the Bodleian, to the Thames, to pubs, or to the Sheldonian's steep wooden seats to hear Handel or Bach, or bicycled around the Cotswolds to villages with improbable names like Aston Magna and Evenlode.

At summer's end I went to London to stay a few days at the grandly historic Athenaeum club and visit *The Economist*. I'd been a contributor of occasional pieces from the Third World for fifteen years (from Jakarta: "Sin City is a pressure cooker"; Kathmandu: "Pottering into the Himalayas"; Cairo: "On the rooftoops, in the cemeteries"; Seoul: "Confucius rules in Swallow Valley"; Bamako: "Even the vultures have fled").

I met the editor, Rupert Pennant-Rea, for the first time. I was astonished when he asked, "How would you like to write a survey on Britain for us?" They'd not done one before. They wanted fifteen to twenty thousand words. Aside from a generous fee, *The Economist* would pay all my expenses to travel about Britain and interview people for six weeks and write it all up in two weeks. It would suggest people to see.

My reaction was sheer fright. "Oh, no, it's impossible," I protested. "I know nothing about Britain."

"Exactly. That's the point," said Pennant-Rea. "We want a fresh look. An outsider's view."

More protests that it was impossible did not get me far. This was England.

> Alice laughed. "There's no use trying," she said: "one *can't* believe impossible things."
> "I daresay you haven't had much practice," said the Queen.

Brenda Maddox, the biographer of Joyce's wife (*Nora: The Real Life of Molly Bloom*) and an American who once edited *The Economist*'s Britain section, told me that just before she joined the magazine's staff in the early 1960s an edict had gone out—no more *Alice* quotes. Third World economies, it seems, were all like the Red Queen, forever running to stay in the same place. But I'll risk another one: walking out of Rupert Pennant-Rea's office that day was just like falling down the rabbit hole.

> Either the well was very deep, or she fell very slowly, for she had plenty of time as she went to look about her, and to wonder what was going to happen next . . . She tried to look down and make out what she was coming to, but it was too dark to see anything.

How does an American with no special expertise on it write about Britain? A foreign country and not a foreign country. Where does one culture end and the other begin? Tweedledee and Tweedledum, the White Rabbit, the Mad Hatter, and the Cheshire Cat were just as much part of my childhood in North Dakota as they were of someone's in Oxfordshire. My favorite country walk at Oxford was along the Thames towpath a couple of miles to Godstow. I was happy to discover that this particular stretch of the Thames was where, on the "golden afternoon" of July 4, 1862, while rowing up to Godstow with the Liddell girls, Lewis Carroll composed his *Alice*. Alice Liddell's son, Caryl, quoted his mother half a century afterward:

> Nearly all of *Alice's Adventures Underground* was told on that blazing summer afternoon with the heat haze shimmering over the meadows while the party landed to shelter for a while in the shadow cast by the haycocks near Godstow.

I had done it myself on hot summer days and the setting had hardly changed at all.

Mark Twain often compared the two cultures. When it came to humor, he wrote,

> Americans are not Englishmen, and American humor is not English humor; but both the American and his humor have their origin in England, and have merely undergone changes brought about by changed conditions and a new environment.

We are all slaves of our backgrounds. I happen to be descended from two eighteenth century British migrants to America: a Quaker doctor from Lancashire and an escaped indentured sailor from Wales (convict? debtor?). A Scots Presbyterian grandmother's family came later, as did an Irish grandmother whose parents fled County Cork in the potato famine. (Asked our origin, my mother always said, "English, Irish, Welsh, and Scots.") How much less claim to the British past does one have if his family spent six or seven generations on the other side of the Atlantic? As John Greenleaf Whittier wrote, "We too are heirs of Runnymede / and Shakespeare's fame and Cromwell's deed." But not quite. The Puritans set sail in the Mayflower to enjoy religious freedom in the New World (and, as humorists say, to prevent everybody else from enjoying his). And about two thirds of the Pilgrims were just looking for adventure or to improve their lot. Robert Frost put it very well:

> The land was ours before we were the land's.
> She was our land more than a hundred years
> Before we were her people. She was ours
> In Massachusetts, in Virginia,
> But we were England's, still colonials

To Frost it took "many deeds of war" to make us a distinctly separate nationality with our own ties:

> To the land vaguely realizing westward,
> But still unstoried, artless, unenhanced,
> Such as she was, such as she would become.

After six frantic weeks of trains, buses, tubes, and planes; B&Bs and upmarket hotels; and interviews in Parliament, the City, coal mines, housing estates, movie studios, and bishops' palaces, "Britain: A View from the Outside" was published in *The Economist* on February 21, 1987. We used the famous opening passage from *A Tale of Two Cities* for our cover. It seemed to me that as postindustrial technology worked its way through British society, people were just as hopeful and despairing as they had been in Dickens's best and worst of times.

It had all gone so fast, I was left with a strong sense of something left undone. So many people left to see, so many places left to go. When the chance came to expand the survey into a book, I went back, taking a flat on Richmond Hill for a year, just beside the famous view of the Thames and Richmond Park with its herds of royally-owned deer, ancient oaks, and views of London in the faint blue distance (especially from the mound where legend has it Henry VIII stood and gazed mournfully in the direction of Tower Green as Anne Boleyn lost her head).

The park, 2,470 acres, two and a half miles across, is one of the last survivors of London's old medieval forests. "Heavens!" wrote James Thomson in 1727. "What a goodly prospect spreads around, of hills, and dales, and woods, and lawn and spires and glittering towns and gilded streams." The view from Richmond Hill glitters still. As a lively old lady from Liverpool sang to me on the train after I mentioned where I was living:

> I'd crown resign to call thee mine
> Sweet lass of Richmond Hill

Just up the hill from my glass-walled, balconied flat, all ferns and ivy, and overlooking the Thames, was Sir Joshua Reynolds' stately old house; Virginia Woolf had lived for a time just down the hill. It was a five-minute walk along the river's banks to Richmond Green, where Henry VII held a jousting tournament with knights in armor in 1492, a date we have reason to keep in mind as well. Just south of the Green are the ruins of Richmond Palace where Henry VIII was born and Elizabeth I, ailing, heeded her astrologer's advice and came to die of distemper. The palace was mainly destroyed after Charles I, its last royal occupant, was executed in 1649, the only English king to lose his head. The oaks in the park are very old. Owls hoot in them at night; there are ponds full of geese, ducks, cooties, and swans. Hares and foxes can be seen in the bracken, and the deer are friendly if wild—and startling to come upon in a dense fog when you may find a group of stags with huge antlers have you surrounded. I could look down on a riverbank farm where cows and sheep still graze in green meadows. Yet Waterloo Station was just eighteen minutes away by fast train. It was a perfect place to spend a year and write. I walked in the park every day. The oaks lost their leaves in autumn but it rarely freezes in London and English grass stays the same wet, luminous green all the year.

"Be acerbic," said an English friend. "Play God," said another. I

will let the British, in their sharp, keen, trenchant way, do as much
of the talking as I can. As Damon Runyon once said, the race is not
to the swift, nor the battle to the strong, but that's the way to bet.
The British are the articulate ones. And it's their country. Even after
meeting a couple of hundred people more, this is still very much "an
outsider's view."

The decline of Great Britain, its loss of empire, loss of morale,
was very much the theme in 1986 when I was at Oxford and during
the winter when I was doing *The Economist* survey. Everybody was
asking: will Thatcherism reverse the decline or just interrupt it?
Margaret Thatcher's third election victory in June 1987 changed the
mood. By 1988 the talk was more upbeat, of recovery and Britain's
promising future in an ever-stronger and more unified Europe of
the 1990s, a Europe potentially richer than America, Japan, Russia,
or anybody. And this was before anyone dreamed Eastern Europe
was about to throw off Communism, and Leninist one-party rule
and a "planned" economy would look pretty much doomed in Russia, and China too. Yet somehow Britain's buoyancy rang a bit hollow out in Richmond where I lived. Unlike cosmopolitan central
London, one of the great crossroads of the world, a suburb in Surrey is as English as can be. Economics and politics may bubble en-
couragingly on the national surface, as reported on the nightly
news, but the deeper, slower currents of ordinary English life reveal
a lot of bleakness and despair. What is a loss of morale, a deep failure of the nerve, is partly obscured by the cultural momentum of
the great British past, which keeps rolling on. It is partly obscured
also by English stoicism, humor, and grit.

But it is there. Even the gains of Thatcherism have not restored
British self-confidence in its old form. The doubts and fears from
the aftermath of two world wars and the loss of empire are too
deep-rooted. The European future too uncertain. So if this outsider's
view of Britain has one unifying thread, story line, underlying principle—call it what you will—it is this: Britain is indeed paying the
price for its cultural and class divisions. The way out, as everybody
agrees, is education, the very best possible for everybody, based on
merit, with plenty of science and math and computers and lab
equipment, but humanities and literature too. But the public school
Oxbridge elite that still runs most things cannot bring itself to do
what it knows it must do. It says it is doing it. It isn't. Its own privileged social and financial future is at stake.

So Britain pays the price. So does the elite itself in its loss of a sense of purpose. To put it very crudely, and if you'll accept that I'm painting with a very broad brush, I think there has been a drop in the emotional authenticity of Britain. That is, a thinning of the kindness and good nature and all the things that you and I so much admire. Its people are lonelier and less nourished and more separate from each other than they used to be. My guess is that it is temporary, a passing phase. The loss of empire was a colossal shock and it is hard for any society to adapt to our new fiercely competitive, single world economy. I did keep asking: could this happen to us? I think it could. We're not investing very well in education either. Nor in the future of lots of ordinary young Americans. We, too, have a shrinking industrial base, failing schools, better scientific research than application, a polarized society, rising crime, drugs, homelessness and underclass, and the rest. We, too, have reason to worry about decline. Is Britain's story a warning of things to come?

I'm not, I hasten to say, one of those wickedly delighted people who predict that Britain will go smash, that one way or another it is tottering toward its fall. If anything, I'm a reasoned pessimist, much of the time feeling Britain is going great guns . . . And yet . . . And yet . . .

One proceeds with trepidation. It is amazing how many Americans feel their cultural understanding is somehow measured in their knowledge of Britain. Maybe it is because in our imagination it somehow bursts on the scene full-blown in all its Elizabethan-Victorian glory, the epicenter of so many great revolutions: scientific (Newton and Darwin), liberal government (Cromwell and Locke), market economics (Adam Smith), industrial (James Watt, Blake's dark satanic mills), and imperial (filling up empty continents like North America and Australia; conquering savage tribes and docile peasants in India, half of Africa, bits of East Asia, the South Seas). Of course all the admiration and affection is mixed with a little rivalry and threatenedness (George III and the redcoats); we did fight two wars.

Sadly, few would disagree with the *New York Times,* which reported on its front page in 1985 that "proud old Britain—birthplace of the Industrial Revolution, master of a third of the world in the 19th century, a Great Power only four decades ago—remains a nation in decline." Even so, in wisdom if not in power, Britain, to me, is still the fulcrum of that North Atlantic liberal world which stretches from San Francisco to West Berlin. And now, with the Berlin Wall down, farther still.

To chart the way ahead, let me give the reader a kind of road map as we set out. My outsider's look at Britain is divided into seven parts. I've kept pretty faithful to the original *Economist* survey. I felt that with such a big subject, fundamentally this book should reflect the things that presented themselves to me as the most salient when I first set out to interpret Britain in a hurry. If I jump around a bit at times it is not because the topics are chosen at random but because this is the way they forced themselves on my attention from the start. In the main I have kept to the preoccupations of the highly intelligent people to whom I talked and the preoccupations of the man in the street.

The opening section, "An Island, and Old," goes into Britain's setting and history. The nineteenth century was the British Century. Queen Victoria outlived it by three weeks. She left behind the biggest, richest empire ever known. But industrial decline going back to the 1870s, two world wars, and the loss of empire itself took their toll, as did postwar setbacks to the smokestack industry, the Labour Party, and the welfare state. Our curtain rises, so to speak, on Thatcherism, as the computer age, an aspiring lower middle class, and a single global market explode the old agenda of the left. And as Britain is being asked to relinquish part of its sovereignty to the European Community as a step toward a still unknown, possibly unstable "common European home."

Even fifty years ago I might have been very critical, seeing the British as immensely rich, arrogant, predatory, formidable (except fifty years ago probably nobody would have asked my opinion). Now one complains in frustration: Why can't they do it better? Why can't they live up to our memories and expectations? If this is what happened to the Mother Country on the minefield of world power, what's going to happen to us?

Is Britain's social fabric starting to tear? Is the old accommodation of civility and goodwill wearing through? Just as when I go out and live in and write about a village, I start here with religion, the core of any society's culture. And then I move to how things looked to other Americans in the past, ending with a look at accent and class. The closest cultural tie is of course the common language, closest of all in the literary language of childhood; a review of children's literature and Shakespeare, besides just being fun, is a reminder at the outset just how deeply English an American's roots are.

Since this is really a book about British culture and what is happening to it, I turn next to its economy, the basis for it; if new technology changes the economy, so will British culture change too. We find that Britain's South is adapting to this technology and prospering and its North, having a harder time adapting, is left blighted and behind. Parts II and III follow the "Two Nations" divide. "South: The Best of Times" goes into how advances in electronics, biotech, and information services are transforming Britain's industry, science, health, unions, education, finance, retailing, and farming. "North: The Worst of Times" looks at problems closely tied in the British mind to the old industrial North and slum cultures of its blighted cities: an old coal-mining valley in Wales, low income housing in Scotland, the rise of violence all over. In Liverpool it is asked: is a permanent underclass being created? In Bradford, we look at the culturally uprooted. And in Northern Ireland, at the way Irish myth plays a role in the cycle of killing and revenge.

Britain's last, great preeminence is literary. In "Mastery of Words," Parts IV and V, we also see signs of trouble. "Letters" discusses British articulacy. If some of the best writing in English is being done by non-English writers, Britain is still supreme in criticism and as the custodian of the language. It remains unrivaled in such popular forms as the spy thriller, historical romance, and mystery. "Performing Arts" looks at Britain's golden age of acting as it draws to a close. Part VI, the story of a team of filmmakers who go to India to portray the last days of the British Raj, is about the psychic shock that came with the end of empire.

The last section, "Your Greece to Our Rome," goes back to politics, first taking up postimperialism, Anglo-American ties, Britain's twenty-first-century future, in a Europe transformed, and the Royal Family. Before the conclusion, three chapters are devoted to Mrs. Thatcher, her style, her record, and what I see as her most important role: trying, just as King Canute's courtiers wanted him to do, to turn the tide and restore Britain's sense of purpose and the enterprise that goes with it. Canute was happy to show, as he said, "how empty and worthless is the power of kings." For, as all those nameless millions who changed history in 1989 in Russia, China, Eastern Europe, and so many places showed, who can command the waves to stand still?

And what should they know of England
who only England know?

Kipling

I

AN ISLAND,
AND OLD

This Little World

A T THE OUTSET it should be mentioned that for such a precise
people, the names for their land are oddly imprecise. True,
"the United Kingdom of Great Britain and Northern Ireland"
is such a mouthful. And "Great Britain," favored by atlases, turns
out to be a geographical designation as much as anything *(Grand
Bretagne* as opposed to the Normans' Britanny, both from the Roman *Britannia)*. One settles for "U.K." or "Britain." And "the British." But what about the singular? The British on the whole don't
like "Britisher" or "Brit." "Briton" is undoubtedly correct. But used
in conversation it has vague overtones of patriotic posturing (Never,
never, never shall be slaves). The singular is defeated by cultural
identity. People regard themselves as specifically English, Irish,
Welsh, Scots, or Cornish. *Cornish?* an American might well ask. Cornish only died out as a language in the eighteenth century; like
Wales and Scotland, Cornwall's Celtic society was never conquered
by the Anglo-Saxons.

So while we talk of British politics, the British economy, and
British government, it tends to be English food, English literature,
English theater, and English habits. The distinction gets blurred. Asa
Briggs in his *Social History of England* deals, certainly in its later
chapters, with Britain. Kipling was inspired to write his poem "The
English Flag" by a newspaper account that a crowd of London
rabble had cheered at the sight of a burning Union Jack. It is a delicate question, like saying "Holland" when you mean the whole
Netherlands. Shakespeare just used "Britain" for plays like *Cymbeline,* set in the Roman period. And Robert Burns and Sir Walter
Scott, like Oscar Wilde or James Joyce, are undeniably part of English literature. To further confuse us Americans, neither of Britain's
two greatest—pre-Thatcher—Prime Ministers of this century were
pure English. Lloyd George was Welsh and Churchill had an Ameri-

can mother. Harold Macmillan, Ramsay MacDonald, Alec Douglas-Home, and Bonar Law, to name a few, were Scots.

One finds the same linguistic sensitivity the world over. Brazilians, Peruvians, and Mexicans, for example, think of themselves as Americans; inhabitants of the United States to Latins are specifically *North* Americans, they live in *el norte.*

"England," writer Paul Theroux told me, "in a sense does not exist, except in the talk." Hugh Kenner in his 1988 book on modern English writers, *A Sinking Island,* seems to go out of his way to provoke Scottish and Welsh wrath. He mischievously begins:

> "English," formerly "Anglisc," was the tongue of the Teuton "Angles" who invaded and then settled Northumbria and Mercia amid cries that the savages had come. Until recently it implied the culture of an island called England . . .

Kenner, tongue in cheek, knows perfectly well that geographically England is just part of an island, Great Britain, bounded as it has always been by Wales and the Irish Sea on the west and Scotland on the north. But with about 5 million Scots, 3 million Welsh, and 1.5 million Northern Irish, most of the just under 57 million British are English living in England (though many are of Scots, Welsh, or Irish birth or descent, Irish greatly affecting the character of Liverpool and Glasgow).

To Americans, the British live in a very small place; you could drop the whole of the United Kingdom inside the state of Oregon. The United States has four times as many people as Britain but thirty-five times as much territory. ("This little speck the British Isles?" asked Oliver Wendell Holmes.) Its smallness makes Britain a very focused country. You can somehow *see* it all in your mind in a way you can't America. Its hierarchy seems natural because the center is so close. Its ruling groups, even institutions, are much more coherent; the British Who's Who is a handy tool, everybody is inside. Harvard, Princeton, and Yale have to work hard at being national universities; for Oxford and Cambridge it's effortless. Size and density go a long way to explain the famous reserve and careful manners, and all the understatement, conscious coolness, and dry, deprecating humor. Maybe Americans are so loud and brash because it is the only way to get heard in all those wide-open spaces.

There is such a different sense of time and space. In Britain you are rarely more than two or three hours from London by a fairly good train, nor do you need to wait more than an hour or so to catch one. It is indeed a right little, tight little island, just as the song says. You are almost always within walking distance of a news agent that sells that morning's London papers. And, with only four channels, everybody watches the same few television news broadcasts at night. Three-fourths of the British people also read at least one national daily every day, posh or gutter. Nothing so gives away class as the papers people pick at the local news agent's on Sunday mornings. The full range of London papers is laid out for you. "RANDY SPOUSE FROLICS WITH VICE GIRLS," "LADY SARAH'S NEW LOVE IS A SEXPOT," and bare-breasted Page Three Girls beckon salaciously from one side. A clergyman has been charged with seducing choirboys, a twelve-year-old boy is on trial for killing an infant girl, a rock star is busted for drugs. On the other, good gray pages promise nothing more exciting than "Airlines face punctuality test," "Thatcher in Africa," excerpts from a biography of Graham Greene. Conservative Party chairman Kenneth Baker, the morning I interviewed him, had all the London papers spread out on his desk, including the tabloids. "Oh," I said, "I see you've got the fun ones. I get the *News of the World* on Sundays. I feel I should take it home in a plain brown wrapper." He laughed. Going from Richmond to Waterloo by train during rush hour with all the stockbrokers in their dark blue pin-striped suits, heads stuck in the *Times, Telegraph, Independent, Guardian* or *FT*, reminds one of T. S. Eliot's "They know what they are to feel and what to think / They know it with their morning printer's ink." When Mrs. Thatcher astonished Americans by saying on a Washington visit that the cold war was over, practically everybody in Britain knew about it and had an opinion, often disputatious, that same day.

In America, in contrast, once you get outside the big cities, trains are mainly terrible, buses slow and too few, and if you go at all, you mainly go long distances by car or plane. American book sales are twenty-fourth worldwide. In newspaper sales per thousand people, Britain has 421, Germany 408, Japan 575, but America just 269. Timothy Dickinson, a widely consulted Englishman long resident in Washington, has his own explanation for this:

> With all respect, once you're outside major American cities, you get *terrible* newspapers! Britain is a compact country. Apart perhaps from the top end of Scotland, you can always get fifteen to twenty very decent London publications. Here you go to a city as important as Austin, Texas, let us say, and the newspapers are not fit to wrap fish. *The Des Moines Register* is a fine paper, but get a hundred miles away and

you're reading dreadful stuff. I would argue that only about a third of the United States is in the catchment areas of really decent papers. No wonder people don't read them.

It is not surprising so many American writers see their society as Jack Kerouac did in *On the Road:* a chaos of individuality, where one encounters endless types of people, endless new situations. The British find it easier to conceive of a stabler world in which things can be taken for granted.

It is also as if on an island—a society without frontiers—people think in much more zero-sum terms (what anthropologists call the idea of "limited good"; anybody who gets rich does so at his neighbor's expense). Despite the announcement in the 1890 U.S. census that the frontier was closed, different frontiers keep springing up in America—irrigated deserts, air-conditioned Sun Belt cities. If you do not like your job in Newark or Oshkosh or Schenectady, move to San Diego or Dallas or Orlando, Huck Finn lighting out for the territory. (Americans are eighteen times more likely to move to find or keep a job than Britons, one study found.) The economy comes to be seen as a deep well to be forever primed and pumped, and not, as it did to so many British workers, not so long ago, proud of their place and their union, as a fixed pie.

One guesses that ever since the last shaggy band of hunters waded across the submerging Channel at the end of the Ice Age, the British have been conditioned by physical insularity ("I do not say they cannot come. I only say they cannot come by sea."). It is after all in living memory—France's Louis Blériot first flew the English Channel on July 25, 1909—that British seapower has diminished. Among the barrows at Land's End, where gigantic breakers crash against the granite headlands, one learns that man has been in Britain at least 250,000 years. From caves on Caldy Island and at Hoyle's Mouth near Tenby in South Wales, you can crouch under the same rocks and see the same dunes and sea that Old Stone Age hunters did when they preyed with spears on mammoths. When the Roman legions first laid eyes on Stonehenge, it had been standing for over two thousand years, no doubt the same puzzling ruin we see today. The tattooed yobbo carries on tradition: Julius Caesar wrote, "All the Britons dye their bodies with woad, which produces a blue color . . ."

Where is Britain most and least like an island? Certainly most on the Atlantic shores, described by Tacitus as "beaten by a wild and open sea." (I'll say, after getting caught on a coastal path in Cornwall in a storm.) This was truly land's end for the Romans. Tacitus:

> Men coming from these remote regions told strange stories—of hurricanes, unknown birds, sea monsters, and shapes half-human and half-animal.

They tell them still in Cornish villages. (Tacitus, after sunny Italy, found the British climate "horrid because of the frequency of rain and mist.")

I asked Paul Theroux, who traveled around Britain's coast, much of it on foot, while writing his 1983 book, *The Kingdom by the Sea.* "Most like an island?" he said. "I'd say the coast. Very much. You feel as if there's nothing behind you. That it's very insubstantial. They're sort of clinging to the wreckage, these people. For better *and* worse, it's an island." He said his best and most haunting images of the British were of people near the sea. I thought of a passage in *Kingdom:* "The British seemed to be people forever standing on a crumbling coast and scanning the horizon."

"Les Anglais s'amusent tristement," wrote the Duc de Sully in his seventeenth century memoirs. The English take their pleasures sadly, something Theroux captured well. (They also take them gaily; think of Sir John Betjeman's "Miss Joan Hunter Dunn, Miss Joan Hunter Dunn, / I can hear from the car-park the dance has begun." Sheer fun on a Surrey Saturday night; one saw a lot of it in Richmond.)

To me, Britain is most like an island when a Gaelic-speaking crofter in his Highland glen laments the clearances as if they happened yesterday. Or in the bilingual signs in Britain's archaic tongue and the us-and-them feeling you get all over Wales. There is a sense of island, too, along the Scottish ports; I remember a wintry day in Oban when the wind blew so fiercely the breakers of the Firth of Lorn crashed right across the pavement of the street. In the pub the locals quietly reckoned how many of Oban's trawlers were still out there at sea. All Celtic examples, but there were plenty of Anglo-Saxon ones too. Nobody tugging at a forelock any more, to be sure. But there was that old man in his village on Salisbury Plain, glimpsed tipping his cap to a grand-looking lady as she stepped into her big black car. Author Jessica Mitford, who now lives in California, says the English are "simply besotted with the sea." As on any island, she says, "It's all around them; they're sea people. People confront these horrible dangers whenever there's a storm, and the wives stay behind worrying."

English poetry is full of imagery of the sea. The sense of it is powerful in Matthew Arnold's "Dover Beach":

> Listen! you hear the grating roar
> Of pebbles which the waves draw back, and fling,
> At their return, up the high strand,
> Begin, and cease, and then again begin . . .

Arnold's great poem, written in the 1850s, struck what has been a continuing theme in English writing, the loss of spiritual belief; he uses the image of the sea as a metaphor for the Sea of Faith, ebbing away from the shores of the world. Arnold's response was to seek in human love values lost elsewhere ("Ah, love, let us be true / To one another!"). Robert Browning's "A Toccata of Galuppi's" does not offer even that hope ("What of soul was left, I wonder, when the kissing had to stop?"). Dust and ashes, a Venice that spent what it earned, a darkling plain where ignorant armies clashed by night, all were prophetic. Both poems were written at the peak of Victorian progress and material wealth.

Another island kingdom, Japan, suggests clues to Britain's character. Densely crowded, industrial archipelagoes at either end of Eurasia, both Britain and Japan have a cyclical sense of history, both have cults of manners, both have gone a-conquering, both are shaped by the sea. And both are overshadowed by America as the world's great star-spangled all-purpose dynamic society. The Japanese, too, tried to have an empire; they were stopped. Full of ceremony and dignity, prewar Japanese society was immensely deferential and hierarchical. Just as class-ridden as Britain, with royalty and noble families, Japan even had its own Eton, a special school for peers. Subordination was reinforced by Confucianism and its adage, "Filial piety is the basis of all conduct"; son obeys father, wife husband, worker manager, subject the state, everybody knows his place. To put group over individual interest, the Japanese find, gives them a technological edge. Today, like the British, the Japanese put money into assets and land. There is the same ex-working-class frustration, in the age of robots and microchips, over the unequal benefits from high tech. All this has left the Japanese even more uptight, rigid, and brittle, even if the time is long past when a Japanese intellectual would propose, as one did in the late Tokugawa era, that the capital of Japan be moved to the latitude of London so that geomantically the Japanese could emulate British success.

Blindfold somebody and parachute him into the middle of the shopping mall in Milton Keynes, a postwar New Town northwest of London, and he won't know but that he's been dropped into St. Paul or San Diego. Britain is least like an island when, with the same Crest toothpaste and Michael Jackson videos and Jeffrey Archer novels, it is so transatlanticized, Americanized, McDonaldized that it cheerfully fits what Gertrude Stein said of Oakland: "There's no there there." Never mind, we Americans feel right at home. Stroll down Midsummer Arcade and it looks like every shopping center you've ever seen—Boots, Woolworth's, British Home Stores, Barclays and Midland for banks, W. H. Smith for paperbacks and newspapers, Wimpy and McDonald's for burgers, a Superdrug. In case anybody doubts what kind of theme park this is, the next attraction at the Stantonbury Theatre is—what else?—"AMERICA!" An ex-welder turned mime will do hyped-up imitations of those representative American types—"Crooks, apaches, hard-hats, vultures, joggers, businessmen, presidents, psychopaths, Shirley Temple lookalikes, beachboys, hookers, easyriders, superheroes, assassins . . . !" And just ahead, a billboard proclaims, is 1992 when all over Europe the last tariff barriers fall and a year later, if all stays on schedule, the Channel Tunnel, talked about since 1825, will at last whoosh you from London to Paris, via Dover and Calais, in just a little over three hours. (Dover-Calais takes thirty minutes by hovercraft now.) What is now a narrow river won't really matter at all and the physical insularity of Britain will be just about totally gone.

I've mentioned size or being such a small island; time differs too. In Stephen Jay Gould's *Time's Arrow, Time's Cycle,* the Harvard paleontologist deals with our two ways of seeing time—as a unique arrow, flying from progress to progress, and as an endlessly repetitive cycle. We live amid recurrent days and seasons, unique battles and disasters, and lives going from birth and growth to death and decay. Gould calls "time's arrow" history "an irreversible sequence of unrepeatable events." "Time's cycle" is when:

> events have no meaning as distinct episodes with causal impact upon a contingent history. Fundamental states are immanent in time, always present and never changing. Apparent motions are parts of repeating

cycles, and differences of the past will be realities of the future. Time has no direction.

Time's arrow, says Gould, is the metaphor of the Bible: God creates the earth once, tells Noah to build the ark, hands down the Ten Commandments to Moses on Mount Sinai, and sends Jesus to Calvary to die on the cross. But the Bible also, he suggests, has an undercurrent of time's cycle, as in Ecclesiastes:

> One generation passeth away, and another generation cometh; but the earth abideth for ever . . .
> The thing that hath been, it is that which shall be; and that which is done is that which shall be done: and there is no new thing under the sun.

(Gould quotes a modern version but I've used the King James language of 1611 which I was brought up on and find congenial to time's cycle in any case.) Novelist John Fowles, who brought *Time's Arrow, Time's Cycle* to my attention, suggests that while Gould's book is in the context of geology, there is no better way of summarizing the sense of time that is perhaps the greatest difference between our two cultures.

Fowles:

> For America time is the linear arrow, full of advance and progress (at least potentially); for us, it is circular, always returning (whence our—often foolish—love of ritual in countless social and cultural matters) and why we remain a deeply conservative nation, despite all our celebrated breakouts into liberalism, democracy, and the rest in religion and politics (above all, that marvelous seventeenth century exodus to America). For us, time is obscurely cyclical, not really springing into a future. I suspect this comes anthropologically from our peasant origins and our island past, and in a sense makes us the *most* European country in Europe.

This helps explain why Britain seems so orderly, predictable, while America is a kind of chaos of individuality. "America is total possibility," says critic George Steiner. "And Britain is total remembrance." These words, during a talk we had in Cambridge, suggest Steiner's views on time are the same. He went on:

> There is nothing thought or done or felt here which does not have a conscious and enormous weight on its back of the past. And that is a constraint. It's also an advantage—it gives a certain ironic density, it gives a tolerance which Americans don't have, it means you don't shoot

your rulers, it means you don't have 49 million fundamentalists who believe that the blood of Lord Jesus . . .

"Why *doesn't* Britain have fundamentalists?" I interrupted.

"It's much too ironic, much too tired. They've known too much history. The Messiah has *not* come."

The Weight of the Past

W E CAN SEE this cyclical sense of time in the way the British
look back. Historian Asa Briggs (authority on the Victorian
age, official BBC chronicler, Chancellor of the Open University, Provost of Worcester College, Oxford, a man who likes to
keep busy) finds a few people who will say, "Let's scrap history altogether," but fewer than in any country he knows. (One, an insurance
executive for Norwich Union, met in the dining car of a East Anglia-
bound train, confided, "We are afflicted with this *dreadful* imperial
past.") Lord Briggs finds the affliction widespread: Marks and Spencer published a centenary history of its department store chain a
few years ago; towns like Wickham in Yorkshire celebrate their
1,100th year; in a switch from America, books about the past outsell
books about the future. It may be, he says, because history, good
and bad, is so visible in the present—Buckingham Palace, Westminster Abbey, the Tower of London, the great castles and cathedrals,
but also the derelict dockyards, soot-blackened empty factories, deserted churches, abandoned pitheads. There is a museum quality to
so much of British life. As Archie Rice says in *The Entertainer:*
"Don't clap too hard, lady, it's an old building."

"The visual inheritance of the past is obvious as is our preoccupation with history," Lord Briggs told me one evening as we talked
in his BBC office atop a house on Cavendish Square where Lord
Nelson once lived with Lady Hamilton. "Now when you go beyond
that and ask about how the past and present and future relate, I am
very worried that many of the futures canvassed from time to time
are very unlikely to make Britain any better than it is now."

Lord Briggs takes the long view. In *A Social History of England*
he gives four reasons why Britain failed to keep up industrially with
the United States and Germany after the 1870s and entered its long
decline: the City of London diverted investment abroad and away
from home industry; Britain lagged behind in investment in scien-

tific knowledge and research; as productivity fell, management, trade unions, and education were loudly and justifiably blamed; and there were low incentives for workers—wages and expectations were too low. Lord Briggs puts the blame on the class system.

All true today, a century later. This makes Thatcherism look more like part of what Anthony Sampson in *The Changing Anatomy of Britain* calls "a very old cyclical trend—of reform followed by reaction, of concessions to the poor followed by the reassertion of the rich." Lord Briggs told me:

> A lot of things seemingly being done with success are only superficially successful. Management and ownership of British industry leave a good deal to be desired. Old people are living so long; what are you going to do to make them feel life is meaningful? Computers and robots can take over work, but you've got to find a new pattern of life. The social divides are greater, the confrontations sharper. The differences between South and North, rich and poor, owners and unions, whichever way you choose to put it, are still in conflict.

Sampson concluded that Britain's lasting historical achievement has been "to hold its people together in peace with a sense of identity and mutual respect, to accommodate social change and to provide the political stability on which everything else rests."

Being an island helped, says American historian William H. McNeill. In *The Pursuit of Power* McNeill argues this allowed Britain to do without an expensive, up-to-date, or very large army, as was needed on the Continent. "A navy," he told me on a visit to his Connecticut country home, "when it comes ashore, is no threat to established regimes." Orwell had the same idea. "We hear about military dictatorships," he said, "but when did we hear of a naval dictatorship?" Francis Bacon's notion that a seapower may have "just as much or as little of the world as it wishes" is an old British maxim. The verse, "Cherish merchandise, keep the admiralty / That we be masters of the narrow sea" goes back to Henry V's day. One suspects that their discovery that Britain couldn't have as much or as little of the world, let alone of war, as it wished, is still a grievance to the British.

In *A Social History of England*, Lord Briggs says, "The greatest Victorian boom had ended by 1875, but while it lasted it was striking enough for Disraeli to describe it as a 'convulsion of prosperity.'" Professor McNeill sees its cultural momentum continuing long afterward. He told me:

Britain genuinely ruled the waves until the 1870s. From then on it had trouble keeping up with Germany and the United States. The great days of Oxford and Cambridge lasted longer, up to 1914. They kept sending men around the world to rule it, and of course to rule Britain itself. The Empire was there. The cultural momentum was very strong. Very strong indeed. In some fields Britain is still preeminent in the English-speaking world.

If we look at why Britain had the first industrial revolution, we find a lot of things came together. By 1800, when subsistence peasant agriculture still blanketed much of Europe, Britain was a pioneer in modern commercial farming. Soil liming, irrigation, drainage, and such inventions as Jethro Tull's seed drill banished the old fear of famine. New crops from America, like the potato, maize, and beans, together with horse-drawn machinery, helped make Britain a food exporter. By 1811 only a third of the work force was engaged in farming; huge numbers of country people were free to go to work in the new mines, ironworks, and textile factories.

In 1765 James Watt invented the first steam engine, originally used just to work pumps. His rotative engines, which could turn a shaft and drive machinery, followed in 1781. Small workshops became big factories, powered by steam. Britain had farming (food and fiber for weavers, millers, brewers, leatherworkers), raw materials (coal, iron, tin, copper, stone, and salt), navigable rivers (Thames, Clyde, Severn, Trent, Ouse, Humber), good harbors (London, Bristol, Liverpool, Newcastle), and networks of roads and canals. Industries grew where coal and iron ore could be mined near ports. By the 1830s Britain saw huge rises in the output of coal, pig iron, engineering products, and textiles as its uprooted villagers became miners, dockers, and factory hands.

It was this Industrial Revolution that thrust Britain into its Empire, seeking trade. At first the British just seized strategic points commanding sea routes, especially to India, its most valuable overseas possession. British India and the Princely States under British tutelage were colonized by 1858, Singapore in 1819, Malacca in 1824, Hong Kong in 1842, Natal in 1843, Lagos in 1861, Sarawak in 1888. As early as 1852, Disraeli called the colonies "millstones around our neck."

Queen Victoria's sixty-three-year reign (1837–1901) roughly fell into two phases, each about thirty years long. The first saw political suffrage extended (not without misgivings; Victoria herself declared she would "never be Queen of a democratic monarchy"). As industry grew, so did population; it more than tripled in the nineteenth century, from 12 million to 38 million. (At the height of the Empire in 1861 there were fewer than 25 million Britons, less than half of today's population.) An industrial middle class, confident of progress, came into being, even if by 1867 those with incomes over five hundred pounds a year still numbered only 20 percent of the working population. Its conflict with the working classes (generally those earning below a hundred pounds a year) was the main theme of Victorian literature, as in Dickens's *Oliver Twist* and *Hard Times* or Thackeray's *Vanity Fair.*

In the second phase of Victoria's rule, the birthrate fell. Britain industrially held its own in coal and cotton, but dropped behind America and Germany in the newer industries of chemicals, electrical engineering, even steel. The old coal-fueled steam engines were giving way to new sources of power: electric generating stations and the oil-fueled internal combustion engine. Perkin's synthetic aniline dye, the Bessemer steel converter, the Gilchrist-Thomas basic steel process, and Parsons's steam turbine were British inventions, but by 1914 Germany was producing twice as much steel. Unemployment loomed; in the nineteenth century nearly 13 million left Great Britain for America, Canada, and the colonies, 4 million more from Ireland. Patriotism became more jingoistic in a European mad scramble for colonies; Britain added Nigeria, Kenya, Uganda, the Rhodesias, Egypt and the Sudan, Fiji, and parts of Borneo and New Guinea. Science began to challenge faith. It was the great age of the English novel.

The ruling classes still ruled. The old Whig doctrine kept proving true: concessions can be made without harm to those who make them. Labour elected just two members to Parliament in 1900. British red colored the world map; time all over the world was set by Greenwich, so were maps. Most countries went over to a gold standard run by the Bank of England. Newly popular tennis, golf, and football were British games.

The "Great Exhibition of the Works and Industries of All Nations," held in London in 1851 under the glass arch of the Crystal Palace, was intended by Prince Albert to celebrate Britain's superiority. Instead it marked the start of Britain's decline. It was no longer the workshop of the world. There was an Indian summer of sorts, though. As the British lost their lead as makers and exporters of goods, they found a new way of making money in the export of money itself. Exporters became foreign investors. The typical British capitalist in, say, 1837, the year Victoria came to power, was a factory owner or a railway king. By 1901 the typical British capitalist was, as he is today, a financier, floating limited companies in the City.

In the first half of Queen Victoria's reign there was pride in stable constitutional government, optimism fed by industrial prosperity, and an as yet unshaken belief in industry, self-reliance, moral propriety, charity, and rectitude. Lord Macaulay wrote in his *History of England* (1848–61):

> For the history of our country during the last hundred and sixty years is eminently the history of physical, of moral, and of intellectual improvement.

(So many statues and memorials of Queen Victoria are scattered about Britain, or the world for that matter—two grandiose ones in palm-lined colonial squares in Mauritius and Nassau come most readily to mind, and a very grand one on Calcutta's Chowinghee Road if rioters haven't got to it by now—that one tends to envisage her as larger than life in bronze or marble or stone, plump, looking sternly disapproving, scepter and orb in hand, on a pedestal surrounded by maidens symbolizing "justice" or "dominion" or "motherhood.")

The failures of the late nineteenth century, if Lord Briggs is right, do much to explain Britain's long decline—not a post-imperial one as we often think, but one which began long before that—and the prolonged difficulty of the British in coming to terms with a new place in the world. Few societies have been so class-ridden. Few have been so divided into "haves" and "have-nots." Disraeli first came up with the "two nations" theory in his novel *Sybil, or The Two Nations,* published in 1845 (and keep in mind that the minimum age of ten for a child to work in a factory, set in 1833, was not changed until 1891, when it was moved up a year to age eleven). *Sybil* is much quoted today:

> Two nations; between whom there is no intercourse and no sympathy; who are as ignorant of each other's habits, thoughts, and feelings, as if they were dwellers in different zones, or inhabitants of different planets; who are formed by a different breeding, are fed by a different food, are ordered by different manners, and are not governed by the same laws.

Disraeli meant the very rich and very poor (one guesses the *urban* very poor; Disraeli did not know much about the rural very poor and since he wanted to lead the Conservative Party he did not discuss them). Roughly, with pockets of prosperity and blight on both sides, Britain today is split by a North-South divide running from Bristol to the Wash. It is a bit better in 1990; and it's not new—William Caxton talked about it in the fifteenth century:

> Men of the South beeth esier and more mylde; and men of the North be more unstable, more cruel and more uneasy; the myddel men beeth some dele partners with both.

Indeed, it really goes back to the Romans, who divided occupied Britain into two provinces: a docile South run by civilians and an unruly North held down by soldiers. The victims of decaying smokestack industry today live in the North; the beneficiaries of new high-tech, finance, scientific, and service industries, plus London's cultural and political elite, are in the South. Cross the divide, going north, and visibly the cars get fewer, the clothes shabbier, the people chattier. (You can even see it at the railway stations; compare the crowds at Euston and Waterloo.)

Tony Benn, the grand old man of the Labour Party's left wing, is a compulsive archivist who records and files everything; he would certainly have been a historian had he not become one of Britain's most durable politicians. Anthony Sampson says Benn's populist appeal owes much "to his ability to always appear thoroughly English, reasonable and Christian." I liked him, if not his politics, enormously. Benn, who came up through Westminster public school and Oxford and gave up his hereditary peerage as Lord Stansgate to sit in the House of Commons, devoted a whole morning to giving me his historical views over coffee (which he made himself and served in soup bowls) in the shabby, comfortable drawing room of his house on London's Holland Park Avenue. His father, also a Labour minister, bought it, Benn told me, for £4,600; it is now worth over a million pounds. Thatcherism, with some irony, has made Britain's leading socialist very rich. Tony Benn:

> I think the first thing, when you look at any society, is to take a very long historical perspective. When Mao Tse-tung was asked to comment on the French Revolution, he said it was a little too soon to say. You have to start with the characteristics of this country. First, we're an island. And unlike Continental countries, we've only ever really had three foreign armies on our territory: the Romans in 55 B.C., the French

in A.D. 1066, and the Americans in 1945. Second, we are probably the
only unreconstructed feudal society in Europe.

Britain's feudal inheritance is a favorite Benn theme. No wonder. In a 1989 survey of Britain's two hundred richest people, *The
Sunday Times* found a hundred and fourteen had inherited their
wealth. A quarter of the total were landlords with huge holdings.
Much of central London (all of Belgravia, half of Mayfair) belongs
to the Duke of Westminster. Outside London, hereditary landowners
possess at least 3.3 million acres, about 7 percent of the entire
United Kingdom. (The Duke of Buccleuch still has 258,000 acres, the
Earl of Seafield 184,000, the Dukes of Northumberland and Atholl
and the Countess of Sutherland over 100,000 acres apiece.)

Fifty-five of the richest two hundred went to Eton. Twenty-five
served in the Brigade of the Guards. The two hundred included
eleven of Britain's twenty-five dukes, plus six marquesses, fourteen
earls, and nine viscounts. "The list is absolutely predictable," commented Sir John Harvey-Jones, a retired industrialist we'll talk to
later. He told *The Sunday Times:* "You won't find hard hacks like me
on it. There is no way you can make it into the top two hundred if
you are a professional manager. There are only two ways of getting
onto it: either you have got to have money in the first place or you
build up a business and sell it."

Queen Elizabeth is listed as the richest Briton, with assets of
£5.2 billion (nearly $9 billion), but nobody really knows her wealth;
it could be five or ten times that. The Duke of Westminster came
second (£3.2 billion, or $5.4 billion). The richest entrepreneur was
Lord Sainsbury, whom we'll also interview; one of fifty-three retailers in the top two hundred, his family's holding in Britain's top grocery chain is valued at just under £2 billion.

The Sunday Times compared the occupations of the richest top
ten in the United States and Britain. The Americans included five
industrialists, two financiers, two media families, and one retailer.
Britain's, aside from the Queen, the Duke of Westminster, and Lord
Sainsbury, included a football pools boss, a car dealer, an (American) oil magnate, three food producers/packagers, and a financier.
Said the *Times* editorially: "Not one has grown rich from making
things." It went on:

> No wonder Japan, America and West Germany continue to beat the
> pants off us . . . In these countries people have grown rich through
> industry; in Britain the rich still come disproportionately from those
> who have managed to hold on to their ancestors' land and property.

The newspaper warned that Britain was repeating all its mistakes of the late Victorian age.

Fortunes have been made under Thatcherism. *The Sunday Times* said the number of British millionaires had gone from about five thousand to twenty thousand in 1984–89. But it was not the same story with jobs:

> American society, with its rich, largely self-made industrialists, created 19 million new jobs in the Reagan years. British society, with its wealth still too much in the grip of Eton and Oxbridge landowners, has managed a net increase of fewer than 1 million new jobs in 10 years of Thatcherism.

Another obvious feudal legacy is the House of Lords. Just over eight hundred hereditary peers get seats (no new ones have been named since Churchill, who turned his down). There are about three hundred and thirty lifetime peers and peeresses, a few of them showbiz tycoons and political cronies, but mostly distinguished older professional people and academics who raise the tone of its debates.

Along with all those old Etonians inheriting huge estates (the rapidly appreciating value of land, art, and antiques has evidently offset high past taxes) and its insularity, Britain's political character is also shaped, says Tony Benn, by "a strong sense of class conflict between rich and poor, peasant and landlord." He says we are not as far away from the Peasants' Revolt of 1381 or the English Civil War of 1642–49 as we might think. "Radical upsurges that owe more to Christian liberation theology than to Marxism," Benn told me, "still boil and bubble away just below the surface."

As do many Labourites, Benn blames Britain's post-1870 decline on the Empire. It created "a market-oriented economy in which redcoats kept the market and colonials obligingly bought our goods and sold us cheap raw materials. You went to India and they bought cotton cloth from Birmingham and sold you tea." Benn says British industry slumbered behind this protected market, steadily losing ground.

The British have long memories. Some Scots told me that Scotland is only now recovering from its decline in the 1920s after so many of its scientists and entrepreneurs died, along with the Glasgow Light Infantry, in the trenches of the Somme. For the English, Welsh, and Irish it is the same. Britain is a land of memorials for the fallen dead; you see them everywhere. (I counted twenty-one for the two world wars in London alone, plus many others from the Afghan, Zulu, Boer, Indian, Chinese, Crimean, and other colonial conflicts.)

You hardly meet anybody over sixty or seventy who didn't lose a relative to the mortars, trenches, barbed wire, artillery, machine guns, and mud of the Great War. Or who hasn't heard old men tell of how in Flanders a hundred men with fixed bayonets, who jumped off into the open country of no-man's-land behind an artillery barrage, were no match for a single entrenched man with a machine gun. Or how they would put on gas masks as they got swallowed up in a poisonous greenish-yellow cloud of phosgene or mustard gas. It was pack up your troubles and a long way to Tipperary for three bloody, hellish years of stalemate and attrition. About a million British soldiers died, 60,000 of them on the first day of the Battle of the Somme, July 1, 1916; another 150,000 on March 21, 1918; twice that many were wounded or shell-shocked. (The Americans lost 125,000 lives in the war.)

Remember F. Scott Fitzgerald's description of the Somme in *Tender Is the Night?* Dick Diver, going about the battlefield, stares sadly out at the old trenches and says:

> See that little stream—we could walk to it in two minutes. It took the British a month to walk to it—a whole empire walking very slowly, dying in front and pushing forward behind.

Somebody says General Grant invented this type of warfare in 1865. Dick objects:

> No, he didn't—he just invented mass butchery. This kind of battle was invented by Lewis Carroll and Jules Verne and whoever wrote *Undine* and country deacons bowling and marraine in Marseilles and girls seduced in the back lanes of Würtemburg and Westphalia. Why, this was a love battle—there was a century of middle-class love spent here . . .

The great nineteenth century culture that made Britain what it was had ripened by 1914 and all the sense of obligation, duty, and goodness was turned into pouring armies against barbed wire, machine guns, and shells. The war was three quarters of a century ago. The sense of obligation is still at issue.

It was different in World War II. This was mechanized warfare; the horrors of the trenches were left behind. After Dunkirk, nightly battles were fought in Britain's skies between RAF Spitfires and three hundred-mph Hawker Hurricanes and Germany's Messerschmitts and dive-bombing Stukas. In the Blitz up to four hundred and fifty Luftwaffe bombers a night rained TNT bombs down on London, while its people huddled in air-raid shelters deep in the Underground. In the Battle of the Atlantic, convoys with detecting devices, destroyers, and cargo ships were pitted against Nazi U-boats and bombers. America, "the arsenal of democracy," poured out its Flying Fortresses, Sherman tanks, Liberty ships, trucks, jeeps, armored cars, rifles, machine guns, artillery. American productivity was matched by British invention: Liddell Hart's weapons strategy, Norden gyroscopic bombsights, Sten guns, eight-thousand-pound blockbuster bombs. Scotland's Robert Alexander Watson Watt invented radar, Sir Alexander Fleming penicillin (firmly established by Sir Howard Florey). At Bletchley Park, Alan Turing laid down the theory of the computer while using electronics to break the German code. (Also working side by side at Bletchley were Englishmen like Asa Briggs and Americans like William Bundy, part of the wartime Anglo-American closeness not seen before or since.) Like the Germans' jet engines and the guided and ballistic missiles of their V-2 bombs, radar, penicillin, and the computer were to radically change our lives.

World War II claimed at least 15 million soldiers, 35 million civilians (20 million of them Russians, 4.5 million Poles, 6 million Jews in the Nazi death camps). Britain's manpower losses were great—420,000 (compared to 400,000 American dead), but well below the mass slaughter of World War I. This time the economic blow was shattering: overseas investments went to pay for the two wars; leadership in world trade, shipping and banking passed to the United States.

Slowly in the postwar years came the astonishing discovery that countries that had been turned into piles of rubble were getting more prosperous than Britain. Up to, say, the mid-1950s Britain looked remarkably good. It had shown the world that it knew how to run a great empire with liberty and style and was liquidating it with good grace. Europe was in ruins, scarred by Nazism and communism. Britain, if badly knocked about, had come through with the monarchy and Parliament and all the great buildings intact, and habeas corpus and people not being shot by firing squads and all that. Its welfare state promised a less class-ridden society with better health and education for everybody. The high point was probably Queen Elizabeth's coronation in Westminster Abbey in 1953 (the first live television I and about 20 million other people around the world ever saw; the gritty young Queen, asked if it was too strenuous, famously replied, "I'll be all right. I'm as strong as a horse"). Britain had shown it could keep the leisurely, lovely graces of life and still prosper and be a power in the world. It even, at last (with help from New Zealander Edmund Hillary and Nepali Tenzing Norgay), conquered Everest.

In 1945 the Germans were cold and looking for scraps in their bombed-out cities; by 1960 everybody was talking about the German economic miracle. British young people going abroad started to notice that the Germans and French and Italians were getting better off (the Italians, admired for their *vino* and *La Traviata* and the Sistine Chapel, alarmingly were richer per head by 1985, declared the IMF). Its young also knew that not very long ago Britain had been a great nation. They were surrounded by reminders of it: memorials, monuments, great houses. They knew that glory had departed. *Something* had departed. There was a vague, baffled feeling they were slightly failures themselves.

Timothy Dickinson, then at Oxford, compares the change to a slow loss of oxygen: "There's been no specific catastrophe. It's been like looking into a room where everyone is nodding off and you say, good God, there must be an oil leak or the air supply is running out." Britain, unlike France, Germany, Russia, Spain, Italy, China, or Japan, had never lost a major war. Yet as early as 1940, when it still had its empire and its allies, after Germany knocked out France, it was "brave little England" which was seen as the underdog. "Tremendously telling," says Dickinson. "There has been an impalpable loss of ground, like the encroachment of the sea, come on bit by bit. It's only when you notice that the tree that stood on shore is now deep in salt water and dying, that you know it."

Tony Benn, too, feels the postwar promise came and went. "After the war, with the empire gone," he says, "British capitalism had a short burst of life. Everyone was employed. Tax revenues were buoyant. We could afford the welfare state. We had a short period of welfare capitalism. Which has now long since departed."

We turn now, in the coming pages, to the Mrs. Thatcher phenomenon. To me, her rise to power partly reflected a failure of the nerve. When the postwar social fabric started to tear, amid a stagnant economy and global decline, the public school Oxbridge elite, those of it who were Conservative Party leaders, turned to Edward

Heath, the son of a builder, Balliol-educated on a scholarship, a technocrat who was supposed to save the day. He failed to deliver. Mrs. Thatcher was the result of the feeling by Britain's ruling classes that they really had to strike out. They'd taken Heath, a self-made, lower-middle-class man and that hadn't worked. Now they'd take a self-made, lower-middle-class woman who was considerably shriller and fiercer and more absolutist than Heath.

It transformed the Conservative Party. Formed from the remnants of the old Tory Party (1640–1832), largely made up of Anglican and royalist landed gentry plus their more deferential rural following, the Conservatives in modern times mainly spoke for the interests of business, the aristocracy, the professional and white-collar classes, and farmers. It is often said that Mrs. Thatcher hijacked the Conservative Party from the "estate owners" and gave it to the "estate agents." When people talk about the "new Tory Party," they mean the radical populist voice of the aspiring lower and middle class, the kind of Conservative that gives Mrs. Thatcher 40 to 45 percent of the vote time after time and whom she means when she says "our people" or "one of us." The "old Tories," who are still royalist, Church of England, and aspire to aristocratic tradition—Mrs. Thatcher's codeword for them is "snobs"—have nowhere else to go and while a few have defected, most have to swallow hard and back Mrs. Thatcher too, if uneasily.

This political shift can be seen in the 1987 voting pattern. The Tories got 36 percent of the manual workers' vote, 43 percent of the skilled workers' vote and 54 percent of votes from the self-made, non-college-educated aspiring lower middle class. Among university graduates, the Tory vote actually dropped 9 percent. Moreover, these pro-Thatcher voters were heavily concentrated in the South of England.

The Labour Party on the other hand, founded in 1900 after Reform Bills in 1867 and 1884 gave the vote to urban workers, is the party of trade unions and workers in the mines, ports, and factories of the industrial North and Scotland and the Welsh mining areas. Unlike America's Democratic Party, which also recruited vastly from working men and women, Labour has been unable to hang on to its members as they become middle-class. (Union membership has dropped from 54 percent to 42 percent of the working force over the past decade; this is still way above the 18 percent of American workers who belong to unions.) As the number of miners and port and factory workers drops, so has Labour's membership, down from 650,000 to 295,000 members in 1979–89. The Labour Party's heyday was in the early postwar years when its governments created the welfare state and National Health Service and nationalized the Bank of England, coal, electricity, gas and atomic energy, railways, airlines, and most of the iron and steel industry. Labour's first response to decline was a lurch to the left, then it swung back to pragmatism and the old Keynesian formulas; it was badly split over unilateral disarmament, an issue now clouded by the radically changed future of Europe. Labour's victory over the Conservatives in elections for the European Parliament in June 1989, forty-five seats to thirty-two, put it back in the running, though in spite of a prolonged policy review it still has to fully decide what kind of a party it is going to be.

Middle-class British voters who find the Conservatives too abrasive and too much the party of pushy and shortsighted businessmen, and Labour too working-class-bound and too wedded to archaic leftist nostrums, support the Liberal Party—now confusingly renamed the Liberal Democrats—or David Owen's Social Democratic Party (SDP), which tried and failed to merge in 1985–86. In both the 1983 and 1987 general elections, their alliance got more than 7 million votes. But after setbacks in 1989 local elections, Dr. Owen was left with just eleven thousand party members and three members of Parliament. He admits he can no longer pretend to be a national force. To me, David Owen, in 1990 just fifty-one, is the fallen prince of the piece; a pragmatic moderate, he would get my vote. To face the changes in Europe and the world, Britain badly needs someone like him. But unless he can rejoin the Labour Party he bolted a decade ago, Dr. Owen is a leading actor who no longer has a role on the British stage.

The Mrs. Thatcher Phenomenon

ALL THE BRITISH—left, right, and center—agree that by 1979 Britain's fortunes were at low ebb. The welfare state had failed to fulfil its early promise. In an era of harder economic times, socialism was almost universally in retreat. There was a questioning, if not yet a dismantling, of Labour's postwar social gains. Strikes, lockouts, and turbulence swept Britain as displaced miners, dockers, and factory workers struck back.

"We assumed," says Norman Tebbit, long Mrs. Thatcher's closest political adviser, "that Britain was in a state of decline. We assumed for a long time before Margaret Thatcher came into office that the progress of British society was going to be steadily to the left."

The belief was widespread. Max Hastings, editor of the conservative *Daily Telegraph*, a man in his forties, says:

> I and most of my generation grew up in this country believing that we were going to live in a nation in a state of chronic decline. And that sooner or later socialism would prevail. What is extraordinary today is that far from *Guardian* readers inheriting the earth, I think now it seems more likely, without being too partisan, that *Daily Telegraph* readers, or at worst, *Independent* readers, will inherit the earth.

"Nobody can quite get at the Mrs. Thatcher phenomenon. None of us can," says David Owen, still described, at the time of our interview, as the only opposition politician who looked like an alternative Prime Minister to Mrs. Thatcher. Dr. Owen recalls how bad things had got as she arrived on the scene:

> Certainly I believe that trade union power in Britain had got way beyond itself by the Winter of Discontent in 1978–79. Fuel couldn't get into hospitals. Children couldn't go to school. The garbage wasn't collected. We couldn't bury our dead. The unions were deciding everything.

Dr. Owen, who was Foreign Secretary in Prime Minister James Callaghan's government at the time, said the Labour Party leader couldn't bring himself to crack down on the unions, as the situation demanded.

> Jim Callaghan just couldn't turn against the thing that made him. The idea of rolling back some of the existing trade union powers, particularly the closed shop, was absolutely right. It had to be done. The intimidation, violence, and mass picketing in the coal strike was a fight the government had to take on and had to win.

Dr. Owen, who, like Tony Benn and Norman Tebbit, generously gave me a long discursive interview, said at one point, "In some ways I'm Mrs. Thatcher's out-and-out supporter. The country was right to throw us out in 1979. We could not do what was needed." He explained:

> Jim Callaghan himself personally had many strengths. His one weakness was the trade union movement. It had built him up and was a crucial influence in making him Prime Minister in 1976. That whole traumatic period, January–February 1979, the Winter of Discontent, was like the death throes of a whale really. The Labour Party, the trade union movement, the whole postwar consensus on where Britain should be going, was thrashing around.
>
> Callaghan wanted to reverse the decline of Britain. He wanted Britain to stand tall. He's deeply patriotic. I'm a fan of the man. I love the man. I mean, he made me Foreign Secretary for goodness sake, God knows why. I saw him from very close quarters. There was a moving moment in January '79, when some of us were urging him to go on television. And say something like: "Look, I've been a trade unionist all my life. I'm dedicated to the concept of collective action. But there is no way that as the Labour Prime Minister I can sit back. We can't bury our dead. The ambulances are striking—people can't get to the hospital. And I am prepared to use the troops just to put this thing together." That's what he should have done.
>
> I thought he became a better man in office. He grew in office. She has not grown in office. Jim became more generous, broader in office. But still, politics is a rough, tough business. And he had his moment.

When I met Lord Callaghan himself, one afternoon at the House of Lords, he made much of Britain's need, over the long haul, for a political consensus, based on mutual obligation and trust, between the Tory and Labour parties, industry and the trade unions. The orthodoxy of the postwar consensus was to maintain full employment, with industry and unions cooperating. Mrs. Thatcher confronted the unions and beat down inflation by holding down the money supply and letting unemployment rise sharply. "You see what Mrs. Thatcher has done," Callaghan said, "is to sweep away the old consensus in Britain. But she has not been able, nor has she tried, to establish a new consensus."

Both Max Hastings and David Owen applauded her for this. "Mrs. Thatcher's greatest achievement," Hastings told me, "is that she has broken the postwar consensus that brought us to the dreadful pass in which we found ourselves in 1979." The very word "consensus," much used in Britain, makes Owen feel uncomfortable. His analysis:

> I think this word, "consensus," is a dangerous word. Whether it's right or not historically, I'll leave for historians to judge. But consensus is different from compromise. I think compromise is essential to the art of politics. It's certainly an essential part of the British political heritage. But compromise is when you actually, knowingly, decide to stand down a belief for a wider good or for a wider agreement.
>
> Consensus, I think, is almost stifling of conviction. And it is part of the British decline. I do not think that consensus is a marvelous political virtue. I think compromise is an essential political virtue. I think this country's economic decline could *never* have been reversed by a consensus politician. You had to have a capacity, like Margaret Thatcher did, to take on the establishment.

Dr. Owen is one of Mrs. Thatcher's most balanced critics. He laments much about her personal style and social policies, but gives her full credit for arresting Britain's economic decline.

> One of the reasons the center of British politics has not been able to make so much headway is the implacable opposition of so many moderates toward the Prime Minister. There's a pathological hatred of all things Thatcher. It's a refusal to face up to the fact that reversing the economic decline of the 1960s and '70s did mean some quite difficult, unpopular choices. Things had to be forced down quite a lot of unwilling throats. There was bound to be blood on the carpet. And a certain abrasiveness. But it didn't have to be accompanied by such shallow coarseness.

Early on, one supposes, Mrs. Thatcher spotted the sea change: as smokestack industry died away, so did the Labour Party's support. Between 1945 and 1990, its working-class constituency dropped from about 70 percent to just about a third of Britain's voters. What has grown fastest is Britain's lower middle class. In 1979 it must have looked as if a Conservative Party that neutered union bosses, cut income taxes, slowed inflation, sold public housing to the people who lived in it, and preached self-reliance was just the thing for them. With that 40 to 45 percent of the vote every time, and with the opposition split, she won three elections in succession.

Mrs. Thatcher's brand of radical populism has created tensions within the Tory Party and Britain's establishment, the public school Oxbridge elite. Harold Macmillan, if the grandson of a Scottish crofter, was the son-in-law of a duke. His government, like the old Tory Party, was Etonian and paternalistic. I was in London when Macmillan died; they reran several of his old television interviews. In one, Lord Stockton, as Macmillan later became, said Labour's trouble was that its objective was to turn Britain's proletariat into a middle class and it succeeded. He felt this left it "out of date" and "talking too much about the have-nots." His kind of Tory, formed by a privileged Eton-style youth in the upper classes just before World War I, felt a strong obligation to look after those at the bottom. In 1984 when there was violence on the picket lines at the coal mines, Macmillan spoke in Parliament of "this terrible strike, by the best men in the world, who beat the Kaiser's and Hitler's armies and never gave in."

Mrs. Thatcher, the grocer's girl from Grantham, lower-middle-class, a woman, provincial, had no such qualms. She gave the miners as good as she got. Many British see the 1984–85 coal strike as a seminal event. She accepted high unemployment in the old coalfields, ports, and factory towns to keep real wages going up in London and the Home Countries of Southeast England where her core constituency lies. This enabled Britain to play a major role in international oil, investment, and finance, which it is doing. A memory sticks: the old grandee in his rundown club with its priceless artworks who rings and rings for tea and no one comes. Mrs. Thatcher is right: a great past and a great pride and a great style is not enough in today's tough global economic fight. So she is out there, a Lopahin chopping down the cherry trees.

And the old sense of obligation? "It is not only missing," says Sir Michael Howard, Regius Professor at Oxford when I talked to him and since at Yale, "it's been deliberately thrown overboard." He explained:

> We were *noblesse oblige* like crazy for about three decades. At last there was nothing left to *oblige* with. Where has it got us? By being soft and wet and conciliatory to the unfortunate, we beggared ourselves.

I thought: by being hard-nosed and Adam Smith-like and appealing to individual selfishness as the way to enrich society you can do a lot worse than that. I asked Norman Tebbit about it. We met at his large office in the Palace of Westminster; most MPs are jammed into cubbyholes. Tebbit, whom the *New Statesman* called "MR. NASTY," is a soft-spoken, pale, and ascetic-looking man with granny glasses and a whispery laugh. Somehow his words, which can be crudely put, have a way of going for the jugular. He used to be described as Mrs. Thatcher's most probable personal choice to succeed her until they fell out after he seemed to be endorsing Thatcherism without Mrs. Thatcher. In a 1988 speech to the Radical Society, the Thatcherites' answer to the old Fabian Society, Tebbit took on both Labourites and old Tories:

> It is certainly safe, in the view of the movement to the right of intellectuals and political thinkers, to pronounce the brain death of socialism . . . The middle-class, middle-aged membership, deferential to the class-based structure of the prewar Conservatives, has been pushed aside by younger, sharper meritocrats of working-class origins . . . One by one the bastions of class privilege, intellectual snobbery, producer monopolies, and cartels are falling to the onslaught of that remarkable animal: a radical, populist Conservative Party.

Like Mrs. Thatcher with her "one of us" mentality ("Is he one of us?"), Tebbit talks very much as one from a beleaguered minority, intent on repudiating the established orthodoxies of men like Callaghan and Macmillan alike, above all those voiced by "academic snobs." He has the same hang-up about class; his real enemy, one senses, is the old Britain of Eton and Oxbridge landowners and the "snobbish" intellectuals of the chattering class.

Tebbit told me that the base of Tory support has gone from older professionals and the upper middle class to Social Categories C1, C2, and D, the census classifications for skilled and unskilled lower-middle-class and blue-collar workers. "So there *has* been a social revolution," he said. "And by judgment and luck the Tory Party has ridden it." Tebbit said if Labour ever gets back into power it will have to live with Mrs. Thatcher's achievements. "Tory doctrine for thirty years after the Second World War was that we must take edges off the changes introduced by Labour governments," he said. "Now that's been reversed."

Even if he is way to the right of a socialist like Tony Benn, or even a moderate centrist like David Owen, Tebbit has the same frank and up-front quality; I liked him for it. He is a former airline pilot and the son of a shop manager. Anthony Sampson calls him "the hardest of the hard men" and critics talk of his "Machiavellian machinations." Columnist Peter Jenkins in his 1988 book, *Thatcher's Revolution,* describes Tebbit with relish as somebody the public perhaps "loved to hate, like a pantomime villain . . . He was there to be hissed. 'Oh, no you won't,' 'Oh, yes I will.' "

Tebbit's remark in the aftermath of inner-city riots in 1981, "My father didn't riot. He got on his bike to look for work," became Thatcherism's best-known maxim, "Get on your bike." The London-bound train from Liverpool, with that city's high jobless rate, is locally known as the Tebbit Express. Tebbit has attacked Prince Charles for dabbling in politics, lashed out at Labour leader Neil Kinnock ("a boy doing a man's job"), warned "our European friends" that they are "dangerously weak" on terrorism, and dismissed the use of "Ms." (an "unattractive designation of frequently unattractive women").

When I asked Tebbit what Mrs. Thatcher was most likely to leave behind, he said:

> She will leave when she goes a much more prosperous country. A country in which, contrary to what the socialists say, wealth is far more widely spread. A less class-conscious country with a much less rigid class structure. I love to see those kids from the East End who've become yuppies and got their Porsches, upsetting their elders and betters from the upper classes. To me that's meat and drink.

"What we're really seeing in Britain is what I would call the revolt of the lower middle class," says Peter Jay, the former ambassador to Washington.

Jay told me:

> From very early this century until Mrs. Thatcher, the lower middle classes were a group who came at the end of every queue. And not only did they come at the end of every queue, they were regarded with contempt, both by the aristocrats and professional classes, and by the true working class. Both Conservatives, representing the first, and Labour, representing the second, looked down on this "taxi-driving class," the poor shopkeepers and so on, with contempt. Both ends of the social spectrum looked down on them as nasty and undeserving people with very little education and appalling artistic and cultural standards. They themselves were afflicted with a sort of pathetic snobbery which made them feel it was terribly important to represent themselves as superior to the working class.

Then Mrs. Thatcher came along to champion them. "She is one herself," Jay said. "So is Norman Tebbit. She has been very strident about articulating their attitudes, their values, their interests. And there are one hell of a lot of such people."

Jay said this class revolt wasn't the only reason for Mrs. Thatcher's electoral success. "Politics is like two blades on a pair of scissors and Labour was in an unholy mess." But he felt Thatcherism was a genuine political phenomenon, likely to have lasting social impact.

> She has tapped this lower-middle-class, petit bourgeois feeling that they have been the Cinderella at the feast, they have been regarded with contempt by everybody. And yet they continue to believe in the values she expresses, of hard work and thrift and education.

So in 1979 Britain voted in a more consciously radical government than any that had held power since the 1940s. North Sea oil income, £60 billion ($106 billion) in the ten years from 1979 to 1988, came about the same time. In tune with much of Thatcherism, spending went on the here and now; little was invested in Britain's long-term future. Yet most Britons, if uneasy about it, feel like Sir John Harvey-Jones, the earlier quoted industrialist who has been an outspoken critic of the government; he told me:

> The country has stopped getting worse. This is Mrs. Thatcher's great achievement. I don't like her style and I don't like the price of divisiveness that we are having to pay. But she has done a number of things that even her most bitter enemy, which I'm not, would have to acknowledge have been good for Britain.

Before turning to look at Britain under Mrs. Thatcher, let me say that her aura of invincibility, bolstered by her sure populist instincts and famous confidence that what she does is right, pretty much lasted up to her tenth anniversary on Downing Street, May 4, 1989. Indeed, at the time it looked merely like a signpost flashing past a Thatcherite juggernaut that in her own words would just "go on and on and on." She was brimming with ideas to further reform the National Health Service, privatize the water industry and whatever else the state still owned in Britain. She wanted to spread local Tory control and do something, at last, about Britain's inner cities, welfare, and environment. Never mind faint hearts who worried about the big rise in social inequality and who felt unfettered private enterprise and "get rich quick" market economics in Britain had gone about as far as they could go. There was to be no stopping her.

Then came inflation and a worsening economy, poor polls, Cabinet squabbles—but above all, the collapse of Communism in Europe. Mrs. Thatcher was the first of anybody I heard to say, "The

Cold War has ended. Marxism's had it." The transformation of a revolutionary Soviet Union out to bury us into a nationalist Russia out to copy us has been going on with dizzying speed. Nobody saw the upheaval in Eastern Europe coming. One day the Iron Curtain looked there to stay, impregnable. Then suddenly, it was like the storming of the Bastille in Dickens: "With a roar that sounded as if all the breath in France had been shaped into the detested word, the living sea rose, wave on wave, depth on depth, and overflowed the city to that point. Alarm-bells ringing, drums beating, the sea raging and thundering on its new beach, the attack began." Within the last six months of 1989, at first peacefully, at the end bloodily, Communism crumbled in Poland, Hungary, Czechoslovakia, East Germany, Bulgaria, and Romania, taking with it the postwar order.

Mikhail Gorbachev, when he got it all started, certainly at the time he proclaimed unilateral arms cuts in Europe at the United Nations in December 1988, while pulling troops out of Afghanistan, wanted to buy time to deal with Russia's failing economy and internal stability. With *glasnost* and *perestroika*, letting Eastern Europe move toward free market democracy and trying to bring pluralism into Soviet politics, he set Russia out on an uncharted, perilous path. The Baltic states, Georgia, Azerbaijan, Uzbekistan, and the other non-Russian republics, demanded freedom and an end to Communism too. The British, familiar with the decline and fall of exhausted empires, know how irreversible, if grindingly slow, these things can be.

Marxism won't turn into Thatcherism overnight either. Change, from the astonishing summer of those brave Chinese students and their Goddess of Liberty in Tiananmen Square to the grim winter of hardship to keep Eastern Europe's factories, farms, mines, and schools going, was of such speed and magnitude as to leave anybody cautious. However thrilling its wonders and perils, you can't eat politics.

Think back to 1789. In the beginning of *A Tale of Two Cities,* Dickens seems just as excited and enthusiastic about what is happening in France—the revolt of the hungry against the well-fed, the oppressed against the oppressors—as we are about what's happening in Eastern Europe. We all applaud the rising of the people against the tyrant. Then, to everybody's surprise, the guillotines come out. Dickens despised the Terror; heads never rolled in Trafalgar Square. Disillusioned with the whole nasty business, he turned the Defarges into villains. So we need to reserve judgment. Watch out for the guillotines.

Again David Owen has it about right. He told me at the time of Gorbachev's U.N. speech, "We ought to watch Gorbachev with care. If I were Prime Minister, I wouldn't go over the top the way she's done. Gorbachev is out to make the Soviet economy strong." Russia is still the land of Lenin; capitalism and Communism make what Leninists like to call an internal contradiction. Gorbachev or a successor has to resolve it and shed Communism or he won't be able to revive the Russian economy. Can it be done?

Mrs. Thatcher's post-1989 contradiction, which just may decide her political life, is how to resolve Britain's role in the post-1992 European Community, dreaded monetary system and all, with her own Little Englander instincts to cling to the sovereign nation-state. Everybody wants to wrap up the big new Germany, soon to be united in fact if not in law, inside Gorbachev's "common European home." It could be something like Churchill's "United States of Europe," with a common currency, a common passport, a common parliament, and a common defense. This would go well beyond the highly integrated regional supermarket and trading bloc planned for 1992.

It could take some time in coming. At the last minute, Germany, France, Belgium, Holland, and Luxembourg decided they could not, after all, allow passport-free travel within their borders. It was to happen last January, but all the non-Germans feared a flood of East German settlers. Mrs. Thatcher is against a United States of Europe: "I believe it will work far better if we cooperate together as twelve sovereign states." She wants to go ahead and eliminate Western Europe's last trade barriers in 1992, but without surrendering any more British sovereignty to the European Community's Brussels headquarters. Like every liberal-minded Westerner, Mrs. Thatcher applauds the rising of Eastern Europe's people against repressive Communist regimes. But deep inside her, like the Victorians whose values she extolls and her favorite English writers from Dickens to Kipling, she has no love of foreigners. Her much-revered grocer-alderman father told her in 1942 that France was "corrupt from top to bottom"—for hardly anybody went to church on Sundays—and the Germans were worse still. "That sweet enemy, France" and the Hellish Hun at the gate live on in English minds.

Margaret Thatcher's dilemma is that Gorbachev and George Bush and practically everybody else see the European Community as the core of a future peaceful "common European home." Only by playing its role in Europe to the hilt is Britain going to have big-power influence.

So 1989 was a great year, what some called an *annus mirabilis*, Latin for "year of wonders." John Dryden used the term for the title of a poem about the London fire and Dutch War of 1666 ("As one that neither seeks, nor shuns his foe"); Philip Larkin for one about 1963 ("And every life became / A brilliant breaking of the bank / A quite unlosable game"). Perhaps we can compare it to 1968 or 1945, even 1848 or 1789. Almost certainly for Thatcherism and postwar Britain, or post-Cold War Britain, it was a big turning point. And 1990 promises to be just as eventful.

"My view," says David Owen, "is we're on a slow bend, having been in constant decline, we're on the up. The question is whether or not we're permanently around the corner. And on this the answer has got to be: nonproven."

In politics, Harold Wilson said, a week is a long time. And the last weeks of 1989 were long indeed. This book looks mainly at British society itself, coming back to politics and Britain's role in the swiftly changing new Europe and the world afterward. Americans whom you have never met in your life will confide things on trains, aircraft, or in bars that an Englishman would not tell you on his deathbed. Except when it comes to what ails Britain. Who was it who said the English are never so happy as when you tell them they are ruined? H. G. Wells found the Englishman's favorite topic "adverse criticism of all things British." Maybe it is like having a problem member of the family; even an Englishman will tell a stranger about a psychopathic aunt.

It seems the condition of Britain, this long, worrying experience, is something that haunts all its people. One might say joining Europe might be a way out, if what ails Britain were less of a mystery. What explains the bleakness, the sense that the old way of life is curiously unrewarding? I've mentioned the core of any culture is religion, the answer one gets to the old, old question: if the world and life have a meaning, what can it be? Is Britain afflicted by a loss of spiritual belief? In its way of life? In God? Does lack of faith explain lack of purpose? A chance visit to Eton's chapel, combined with a conversation with a left-wing movie-maker and the failure of a West End play, suggested at least the questions to pursue.

In Eton's Chapel

ONE AFTERNOON I went out to Eton to interview the Head Master, Eric Anderson. I was too early for my appointment, so I went in to see Eton's Gothic chapel. Henry VI had laid its foundation stone in 1445. The verger began to show me around until he was called away to the telephone. The chapel's dimly lit interior had wall paintings of medieval figures on the sides, and looked very long and very high, with a great stone-ribbed vault and buttresses. There was little solid wall, but panels of stained glass in mullioned windows, set in stone; a series of them above the altar portrayed the Crucifixion. I was halfway down the aisle when all of a sudden, with a loud peal, someone began to play the organ. It was Bach and the organ, in a mid-pier at the back, swelled to its full volume. For some time the marvelous music soared higher and higher, like a melodic expression of man's spirit. And I stood and looked at the stained glass and the fan-vaulted roof and the stone art all about and I thought: if there is a center to Western civilization, it must be a place like this.

The next day I was having lunch with playwright David Hare in the canteen of Twickenham Studios where he was editing and cutting a new film of his to star Charlotte Rampling, *Paris by Night*. I told Hare, "People at Eton were extremely nice. Probably the great moment of my stay in Britain so far came as I walked into the chapel. The verger, who was taking me around, was called away. So I was in this marvelous fifteenth century chapel alone. And just at that moment the organ blasted out with Bach. It was like God saying, here you are. And I thought: 'This is the center of Western civilization, if there is a center.'"

Hare looked amazed. "You felt that? I wouldn't locate it there. I wouldn't locate it there."

"Then where?"

"I would have thought the center of Western civilization was more likely to be . . . Well, I would have thought of the NASA space agency. If you actually said, 'Where are the cleverest people in the West, doing the greatest things, and putting them into practice and actually achieving something extraordinary?' What we admire *you* for, what English admire Americans for, is your ability to put intellectual ideas in practice."

"That's science, not religion," I countered. "That's why I said I was in the center of Western civilization. I was in a church. If Western civilization doesn't have spiritual faith at its center, it's hollow. Empty."

"I'd say you'd find more religious sense among men who explore space," Hare argued. "There is a spiritual dimension to the lives of scientists and astronauts which excites me because you can't work in a space probe without it raising all the most fundamental questions about human life. To me Eton is so locked into a particular social system and a particularly narrow way of looking at the world, I can't see it as truly civilized."

When I told this story to David Jenkins, the Bishop of Durham and perhaps Britain's most controversial religious figure, and asked, "Isn't that putting science and technical advance as the final good?" he replied:

> That is indeed so. And that, of course, is the practical atheism that doesn't even know it's atheist. And is possibly somehow the lie in the soul of modern man.

John Habgood, the Archbishop of York, hearing the same episode, looked for the middle ground:

> There needs to be a bridge. If you're simply there for Cape Kennedy and forget Bach, you will misuse your technical expertise in frightful ways. If you simply stay with Bach in the Eton chapel, you're stuck in the past.

I later saw some of Hare's plays and learned he was left-wing— *fashionably* left-wing, "Hampstead left," or what we used to call "radical chic." Even so, his words seemed to exemplify what Reinhold Niebuhr warned about some years ago: "Modern civilization may perish because it falsely worships technical advance as a final good." Hare's plays, like his 1985 hit *Pravda*, or his 1988 *The Secret Rapture*, are about self-interest, sex, power, and money. The most extreme example of this genre, going even beyond Hare's work, was Caryl Churchill's 1987 play, *Serious Money*, an enormously success-

ful satire of corruption in the City of London. *Serious Money*'s final
chorus celebrates Mrs. Thatcher's 1987 reelection and continuance
of her "enterprise culture":

> Five more glorious years, five more glorious years
> We're saved from the valley of tears
> For five more glorious years
> Pissed and promiscuous
> The money's ridiculous
> Send her victorious
> For five fucking morious
> Five more glorious years.

Serious Money, like Hare's satires, packed them in. In contrast,
Ronald Harwood's *J. J. Farr,* a deeply serious play, closed in late
1987 after barely half-filling its theater for five weeks. As columnist
Bernard Levin, who tried to save the play, wrote in *The Times:*

> It is set in a curiously suspended world, a kind of rest-home where
> Catholic priests who have lost their faith, or are seeking it, may talk,
> reflect, explore, suffer, be healed—all without commitment or obliga-
> tion.
>   When I saw *J. J. Farr,* the Phoenix Theatre was far from full. . . .
> The reception of the play has emphasized what anyone who ever treats
> of matters of the spirit will now; that for many, in our enervated day,
> God is a four-letter word.

The play's hero, played in the 1987 production by Albert Finney,
is an ex-priest who has been kidnapped by Arab terrorists and kept
hostage for months, being beaten and tortured in his captivity. Released and back in England as the curtain rises, Farr gradually re-
veals to the other priests how he returned to belief after performing
the final sacrament for a dying colleague in conditions of appalling
horror. He finds them unable to deal with it.

In the play's climactic scene, Farr tries to calm an atheist among
them (Bob Peck), who when Farr recants his atheism, goes to pieces
and tries to kill himself by slashing his wrists. (A bit of the blood got
spattered on my shirt down in the front row.) The injured man, half
in shock, murmurs broken phrases like "Bleak world, mine. And
yours. Don't say anything. Don't want arguments. Or comfort. Or
help. Or forgiveness. Or creeds. Or salvation . . ." But Farr does try
to comfort him in a moving statement of regained faith. Finney is
such an intense, mesmeric performer, even from just a few feet
away you couldn't tell he was acting:

> In a cage, an animal tortured by animals, I had this—I don't want to
> make too much of it—but this—image: in the world, with all its terror
> and pain and horror, there are scales tipped in favor of harmony,
> beauty, love, goodness, all the things you affect to deny . . . The bal-
> ance of goodness is slight but it exists outside of us, not our making—

Bernard Levin wrote in his *Times* piece, "If London lets *J. J. Farr*
go, London ought to be ashamed of itself." He told me over breakfast one morning at Selfridges Hotel that he believed "a first-rate
playwright, grappling with themes as important as that, ought to
find an audience." Levin felt it might do better in Chicago or New
York. "The American attitude toward religion is quite different from
the British. I suspect it would interest Americans far more."

Ronald Harwood himself, who also wrote *The Dresser*, interviewed in his Chelsea home, was baffled by the play's reception. "It
seems to me," he said, "that most people have a longing to experience or sense something outside themselves, however that's described or imagined. Not necessarily a God figure, but some spiritual dimension." Harwood, who is Jewish and South African—he'd
come to England as a young man and once was the dresser of Sir
Donald Wolfit—said *J. J. Farr* grew out of an interest in all forms of
extremism.

> Obviously terrorism is an extremist theme. But so are certain religious
> attitudes extreme. What I was trying to do with *Farr* was to say there
> was perhaps a way of approaching the world where spirituality can be
> detected in all things. I mean it's an ancient human trait, isn't it, that
> everything man did he believed had spiritual value? Whether it was
> planting seeds, harvesting crops, or asking for rain. They were all im-
> bued with spirituality. Now that's been lost over thousands of years.

"For us," I said, saying it was still true of most villagers in the
poor two thirds of the world.

"Yes, for us. A majority of mankind still has that spiritual faith. I
meant in the West, this harsh West."

J. J. Farr seemed like an important failure. Like Levin, I'd been
gripped by the play and Finney's performance and went back to see
it again. In Cambridge I asked critic George Steiner about *J. J. Farr*,
saying, "It's about a fallen priest who's lost his religion and becomes
an Arab-terrorist hostage, and he regains his faith."

"We're not in the mood at the moment for people who regain
their faith," Steiner said.

"There's a final beautiful scene . . ."

"Yeah, I know. This strikes English as kitsch. They're not very strong on regaining faith." I said Harwood had made a point of his being South African and Jewish.

"That's right, that's right," Steiner said. "He has seen the real horror. Nobody in this country has. Nobody's knocked on our door at night in a very, very long time, if ever. *Shoah*, the film on the Holocaust, was a nonevent here. I have colleagues in this college, who if they were in this room would say, 'Shut your mouth. I was on the Death Railway. So don't tell me about suffering.' They'd say it was British troops who liberated Bergen-Belsen. They'd say, 'We didn't make any camps. Don't come to us with your bloody *Shoah* stuff. It's not our business. We beat Hitler. We fought on. We held out.' "

"Isn't there a spiritual vacuum here?" I asked.

"It may be there's a vacuum," Steiner said. "But here the vacuum is experienced ironically. In this country growing old, being sick, and dying is not thought to be a mistake or being an unfairness as in America. Here you can be ugly, old, sick and it's generally felt that's what life is all about. And that a day which hasn't gone badly is a very lucky day."

Mrs. Thatcher has called for a return to Victorian values. Many churches that once preached them stand empty, even derelict. Official Christian church membership has fallen below 7 million, down by 1.5 million since 1970. In 1980–85, the number of ministers dropped by nearly 1,500 and over 750 churches closed their doors, or became old folks' homes, restaurants, warehouses, or, in a few cases, mosques. Islam is Britain's fastest-growing religion. In 1986 Muslims, for the first time, outnumbered Baptists and Methodists combined. Some 1 million to 1.5 million Muslims prayed to Mecca in 314 mosques. In 1960 there were just six mosques in the whole of Britain.

Church of England officials say they can no longer count on drawing more than 1.5 million people to Sunday services. (About 3 percent in Britain go, 40 to 45 percent in America.) All told, about 20 million British have some tie to a church (4 million of them Catholic, mainly Irish). For many of the Protestants it is just a matter of baptisms, weddings, and funerals. Why is there no fundamentalist revival, as in the United States?

"Britain's a country more at ease with itself," says Brenda Maddox. "I mean what Britain doesn't have is the Bible Belt, it doesn't have the terrible Puritanism of America." She went on:

I don't think Britain is riven with questions of good and evil. You've got this established Church and the Queen and it's all sort of okay and doesn't demand an awful lot from you. The Church of England has always been lukewarm. It's watered-down Catholicism. It's part of the establishment. It's supposed to marry you and bury you and give you Christmas carols. Not make life difficult. They're not supposed to say: you can't use contraceptives even if you have a pregnancy which will kill you. None of that hard stuff. The C of E is not supposed to make life miserable.

I feel the absence of interest in religion and contention about religion is one of the nice things about British life . . . People enjoy the countryside. Which gives you an enormous feeling of continuity with the past. When you go to Dorset and see the Romans were there and the Beaker Folk and the Bronze Age . . . I mean, you know, the fact that you're just a temporary resident on this planet is always with you.

I said Asa Briggs had talked about feeling the past all about you. "I feel it constantly," she said. "And I find it very enriching. Whereas in America I go to a place and I think: where am I? I can see that person probably needs God. But *here*, living on this island, I just feel part of this great human pageant."

When I repeated Brenda's remarks to the Bishop of Durham, he said, "This has been the educated bourgeois and upper-class approach for years and years and years. It's like Lord Melbourne's remark: 'Things have come to a pretty pass when religion is allowed to invade the sphere of private life.' " The Bishop said:

There is a sort of cross between the dilettante approach and the esthetic approach to religion which the Church of England is supposed to be particularly good at providing. And it has a negative, minimalist end. It also has a more positive though still not adequate end for the people who don't merely go to Christmas service for the carols but because there's somehow more to it than that, but they don't know what the more to it is.

So in the land of Wesley, Fox, and the Salvation Army, religious belief has waned. Moral leadership sometimes seems to fall on the Queen; her yearly Christmas message echoes the Golden Rule: "Treat others as you would like them to treat you."

What happens, I asked Jenkins, when somebody gets sick or old? He said:

You can't tell, can you? Sometimes he or she pulls on the experience of their youth. Often the elderly find they can suddenly remember what they were taught. Or some people panic and go in for what I call superstition. But modern medical science can keep people healthy to quite a late age and oddly enough, a whole lot of people are like Voltaire, but in a twentieth century sense.

"You mean, 'That is all very well, but we must cultivate our garden.' "

Yes, the end is the end. You've lived as long as you can live. Life has always been a combination of sorrows and accidents. Many people, I think, come to terms with that combination of stoicism and mysticism. It gives a certain sense of comfort and purpose . . . But it's very destructive of humanity. It *does* leave people in a vacuum.

While Americans are faced with the same doubts, their churchgoing is rising. The official claim is to 112 million "Judeo-Christian members" in the United States. In the Midwest where I grew up, many rural areas report fully three fourths of the population going to church on Sunday; looking around, except in baseball season, you can believe it. But membership is falling among the mainline Lutherans, Methodists, Presbyterians, Baptists, and Congregationalists, rising in support of fundamentalists. This seems to be an American lower-middle-class reaction to such perceived threats to traditional values as feminism, divorce, pornography, drugs, and abortion. Somehow mainstream intellectuals are failing to articulate their spiritual needs and hopes.

I thought of this in a talk with Hugh Montefiore, former Bishop of Birmingham, when he said, "What worries me most about Britain is the breakdown of the consensus on values." Montefiore spoke of Britain as a "postreligious" society. Later at his palace near York, John Habgood, the Archbishop of York, described Britain as a "secular" society.

Another church leader interviewed, Ronald Bowlby, Bishop of Southwark, in the southern half of London, saw crime, drugs, and family breakdown as a sign that if you take away religion, Britain has nothing to put in its place.

I think we now have a society where a great many people no longer have any basic Christian knowledge or awareness. How many there are, and how much there is still some innate religious sense imbedded there, that's harder to put your finger on. There's been an enormous drop in churchgoing. The core of committed people will soon be too small to enable us to go on being a national church. Soon, unless we make new Christians in a society where people know little about it or reject it and say it's all out of date. There is something hollow about our society. It's not just religious figures saying it. Artists and writers and many others are saying: There's something wrong. There's something missing. There's no heart in our society anymore.

This bleak, rather despairing picture of Britain, says the Bishop of Durham, is rooted in history:

> The industrial revolution and now the pressures of the electronic age mean that the British Isles, perhaps more than anywhere else, are on the leading edge of the breakup of the old communities . . . We have now stopped being a Christian country.

To me, this side of Britain, the progenitor of the English-speaking world that makes up so much of the West, was a startling and depressing contrast to the non-Western two thirds of the world. I'd spent over a quarter century outside the West and in China, Africa, India, Indochina, Indonesia; one hardly ever, and in Muslim villages never, met anyone who had lost their spiritual faith this way. Why in the rich West, and in what to me was its most civilized country, did one find this bleak, hollow disbelief at the center of life?

> I inform the proud Muslim people of the world that the author of *The Satanic Verses* book, which is against Islam, the Prophet, and the Koran, and all of those involved in its publication who were aware of its content, are sentenced to death. I ask all the Muslims to execute them whenever they find them.

In this statement on Teheran Radio February 14, 1989, Iran's fanatic Ayatollah Khomeini—he himself would be dead within months—called for the excommunication and destruction of Salman Rushdie as a *mahdur ad-damn*—one whose blood is unclean. It was the kind of edict not heard in the West since the Middle Ages when devout Christians sentenced heretics and their books to the fire.

Salman Rushdie, born a Muslim in Bombay in 1947, emigrated to Britain when he was fourteen. At public school and Cambridge, and in London's literary set, he was subject to the devaluation of religion by the public school Oxbridge elite. Indeed, the vehemence of the antipathy so many English intellectuals show Mrs. Thatcher may partly be because they have lost their sense of purpose and she has not. A Thatcherite is the villainess in David Hare's *Rapture*. In *The Satanic Verses* an effigy of "Mrs. Torture" is melted at the "ethnic" Club Hot Wax to cries of *"burn, burn, burn!"*; both Hare and Rushdie helped to found, in Lady Antonia Fraser's Kensington drawing room, the anti-Thatcher "June 20th Group."

Just after his books were put to the match in the West Yorkshire city of Bradford in January 1989, Rushdie responded:

Dr. Aadam Aziz, the patriarch in my novel, *Midnight's Children,* loses his faith and is left with "a hole inside him, a vacancy in a vital inner chamber." I, too, possess the same God-shaped hole. Unable to accept the unarguable absolutes of religion, I have tried to fill up the hole with literature.

This is very English. The tradition to substitute literature for religion goes back to Matthew Arnold. In a 1987 interview in San Francisco when he was still relatively little known in America, Rushdie described this loss of faith:

I think really that writing for me fills the place that would perhaps have been filled by religion. That's to say I don't have any religion. And I used to. I mean, I recall as a teenager, when I was about fifteen, you know, it's the football hooligan age, I remember quite clearly the day I ceased to believe in God. And went and ate a ham sandwich to celebrate . . . uh, to ritually consume the flesh of the swine . . . It tasted sensational because it was forbidden meat, you know . . . I ate ham. And the thunderbolt did not strike me and so I proceeded to cease to believe in God the rest of my life.

Which means Rushdie stopped being a Muslim a year after he came to Britain, nearly thirty years ago.

Bradford's fifty thousand Muslims are somewhat distinct from Britain's other two million nonwhite postwar arrivals. Just about all of them are ex-Pakistani peasant villagers, either Kashmiris from around Mirpur or Pathans from the North-West Frontier, brought in during the 1960s as cheap labor to keep Bradford's dying wool industry going for another ten years. Bradford's Mohammed Ajeeb, who in 1985 became Britain's first Asian lord mayor, was present at the book burning. I met him earlier and he told me many of Bradford's immigrants were illiterate and got left high and dry once the wool mills automated or closed. He said, "Despondency and disillusionment are quite common among them."

Unusually for Pakistanis in Britain, the Bradford Muslims cling for dear life to their old peasant dress, village customs, and Islamic values. This may be easier because Bradford is so cut off by the West Yorkshire moorlands (you have to go up to Leeds and backtrack by train to get there). The most popular item at Bradford's Panorama Stores, the only Asian supermarket in Europe (endless bins of saffron and lentils and rice) is a large framed inscription in Arabic of the Islamic reaffirmation of faith: *"La illaha iuallah Muhammadur rasullah."* It was Rushdie's substitution of the derogatory and satanic, medieval Christian "Mahound," a conflation of "Mahomet" and "hound," that set off the book burners. (You get, "There is no God but Allah and Mahound is his prophet.")

Plenty of Muslim writers themselves have been this blasphemous, just as plenty of Christian writers have denied the divinity of Christ and said the Gospels were fiction. It was Rushdie's fate that the passionate but orderly Bradford protests set off much bloodier riots on the Indian subcontinent and these caught the eye of Iran's fanatic imam.

Ayatollah Khomeini, of course, has about the same relation to true Islam as Torquemada did to the Sermon on the Mount. The clergy of Cairo's Al Azhar mosque, the Sunni Muslim world's theological center, hastened to say that while *The Satanic Verses* are "an insult to Islam and a threat to sectarian harmony," Rushdie, like Christian heretics in the Inquisition, should have been given a chance to repent before he was condemned, and should have been condemned only by a court of clergy.

The issue for the West was the principle of free speech; for the Islamic world, blasphemy. Somehow when it comes down to rule of law and respect for human rights, the British seem instinctively to get it right. The free speech defense was best put by Sir Geoffrey Howe, speaking for the British government:

> I do emphasize that we are not upholding the right of freedom to speak because we like this book . . . It compares Britain with Hitler's Germany. We do not like that . . . We are not sponsoring the book. What we are sponsoring is the right of people to speak freely, to publish freely.

Unlike that of many English intellectuals, who stayed silent for some days, as did the Bush Administration, the Thatcher government's response was quick, upright, and unequivocal. Even if one of Mrs. Thatcher's close aides commented wryly, "The thought of Salman Rushdie, who accuses us of running a police state, being under police guard and our protection is a hard one for me to handle." I found myself agreeing with Russian poet Joseph Brodsky, who commented in New York, "I'm afraid the book itself asked for it. It was bound to create a stir among Muslims." In February 1990, after a year of hiding out under police protection, Rushdie appealed to Muslims in a newspaper essay, saying his book was not an attack on Islam, but "a secular man's reckoning with the religious spirit."

The Satanic Verses itself is such a big book (547 pages) and so crammed with fables, folk tales, and savage commentary, it is hard to know what to make of it. ("This is imagination working at quite a pitch," *Granta*'s Bill Buford said in his review. "Joyce has been here before, but not many others.")

Just after the Bradford burning, Rushdie commented, "How fragile civilization is; how easily, how merrily a book burns!" It depends, I suppose, on the civilization. If spiritual faith is what creates and keeps going a civilization, some of the Muslim villages I've visited in the Khyber Pass or Kashmir look a lot less fragile than Rushdie's alienated intellectual set in London. Somebody said of Britain in the 1960s, "Well, the Romans turned into Italians one day." One might say Rushdie joined a set of rather cut-rate Romans turning into a set of highly intelligent Italians, but still Italians, if you know what I mean. The Romans might not have been particularly brilliant, but they had a certain quality of discipline and confidence and adequacy; they didn't give up.

In Rushdie's defense, remember what Pierre Cauchon, the Khomeini of the piece, had to say in the 1431 trial scene in Shaw's *Saint Joan.* He warned that the most dangerous heresy is that which "sets up the private judgment of the single erring mortal against the considered wisdom and experience of the church." What kept Bishop Cauchon awake at nights was the coming Reformation and its freedom of individual dissent. The foundation stone of Eton's chapel was laid just fourteen years after the English soldiers and French clerics at Rouen burned Joan of Arc at the stake.

Rushdie complained that Iran's "clerics" had taken over Islam from "the faithful." I was reminded of American anthropologist Robert Redfield's idea that every culture has its Great Tradition cultivated by philosophers, theologians, and literary men ("clerics") and a Little Tradition that works itself out in the lives of ordinary people ("the faithful"). A gap between the two doesn't matter, said Redfield, as long as everybody shares a common consensus of values. Faithful and clerics have to share "a single cultural universe where people hold the same things sacred."

This applies to Islam, but it can also apply to Britain. The Bishop of Southwark told me he feels alienation from their old values and behavior has affected large numbers of British urban dwellers:

All the people who flooded into the English cities during the nineteenth century were rural. They had an ingrained kind of religiousness. It wasn't particularly formed or churchgoing. But it was there. And it is that which has finally drained away. People say the Church ought to work harder to reclaim the working classes. The truth is it never had them.

What makes a civilization fragile anyway? Historian William H. McNeill, a student at the University of Chicago when Redfield was teaching there, quotes him as saying that any civilization has "psychic limits, which if transgressed, will lead to social breakdown." These destructive forces, says McNeill, are "too many changes, too much buffeting from outside, too many strangers within the gates, too little time to reduce novelties to routine and ritual." I was reminded of Mrs. Thatcher's controversial remark: "People are really rather afraid this country might be swamped by people of a different culture." McNeill has written:

> Perhaps consensus was bound to fail sooner or later in civilized societies, whenever the garment of the sacred became too threadbare to cushion collisions among social classes and other interest groups.

With religion on the wane and so much class division, this, I think, is also highly relevant to Britain.

And so, as the whole Rushdie business suggests, are the ideas of Arnold Toynbee. Let me say, I came across the works of Toynbee very late. I was once in the remote Mexican highland town of Pátzcuaro with nothing to read and it turned out the local library was sort of a literary Rip Van Winkle. It had a lot of books in English, but all published before the 1960s when some UN funding evidently gave out. But all twelve volumes of *A Study of History* were there, as were many of Toynbee's other books of the 1950s, like *Civilization on Trial.*

To anyone coming to Toynbee's ideas several decades late and ignorant of all the disputes about them, he seemed amazingly prophetic. Just as he said was likely to happen, we now have an Islamic revival, a Confucian cultural-economic challenge, and expanding Latin influence. A quarter century spent reporting the Third World, much of it from villages, taught me that Toynbee was right: cultural groups matter more than nationalities. And the core of any culture, its religion, affects everything: how hard people work, how inventive they are, how much initiative they take. Somehow, I suspected, Britain's loss of a sense of purpose and enterprise was related to the loss of religious faith the Anglican bishops described.

And crucial to today's world is that Confucians like the Japanese, Chinese, and Koreans are adapting to modern technology so quickly and the Islamic world from Morocco to Indonesia so slowly (except in arms), even if Islam is the more vital religion in other ways. Toynbee, unlike Oswald Spengler in the 1920s in *The Decline of the West*, saw that such psychic factors matter in the rise and fall of societies in much the same way as material forces do.

Toynbee's ideas on religion, I later learned, were formed both by formidable erudition and by personal experience. In 1912, ignoring the warnings of Greek shepherds, he drank bad stream water and came down with dysentery. It kept him out of World War I. Many of his Oxford classmates died. This left him with a deep ambivalence, both guilty survivor and man saved for a purpose.

His ideas about history, the role of the West, and man's ties to God, while much criticized in Britain, found a receptive audience in America, most notably in Henry R. Luce, publisher of *Time* and *Life*. The first half of *A Study of History* was condensed into one volume by D.C. Somervell and published in the United States in 1947, just after the Truman Doctrine was proclaimed. Luce had already declared this to be the American Century. Toynbee's work suggested that this might be predestined by historical pattern. If so, in its struggle with the Soviet Union was America Rome or Carthage? Luce put Toynbee on the cover of *Time* and *A Study of History* became a bestseller.

It still looked, in those days, as if an American imperial era had begun. In 1960, when I was teaching journalism in India, Henry Luce visited Delhi and invited my students and me to meet him in his palatial suite at the Ashoka Hotel. After an hour's grilling from the determinedly nonaligned Indians, Luce got the last word: "The Russians are out to get us, boys and girls, and we're not going to let 'em. And that's that."

(Another example of how ideas go and come across the Atlantic, getting cross-fertilized and stronger in passage: the day after Kipling's "White Man's burden" was published in American newspapers for the first time in 1899, Congress voted to take over the Philippines, starting us down the long road to Vietnam. "Take up the White Man's burden— / Send forth the best ye breed—.")

Luce tried to get Toynbee to prophesy. He was unwilling. He did argue that the West could save itself from decline if it established some sort of world government (the United Nations, World Bank, IMF, and such are a start), found working compromises between free enterprise and socialism (look what is happening in Britain, Russia, and China), and regained its religious faith (not happening, or not yet; maybe it's going to be the big post-Cold War development now that there is such a yawning ideological vacuum).

William McNeill, who worked with Toynbee in London at Chatham House when he was helping to write and edit *A Survey of International Affairs* in the 1950s, later wrote his obituary for the British Academy after Toynbee's death in 1975. McNeill brought out a new biography of him, *Arnold J. Toynbee, A Life* to mark the centenary of Toynbee's birth on April 14, 1889. In McNeill, I think, Toynbee found his perfect disciple—American, very bright, with serious scholarly capacity, and possessing the same conceptualizing ability. Once famous, Toynbee found himself admired by businessmen and journalists, but not by his fellow British scholars. Still true, I guess. When in 1988 I asked the late Sir Alfred Ayer, the noted philosopher, if he didn't feel Toynbee's prophecy was right, that great Eastern religions like Islam were rising to challenge the technologically superior West on a spiritual plane, he said, "I don't think it's happening at all. Not intellectually. No."

When I asked Professor McNeill about his Toynbee biography, he said that now, forty-two years after Luce launched Toynbee on the American scene, he wanted to give him his due. "What Toynbee did in my view," he said, "was to enlarge the field of history to make it embrace the whole of humanity. In a way that had not been done before. And this was one of those seismic changes."

I asked him if Toynbee's work influenced his own book, *The Rise of the West*, which many consider the best world history by an American. "Oh, it made *my* mind over," he said. He said the difference in his work was that it focused on technology and ecology, not religion. He said he also failed to interest Toynbee in the cultural findings of American anthropology.

"It isn't true that the history profession has followed in his path," McNeill said. "But no one now can think there was no independent history of Asia or any other part of the world before the Europeans discovered it. That's the way it was treated. The timeless East. And he broke that down."

Americans have gone to Britain to confirm their worst fears, learn from its manners, absorb its culture, study its traits, or, like William McNeill, to honor a prophet. What can we learn from them?

Through Our Eyes

RY FREE ASSOCIATION. Think of "England" and say the first ten words that come into your head. I'll give it a go: Rain . . . Oxford . . . theater . . . Magna Carta, cricket, tea, vicar, Scrooge, Mad Hatter, heather . . . It's all part of our lives. Nathaniel Hawthorne's Edward Redclyffe described feeling "the deep yearning which a sensitive American, his mind full of English thoughts, his imagination of English poetry, his heart of English character and sentiment—cannot fail to be influenced by." Henry James, after long years in England, wrote home, "I can't look at the English-American world, or feel about them, any more, save as a big Anglo-Saxon total . . ." Historian Henry Steele Commager in his splendid 1974 anthology, *Britain Through American Eyes*, wrote, "Certainly England (and it was almost always England rather than Scotland, Ireland or Wales) troubled and confused America and the Americans." He asked, "How account for this interest, this anxiety, this passion?"

Commager did find a changing pattern in it, starting with the resentment of the post-Revolutionary era. We often forget how deeply this split families and friends. These words were sent from London relations to one of my Quaker ancestors in New England in 1774:

When men give themselves up to the guidance of their fears, their fashions and their interests, observe the injunction of our Lord, "When ye hear of wars or rumours of wars, see that ye not be troubled." . . . Tenderly we advise . . . Mix not in the various consultations . . .

Then came long years of affection when Americans were still mainly English in origin, as reflected in Nathaniel Hawthorne's *Our Old Home*:

. . . in visiting such scenes as I have been attempting to describe, I had a singular sense of having been there before. The ivy-grown English churches were quite as familiar to me, when first from home, as the old wooden meeting-houses of Salem . . .

The letters of my Quaker ancestors in New England in these years continue to sound very English. One of them writes in 1836 to my great-grandfather, who has gone west to clear new farmland in New York State: "We think thou has made rather a bold shake at last." Back home, someone has come and gone "in the stage," the tavern in the Hollow is being repaired, and

> Elder Eaton has hired a gentleman from Hamilton to teach school in the basement story of the meeting house so this summer there will be six schools in the Hollow, quite a seat of literature, we think.

Another goes west and sees progress all about:

> Stage twice a day and has been for 2 or 3 years. We are approximating the center of civilization and who can say we are not in the focus . . .

Commager says the "Mother Country" syndrome gave way in the 1850s and 1860s to proud independence. This coincides with the settlement of America's Great Plains. From the family letters it is evident that once the uprooted New Englanders migrated to the farmland of the Midwest, they lost much of their English diction and began to take on an American twang. An 1860 diary entry:

> When I was a boy I went to the school of "Lickin' and Larnin'." Our teacher would wield a birch in the air and cut it to make a figure 8, but he couldn't tell the difference between Simon Barjona and Simon Jobarny.

By the time we get to my grandfather, who came to Iowa with his Quaker family in 1859 at age five, we get:

> Good land a mercy! The world can't wait one minute before it changes ten thousand ways. I'm handy enough with a dripping faucet and can tinker with a lawnmower and put the storm windows on. But how in the blazes would you fix one of them new-fangled automobiles?

By now the voice—it is 1905—is unmistakably American. As Americans changed, so naturally did their perception of Britain. What Commager calls "the almost sycophantic veneration of the Brown Decades" was balanced by American disapproval of the class system and of the Church of England as part of it; bishops sit in the House of Lords, while the Queen is the Church's nominal head. To Americans it was an affront that transmitted wealth was more respected than money a man earned with his own hands. If they went to Liverpool or Glasgow or the seamier parts of London, Americans were disturbed—and still are—by the contrast of this poverty and the glittering wealth of the rich. And by the envy that goes with it. Eric Sevareid, who spent many years in Britain for CBS, told me, "Say an American factory worker standing on a street corner sees a guy go by in a Cadillac. He says, 'Boy, one of these days I'm going to be riding around in one of those.' An English worker seeing somebody go by in a Rolls-Royce will say, 'One of these days that son of a bitch is going to be driving a Volkswagen like me.'"

Commager argues—I'm not sure I'd agree—that in the past century the pattern has gone "from the practical disappearance of rivalry between the two great branches of the English-speaking peoples, and the long search for an American identity, to a decisive shift in the center of interest, away from Britain and to the Continent." The search for identity, Commager says, was itself an essential part of the American process of self-identification.

> It was Britain that provided Americans with a meaningful standard either for comparison or for contrast; it was in the approximation to or the departure from things British that the Americans discovered their character.

British decline has always been a favorite American theme. James Fenimore Cooper confidently predicted that "should England give up her dependencies . . . she would sink to a second rate power in twenty years." Hawthorne saw Westminster Abbey as the "glory of a declining empire." Ralph Waldo Emerson in *English Traits* prophesied that "England, an old and exhausted island, must one day be contented, like other parents, to be strong only in her children." Even at the height of Empire many agreed with Kipling, who wrote Cecil Rhodes in 1901: "England is a stuffy little place, mentally, morally and physically."

In Commager's anthology, we have George III, from his throne in the House of Lords, conceding the North American Colonies to be "free and independent States":

> Religion, language, interests and affection may, and I hope will, yet prove a bond of permanent union between the two countries.

The "special relationship" was born, though Abigail Adams, as the American minister's wife, found the London court frigidly polite. "Studied civility and disguised coldness," she wrote a friend at home, "cover malignant hearts." Many were to feel of the Englishman, as did George Santayana in 1920, "He carries the English weather in his heart wherever he goes . . ." But Samuel Eliot Morison bid a moving 1925 farewell to Oxford:

> There will be many moments when I shall regret the soft and sheltered days within Oxford walls, the conversation and the company of the most humane and intelligent group of people I have ever known. My days of wine and roses are over.

A funny, if caustic observer was Margaret Halsey, who went with her husband, a visiting professor, to Exeter in the 1930s. Her *With Malice Toward Some* was for a time must-reading among American academics who taught in England. Mrs. Halsey, who complained about "the relentless subservience of the lower classes" and "that death-in-life which the Britons, with characteristic understatement, like to call English reserve," decided, "What makes an American realize sinkingly that this, by God, is alien corn is the relative scarcity of laughter."

Journalist Vincent Sheean in 1939 describes a Pall Mall club, today, fifty years later, in many ways unchanged:

> These huge, comfortable monasteries where you can eat a very bad lunch and drink magnificent wine with it, in the best English tradition, and sit over your coffee afterwards in a lounge where everybody talks in a discreet undertone, and all the papers published in London, daily and weekly, are to be seen . . . These are the political clubs, the clubs which date from the nineteenth century; the purely aristocratic clubs are further away, in St. James's . . .

These clubs can become part of one's days in London. If a play or opera or dinner ran late, I stayed at various times at the Athenaeum (bishops, scientists, judges), Travellers' (Foreign Office, ambassadors) and Reform clubs (the last the scene of Phileas Fogg's bet in Jules Verne's *Around the World in Eighty Days*). Or had lunch or went for tea, a drink, and an interview at these and the Garrick (actors, journalists) and Brook's on St. James's (intellectual politicians), if not the really aristocratic White's and Boodles. The Athenaeum's hushed atmosphere reminded Kipling of a cathedral between services. Over seventy of its past members are buried in Westminster Abbey. Today the Athenaeum is still an imposing Regency edifice with its gilded statue of Athena, majestic central staircase, and great Victorian library. It is still a gathering place of what the British, half-banteringly, call "the good and the great." But in all the clubs there is an air of musty decrepitude about the dusty bookshelves, tall green leather chairs, and the huge oil paintings of the

Palmerstons and Gladstones, Asquiths and Peels. They have seen better days. The time is gone when someone would say, as did John Fiske, a Harvard Anglophile quoted in Professor Commager's collection, after visits to the Athenaeum and an Oxford high table in 1873, "What could be more grand than the life I have led here?"

Commager also found "resentment against what appeared to be, and often were, calculated snubs, slights and discourtesies; and simply exasperation with the conventionality and complacency of the English mind . . ." He quotes, however, a sentiment of Henry James many visitors to Britain have shared:

> Considering that I lose all patience with the English about fifteen times a day, and vow that I renounce them forever, I get on with them beautifully and love them very well.

Few have been so preoccupied with the English, in mixed admiration and contempt, as Mark Twain, that most American of writers. Commager, who doesn't quote Twain, refers to *The Prince and the Pauper* as "savage caricature," though *A Connecticut Yankee in King Arthur's Court* and the English con men in *Huckleberry Finn* are fonder portraits; all are popular with English children. In *Following the Equator,* visiting the New Zealand town of Christchurch, Twain observes, "If it had an established Church and social inequality it would be England all over again with hardly a lack."

Some fictional portraits are loving. J. D. Salinger's short story of an American soldier who encounters a charmingly self-possessed titled little English girl and her younger brother in a tearoom on a rainy Devon afternoon in 1944, "For Esmé—With Love and Squalor," is a classic example.

Paul Theroux, who has written about England in such novels as *The London Embassy* and *The Black House,* has deeply mixed feelings about it. He may say Britain is living in and off its past, but his wife is English, two sons were educated at Westminster, a famous public school, and one is at Oxford and the other at Cambridge. He wrote *The Kingdom by the Sea,* Theroux told me, because "I was really trying to make an effort to unburden myself. I'd lived here for eleven years then. I was trying to see: Who are these people? What are they all about? What goes on here? Who are they?"

. . . The English were great craftsmen but poor mass-producers of goods. They were brilliant at running a corner shop, but failures when they tried their hand at supermarkets. Perhaps this had something to do with their sense of anonymity? Person to person, I found them truthful and efficient and humane. But anonymity made them lazy, dishonest, and aggressive. Hidden in his car, the Englishman was often impatient to the point of being murderous; over the phone, he was unhelpful and frequently rude. They were not timid, but shy; shyness made them tolerant, but it also gave them a grudge against foreigners, whom they regarded as boomers and show-offs . . . But the same qualities that made English people seem stubborn and secretive made them, face to face, reliable and true to their word.

Often Theroux is lighthearted:

. . . And I thought: . . . They don't give you bags in supermarkets! They say sorry when you step on their toes! Their government makes them get a hundred-dollar license every year for watching television! They issue drivers' licenses that are valid for thirty or forty years— mine expires in the year 2011! They charge you for matches when you buy cigarettes! They smoke on buses! They drive on the left! . . . They call their houses Holmleigh and Sparrow View! . . . They live in Barking and Dorking and Shellow Bowells! They have amazing names, like Mr. Eatwell and Lady Inkpen and Major Twaddle and Miss Tosh . . .

He might have added those TV weather forecasts which are always the same: "A little rain and drizzle from time to time." (Just like so many American weathermen tend to be black, in Britain many are Scots.)

Henry Steele Commager himself, in a 1948 essay written for the centenary of Emerson's *English Traits,* warmly analyzed the English character. By then he had taught American history at both Oxford and Cambridge. He put tenacity first: "Come hell or high water, the Englishman remains imperturbably English . . . Nothing will make him false to his word or discourteous to his guest; nothing will keep him from his tea or change his cooking."

Emerson had written, "England is the land of mixture and surprise." Commager listed such paradoxes: the English are globetrotters and gardeners; democratic but class-conscious; peaceful but bad enemies; allegedly humorless, but gave us Gilbert and Sullivan; law-abiding but the best crime and mystery writers; conformists but passionate individualists.

They do not smoke where smoking is forbidden, or walk on grass in defiance of signs, nor do they dabble in the black market or try to evade payments in their income tax, or get out of place in a queue.

Indeed, Commager tellingly observes, "It is sometimes hard to avoid the feeling that the Englishman likes standing in queues, and that a single Englishman forms a queue automatically."

Another of his insights is the English paradox of being intensely conservative (judges wear wigs, the feudal customs of Oxbridge) and yet the most adventuresome of people (exploring remote islands, mountains, deserts, discovering the sources of the Nile), while carrying with them their Englishness, even their afternoon tea.

Kingman Brewster, ex-president of Yale, a lifelong Anglophile who served as our ambassador to the Court of St. James's and who died while Master of University College, Oxford, had told me the English still feel assured of their "superiority." Commager found, in a land where tweeds and the umbrella are national symbols, the highest compliment was that a thing was "so English"; he also noted, as the English themselves complain about, a suspicion of success. To Commager, England is a masculine country, "a society made for men and run for men." Still true. George Steiner told me at Cambridge, "You're sitting in a university where there are now 40 percent women and even those 40 percent are in many ways a token." Few Oxford dons bring their wives to dine in a senior common room nor do London clubs generally admit women to lunch (most do for dinner). Yet there are more women MPs than congresswomen (if just 49 of them compared to 609 men in Parliament in 1990; American-born Nancy Astor was the first, in 1919), and ever since Jane Austen and George Eliot women have been among the best novelists.

Americans also voice chagrin at what they call "snobbism" (as does Mrs. Thatcher). Eric Sevareid, who is a native of North Dakota too, told me about going to Britain in 1937 when he was just twenty-four and how, after studying so much English history and literature, he felt "almost like a pilgrim going to a shrine." He was surprised to find Oxford had only one or two chairs in American history.

> This rather astonished me. I was aware that I came from this rather raw place on the globe, but after all my country was already quite clearly destined to be Number One in the world, the richest and strongest. The indifference of the average Englishman to the United States dismayed me. Some of it was reserve and shyness.

Later, Sevareid said, he learned how to cope with the British:

> When I was working for the Paris *Herald* I knew Louis Bromfield, the author, fairly well. He was a big farmer, built like a farmer too, but

still he was a famous man. He said, "Oh, the secret of Britain is when you walk into a drawing room, don't ever ape their clothes or their accent or anything. Just be as goddamn American as you know how to be. That's the only way that they'll respect you."

Once, during the 1960s, a woman at a party asked Sevareid, "What might you be?"

> She was a big horse-faced Englishwoman of formidable appearance and I said, "I'm an American." "That means you're a second-class Englishman," she said. "No, ma'am, it means I am a first-class American." After that she was terribly nice and pleasant, but with some of them you have to do it. Most of them aren't that way at all. But there's still some of that.

Sevareid, who as a CBS correspondent in Britain during the war saw it all firsthand, feels the British handled their loss of power with reasonable grace. "It would be a worse world without them," he says.

But it is the way the English accept social inequality—their class and cultural divisions—that to many Americans is almost a personal affront. Remember how Dickens satirized class-consciousness?

> O let us love our occupations
> Bless the squire and his relations
> Live upon our daily rations
> And always know our proper stations

Class is as deeply a part of the English psyche as the saloon bar and public bar that divide every English pub. If class is a rank or order of society, how many classes are there in Britain? The census, which classifies everybody by the head of household's occupation, gives five, from "I-Professional" to "U-Unskilled," with skilled workers divided into manual and nonmanual. Another market research version, with categories A (high managerial, professional), B, C1, C2, D, and E (manual laborers, dole queue), is used by advertising and the media; Tory politician Norman Tebbit used it in our interview. Professor Alan S. C. Ross, an American, in a 1954 essay, first divided the English by accent and vocabulary into "U" and "Non-U." Ross intended the abbreviations to stand for "University Speech" and "Non-University Speech." The idea was picked up and popularized by Nancy Mitford and U and Non-U entered folk etymology, it just being assumed they meant Upper Class and Non-Upper. Most British probably think in terms of six classes, entertainingly described by

Jilly Cooper in her 1979 book, *Class:* the Stow-Crats (aristocrats), Upwards (upper class), Weybridges (middle class), Teales (lower middle class, the wife is Jen Teale), Definitely Disgustings (working class), and Nouveau-Richards (whom Cooper meanly puts at the bottom). It is a funny book, showing how class attitudes vary to work, sex, houses, food, drink, religion, but above all, language. For example, working-class people often call strangers "dear," "love," or "mate." If the lower middle class says "gentleman" and "lady," for the upper class it's "man" and "woman." Journalist Norman Gelb, a veteran American observer in London, in his 1982 book, *The British*, quotes Tony Benn, born Lord Stansgate, as having told a working-class supporter, "Don't call me sir, my good man."

Accent betrays class, even in the cases of Margaret Thatcher and Edward Heath, who have taken elocution lessons; everybody still knows they come from lower-middle-class backgrounds (the Teales). Tony Benn's accent, no matter how hard he tries to sound like a working man, is irredeemably upper class (he pronounces, for instance, "valet" to rhyme with "mallet," as in croquet, and not as the French or crasser people do). There are two or three upper-class speech defects, such as a lisped *r* so it sounds like *w*, the dropping of *g*'s as in the gentleman's sports of huntin', shootin', and fishin' (as with Dorothy Sayers's Lord Peter Wimsey), and a stridently loud and arrogant bray, almost a shout.

Upper-class accents can be learned; Baroness Blackstone, a Labour life peeress whose mother was a dancer, sounds to the manor born; Lord Jenkins, the son of a Welsh miner, has mastered the lisp. Some, like Mrs. Thatcher with her finishing-school ironed-out vowels and slow, affected enunciation, never quite learn the trick; Sir Ernest Parker, the noted historian, spoke a Yorkshireman's Geordie to his dying day; Lord Curzon, despite years at Eton and Balliol, had a marked Derbyshire accent and never mastered the broad *a*.

When I told author John Ranelagh, who was once on Mrs. Thatcher's staff and is a member of one of England's oldest families, the Oburns, that I thought Mrs. Thatcher and Heath were mistaken to assume such artificial-sounding accents, he said, "Neither would have been Prime Minister if they hadn't. They were paying their dues very publicly." Ranelagh said British society welcomed outsiders; there was a good deal of social mobility "provided they make it very clear they want to play the game." This has been going on a long time. Daniel Defoe's satirical poem "The True-born Englishman" points out what a mongrel people the English have always been, accepting newcomers if they respect the system. The right accent, like the right school and right family, has always been the ruling class's way to let a few new members in and keep the rest in their place. ("We few, we happy few.") One need not be born into it; for the British, to paraphrase Tiberius, high merit is its own ancestor.

At the top of society, after the Queen and the princes and princesses of the royal family, is the aristocracy. It is best defined by ownership of land. Elizabeth herself owns 280,000 acres of Crown Estates, plus another 70,000 acres personally, mostly in stud farms. The aristocracy includes 4 royal dukes, 25 other dukes, 29 marquesses, 159 earls, and 103 viscounts. Then come 550 barons who, like all of the higher peers, are addressed as "Lord."

Below the peerage proper are some fourteen hundred hereditary baronets, with the title, "Sir"; about a third of the baronet families are regarded as really aristocratic. Then come the knights, who just hold titles for life.

The House of Lords today has just over eleven hundred members, a third of them life peers. Most peers, to complicate things, are not part of the aristocracy. And some aristocrats who own vast hereditary estates going back centuries have never held a peerage, or their peerage is long extinct. For instance, the untitled Gatacre family has lived at Gatacre for eight hundred or nine hundred years and is definitely part of the privileged uppermost class. (In Britain if you meet somebody who has the same name as the place he lives it means his family was there before the age of surnames and acquired the place name when people started using them.)

In 1965 the House of Commons vowed it would recognize no new hereditary peerages; none has been created in half a century. The rise in the value of land, antiques, and old masters, and success in overseas investment and banking in the Thatcher years, have made many rich families much richer and offset Labour's punishing taxes of the 1970s. You don't see much of the aristocrats; unlike the royals, always on display, many aristocrats go straight from Eton to Christ Church, Oxford, to their country estates. A few of the old nobility, like the Devonshires, Londonderrys, or Lansdownes, still live very grandly. They do have their stamping grounds in London, clubs like White's or Brook's; at a party at Brook's I met several hereditary peers.

But high-achieving life peers matter more in House of Lords debates; it is famous that in 1911 when an unusually large number of hereditary peers turned up to vote on the Parliament Act, lots of them had to ask the way to the House of Lords; they'd never been there in their lives. People say the House of Lords is little more today than a gentleman's debating society; House of Commons members just call it "the other place," and columnist Hugo Young has dubbed it "the museum of extinct volcanoes." I used to go and listen for hours. It is just as if you took the three hundred or so most eminent elderly Americans, all unelected, and had them debate whatever is before Congress; it can be very edifying.

A peerage is objective fact. What makes an aristocrat is subjective judgment. For instance, the second Earl Attlee, Clement Attlee's son, who went to Southampton University and runs a public relations firm, is not an aristocrat. It seems a matter of land and generations. Lord Sainsbury's great-grandfather ran a milk, butter, and egg shop in Drury Lane. But as Britain's third richest person, chairman of the Royal Opera House, and owner of country estates, Sainsbury probably qualifies. Upper class would be a high-ranking official like a Cabinet Secretary or any hereditary millionaire who came up the public school Oxbridge route.

Links between the old aristocracy and politics pretty much went out with Harold Macmillan. You still have the occasional "grandee," such as Lord Denham, the Conservative whip in the House of Lords. Landed, rich, comes from a long line, writes thrillers, is an expert fly fisherman. Just what is a grandee? A fellow lord explained, "Bertie Denham's word in somebody's ear can get you elected." That is how it works. There are still close ties with the army. The Guards, two elite regiments of cavalry and five of infantry attached to the household of the Queen, are still heavily officered by the aristocracy.

In its day the aristocracy produced some people of great eminence, like Victor Rothschild, the scientist. Bertrand Russell, the younger son of the Duke of Bedford, ranked the same as an earl. His grandfather, Lord John Russell, was one of Queen Victoria's Prime Ministers. A great-great-grand-uncle was the admiral Voltaire had in mind when he wrote in *Candide* that in England "it is thought well to kill an admiral from time to time to encourage the others *(pour encourger les autres)*." A sign of the times is that the Bedfords, after numbering one eminent personage after another from 1530 to 1970, the year Bertrand Russell died, are today just another pleasant upper-class English family.

The real class division—I would even say class antagonism—in Britain today is between the public school Oxbridge elite and everybody else on down. Alan Ross was right back in the 1950s to make the U and Non-U dividing line a university education, even if few universities make the grade. This establishment, overlapping a bit with but mainly a notch down socially from those I've been describing, is an essentially upper-middle-class group of people, often related, who all know each other, went to Eton or another public school, studied at Oxford or Cambridge (or a very few other places in a very few fields), are engaged in the professions or public life, call each other by their first names (Bertie or Tessa, Dickie or Neville, never by their titles, though many of them have them), and are instilled, presumably at a young age at school, with a firm sense of their own moral and intellectual superiority.

It is this establishment, or public school Oxbridge elite, which makes Britain seem so small and focused. It would be a crowded little island anyway. But superimposed on its 57 million people, as one of the elite put it to me, are "probably no more than five or six thousand people *who matter.*" I believe it. Just the small fraction I met have astounding national influence. They constantly air their ideas in books, newspaper columns, reviews, and television chat shows. There is nothing quite like it in America. If somebody comes up with something new, before a day or two is out, everybody hears about it, from Margaret Thatcher to the beer drinkers at your local pub.

One would expect an elite to go into the top A stream of the civil service, into the Foreign Office, the Home Office, the Treasury. Or into finance in the City or teaching at Oxford or Cambridge or a good public school. What is surprising is the way so many go into television, journalism, advertising, publishing, the arts. It is as if Harvard men took over showbiz. This narrowing down of opinion-making helps give London its small-town feeling. Everybody knows everybody else (within that charmed circle of five thousand to six thousand, and my guess is it's much smaller). Things get done in notes, phone calls, a word at lunch along the old boy network. It makes Britain far more concentrated than people outside the country understand. And in many ways shapes our view of it.

In structure, it is not a layer cake—more like several mountain peaks shouting at each other: law, science, finance, the higher civil service, the media, the military. At the top are "mandarins," the professional managers. Never mind managing what. A mandarin moves with ease from running a ministry to an embassy abroad to a bank to an Oxford college to a television channel to a newspaper, even to the Royal Opera at Covent Garden; he runs things (but rarely factories). Mandarins come from the right schools, are highly articulate, often have knighthoods; close to a dozen will be interviewed in this book. Indeed, David Owen chided me for talking with so many. The best way to understand most countries is to focus on a few ordinary people. Somehow this doesn't work with Britain.

Perhaps it has to do with the chattering class (sometimes referred to in the plural though there is only one), an establishment subgroup of journalists, writers, poets, critics, academics, people in the arts—Britain's intelligentsia really. We'll hear a lot from it in these pages. Its continuous public debate is trenchant, fluent, elegant, skeptical, witty, if for Americans a little sharp-edged and flippant. British intellectual life is much less purposeful than American intellectual life, where ideas are expected to issue in consequences. There is a lower level of earnestness; it's like an endless game of tennis. What matters is that it sets the tone and "makes the going" for the whole of British society, to use an English racing phrase about the pace set by the horse to beat.

The chattering class embraces, perhaps surprisingly, both Labour and Tory members of Parliament, if they came up the public school Oxbridge route. And while the establishment espouses enlightened ideas, even its Labour left-wing radical faction is not itself democratic. As I mentioned, a few gifted non-Oxbridge people are let in from time to time. But participation is not generally widened. To make itself more democratic would be to loosen the public school Oxbridge elite's grip on British society. Its members are all very exceptional people. Very able. In no sense must they be underrated. But their instinct for self-preservation, as a group, as a way of life, is very highly tuned.

In his informative book, *The British,* Norman Gelb argues the class system has staying power. He says:

> It is hard for anyone familiar with the British to believe that they are about to shed their class mentalities. Most Britons have too many firm, distinctive, reassuring tribal commitments—to the jobs they do, the words they use, the clothes they wear. But there is a growing realization among them that the antagonisms and cussedness their divisions have stoked up are responsible for Britain's costly inability so far to cope with today's world.

Is there any sign class barriers are breaking down? Jilly Cooper tells how romance novelist Barbara Cartland, a grande dame who is

Princess Diana's step-grandmother—we shall meet Mrs. Cartland later—was once asked the question on British television's *Today* show. "Of course they have," she replied, "or I wouldn't be sitting here talking to someone like you."

From Froggie to Guts and Blood

WHERE CLASS DIVISIONS matter hardly at all, and even cultural differences between the British and Americans narrow to almost nothing, is in the shared literary language of early childhood. "A frog he would a-wooing go" and "This little piggy went to market" are just as familiar to the grandee in the House of Lords as to the Liverpool football hooligan, and as they were to me half a century ago back in North Dakota.

As children we all rode a cock-horse to Banbury Cross, asked, "What are little boys made of?" and formed a church and steeple with our fingers. From our mothers we learned about Dick Whittington ("Turn again, Dick Whittington, turn again!"), King Alfred burning the cakes ("Yet you're quite happy to eat them!"), and the coming of the Vikings. Both British and American schools rang out with children memorizing the same lines: "The curfew tolls the knell of parting day . . . ," "It little profits that an idle king . . . ," "Listen, my children, and you shall hear . . ." Americans read *David Copperfield* and *Treasure Island* and British children *The Wizard of Oz* and *Huckleberry Finn*. Even the authors crossed over; Robert Louis Stevenson lived for a time in California's Napa Valley and Kipling wrote *The Jungle Book* in Brattleboro, Vermont.

It is these shared remembrances of culture and language, much more than history or geopolitics, that really explains the Anglo-American special relationship. What we learn by heart as children—nursery rhymes, poetry, bits of the classics, Shakespeare, and the Bible—makes up a lifelong common body of reference in our minds. As children grow older there's a parting of the ways and even in nursery rhymes there are some transatlantic differences. Here I turn to those splendid sources, *The Oxford Dictionary of Nursery Rhymes* and *The Classic Fairy Tales*, both edited by Iona and Peter Opie. For instance, the English "Ring-a-ring o'roses" becomes the American "Ring around the rosy," just as "Pat-a-cake, pat-a-cake, baker's man" becomes "Patty-cake." While everybody would have early memories of "Four and twenty blackbirds baked in a pie," the Americans would not know, as the British would, "A slipkin, a slopkin, a pipkin, a popkin" or "Over the hills and far away."

The English know the verses as nursery rhymes. We think of Mother Goose, a wholly American legendary being. In the mid-nineteenth century somebody did advance a claim that a Mistress Elizabeth Goose, born in Boston in 1665, was *the* Mother Goose. Just as apocryphal was *The Real Personages of Mother Goose* by Katherine Elwes Thomas, published in Boston in 1930. It claimed, entirely without historical foundation, that Bo-peep was really Mary Queen of Scots; Jack Sprat, Charles I; Simple Simon, James I; Old Mother Hubbard, Cardinal Wolsey; and the lady who rode to Banbury Cross, Queen Elizabeth. MGM even made a short film of *The Real Personages*. I saw it as a boy and for years, until I read the Opies, who disprove the whole thing, I went through life thinking that "Rock-a-bye, baby, in the tree-top" was originally doggerel sung in the London slums about the supposedly shaky reign of James I ("Down will come baby, cradle and all"). I expect many Americans still believe it. ("I've given up protesting at all," said Mrs. Opie when I met her.)

It is true that few of the nursery rhymes were originally composed for children. The Opies say they variously come from old folk ballads ("Old woman, old woman, shall we go a-shearing?"); remnants of ancient ritual ("Ladybird, ladybird, fly away home," in America "ladybug"); echoes of long-forgotten evil ("London Bridge is falling down," which may relate to ancient human sacrifice); old street cries ("Young lambs to sell!"); proverbs ("Jack Sprat could eat no fat" or "If wishes were horses beggars would ride"). Others are legacies of prayers, tavern songs, relics of wars and rebellions, rude jests about religious practices, or romantic lyrics, some decidedly obscene.

A few of the rhymes are definitely of American origin. "There was a little girl and she had a little curl" is usually attributed to Longfellow, an unenthusiastic claimant; his juvenile poems, he said, clung to him "with a terrible grasp." "Mary had a little lamb," perhaps America's most notable contribution to the nursery rhyme, was written by Sara Josepha Hale of Boston in 1830. Several others later claimed to be its author, most notably a Mary Sawyer Tyler, whose spurious case was supported by Henry Ford.

During the Revolutionary War (the War of American Independence to British readers), both colonial and British troops sang

> Yankee Doodle came to town
>   Riding on a pony;
> He stuck a feather in his cap
> And called it macaroni.

It evidently entered the English nursery that way.

The Opies say we know from the Bible and Roman writings that nursery rhymes existed two thousand years ago, even if few have survived.

> I'm the king of the castle,
> And you're the dirty rascal.

is quoted by Horace in 20 B.C.:

> *Rex ecrit qui recte faciet;*
> *Qui non faciet, non erit.*

And Humpty Dumpty appears, of all places, in an ancient Swedish version: *"Humpelken-Pumpelken sat op de Bank."*

A ballad the Opies say was registered in 1580, " A moste strange weddinge of the ffrogge and the mowse," is almost certainly the ancestor of verses my mother was still singing at age ninety-four, not long before her death in 1982. The English version starts: "A frog he would a-wooing go, Heigh ho! says Rowley . . ." My mother's version:

> Froggie would a-courtin' ride
>   Uh-hum, uh-hum
> Froggie would a-courtin' ride
> Sword and pistol by his side
>   Uh-hum, uh-hum

The frame of reference is specifically American:

> He put Miss Mousie on his knee
>   Uh-hum, uh-hum
> He put Miss Mousie on his knee
> Said he, "Miss Mousie, will you marry me?"
>   Uh-hum, uh-hum
> "Not without Uncle Rat's consent."
>   Uh-hum, uh-hum
> "Not without Uncle Rat's consent
> Would I marry the President."
>   Uh-hum, uh-hum

The Opies say the song goes back at least to 1549. In the earliest extant version, it is closer to the American:

> The Frog would a-woing ride
> Humble dum, humble dum
> Sword and buckler by his side . . .

Iona Opie, who, now widowed, lives in what she calls "a Victorian edifice" in the small Hampshire farming village of West Liss, told me, when I visited her for lunch one day, that Americans often have older versions of words and rhymes than the English do:

> Words like "kid," you see. Which is Elizabethan English. "Kid" was a little Elizabethan endearment for a child. My mother in the 1920s, she used to get really annoyed when she heard it. She'd say, "These dreadful American words are coming over with the movies. Kid. They call each other kid." She didn't know it was old English.

Mrs. Opie said my mother's version, more or less what Burl Ives also sang, was likely to be old English, though without the "uh-hum." (Her huge house was unheated and so chilly she kept hospitably asking if I wanted a "jumper," which vaguely brings to an American mind a kind of skirt with bib schoolgirls wear; in England it's a sweater.)

Just why the rhymes change the way they do in the transatlantic crossing is a mystery. For instance,

> Eeny, meeny, miney, mo
> Catch a nigger by his toe,
> If he squeals, let him go,
> Eeny, meeny, miney, mo.

In America becomes:

> Eeny, meeny, miney, mo
> Catch a nigger by his toe,
> If he hollers make him pay
> Fifty dollars every day.

While "nigger" survives in nursery rhymes, the Americans are more squeamish about racial slurs. *Little Black Sambo* has vanished from sight. Agatha Christie's *Ten Little Niggers* became *Ten Little Indians* in America; Hollywood further sanitized the film version into *And Then There Were None*.

"The denigration thing has come over from America," Mrs. Opie says:

> It was you that started feeling guilty. And now we must behave too. We had somebody tearing a page out of our rhyme book when we had *Ten Little Niggers*. But taking *Little Black Sambo* out of libraries is going too

far. And they're taking the rather jolly African chief out of Doctor Doolittle. And he was such a nice character.

In Britain Little Bo-peep's sheep come home "bringing their
tails behind them," while in America they come "dragging their tails
behind them." The American Billy Boy cannot leave his mother, the
British his mammy. In Britain Little Boy Blue sleeps under a hay-
cock; in America it's a haystack. The little pig that goes to market in
Britain becomes a little piggy in America.

One mystery is why Robert Louis Stevenson's *Child's Garden of
Verses* has attained nursery rhyme status in America but not in Britain. Many American children know about the birdie with a yellow
bill who hopped upon the window sill, or:

> Of speckled eggs the birdies sing;
> The sailors sing of Spain.
> The organ and the organ man
> Are singing in the rain.

Brenda Maddox says she read Stevenson's poems to her children in London, adding, "Maybe that was because I was an American wife." (Her husband John, the editor of *Nature*, is English.) "I
always feel now," she says, "and I did with my kids, that I'd never
understood *A Child's Garden of Verses* because you need to be English to know what it meant, you know, in winter to get up by night
and dress by winter candlelight, and all that." Or Scottish since he
was a Scot. But it is true of so many English allusions in the rhymes.

> As I was going to St. Ives
> I met a man with seven wives.

It was a great surprise to go to Cornwall and find St. Ives really
existed (as did Virginia Woolf's lighthouse just offshore). Our Boy
Scout troop in North Dakota roaringly sang, "I've got sixpence, jolly
jolly sixpence!" without anybody knowing what a sixpence was. Millions of American mothers have been at a loss to explain "curds"
and "whey." There was a real Bobby Shafto who died in 1737 and
there was probably a real Jack Horner too. And Banbury is in
Oxfordshire (the Opies suggest it is mentioned in so many rhymes
because Rusher, the printer of the most common chapbooks, came
from there).

The Opies say of "Yankee Doodle," Longfellow's "There was a
little girl and she had a little curl," and Sarah Hale's "Mary had a
little lamb":

Most Englishmen would probably be as ready to swear that they were English rhymes, as would many Americans that "Mother Hubbard" and "Twinkle, twinkle, little star" were genuinely American. Indeed, most English nursery rhymes are better known in the States, and in the case of the older ones, often known in versions nearer the original, than they are in their home country.

Most Americans are sure that Benjamin Franklin is the author of

> Early to bed and early to rise
> Makes a man healthy, wealthy and wise.

In fact, say the Opies, it goes back to England in 1639.

"Oh, where, oh where, has my little dog gone?" is American, originating in nineteenth century Philadelphia as a song for adults. "Three little kittens they lost their mittens, and they began to cry . . ." may be of New England origin. But "Where have you been, Billy Boy, Billy Boy?" popularly assumed to be an American folk song, has English origins as a sea-chanty. (The Republicans used it to taunt William Jennings Bryan in the 1900 presidential campaign.)

> Hot cross buns!
> Hot cross buns!
> One a penny, two a penny
> Hot cross buns!

This old London street vendor's cry is still chanted by children in Minnesota and Kansas who have never tasted a hot cross bun in their life. Mrs. Opie says the buns are a survival of medieval communion wafers. She said children don't really need a meaning: "It leaves a strange wonder in your mind." Hardly anyone would suspect that Gotham, home of the three wise men who went to sea in a bowl, is a present-day village near Nottingham. Or that London Bridge still stands. (An older version, when replaced, was sold to an American and now is out in the Arizona desert.)

> Ladybug, ladybug
> Fly away home,
> Your house is on fire
> Your children will burn.

The Opies say this is a very ancient incantation. In both England and America the little magic-looking insect, black and orange in the United States, is set on a finger while being addressed and blown off; it turns out to have wings and flies away.

During the Depression, American playwright Clifford Odets titled a play *Saturday's Children:*

> Monday's child is fair of face,
> Tuesday's child is full of grace,
> Wednesday's child is full of woe,
> Thursday's child has far to go,
> Friday's child is loving and giving,
> Saturday's child works hard for a living,
> And the child that is born on the Sabbath day
> Is bonny and blithe, and good and gay.

The Opies tell an amusing story about this. It seems when Princess Elizabeth gave birth to a son—Prince Charles—in 1948, the First Lord of the Admiralty, Viscount Hall, declared in the House of Lords: "The baby Prince . . . has come amongst us as a Sunday's child, and we remember the good omen of the age-old saying:

> " 'The child that is born on the Sabbath day
> Is fair and wise, and gay.' "

Oh, no, the Lord Bishop of London corrected him; it should have been, "Sunday's child is full of grace." The Opies: "This started practically a national controversy on what was the correct wording of the rhyme. Many newspapers and readers took pleasure in saying that both of their Lordships were incorrect."

Though the Opies don't deal with it, an extraordinary number of nursery rhymes have been used in the titles of murder mysteries. This does not seem to have happened just by chance. It might be argued that excepting Shakespeare, the Bible, and probably *Alice in Wonderland,* the murder mystery, or crime novel, follows the Mother Goose rhyme as the most widely shared item in our common literature. Titles quoting rhymes, intuitively or by design, really resonate.

Agatha Christie holds the record on this, as in so much else. *Three Blind Mice, Crooked House, Five Little Pigs, Hickory Dickory Dock (Hickory Dickory Death* in the United States), *One, Two, Buckle My Shoe, A Pocket Full of Rye,* and *Ten Little Niggers (Ten Little Indians, And Then There Were None)* most readily come to mind.

Some rhymes get quoted more than others. "The house that Jack built" appears as *The House That Hate Built* and *The House That Fear Built,* plus at least three other variations. "Ride a cock-horse to Banbury Cross" becomes *Ride a Dead Horse* and *Ride a High Horse.* We have *Cock Robin, Who Killed Cock Robin?* and *Who Killed Robin*

Cockland? The child's prayer has yielded *Now I Lay Me Down to Die, My Soul To Keep, If I Should Die,* and *Before I Wake.* Besides Christie's *Crooked House,* there are *Crooked Mile* and *Crooked Sixpence.* Three other authors have used *Three Blind Mice. And Then There Were None* also appears as *And Then There Were Nine* and *And Then There Were Three.* The *Queen of Hearts* has been used twice; *All on a Summer's Day* and *Knave of Hearts* once each. There have been *Ring Around a Rogue/a Murder/Rosa/* and *Rosy. Thirty Days Hath September* has titled three novels, not all of them crime. There have been four *Sing a Song of Murder* titles, plus *Sing a Song of Homicide, Sing a Song of Cyanide, A Pocket Full of Clues, Four and Twenty Blackbirds,* and *Four and Twenty Virgins.*

Then we have le Carré's *Tinker, Tailor, Soldier, Spy,* plus *Rich Man, Dead Man. The Tea Tray Murders* comes from Lewis Carroll's parody of "Twinkle, twinkle little star" ("like a tea-tray in the sky"). There are *Little Miss Murder, One for My Money, Pick Up Sticks, To Market, To Market, The Blood of an Englishman, King of the Castle* (used twice), *The London Bridge Mystery,* and *Eenie, Meenie, Minie— Murder!*

I asked Iona Opie why so many crime writers use nursery rhymes in their titles. She said:

> Everybody uses nursery rhymes for everything. 'Cause they're the most readily available rhymes in everybody's head. They have a deep appeal in some way to everybody. So if you want an example of an old woman or a funny pig or something, the first thing you think of is a nursery rhyme. I mean, people quote them in Parliament because they know every other member will know the allusion.

Not surprisingly, several crime titles come from that most sinister of nursery rhymes, which Mrs. Opie says gives children nightmares:

> Oranges and lemons
> Say the bells of St. Clement's.
>
> You owe me five farthings,
> Say the bells of St. Martin's.
>
> When will you pay me?
> Say the bells of Old Bailey.
>
> When I grow rich,
> Say the bells of Shoreditch.
>
> When will that be?
> Say the bells of Stepney.

I'm sure I don't know
Says the great bell at Bow.

Here comes a candle to light you to bed.
Here comes a chopper to chop off your head.

Bells of Old Bailey, Here Comes a Candle (used twice), and *Here Comes a Chopper* appear as mystery titles. American visitors to London, especially if they are mystery fans, are thrilled to find these churches, mostly in and around the City and East End. Shoreditch, Stepney Green, and Bow Road are stops on the Underground. The Opies say Bow is St. Mary-le-Bow in Cheapside, whose bells might have told Dick Whittington to "Turn again" (so he became Lord Mayor of London).

When we leave nursery rhymes (reluctantly) and turn to fairy tales, we find only a few of the most famous ones are indigenous to Britain: "Tom Thumb," "Jack the Giant Killer," "Jack and the Beanstalk," and "The Three Little Pigs" (with the big bad wolf who huffed and puffed his way to become a popular Walt Disney cartoon character). The poet Robert Southey wrote up "The Three Bears" in 1837, though the story is much older. But "Sleeping Beauty," "Red Ridinghood," "Bluebeard," "Puss in Boots," and "Cinderella" all go back to Frenchman Charles Perrault's 1697 collection of fairy tales. The German Grimm brothers brought us "Snow White," "Hansel and Gretel," and "The Twelve Dancing Princesses," folktales collected in Hesse. And Denmark's Hans Christian Andersen himself wrote, among others, "The Tinder Box" and "The Princess and the Pea." The Grimm and Andersen stories spread to Britain and America in the nineteenth century, Perrault's French tales, some of ancient origin, about a century earlier. The first published version of "Jack the Giant Killer," the Opies say, was most probably in the 1760s.

Fee, fie, foe, fum
I smell the blood of an Englishman
Be he alive or be he dead
I'll grind his bones to make my bread.

This version I carry in my mind from childhood. In 1596 Thomas Nashe in *Haue With You to Saffron-Walden* had it:

O, tis a precious apothegmaticall Pedant, who will finde matter inough to dilate a whole daye of the first inuention of fy, fa, fum, I smell the bloud of an Englishman.

Nine years later in *King Lear*, probably published, according to the Opies, in 1605, Edgar, mouthing snatches of old verse in his pretended madness, voices the lines:

> Child Rowland to the dark Tower came
> His word was still: fie, foh, and fumme,
> I smell the blood of a British man.

The Opies call "Fe, fau, fum" "perhaps the most famous war cry in English literature." (It also appears in some versions of "Jack and the Beanstalk.")

"Little Red Ridinghood" in Perrault's version is eaten by the wolf. The Opies amusingly report:

> Subsequent tellers of the tale, however, have disagreed about whether Red Ridinghood should be killed or saved, and if saved by whom, and if swallowed whether she alone, or her grandmother as well, should be allowed to survive the ordeal.

In the Grimm Brothers' version,

> A huntsman passing by hears the wolf's thunderous snores, goes into the house, sees the wolf in bed, guesses what has happened, and rips open the wolf's stomach with a pair of scissors. Out jumps the little girl ("How dark it was inside the wolf!") followed by the exhausted, but otherwise unharmed, grandmother, and the wolf is then dispatched.

Snow White, in the 1938 Walt Disney version, got a new lease on life when it was rerun all over the world to celebrate its fiftieth anniversary. I saw it first at age seven and again at age fifty-seven. It was intriguing, the second time, to see how Disney chose not to gloss over the more gruesome bits: the queen not only orders Snow White to be killed but wants her heart cut out and brought back as proof; in the woods the trees snatch viciously at Snow White and, again, when the witch is struck by lighting and falls to her doom, Disney chose to linger on the shot of the two hideously grinning vultures descending to presumably eat her remains. Mrs. Opie remembers those vultures. She says, "I have a tremendous admiration for Walt Disney. He knew children needed something frightening as well as having everything happy. For a happy ending, you see." I also noticed, seeing *Snow White* again in a London theater full of English children, how well Walt Disney understood that age of audience. They responded with enthusiasm to the slapstick antics of the dwarfs which to me were corny and humorless but which they found funny and very jolly indeed.

It is interesting that in Southey's version of "The Three Bears"

the intruder is an angry old woman. She jumps out of a window
when discovered and "the Three Bears never saw anything more of
her." In other early English versions the bears debate whether to
hang her, drown her, or throw her out the window. In a rhymed
version, the bears throw her on a fire "but burn her they couldn't,"
and put her in water "but drown there she wouldn't." So they "chuck
her aloft on St. Paul's church-yard steeple" (the same one Prince
Charles in 1988 complained was being hidden by ugly new high-rise
buildings). The Opies say "Silver Hair," an old crone, was transformed into "Silver-locks" (1858), "Golden Hair" (1868), and
"Goldenlocks," before finally emerging as Goldilocks in 1904.

After nursery rhymes and fairy tales, there is less common literature between us. Sometimes, visiting primary schools in Britain, I'd
ask children what they read. Typical was a class of seven- and eight-
year-olds at St. Andrew's Primary School in a suburb of Cambridge.
The slow learners sat around tables on one side of a large, pleasant
room, the fast learners on the other. The headmaster, Derek Nightingale, took me around. Among the slow learners was a little Ban-
gladeshi girl, bright enough but her immigrant parents spoke Bengali at home. Several children were from a gypsy caravan.

Among the fast learners we found everybody knew *The Wind in
the Willows* and *Winnie-the-Pooh*, a few *Alice's Adventures in Wonderland*. Most went to Sunday School. Their parents, who largely
seemed to be professional or white-collar workers, sometimes read
to them.

The smallest children were shy but forthcoming. When I put a
standard query about who read *Alice, Wind,* and *Winnie* to some
unshy twelve-year-olds, there was a chorus of "Yeah!" One boy
asked: "Do you know *Guts and Blood?*"

"*Guts and Blood?*"

"*Fangs of the Werewolf!*" shouted one child.

"*Flesh Creepers!*" cried another.

It turned out all these Horror Comics addicts were also television soap opera fans although one little boy said he was forced to go
to his room upstairs to escape TV if he wanted to read. Another boy,
asked what he wanted to be when he grew up, said, "A shark fisherman and go to Key West." Their favorite actor? "Clint Eastwood!" I
told the headmaster, "A very sophisticated little group. No little
sweet and innocent ones like the seven-year-olds. These are the guts-
and-blood crowd." Mrs. Opie, when I told her about the St. Andrew's
kids, replied, "A parent who is worried about a slow learner will not

mind if they read *anything*. They just want them to read *something*. If one of your children is a slow learner, you're grateful for comics. It's very much a toss-up. A child has no power really. It very much depends on who gives them the books."

London librarians say that many parents no longer send their children to Sunday School; allusions to David and Goliath, Samson and Delilah, Moses in the bullrushes, Hagar in the wilderness, long such a part of the warp and woof of English life, can no longer automatically be assumed.

Yet English articulacy starts young. Brenda Maddox noticed her children, growing up in London, used good strong English from an early age. "She'd say, 'He trod on my foot' and he'd say, 'She spat at me.' Can you imagine kids saying that in America? They'd use three or four times as many words." What struck me was the way mothers, and sometimes even fathers, could be seen engaged in long conversations with very tiny children. They wouldn't just say, "Do this," but explain at great length why. There is just plain more talking to children.

> "I want a clean cup," interrupted the Hatter: "let's all move one place on."

I remember going to St. John's College at Oxford to dine one night; between the main course and dessert we all rose, went into an adjoining room, milled about, and returned to the table again to be assigned different seats as was the custom. One really needs some experience of England, particularly of Oxford's idiosyncratic ways, to fully comprehend *Alice*. At Wadham's high table, when I mentioned "You are old, Father William," I was asked, "Southey or Carroll?" If the Mad Tea-Party and its conversation were donnish, the Queen's croquet ground, the knitting Sheep in her dark little shop, the train carriage all seem terribly English.

> "Now then! Show your ticket, child!" the Guard went on, looking angrily at Alice. And a great many voices all said together ("like the chorus of a song," thought Alice) "Don't keep him waiting, child!"

Hurrying about London on a crowded sidewalk or in the Underground, some phrase from *Alice* would come to mind:

> "Will you walk a little faster?" said a whiting to a snail,
> "There's a porpoise close behind us, and he's treading on my tail."

Or if someone was indecisive at the ticket booth:

Will you, won't you, will you, won't you, will you join the dance?

Again, for the American childhood reader of Kenneth Grahame's *Wind in the Willows* there is the same shock of recognition in first seeing the Thames.

> He thought his happiness was complete when, as he meandered aimlessly along, suddenly he stood by the edge of a full-fed river. All was a-shake and a-shiver—glints and gleams and sparkles, rustle and swirl, chatter and bubble.

Mr. Toad, for me, has always embodied the zest for travel:

> ". . . The open road, the dusty highway, the heath, the common, the hedgerows, the rolling downs! Camps, villages, towns, cities! Here today, up and off to somewhere else tomorrow! Travel, change, interest, excitement!"

Not all the English children's classics work for everybody. I'm not much of a *Winnie-the-Pooh* fan myself, though the brown and furry little bear has won over generations of children, as have Eeyore, Piglet, Rabbit and Owl, Kanga and Roo. They live, like Toad, Badger, and Ratty, in a fantasy world, only A. A. Milne's is presided over by his own son, Christopher Robin.

William McNeill says he doted on the *Pooh* stories, even more than on *Alice*. "They were a very powerful influence on my youth," he says. "But it's probably faded from the current generation. From our nurseries and our primary schools. *The Wind in the Willows* too."

Brenda Maddox takes another view. *The Wind in the Willows?* "Hate it! Hate it!" she cries. "It's because of the Toad business. Mr. Toad and his wonder car. I mean, it's the Toad part I can't stick." A lot of Americans share Dorothy Parker's famous feeling about *Winnie-the-Pooh:* "Tonstant Weader Frowed Up."

"Well, I'm with her," says Maddox. "My kids liked a lot of stuff which I still can't stand."

English minds are full of phrases like Sylvie and Bruno's screams of "Less bread! More taxis!" or "Hellish dark and smells of cheese." A favorite of mine is Ethel's "I am very pale owing to the drains in this house." And once read, who can forget the levee in Daisy Ashford's *The Young Visiters:*

> The earl and Mr. Salteena struggled through the crowd till they came to a platform draped with white velvet. Here on a golden chair was seated

the prince of Wales in a lovely ermine cloak and a small but costly crown. He was chatting quite genially with some of the crowd.

Up clambered the earl followed at top speed by Mr. Salteena.

Hullo Clincham cried the Prince quite homely and not at all grand so glad you turned up—quite a squash eh.

Somehow nine-year-old Daisy achieved universality while Robert Surtees, with *Mr. Sponge's Sporting Tour* and *Mr. Facey Romford's Hounds*, remains a very British comic author. Lord Scamperdale, Master of the Flat Hat Hunt, and his toady Jack Spraggon, hilarious to an Englishman, are somehow too far from our experience:

"Yo-o-icks—wind him! Yo-o-icks—pash him up!" cheered Bragg, standing erect in his stirrups, eyeing the hounds spreading and sniffing about, now this way, now that—now pushing through a thicket, now threading and smelling along a meuse.

It may be that on both sides of the Atlantic we have now seen a generation in which there are no longer a set of sacred texts, core classics that everybody knows. Rudyard Kipling's story "The Janites" tells how all over the world people met each other, akin by the freemasonry of being able to allude to Jane Austen in intimate detail. After Shakespeare, the Bible, and *Alice,* for us this also would be true of Dickens. Such lines as "Barkis is willin'," "God bless us every one!" and Uriah Heep's "I am well aware that I am the 'umblest person going" or Micawber's "in case anything turns up" are part of the American psyche. After seeing the two-part film of *Little Dorrit* in London in 1988, for days people I'd meet reminded me of Flintwinch, Mrs. Clennam, Affery, Flora, Mr. Casby, and Mr. Meagles.

Kipling is another *core* writer ("You're a better man than I am, Gunga Din!"), above all with his masterpiece, *Kim.* I shall never forget the thrill, when I lived in India, of going to Lahore and finding that the old cannon Kim straddles in the opening passage is still there.

He sat, in defiance of municipal orders, astride the gun Zam-Zamah on her brick platform opposite the old Adjaib-Gher—the Wonder House, as the natives called the Lahore Museum.

A few paragraphs later Kim—"Little Friend of all the World"— meets the Tibetan lama who comes to dominate the book:

He was nearly six feet high, dressed in fold upon fold of dingy stuff like horse-blanketing . . . His face was yellow and wrinkled . . .

"Who is that?" said Kim to his companions.

"Perhaps it is a man," said Abdullah, finger in mouth, staring.

Beatrix Potter's *Peter Rabbit*, Albert Payson Terhune's *Lad: A Dog*, Eric Knight's *Lassie*, Anna Sewell's *Black Beauty*, and Thomas Hughes's *Tom Brown's Schooldays* still cross the Atlantic, with *Tom Sawyer*, *Little Women*, and *Uncle Tom's Cabin* coming the other way. But not, I'm told, as once was true, the Leatherstocking Tales, Davy Crockett, or B'rer Rabbit. Franklin Dixon's Hardy Boys and Carolyn Keene's Nancy Drew mysteries, hardy American perennials, have caught on in Britain, but not the equally popular Bobbsey Twins of Laura Lee Hope (Freddie and Flossie, Bert and Nan); nor is Enid Blyton (Noddy and Big Ears) read in America. L.F. Baum's *Wizard of Oz* (and Judy Garland's Dorothy), Walt Disney films (Mickey Mouse must be our best ambassador), "Peanuts," "Garfield," and "Calvin and Hobbes" are popular in Britain, as are Judy Blume's stories of adolescence, Richard Scarry *(The Great Big Airport)*, E. B. White's *Charlotte's Web*, and Maurice Sendak's *Where the Wild Things Are*. But you have to talk to women in their seventies to find English readers of Gene Stratton Porter *(A Girl of the Limberlost)*. Dame Wendy Hiller told me, "I've just caught up with Willa Cather."

Reading itself is in decline just as books themselves are selling in greater numbers than ever before. This paradox came out when the International Publisher's Association met in London in 1988; in the keynote speech George Steiner voiced the theme that over a very short span of history—1550 to 1950—literature was mainly associated with the solitary, silent reading of books. Modern media, he argued, had brought that period to an end.

When we met in Cambridge, I mentioned how the semiconscious use of Shakespeare and the King James Bible in the language of older people, both in America and England, seemed to be fading away.

"Oh, completely," Steiner readily agreed. "There is now a television culture; the book itself is fading. Not just Shakespeare. The habits of long silent reading, of memorization. The habits of being able to parse a sentence. The habits of caring very much about grammar. These are rapidly fading away.

"I don't know the answer to this one. Whereas in most countries —France, God help us—television goes to the lowest common denominator, the quality of much—I don't say 'all' at all—but the quality of much British television is relatively so high there is still in it a kind of literacy. It isn't the old literacy. It isn't the referential and memory literacy. It isn't the literacy of quotation. But in science, politics, social affairs, it's not abject. It may become so. But you can't put the simple equation that television is junk after literary quality." The same may be true of videos. Mrs. Opie says *Richard III* and Olivier's *Henry V* are big hits in her village's tiny video shop. "People are very surprising," she says. "One local plumber is just as likely to be a Shakespeare addict as the grand old lady up the road is to watch Elton John."

My mother, who was born in 1887, the year of Queen Victoria's first jubilee, used colorful language I long assumed was Midwest folksiness. I realize now she was quoting phrases from Shakespeare and the King James Bible, mostly quite unconsciously; they had somehow seeped into her ordinary usage. Often those from the Bible didn't sound Biblical—"eat off the fat of the land," "stiff-necked people," "after my own heart," "no respecter of persons," "fear and trembling," "fight the good fight." It was the same with Shakespeare. He was truly universal. As Steiner told me, "Shakespeare, like Homer. Like the Bible. Like a very few works. It's the English language that carried them with it. It's a fact that in the primary schools of the lower Zambesi and where I've been in China and Japan, you'll study a Shakespeare play. And you study *Alice in Wonderland* and you study a Dickens novel. The language has brought with it its great treasures."

I remember once spending some months in a fishing village on the southern Indian Ocean island of Mauritius. We sailed out into a cove each morning to dive underwater with spears for octopus. The fishermen were Africans but my interpreter, Prem, was the son of a Hindu cane cutter. Though very poor, Prem had memorized lines from Shakespeare at the village school. Sailing to and fro, he used to quote what he remembered as Juliet's words on her balcony, "It is the dark of night. How come you here?" and Romeo's reply: "For stony limits cannot hold love out." Prem liked to compare the island's pudgy Hindu prime minister to Julius Caesar: "Why does he bestride the narrow world like a colossus? We petty men under his huge legs peep about to find ourselves dishonorable graves." Sometimes Prem's memory was a bit faulty, so that Milton's sonorous passage became domesticated in an Indian way by adding "the," with Adam telling Eve, "With thee conversing I forget all *the* time." Many English librarians said children are losing the habit of memorizing poetry. In Milton Keynes I visited a class, "Introduction to Information Technology," at the Lord Grey Comprehensive School. The teacher told his twelve-year-olds, all of them seated at word processors, things like "The machine is not wrong. You are wrong. Press escape to edit mode and go back to command." Green letters darted about the screens. I asked several of the children if they knew any poems by heart. None did. The teacher interrupted, "We want the children to learn how to retrieve and use knowledge, not just keep it in their heads."

Bernard Levin agreed this was an alarming trend:

> I think it's true that for centuries Shakespeare and the King James Bible were the two currents that seeped into the English language. Until fairly recently a literate person—and I don't mean a highly educated person, I mean a person who reads books and can describe his ideas in intelligible language—would recognize a biblical quotation immediately. You didn't have to be an expert biblical scholar to know the holy work; the familiar texts would be part of any educated Englishman's mental baggage. Automatically. And so would Shakespeare. I now find —I quote quite a lot in my writing—I now find even in *The Times* where I write, I get letters from people making clear they did not understand an allusion, Shakespearean or biblical. I couldn't put a finger on it, but it is obviously from younger people.

Levin in 1983 published a book, *Enthusiasms*, which devoted a chapter to Shakespeare. "Towards the end of the chapter," Levin said, "there's a gigantic paragraph which consists entirely of the familiar phrases of Shakespearean origin which most people don't know are of Shakespearean origin. I catalogued some." The paragraph:

> . . . If you cannot understand my argument, and declare, "It's Greek to me," you are quoting Shakespeare; if you claim to be more sinned against than sinning, you are quoting Shakespeare; if you recall your salad days, you are quoting Shakespeare; if you act more in sorrow than in anger, if your wish is father to the thought, if your lost property has vanished into thin air, you are quoting Shakespeare; if you have ever refused to budge an inch or suffered from green-eyed jealousy, if you have played fast and loose, if you have been tongue-tied, a tower of strength, hoodwinked or in a pickle, if you have knitted your brows, made a virtue of necessity, insisted on fair play, slept not one wink, stood on ceremony, danced attendance (on your lord and master), laughed yourself into stitches, had short shrift, cold comfort or too much of a good thing, if you have seen better days or lived in a fool's paradise—why, be that as it may, the more fool you, it is a foregone conclusion that you are (as good luck would have it) quoting Shake-

speare; if you think it is early days and clear out bag and baggage, if you think it is high time and that that is the long and short of it, if you believe that the game is up and the truth will out even if it involves your own flesh and blood, if you lie low till the crack of doom because you suspect foul play, if you have your teeth set on edge (at one fell swoop) without rhyme or reason, then—to give the devil his due—if the truth were known (for surely you have a tongue in your head) you are quoting Shakespeare; even if you bid me good riddance and send me packing, if you wish I was dead as a doornail, if you think I am an eyesore, a laughing stock, the devil incarnate, a stony-hearted villain, bloody-minded or a blinking idiot, then—by Jove! O Lord! Tut, tut! for goodness' sake! what the dickens! but me no buts—it is all one to me, for you are quoting Shakespeare.

After *Enthusiasms* came out, Levin was asked to organize a program for the annual dinner of the Folger Shakespeare Library in Washington.

"It was great fun," he says, "and I got Maggie Smith and Ian McKellen to perform. In effect I wrote a script which was that Shakespearean chapter. And it ended with the two of them tossing these phrases back and forth. What was astonishing is the gasps from all over the room as people began to realize all these phrases were from Shakespeare. They had no idea at all. I was much struck that this was *le tout* Washington and you could hear all over the room jaws dropping as they discovered for the first time that phrases they'd been using all their lives came from Shakespeare. I thought: would it have the same effect in Britain? And my answer was: there's an age line when it would or wouldn't. Because something that gets in your head at age twelve stays there forever."

Aristotle's Rule

ARISTOTLE GOT IT RIGHT. In his view, what matters most for a society's health is its fundamental institutions of marriage, family, and property. He had few illusions about human nature: "Man, if perfected, is the best of all animals; but when isolated, he is the worst of all." Man could change, but only by changing his environment, which in turn would change him: "We cannot directly will to be different than we are." If we look at the family and how it is doing and what kind of houses it lives in, Britain is not doing too badly.

In the United States in 1960–75, there was a huge rise in post-pill premarital sex. The birthrate fell by 38 percent. (In the 1980s the birthrate never got above 15.9 percent or below 15.5 percent.) The divorce rate more than doubled. Full-time homemakers dropped from three quarters to just a quarter of all married women. In 1973, half of all young American women were married by twenty-one, men by twenty-three; by 1990 the age of marriage for both men and women was up by two and a half years. Fewer than one American family in ten fits the old Norman Rockwell image of dad at the office, mom in the kitchen, and tiny tots or schoolkids at home.

In Britain in 1990, more than a fourth of births were outside marriage, nearly five times as many as in the permissive 1960s. A quarter of couples were unmarried cohabitants. The birthrate for women in their early twenties fell nearly 40 percent in 1971–88. One marriage in three ended in divorce by 1990 (one in two in America). Marriages are later; young singles are multiplying. At least 70 percent of British women between age thirty-five and retirement now work, virtually all until babies come, about 50 percent part-time after that. Two-parent families with dependent children now make up just 28 percent of households. And so many mothers work, John Ermisch, the demographer of Britain's National Institute of Economic and Social Research, himself an American transplant, reckons that even fewer than 10 percent of British families fit the old image.

Dirty Den and Angie aside (part of the original *Economist* assignment was to watch the British soap opera "EastEnders" faithfully), British couples stay together better. One explanation for the higher divorce rate in America could be that Americans have a higher standard of conscious happiness. Marriages fail when people feel they are not specifically "happy," a discovery that has broken up tens of millions of American homes. Not that a British marriage is such a dogged partnership, but the British have a much lower impulse to lift up the stones and see what is living underneath in their emotional lives. Hence the American fascination with psychotherapy. A marriage in Britain has to make its way, in the words of Paul Theroux, in "secretive, rose-growing, dog-loving, window-washing, church-going, law-abiding, grumpy, library-using, tea-drinking, fussy and inflexible England." The one-big-happy-family myth was never quite true; as early as 1961 fully 41 percent of British households were made up of couples alone or single people. A quarter of all the British now live alone; 40 percent of adult Americans do.

The enormous viewer appeal of "EastEnders," despite one dreary family crisis after another (its Cockney characters tend to whine a lot), suggests it has a substratum of real angst to work upon. Here's some sample dialogue from a show that ran March 13, 1988. (It is taken not from the script by Gilly Fraser, but is taped and transcribed from the actual broadcast, which varies a bit.) Pauline, her husband Arthur, her elderly mother, and Ken, a visiting brother from New Zealand, are all crowded around the dining table, drinking tea, as they do endlessly.

ARTHUR: *(entering)* Oh, charming. Every time we go in the bathroom, there's no hot water. 'Chelle's washing her hair again. [Michelle, their daughter, lives at home with her illegitimate baby.]

MOTHER: What do you expect me to do? Buy a second bathroom? [Arthur, long unemployed, now has a job in a "convenience" grocery store, open all hours, which is run by a Pakistani family. He says they are having family problems.]

MOTHER: *They've* got family problems! *(She makes a face.)* You let them exploit you.

PAULINE: Yeah, but I don't hear you worrying about all the food he brings us though.

ARTHUR: *(defensively)* They're very good to me. What's the matter with you this morning?

MOTHER: Nobody's got any time for me anymore. You both work. And that girl upstairs . . . No one to talk to.

PAULINE: Honestly, Mum, you're impossible. You did enough talking when Arthur *didn't* have a job.

MOTHER: Well, it's not a proper man's job, is it? Oh, nobody cares for me these days. You'll be sorry when I'm gone.

PAULINE: Will you stop whinging, Mum? I tell you, I wish I was your age. I'd put meself in an old people's home just for the peace and quiet.

ARTHUR: You should be so lucky. When it comes to our turn there won't be any left. They'll all be *privatized*. [He means sold by the Thatcher government to private companies like other state-owned enterprises.] And we'll be in a dust bin. Won't it?

[Pauline, who is a charwoman, goes off to work.]

KEN: She shouldn't have to go out cleaning. Not on top of the rest of it. What sort of life is that for a woman?

Too many people have to scrape by on such menial jobs or live on the dole. Yet they all seem to be proudly British. In 1982 Norman Gelb found that if the TV license was paid up, a racing bet could be made now and then, there was a candy bar for "elevenses," a friendly local pub, and two weeks by the seaside each summer, "most Britons are, despite everything, well enough pleased, thank you, not to be numbered among the foreigners." Today, still living in London, he sees a lot of change. "Though pubs retain a distinctive British flavor," he says, "the increasing, stultifying pervasiveness of the television culture, a sharp rise in the cost of pub drinks compared to supermarket six-pack prices, and perhaps the spread of yobbism have dented the image of pubs as the center of British social life. As for the seaside, though reports indicate the British are beginning to turn once more to domestic holidays, during the last few years they have instead flocked abroad in droves come vacation time, particularly to the Mediterranean coasts of Spain."

In America the baby boom peaked in 1960; in Britain, 1964 (making twenty-six the worst age to be in 1990 when looking for a job in Britain). The post-1971 drop in Britain's birthrate should mean, besides closed schools, fewer petty criminals and fewer football hooligans. It will also mean more badly needed places in colleges and universities, allowing Britain to meet the expanding demand for scientific and technical skills, the shortage of which is one of the big weaknesses in British society. Only in primary schools is the population growing, the baby boom's "echo effect." A big shortage of teachers is expected until the mid-1990s as there are not enough eighteen-to-twenty-one-year-olds. The number of first-time voters will soon fall. There will be intense competition for first-time workers.

Like America, Britain will keep growing as long as babies outnumber old people and immigrants keep coming in. Now with a population of 56.5 million, or a little more, Britain is officially projected to reach 60 million by the year 2025. But Ermisch notes its present birthrate is stuck at 1.8 percent; replacement level is 2 percent. Though 250,000 new residents flowed into the United Kingdom in 1986, enough others left so that the net gain was just 37,000. The present growth may not be for long. If immigration is cut off and the birthrate stays down, Britain will start to shrink (as West Germany already had until the East Germans started pouring in and Denmark and Sweden soon will). For whatever reason (more working women, consumerism, the bomb) enough individual decisions are being made not to have children that the West is no longer replacing itself. America alone seems likely to grow, not from births but from the continued huge influx of Hispanics across its two-thousand-mile southern border and other, legal immigrants. Native-born white Americans stopped replacing themselves in 1972.

In home ownership, Britain is catching up. Thatcherism has made nearly two thirds of British householders owner-occupiers; the number of owner-occupied dwellings has doubled since 1961 to over 14 million. Since Mrs. Thatcher came into office in 1979 private sector houses (169,000 in 1986) made up 82 percent of all house completions. Britain's postwar heyday of public housing is over. Vast, barracklike council housing, some of it high-rise, blights many British cities; Le Corbusier has a lot to answer for. The 27 percent of British households who still live in council housing—58 percent in Glasgow—are stuck—house prices have soared so high in London and the Southeast, it's too expensive to move. One can't live in London on a nurse's salary any more, part of the crisis in the National Health Service.

A difference with America is in style. The American postwar housing explosion was due to veterans' low-interest federal housing loans, cheap new prefab and jerry-built methods of home construction, and the interstate highway system, which ringed many cities with what Americans call beltways. These combined to circle the American cities with sprawling conglomerates of detached, look-alike, "ranch-style" bungalows grouped around glass-and-concrete shopping malls. In Britain, with far less space, the boom took the form of semidetached or terraced houses (the last what Americans call "town houses," now widely catching on in the United States, especially as single-occupant dwellings).

The home in the country is still the ideal in both Britain and America. Most British settle for a house and garden. Here, perhaps, is another cultural difference. In his classic *English Journey*, written in 1933, J. B. Priestley railed against the monotony and "same squat rows" of English housing. He found Birmingham "beastly":

> Possibly what I was seeing was not Birmingham but our urban and industrial civilization . . . It was so many miles of ugliness, squalor, and the wrong kind of vulgarity, the decayed, anemic kind . . . I loathed the whole array of shops, with their nasty bits of meat, their cough mixtures, their *Racing Special*s, their sticky cheap furniture, their shoddy clothes, their fly-blown pastry, their coupons and sales and lies and dreariness and ugliness.

Yet Priestley was no champion of the freestanding home, maybe because he knew England simply lacked enough space for every-body. "I do not understand this passion for being detached or semi-detached," he wrote, "for you can have gardens just the same if the houses are built in little rows." Like all English, though, it is the rural village that he truly loved; he described one in the Cotswolds:

> In this valley was a hamlet, an old church, and the manor house that was our destination, all of them clustered together in a lovely huddle of ancient tiled roofs. The moment we were inside the gate and could see that manor house, I knew that anything might happen now, that we were trembling on the very edge of common reality, that life might turn into a beautiful daft fairytale under our very noses.

Remember the first line in Daphne du Maurier's *Rebecca*, one of the most famous in all fiction? "Last night I dreamt I went to Manderley again." The English manor house, all roofs, gables, chimneys, windows, and doorways, with its rose garden and great elms and oaks, seen across a green lawn or deer park, still has its magic.

In Britain, for most people, housing is politics. A mortgage goes with being a Tory. Pay council rent from a housing benefit and you are Labour, or so it is supposed. Aristotle, the original Thatcherite, argued the stimulus of private ownership is needed for pride and care. He should have seen the vandalism and graffiti of some of the British council-owned estates. (Aristotle had a low opinion of welfare; helping the weak and lazy with state subsidies, he wrote, was "like pouring water in a leaking cask.")

Age affects family and home. When Browning wrote, "Grow old along with me! / The best is yet to be," he never dreamed that life expectancies in Britain and America would rise over the next century from the mid-forties to seventy-four in both countries, averaging out men and women. This was due mainly to falls in infant, childhood, and maternal mortality. The trick in Victorian times was to survive into adolescence. The average sixty-five-year-old Englishman or American in 1990 can expect to live just three years longer (six years for his wife) than he could in Browning's day.

So he wants to retire as soon as he can, a trend that may be reversed as the working-age population falls. In 1988 only 75 percent of American men aged fifty-five to fifty-nine and just over half of those aged sixty to sixty-four were still working. In Britain they are staying in harness steadily less longer; between 1971 and 1988, the sixty to sixty-four age group still working dropped from 83 percent to 53 percent. Of those aged fifty-five to fifty-nine, 83 percent were still at their jobs or looking for one. Earlier retirement is one way to cut down employment. Just 3 Americans and 2.7 British now work for every retiree. In 1910, 10 percent of Britain's people had reached retirement age. Close to three times that have now. Still, Britain is going to get a breathing space. A big fall in the birthrate in the 1920s means the numbers of old people will stop growing (in America the fall came later, with the onset of the Depression in the 1930s). Britain will not start aging again until the twenty-first century.

Work itself is changing. Full-time jobs are disappearing. A third of working Britons are already self-employed, part-time, or temporary workers. In time, some predict, most people will work for themselves and not for companies. This is one of those unpatterned, unsettling, and confusing changes brought by advancing technology, particularly computers and biotechnology. To see what a radical shift of approach is going to be needed, let us take a look at how Britain is adapting to the microchip age.

II

TWO NATIONS–
SOUTH:
THE BEST
OF TIMES

Going Micro

THE BRIGHTEST FUTURE for Britain, says a senior Japanese economist I met in the City of London, lies in electronics, biotech, and information services. One thinks at once of the South. Disraeli's "Two Nations," as stated earlier, still affects the way you see Britain—South and North, rich and poor, haves and have-nots—a state of mind as much as geography.

But it is also true that the old grimy, metal-bashing Britain that harnessed steampower to railroads and steamships at its ports, to water pumps in its deep-shaft coal mines, and to factory machines, what is left of it, is mainly to be found in Scotland, Wales, and the North of England. A newer Britain that harnessed electricity for lighting and power for turbines, and chemistry to make synthetics, petrochemicals, and plastics, can be seen all over. The newest Britain, with its joining of computers, semiconductors, and telecommunications in robotics, electronics, and information systems, with the exception of Scotland's "Silicon Glen," is mainly in the South, best seen along the M4 motorway from Slough to Swindon west of London or up the M11 from London northeast to Cambridge.

One gets so conditioned in Britain to think of industries as aging and ailing, it is perhaps a good idea to start out with many that are doing well. I've called this section the South; it is really about, with the exception of education, what is going right in Britain. The next section, North, is, by and large, about what is going wrong. But computer-integrated manufacturing with its microelectronic products and processes is spreading up and down the country, transforming even the oldest industries with automation, robots, microchips, computers, sensors, software, and telecoms. It is the only way to stay competitive. Before looking at this "white-hot technological revolution," to use Harold Wilson's old phrase, in the rest of Britain's industry, and its science, health, services, education, finance, retailing, and farming, let me sketch some random examples:

• At Plessey's semiconductor plant near Plymouth—vibration-proof, its air swooshed clean six hundred times an hour—engineers in blue space suit outfits, their faces hidden by surgical masks, bend over scanning-electron microscopes to put together integrated circuits. Plessey, since taken over by Britain's General Electric Company and West Germany's Siemens, was Britain's biggest microchip manufacturer; this plant, which I visited when it opened in 1986 and again in 1988, looked to me like something straight out of Arthur C. Clarke's science fiction. But I've never seen a comparable Japanese or American plant; the British engineers say the frontiers of science are being pushed back so fast, they really have to scramble to keep up. The Plymouth plant makes six-inch wafers at geometries ultimately down to the submicron level (a human hair is eighty microns) and aims to get 500,000 to 1 million transisters per chip by the late 1990s. Such ultra-miniaturization means complex information can be moved at superfast speeds on one tiny piece of silicon.

• What does it all do? Almost anything, you realize when you look down the assembly lines at Austin Rover's gigantic Longbridge plant near Birmingham. At first, inside Britain's biggest factory, it looks like nobody is there. In a space the size of ten football pitches, a buzzing, clanking army of computer-run automated welders and robots rush about at frantic speed assembling car bodies and suspension systems. Robots are whipping around, fitting dashboards, front and rear screens, putting together seats, bumpers, and wheels. I'd been down assembly lines at big avionics and tractor plants at home; none were this automated. Rover's even had driverless, flatbed carts moving about on tracks; if you happened to be in the way of one it nudged you in the shins, stopped, and gave you four seconds to get out of the way. In all the frenzied noise and motion there were just a few humans, supervisors in white coats (some of them Japanese from Honda) riding about on bicycles. It outdid Charlie Chaplin's *Modern Times*.

"What will the people do?" a group of visiting schoolgirls from Bristol kept asking their teacher. I wondered too. The machines are taking over. I suppose it's like hearing in 1900 that hardly anybody will have a servant in 1990. (Some 15 percent of Londoners were servants in 1900.) It turned out not to mean that the average middle-class person would be a lot poorer in 1990, but that machines are performing the servant's functions: a washing machine, not the slavey scrubbing laundry with chapped red hands; a modern kitchen, not the toiling cook. Still, introduce a bulldozer that does the work of sixty men with shovels, what do you do with the sixty men? Hardly anybody wants to go back to the technical level of goods and services available in 1900. Computerized automation, with its much lower break-even point when it comes to earnings, is here to stay. But there's a lot of dislocation. Ford's big Halewood plant outside Liverpool in 1980–90 expanded car production over 40 percent while it trimmed its payroll by a third. Smart machinery cuts off unskilled people who are a little too old or a little too unskilled to keep up with it. It is worrying that unlike their American counterparts, 45 percent of British entrepreneurs in 1988 had left school at sixteen; industry lacks whiz kids.

• That is what Larry Rowe, who learned electronics in the Royal Air Force and later at university, reasoned too. And you cannot learn high tech with a blackboard and a piece of chalk. So in 1949 on a £140,000 loan, Rowe set up a teaching systems company in Norwich. His L.J. Electronics makes robots, digital systems, and other micro teaching aids. Typical of the new, small high-tech industries starting up all over the South, Rowe's firm, with seventy employees, finds it has to sell in Europe and America to have a big enough marketplace. Larry Rowe says salesmanship is half the battle. So does Datron Instruments down the road, a Norwich pioneer in autocalibration. Set up in 1971, it now has branches in Florida and California; three fourths of its turnover is in exports.

• New electronic dealing systems and computer information services made the City of London's 1986 deregulation, the "Big Bang," inescapable. A computer system's eight thousand terminals now allow London's traders to update prices for shares on the machines instead of through the old face-to-face dealing on the Stock Exchange floor. Computers are now programmed to analyze investments, pick winners, compile portfolios, manage them, and, as dramatized by Wall Street's 1987 crash, trigger buy-and-sell orders. Global stock trading, despite a slowdown, is here to stay with a single world economy, deregulation of financial markets, and continual advances in communications and computer technology.

• Biotech is harder than the microchip to grasp but may change society more. Ever since two Cambridge scientists, American James Watson and Englishman Francis Crick, worked out in 1953 the double-helical structure of DNA, the chemical blueprint of all living creatures, the biotechnology business was born. A step toward cloning animals came in Edinburgh in 1986 when foster ewes gave birth to lambs with genetically manipulated embryos. The Institute for Animal Physiology and Genetics Research is also breeding sheep that produce milk containing a clotting agent by introduction of a human gene; pharmaceutical companies may soon be establishing herds to make insulin, anticlotting agents for stroke victims, and other drugs. At Nottingham University in 1986 DNA was put into a single cell of rice; the Japanese have now gone further, getting whole plants.

Among British biotech breakthroughs, aside from DNA, were the isolation of interferon in 1957 and the development of monoclonal antibodies in 1975. The antiulcer, anti-Parkinson's syndrome drug, Tagamet, and heart-protecting beta blockers also came from Britain. It may be that a century from now contemporary Britain will be most remembered for its science. Where it falls down is in the practical application of science as technology. DNA was largely a British discovery, but once it was unveiled the whole planet went to town on it. Scientists hit the ground and ran with it all over the world.

Mrs. Thatcher's government gives grants to encourage British industry to adopt semiconductors, computing, and high-tech communications. Microchips are used in about half of all production processes. Fiber optics are catching on. Factories using robots doubled in 1984–88. High-tech industry tends to be in aerospace and defense—missiles, spacecraft, aircraft, electronics and telecoms, ordnance and instrument engineering—plus engines and turbines. Plastics, rubber, and synthetic fibers are counted among British high tech, as is medical, optical, and filming equipment. As everywhere, there has been fast growth in office automation (computers, calculators, storage devices, duplicating machines).

Britain's two giant oil companies, British Petroleum and Shell, tower over other corporations in turnover, capital, and profits. Eighteen oil fields in its part of the North Sea have made Britain self-sufficient. Forty-three towering offshore oil or gas platforms pump oil up from spongelike pools as much as six hundred feet deep in the earth's crust. Their giant steel frames are anchored in the seabed to allow the North Sea's hundred-mile-per-hour winds and sixty-foot waves to crash through them. One such platform, Occidental's Piper Alpha 127 miles off Scotland's coast, exploded into fire in July 1988, killing 166 men in the worst disaster in the history of the offshore oil industry. Britain's oil production was yearly averaging 2.5 million barrels a day from 1984 to 1987; it fell to a low of 1.4 million in June 1989, but was back above 2 million, where it is expected to stay, by early 1990. With estimates of known reserves of 4.3 billion tons, present production, depending on prices, may be held past 1995, maybe even to 2000. BP is now half-nationalized. Shell, with Anglo-Dutch ownership, is more truly multinational, as is Unilever, another Anglo-Dutch giant, with soap and food products.

Another worldwide but very British giant is Imperial Chemical Industries, which together with BP, Shell, and British American Tobacco is one of four British firms that rank among Europe's top twenty industries in terms of sales. ICI was put together out of five companies in the 1920s to counter the German chemical combine, I. G. Farben. ICI now ranks fifth among the world's chemical manufacturers, making plastics, pharmaceuticals, and pesticides. It is Britain's fourth biggest industry.

I asked ICI's former chairman, Sir John Harvey-Jones, about the future of British industry. He said:

> The worry is that our basic industrial foundation may be too small to carry our aspirations. We suffered a horrendous loss in 1982 when the pound was allowed to go too strong for too long. That knocked out something between a third and a fourth of all British manufacturing companies.

Sir John felt that perhaps 10 percent of them were outmoded.

> But the others, I think, went because of this government's belief in a particular economic system. It caused immense harm. What people don't understand is that if you lose an industrial position it doesn't come back. Once you lose your market position, you won't invest. It's too much of a risk both to invest in the technology and the market. If you hang on, even by the skin of your teeth, there's a chance you'll come back. I mean the shoe industry is a good example. It bloody nearly went to the wall but didn't quite. With modern technology you can now make shoes in Britain competitively. But consumer electronics completely went out, as did the earlier stages of textiles. There's only one spinning factory left in Britain. Once you disband the troops, you've lost your marketing position for good.

Sir John is a supporter of David Owen's Social Democrats and a onetime Labourite. But Lord Prior, a Tory, former member of Mrs. Thatcher's Cabinet and, when I interviewed him, chairman of General Electric in Britain, felt the same way.

I don't think one can be under any illusions. Certainly Britain's manufacturing base has declined. This partly comes from the heavy industries going out—shipbuilding, steel, heavy engineering, to some extent,
foundries and forgings. All that has declined. There has also been a
good deal of uptake from the newer high-tech industries.

But we've lost out on whole markets. We no longer have a major
home car industry. We don't export many cars. We don't make many
television sets. We don't make any video recorders of our own; the Japanese make some here is all. In a number of fields, we really have lost
out very badly.

Lord Prior, too, blamed the high pound of the early 1980s.

Some industries needed to go out. They were just hanging on by their
bootstraps. And as soon as the pound went up, export markets just dis-
appeared. And they don't come back. A number of those which just
hung on have expanded now that the economy's picked up.

John Redwood, an MP who headed Mrs. Thatcher's Policy Unit
at Number Ten Downing Street in 1983–85, admits setbacks in
Britain's electronics industry, but argues that the aerospace and defense industries are strong. He told me:

You can't have everything. British industry was totally demoralized by
1979. Its profitability was very low. It was strapped for cash. It had lost
a lot of talent overseas because of high tax rates. It had got used to
failure. It had to spend all its time discussing trade union problems.

British industry now is in a very different position. It has the highest return on capital it's enjoyed in twenty years. It has a strong cash
position. It has adequate banking facilities. It is beginning to attract
talent back. People are coming back from abroad. The tax rates are
low. Salaries are going up. Some industrialists are beginning to understand that successful industry is about innovation, research, and investment. And they are things which industry, in its profitable state, has
jolly well got to pay for itself.

We have world-leading companies and products in aerospace, radar systems, electronics, engines, some defense products, including
planes, weapon systems, and naval ships, some aspects of telecommunications and radio-telephones and one of the world's three largest
stock exchanges, with leading edges in many areas of financial advice,
insurance, and banking. So we have a lot of leading edges as well as
some bad bits. Vehicles has been a disgrace. The only way we'll get that
right, in my view, is to invite even more Japanese in to reorganize the
industry for us; with their technology and management skills, we can
produce a formidable offshore manufacturing base with British workers and British investment to export into Europe.

Harvey-Jones claimed most government scientific research
money went into defense ("extremely inefficient and gives us no in-

dustrial feed-off at all"). The conservative-leaning Confederation of British Industry has repeatedly called for greater manufacturing investment, reporting it was just £1.950 billion ($3.315 billion) in 1986, well behind Germany, France, and the United States and less than half what Japan was investing. From 1979 to 1987, Japan's industrial production went up 31 percent, West Germany's 11 percent, and America's 11 percent. Britain's declined the whole time. It was not until mid-1987 that unemployment dropped below 3 million. The CBI has also steadily argued for internationally competitive exchange rates. Its complaints about low industrial investment and poor education in Britain go back a century.

An example of a defense industry would be Vickers Defence Systems, like ICI a survivor from the nineteenth century. The British Tommy had a Vickers machine gun in World War I and Vickers made the world's first tank. Today the company turns out a whole range of tanks, armored vehicles, bombs, and munitions. Vickers Shipbuilding and Engineering has been building Britain's submarines since 1902 when one could make seven knots and was steered with a periscope from twelve feet under water; today's nuclear subs go for thousands of miles at depths of 500 feet or more.

All through the 1980s Mrs. Thatcher pursued her program of "privatization," working with bankers to sell off to private shareholders such nationalized businesses as airlines, aerospace, automobiles, gas, steel, and telecommunications, thirteen of the eighteen old nationalized industries in all. By 1990 she was moving on electricity and water; just the railway system, coal, and the post office were left.

While many industries were nationalized by Clement Attlee's Labour government in the forties, the issue has never been as clearcut as both Tory and Labour ideologies would make it. Most of the oldest industries—beginning with coal and railways—had to be taken over by the state as they became too costly for private shareholders. The Tories, for instance, created British Overseas Airways Corporation, the old BOAC, as a state-owned airline in 1939. Sometimes it's gone back and forth. Steel was nationalized by Labour in 1950, denationalized by the Tories in 1953, renationalized by Labour in 1967, again denationalized by the Tories in 1979.

In 1979–88 Mrs. Thatcher's government made seventeen major public offers of shares, widening the number of shareholders among Britain's people from 7 percent to close to 20 percent, and earning the government nearly £20 billion ($34 billion). British Aerospace, the result of a steady amalgamation of smaller aircraft engineering firms, was formed in 1977, privatized in 1985. It, in turn, has since bought Royal Ordnance, an arms producer, in 1987 and the Rover Group of car manufacturers in 1988 (promptly announcing nearly five thousand jobs would be lost). British Aerospace makes Harrier and Buccaneer jets, updates Phantoms, and its new EAP (Experimental Aircraft Programme) with Germany and Italy is turning out what is expected to be a truly Space Age fighter; it also manufactures components of the European Airbus.

The great triumph of British Airways is, of course, the Anglo-French-built supersonic Concorde, which, flying ten miles high at 1,500 miles per hour, gets you from London to New York in three and a half hours. Long dubbed a white elephant (the British government had to write off £1.2 billion in development costs), the Concorde is now just as accepted as the majestic, four-engined biplanes built in the early 1930s by Handley Page, the HP-42s. These carried the intrepid passengers of Britain's old Imperial Airlines from London to Cairo and Karachi at 130 miles per hour, the kind of adventurous flights that helped inspire James Hilton's *Lost Horizon.*

Britain is struggling to hold its own at the top end of the car business. Rolls-Royce, rescued from receivership in the early 1970s, still produces its Silver Shadows. (A separate Rolls-Royce corporation makes jet engines.) Jaguar, born in 1931 at the height of the Depression, has stayed with low-slung, stylish lines right up to the present XJ6 model. Soon after it warned a strong pound made its sales too expensive in America, its best market, it was taken over by Ford. Like other specialist, classic European names, Rolls-Royce, too, seems in constant danger of being gobbled up by the Americans or Japanese.

British Gas is an offshoot of the North Sea Oil bonanza; companies like BP, Amoco, Philips, Shell, and Total developed methane-producing fields. A nationwide "gas grid" now supplies 60 percent of British homes and 40 percent of industry, making the old "gasworks," with their grim heaps of coke and coal, rail tracks and shunting wagons, a thing of the past.

British Telecom goes back to Scotsman Alexander Graham Bell, who in 1876 summoned his assistant with a strange apparatus he'd invented, "Watson, come here. I want you." Today his telephone has grown into a vast network of underwater cables (increasingly made from lightweight optical fiber) and satellites which cover the world, carrying both sound and sight (ocean bed cables still carry most phone calls). A very British public fracas is indignation over the replacement by stainless steel booths of the old-fashioned red call boxes; 78,300 public pay phones are to be replaced by 1992. British Telecom has agreed to leave a few red ones around for old times' sake.

Less photogenic are British Telecom's huge satellite dishes on the Isle of Man and at Britain's first earth satellite station at Goonhilly, part of the world's global network of telephonic and televisual communications. They fit right in with Cornwall's many giant megaliths, which share the same Atlantic coast.

The Central Electricity Generating Board, which runs all Britain's power stations, has long been earmarked for privatization. A few years ago, faced with an urgent need for backup supply to the National Grid—what if everybody made a cup of tea at the same time?—the British came up with an ingenious power station. Their engineers built it under Snowdonia, a National Parks area in Wales with Britain's most spectacular mountain. Nothing to see. The whole complex—ten miles of tunnels and shafts, a rock-filled dam, turbines, generators, and all—is housed in the biggest subterranean hydroelectric plant in existence. Water from two mountain lakes plummets down to fuel the power plant before being pumped back up again. Tourists are often unaware anything is there.

Britain is an island of coal; it is its oldest industry. But since Mrs. Thatcher put down the miners' strike in 1984, mine after mine has been closed down. Automation affects mining too, as at the new Selby coalfield in South Yorkshire where six modernized collieries mine the Barnsley Seam with power-loading shears and automatic cutters. Even so, hidden underground gas and water courses still make mining dangerous. Coal is still used in Britain to generate steam and electricity; coking coal is used to make steel. The British Steel Corporation, its work force halved to less than 130,000 since 1967, is still the world's fourth largest company. The 14.3 man-hours needed to produce a ton of liquid steel in 1969 has gone to just over six hours, in a few places four hours. Steel was privatized in 1988.

The government still runs Britain's postal system; it is amazingly good. Most first-class letters in London reach their destination the next day. Within Britain a stamp costs eighteen pence (about thirty cents), but you can stuff as much in the envelope as you like up to sixty grams; the cost is fixed. Some packages must be tied with string, confusing as it's banned in America. A big difference is that you can pay your phone or electric bill, deposit money in a savings account, apply for a passport, and do no end of things in a British post office. There are the same ever-longer queues on both sides of the Atlantic.

The East Midlands Airport at Derby is Britain's night postal hub. Eighteen planes fly in every night from all over Britain carrying first-class U.K. mail. Even with electronic and computerized sorting, there is a hangar full of postal workers. Some years ago when I lived in Nagpur, the centermost town in India, the same thing happened there. Every night, planes flew in from Delhi, Calcutta, Bombay, and Madras and passengers got herded into a terminal to wait a couple of hours while they and the mail got sorted out; if you told somebody you were from Nagpur, you had to be ready to hear a horror story. Since Britain has the same system the one in India must be a legacy of the British Raj.

Derby also gets Britain's Traveling Post Offices, trains where all the bagging and sorting is done aboard. The secret of London's fast delivery is an ingenious miniature railway network, six and a half miles long, dug deep under the center of London, as much as seventy feet down and well below the Underground. Little unmanned trains—an engine with wagons full of mailbags, each one about four feet tall and twenty-five feet long—zoom around as blue dots on a control room panel keep track of their whereabouts. A company in Leeds builds the trains, keeping to the original 1927 design. The system of nine-foot-high tunnels was dug in 1914 in the expectation London's surface traffic wouldn't get faster than eight miles an hour (about par for rush hour now). The tunnels housed the art treasures of the Tate and National galleries during the Blitz. And not a microchip or a computer in the system. Like British Rail itself, with its fast and frequent trains, Britain's postal system impresses an outsider.

As with many of the industries just described, some things in Britain are going right. British Steel, for example, has increased its productivity up to 13 percent a year in 1979–88. In 1989, ten years after Mrs. Thatcher came to office, new labor laws, a shift of roughly 5 percent of Britain's gross domestic product out of the public sector and back to private hands, a drop in the top rate of personal income taxes from 83 percent to 40 percent, deregulation, and the rest have made a difference. The British economy in 1989 was expanding at nearly 5 percent in real terms, faster than any industrial nation but Japan. Unemployment fell, at last, to below 2 million, 7 percent of the labor force. Company profits rose to record levels. All this is a radical change from 1980–81 when, as Sir John Harvey-Jones and Lord Prior said, recession and a high pound left hundreds of British firms bankrupt, gravely cutting the size of Britain's industrial base. Not all the news was good. Manufacturing output passed the 1979 level only in 1987. Investment in industry did not reach its pre-1979 level in real terms until 1989. In 1979–88 Britain's share of world trade in manufactures fell from 8 percent to 6.5 percent, a far cry from the 40 percent of a century ago.

Is British industry lifting itself out of its old demoralized state? Bill Emmott, *The Economist*'s business affairs editor, says:

> In the 1970s Britain was assumed to be a land of mediocre management, adversarial industrial relations, old-fashioned industries, second-rate schooling, poor marketing, insufficient research and development, a disdain for business, and a liking for tea breaks.
>
> If that was so, then even allowing for the British penchant for exaggerated self-denigration, it is not going to change in just a few years.

Too true. Nowhere is this more evident than in Britain's chronic failure to cash in on British breakthroughs in science.

Faraday's Day Off

T ALK TO ENOUGH people in Britain and you find so many troubles stem from a long-term inability to apply science to technology. Asa Briggs gave it as one reason Britain failed to keep
up industrially with America and Germany after the 1870s. Anthony
Sampson calls it Britain's "century-old problem."

Britain, home of Newton and Darwin, split the atom, gave the
world radar, penicillin, and the test-tube baby and determined the
structure of DNA. Her scientists win Nobel Prizes with striking continuity, and those like Cambridge's Stephen Hawking probe the mystery of the origins of the universe. The problem is to put the discov-
eries in physics, chemistry, and physiology to use. That takes
engineers and entrepreneurs and Britain just doesn't have enough of
them.

In April 1988, Sir George Porter, himself a Nobel prizewinner
and president of the Royal Society, the highest body in British science, made a bitter public attack on the Thatcher government:

> There now seems to be a deliberate policy of downgrading the pur-
> suit of knowledge in deference to the pursuit of affluence.

It was an old story; the Royal Society, where Newton, Halley,
Dryden, and Pepys gathered to talk about telescopes, gravity, and
comets, was once again voicing the scientists' resentment of the politicians. Sir George recalled how during World War II Britain's survival depended on those who came up with radar, the jet engine, the
mathematics of code breaking (which produced the computer), and
antibiotics. Now fewer than half the scientists who applied for funding for research projects could expect to get a grant. Some gave up
applying. The brain drain had become a hemorrhage. Of thirty-three
British scientists elected to the Royal Society in 1988, he said, eight
lived and worked abroad.

Despite such great scientific breakthroughs the past half-century as radio astronomy, molecular biology, and solid state physics, and such technological advances from them as space satellites, transistor radios, computers, and rockets, British politicians, whether Labour or Tory, and the scientists are as far apart as ever. Many thought Margaret Thatcher, herself a chemistry graduate from Oxford, would bridge the gap; she cut scientific funding instead.

I asked Norman Tebbit, long Mrs. Thatcher's closest adviser, why. He said:

> Over the years we've won so many Nobel Prizes for pure science. And the Japanese and the Americans have taken up those ideas and used them to create goods on the shelves. I'm not decrying the wild-blue-yonder stuff. But what a number of us feel very strongly is that universities are still very resistant to hearing market signals about what is needed.

Many agree the Universities were too complacent; they did need a shake-up. Nuclear power stations, commercial jets, vertical takeoff aircraft, brain scanners are other examples of British inventions somebody else turned into commercial products better. But one finds serious hostility toward the government from sensible, wise scientists. David Owen found the same thing; he told me, "These are not people who sit on their duff, expecting a handout. Many of them have very good relations with industry and have had them all along."

The politicians ought to take a closer look at the Cambridge Science Park, formed in 1970 to generate new scientific ideas with industrial potential. Nearly thirty British universities now have them, with Edinburgh, Warwick, and Surrey outstanding. An American invention, the biggest science park is in North Carolina, linked to Duke and the University of North Carolina at Chapel Hill. Parks around Harvard and MIT have transformed Boston. The most famous of course is Stanford's Silicon Valley, aped by the Bavarians' *Silizium Tal,* the Scots' Silicon Glen.

The Cambridge Science Park, by far Britain's biggest and best, is a 130-acre grouping of sixty-five high-tech and research companies. Its moving spirit is Dr. John Bradfield, a zoologist who is senior bursar at Trinity College, Cambridge. The university has a few old ties with industry; both Pye and Cambridge Instruments built world reputations on work done for the Cavendish Laboratory. But generally, industrial links were discouraged; IBM was turned away in 1960. In time the mood began to change. Prime Minister Harold

Wilson's "white-hot technological revolution" promised a closer relationship. As Dr. Bradfield explained over lunch at Trinity:

> The government in the late 1960s wrote around to all the universities, saying, "Do reexamine your links with science-based industry. See whether you are giving them sufficient access to libraries and apparatus and ideas." At Cambridge a small committee presided over by Sir Neville Mott, the head of the Cavendish, thought about this a year or so and recommended that there should be a modest area of science-based industry. On seeing the report and getting the idea, we decided to have a go.

Trinity happened to own a derelict wartime tank yard on the edge of town near the proposed junction of two major highways. When the park opened on that site in 1973, it had just one tenant, Laser-Scan, a spin-off from Cambridge's High Energy Physics Group; it developed a computerized laser-scanning gadget to analyze the tracks and collisions of nuclear particles, then adapted it to computerized map-making. Laser-Scan is now quoted on the New York Stock Exchange.

Dr. Bradfield's acres stayed pretty empty until 1979 when a local banker, Matthew Bullock, helped set up something called the Cambridge Technology Association, which gives credit to small businesses spun off either from the university or slightly older companies. The park took off. So, beyond anybody's expectations, did the whole Cambridge area. Firms within the science park account for just a tenth of some fourteen thousand new jobs; about £1 billion was generated in 1988 by Cambridge's applied-science explosion. Real estate values, wages, and retail sales have shot up. Two more local science parks are in the works, plus another in Kent which will be near the Channel Tunnel supposed to open in 1993. Stansted Airport, halfway to London and with fast rail and highway links, could become London's third big airport.

The Cambridge Science Park is a model the rest of Britain should follow. Its tenants now range from Napp Laboratories, with over three hundred employees, to small spin-off businesses like Synoptics or Data Analysis and Research that tend to be technological pioneers and job creators. Mrs. Thatcher has cut taxes, a needed step, but she has also moved to reduce, not increase, local revenues; in Cambridge local government played a big role.

Does this success mean Britain's scientists can move from the kind of research that probes the riddles of nature and wins Nobel Prizes toward the kind that comes up with microchips, computers,

software, sensors, and telecoms? Just a tiny percent of British graduates find their way into small businesses (compared to Harvard
Business School graduates; three fourths of them run their own
businesses within ten years). Dr. Bradfield is confident, though wary
things might go too far:

> I am a keen Conservative and a great supporter of Margaret Thatcher
> myself. And I'm very keen on applied science. But the tail must never
> wag the dog. Sir George Porter is perfectly right. The basic purpose of a
> great university, wherever it may be, Cambridge or Berkeley or any-
> where else, is to pursue pure learning. And that must never be distorted
> by practical application. There's plenty of time in the day to do both.

Everyone at the Cambridge Science Park agrees marketing is
the big problem. Peter O'Keefe, who heads Qudos, a firm that makes
silicon chip design and manufacturing technology available to students in Britain and as far away as India and China, says it all
comes down to markets:

> It's the big limiting factor, whether for microchips or electronics or
> biotechnology. British companies are notoriously bad at getting their
> products down the sales pipes. If you go to a board meeting and say,
> "We've got projects X, Y, and Z, and we need £300,000 to take on a team
> of six engineers for a year or we need a megacomputer," it goes
> through as fast as you can snap your fingers. But if you say, "I want to
> penetrate the Mexican or the Scandinavian market and need £300,000
> to spend on advertising and promotion and seminars and exhibitions,"
> well, that's another story.
>
> It's still an act of faith for a small company which is trying to make
> the transition from a £5 million to a £100 million company to go out-
> side the U.K. and really invest heavily in developing overseas markets.
> The U.K. market just isn't large enough in its own right to turn creative
> small companies into worldwide forces. So what you do is grow a com-
> pany and the first time somebody comes along with a bag of dollars to
> buy you out or merge you, you take the money and run. And get into
> something which is more interesting than selling, which is inventing
> new products.

Norman Tebbit is right, O'Keefe says, that an association with
Cambridge can be "the kiss of death" in some microchip fields:

> Cambridge is still number one in computer science, but there's a
> clear division in the minds of Americans who buy products between
> research and manufacturing skill. The association with Cambridge is
> great when it comes to research, but cuts no ice if you're talking about
> delivering products at the right place at the right time. Whereas in

parts of the old British Empire, as in Russia and Europe, it's a real plus for you.

A problem for applied science, Mike Skidmore of Altek Automation, which makes assembly automation systems, told me, is the low standing of engineers in Britain, which trains just half as many as France or Germany:

> Outside of Scotland, it's been almost an apology to be an engineer. In Japan or Germany to be a diploma engineer is high-status like law or medicine. Not here.

British industrialists have long urged that the education and licensing of engineers be completely overhauled; most engineers are organized in antiquated Victorian professional institutions.

Another problem, according to Michael Foxe of Twyford Plant Laboratories, which does a big business cloning plants, such as date palms, is that Mrs. Thatcher's government, in its zeal to privatize, sold Cambridge's Plant Breeding Institute to Unilever. Its head went off to Rutgers and its molecular biology unit shifted to the John Innes Institute in Norwich. Dr. Dick Flavell, a molecular biologist from Cambridge who heads the John Innes Institute, agreed with me this makes it more difficult for some of the biotech companies in the science park. "They moved to Cambridge to be in the swim of things," he said, "where there was a high concentration of plant scientists."

Perhaps the best example of a science park company is Cambridge Life Sciences, which works with thirteen British universities to find new applications of enzymes in medicine and industry. At the time of my visit the company was just getting ready to market its first biosensor product. Howard Thomas, a former student of Sir George Porter, said biosensors had become his firm's key technology; it had eleven patents then and things were moving so fast in electronics, physics, electrochemistry, and immunology, it was filing at least one new patent a month.

The breakthrough, Dr. Thomas said, was coming in small handheld instruments which allowed a diabetic to prick his finger and within ten seconds tell his own glucose level, or a heart patient to tell his own cholesterol level.

> We see biosensors being very much a common first-line situation in health care. Certainly by the late 1990s people will be accustomed, I think, to monitoring their own health on a routine basis. If you look at health care around the world, every system, whether it's state-funded

or privately funded, is straining under intense financial pressure. People now expect, as a right, to get heart and lung transplants, organ transplants, the most advanced treatment there is. And as technology keeps advancing, it all gets inordinately expensive. Biosensors will cut costs by making the consumer more responsible for his own health.

Interestingly, says Dr. Flavell, Britain is moving much closer to Europe in science:

Ten years ago if I thought of devoting some days to exciting science, I'd be getting on a plane and flying west to America. Now there are many more centers in Europe in plant science. We have common scientific funding programs in the EEC. In science, everybody speaks English so that's no problem. Europe is undoubtedly going to form a stronger scientific base for Britain.

In his Royal Society speech, Sir George Porter spoke of Mrs. Thatcher's favorite scientist, the Victorian Michael Faraday:

One can understand her admiration of this great individualist, largely self-taught and self-supporting. But there is another lesson to be learned from his life. His survival to do his greatest work was a close-run thing.

Faraday, Sir George said, had to fund his laboratory by doing short-term applied work to improve the quality of optical glass. After nearly five years of this, he asked for permission to lay it aside "that I may enjoy the pleasure of working out my thoughts on other subjects." That was on July 4, 1831. On August 29 Faraday discovered electromagnetic induction.

A Slow Cure

A S BIOLOGICAL SCIENCE advances in medicine and diagnostics —curing more diseases, replacing more organs, prolonging life—the demand for better health care seems infinite. Britain's National Health Service, forty-two years old in 1990 and with about a million workers Europe's largest employer apart from the Red Army, has done well in containing cost and providing access for 30 million patients a year. There is none of the runaway cost inflation of America, with money going to doctors and hospitals. But Britain shares the universal health problems of richer countries: how to subject doctors and hospitals to financial discipline, how to get adequate treatment for the poor and old, how to get enough young women to enter nursing.

America is looking hard at switching more to public financing (Canada did in the 1970s) and aping Britain, just as Britain is going our way. Margaret Thatcher, in her free market zeal, wants to inject competition and choice into the NHS. Some experts agree. They say health care would be improved if hospitals, doctors, and patients got the right incentives. In early 1989 the Thatcher government published its white paper on plans for reform, mainly to come into effect in April 1991 (the betting is on general elections in May or June). Mrs. Thatcher stuck with tax-financed free health care, but set down the new principle that spending should follow patients. She reassured Britain:

> The National Health Service will continue to be available to all, regardless of income, and be financed mainly out of general taxation. We aim to extend patient choice, to delegate responsibility to where the services are provided, and to secure the best value for the money.

Dr. David Owen, who once practiced medicine, says Mrs. Thatcher has put British health care "on the primrose path down which inexorably lies American medicine: first-rate treatment for the wealthy and tenth-rate treatment for the poor." He told Parliament, "The NHS is not safe in her hands because there is no place in her heart for NHS."

Nobody really knows how it will work out or whether it will lead to better or worse quality or higher or lower costs. Mrs. Thatcher wants to both improve health services and restrain public spending, already low by European Community standards (only Portugal, Spain, and Greece have fewer hospital beds per head). Hospitals will be encouraged to compete for patients. They can opt out of local control if they want to be "self-governing" trusts. The idea of giving doctors more responsibility gets round the problem of applying market principles to health care: how can patients decide what is best for them?

It still leaves the NHS open to all, free, and financed mainly from general taxation. The big criticism, as with Mrs. Thatcher's 1988 educational reforms, is that the health reforms are being proposed as a national plan, but were conceived in secret and are untried, incompletely worked out, and with unknowable consequences. More of Mrs. Thatcher's daring. But the British Medical Association, which speaks for three quarters of the country's doctors, strongly opposes the reforms.

Everybody agrees about the urgent need to make Britain's health care system more effective and less costly. Polls show it is one of the British people's main worries. For good reason. Close to 700,000 people are on waiting lists for non-emergency surgery. Half of the local health authorities claim they are badly short of funds; thousands of hospital beds were eliminated in the 1980s. Trying to keep up with all the new advances has meant a steady shutdown of capacity. The snag is that Mrs. Thatcher's core constituency, unlike richer Tories, depend heavily on the NHS; they are nervous about her schemes to bring tighter management, contract privately for services, or have higher user fees. Unusually for Mrs. Thatcher, she has zigzagged on the issue, first defending her record and denying the NHS was short of funds, then increasing its budget to £22 billion ($37.4 billion) a year, raising nurses' wages, and finally proposing the most radical changes in the NHS since Clement Attlee's Labour government introduced it in 1948.

A big problem is delay: patients can wait ages for heart surgery, cataract removals, hip replacements, hernia operations, and surgery for other afflictions of aging. To avoid this, one fourth of surgery in

Britain is now done privately. (Waiting lists in the United States or Germany are rare.)

British television is constantly showing some harrowing tale where death might have been avoided by a timely operation. In February 1988 four-year-old Matthew Collier died; the month before he had at last got his open-heart surgery but it had been delayed three months by "a shortage of nurses." Matthew's grieving young mother told British viewers:

> He was ever so weak and he kept going blue, I mean, all day long we were giving him oxygen. He couldn't do nothing. Matthew couldn't even walk. I mean if you sat him there for a second, you'd see his head flop. And you'd have to go pick him up and give him more oxygen.

Shots of Matthew's family visiting his grave came the following July, on the NHS's fortieth anniversary. Hardly a week goes by without television showing some old man in agony for lack of a prostate operation, or an old woman desperately crippled for lack of a hip replacement. There are much-publicized deaths of babies with "a hole in the heart" who didn't get it surgically repaired in time. Some of it rubs off on Mrs. Thatcher. Her British image as "uncaring" and "heartless" has a lot to do with such sob stories being standard fare on the evening news. After all, who is to blame?

Aside from raising their pay, as she has done, it is hard to see, as the number of eighteen-year-olds falls, what Mrs. Thatcher can do about the shortage of nurses, most critical in the Southeast. Nurses make up much of the NHS's work force of 800,000 in England and 200,000 in Scotland and Wales.

David Willis, a Thatcher adviser, says, "One of the dangerous features of the NHS debate is anybody who doesn't want any change at all—the reactionaries—denounce any reform and claim she simply wants to dismantle the entire system." Tory MP John Redwood says, "What we're saying is that it's about time that patients as the consumers of health care have more choice to decide where they want to go and how they want to be treated."

In Germany, the better off can opt out of paying state contributions in favor of private insurance. They get better care than those left behind, but some try to return when income falls or need for treatment rises. The French have a social insurance system but also make high direct payments. Most of the French now pay nearly £9 ($15) to see a general practitioner. In Britain it is free, though as a foreigner I paid £15 to £20 ($25 to $34) per visit and once, to see a Harley Street specialist, £50 ($85). The local general practitioner, a neighborhood family doctor, though overloaded with NHS patients in a run-down, old-fashioned surgery, turned out to be very good.

All the stress on competition makes Labour's health spokesman, Robin Cook, uneasy: "I really cannot accept the government's vision that the day may come in which busloads of people with certain hip operations pass busloads of people in search of an eye operation going in the opposite direction." Yet this has happened already, even across national borders. Sweden sends heart patients to London; patients fed up waiting for three or four years for a hip replacement in Britain may go to West Germany where they are entitled to treatment under the EEC's reciprocal health care rules. (Free care used to be extended to visiting Americans in Britain; no more, now Yanks pay through the nose.)

Three of every four Americans have private health insurance, compared to one in nine in Britain. But this is getting uncontrollably expensive in the United States, and for a middle-aged single person can run $3,500 a year (something over £2,000). In North Dakota, for example, where standard medical insurance now costs a farm family $3,800 a year, more and more rural people are going without. The state pays just for the over-sixty-five and the very poor, which means a two-tier system. Actually, some of the best urban hospitals in America treat the poorest people. If a patient consults a specialist at the University of California's medical school, he may pay anything from $40 to $220, whereas the same doctor may see a group of indigent patients at a "free clinic" down the hall. The top doctors are often at the teaching hospitals, whose patients tend to be both paying and public.

A British television documentary, after showing scenes of luxurious private care and hearing from a smug-sounding American doctor ("We don't put surgery off for three months if it has to be done now. And it has to drive the cost of care up. And it does"), went to the squalid emergency room of a publicly funded hospital in Newark where a derelict black man on a stretcher had overdosed on drugs. It looked nightmarish. A doctor grimly warned in a voice-over that if Britain's private sector expands, its public hospitals will increasingly be seen as a place of last resort like this.

An American pitfall is that most doctors work in clinics that tend to encourage extravagance: lots of unnecessary tests may get repeated, too many X rays, too much expensive new equipment to keep in use. The level of treatment is far higher than in Britain. Is it all essential? A woman is three times likelier to have a hysterectomy in America, a baby twice as likely to be born by cesarean section. Americans spend twice as much per person on health care as do the British, yet statistically no more lives are saved. And no one in Britain need fear financial ruin from catastrophic illness.

Debate on the NHS will get hotter as 1991 approaches. It has become unable to satisfy the demand created by medical advances. Whatever Mrs. Thatcher does, as people get more money more of them will go in for private medicine, just as they do now. Mrs. Thatcher's approach to health is like her approach, as we'll see in the next chapter, to education—she wants to see more competition and choice. But she also knows what the British public will think if she backs away from tax-financed free health care. Better to look like Florence Nightingale, not Typhoid Mary.

The Gods of the Copybook Headings

> But though we had plenty of money, there was
> nothing our money could buy.
> And the Gods of the Copybook Headings said,
> *"If you don't work, you die."*
>
> KIPLING

AN INDUSTRIALIST WORRIES how Britain can stand "the stresses and strains of getting to the future." "The problem is not inventiveness," says another, "it's drive." A vicar warns, "The whole system is cracking at the seams." What's wrong? The common problem, yours, mine, everyone's, to use Browning's phrase, is education. As David Owen put it to me, "Our whole system needs substantial change."

Britain's educational system perpetuates the class and cultural divisions that hold the country back. Social and financial standing, not merit, by and large, still decide who gets the education at the top public (that is, private) schools like Eton, and Oxford and Cambridge universities. It weakens the average pupil. It strengthens a prejudice against industry among the above-average.

There is nothing new or original about this perception. The British themselves have been complaining about it for thirty, forty years. Nonetheless, not much changes.

The most telling fact about Britain is that over 40 percent of its youth leave school at sixteen with no really useful qualification to make a living (in West Germany just 10 percent). Take virtually any measure and Britain gets placed way behind. In standardized mathematics tests, the average British secondary school pupil scores 12.9 points compared to 22.4 points for the average German. Ten times as many clerical applicants in France are shown to be proficient on word-processors and data processors. Half of school-leavers in America go on to college, just 14 percent in Britain do.

Of these, 8 percent go on to forty-two universities, 92 percent to thirty polytechnics. In Germany 22 percent go to university, but so many drop out that fewer get degrees than in Britain. Britain greatly expanded higher education in the 1960s and 1970s, creating eight new universities and increasing the enrollment of some of the older ones; the University of London went from 16,000 to 46,000 in 1961–81, the University of Wales in Cardiff up to 17,000. But a sharp cut in university budgets since Mrs. Thatcher took over in 1979 has left a lot of unmet demand. How much can be seen, for example, at Plymouth's polytechnic; the head of its statistics and computing department told me that in 1988 it had more than 2,500 applicants for 90 places; there were 1,400 applicants for electronic engineering's 95 places. Oxford, in contrast, where 40 percent study science, gets about 7,000 to 8,000 applicants for 2,800 places. This self-selection, implying as it does low expectation—you'd think everybody would want to go to the great university—is one of the most dispiriting sides of the public school Oxbridge elite's grip on things.

Whether you look at education or at vocational training, it is getting worse. The 1987 Labour Force Survey found that 80 percent of men aged twenty-five to twenty-nine in Britain had no educational qualifications, compared with 65 percent of those in their forties. In a poll of nearly a thousand people in 1988, Britain's authoritative Market and Opinion Research International (MORI) found nearly half could not read a railway timetable. Two out of three could not spell "embarrass." A quarter did not know what happened in 1066 (the Battle of Hastings). One in six could not find Britain on a map. "Depressing, isn't it?" Kenneth Baker, who was still Education Secretary when I interviewed him, had to say.

America is no better. A 1987 poll of high school juniors, the First National Assessment of History and Literature, done in cooperation with the National Assessment of Educational Progress, found three fourths did not know what the Magna Carta was, a third did not know Columbus discovered America in 1492, and 80 percent had never heard of Joyce, Dostoevsky, James, Conrad, or Melville. The 1986 census found that 23 million American adults are now functionally illiterate; 40 percent of adults in the United States have trouble using menus and road maps. The worst was a 1988 poll that found 52 percent of Americans thought the sun went around the earth.

How, in an age when education, skills, and ideas make people productive in offices and factories, and computer-run machines are taking over so much of the old manual labor, are these semiliterates on both sides of the Atlantic going to make a living? In Britain they will be helped by a 26 percent drop in the number of fifteen-to-nineteen-year-olds in the ten years leading up to 1995 (43 percent in Germany, just 5 percent in Spain). The downside of this is that labor shortages, meaning higher wages, make it more tempting to give up school and take a job instead. Already eighteen-to-twenty-year-olds can earn two thirds as much as the average man. Three fourths of sixteen-year-old girls now leaving school go into clerical, sales, catering, or hairdressing jobs, all areas likely to face shortages if, as hoped, more girls stay in school or become more technically skilled. Demand for computer-literate office workers is growing at 5 percent a year. To meet expected demand for nurses, Britain's hospitals would have to recruit 30 to 40 percent of all girls leaving school with fairly good grades.

Higher education in Britain is virtually free, one of the welfare state's direct subsidies. Grants are subject to a means-tested contribution from parents. A 1986–87 survey of student spending showed a 30 percent income rise from the mid-1970s offset by a 35 percent rise in student housing costs. An average college student gets just under £2,500 ($4,250) a year in government handouts. He or she borrows in a year just £99 ($168), earns £119 ($202) during short vacations, and spends £96 ($163) in savings from summer earnings. These low average amounts suggest many students do not borrow or earn at all; in recent years there has been a sharp rise in money from parents. I was amused to hear British students complain about having to take menial jobs. In college I washed dishes, mowed lawns, cleaned windows and worked as a fire fighter, a gardener, even a bartender. Indeed, the only written comment I ever got on my master's thesis at New York's Columbia University was "Pretty good for a bartender."

Mrs. Thatcher's government is trying to reform Britain's thirty thousand schools, a huge task involving close to 10 million pupils. In July 1988, Parliament passed, after much Tory ideological fervor and Labour cries of indignation, measures that seek to improve education by introducing more competition and choice as well as a national curriculum, and by changing the way higher education is financed. It was the latest in a series of reforms, most notably the Butler education act of 1944. All have been intended to escape from the class-ridden past and make schooling more meritocratic.

Mrs. Thatcher herself held the education portfolio in the Heath government. Budget cuts were being levied at the time and she chose to cut free milk for young children. There was a huge outcry and "Mrs. Thatcher, milk snatcher" was a label that stuck. (Even more memorable were cries of "Ditch the bitch!" from Labour back benchers when she got up to defend herself in the House of Commons.) The raucous give-and-take of parliamentary debate, with frenzied shouts and jeers of "Question! Question!" "Reading!" "Hear, hear!" as the Speaker furiously cries, "Order! Order!" is something totally out of the American experience. A year ago a group of rowdy Labour backbenchers broke into a speech by a Tory minister by barking like dogs. Commons debates have been televised since late 1989 and watching Mrs. Thatcher flatten the unruly Labourites with a steamroller of fact and argument makes rattling good TV.

Mrs. Thatcher has the seats in Parliament to pass almost any legislation, but skeptics already wonder if the new school reforms will help much. Under the new curriculum, all British children aged five to sixteen will be taught science, math, and English, plus history, geography, technology, music, art, physical education, and religion, getting tested every three or four years and being continually assessed on classwork. Eleven-year-olds, for instance, will be taught to multiply seven by nine. But Professor S. J. Prais, who at the National Institute of Economic and Social Research in London did the earlier-quoted studies comparing skills with France and Germany, says other countries teach that to eight-year-olds. He resigned from Baker's maths committee once this became clear.

Baker, whom I met just after his measures became law and when he was still Education Secretary, says schools can now opt out of local authority control if enough parents want it. Schools now manage their own finances. He said, "It's more revolutionary than anything that's gone on in America." Baker claimed enrollment in higher education had risen by 200,000 under Mrs. Thatcher. He also set up new city technology colleges linked with industry, explaining, "I want them to act as beacons in the inner cities. You can't leave the old manual worker high and dry so he gets disgruntled and fed up. The whole nature of work is changing. We've got to show young people how to get technology on their side, not working against them."

Together with new laws on housing and a poll tax, Mrs. Thatcher has made the most radical changes in the way locally elected councils govern cities, districts, and counties since the Poor Law of 1601. Out have gone the ancient rights of local councils to raise their own taxes on property and businesses and run their own schools as they see fit. The poll tax, with a flat rate payable by all adults, went into effect in 1990. Tenants in council-owned public housing, usually low-rent and on the outskirts of a city, can now opt out in favor of a housing association. Since most local councils in the Northern cities and Scotland are Labour, Mrs. Thatcher seemed out to break their power.

British education has come a long way from the old ruthless segregation of children in the "eleven plus" exam, sorting them out at age eleven for academic or vocational schooling. Britain's comprehensive schools, which came in during the late 1950s and 1960s, offering subjects from Latin to typing, mathematics to metal shop, gave more hope of eroding class barriers. The West Germans still stream a third of their pupils into technical or commercial schools that lead to an apprenticeship. Another 45 percent choose between mechanical technology, electronics, textiles, or household studies at age thirteen, specializing still more at fifteen. I much prefer Britain's new emphasis on basic English, science, and math for everybody until sixteen; high technical training is one thing, but young people need arts and literature too.

Constant reform does cause a lot of turmoil. Baker appeased his critics in the education debate, seemingly backing down to let noncompulsory courses be taught 30 percent of the time, winning over the churches by finding time for religion (a hot issue among the Muslims), and pacifying the universities, stirred up by the many retired professors in the House of Lords, by modifying government control of their finances. I visited twenty or so primary and secondary schools in Britain. Their undervalued, underpaid teachers were very dedicated. In the confusion of the Baker reforms I kept thinking: why don't they just give them more money and let them get on with it? Raise their pay and give them status. In subjects like math and physics, crafts, design and technology, good teachers keep going off to higher-paying industry. Schools make do; it is said 13 percent of math teachers and 18 percent of physics teachers lack higher education in their subject, while less than half have a degree in it. Real educational reform does not square with Mrs. Thatcher's lower personal taxes. Her free market zeal works against her wish to enable more lower-middle-class families to better educate their children.

I asked Baroness Blackstone, the Master of the University of London's Birkbeck College, what she thought of Baker's reforms. Together with Lord Callaghan, she is Labour's watchdog on education in the House of Lords. The baroness, a dark-haired woman of striking good looks familiar from TV chat shows, said, "There is nothing in them which focuses on the real problems in British education: the quality and performance and morale of teachers. And tied in with that, status and pay."

"Higher pay?" I asked. She went on:

Money is part of it but it's also recognition of the value of their work. The other serious problem in Britain is that we don't keep as many children on after the age of sixteen as we should. We have a very, very small system of higher education. So we're in danger of having a rather uneducated population who won't be able to grapple with the problems of the twenty-first century.

To me, Britain also faces the problem, just as America does, that, as George Steiner says, children simply don't read the way they used to. I told Baker I noticed in talks with pupils at the schools I'd visited that how their parents acted seemed to make all the difference.

"Well, that's Plato, isn't it?" he said. "Plato said if you want to get children to be equal you must take them away at birth from their families. If a family listens to rather more serious programs on television and they take the more thoughtful newspapers, that will rub off on the children. Isn't it true in America?"

I said it was. Still it is worrying how many people are earning so much money to entertain the very young. When kids can switch on a TV set, I told Baker, their *own* TV set, and watch shows million-dollar talents are toiling away to give them, how is the nice old schoolmarm going to compete? What chance does Mr. Chips have against *Guts and Blood?*

Baker said, "Bright children will survive almost anything. Their talents come out almost by themselves. But every person has something in them. What was it Shakespeare said? 'The fire in the flint / Shows not till it be struck.' There's a flint in everybody. What education has to do is find and spark it."

Like all politicians, Kenneth Baker was a hurry, probably trying to make his mark too quickly. (He has since become, in Mrs. Thatcher's 1989 Cabinet reshuffle, chairman of the Conservative Party, a position which gets him spoken of as one of her likely successors.) And despite all the talk of really reforming education, Thatcherism has a tendency to substitute gimmickry for breadth and vision. In higher education the idea of imposing business-style efficiency has actually hurt universities with budget cuts, frozen professors' salaries, unfilled vacancies, and trimmed funding for libraries, laboratories, and graduate assistants. I found the polytechs especially starved for high-tech equipment. It is not surprising the British brain drain of the 1980s sometimes looked like a flood. David Cannadine, a Cambridge historian who went to Columbia University, told *The New York Times* it was "perhaps the largest single influx into America from a single source" since Jewish professors were forced to flee Germany and Austria in the 1930s. With American universities offering two or three times the pay of an Oxford don, any British Education Secretary—and Baker's successor, John MacGregor, was not very effective in previous jobs—is left holding a finger in the dike.

Baker wanted to turn to British industry. Industry in the United States spent $600 million in university-based research in 1986, much of it going to graduate students. Stanford University, whose industrial park led to Silicon Valley, gets about 6 percent ($10 million or so) of its yearly research budget from private companies. It needs to: a year at Stanford, compared to Britain's free, state-paid education, costs about £12,000 a year (over $20,000). Professor John Ashworth, a combative young biologist who is vice president of Britain's Salford University, has taken the lead in battling for industrial support. All told, Britain's universities turn out 76,000 graduates a year at a cost of about £2 billion ($3.4 billion); nearly 44 percent study science, technology, engineering, or management.

But look at this statistic: in 1979, 16 percent of new graduates from Cambridge University went into "industry," a category that includes manufacturing, civil engineering, and some services, but not the City or banking. By 1988, after a decade of Thatcherism, the figure had fallen to 9 percent. Those going into "commerce"—stockbroking, other financial services, advertising, and management consultancy—rose from 8 percent to 13 percent, probably partly at industry's expense. Historians have long noted that the elite has disdained industry since the 1850s. Not much has changed.

Sir John Harvey-Jones, as the former chairman of Imperial Chemical Industries, feels it is hard to compare industry's involvement in education in Britain and America. Over drinks one evening in the bar of London's Mayfair Hotel, Sir John explained:

> You Americans start with a very healthy position of (a) a very high profit in business and industry and (b) an enlightened situation where businessmen give of their companies' money to support universities or charities stimulated by tax breaks. And it's socially respectable. In Brit-

ain I was always very conscious as chairman of ICI that I was actually giving away the stockholders' money. My view was that it was better to give the stockholders the money to make their own bloody choice where they wanted to put it.

When I quoted Sir John's remarks to Kenneth Baker, he bristled. Baker told me:

> I'm going to change that philosophy. I'm saying, don't say to me, "Baker, or Thatcher, or Tory government, get it right for us, improve our schools." I say to you, Mr. Harvey-Jones, "What can you do to help to improve the schools as well? Because you're employing these kids. When did you last go to a school and see what's being taught in English, Mr. Harvey-Jones? When did you last go around with the other industrialists and see what's happening in the physics departments of universities? Go and see what's happening. See if you can contribute in some sort of way to help refashion the curriculum. Make it more pertinent. Make it more relevant.

Lord Prior, who heads Britain's Council for Industry and Higher Education, told me that if he had to put it in a nutshell, he would say the two main problems are a lack of teaching ability and a sheer lack of numbers of instructors to teach math, physics, and the other sciences to pupils age thirteen to sixteen. "That's one thing," he said, "The other is demography." He explained:

> The number of children reaching eighteen now is down by a third from five years ago. The number of people in higher education between now and the year 2000 is only going up by 4 percent. At a time when we desperately need better-educated people. I don't just mean better scientists or better mathematicians. I mean better-educated people. We'll have nothing like enough for a society which needs to expand at the rate of 3 percent a year. What we're going to have to do is retrain and reeducate large numbers of mature people, get them back into higher education and then into industry.

I felt Lord Prior put his finger on it. Britain didn't have *enough* education; not enough people were studying, particularly at the university and polytechnic level. When I met Norman Tebbit, Mrs. Thatcher's close colleague, I asked him why she didn't make education her top priority and back it up with money; all the free market emphasis on injecting more choice and competition into education, of letting a youngster choose what was "best suited" for him, not just what his parents could afford or what local politicians thought he should have, was fine. It just didn't solve the problem. Tebbit responded:

There will always be an unmet demand for things that are given away. If I stood on the corner of the road giving things away I would have an enormous demand for them. But education in Britain is run for the people that work in it, not for the customers.

What we need is to say to parents: there is a choice of schools, just as there's a choice of supermarkets. And you must make your choice. Now the educationalists of course regard this with complete horror. To talk about education in the way you talk about groceries is to demean it. But the fact is over the last thirty years the standard of groceries has been going up and the standard of education has been going down.

He was right. Baroness Blackstone regarded his remarks with complete horror when I repeated them to her. She fumed, "That would be his view. A barbaric view. It's very sad that a man as intelligent as him makes such an inept comparison. Schools are not grocery stores." (Sometimes I felt guiltily mischievous, repeating views back and forth, stirring up argument. *En garde, rally, thrust!)*

Tebbit was unfazed. He strongly supported the idea of everybody going back to a core curriculum of English, math, and science.

It's much easier to teach kids to use a computer than it is to teach them to add and subtract. And yet if they don't understand the basic concept of numbers, they'll never ever really be able to use the computer intellectually as a tool. In the same way it's very easy to give them free expression and it's very difficult to teach them the rules of grammar. Teachers are eager to teach easy things. Their own professional standards have fallen.

I agreed with Tebbit about computers. Ever since I found the twelve-year-olds at Lord Grey Comprehensive School in Milton Keynes were whizzes on computers but didn't know a single poem by heart, one of my stock questions was to ask about memorizing poetry. When I mentioned to Dr. Bradfield, the founder of the Cambridge Science Park, how few children I met were learning poems, he was alarmed:

Is that so? That's tragic. Terrible. Wicked. It's a profound mistake. You can't really make friends with a poem, as it were, unless you commit it to memory. Then you can say it over to yourself as you go for a walk. During holidays my wife and I recite things to each other a great deal really, for old times' sake. It's great fun.

Dr. Bradfield was also concerned that studies of the classics hold their own. He later wrote me that at Cambridge there were about two hundred fifty undergraduates—2.5 percent of the total—and forty graduate students. "It has fallen slightly," he wrote, "but is still strong."

When I told Kenneth Baker that Dr. Bradfield voiced alarm that children weren't memorizing poems, he said, "So do I." Baker said, "I'm trying to reestablish respect for the old acquisition of basic facts and knowledge, and not just the processes of learning. We have to implant into these young minds basic facts about our history, about the rules of mathematical law . . ."

"Ah, you say you want children to memorize mathematic tables and poetry. Why can't you tell teachers to do this?" The more I saw of British schools, the more I was sold on the old-fashioned system where you learned by heart facts, dates, places, history, names, and, above all, poetry.

"I can't because then I would be Napoleon." What he could do, Baker said, was to reinforce the instincts of many teachers that memorization was the right thing to do. He explained:

> When teachers have people going around the schools saying, "We ought to teach them access to knowledge, not knowledge itself," they get demoralized. They get worried and they say, "Well, maybe we're wrong." Well, the Secretary of State is saying, "You're not wrong. Stick to the verities. Learn our tables by heart. Worry about grammar and punctuation and spelling. Just like you and I did."

I told Baker about one school I visited, where the drama coach had several girls screaming and shouting at each other, "acting out aggression." I said, "The teacher seemed to think it was a good idea. I didn't."

Again Baker agreed. "You're absolutely right." He said he'd been to ghetto schools in America where children were learning Shakespeare.

> And that's good. It's structured, beautiful language. You have to have structured education. You want to stimulate the imaginative side of a child. But you can't let it all be free form, everything hanging out.

What people like Baker and Tebbit, Dr. Bradfield, Baroness Blackstone, Lord Prior, and Sir John Harvey-Jones are working for, all in their different ways, like so many of the teachers I met, and Mrs. Thatcher herself, is a change in attitude. They are trying to combat the kind of attitude that puts a ceiling on human enterprise and expectation for the great mass of people. It will be a big task, possibly one taking generations, not just years. Without it, there are real limits to what British society can do.

This attitude is rooted, above all, in the education system, particularly in the top public schools like Eton, and at Oxbridge. I had a vague feeling when *The Economist* asked me to do the Britain survey that somehow my spending the summer at an Oxford college had played a role in my getting the assignment. I see now why it was essential, indeed, close to being the heart of the matter when it comes to trying to understand what ails British society.

Eton and Oxbridge

THE MOST NOTABLE school of all is Eton College, founded by Henry VI in 1440 on a plain below his royal residence, Windsor Castle, now an hour's rail trip from London. Earlier I mentioned visiting its Gothic stone chapel. And how its art and architecture, music and religion, seemed to epitomize our whole Western civilization.

Eton's Head Master, Eric Anderson, a practical Scotsman who was educated in St. Andrews, Scotland, and at Balliol, Oxford, said Eton today tries to strike a balance between science, math, computing, and economics, and the more traditional history and classics. He told me:

> It may be more important to teach the boys to weigh up issues, to argue them. In many ways we are still an old-fashioned school. You can sum it up pictorially almost by looking at a boy wearing a white bow tie and gown sitting at a computer. In a way that does describe Eton today.

Traditions are kept. "What we still do, which not all other schools do," Anderson said, "is to insist on Latin for the first two years on the ground that it is the basis of Western civilization, which to a large extent is based on the Greek and Roman world. We don't want to throw that part of our heritage away." As I expected, great emphasis is given articulacy, both spoken and written; it sets the patrician manner. In Britain, as anywhere else, it is plain to see, culture and above all how one speaks, not money, decides class. Anderson:

> We still have what we call "private business," which is unique, I think, to English schools and is really a kind of tutorial system. Boys of all ages, in small groups of five or six, twice a week go to the master's house. There they sit in the evening for an hour and talk about whatever the master decides. The only rule is it should not be part of the syllabus. They may discuss astronomy or an opera or play records of it. A lot of people say it was the best education they got at Eton.

Eton's pupils, who go from thirteen to eighteen, also write a good many essays in the course of a year. Anderson said he found the biggest difference between a school like Eton and schools he visited from time to time in America was the amount of English composition. "A quiz or test in your country will very often be a one-word answer or a very short sentence. Here it's nearly always an essay."

I asked about memorizing poetry. It was one tradition not being much upheld. Anderson apologized.

> I regret to tell you, because I am very much a believer in memorizing poetry, that we do it much less than we did. A couple of generations ago most young boys learned a poem a week. Now I'm afraid the pressure of getting everything else into their curriculum has ended that habit. *Some* poetry is still memorized by the little boys in their first two or three years.

Yet Shakespeare and other great English authors are taught more at Eton today than in the past, when more reading was done for fun. Familiarity with the Bible—King James version—and the Book of Common Prayer comes from going to chapel every morning the first two years, later just twice, then once a week. Nonetheless, Anderson finds, Biblical allusions are already fading. "Boys brought up on the New English Bible," he said, "don't understand what the 'talents' are anymore. A whole part of your heritage gets stripped away; you lose the nuances of what you read."

Aside from its (rather aesthetic) Anglicanism, its games (football, cricket, rowing, and its own muddy Field Game and Wall Game), its hierarchy and authority, Eton's most enduring asset is self-confidence, based on a fixed belief in an Etonian's superiority. As Lytton Strachey wrote in *Eminent Victorians*, worship of athletics and good form were the poles on which the English public school turned.

Over tea one rainy afternoon at the Garrick Club, Sir Peter Ramsbotham, a former ambassador to Washington, recalled his own days at Eton:

> You studied history and Greek and Latin, the classics. No virtue in a dead language but it trained the mind. It was a means toward very clear thinking, sparse, succinct thinking. Under eighteen you don't remember other than what it was that equipped you to use your mind.

Sir Peter, the son of a viscount and one of the few authentic aristocrats I interviewed (he was going off that evening to Clarence House to dine with the Queen Mother), still feels it is important to get young people to memorize poetry.

> The best teacher was the man who gave you some love of poetry, who taught you how to handle a book, what value was a book, how to use a book. When you leave school you should carry with you a store of things you love in your mind. If you are lucky you absorb, from your parents and your school, some things of lasting value.

It is an old, but evidently true, generalization that nine tenths of Britain's traditions were invented in the nineteenth century. Most of them were designed to equip Britain to rule its vast empire. For example, the great public schools like Eton and Winchester (or Westminster, where Brenda Maddox and Paul Theroux sent their sons) do go back of course for centuries, educating not just the aristocracy but quite large numbers of the middle class. The poet Thomas Gray went to Eton and his mother was a hatter.

It was between 1835 and 1885, as Britain trained more and more Victorian civil servants and colonial governors, that things started getting codified. Class became more rigid. From this period dates the mechanism to form boys in adolescence to become the future rulers of empire, of compulsory games, of hierarchy and authority, of starchy Anglicanism, of the stiff upper lip, of "not going into trade." Many are associated with Matthew Arnold's father, who at Rugby established a whole system to educate a specialized elite. Part of Britain's problem is so much of the mechanism lives on, even if it has lost its original purpose.

Clifford Davies, the Sub-Warden at Wadham College, where I stayed in 1986, says most of the present public school Oxbridge ways date back to about 1860, even if the universities themselves are very old (Sir Walter Raleigh went to Oxford and Elizabeth I saw plays at Cambridge).

> Although our buildings and our institutional history are very ancient, practically everything else you can think of that is typical of the English public school or the Oxford-Cambridge university system in fact goes back to the mid-nineteenth century. I mean the tutorial system as it is presently practiced, the accent on games which is now dying away, all the subject classifications in the syllabuses, they all date from then.

When I asked Eric Anderson about Eton's contemporary role, he replied:

> Exactly what it's always been. King Henry VI founded the school in order to provide himself with people to run the church and the state.

We still largely help to do that. I don't know how much of a role Eton played in the service of empire by creating inquiring minds and a willingness to take responsibility. It wasn't just Eton; I think it was all the public schools of the day. Relevant to that, I think it was extraordinary chance that this school was founded by the monarch right next door to his residence, Windsor Castle. Because what happened was that the top people in the country felt that to have their sons educated almost under the king's eye was a good idea. That no doubt gave them a chance to come and see the son and to pay a visit to the court at the same time. And in a curious kind of way, once that tradition was established, as society changes, whoever are the top people in society tend to follow their predecessors even when the top people are no longer the aristocracy.

"Where *is* the aristocracy?" I asked him. Sir Peter Ramsbotham certainly belonged to it, I'd met some hereditary peers, and *The Economist* had a few of its members on its staff, though you had to know who was who. Generally you got the feeling in Britain most of the eighty thousand or so aristocrats were off farming their estates.

"They're very invisible," I said.

"My point is: once you've got a reputation and the top people send their sons there, then generation after generation, society changes and Eton people come to the top." Even in Mrs. Thatcher's populist government, Etonians survive: they include Foreign Secretary Douglas Hurd, Environment Secretary Nicholas Ridley, William Waldegrave, son of an earl, and, until his retirement in 1987, Lord Hailsham, the former Lord Chancellor and the last link with the predominately Etonian Macmillan government of a quarter century before. But there hasn't been an Etonian Prime Minister since Alec Douglas-Home was defeated in 1964, though he was the twentieth. There are about fifty Etonians in Parliament; one ran into them in diplomacy, banking, the Guards, and, as we have seen, fifty-five among Britain's richest two hundred.

Hurd, in a 1988 book of interviews by Danny Danziger, *Eton Voices*, said he was embarrassed if introduced as an old Etonian. But he confessed:

I dream of Eton. Of particular rooms rather than of people. If you lived in college, which is alongside Lupton's Tower, the clock looms very large in your life. I went through a phase when I couldn't sleep, which I think teenagers do, and you could measure the passing hours when you weren't sleeping by the clock which never stopped . . . I still dream of it.

Having slept in a room at the top of the Keep of Durham Castle, just across a yard from Durham Cathedral and bells that tolled quarter-hourly all the night, I know exactly what he means.

Waldegrave, also quoted in *Eton Voices*, describes the same influences I felt in Eton's chapel:

> I think there was a very powerful sense in which a tradition of England —which is in danger of collapse—was strongly represented by the Eton of my day, with the mixture of the Anglican Church and of high English culture. I think Eton did have a shot . . . at representing a kind of tolerant high-culture tradition, which was very powerful, mixed in with the fabric of the buildings, the fabric of the connection between the Church and the school, the music, the literature.

It is true that Hurd and Waldegrave—Ridley seems harder-edged—come off as the two most liberal or "wet" members of the Thatcher government. This was noticeable in an interview I had with Waldegrave when he was still a junior minister for the environment, where he safeguarded the Tory green vote. In America, to meet competition with Japan and East Asia, there had been a fall in real wages. In Britain this hadn't happened. Real wages kept going up, at the time I interviewed him by around 3.4 percent, and companies kept closing down. Waldegrave made no attempt to sidestep the issue. He said the cost in Britain had "been borne by rather few people":

> We took the whole of this last recession by putting it on the unemployed. At no point did the real personal disposable income of people in work fall, as an average for the nation. If you take the average employed worker, he steamed through the hard times, not moderating his pay demands, taking real pay increases every year, and his standard of living went up.

Over the years Eton, like Winchester, Rugby, Harrow, Westminster, and the other public schools, has become both more expensive and more intellectually competitive. At the time of our interview, a year's tuition was the equivalent of $13,000, Anderson said. (Just about the average yearly cost of college education in America—$12,000.) About 30 in an enrollment of 1,270 were deemed sons of aristocrats. There were 250 pupils on reduced fees, 30 paying no fees at all, just as in Henry VI's day, 40 more very little. Fee-paying "Oppidans," or boys not on scholarship, still form the great body of students; in that sense, unlike Oxford and Cambridge, Eton and the other public schools are still mainly for the rich. Top hats went out in the 1940s, but white tie, tails, and striped pants is still very much the school dress. Anderson himself and most of the boys and masters were wearing it, except for a very muddy horde in shorts, shirts, and knee socks coming in from a Wall Game.

In Britain, the issue keeps coming back to Oxford and Cambridge. The old saw about Oxford educating people to run the country and Cambridge to advance the frontiers of science is still true. An amazing proportion of those I interviewed in Britain turned out to have been at Oxford, fewer, unless scientists, at Cambridge. What of their disdain for industry? It is true, Clifford Davies told me:

> I think Oxford and Cambridge mirror, in an exaggerated form, what is true of the country. It's hen and egg, isn't it? I mean we successfully adapted from training clergymen, which was what we were founded for, to train Victorian civil servants and colonial governors. Now we're adapting to City money. We haven't ever really adapted, it's true, to manufacturing industry or salesmanship.

Yet these are the two things Britain needs to have for a Japan-style "economic renaissance." There *is* a new professionalism, says Davies. The old gentlemanly amateurism—Kipling's "flannelled fools at the wicket or the muddied oafs at the goals"—when an Oxbridge education prepared Britain's brightest young men for a glittering career in the civil service or when a clever undergraduate's highest ambition was a university chair in medieval history or classical Greek, are gone. Davies:

> The City used to recruit very much on the old boy network. You had to be from the right school and socially acceptable. Now it's much more ruthless and competitive. In that sense the phenomenon of Thatcherism is working and changing our society.

The aim of the historic 1963 report of Lord Robbins, then chairman of both the *Financial Times* and the London School of Economics, was to expand by the early 1980s the number of full-time students in higher education from 216,000 to 560,000; this has nearly been achieved, though far fewer students headed for science than hoped. Lord Robbins worried about the Oxbridge monopoly:

> It is not a good thing that Oxford and Cambridge should attract too high a proportion of the country's best brains and become more and more exclusively composed of a certain kind of intellectual elite.

Interestingly, Britain's industrial decline, compared to America or Germany, goes back to the mid-nineteenth century, when the present Oxbridge system emerged. Anthony Sampson, for one, blames Oxford and Cambridge for Britain's failure to face up to her economic predicament:

> They are certainly less contemptuous of industry, more worldly and realistic, than they were twenty years ago; there is much more to-ing and fro-ing between Oxbridge and London; and behind the more glittering surface of balls, debates and exhibitionists there is another Oxbridge of industrious and often penurious scientists and engineers who spend their afternoons in labs and their evenings at books. But the spells and enchantments which these universities cast on many of their graduates still, I believe, exact a high price.

Another Oxford don told me:

> It's true there's a tendency to despise manufacturing industry and that what has always been considered smart is to go into the civil service or media or the City. Oxford and Cambridge for ambitious students are exciting and metropolitan; you can continue this sort of life if you go to live in London. But manufacturing is likely to send you to Middlesbrough or somewhere tedious. A complaint you hear from a lot of students who have gone off to industry is that it doesn't give you much opportunity for the first few years. It can be boring.

"I've never despised industry," objected Lord Briggs, when I brought up the matter with him. "You see, at Oxford we didn't despise industry. But we never attached as much importance to it as to links with government—the Foreign Office, the Treasury. Then there was the media, the City, the law. Oxford has had very, very firm and secure links with London." Among his own students at Worcester College, Lord Briggs told me, were men who became chairmen of Courtaulds, British Oxygen, and ICI, all industrial giants. "I think now, however, it may be worse than twenty-five years ago. These days they all want to go into merchant banking. They want to get money."

Sir Michael Palliser, vice chairman of the Midland Bank, one of Britain's Big Four, after a career in the Foreign Office, said, "To my mind, the fundamental weakness of this country over the past forty years has been in education. We haven't educated our people properly. We haven't succeeded in mounting the class divisions. They're still too prevalent in Britain. I'd preserve Oxford and Cambridge as centers of excellence, but I'd give them—particularly Oxford, my own university—a considerable kick in the pants."

Playwright Ronald Harwood, who spent a year at Balliol as Visitor in Theatre, told me students would come up to him and ask, "Should I be an actor or should I go into merchant banking?" He said, "I always gave them the same answer: 'Go into banking. Because if you don't feel it to be a compulsion, an absolute obsessive need, you don't want to go into the theater.'"

Denis Healey, the veteran Labour Party leader and its shadow foreign secretary, when I interviewed him, was also outspoken. "Our educational system for the masses is based on nineteenth century public school values of Matthew Arnold and *Tom Brown's Schooldays.*" (Arnold characterized the business classes as money-grubbing "Philistines.") Healey, who went to Balliol, said:

> We just do not produce enough people with the skills a modern economy requires. People in Britain feel they're failing if they go into industry. If they go into the professions or into the financial sector, they're a success. In the City, as in the States, you can earn telephone number salaries when you're twenty-seven. And in manufacturing industry you can't get to that level ever.

How to change this attitude? Two thirds of Oxford and Cambridge students now want to work in the private sector, one survey found. Only a fifth chose government, mainly for ideological reasons or because it was "worthwhile"; just 3 percent are attracted by prestige, pay, or perks. But the City was still the big magnet. The survey found fewer students, however, choose careers for pay than for job satisfaction, promotion prospects, and good training facilities. Though 44 percent expect to spend some time in industry, low pay there put off 36 percent of the men and 18 percent of the women polled. And 28 percent thought jobs in industry had low status or were dirty.

Roy Jenkins, who has become Lord since we talked, and chancellor of Oxford ("put out to graze," a political rival said), thought full employment in Britain will only come when its people get more technically qualified. "I don't want the technocrats to take over Oxford," he said, "but our university population is too small. We need more people going and we need more apprenticeship schemes."

Oxford and Cambridge are steadily becoming more competitive; in 1981 for the first time Oxford took more new undergraduates from state schools than from public schools, though there is still too much self-selection out. Two in five applicants get admitted. But the route to fame and fortune in Britain is still from public school to university to the Bar to the House of Commons or a slight variation; for Sir Michael Palliser, for example, it was public school, Oxford, Brigade of Guards, Foreign Office, Midland Bank. Sir Antony Acland, who became ambassador to Washington in 1986, fits a similar pattern: Eton, Christ Church, headed the Foreign Office. Acland himself, in an interview I had with him in Washington, suggested the old route is too limited:

> I got onto the tram line at the first stop when I left university and I suppose I'll go to a stop called Retirement at the age of sixty. And I rather wish I'd done something else. Been a Reuters correspondent, been a lecturer, run my own business. But we're getting people in the Foreign Office now from other walks of life. I put up the age so that you can apply to join until thirty-two rather than twenty-seven. Start off your career at thirty-two. They'll be people who have *done something else.*

It is hardly surprising that Oxford and Cambridge have produced so few tycoons. They represent stability and continuity: the ideals of the mid-nineteenth-century Victorian gentleman. Sir Michael Howard says the old route to the top—public school, Oxbridge —is no longer true of Mrs. Thatcher's ministers. "You are starting to get upwardly mobile lower-middle-class people. She's got all these young people who have come from practically nowhere to make it on their own." But Senator Daniel P. Moynihan, who was at the London School of Economics, says, "The way the English still conjugate the verb 'to be' is: *I* was at Oxford, *you* were at Cambridge, and *he* was at the LSE."

Though she herself went there, Mrs. Thatcher and Oxford have been mutually hostile ever since the university voted against giving her an honorary degree. "She pretended she didn't care," said one don who was involved, "but it was a devastating insult. It was a coalition of left-wing arts people and scientists who were annoyed that their research grants were being cut by the government."

"I'm afraid Mrs. Thatcher isn't terribly popular with academics," says Howard. "She is seen as being extremely unsympathetic to intellectuals, anybody who doesn't make money."

Sir Oliver Wright, her former ambassador to Washington, says:

> The universities and the teaching profession, like the trade unions, the industrialists, the working people, had been cocooned by the welfare state. Unlike American universities, all our universities rely on state funds. They've grown used to it. They make no effort at all. Whereas private universities in the United States have to make tremendous efforts. Even some of the state universities, if they want improvements, have to get out and get money and sponsorship. Mrs. Thatcher is getting rid of the welfare state mentality and making us stand on our own two feet and be self-reliant.

Sir Claus Moser, the Warden of Wadham College, where I spent the summer, said in a speech observing the twenty-fifth anniversary of the earlier mentioned Robbins report that Britain could be proud of all the universities and polytechnics opened since then. But he also warned:

> In one sense, we may also be one of the least educated advanced countries. Forty percent of our children leave school after only eleven years and are by then likely to have been poorly taught in some key subjects, notably mathematics. Even if they do stay on . . . they are likely to emerge with either little mathematics or science or with little English, history, or languages. No other advanced country gives the majority of its children so half-baked an education.

In a talk I had with Sir Claus in his office at Rothschild's bank in the City, he said he put all his hopes on improving Britain's educational system: "I would like to live in a society where to go and teach was the highest objective. I'd like the teacher to be the most highly respected citizen in society. I can't think of anything more important, whether it's primary schools, secondary schools, polytechnics, universities, I don't care where." A stunning 85 percent of the eighteen-year-olds, he went on, "get no sniff of higher education." Kenneth Baker, when I interviewed him, said 12 percent rising to 14 percent of these were now doing first degree work, about half at universities and half at polytechnics. The end-of-the-century target, Baker said, was just under 20 percent. Sir Claus told me he found that alarmingly "unambitious." In the United States, where over half the eighteen-year-olds are in higher education, 19 percent of the population have university degrees; it is 13 percent in Japan, 8 percent in West Germany, and just 6 percent in Britain. But the statistics are somewhat misleading as Britain has all kinds of technical colleges offering practical skills such as motor mechanics, welding, engineering, and business studies, which it does not include in "higher education," as American statistics do. Sir Claus was pessimistic:

> Look at this country. Leaving aside things like family life, the arts, what you can't measure. I mean look at this country. Look at our hospitals, look at our schools, look at our airports, look at our railway stations. In none do we now compare with Germany, Switzerland, even Italy and France, which one used to be snooty about . . . We've slipped and I don't understand why.

We were, of course, in a vice chairman's office in one of Britain's greatest merchant banks, the destination so many of its young want to reach. Sir Claus appreciated the irony.

We happen to be sitting in the City but my heart is not here. I think the City is doing its job moderately well. But I don't think the City has an important part to play in society. Nor does Wall Street in America. I think if I were a dictator in charge of Britain, I would divide the work force in the City by ten and I'd move a lot of the best people into industry. I want the ablest people to go into teaching and into manufacturing where a country's real wealth is created. Our industry is slipping. Schools, books, teachers. They have a profound role to play. One shouldn't even have to discuss it. Our economic growth, quality of life, everything depends on education.

What Happened to
the Wheelwrights?

L ET US SAY, just supposing, that Britain's education improves radically and its industry gets the scientific and engineering skills it needs to compete globally in electronics, biotech, and information services. It gets big R&D budgets. Computers fed with electronic impulses run automated machines. Electricity supplies the energy.

What happens, as the girls from Bristol asked at the Rover plant, to the manual workers you don't need anymore? The microchip is like the motor car. That threw blacksmiths, breeders, oat growers, harness makers, wheelwrights out of work. When will there be a like harnessing of the microchip's potential for everybody's benefit?

The problem of displaced labor seems particularly acute in Britain. As a Midwesterner, who has gone back several times during the American farm crisis, I've seen a good many farmer's sons, uprooted from the land, at once go for training in mechanics, engineering, computers, one of the new skills. The same with the sons of factory workers in the towns. In Britain the way so many working-class youth are not more aspiring has to be class-related. You simply do not find the same ingrained discouragement among their American counterparts. About half of British sixteen-year-olds are outside full-time education. Since 1983 the government has tried to keep as many as possible of the rest learning some skill through its Youth Training Scheme, in theory on-the-job training. The YTS trainee gets a £30-a-week ($51) allowance, more than the £20 ($34) he or she would get on the dole. A regular unskilled job pays about £80 ($144) a week.

Britain's unemployment fell from about 3.5 million to under 2.5 million in 1986–88. The government hopes it will fall well below 2 million by 1991–92, the probable time of the next election. The biggest problem is uneducated laborers who once would have done physical work in field, factory, or mine. Somehow they've got to be given new skills; nearly half of all jobless British males in 1989 had been out of work for over a year. Government training programs center on a switch from the old smokestack industry skills to services.

"It won't happen, it won't happen," says Asa Briggs, speaking in his role as head of the Open University. This is Britain's one undisputed success story in higher education, which provides degrees by correspondence course and television. Conceived under the Wilson government and set up by Mrs. Thatcher when she was Minister of Education in 1971, it has taught more than half a million people, over eighty thousand of them earning a degree. It has also trained some thirty thousand managers and engineers in microprocessor technology. Many British companies use its courses to upgrade staff skills in manufacturing, design, new technology, management, and marketing. There are special branches for nurses, teachers, and social workers. Its headquarters in Milton Keynes, commuting distance from London, has about four hundred full-time dons and three hundred broadcasting staff, who make all the films and tape. Here, too, demand exceeds capacity; more than half its applicants every year get turned away.

And yet the Open University, for all its success, does not provide the kind of adult education the displaced laborer needs: on-the-job training to learn a trade. But just how this can be done, Lord Briggs says, is very unclear.

> Everybody talks about them getting jobs in services. It won't happen. If you want to buy a railway ticket at a London station, you've got to stand in a long line, two or three times as long as twenty years ago. They've got to cut the costs of labor. If you do, standards of service undoubtedly deteriorate. It's the same on a London bus; 70 percent now have a combined driver and collector of fares. It takes that much longer to get from one point to another because you've got to wait while the driver's collecting the fares. The bus companies have reduced their labor costs, but the services have deteriorated.

Alan Tuffin, who heads the Union of Communication Workers (UCW), confirms this. There has been a steady drop in the number of communications and telephone workers. Households with telephones have doubled to 60 percent since 1964, but the number of switchboard operators ("telephonists" in Britain) has dropped from eighty thousand to thirty thousand. Fewer maintenance men are needed when high-tech systems go underground.

The post office has over 100,000 postboxes, 28,000 vans, and 45,000 postmen on the streets every day, but computers cut down jobs in the postal service even as the volume of mail grows. As I mentioned earlier, mailing a letter is a lot more efficient in Britain. But it is a lot easier to make a phone call in America; the British telephone system is strangely antiquated. When you dial Information you often find it is busy or a recorded male voice tells you to "take your place in the queue." Both systems in Britain will expand as it gets more telephone lines and open networks, microcomputers, printers, copying machines, and data links. Rival private postal services, guaranteeing overnight or same-day delivery for a higher cost, are popping up in Britain as they are in America.

Tuffin, a moderate who has tried to adapt his union to change, says all union leaders find it the same; he told me, "Old-style work is not going to be available. Services won't absorb enough. People have got to stay longer in school, get better trained, retire earlier, and share what work there is."

Just between 1980 and 1988, Britain lost 2 million manufacturing jobs. In Scotland's depressed town of Dundee, where 15 percent of its adult workers were unemployed and on the dole, an offer by Ford in Detroit in 1988 to put up an electronic components plant, to initially employ about four hundred, was the best news the town had heard for years. Ford's main condition was that it wanted to deal with a single trade union, in this case Britain's Amalgamated Engineering Union. The AEU readily agreed; it has single-union agreements with many companies, including Sony, Dunlop, Nissan, and Komatsu elsewhere in Britain, and Timex in Dundee itself. Gavin Laird, the AEU chief, argued:

> We are able to demand an end to archaic distinctions between blue- and white-collar workers. The petty apartheid of better holidays, sick pay, pensions, canteen facilities, and training for white-collar workers are dispatched to the wastebin where they belong. More than this, we managed to extract a commitment from Ford to pay rates in the upper quarter of the Scottish electronics industry . . . It was an excellent deal . . .

The deal fell through after leaders of Britain's Trades Union Congress (TUC) opposed a single-union agreement. Ford set up its factory in Spain instead. A further fight with the electrician's union led by Eric Hammond has kept the British labor movement split over the issue of whether London labor leaders can tell independent unions what deals they may sign.

Lord Briggs agrees with Alan Tuffin that as computers and robots take over, our whole idea of work will have to change: "You've got to do three difficult things in the long run: change the conception of leisure, share work, and develop a more broken pattern of life. People are going to have a lot of time when they're not at work."

When it comes to information services, Britain enjoys an overwhelming competitive advantage: the English language. Three quarters of the world's mail, telexes, and cables, half its technical and scientific journals, 80 percent of the information stored in the world's computers, are in English; it is the language of high tech from Silicon Valley to Seoul (whose biotech scientists, I found on a visit in South Korea in 1980, are all American-educated). English is the language of aircraft and ships at sea. When I taught graduate students from all over India, plus a few from Africa and Nepal, at Nagpur University in the 1960s, English was the only common language. Triumphant in Asia, it holds its own with Arabic and French in Africa, and is really only embattled in Latin America (if you go to Brazil, learn Portuguese).

As information services expand from books, newspapers, periodicals, radio, and television into computing services, video products, satellites, cable networks, and on-line and off-line information, they make up over 6 percent of Britain's GNP. Industries that employ people who create words, sounds, or pictures, that is, copyright what they do, have an estimated £15 billion ($25.5 billion) annual turnover. Foreign spending for the arts alone accounts for 34 percent of turnover, compared to 27 percent for British manufacturing. The arts, according to London's Policy Studies Institute, earn £14 billion ($23.8 billion) a year, and are Britain's fourth biggest invisible earner.

Is Britain, with English as the global language and the British masters of it in so many ways, realizing its potential in the new techniques? As Sir Nicholas Henderson, a former ambassador to Washington now with the Midland Bank, told me, "I think this government makes a great mistake in not having an English language television service worldwide, which has been suggested. To economize on a world service for the BBC is wrong." Mrs. Thatcher, as we'll see next in the City of London, has done what she can to encourage its bankers and stockbrokers by lowering tax rates and easing exchange controls. But she seems strangely indifferent to the arts. Is her government missing the boat by not investing more in them, in satellite channels and optical cable systems, and in more computers and software for schools and universities? Is it training enough people in all the new telecommunications skills? Arts subsidies have fallen sharply. Are the British once again being penny-wise and pound-foolish?

Is Greed Good?

The British Empire was a cartel.
England could buy whatever it wanted cheap
And made a profit on what it made to sell.
The empire's gone but the City of London keeps
On running like a cartoon cat off a cliff . . .
Serious Money

MENTION THE City of London and you hear it is un-British and full of greedy young speculators at computers chasing quick killings and six-figure salaries. In the heady month leading up to the Big Bang in October 1986, when the London Stock Exchange was decartelized, the City's image was personified by the young champagne-swilling broker who said on BBC, "The stock market will be a car park in five years and I'll have made a fortune." When Wall Street's Black Monday came along a year later, amid the storm of insider dealing scandals, some of the Porsches and BMWs got returned and the City lost a bit of its glitter. A year after that, reality hit the City with an even bigger bang. Its firms' combined losses in 1988 came to around £500 million ($850 million).

The 1980s have seen fundamental changes: an agreement to drop fixed commissions in 1983, merger with international securities dealers in 1985, the Big Bang in 1986, the implementation of the Financial Services Act in 1988.

It is often said that the City ought to invest more in Britain's home market and industry through long-term capital projects and not just look to relative global share prices from day to day, with its frenzy of takeovers and leverage buyouts, making money from money. We have seen the City blamed for treating sterling as a petrocurrency, like the Arab oil-earned dollars that flooded banking in London and Washington with huge cash surpluses and are at the bottom of the Third World debt crisis. In Britain this really got going in 1979–81 when huge earnings were coming in from North Sea oil. The City, with the Thatcher government's blessing, tended to treat this money in the same way it did petrodollars earned by Arab oil and recycled by banks into the industrialized nations. Both London and New York banks became big dispensers of loans.

This kept the City as a powerful force in world banking and finance. Both Tory and Labour leaders complain it gravely damaged British industry. John Davidson, head of the Confederation of British Industry for Scotland and a Tory himself, whom I met in Glasgow in 1986 and 1988, said the City's response to North Sea oil earnings (6 percent of Britain's GNP) in part caused Scotland's continuing depression. After 1979, he said, the value of the pound went way up, thanks to oil, and exports dropped as British manufacturers couldn't stay competitive. He said, "Many British industries were really crippled. We've never recovered from it." We heard the same thing from Sir John Harvey-Jones and Lord Prior. Sir Oliver Wright, Mrs. Thatcher's former ambassador to Washington and Bonn before that, had just as strong feelings about it. Over tea at the Travellers' Club he complained, "All these young men in pink jackets who send currencies whizzing around the world twenty-four hours a day at the touch of a computer got it into their little noddles that the pound is a petrocurrency. A lot of our companies went to the wall."

Bryan Gould, the Labour Party's spokesman for trade and industry, told me, "We still run the economy in the interests of the City." To Gould, in a talk at his office in Westminster, this has its roots in the British Empire and the habit gained then of giving priority to "maintaining the value of our assets." The City, he said, concerned about short-term variance in the value of these assets, won every policy argument. The Bank of England and those worried about inflation, financial orthodoxy, and keeping up the value of assets, not industry, were persuasive when it came to setting interest rates. "They have the government's ear, they win," said Gould. "The CBI [Confederation of British Industry] gets up and says: interest rates are bad for business. But who takes any interest?" Gould warned:

> We're living in a fool's paradise. We have squandered North Sea oil. We have a raging consumer boom financed on credit. We are failing to make any provision for the future. We're not investing in basic science. Or in R&D. We're not investing in straightforward plant technology. We're not training our work force. All this is linked with the short-termism that comes from the predominance of the City.

The City rivals Wall Street in banking, insurance, and securities. After the oil price rises in the 1970s, it became the center of the Eurodollar market (recycled petrodollars) and international lending. The oil companies also made it their de facto world headquarters. With its new regulatory structure, the huge increases in international capital flows, and the microelectronic revolution in financial information, London is a leading player in the orchestra of world stock exchanges (New York, Tokyo, Paris, Frankfurt, and Milan, plus Hong Kong, being the big ones). It turns over $2 trillion a year in stocks, bonds, and options. Mrs. Thatcher fostered this all she could. She liberalized exchange controls imposed by past Labour governments and lowered the top tax rate from 98 percent to 40 percent (25 percent for most people). She has encouraged Britain to play its role in international finance, oil, and multinational conglomerates, even if the City has progressively less to do with Britain itself and its industry.

It does have to do with Britain's geographical location and its financial and dealing skills. Wall Street tends to be preoccupied with America itself, and Japan, despite its growing role in export capital, has no tradition of foreign investment. London has the advantage of nearly five hundred foreign banks, a tradition of free entry and equal treatment, markets in shipping, insurance, commodities, and banking, and an informal system of regulation and benevolent despotism run by the Bank of England, all located within one square half mile.

The charge that the City neglects British industry goes back a long way. The stock exchange and clearing banks rarely provided industry with long-term finance (German banks heavily invested in their industry, late getting started in the 1870s after the Franco-Prussian war; they still do). Britain's industrial revolution was mainly financed by rich farming and London families at a time when the merchant banks of the City were making fortunes buying and selling commodities, gold, and minerals, and financing merchant adventurers like those who started the South Sea Company and the East India Company in the eighteenth century.

John Forsyth, a senior director at Morgan Grenfell, a merchant bank (first established by J. P. Morgan, and sold to West Germany's biggest financial institution, Deutsche Bank, last fall), says, "The City, going back to the sixteenth century, has always been an international entrepôt. It is and always has been an export industry." Over the centuries this has helped make Britain rich, as is seen in the country houses and estates of Southeast England, many of them the present homes of City commuters. In 1987 the City's invisible earnings were running close to £900 million ($1.5 billion) a month, plus the spillover in earnings by hotels, restaurants, and entertainment, the whole life of London. An estimated 400,000 men and women work in the City; armies of them in well-tailored dark blue pinstripes move across London by car, train, and Underground every weekday morning. The bowler hats and umbrellas are largely gone, but the City's high fliers, amid the long hours, stress, and intense competition, look richer and better dressed than they did a few years ago.

Forsyth defended the City over the pound's rise after 1979. "Don't look at emotive phrases like 'young men in pink jackets.'" He said he blamed the government for letting currency get in such short supply it drove sterling though the roof. ("Pink jackets" refers to the pink morning coats still worn by attendants at the Bank of England.)

Forsyth admitted:

> There is great resentment in industry, in Whitehall and political circles, and among the unions, indeed among the press, that the City's main concern should be serving British industry and the British economy. It's like saying an industry should not worry about exports but stick to the home market. The City has been an international entrepôt market, buying and selling, from the start. If you want an international entrepôt market, what do you think Venice was? A giant gambling den.

"And look what happened," I said, quoting Browning: "'Venice spent what Venice earned.'"

Forsyth compared what was happening in the City to the Gold Rush, a huge booming industry generating pop-star-scale salaries for Eurobond and gilts traders, making brokers out of taxi drivers (there have been a few cases)—and turning others into taxi drivers. For an overview from somebody who has been both in government and the City, I turned to Lord Roll, president of Warburg's bank and formerly a director of *The Times* and the Bank of England, and in 1963–64 the senior-most civil servant in the Treasury.

Does the City support industry enough? He said:

> I've lived quite a long time now and I know this question crops up every few years at almost regular intervals. The City's standard defensive argument is that there's never any shortage of money for anything that's worthwhile in terms of profitability. True, I think.

Even for Britain this has changed. "Now that this has all become global," Lord Roll went on, "a chap who's making chocolate in Switzerland might raise money in the Tokyo market. Somebody making bridges in Japan might raise Swiss francs in Zurich. And swap them for dollars and swap the dollars into yen." The Stock Exchange's old motto, "My Word Is My Bond," has given way to legal regulation; a London bank like Warburg's also belongs to stock exchanges in New York and Tokyo; it does a brokerage business and market trading. Building societies lend money and compete with banks; banks lend money on mortgages. "You have a much more multifarious type of financial services industry," Lord Roll said. "Barriers are breaking down."

You can see this just by walking around the City, with its paradoxes of glass skyscrapers and Victorian stone palaces, its banks of computer terminals and bits of the wall the Romans built around their first big settlement of Londinium in AD 43. Among the giants are the big British commercial merchant banks. But Americans are almost as much in evidence as are Japanese and so are many other overseas banks, discount houses, jobbers, stockbrokers, or other financial conglomerates. Anthony Sampson compares the City to an island, whose inhabitants view the world in their own way:

> They can see across the whole globe, but they see it through money . . . They still remain aloof from the real industrial problems; and their business . . . is making money, not things.

Looking at it the way Mrs. Thatcher's government might, the City makes up to a large extent for ailing British industry's trade gap. Britain still has to import a fair amount of food and raw materials to survive.

Lord Roll recalled George Bernard Shaw's *Apple Cart* where Britain's great contribution to world affairs was exporting chocolate creams. Britain's future, he agreed, most probably lay with the microchip, biotech, and information and financial services, plus, when it came to exports, upmarket luxury goods like the Rolls-Royce and Jaguar. The government had come to this, he felt, partly because it fit in with its free-market, private-enterprise ideology, and partly because so many old industries had turned out to be lame ducks. But he also agreed Mrs. Thatcher had been "parsimonious" about funding science and the arts.

"Mrs. Thatcher seems to encourage the City more," I said.

"I think that's probably true. The City is of course par excellence an example of the free market." Lord Roll expects the City to grow, for two reasons:

> Partly, because of our geographical location between New York and Tokyo you can work twenty-four hours a day in all financial markets. Then, even with more regulation, we still have the old tradition of an open door; there's never been any real obstacle to foreign houses setting up here. And there is still a large degree of self-regulation, self-discipline.

Though some of British industry's ills can definitely be blamed on the City, financial services is one of the major props for the whole economy. In 1980–86, the cumulative surplus for Britain's financial services of £38.5 billion ($65 billion) was greater than that for oil (£33.5 billion or $57 billion).

The City's high salaries are sometimes defended as the only way to keep the ablest young people from being hired away by Americans and Japanese. Asa Briggs says: "If British industrialists were prepared to pay as much and give their managerial entrants the same career opportunities when they're young, they'd get better people. I see it very clearly at Oxford." General Sir James Glover, commander-in-chief of the United Kingdom Land Forces, confirms this view. In a talk at his headquarters near Salisbury, he said that young officers tell him so few of their contemporaries are attracted to industry because of its lower pay, less chance of responsibility at an early age, the poor location of some industries, and the possibility of union trouble.

Come Fill the Cup

ONE CRITICISM MADE of the City is that it is more willing to buy up foreign companies than invest in good old Britain. "After all," says Sir Terence Conran, one of Britain's biggest retailers, "it's their country too." And it is true that in the late 1980s, British investors spent £70 billion in America, beating even the Japanese. After Mrs. Thatcher abolished exchange controls in 1979, combined with Britain's oil-fired current-account surpluses in 1980–85, there was a regular flood of capital outside the country.

City bankers get back at traders like Conran by reminding them that the Channel tunnel and the fall of remaining nontariff barriers to trade in the EEC will expose them to a lot more competition. Can they cope? Some worry British salesmen are insular, ignorant, and, besides, can't speak German, Italian, or French. Napoleon's quip, "a nation of shopkeepers," still piques the British (actually Adam Smith used it first and Napoleon said it in French, *"une nation de boutiquiers,"* which only makes it sound nastier).

But within Britain, retailing boomed during the 1980s; consumer spending in 1987 and 1988 rose by 7 percent a year (but just by 4 percent in 1989 and early 1990). Consumer credit more than doubled in 1981–87. So did house borrowing—mortgages on equity loans. So, alarmingly, did the British propensity to import. As Britain's class system got a bit less rigid, it gave newly prosperous yuppies more chance to define themselves by what they could buy rather than by their accent or where they came from; to many this meant buying everything in sight and going into debt.

Sir Terence Conran has been called the Golden Boy of British retailing. A designer-turned-tycoon with outlets in Europe and America, he built up the Storehouse group—Mothercare, Habitat, Richard Shops, Heals, British Home Stores. Sir Terence is one of the few people I met who says when it comes to buying consumer goods, he sees little evidence of Disraeli's "Two Nations," poor and rich, North and South.

"You're talking to a shopkeeper who's got an equal balance of stores in the North and Scotland, and the South of England. We do not really see significant differences." With all the credit, nine out of ten in the work force holding jobs, two earners in most families, fewer children, higher wages, big tax cuts, the dole, a brisk black economy, and plenty of credit, people somehow had money to spend.

I interviewed Conran in his big, studio-like office in Tottenham Court Road. He may have made his name designing modestly-priced furniture, but this had an imported Italian sofa and an expensive Turkish rug. Now fifty-nine, easygoing and affable, Sir Terence has been put to be worth around £120 million (over $200 million). He made it all in less than forty years. A native of Dorset, he came to London to train at its Central School of Art and Design. His bright fabrics and furniture, shown at the Festival of Britain in 1951, appealed to consumers after the drab deprivation of the war years. The first in a chain of Habitat stores, aimed at young couples setting up homes, opened in 1964; Mothercare (mother-and-child clothes) was bought up in 1983; and the company merged with British Home Stores, a big but dowdy department store chain, in late 1985. In four years, like a character in his ex-wife Shirley's bestseller *Lace,* Conran went from a designer with a medium-sized business to a retailing tycoon. (Shirley has done all right too, he said, getting a $3 million advance for a one-page typed outline of her novel *Savages.)*

Apolitical, Conran finds Labour good on welfare ("removes stresses and strains"), the Tories on helping business ("They've got all that sorted out"). He praised the Thatcher government for reducing the power of unions but criticized it for not doing more, as in tax breaks, to encourage industry to invest in new plant equipment. He said:

> The City has always had a very short-term view of profitability. Its investment companies expect a three-year return. This holds back the country. Capital-intensive equipment is a long-term payback. Since the City won't do it, it's got to be underwritten by the government. It's the same the world over. Industry has to modernize and that means investing in machinery that does without people.

A trend to American-style suburban malls is on. In Newcastle, right at the peak of the 1980s recession, with 15 percent of its labor force on the dole, MetroCentre, Europe's biggest shopping mall, was

opened just southwest of the city, with a ten-screen cinema and
funfair. Elsewhere in Britain, over two hundred shopping malls
were under construction in the late 1980s. "Our greatest handicap is
the conservatism of the left," says John Sainsbury, chairman of the
retail chain that has done much to speed the switch since the 1970s
to suburban malls. In 1988 Sainsbury's supermarkets, with annual
sales over £5 billion ($8.5 billion) toppled the department store
chain Marks and Spencer to become Britain's biggest retailer.

In just ten years, a 1986 Sainsbury study showed, British car
ownership per household jumped from 55 percent to 62 percent (17
percent of households owned two). Refrigerators went from 81 percent to 95 percent, freezers from 13 percent to 35 percent. Which
means, with so many women working, families want to shop once
or twice a week by car and really stock up. Consumers are also getting choosier (a Ford Escort, for example, now comes in fifty versions, plus all kinds of colors, trims, and interior designs). Tastes
are influenced by television (twenty-six hours a week average view-
ing) and travel abroad (16 million Britons took overseas trips in
1986, compared to 6 million ten years earlier; midsummer air traffic
to the Continent can cause chaos at airports).

In eating habits, Sainsbury's researchers find, aside from expected shifts from sweets and fat to salads and whole-meal bread,
that there is a marked decline in such venerable British institutions
as the big breakfast, high tea, the Sunday roast beef dinner, or even
family gatherings. More people eat alone outside the house or just
have a snack. Gourmet cooking is in, along with freshly baked bread
and freshly squeezed orange juice. Sainbury's statistics: its lorries
went over 15 million miles in 1987 to 279 stores so that 68,000 employees could sell 10.8 percent of Britain's food and drink.

The Sainsburys themselves are Britain's third richest family,
worth around £2 billion ($3.4 billion). It all began with Lord Sains-
bury's great-grandfather, also named John, who opened a small
shop selling butter, milk, and eggs in London's Drury Lane in 1869.
With sixteen new supermarkets in 1987, eighteen in 1988, and sixty
more planned through 1991, Sainbury's is growing like Topsy. But
Britain should take a good look at what happened in America before
turning its High Streets into wastelands. The world's fifth richest
man, an American named Sam Walton, amassed over $8.5 billion
(£5 billion) by putting discount stores called Wal-Marts just outside
little towns all over the United States. Every time he did so, a Main
Street died. "England is too small to do things in the American way,"

Asa Briggs told me. "If John Sainsbury could put his shops wherever he wanted to put them, and we had roads wherever drivers want them, you'd quickly turn this island into a concrete jungle."

Lord Sainsbury, when I met him in his office at the company's Victorian stone palace near the City, argues:

People say: look what's happening in America. The middle of towns becomes a desert. But there's a side of Britain we're awfully slow to recognize. Thirty years ago the wife would have been home and had time to shop. Now she's working. If it's a family of two parents plus two children, she will need to take away eighty-five, ninety pounds of food, enough to last them for a week. We're very slow to recognize the importance of car parking close to supermarkets. And I'm against multi-story car parks in city centers. You get violence and vandalism.

I found, after I'd shopped in Britain, that it was best to avoid big supermarkets, whether city center or suburban mall, in favor of one of the small grocery shops run by Asians or Iranians. A Sainsbury's checkout stand may have electronic scanners, but you are likely to encounter the same old grumpy, underpaid-feeling salesgirl, who is invariably sitting down, not standing as in America, and unlike American clerks, she doesn't put the groceries in bags for you. She just takes your money, shoves everything into a tumbled pile, pushes it aside, and turns to the next customer, leaving first-time American shoppers with culture shock.

The Asians have also taken over the news agent shops from the English; they stay open all hours while the English tend to shut down for lunch and close for the day at five. (American joke: Somebody who'd visited England was asked how it was. "I don't know," he said. "It was closed.")

Britain abounds in Horatio Alger Ragged Dick-style heroes who got rich in retailing. Sir Terence Conran's gift was designing; but an intuitive sense of what consumers want made him a fortune. Sir John Moores, ninety-two, whose wealth of close to £1.7 billion (just under $3 billion) ranks him just after Sainsbury, left school at fourteen to become a post office messenger; he soon got into retailing. Publisher Robert Maxwell (£700 million) was born in a poor, remote Czech-Romanian peasant village. Alan Sugar, Britain's Amstrad computer czar, started out peddling car aerials from the back of a van. Anita Roddick, like Sugar still in her forties, whose parents run a small Italian cafe, started her Body Shop chain of two hundred fifty outlets for "natural" cosmetics (cucumber cleanser, milk bath, banana conditioner) with a £4,000 overdraft in 1976. Richard

Branson, who is still just thirty-nine in 1990, made at least £100 million in twenty years on cheap records (Phil Collins, Boy George) and transatlantic airfares. His Virgin business has opened—what else?—a super shopping mall in Milton Keynes. And then there is Sir Freddie Laker, who came and went with the speed of one of his bargain flights.

Lord Sainsbury, married to a ballet dancer and in 1988 chairman of the Royal Opera House, Covent Garden, after four generations has the aura of old money; he is no longer "trade." Not the newcomers. Mary Quant, after she opened her shop, Bazaar, in King's Road, Chelsea, used to work, as did her husband, until three or four o'clock in the morning. In due course somebody came with a factory inspector and told them it was illegal. Quant was told: "You realize if you work this hard, other people will have to do it too in order to keep up."

A problem is that the Conrans of Thatcher's Britain, with their jets, phones, telexes, and faxes are finding the future belongs to them—those who work harder, use their elbows, and make more money. David Owen, who has an American wife, feels the market is deeply imbedded into the ethics of the United States. He told me, "In America everybody says, 'Get off your ass. Get going. Get on.' It's quite accepted. In Britain it can be resented." Sir Terence agrees:

> I'm sure you've found this sort of feeling in England: that anything successful is wrong. It's a total reversal of America where it is assumed anything successful is right. When I was struggling hard, doing things well but making no money, I was a hero. The moment I went on to do exactly the same things but made money out of them, I became a capitalist swine.

When I met Sir Terence he was riding high. City stockbrokers were just beginning to take a predatory interest in his Storehouse empire as a takeover target. One suspected, from the way he talked, that Conran would rather be cooking or gardening than running a business empire anyway; he seemed a thoroughly contented man. He told me, "What a fantastic world we live in compared to when I was a boy. Travel, the change in society, the opportunities for enjoying life!" I was reminded of Mr. Toad's "Travel, change, interest, excitement!" Conran even has his Toad Hall, Barton Court in Berkshire; he also has homes in Belgravia and the south of France. So much moving about, one thinks of Mr. Badger too: "I say nothing against Toad Hall; quite the best house in these parts, *as* a house. But supposing a fire breaks out—where's Toad? Supposing tiles are blown off, or walls sink or crack, or windows get broken—where's Toad?"

One rarely meets anyone in Britain, North or South, who, if he makes a fortune, doesn't buy a manor house in some picturesque little village in the Home Counties. It preserves the countryside, I suppose, since it brings a lot of money into villages that otherwise would just depend on farming.

This may be why so much of the English landscape that Constable painted is still around. One minute your train is in an ugly decaying industrial city of tall brick chimneys, blackened factories, and street after street of gray council houses, all just alike. The next minute you enter luminous rolling countryside of hills and hedgerows, woods of broad-leaved oak and beech, flower-strewn meadows, sheep nibbling grass. It's Aston Magna, Mary St. Mead, the poet's England, Blake's "green and pleasant land."

Green and Pleasant Land

A DISTANCING OF the aesthetic side of the rural scene from the facts of farming life has gone on in Britain for ages. The country house was set in its park—the rose garden, the maze, the beechwoods, the well-stocked lake, the riding trails. Early on, the home farm came into being to supply the gentry with milk, eggs, meat, vegetables, and grain. But its barns were kept several hundred yards away. The smell of manure did not waft into her ladyship's window. The Louis Quinze drawing room looked out not on plowland, but on acres of lawn and Capability Brown landscaping.

". . . A bold peasantry, their country's pride, / When once destroy'd, can never be supplied." It was steam power, with factories relying on coal, that packed the British together, herding 90 percent of them out of the Sweet Auburns and into cities and towns. The same steam, in ships and railroads, made imported American and Australian wheat cheap and shattered British farming. If Britain grows three fourths of its own food today (practically everything but soya beans), it is by saying, river, stay away from my door. After submarine blockades in two world wars, farming is subsidized. Less now that the EEC's common agricultural policy has begun to go bust. Farming subsidies, which cost two thirds of its budget, have been cut. Incentives are being tried to reduce production surpluses. Since the war, British farms have got bigger and fewer, farmhands replaced by machines. Milk output has doubled. Fertilizer use is up eightfold. Wheat production has quintupled, barley gone up six times.

As Britain went from importer to exporter of food, hedgerows were ripped up—nearly 190,000 miles of them since 1947—and millions of acres of downs, moors, wetlands, and woods lost. While 10 percent of Britain is wooded, about twice as much as in 1900, the increase is mainly in conifer forests. Native broad-leaved trees like oaks are only half as plentiful as they were in the 1930s. Yet pastoral land is fiercely defended. Unlike the United States, late in realizing even its vast amounts of natural scenery had limits, groups like the Council for the Protection of Rural England have long worked to preserve the countryside. Too zealously, an elderly farmer grumbled to me in a pub in the Cotswolds' Chipping Camden. He complained he needed the county council's say-so just to paint a barn door.

The income of Britain's farm sector has halved and its bank debts doubled in real terms since the boom days of the early 1970s, say officials of the National Farmers Union, the agricultural lobby. Farmers also get blamed for despoiling the countryside's bucolic beauty. Environmentalists claim they reseed wildlife areas, neglect barns or woods, plow up chalk grasslands on the South Downs to grow new crops, or, as in Penwith on the Cornish coast, tear down stone walls. Mrs. Thatcher's government, initially slow to treat the countryside as a public good, now has schemes to pay farmers to safeguard landscape, wildlife, and archaeological features in some endangered beauty spots.

Though the aesthetic issue is much hotter in Britain, its farming crisis is the same as ours: how to arrest the trend toward ever bigger and fewer farms and how to curb overproduction. America has anywhere from 250,000 to 2 million farmers, depending on how you count them, Britain 295,000 to 700,000 (hired hands and all). In both, smaller farmers are being swept away, even if in output per acre, per head of stock, per labor or energy unit, or per dollar investment, smaller farms are arguably more efficient. The National Farmers Union favors voluntary "set aside" schemes to leave land fallow; the Council for the Protection of Rural England wants to curtail fertilizer use, reduce grazing, leave larger boundary headlands unplowed, and go back to rotational fallowing.

Agriculture matters to Britain because the mild, moist climate of its "rainy isles" is just what new laboratory-bred biotech crops need. (Northwestern India, eastern China, the California valleys and the Nile valley are favored too, thanks to irrigation.) Sir Leslie Fowden, director of the Rothamsted Experimental Station, told me average wheat yields have quadrupled since 1950 to six and a half tons per hectare, with the best farmers getting ten tons. (The average American yield: two and a half tons.) Professor H.W. Woolhouse of the John Innes Institute in Norwich, which engages in genetic engineering, predicts: "Science is going to change the face of British agriculture totally in the next twenty years." Gene implantation can make plants resistant to insects and viruses, or nitrogen fixing, reducing the need for chemical fertilizers. Genetic engineering in tubers, trees, and ornamental plants, however, has not been matched in grasses like wheat, barley, rice, and maize.

But already embryo implants enable cows to have five or six times more calves (up to eighteen) and growth hormones increase their milk yields 10 percent. Cloned calves are following cloned sheep. Norman Borlaug, the American plant breeder who won the Nobel Peace Prize in 1970 for his work in high-yield crops, was cautious about biotech in a talk I had with him at his Mexico headquarters in 1989. He saw early breakthroughs in vaccines, insulin, interferon, and growth hormones and in antibiotics. But he said:

> Leaving aside asexually propagated species such as potatoes, there is little evidence as yet that genetic techniques can produce higher-yielding food crops with greater disease and insect resistance in the next ten or fifteen years.

In farming, Britain's biotech outlook seems to be early delivery in new drugs, fertilizer, and pesticides, with genetically enhanced livestock following, but radically improved food crops are a good way down the road.

In *A Writer's Britain*, Margaret Drabble observes it is no accident that Tennyson was so fond of words like "glimmer, wan, dim, ghastly, misty, dusk, chill, dreary, dropping, sodden, drenched and dewy"; they describe "the half-tones, the melancholy, the dim wetness of a Northern world." Paul Theroux told me, "England is the hardest place to write about because it's been written about so much." I've mentioned coming across Virginia Woolf's Godrevy Lighthouse near St. Ives on the wild and magic Cornish coast; on the same hike, eight miles down the path towards Land's End in a lonely landscape of gorse, cliffs and Atlantic breakers, I got caught in a sudden, savage rainstorm. Heading inland—yes, sodden and drenched—I reached a pub in a village called Zennor to discover D.H. Lawrence had lived upstairs for a time. (It was during the war and the Lawrences had to flee when the Cornish fishermen decided Frieda might be a German spy.) Again, walking along the Pennine Way in Yorkshire, that two-hundred and fifty-mile footpath through England's high, wild grassland country, I chanced upon the ruined farmstead at Top Withens.

> The farthest house was one which stood on the highest level of the far pasture land, with large black walls and mossy porch and a planta-

tion of gloomy firs . . . Beyond this house its long-built walls made a line with the November sky, and the path across them led on to an interminable moor . . .

The writer is Emily Brontë's brother, Branwell, who described Top Withens in a sketch he wrote in 1837; it almost certainly became *Wuthering Heights.* An hour's walk in a windswept moor of heather and harebells takes you downhill into the parsonage, church, and graveyard of Haworth, preserved, just like the deserted moor, practically the same as it must have been in the Brontës' lifetime.

In theory, a fifth of England and Wales has been given official protection for its scenery and wildlife so that Arnold's seascapes, Hardy's Dorset, Wordsworth's Cumbria, and Tennyson's Lincolnshire survive. Even in national parks, people complain, moorland gets planted in forests or farmed, meadows get reseeded, stone barns and walls are left to crumble. Military training can be a danger. I found this out early one summer morning near Tenby on the Pembrokeshire coast of South Wales. I'd climbed out on a grass headland to watch hundreds of cormorants feeding out on a rocky outcropping in Carmarthen Bay. I just happened to look back in time to see a helmeted figure hoist a red flag to a mast. I scrambled down the path descending the cliffs, remembering a red flag on an army target range means firing is about to start.

Many British feel too much countryside has already been lost. I asked novelist John Fowles about it. He lives in the coastal town of Lyme Regis, setting of Jane Austen's *Persuasion* and Fowles's own *The French Lieutenant's Woman;* the Meryl Streep-Jeremy Irons movie was made there too. He replied, "I have lived all my life with the strong supposition that England is in grave decline, and is done for." Fowles said this had a powerful parallel in:

> the loss, pollution, and destruction of the English countryside (a tragedy to which Thatcher has been largely indifferent). More and more during my lifetime nature has turned from a living present into a lost past, something gone, alas, forever . . .

In 1947 Parliament set aside 4.5 million acres in England, about a tenth of its land, as greenbelt. Its defenders conflict with those like Sainsbury who would like to see more big shopping malls. One of Mrs. Thatcher's junior ministers, the previously mentioned William Waldegrave, when he was still at the Department of Environment, attacked "giant speculative projects which fly full in the face of long-established greenbelt policy to which this government is fully committed." Nicholas Ridley, who used to be Environment Secretary and now has gone to Trade and Industry, tended to alienate environmental groups with his abrasive style and policy of letting the market lead.

Christopher Patten, whom she made Environment Secretary in 1989, is much more in tune with the Prime Minister's own conversion to the greens. I talked to Patten when he was still a junior minister; like Waldegrave he was openly critical of Mrs. Thatcher's economic policy. Proving that Tories can be green should be to his liking.

Mrs. Thatcher's own conversion seems based on political calculations that as the gap with the Labour Party closes, environmental issues like the Channel Tunnel rail link, or lead-free petrol, or the global "greenhouse effect" might turn out to be electorally decisive. Waldegrave has helped Mrs. Thatcher draft the green passages in her speeches to Tory party conferences; he inspired the line that "no generation has a freehold on this earth. All we have is a life tenancy —with a full repairing lease." Mrs. Thatcher was also said to be influenced by Sir Crispin Tickell, Britain's ambassador to the UN, who spent 1975–76 at Harvard studying climatology.

The greening of Margaret Thatcher has meant treading on ground once left to the royal family. The Duke of Edinburgh has long campaigned to save endangered species and tropical rain forests. Prince Charles has called for a compulsory ban on ozone-damaging chloro-fluorocarbons, implicitly criticizing Mrs. Thatcher, who favors a voluntary approach.

Environmentalists used to find it galling, before Mrs. Thatcher's big 1989 Cabinet reshuffle, that Ridley seemed indifferent to their issues but himself lived in the Cotswolds, the range of hills northwest of Oxford whose carefully preserved and protected landscape comes to many minds as the most English of rural countrysides. Once given to sheep rearing, but now mainly farmed, its villages, manor houses, and farmsteads are built of golden-gray stone; on bicycle trips around the Cotswolds' misty valleys, I found it all beautiful, but self-consciously so. J.B. Priestley in *English Journey*, his classic account of a trip around England in 1933, wrote:

> The beauty of the Cotswolds belongs to England, and England should see that she keeps it. Even if the Church ceased to exist tomorrow, we should not allow Salisbury Cathedral to be turned into a filling station;

and we must see that nobody is allowed to carve and tinker and daub away at these hills and charming villages . . .

Fifty years later the BBC had the inspired idea of sending around another Northern writer, Liverpool-born Beryl Bainbridge, to retrace Priestley's footsteps. Mrs. Bainbridge found herself homesick for the very North England towns Priestley deplored—"the huddle of undignified little towns, the drift of smoke, the narrow streets that led from one dreariness to another." Mrs. Bainbridge, whom we'll meet later, cast a cold eye on the Cotswolds:

> On to Bourton-on-the-Water . . . Tourists wall to wall, cars and coaches parked bumper to bumper . . . More antique shops, more bric-a-brac. More cream cakes and tea cosies and pots of strawberry jam done up with muslin lids and pink bows. The houses were still honey-colored and ancient, but it was hard to see them for the people and the traffic signs . . . No sign of inhabitants . . . Perhaps they come out at a certain time . . . waiting to be photographed, like those sad Sioux Indians . . . on the tourist route through the Badlands . . .

Cotswold villages are mainly inhabited by stockbrokers and accountants and oil men from the City nowadays; the villagers' children often find themselves priced out of the house market. Too many city commuters want fresh air, bird song, rose gardens, and the half-real, half-fantasy village idyll. Once there, they don't want change. It is the latest arrivals from London, once they get settled into some ancient stone cottage, not the natives, who are ferocious about keeping developers and other newcomers out. Paul Theroux in his trip around coastal Britain found the prettiest and quaintest villages to be the most inhospitable:

> Most villages and towns wore a pout of rejection—the shades drawn in what seemed to be an averted gaze—and there were few places I went in England that did not seem, as I stared, to be whispering to me all the while, *Move on! Go home!*

True, I agree, of the South. But go North, to Wales, to Scotland, to the old industrial ports and cities like Liverpool or Leeds, even just to the Midlands an hour out of London, and you are in another country.

III

TWO NATIONS—
NORTH:
THE WORST
OF TIMES

English Journey

THE BRASS IS GONE, the muck remains. What J.B. Priestley called the "sooty dismal little towns and still sootier grim fortress-like cities" of the North must have looked, if a lot smokier and sootier, much the same in the nineteenth century Britain of coal, iron, steel, cotton, wool, and railways. Disraeli's famous "Two Nations" concept is a social perception not to be found on any map. But Britain is economically divided just as surely as if it were. Roughly, as I mentioned at the outset, with pockets of wealth and blight on both sides, we find Britain split into a North-South, poor-rich divide running diagonally up from Bristol to the Wash. North of this line are Wales, the Midlands, the geographical North of England proper (north of the Humber River), Scotland, and, across the Irish Sea, Northern Ireland.

The victims of decaying or extinct mines, ports, and factories live in this North. The beneficiaries of much of the new high-tech, finance, scientific, and information industries, plus London's political and cultural elite, are in the South. Mrs. Thatcher is Prime Minister of the United Kingdom. But the 42.5 percent of Britain's voters who supported her Conservatives in 1983 and 1987 are heavily in the South. After the 1987 election the Conservatives held just ten of seventy-two parliamentary seats in Scotland, eight out of thirty-eight in Wales; they did poorly in the North of England and Northern Ireland too. So the divide is also political.

And it persists, raising the worry that resentment might become, as it has in Northern Ireland, separatism. English-owned homes get set on fire every so often in Wales. The Scottish National Party has long been on the warpath, demanding devolution of power to an elected assembly of Scotland's own. Harold Macmillan spoke of the divide. So does the BBC. So, in his *English Journey*, did Priestley in 1933. He found England itself—he did not visit Scotland, Northern Ireland, or Wales—a divided country, its Northern cities in decline, their people on the dole. Except for modern shopping centers and tower blocks and the way so many Victorian town halls and other brick or stone buildings have been handsomely restored, the old mills, foundries, warehouses, and row after endless row of dreary terraced houses are little changed.

Then as now factories stood derelict and many were on the dole, feeling just as useless and defeated. Workaday factory towns without work, wage-minded men without wages. Unemployment doubled in Mrs. Thatcher's first few years in office to over 3 million, it reached 13 percent of the labor force at peak. By 1989 it was down to 7 percent and below 2 million (5.4 percent in America). But tight labor markets in the booming South tended to obscure the dole queues in the North; high-priced housing keeps many would-be workers out of the London area. So why, with all its problems, is this poorer (and less class-ridden) Britain so often cheerier, somehow more welcoming and real?

As in the South, before looking at an old coal mining valley in Wales, I'll start with some random examples of the North: Liverpool, an old port city; Bradford, once the heart of the wool trade; Sheffield, long synonymous with steel; Newcastle, another decaying industrial city, where Japanese investors, to local enthusiasm but to mixed British emotions elsewhere, are finding the North's unskilled dole queues mean labor that is cheap and easy to find.

• Imagine, late in the year, coming into Liverpool for the first time on a wettish, wintry night. Outside the cavernous old station the streets were jammed with people, thousands of them milling about, with hoods and umbrellas up against the rain. Another Toxteth riot? Loony leftist Derek Hatton on the loose? Militants fomenting anarchy to set the stage for revolution? All of a sudden everybody starts singing "Jingle Bells." A stuntman dressed as Santa Claus scales the front of Lewis's department store. Cheers. Fireworks explode. In the Adelphi hotel, splendidly seedy and grand, a leftover from the heyday of transatlantic liners, outer-galactic monsters and men in silver space suits swarm about, members of a "Doctor Who" fan convention. Down in the Merseyside pubs, pure she-loves-you-yeh-yeh-yeh pop is the electricity of the air, reminding you whose hometown this is. It goes right along with the streetwise Scouse humor ("Nothing growing in the economy? What about museums?") and quirky Liverpudlian pride in the bad old days ("And *here* is where they burned down the Squash Club"). The local accent is so thick if somebody says, "Gisalite," it means he wants a match, while "Boogaroff" is "Get lost." As Alan Bleasdale's Scully explains why there's no more plays at school: "It's not funny or nothin'. Gorra be bad hasn't it, when eight-year-olds throw things at y' an' try an' burn the curtains down." Businessmen may not invest until the city council is rid of Trotskyites, but Britain's worst-case city has bags of character.

• Bradford was, and is, the wool trade, now half its former size, with one man watching forty microelectronic looms. Thirty years ago, it looked much like the metaphor Dickens used in *Hard Times:* a bowl of smoke pierced by mill chimneys. Though the smoke has gone and the jobs with it, there is still a slimmed-down and auto-mated wool industry. I went through the vast Manningham Mills, walled round like a prison, its 250-foot high Italianate chimney one of Bradford's great landmarks. Bradford remains a city of factories, drab streets, and dreary row houses, no matter how clean its postin-dustrial air. But its valley sits just on the edge of the Pennine moors, Heathcliff country.

Priestley, born and bred in Bradford ("grim but not mean" Bruddersford in his novels), remembers:

> However small and dark your office or warehouse was, somewhere in-side your head the high moors were glowing, the curlews were crying, and there blew a wind as salt as if it had come straight from the middle of the Atlantic. This is why we did not care very much if our city had no charm, for it was simply a place to go and work in, until it was time to set out . . . We were all, at heart, Wordsworthians to a man.

Bradford honored Priestley in 1986 with a statue right in the heart of his old city, beside the Edwardian Alhambra Theatre, now restored to its original pink-plush-and-gilt splendor. In bronze, clad in a raincoat, Priestley sets out forever into the Pennine winds. Hap-pily of the northern cities, the Yorkshire moors and the Brontës give Bradford a lead in tourism. Haworth, just twelve miles away, is Britain's second most popular literary pilgrimage after Stratford-on-Avon. In mist and purple heather one sees the Brontë parsonage as stark as ever against its moor.

You can go to see Bradford's working mills: one mill has been turned into a museum for the works of painter David Hockney, an-other native son. As Britain markets its past, fictional and real, tour-ism has come to be its biggest industry and biggest employer, bring-ing in £13–£14 million a year. Close to 15 million overseas tourists spent 60 percent of their nights outside London; 1.5 million British make their living looking after them. But it is Britons touring Britain who matter most to cities like Bradford.

• The left, businessmen all over the Midlands complain, is better at spending money than making it. Higher rates set by Labour-led local authorities, they say, drive investors away. Demolishing local government, as mentioned, has been a main thrust of Mrs. Thatcher's poll-tax, housing, and educational reforms; out have gone rights, going back for centuries, of local councils to levy domestic property rates or raise their own taxes on business. A prime example of the big leftist Labour spender is David Blunkett, who was the leader of the Sheffield city council when I interviewed him; he has since been elected to Parliament. While he ran Sheffield, Britain's traditional steel city, its council spent £75 million ($127.5 million) more than its £335 million ($560 million) budget to provide seven thousand new jobs. With a payroll of 33,000, Sheffield's biggest employer is local government. Blunkett, in turn, blamed Sheffield's troubles on its steel firms for not redesigning their cutlery, silverware, and pewter nimbly enough to compete with Sweden and South Korea. He feels there is still a market for Sheffield craftsmanship.

Blunkett helped Neil Kinnock oust extreme-left militants from the Labour party. He exemplifies Labour's realist left wing and feels strongly there are two Britains: "I think the Tory notion of unregulated private enterprise without dealing with the social consequences has led us into a divided society." Take a look, he says, at the City's stock exchange boom, British investment abroad, and London's real estate values ("A house that forty years ago cost £2,000 is selling for £350,000").

> People are living like this while our manufacturing base disintegrates under us. People say, look, this is the kind of society we live in: you make a quick buck where you can. That you can make more by playing the stock market or being in the right place in property than by slugging your guts out in a factory.

Blunkett, a youthful-looking, black-bearded man in his forties, blind from birth, personifies a kind of left-wing ideology peculiar to Britain. It is shaped not by Marxism but rather by Christian non-Anglican or what the British call "nonconformist" Protestant creeds —Methodist, Baptist, Congregationalist, Presbyterian—all of them associated, unlike in America, with the poorer working classes. This leftism is the kind of muscular Christianity of the night classes and YMCAs, gymnasiums and choirs, camping clubs and debating societies, that grew up in the industrial cities of Britain's North. (Blunkett: "I went to church with my mum on Sundays. I had built into me a fundamental morality. I don't mean a sexual morality. I mean a morality about the world, about our part in it, about what we must contribute if we want to get something back out.") Mrs. Thatcher's radical populism—she was brought up a Methodist—shows a streak of this, though with her it takes a second place to free market principles.

We talked about unemployment, which has fallen from about 3.5 million to 2 million since our interview. Half of the remaining jobless are long-term unemployed. The longer people are out of work, the more despondent they become and the worse they are at finding jobs. In 1988 over 1.2 million people had been out of work for over a year. Said Blunkett:

> A big problem, potentially dynamite, is the young person getting up in the morning and not feeling that work is worthwhile. You get this psychology if you're unemployed long enough. Two or three months and then you find a job, you can treat that as a break. Anything longer and people start to lose their will; they also start to ask: why bother?
>
> I think the political right in Britain has misunderstood the North American enterprise psychology. You have a different culture, different history, different makeup in society.

In the old days, he said, Sheffield's people had pride in producing their special steels, alloys, and stainless steel; now they've seen their jobs go and their status and dignity go with them.

> They were producing steel before, creating wealth. All that gave people pride even if the North of England and Scotland were not as environmentally desirable as the South. We were the heart of Britain's economy. You know the saying, "Where there's muck, there's brass." Which is: "Where there's dirt, there's cash." So we have a lot of pride and we're desperately trying to hang onto it.

• "DON'T BE A FORK FIEND," "DO IT RIGHT THE FIRST TIME," "QUALITY IS PAY ATTENTION TO DETAIL." The gung ho signs posted about (the first meant a fork*lift* fiend), dedicated Japanese managers bustling in and out, and Swedish-style physical exercises at the start of each shift give the Kotmatsu earth-moving equipment plant just outside Newcastle a distinctly un-British air. Its robots, though, seemed to be doing a lot of old-fangled metal bashing without the ultratech frenzy of Birmingham's Rover factory.

The Komatsu plant is just one of twenty-one Japanese manufacturing companies in northeast England. The biggest, Nissan Motor

Company's giant plant in nearby Sunderland, plans to double output to 200,000 cars a year by 1992; the firm has hinted it may go up to 400,000 by the late 1990s. Evidently encouraged by this, Toyota, Japan's biggest and the world's third-biggest carmaker, plans to build a new £700 million factory in Derbyshire that will employ three thousand people and make 200,000 cars a year by 1994. With Honda, Nissan, and Toyota aiming to produce over 500,000 vehicles a year at British plants by the mid-1990s, Britain is Japan's investment favorite in Europe, with $2.5 billion by March 1988, more than six times the Japanese investment in Germany, eight times that in France.

It is welcome, even if it implies Britain has the best skills at the cheapest price. When Nissan came into northeast England in 1984, it gave one of Britain's most depressed areas a badly needed boost of confidence. In 1988, when I was last in Newcastle, unemployment was still running at 13 percent, the highest outside Northern Ireland, and along the Tees and Tyne rivers, derelict plants looked like an industrial museum for steel, shipbuilding, and coal (more of Britain's peculiar museum quality). Swan Hunters shipyard announced layoffs of seven hundred the day I was there; a few frigates for the Royal Navy aren't enough to keep even a much-reduced shipyard fully occupied. Foodstuffs, engineering, electronics, and electrical engineering firms don't begin to employ all those let go. The British steel plant at nearby Consett, when it closed in 1981, laid off five thousand workers in a single day. Between 1971 and 1984 people employed in manufacturing on Tyneside almost halved from 147,000 to 77,000.

So the Japanese invasion has been a blessing. There are ninety-seven Japanese firms in Britain so far, employing about twenty-five thousand workers (still small compared to big American outfits like IBM and Mars). What is it like to work for the Japanese? All brainwashing, morning calisthenics, and company songs? English workers at the Komatsu plant, who seemed happy to be there, told me the biggest difference was that while the Japanese have their own pretty rigid social hierarchy, they do their best to remove the old British class barriers, the "us and them" mentality dividing worker and manager. (Not that the Japanese preach equality; far from it. In their post-Confucian system of subordinate relationships, workers enter according to their schooling and get promoted according to age. But everybody does have some sense of being on the same team.)

"They try to make people feel they belong," one worker told me. "So there's nothing to stop the guy on the shop floor who's got a bloody good idea. Not like the traditional-type English boss who says, 'I don't know why he's talking to me about that. It's *my* job to think of ideas.'" Komatsu has an open-plan office; everybody can see everybody else and the blue jackets they all wear means managers look the same as workers on the shop floor and the old blue- and white-collar divide is less. "It's not the old-style company where the manager has an office and there's a tap, tap, tap on the door," said another worker. "They remove the barriers."

What is the Japanese secret? A long-term view instead of quick City profits? A government, unlike Mrs. Thatcher's, that really invests in industry? The English workers at Komatsu say Japan's industrial genius really lies in efficient production. They modify good conceptions and produce them, not invent or create something new. Mike Leithrow, a foreman, told me, "They're very good at looking at something and if it's good they adopt it."

> They don't reinvent the wheel. Look at the motorbike industry. I think Britain built the best motorbikes in the world twenty years ago. You couldn't touch us. But we priced ourselves out of the market. The Japanese couldn't invent the motorbike. But they could sure as hell build a cheaper one. Every motorbike, maybe barring one in a hundred, in the U.K. now is Japanese.

Not everybody is happy about assembling Japanese products at European plants. Last winter the European Community put pressure on the Japanese to accept "voluntary import restraints" and include cars made in Europe in Japanese quotas. The British disagree. "Our cars should not be considered imports because they are assembled in Europe," says an official at Nissan's Sunderland plant. France's Peugeot and Italy's Fiat are leading the battle to freeze the Japanese to below 10 percent of the European market, while Britain heads the free traders. Since 1985 the Japanese voluntarily sell just 2.3 million cars a year in the United States, but this does not include American-built Japanese makes. Yet if Britain learns how they do it from the Japanese, it just might again be the workshop of Europe. That will take energy, and when the North Sea oil runs down in a decade or so, it could mean going back to coal.

How Green Is My Valley

"I N THE 1820s," said Tony Roberts, borough council secretary for the Rhondda Valley in South Wales, as we drove along the green hills, "this was moorland and trees. Speckled trout in crystal-clear streams. By 1900 it was all pits. Teeming. Coal was king. In a hundred and forty years you've gone from four thousand people up to a hundred and eighty thousand and back down to eighty thousand. Full circle."

I was seeing the Rhondda with Roberts and its Labour member of Parliament, Allan Rogers, himself an ex-miner. That day, in December 1986, the Rhondda's pit wheels and shunting trains stopped for good. The last of its sixty-six mines shut down, ending a chapter of Glamorgan pits that stirred the world's imagination in such novels and film classics as *How Green Was My Valley* and *The Corn Is Green*. The mines changed a pastoral landscape of heather moorland and wooded valleys into a teeming, blackened, profitable industrial belt. A plaque on the wall of the Fern Hill Hotel, which was once a colliery agent's villa, reads:

> In 1913 53 large collieries were at work in the Rhondda Valley. Of these 44 employed over 500 underground and 21 employed over 1,000. In 1913 Rhondda's 41,000 miners manually produced a coal output of 9.5m tons.

Now it is green again. The mines are capped, their slag heaps leveled and grassed over. About all that is left of the once-celebrated miner's towns like Treorchy and Tonypandy are their bleak terraced houses, deserted chapels, and the valley's upward winding railway tracks where a diesel passenger service has replaced the old coal-laden wagon trains. Britain's coal now comes mainly from more modern fields in Nottinghamshire and South Yorkshire. Mining jobs in the Welsh valleys have dropped from nearly 300,000 to below 9,000 and these, too, will eventually go as deep coal mining disappears altogether. Unemployment in the late 1980s was about one man in four; about two thirds of school-leavers failed to find steady work.

Already gone are the old pick and shovel, replaced by automatic cutters. Gone, too, the old timber pitprops; now there are hydraulic roof supports. The miners still have their lamps, and after a shift below you still get coal-blackened faces and tired eyes when the lift brings them back up into the daylight. In his 1988 novel, *Underworld*, Yorkshire writer Reginald Hill graphically captures the feeling of a coal mine: "Water dripped, earth dribbled, pebbles clinked, and from time to time there were creaks and groans as a hundred thousand tons of ancient rock tried to close this wound savagely ripped along its guts." But the women in filthy rags and the small children, a few just four or five years old, who in the 1830s and 1840s pulled loads along underground tramways in twelve-hour days are now just faded engravings in the Rhondda's local museum, once a mine owner's hilltop mansion. In 1837–1934 there were more than seventy disasters in the Welsh mines alone; the worst, the Senghenydd explosion, took 439 lives in 1913. In Aberfan in 1966, 144 died when a slag heap slid into a community school, all but twenty-six of them children. Now a new industrial site is coming in there. "We don't live in the past," said Roberts. He hoped, like everybody else in Britain where a way of life has died, that enough light industry and tourism would be coming in.

"That verge is a capped coal mine," said Roberts. "We're hard-pressed to show you all the scars, all the tips, because the land is landscaped, grass is planted, and they'll be used for housing or light industry."

"What we have here in South Wales," Rogers said, "is very high quality bituminous coal which was used for steam generation. We also have high-grade coking coal used in steel production." But Britain's steel output had dropped by a third in the previous ten years, he said. South Wales alone has enough coal to keep Britain going for two hundred years. When oil runs down in a decade or two, it may need it. The Welsh say: sink a pit and you dig a well. Rogers explained: Once pumping is stopped, a pit anywhere from five hundred to fifteen hundred feet deep gets flooded. It is easier to dig a brand-new shaft and start from scratch. Rogers felt some of the Rhondda pits should have been put in cold storage, not shut down for good.

"One hears some Tory say, 'Well, let's just move everybody out.

Why should they be there? The pits are closed. The raison d'être is gone. Let's just flood the valleys.'" What people in London didn't understand, Rogers said, was that many Rhondda families had been in the valley for four or five generations. Something like 80 percent owned their own homes; hard, tough, independent people, they made their own world, rather like the small mining towns of Pennsylvania.

The dangers and tough life underground forced strong bonds among these Welsh miners, who often played rugby together, drank at the same workingmen's clubs, and sang in one of the famous Welsh male voice choirs. A powerful nonconformist Protestant church movement in the mining valleys—Methodist, Baptist, Wesleyan, Congregationalist, Church in Wales—helped build the rich Welsh singing tradition. Today many of the Rhondda's chapels have been boarded up or converted into old-age homes or community shelters. The rugby clubs, brass bands, and men's choirs like those in Treorchy and Penderis still exist, but without the old neighborhood and mining ties.

The Rhondda was the last place in Britain where army troops were used to quell a riot. Winston Churchill sent them into Tonypandy in 1911. During our tour of the valley, we saw Tonypandy now has a big new supermarket; one in Treorchy had done so well the company expanded. Somehow the consumer boom was reaching Rhondda too, even if one in three men was unemployed. There is a steady exodus of young people down to Cardiff and London to look for jobs.

It was the same way in another mining area I visited, South Yorkshire's Rother Valley. Here, where lower-grade coal is used to generate electricity, some mines are still open. But Kevin Barron, another ex-miner MP, who took me around the coal pits, said the number of miners had dropped to one third of what it was before the 1984–85 strike: eight thousand had taken redundancy payments. Unemployment in the coal valleys must be the highest in Britain. Barron said a study he made showed only 11 percent of the Rother Valley's 1986 school-leavers had work to go to. (One study found only sixty-one of the Rhondda's twelve hundred school-leavers had, three years later, found jobs.)

Barron, a miner for twenty-three years until he was elected to the House of Commons in 1983, was parliamentary private secretary to Neil Kinnock, the Labour Party's leader (just as Rogers used to share a flat in London with Kinnock, a fellow Welshman). Barron said that in 1961 in Maltby, his hometown, he was given a choice of jobs in mining or a steel plant or joining the army, having failed his eleven-plus exam.

> So I ended up a coal miner at fifteen years of age. That was just how it was. I did what was quite natural in a coal mining town, which was that sons followed fathers and brothers into the mines. The sad thing about South Yorkshire now is those options which I never thought were very good anyway are not even available to young kids in our area.

In South Yorkshire's small town of Dinnington, Barron keeps his MP's surgery, a tiny back room behind a lawyer's office, where he meets constituents; a few black chimneys and winding gears at a pithead showed that one nearby colliery was still going. A poster in the Jobcentre window read:

> Wanted: anti-vandal patrol. Men aged 30–50 needed to patrol Dinnington Comprehensive School to deter vandalism.

Barron said people in mining communities didn't like to leave. I asked about his own children. His daughter, fifteen, was studying computers.

"Will she go to college?"

"That's up to her."

"Aren't you urging her to go?"

"No. Look where I got on my own. I was a miner at fifteen years of age."

Later in Sheffield I asked David Blunkett about the generally low expectations in the mining communities; it seemed to go right along with a taciturn suspicion of outsiders and pride in the old way of life when boys joined their fathers "down in the pits."

Blunkett said that in Parson Cross, the large council estate where he grew up, nobody went to college:

> I was probably the only person at university within a square mile of where I lived. The parents don't think about their kids are going. They don't have books in the houses. At university I found a lot of well-off kids much thicker and less intelligent than some of the kids I'd been brought up with. But their middle-class parents expected them to go, they'd pushed them. Working people in this country have a low expectation of what life is going to offer them.

When I went back to Rhondda in 1988, I found men still going down in a mineshaft at Maerdy by bringing coal out at Tower Colliery in the next valley; all the Rhondda's mines remained closed.

The bartender at the Fern Hill in Treherbert told me, "Within a radius of one mile from here there were eight mines." Now fifty-one, he'd worked in the last to close; it was the one which shut down during my 1986 visit. For thirty-five years he rose at five-thirty to be two hundred feet below ground to start work by seven in the morning; his shift went until two-fifteen.

> When I left school, I failed at the factories. Couldn't get a job. I could go to the pits. I didn't want to go down. My father didn't want me to go down. Then after the war, when I came out of the army, it wasn't a question of finding a job. It was a question of choosing one. But I knew nothing else. And there was some good times, there was.

His pub was a hangout for ex-miners. They started coming in after supper, ordering their pints of bitter.

"We went to chapel," said an old man wearing a cloth cap. "We went to Sunday school. The chapel was the center of village life. Now people are simply not interested." Everybody had something to say.

"The war had an adverse effect."

"It was television."

"Coal from Rhondda made Cardiff what it is. There was a coal train every ten minutes."

"Welsh coal was very, very much in demand by the British Navy."

"The miner used to come home black. He'd take a bath in front of the kitchen fire." The men criticized Mrs. Thatcher for shutting down the last of the mines. Maybe two hundred small businesses had come into the valley; they made seatbelts for cars, fire extinguishers, furniture, metal components, one company, slot machine covers for Las Vegas. People were determined to hold on, see the hard times through. The barman said that the Russians and Americans put genes into a cow and got so much milk. "And the English took a cow and put her in Downing Street and we got three million unemployed."

"There was no answer for it than closing the mines," one of the men chided him. "They were being subsidized for millions and millions of pounds."

"Rhondda used to send preachers and teachers all over," said somebody else. Migration was nothing new. "Parents didn't want their sons to go down in the mines. Some of them put a great store in education." Actor Richard Burton, pop singer Tom Jones and

1930s heavyweight contender Tommy Farr are all, Rhondda's people say with pride, the sons of coal miners who used their talents to escape the mines; all stayed proud of their mining valley roots.

And what about *How Green Was My Valley?*

"Walter Pidgeon and Maureen O'Hara. I remember the father. Donald Crisp. He talked with an Irish accent." They all grinned.

"The miner's house was something they made in the Hollywood studio. Polished floors. Big rooms. No miner lived like that."

"And who would have thought that the last dram of coal has been taken out."

Last Exit from Easterhouse

"WELCOME TO THE BRONX" is the graffito that hails visitors coming into Easterhouse, Britain's biggest council-housing estate, on the edge of Glasgow. If in Wales there were rows and rows of drab miners' houses in the bottoms of the old coal valleys, in Scotland public housing built for now-redundant dockworkers and factory hands seems to go on forever. Easterhouse, with fifteen thousand units for sixty thousand people and just two pubs for the lot, is a battle-scarred reminder that the best-laid plans "gang aft a-gley." *The Economist* has called it and Glasgow's other three vast outer estates, with forty thousand units between them, "the biggest single housing horror story in Europe."

There are eleven such estates—human dumping grounds really —in the whole of Scotland. Small wonder that to Scots, housing is politics. Or that an alarming number of them say they loathe Mrs. Thatcher and have lost faith in union with England.

Scotland is a land of paradox. Except for its truly terrible housing and high unemployment—the two go together as people get trapped on the estates—it has a lot going for it: Britain's cheeriest and friendliest people, its best school system, and a hinterland of wild, rugged, mountainous landscapes and surpassing beauty ("My heart's in the Highlands, my heart is not here").

Edinburgh, if you stay out of the slums, is perhaps Britain's most beautiful city, a place of rocky crags and ridges, a notable fortress-castle, and stately slate houses. Plus the Festival. Glasgow, too, is blessed with fine old stone buildings in the city center. Even so it came as a surprise (most of all in Edinburgh) when Glasgow was named European City of Culture for 1990. (So much for haggis jokes and tales of razor fights in the Gorbals.)

"We've really got only two big things," says John Davidson, the Confederation of British Industry's director for Scotland. "Educated young people from eight universities or technical colleges with an industrial heritage, and North Sea oil." It is true that after seventeen, twice as many Scottish children stay in school as do English children. Scotland has proportionately more apprentices than anywhere in England, and the most college graduates. The Scot engineer was an empire stereotype. The Scots take seriously the idea of education for all.

So why the housing problem? As the Scots are first to tell you, the mythology of kilts and bagpipes, Robert Burns and Sir Walter Scott, obscures an embattled history. In the enclosure actions of the late eighteenth and early nineteenth centuries, the "clearances," landlords dispossessed much of the population in the Highland grazing lands. So many Scots went to the United States, Canada, and Austria, parts of Scotland were virtually depopulated. This coincided with expanding trade within the British Empire, and the Industrial Revolution, which absorbed some of the uprooted Highland crofters as port and factory workers.

Glasgow, which had just eighty thousand people when Scottish engineer James Watt invented his steam engine in 1765, grew to a million by 1900. Iron and coal were found near Glasgow and by 1910 it was making a quarter of the world's ships and rolling stock. Its rails crossed America, India, and South Africa. The decline of this heavy industry has led Scotland to diversify. Electronics (over half of the firms American-owned), light engineering, and Scotch whiskey are today's big money earners. The nearly forty thousand electronics workers in Silicon Glen now exceed the numbers left working in Scotland's old staples of coal, textiles, and shipping.

Glasgow's population kept growing until the postwar years with a continued exodus from the Highlands and many Irish immigrants pouring in. Since the mid-1950s it has dropped by half a million. But half of Scotland's 5 million people still live within a twenty-five-mile radius of downtown Glasgow. Edinburgh, with another 420,000, is just an hour's train ride away. So Scotland is an abnormally empty land whose people are mainly crowded around the two cities, plus the oil boomtown of Aberdeen.

The big housing estates like Easterhouse are the hellish results of good intentions. The Labour-led councils that ran Glasgow after World War II wanted to demolish the dark bog of the city's century-old slums, mostly dank stone tenements, and move at least a quarter of a million Glaswegians out into the fresh air on the edge of the city. Ex-gangster Jimmy Boyle, whom we will meet, describes these slums:

> The Gorbals was full of old tenement buildings three stories high, each floor containing three houses. Two of the houses were one-room-and-kitchen, the other in the center was a single end. The toilet was on the stairway, shared by the three families on each landing . . . The backcourts and streets were our playgrounds.

Many of these tenements are now being redone into comfortable modern apartments, but I saw some of the old ones still in use, with whole families sleeping in shelflike beds in the wall. In his book *A Sense of Freedom*, Boyle tells about raids on the rubbish bins of better-off people living near the Gorbals, those he calls the "toffs":

> Groups of us, usually with the arse torn out of our trousers, snot running down our noses and filthy, would head for Queens Park, a "toffy" district . . .

Sometimes they were chased by householders "disgusted to find scruff such as us." But Boyle also mentions the way the old slum neighborhoods held together:

> The Gorbals streets had their own warm blend of character that was very comforting to the locals . . . The women of the district would either lean out of their windows or, if the weather was good, take chairs down to the streets to sit and gossip about anything and anyone. Everyone was very familiar with each other and we kids were out and in each other's houses as if they were our own.

Glaswegians now say the old Labour Party bosses were "Stalinists"—they ran the city in totalitarian style. Nobody was asked whether he wanted to move to a new barrackslike flat in the outskirts; he got moved.

If joblessness, frustration, and bad housing make a powder keg, Easterhouse is it. The flats are damp and leaky, thin-walled, and hard to heat. Open decks, intended to be airy, invite vandalism, graffiti, and crime. Repairs are left undone. Drunken fights, murders (over twenty-some years), gang brawls, sons in jail, are routine.

In 1984 a record eight thousand people applied to go elsewhere. In 1989 close to two thirds of the households were living on less than £75 a week ($127.50), but bus fare into downtown Glasgow and back was £1.40 ($2.38). Many people are confined to its ugliness— the broken or boarded windows, the grassless lots littered with fast-food packaging, the mile after mile of treeless, shoddy buildings, the drug culture. "That's not to say a lot aren't making a go of it," one cheery old lady, a survivor of the Gorbals, told me. At least diets have improved. She recalled how many poor Glaswegian children in prewar days had rickets, bow legs, bad teeth and were stunted from lack of vitamins.

An independent 1986 inquiry led by Professor Sir Robert Grieve, which had follow-up hearings during another trip I made to Glasgow in 1988, proposed that the Glasgow district council, which owns 170,000 of the city's 280,000 housing units of all kinds, sell off at least a fourth of them, with up to half of the units on council estates being sold. Flats and houses could go over ten years, the inquiry said, to housing associations, cooperatives, developers, or private owners.

Paul Mugnaioni, who used to run Glasgow's housing and now works for a private building firm, told me, "The big issue is power. Is the council going to behave in the old paternalistic way? Or do we look on housing not as a charity, but as a business? I say the customer comes first." Mugnaioni recalled how in the old days the council used to send "green ladies" (they wore green uniforms) out to inspect public housing ("You'd better tidy this up"). Such humiliations are a thing of the past.

"Everybody wants to be an owner-occupier," says Professor Duncan Maclennan of Glasgow University. "People are fed up with relying on an overcentralized, bureaucratic local authority for repairs and service. They want out from under the heel." It is ironic that Mrs. Thatcher's sale of council houses to tenants seems to be working best in Labour-controlled Glasgow. Maclennan says 58 percent of the city's housing is still in the public sector compared to 30–40 percent elsewhere. (In a new town like Milton Keynes, they have so few rental units they don't know where to put the desperately needy.)

The Scots' can-do spirit to remedy past mistakes has boosted Scotland's GNP per head. Held up as models are the way its Labour-run councils work so well with Scotland's private sector and the government-funded Scottish Development Agency; the fact that 45 percent of pupils stay in school after seventeen (just 27 percent in England); and how Silicon Glen has become Europe's largest center of microchip production. There are lots of encouraging signs for the future. Tourism is growing in Glasgow and Edinburgh, attracted by opera, ballet, symphony orchestras, and art, plus some of Britain's liveliest theater, such as touring rep companies like Wildcat and 784 (which claims 7 percent of the Scots own 84 percent of the wealth).

But while all this looks good, Scotland's industrial base, like England's itself, has worryingly narrowed under Mrs. Thatcher. It cannot live on making microchips alone. The Scots blame her for it. Even the CBI's Davidson, a Tory, was critical. He went so far as to say Scotland's union with England, which goes back to 1707, was at risk. Davidson explained:

> The Prime Minister in June 1987 won a huge victory in Britain. But what happened, on that morning after the election, she looked around and she saw essentially that the South of England backed her and the North of England, Scotland, and to an extent, Wales, said, "Go and get knotted." Now what does Margaret Thatcher do in those circumstances? Does she say, "I have no time for them because they didn't vote for me"? Or does she say, "That part of the country is clearly a major problem. And if I'm going to retain the union of the United Kingdom, we're really going to have to do something about that."

"You mean Scotland could pull away?" I asked.

"And even Northern England. A sort of anarchy thing. It could happen." The one good sign, Davidson felt, was that Thatcherism had persuaded many Scots of the practicality of public and private sector working together. Unless you played by Mrs. Thatcher's rules, you didn't get anywhere. The days of big government spending were over.

This was the first time I had heard that the union of England and Scotland might be in peril. Many Tories are now saying it. Some argue Scotland's embattled Tories haven't been Thatcherite enough, accepting pleas for special treatment (to save airports, smelters, and steelworks). Another wing maintains Scotland is a place apart; it needs its own assembly to focus its sense of nationhood.

I asked Jim Hastie of Glasgow's housing corporation, a genial Scot I met on all my visits, when we went for a pint at the pub, just what did he feel was the true Scotland. For instance, I said, James I was a Scot who'd ruled the whole of Britain.

"That's just fairy-tale stuff," he objected. "That's just a Walter Scott-type version, a heather-and-kilts image of Scotland."

"Like Robert Burns?" I'd been rereading his poems. One forgot how familiar so much of it was—"But to see her was to love her," "Should auld acquaintance be forgot," "Bonnie wee thing, cannie wee thing," "Gin a body meet a body / Coming through the rye," "Flow gently, sweet Afton," "A man's a man for a' that," "Oh, my Luve's like a red red rose / That's newly sprung in June," "O wad some Pow'r the giftie gie us / To see oursels as others see us!" Our heads are full of Burns.

"No, he's not," objected Hastie. "Robert Burns isn't heather and kilts. Burns is the tradition of brotherhood. He's family. People mattering. His poetry is about . . . There's a small town coziness . . ." He searched for words. Burns was the son of a farmer. His many songs, some based on old verses and folk tunes, were a labor of love. He got no payment. His rollicking "Tam o' Shanter," reckoned his greatest long poem, he wrote in a single day. A hard drinker, he was dead at thirty-seven. Whatever Scotland was, Burns was at its heart. Hastie found what he wanted to say:

> The Scottish soldier was going off to fight two world wars, bagpipes playing, dressed up in the Highland regiments in kilts . . . I mean, this identity myth Scotland's left with. The kilts and Edinburgh Castle and Scott's novels, they're not important. If people want to come and see these things, fine. Hear about the clans fighting, hear about Robert the Bruce, hear about the stories of Bannockburn. Fine, give them all that. But for heaven's sake, don't confuse that and Scottish culture. Scottish culture is about family and friends and singing and humor and wit and taking people as important. That's what Scottish culture's about, aye.

Mrs. Thatcher, in her way a South English nationalist governing from London, doesn't seem to be able to understand this sense of being Scottish. There is no question but that Scotland should have its own national assembly and be given far more legislative and economic independence. So should Wales and Northern Ireland. Mrs. Thatcher keeps going the other way, centralizing political power, gathering it in her own hands. This may mean trouble. As Walter Bagehot warned in 1869:

> A Scotch mob is exceedingly dangerous, because it will not rise till it knows what it wants, and will then go straight forward to that even if the path lies over human lives.

The Scots, like the Welsh and Irish, are just different than the English. The open Scots cheeriness wins you every time after London's reserve. I mean, you go for an interview in Glasgow or Edinburgh and you end up having a meal or a pint at the pub. Rarely in England. One has English friendships, some of them close and lasting for years, but never struck up casually. Just about the only time at Oxford we moved from interview to pub was with Professor Norman Stone and he turned out to be from Glasgow.

The Scots do have that mad sectarian streak that so afflicts the Irish. Glasgow is famous for its football teams. To incite Celtics fans, whose badge is a shamrock, Rangers' supporters sing, "The Sash My Father Wore." It refers, incredulous Americans get told, to sashes worn by William of Orange's Protestant soldiers when they defeated

James II and his Irish Catholic troops in the Battle of the Boyne in 1690, a full three hundred years ago. Paul Theroux quotes a Glaswegian:

> We got our Catholics. Ha' ye nae heard of the Rangers and the Celtics fitba matches? They play each other a guid sux tames a year, but there's nae *always* a riot.

"A couple of Celtics players cross themselves before playing to incite Protestant wrath," a Rangers fan told me. "They say the Catholic religion is seven days a week while for us it's just weddings and funerals." "Sectarian strife," as he called it—the Rangers fly the Union Jack, the Celtics Ireland's tricolor—and the often bloody clashes between the two teams' fans, was nothing compared to Northern Ireland's civil war. "Here it smoulders away, this religious divide. Quite dangerous, to have it so." He knocked wood.

Glasgow has its middle class. But half its people are living on family incomes of less than £5,200 ($8,440). Easterhouse's infant mortality is four and a half times the national average. Glaswegians learn survival techniques early. One afternoon I was walking with a city architect through Possil, the worst of Glasgow's inner-city slums. We came upon two very little boys squatting by a car. Possil, its ground strewn with glass and broken chunks of concrete, its windows boarded, looked as if it had just come through a bombing raid. I thought the boys were changing a tire. The architect, a Glaswegian, said more likely they were stealing it. "Boys, what are you doing?" I called. "Fuck off," said the smallest one. He looked about five.

You get glimmers of hope in self-help projects. At Calvay Crescent in Easterhouse, the local people took an almost derelict building of nearly four hundred units and were making it look like new. I went back two years after a first visit and was amazed at what they could do. But when it came to jobs, nothing much had changed. Alex Sinclair, a sturdy, retired workingman, told me Calvay still had one of the highest unemployment rates in Easterhouse, close to 70 percent. "I donnae see any way out," he said. "There's certainly not going to be enough jobs here. This landscaping and construction we're doing at Calvay. There's nae money being generated. We don't produce anything that we can sell outside. We're just passing the same money around and around again."

Patricia Phillips, another neighbor, said plenty of Scots would like to emigrate, but it wasn't as easy as it used to be.

"If you're going to Australia," Sinclair said, "you've got to have a job there. You've got to be spoken for. Och, aye, ye must hae money in the bank to go." They said some local boys had spent three or four years learning several skills in government training schemes but still could find no job. There was plenty of work in London and the South, but who could afford to stay there?

"How," I asked, "do young people keep their spirits up?"

"Very hard."

"Very difficult."

"Ye can only be supported by the youth culture for so long," said Sinclair. "Ye get to a stage when you want to get married, but ye cannae afford to raise a family. Ye hae to live with your folks. Och! that's the ones that will revolt."

It turned out that since my earlier visit, Prince Charles had come to Calvay. Mrs. Phillips, the neighbors said, even gained a splash of notoriety by giving the Prince a kiss and a hug in front of the television cameras. They all felt the Prince took their problems seriously. He has denounced postwar council estates like Easterhouse as "thoroughly inhuman." He says "too many people's lives are being wasted."

Prince Charles probably meets and talks with more people in Britain than most politicians. He told an audience in Pittsburgh that bringing cities back to life took more than "just money or market forces," a jab at Thatcherism. The Prince blames the "anonymity of postwar design" for some of the "breakdown" in communities like Easterhouse.

In spite of all the aristocratic and social paraphernalia that surrounds him and the media following his every step, Prince Charles can help set a socially concerned tone. But what he can observe and grasp with his mind, it takes a Scot born and bred in the slums to feel in his bones. For that we'll turn to Jimmy Boyle, who sees evidence of the same breakdown in rising crime and violence.

"Everything's Breakin' Up"

E DINBURGH MIGHT SEEM like an odd choice for a look at social breakdown and crime. If you brave the winds and climb the green crags of Arthur's Seat, an extinct volcano right in town, you can see all the ancient stone skyline dropping down from the castle rock to Netherbow and the port, with the Firth of Forth spread out below. Scotland's capital, whose fortunes rose and fell with the Stuarts, is now a gentle-looking city chiefly known for its festivals and finance, bureaucracy and breweries.

Since 1982, when he ended his fifteen-year sentence for a Glasgow gangland murder, it has also been home to Jimmy Boyle. In and out of jails from ages twelve to thirty-eight and working with ex-cons or needy kids ever since, Boyle is, in his way, an expert like no other. I was lucky he took the time to show me around Edinburgh's dimmer and darker side for a day. I had, when we met, not yet heard of Jimmy Boyle. In Britain that is like not knowing who Mike Tyson or Joan Collins is, confessing you can't keep up with the world of stars.

Americans, when they think of crime in Britain, have an image long instilled by the movies of a benevolent, unarmed bobby with an old-fashioned helmet and stick, probably blowing a whistle at fading footsteps in a fog. Television shots from Northern Ireland, the inner-city riots of 1981 and 1985, and all the football brawls in Germany, Belgium, and at home bring more an armed, shielded riot policeman to mind. Douglas Hurd, when he was still Home Secretary, told me, "All the police organizations are passionately keen on keeping the unarmed bobby. There are actually fewer firearmed officers in Britain than there used to be. And they use firearms less." Under Hurd the total number of police in England and Wales alone rose to a record 138,000, if by American standards Britain is still remarkably law-abiding.

In 1988 Britain had 624 killings; America had over 21,000 (even this was not a record year). Four times Britain's size, the United States had nearly thirty-five times more murders. (More than thirty thousand Americans died of gunshot wounds last year, nearly half of them suicides.) Americans were shocked to learn that in Detroit in 1986, 38 people were killed and 333 injured by handguns. But shocked because this was just the number of children *under seventeen.* ("KIDS KILL KIDS," said the headlines.) Count adults, and Detroit's deaths from handguns alone that year were over 500. Bodies were even piling up in Washington, D.C., with 372 murders in 1988, 438 in 1989, and even more predicted for 1990, an offshoot of the trade in illegal drugs. Even so, it is something when America's capital city alone has more murders than the whole of Britain. The British take a sort of ghoulish vicarious glee in crime, especially if it is local ("OXON MAN IN HORROR STABBING"). But Americans are rightly more afraid of walking city streets at night.

What is alarming in Britain, even if handguns are illegal and licenses hard to get, is how fast violent crime is rising. Since Mrs. Thatcher came to power in 1979 recorded crime has gone up 40 percent. There were 3.7 million crimes in 1988. Hurd says more is getting reported:

> People are more inclined to report that black eye, that row at home between husband and wife, which in the old days would never have gone to the police. So much rape is within the family. A woman didn't report that. Now she does. A wage earner maybe came back on Friday night after he'd had too much to drink and socked his wife. Now she'll ring up the police. Now people have been made more conscious by the media just what is a crime.

I asked Hurd, whom I interviewed at the Home Office: "You have this curious thing in Britain. People attacking cars. Robbing cars. It's so high in proportion to other crimes. Is it that car ownership was originally middle class and poorer people got in the habit of ripping off cars to get even?"

Hurd:

> I don't know. It's an unsolved question. It's falling. There were under twenty-five thousand last year. But car theft is still very bad. One in five cars has been robbed. I think part of it is our car radios are so ludicrously easy to steal. Defects of design.

The cost of policing Britain is also going up, generally per head per year £58 (just under $99), but up to £71 in Liverpool ($120) and £117 ($199) in London. For all of England and Wales it is about £3.5

billion ($5.1 billion). In Scotland it is £400 million ($680 million). Britain sends more men to prison than any other European country —49,800 in 1988. A building program aims to provide sixteen new British prisons in the 1990s. Britain should look twice at this punitive approach. Almost 1 million Americans are now locked up in prisons and jails, one of every *ten* adult black males, and the cost of it, including jails, police, and courts, came to $25 billion in 1988, ten times what was spent a decade earlier. Yet two-thirds of ex-prisoners go back to crime and are jailed again within three years.

Mrs. Thatcher tends to relate crime prevention to more police with wider powers and tougher prison sentences, just as her Labour opponents link it almost solely to unemployment and poverty. One survey of crime in Merseyside, the Liverpool area, undertaken by the Center for Criminology in Edinburgh University and London's Middlesex Polytechnic, confirmed most American experience. Poor people saw crime as their third most pressing problem, after unemployment and lack of facilities for teenagers. The poorer you were, the more you worried about it and the likelier you were to be a victim; crime and fear of crime hit working class women worst of all. So did sexual harassment on the streets, bag snatching, and fear of going out after dark; in the poorer parts of Liverpool over half the people questioned said they either "always" or "often" did not go out at night.

A book that grew out of the Merseyside survey, *Losing the Fight Against Crime*, coauthored by three academics involved, Richard Kinsey, John Lea, and Jock Young, noted that for every 100 crimes known to the British police at the outbreak of World War II, there were 550 in 1950 and close to 900 in 1980. They also interestingly observed that as real crime goes up, so does its fictional portrayal; British television averages five hours of peak-time crime and police dramas per night. Crime headlines keep the tabloids going. Real crime, the authors say, is consistently misrepresented. Most thefts are committed by amateurish adolescents acting on impulse: "Today's offender will be law-abiding tomorrow, and a victim the day after."

The reason they give for rising crime is a breakdown in stable working-class neighborhoods; 90–95 percent of serious crime in Britain is reported by the public to the police (which makes random killings, from Jack the Ripper to the Yorkshire moorland murders, so hard to solve, because they involve more than one locality, making clues harder to come by). With long-term unemployment rising in the inner city, the social basis for policing starts to crumble. As the police adopt high-profile methods such as quasi-military units, surveillance, and intelligence systems, and gain wider powers to detain and interrogate, the flow of information from public to the police gets less. Crime prevention gets locked into a vicious circle. The solution, say Kinsey, Lea, and Young, is what they call "minimal policing," or whatever increases the public's flow of information to the police and the police's ability to collect, interpret, sift, and act upon it.

I went to Edinburgh to meet Kinsey at the university; we had lunch with Lea, who was visiting from London. Kinsey felt neither Mrs. Thatcher's Conservatives nor the Labour leaders were facing up to the collapse of Britain's manufacturing base. "It's all going down, down, down," he said, and with it the conditions of the old working class. He said the biggest difference between Britain and the United States was in police powers: in Scotland the police can detain people without arrest for six hours, in England and Wales for thirty-six hours, when they can be questioned without legal advice. Detention is renewable up to ninety-six hours, but with the right to a solicitor.

Kinsey arranged for me to meet Jimmy Boyle, whom he described as "somebody who did time for murder and was known as a violent, very hard man in Scottish prisons." Anyone British would have known Jimmy Boyle's two books, *A Sense of Freedom*, published when he was still in prison, and *The Pain of Confinement*, in 1984; both were bestsellers. Born in Glasgow's Gorbals in 1944, the son of a safe-blower, Boyle was in and out of borstals from age twelve until 1967, when he was sentenced to life imprisonment for murder. I've quoted from his picture of life in the Gorbals; it was not all that bleak:

> The best nights of the whole week in our district were Friday and Saturday at pub closing time . . . This was when all the fights took place and it was great fun watching them, the funny part being that there was hardly ever a policeman in sight at this time. One of the best fighters on our street was a guy called Big Ned and he was always fighting although he didn't always win . . . When he got to the chip shop he would take us in and buy us bags of chips without paying the man for them and this really delighted us. . . .

When his father died and his mother got a job cleaning out trams, Boyle became a petty thief, leading a gang called the Skull. Violence was part of street life and even after he turned sixteen, "I was busy thieving and fighting, still trying to gain a position for my-self." Soon "I was walking the streets with a revolver and a knife, ready for anything." His gang turned to break-ins and lending money at 25 percent interest a week, terrorizing anybody who didn't pay. It was at this time, it is commonly claimed in Glasgow today, that Boyle's gang nailed a man to the floor.

At Peterhead, Scotland's maximum security prison, Boyle fought his way into five and a half years of solitary confinement. Once, put into a three-by-eleven-foot cage, he rubbed himself with his own excrement to scare off the warders if they came to beat him.

> The screws obviously thought I was insane but I wasn't going to lie there naked and helpless while they beat me up.

By the time he was in his early twenties, Boyle had been tried for murder twice, once when just eighteen, and both times been ac-quitted. His gangland ties now reached to England.

> By now we had a strong friendship with the Kray twins in London, and we would go down there to big fights or get a few days away from the Glasgow scene . . . I have always noticed an innate disdain by lots of Scottish guys for the English criminals—most of them thought they were a bit soft. This is certainly far from the truth.

Ronnie and Reggie Kray, ex-boxers who in the sixties were slum landlords and ran protection rackets in the East End, were notori-ous for gangland killings, razor slashings, and running nightclubs where they mixed with showbiz stars; Ronnie Kray, a predatory ho-mosexual who preyed on teenagers, once boasted of a gangland kill-ing, "I felt fucking marvelous. I have never felt so good, so bloody alive, before or since. Twenty years on, I can recall every second . . . I had killed a man. I had got my button, as the Yanks say . . ." After a forty-day trial in 1968, ten of their gang went to jail, the Krays getting sent up for thirty years apiece. A year earlier Boyle was given his fifteen-year-minimum sentence for the murder of Glasgow gangster Babs Rooney. As Boyle told writer John Morti-mer:

> You know I didn't kill Babs Rooney? Babs was someone I'd met in prison and once or twice on the outside. We quarreled that night and I cut him. I know who actually did the murder and we tried to cover up for him because he was a friend of mine.

Mortimer asked him about the Krays, widely regarded as psy-chopathic thugs: (Ronnie Kray, today judged insane, is now committed to Broadmoor asylum, though a new film, starring pop musicians Gary and Martin Kemp from the group Spandau Ballet, mythologizes the Krays).

> I think the Krays were highly respected around the East End of London. People there thought they'd done very well. It's the culture, you see.

Mortimer wondered why "all reformed criminals start to talk like sociologists." Boyle's reform began with an experimental Special Unit in the Scottish penal system. A few long-term inmates at Barlinnie Prison were set apart to live in fairly humane conditions and, within limits, to run their own affairs. Boyle spent eight years there, producing sculpture which was exhibited in Edinburgh, writing his first book, and meeting a pretty psychiatrist, Dr. Sarah Trevelyan, whose father at the time was Britain's film censor. They got married while Boyle was still in prison.

After his release, Jimmy and Sarah Boyle opened a social center, the Gateway Exchange, just a short distance from Edinburgh's Holyrood Castle, once home to Mary, Queen of Scots. They offer help to ex-convicts, homeless teenagers, and drug abuse victims. The center also houses a café and an avant-garde theatre, the Mandela.

Jimmy Boyle himself, when I met him there, was blond, athletic-looking, and affable; he was in sweat clothes, having just jogged four miles that morning up to the top of Arthur's Seat and back. His Scots accent was heavy. He was very obliging. After we talked over coffee an hour, he offered to take me around Edinburgh's most problem-ridden housing estates.

What makes somebody turn to crime? If you're sympathetic, you can say a poor man, if he's jobless long enough, maybe with a hungry family, can get desperate enough to try anything. If you're hostile or afraid, you blame criminality on childhood experience, psychic debility, or even derangement. Or you put it down to the cultural breakdown of a society. Jimmy Boyle did the last.

> Everything's breakin' up. The dyin' traditions. The unions. Churches. The old mold's been broken. And it isn't necessarily a bad thing. We'll maybe get through it. Become a healthier nation. There's no doubt we're well into the Thatcher Revolution. She's got in there three times. If things continue, she'll probably get in a fourth time. She's changed all the big institutions. Housing. Schools. The BBC. The poll tax. All that. She's revolutionized the country. They all hate to admit it. Everybody's been affected by Thatcherism.
>
> It's not all bad. Some aspects of it are quite healthy. I don't say that

easily because I don't particularly like Thatcher or many of her policies. But she did what she said. Absolutely no doubt about that. She's
done it. Some of those who put her in, now they're squealing like pigs.
And what I say is, well, you fuckin' deserve what you get. Because you
voted for her.

She's privatized everything. She's rolled back the welfare state. You
can't take it away from her. But in terms of the people at the bottom of
the ladder, they've been crushed even further. They just rot away. That
pile is getting higher and higher. And Thatcherism will be looked back
on and people will say, "How dumb we were. We wasted all those
lives."

Pressures kept building up in the low-income families, he said.

At one time it was unthinkable for parents to abandon teenage daughters. They were more protective. Now we're seeing more and more girls
thrown out of the house because it doesn't pay the parents, benefit-
swise, to keep them. It's not a cold, calculated act. But poverty and
hardship create tremendous conflicts within the families. And so
they're biting each other. And so the kids are movin' out, movin' out
quickly.

We drove past high-rise publicly owned apartments which Boyle
said were full of "single parents," a euphemism for unwed girls living with two or three young children. "Most of them are heavily into
tranquilizers," Boyle said. "They're isolated up there. They've lost
confidence. They're bringing up kids and the kids are badly damaged as the result of the mother not being able to cope." (Homelessness is also growing at phenomenal rates in Britain and America,
the man sleeping under a bridge or the woman mouthing angry
abuse as she goes down the street now familiar sights in both. Estimates of American homeless, about a third of them mentally ill, go
from 350,000 to over 4 million. The *New York Times* has reported
that more than 430,000 beds in American mental hospitals, about 80
percent, were eliminated the past thirty years. In Britain, mental
hospital beds dropped from 90,600 in 1978 to 71,200 by 1986. Some
estimate a third of the homeless are military veterans, another third
families; there are large numbers, in both Britain and America, of
destitute elderly, runaway teenagers, drug addicts, and alcoholics, as
well as young mothers with children and single men with low-paying jobs. Local authorities in both London and New York spend ex-
orbitant amounts renting temporary accommodations for homeless
who qualify. Why homelessness is happening all over the West at the
same time is one of its more baffling aspects. Even Paris has between 25,000 and 40,000 *sans abri,* those without shelter.

After London, Edinburgh has Britain's highest incidence of AIDS. Close to 60 percent of the city's drug addicts are believed to carry the AIDS virus. Jimmy Boyle explains: "In Liverpool, for instance, most people chase the dragon, they either snort it or smoke it. Here people inject it. Now it may be you can attribute that to the meanness in Scottish people. You get more value for the money if you inject it with a needle."

We entered Pilton, a bad housing estate. "BALL GAMES PROHIB-ITED," read a sign. There was a lot of graffiti. We turned into a street where every housing unit was barricaded or boarded up. "Isn't there a pub?" I asked.

"That was it down on the corner. It got blown up."

"By who?"

"Just guys. They put it under new management and the new management wasn't going to continue the old . . . um . . . games. No games." Boyle grinned. "They're anti-ball-game, as you can see, in this area."

A bus came by. The fare was fifty pence, half a pound. With the going wage for a woman's part time job just a little over two pounds an hour, she'd work the first half hour to get there and back. "A lot of people are locked into these areas," Boyle said. "They can't afford to go downtown on the bus." It was the same as Easterhouse or any of the outlying estates; inner cities might be huddled and decayed, but you could walk where you had to go. As we drove, we saw many teenage boys standing idly about. Earlier Police Detective Superintendent Tom J. Wood told me, "If you look at Edinburgh, you'll find an awful lot of young men fall into criminal tendencies between about fourteen and nineteen years. And then, from our view, they disappear. The whole crime scene drops off. They mature."

"Aren't there people to teach these kids skills?" I asked Boyle.

"Okay, you teach somebody welding and joining. What do they weld and join? There's no jobs. Thatcher's right that people have to learn to do things by themselves. But she forgets there are a lot of people not capable of it. Norman Tebbit says get on your bike and look for work. But where do you pedal to?"

We came out of the slums into a street of handsomely restored old stone tenements. There was no graffiti here; some shops were open.

"This was an old poverty-stricken area. Now on the way up as a result of Thatcherism."

"You have mixed feelings about Thatcherism, Jimmy."

"When I say it's on the way up, the people who lived here just go to some other ghetto. The people who come in are yuppies."

Even in Edinburgh it was a relief to see the roofs of the Royal Mile and the great old castle on its ridge just ahead; I was glad to get back to sedate and reassuring George Street, with its Victorian monuments and air of prosperity. So many slums in Britain are living on a short fuse that could explode at any time.

"It's scary," I told Boyle. "Nobody's teaching those kids anything. The whole culture starts to go."

Weeks later I read Boyle's account in *A Sense of Freedom* of how he looked back on himself, at the lowest depths of the penal system, naked in his prison cage:

> . . . I often thought of the vicious circle of staying in places in the
> Gorbals and how I always looked up to all the hard men in my street
> and district. Then the kids looked up to me and saw me as the game
> guy who would do anything . . . And yet if only they could have seen
> me in that cage. I would hate this to sound as though I'm on the evan-
> gelistic trail for that is not my purpose and I don't give a shit for that
> side of it. I have simply been on a journey and experienced terrible
> pain of a physical, spiritual and emotional nature and I want to stop
> those of my ilk from doing the same . . .

"Nobody cares anymore," he told me that day more than a decade after writing those lines. "That's why we have the violence and everything else. These kids just feel: 'Nobody cares about us. Why should we care about them?' There's areas here every bit as bad as Liverpool or Glasgow. How do these people get out of their misery, their despair? You see, it's okay looking at it from out here. But if you're in there, how do you start?"

"If they could get out of it and get a job and have a normal life, they'd choose it?"

"Everybody I know would choose that."

Ratchet of Violence

O A LOT OF self-confident English in the South, violence is irre-deemably tied to the North and the slum cultures of its blighted ports, factory cities, and coal towns. To them it is per-sonified by the yobbish, jobless, tattooed, and shaven-headed teen-ager, probably speaking in an unfathomable Liverpudlian or Glas-wegian dialect, maybe on drugs, shivering in his torn gear. If one excepts Britain's black immigrants in the inner cities of the South, they are pretty nearly right. As Jimmy Boyle seemed to agree, if nobody teaches these kids anything, the whole culture starts to go.

But the self-confidence of the southern English got shaken to the core in the 1980s. Flashing knives in Soho, racial tensions on Not-ting Hill, "lager louts" raising hell in the Home Counties after the pubs close Saturday nights, brought home that it can happen here. Beer drinking certainly figures in. Fully 39 million of the 57 million British are boozers, government figures say. More of them keep turning to new "super-strong" lagers—a 99p can (about $1.70) packs the punch of two and a half pints of traditional bitter or four pegs of whiskey. In 1989 over 600,000 barrels of this stuff went down British throats. Oblivion is guaranteed for $7 or $8.

I've left this chapter on violence in this section on the North because that region suffers a lot more from the urban decay, jobless-ness, and social breakdown that causes crime, and so it gets more. If violence were ever to be a serious peril to Britain, it would be along the North-South divide. True, smash up people and television cam-era crews, hungry for visual drama, start cranking away. ("Stay tuned for the mutilated dog story!") In America, land of Rambo and Wyatt Earp, you expect it. Somehow in Britain, it's wrong. In our eyes, British society has always shown so much cohesion; it has all the virtues of civility and accommodation and tolerance, it keeps a stiff upper lip, it muddles through.

London and the Southeast especially live up to expectation (the

North is a lot more like America). Orderliness shows up in the patient queues at the bus stop or post office. The girls in the tea shop are courteous when an old lady fumbles with her change. Librarians and book store clerks can be very obliging if sometimes cranky. And there's a surliness about some Londoners; many of the Cockney cab drivers could do with a course at charm school. You do find plenty of English with the old courtesy and civility, if leavened by a kind of glum separateness. This is the England of Barbara Pym and Margaret Drabble novels, of trivial but crucial pleasures—taking flowers to the vicar, pottering about the garden, walking the dog on the Common, the prospect of a cup of tea.

Social cohesion persists. But out in Surrey, especially, there are worrying signs of strain—a new meanness, more verbal or physical abuse in pubs, schools, and the Underground. It is most often revealed in aggression shown in language or driving. Drivers go at maniacal speeds on narrow nineteenth century lanes designed for horses. They can angrily shout abuse at pedestrians who don't get out of their way fast enough to suit them; it's happened to me. Something happens to the British when they drive; put the most mannerly Dr. Jekyll behind the wheel and he turns into a fiendish speed-crazed Hyde. A few drivers have been known to jump out of their cars and attack a pedestrian on the sidewalk; one was fatally shot. Just in my neighborhood in Richmond, a middle-aged woman was killed crossing the street ("I wouldn't be driving like that if it was raining," said her son); another woman, seventy-nine, had just about reached the curb when a speeding motorbike knocked her down and killed her. A young man died when a drunk driver lost control and went up on the sidewalk, sweeping his victim off his feet from behind; the driver only got two and a half years. Walking around Richmond, you had to be ready to jump.

This disregard for the next man—and this is just the South of England, not Britain as a whole—can show up in lack of eye contact and aggressive body language on crowded sidewalks. One of my family, visiting from home, said after several days of exploring Richmond that it reminded him of the old movie *Invasion of the Body Snatchers,* where creatures from outer space inhabit the bodies of humans; what gives them away is they have no emotions. Like tattoos and spiky hair, this kind of death-in-life reserve could suggest anger and alienation. A number of veteran American observers in Britain have asked if all the self-imposed decorum and respectability might not, in the words of Norman Gelb, "restrain and mask fierce aspects of character which were so relentlessly exhibited in former times and which may still lurk not far beneath the British skin."

The British are so various and full of surprises anything is possible. (Like the elegant old lady in a crowded Richmond tea shop who, after chatting a few minutes, leaned over and confided, "I was a Bluebell." Luckily I had seen the Folies-Bergère in Paris and its famous Bluebells, a tall, blond, Rockette-like chorus line recruited entirely from English girls.) But Norman Tebbit talked about an end to the old class deference, a good thing if it didn't get out of hand. And Tony Benn said tension was growing and people were getting anxious; he said that was why they kept voting back Mrs. Thatcher.

One can't, of course, overdo it. But maybe the English were never as nonviolent as we think. Public executions in London, at Tyburn and later Newgate, were public holidays, drawing huge crowds of rowdy spectators; they lasted until the mid-nineteenth century, Dickens describes them. Cockfights, bare-knuckle boxing, bear-baiting, and setting bulldogs against tethered bulls were all popular pub pastimes. Erotic flagellation still seems a peculiarly English kinky thing; I was astonished to enter a shop near Piccadilly Circus and find it sold nothing except switches and whips. Floggings, beheadings, hangings, and burnings at the stake, people like Sweeney Todd, the throat-cutting barber, and Jack the Ripper, are the dark side of English history. And plenty of Mrs. Thatcher's young Conservatives want to bring back hanging and flogging. Hanging, drawing and quartering for treason went on well into the eighteenth century. Technically speaking, it was only abolished in Scotland in 1948 (it hadn't been done for two hundred years). The condemned was put on a hurdle and dragged to the place of execution (hence drawn). He was then hanged, cut down, disemboweled, and beheaded. The body was cut in four bits and stuck on London's different gates; Thomas Cromwell's head was exposed just outside Parliament. And we have Samuel Pepys in 1660: "I went out to Charing Cross, to see Major-general Harrison hanged, drawn and quartered; which was done there, he looking as cheerful as any man could do in that condition." When Harrison was being cut into, he drew back and slapped the executioner in the face. Henry VIII had Anne Boleyn's brother hanged, drawn, and quartered after falsely charging him with incest. King Henry, who summarily executed Sir Thomas More and so many others with little excuse, beheading two of his six wives, sounds a monster. Contemporaries indeed called him "worse than a beast" and "more cruel than Nero." And Dickens called him "that blot of blood and grease upon the History of England." Which makes all the more poignant Anne Boleyn's own words just before kneeling to the executioner's sword at Tower Green; she called Henry the "most goodliest, and gentlest Prince that is."

> At about 6.10 on the warm evening of Friday, April 10, 1981, Police Constable Stephen Marigiotta (PC 643 L) was on duty in Atlantic Road, where he noticed that traffic had come to a standstill.

Thus began Lord Scarman's narrative of the mass violence that in 1981 spread from the inner-London district of Brixton to cities all over England. (Similar rioting, involving blacks against the police, broke out in London's Broadwater Farm council estate in 1985.) In Brixton a fight between neighbors turned into a melee with bricks, knives, firebombs, burning cars, and looting that lasted three days. Skinheads took on Asians and blacks in west and south London. In Liverpool's worst area of Toxteth, known locally as Liverpool 8, blacks and whites together smashed and burned, battling the police. There were riots, arson, and looting in Moss Side in Manchester and in a dozen other cities. "Oh, those poor shopkeepers!" was Mrs. Thatcher's first reaction. Petrol bombs were thrown in Welsh mining valleys like the Rhondda. Only in Birmingham, where Britain's second biggest concentration of blacks lives, was a potential riot damped down by police consultation with black leaders.

Obviously television made things worse. Shock spectacles of burning and fighting and looting, as it goes from city to city, are bound, among troublemakers, to have a copy-cat effect. It's just common sense that the more violence TV carries, the more brutal a society is likely to become. T. S. Eliot said, "An artist has influence over us whether he wants one or not and we are influenced whether we want to be or not." Young men in Rambo-style bandannas and bandoliers have shot people in Britain. Stanley Kubrick made sure his film of Anthony Burgess's *Clockwork Orange* was not seen in the cinema or on video in Britain after youths started dressing up like its thugs, raping women, and beating up old people (". . . we gave him the boot, one go each, and then it was blood, not song nor vomit, that came out of his filthy old rot").

What caused so many blacks to riot? Nonwhite immigrants from Britain's former imperial colonies were brought in during the 1950s to the 1970s to take jobs and live in outworn houses the British-born didn't want. Recession, rapidly worsening in the 1980s, harshly affected their children, isolated in inner cities or the big housing estates. Racism combined with poor schooling to keep the black immigrants and their British-born children out of better jobs and better homes. Verbal and physical abuse heightened discontent. Crime involving personal violence rose. Police crime-control methods focused on young black people, offending all blacks. Lord Scarman, a leading judge asked to investigate, in his report called for a direct attack on racial disadvantage in education and skills.

Since 1981 Britain seems to be repeating the experience of America. There the urban riots of the 1960s have not recurred, even though the social isolation of the blacks is as bad as ever and youth unemployment is worse. What has happened instead is a huge increase in destructive behavior by individuals: vandalism, theft, personal violence, resistance to schooling, drug abuse.

In Britain the 1985 Broadwater Farm riots were more vicious than anything that came before. On a Sunday night hundreds of rioters clashed with five hundred policemen in the large, heavily black housing estate in Tottenham, north London. One policeman, Police Constable Keith Blakelock, was hacked to death. Forty others were wounded, several with shotgun pellets. In the fall of 1988, while I was in London, PC Michael Shepherd, given the Queen's Gallantry Medal, described the scene at the riot:

> I'll never forget it. I was so scared. I didn't realize I was so scared. The youths had covered us in petrol and then sent down some lighted petrol bombs hoping we would go up. But only a few went off.

He helped rescue Police Constable Richard Coombes, who fell injured as his sergeant tried to beat off rioters stabbing Blakelock.

> There was a lot of punching and kicking. I saw PC Blakelock go down and a group surrounded him. But I had to get to Dick as I knew he wasn't dead but lying unconscious and needed help. I covered him with my shield.

In a country that is 96 percent white, Britain's native-born multi-racial population, divided as it is between blacks and Asians, has problems that will not be easily solved. The oldest black community is Liverpool's, about twenty thousand strong. Tellingly this is the most unemployed group in the most run-down section of Britain's most depressed city.

"It's definitely eased," Douglas Hurd said when I met him. A

diplomat by training, Hurd seems more comfortable since he became Foreign Secretary. That day he told me:

> In the 1985 riots the police were in better communication with black
> leaders who were able to establish some sort of control. There was a
> time when I first took over the Home Office when I was expecting trou-
> ble week by week. Was there going to be a major city disturbance? And
> if so, where? I don't feel that now. Touch wood.

Some, like industrialist Sir John Harvey-Jones, feel the image of
the police in Britain has been permanently changed:

> Take the miners' strike. Seeing lines of ordinary police battling with
> pickets night after night on television screens. It's a price I would not
> have paid. Once you've done it, you can't go back. It's a ratchet, a set of
> teeth that catch as the wheel turns. You can't take the great British
> picture of the friendly bobby and say, "From Monday to Friday you
> help little old ladies across the road and on Friday night don riot gear
> and knock seven bells out of a bloody bunch of miners."

The white who shaves off his hair, gets tattooed, wears Doc Mar-
ten boots, and calls himself a skinhead, and the black who wears his
hair in long dreadlocks, speaks an invented dialect, and calls himself a Rastafarian, are alike in seeking to visibly express their disaf-
fection with the larger society. A more baffling cause of violence, the
football hooligan or yob, wears the same haircut, jeans, jogging
shoes, and windbreaker of most working-class young men and is
English to the core. British football, soccer to Americans, was getting more popular again when, at Hillsborough stadium in Sheffield
in April 1989, a massive crush killed ninety-five spectators. It was
Britain's worst-ever sporting catastrophe. New identity cards and
the abolition of terraces, where fans stand, are bound to change the
game's setting.

The Hillsborough horror came after a police officer, fearing in-
juries as a crowd of ticketless Liverpool supporters massed in front
of the stadium's turnstiles just as the game was about to start, ordered some large doors to be opened. The crowd, pushing and shoving, some of them drunk, surged forward into a tunnel and out onto
an overcrowded terrace behind a goal. Fans already there were
crushed or suffocated against a steel perimeter fence.

It was the worst in a string of disasters related to British football's violent culture. In May 1985, thirty-nine fans, mainly Italian,
were crushed or trampled to death in a riot set off by Liverpool
supporters at a European Cup Final at Heysel Stadium in Brussels.
Earlier that same month fifty-six English spectators burned to death

when fire swept Bradford stadium. In 1961 sixty-six Scottish fans died in Glasgow in a crush between people trying to get out of a football match and others trying to return when they heard a late goal had been scored. All reflected the tension around big football matches. The fatal perimeter fence at Hillsborough was only there to keep fans from invading the field or attacking the rival team's fans. At Bradford the fire extinguishers had been taken away for fear hooligans would use them as weapons.

Most of Britain's bleak and tattered stadiums were built between 1880 and 1910. Antiquated buildings or equipment also figured in the King's Cross Underground station fire in November 1988, in which thirty-one died, as well as in a whole series of train collisions, the worst of which killed thirty-five people at Clapham Junction in December 1988. Britain is so small these are not remote happenings to most people; for example, I have seen a match at Hillsborough, changed tubes at King's Cross many times, and passed through Clapham Junction several times a week. It is the same for many people.

The worst of the football violence has come in the North. Yet there are brawls in one stadium or another, even in London and the South, practically every weekend. About half a million fans move about the Underground, intercity trains, or chartered buses every Saturday for nine months of the year. If you use public transport, you run into them.

The first match I went to see was a home game for Chelsea, a club notorious for rioting. The stadium, in a crowded section of London, looked like a maximum security prison. Ringed by steel fences and helmeted, shield-bearing riot police, with armored vehicles and water cannon to back them up, it was not at all like an American-style stadium, but resembled a sooty, sinister old Victorian brick warehouse built around a playing field. Narrow, menacing slits and heavy turnstiles were the only way in; we all got searched for knives. A surveillance helicopter whirred overhead. There were Black Marias and mounted policemen with rearing horses, and others holding back fiercely barking dogs which looked ready to tear you to pieces. Like the zoolike cages of each club's supporters inside, it all created an atmosphere of hysteria and tension. Scarf-waving, chanting Chelsea and Manchester United supporters were jammed into these standing-room-only terraces at each end, which were enclosed by metal barriers and gates and fenced off from the playing field and those in the seated grandstand by iron, spiked fences. Some of the police seemed to be as spoiling for a fight as many of the fans; they say there is no shortage of volunteers for football duty.

When I was in Oxford, after a match, police would herd the visiting team's supporters back to the railway station and keep them in a special pen, much like you would see at a stockyard. When their train came, the police marched them into it, the fans often singing obscene abuse of their jailers to tunes like "Old McDonald Had a Farm." Once I saw a policeman burst into a telephone booth where two meek-looking younger boys were phoning. He roared, "Who are you calling?" "My mother," stammered one of the boys, looking scared. At such times, anybody who looks remotely like a "hooligan" gets treated with suspicion. (The term comes from the name of a rowdy Irish family in London's East End in the 1890s.) Police fear word will be passed to confederates in London that a trainload of fans is coming in. Police with barking dogs straining at their leashes are a not uncommon sight in Underground stations on late Saturday afternoons.

When you talk to the young fans themselves, they are full of bravado. "There's a few stabbings," "People get thrown from trains," "Some like to fight, some don't." A Chelsea supporter told me, "It's a game of cops and robbers. It's not new. It's been going on as long as we've had matches. Somebody always ends up needing stitches or gets a broken nose." The horror of Hillsborough is sickeningly caught in photographs taken through the fence. These are like the much-replayed television footage of the Bradford stadium fire, which shows fans laughing and jumping about on the playing field while the grandstand behind is a mass of flames and a policeman runs right at the camera, his hair on fire. In 1986 about fifty Millwall fans terrorized the Underground itself, attacking a train carrying rival supporters. They shouted, "Kill, kill, kill!" and ripped benches from a station platform to use as battering rams.

Hopes that the English fans would not behave like nihilistic vandals in West Germany in the summer of 1988 proved short-lived. British teams were banned from European competitions after Brussel's Heysel stadium disaster. But as feared, hundreds of English, Dutch, and German fans fought pitched battles with knives, broken bottles, even tear gas, drinking, fighting, vomiting, and urinating in streets, bars, and railway stations. At times Britain's tabloid press seemed to be egging them on. "HOW WE TAMED ENGLAND FANS: German Police Claim Victory," taunted the *Evening Standard*.

A Leeds fan:

We're five years out of date; we fight with fists and feet, but these German blokes have got gas, rockets, flares. They're really tooled up. I saw one of them with a gas mask. It was like fucking World War III.

Another:

We was having a drink, fifteen of us, at the bar round the corner there. This car just drives right up on the pavement at us, and knocks two English blokes down. Then the bastard gets out with a knife and just cuts one of the lads' throats. I tell you, it's bloody *true* . . .

The Sunday Times estimated that of ten thousand English fans who went to Germany for the European Championships, probably no more than five hundred were seriously looking for a fight. This included such heavy-duty hooligan mobs as West Ham's Inter-City Firm, Chelsea's Headhunters, Arsenal's Gooners, Millwall's Nutty Turn Out, and the Leeds Service Crew. Lesser "firms"—include the Exeter City Sly Crew, whose calling cards have the initials KKK (Ku Klux Klan) or AWL (Anti-Welsh League) on them. Birmingham's Zulu Warriors paint their faces with black and white stripes and chant, "Zulu! Zulu!" as they charge opposing fans or even the police. Even the most notorious thugs, in what amounts to a criminal underground subculture, seem to have jobs: clerks, bouncers, construction workers, even market traders, bankers, stockbrokers. "The real hard nuts," police say, "are estate agents, travel agents, that sort of thing"; they sit in the seats to avoid detection.

"God Save the Queen" and "Rule Britannia" are regularly sung, but with Nazi salutes and a shouted climax of *"Sieg Heil! Sieg Heil!"* Most football gangs are white; racists among them grunt, or throw bananas, at black players. Hooligans from the South of England often say they support Mrs. Thatcher, even if her policies are too mild. They say things like "They should scrap the dole altogether. It's only for lazy buggers and idiots." The racist National Front recruits at football matches. When a twenty-two-year-old Egyptian youth was slashed with a knife in Stuttgart, an English fan told *The Sunday Times*, "Well, he was black, and there was nothing much else going on."

Football violence is not new. Ever since football became a spectator sport in the 1880s, crowds have every so often surged onto pitches to attack players or referees, or gone on drunken sprees to celebrate their team's victory. Newspaper accounts of the time tell of "the terraces and railings broken up" and referees driven off by "a howling stone-throwing mob." Now, with cheap fares and higher incomes, more fans can travel and pitch battles in bigger numbers. Lord Carrington, who was in Belgium during the Heysel stadium riot, told me, "It wasn't just what happened at Heysel, it was the behavior of the Liverpool fans before the match. Wholly disgusting."

Lord Carrington admits violence goes way back in Britain. "I think we've always been a pretty rowdy race. Remember the Duke of Wellington's famous remark about his troops during the Napoleonic wars? 'I don't know what effect these men will have on the enemy, but, by God, they terrify me.'" (Wellington called the English army "the scum of the earth," a phrase borrowed by Edward Heath in 1988 to describe in Parliament how Mrs. Thatcher treated her critics.)

When I asked Douglas Hurd about Wellington's remark, he said there was some truth in it:

> In Wellington's time the London mob was the most feared in the world. In 1780 it held London to ransom in the Gordon riots. And in the 1830s, Wellington's time, Bristol was burned to the ground, Nottingham was burned . . . There was rioting on a scale we've certainly never had since. Then, I think, we had a period of social stability gradually building up during the Victorian time and reaching its height during the war. But in the last thirty years we've seen the steady growth of violence again. There's always been a good deal of drunken brawling. But it used to be fists and now it's knives. That's a different matter. Because knives kill people and knives scar people.

Mrs. Thatcher has told the House of Commons, "The survival of football as a spectator sport is in question." It is hard to see what she can do, other than a compulsory national member scheme for football clubs, with entry only for spectators who show their photo on a stamped card (talked about and now ignominiously abandoned), and the abolition of terraces.

Norman Tebbit says young people today are probably no rowdier than he himself was as a young commissioned officer in the RAF, only he and his buddies got drunk in private. "In all human beings there's a violent streak, a destructive streak," he told me. "As well as a constructive and decent streak. And what we've done in recent times is to relax the disciplines to allow that violent streak to come out too easily. And we've not done enough to impose the disciplines that control it."

You can even see it, Tebbit says, in cricket. "Cricket," I exclaimed. "The very name rings with the old empire-building team spirit, the code of fair play between gentlemen."

"No more," Tebbit said. Even cricket players are arguing with the referee or umpire, he continued, something they never used to do.

> Boxers don't. They're disqualified. They lose the fight. Whereas on the football pitch—and I regret to say, increasingly on the cricket field— you can gain an advantage if you intimidate the referee or the umpire. If bad behavior pays, you'll see a lot more of it.

"Soccer," claims sociologist David Robbins, "is everywhere the number one safety valve of young men." That is one theory. Football hooligans, says Robbins, show Mrs. Thatcher's success in breaking down class ties and for some youths, like those working in the South's building boom, putting more money in their pockets. One finds a de facto tolerance of some football hooliganism. "Better they fight each other than us," columnist Simon Jenkins half-joked to me over lunch. This "safety valve" school holds that the excitement and nastiness of football hooliganism prevents more serious social disruption.

Maybe so. But violence in Britain, like anywhere else, grows out of poverty, not prosperity. If you stop to think about it, all the big football disasters—Sheffield, Bradford, Glasgow, Brussels—either involved a city in the North or, in the case of Belgium, fans from a city in the North, Liverpool. The only deeply serious violence in the South, the riots of 1981 and 1985, involved the South's only really poor and left-out group, its West Indian blacks. The more-money-in-their-pockets idea doesn't hold up.

It is funny when London's clubs turn Liverpool's theme song, "You'll Never Walk Alone," into "You'll Never Work Again," while waving credit cards and cash at the poorer, often jobless Liverpool fans. It would be funnier if, for so many of them, it wasn't so likely to be true. In one of the grimmer effects of the North-South divide, Liverpool is the place where young long-term unemployed may be creating a new subculture of their own, one based on crime and drugs.

Chasing the Drag in Liverpool

I N "The Underclass—A World Apart," a public affairs show produced by London Weekend Television, its commentator, Matthew
Parris, warns that "the young unemployed, some of whom face a
lifetime on the dole, have begun to forge a new culture." He says it
turns on family breakdown, drugs, and crime. Parris, a former Tory
member of Parliament, makes it sound threatening:

> If the underclass culture continues to seep into our society, the rest of
> us will indeed be paying a higher price for our security. Many people
> also fear the prospect of more of the sporadic violence and small-scale
> rioting that takes place, often unreported, in our cities.

As Parris's voice continues, "On the drug-infested estates, violence erupts sporadically . . . ," we see youths viciously beating
each other with sticks while a baby shrieks, "Mummy!" and a man
shouts, "Put that away!" This Liverpool slum has seen lots of stealing. A jobless teenager says if a pair of jeans or shoes comes into his
house, his parents say nothing. He has no other way to get money.

> So we go out and knock it. Go out on the rob. It's just the same. You go
> to the shops to buy something. We go to the shops to rob something.

Another says drugs are part of the day:

> You have a snort. Go shoplifting, car breaking. Go home, have a nod.

An unwed mother, who had her first baby at sixteen, is fearful
about her children's future:

> If they're not going to have money they're going to get into trouble,
> aren't they? It just makes me wonder why I brought them up in this
> world. 'Cause it's not any good.

An older Liverpool man is interviewed:

> Well, either there'll be a mass exodus to somewhere else or this will
> finish up like Harlem or the Bronx. Where you have to defend what

little you've got. If you've got a radio or somethin' like that, you'll probably have to sit up all night, watchin' your house. Frightened to go to bed. This is the way I see the future. Not just here. This is gonna happen all over.

The argument is that if children grow up without a stake in society, they won't abide by its moral code of what's right and wrong. And that this can be passed on from generation to generation. We talk a lot about an underclass too. American anthropologist Oscar Lewis, based on his fieldwork in Mexico and Puerto Rico, called this the "culture of poverty." English geographer Peter Hall says it is happening in Britain's North, where some of the cities are developing "an alternative culture of a very vicious kind."

> One based on crime. One based on drugs. One based on any kind of illegal activity that brings you an income, some kind of interest, some excitement to your life. And this culture will rapidly create "no go" areas. You might as well put barbed-wire fences around them surrounded by armored police.

Criminologist Richard Kinsey, whom we met in Edinburgh, strongly denies an underclass is being created. He says the poor just need jobs. Kinsey argues drugs are an addiction, pure and simple. Jimmy Boyle is less sure, saying once you drift into a life of crime and drugs, it is hard to get back out again. Tony Benn, when I mentioned an underclass to him, was vehemently opposed to the idea.

> Mrs. Thatcher's invented, very cleverly, as anyone would try to do, an analysis of the structure of British society that gives her a permanent majority. She says, "Oh, there is an underclass. We won't bother about them."

Others argue an underclass does exist in Britain. Paul Barker, the respected long-time editor of *New Society*, Britain's best sociological journal, which sadly shut down in 1988 after twenty-five years (if it sort of lives on merged with the *New Statesman* as the *New Statesman and Society*), says the underclass has been gradually forming for years.

> It hasn't just happened under Mrs. Thatcher. I think she has helped it along. She's like a bull in a china shop, you see, breaking a lot of crockery. A lot of her policies, like selling off council houses or narrowing down the distribution of social services, increasingly leave this residue group who are stigmatized by their housing conditions, stigmatized because they take welfare.
>
> Mrs. Thatcher's education changes mostly won't actually take place

for years. She is trying to get some of the brightest kids out of the underclass. But of course that leaves the rest even worse off.

Barker, a Yorkshireman, has mixed feelings about Thatcherism, as most thinking Britons do.

I mean her line is: if you don't get business right, nothing else will be right. And that's a very ungentlemanly thing to say. A lot of your people having tea at the Athenaeum have gentlemanly values. They don't want to be contaminated by trade. Mrs. Thatcher *loves* trade. That's what she's all about.

Remember Scott Fitzgerald's remark about the rich: "They are different from you and me," and Hemingway's rebuttal in "The Snows of Kilimanjaro," "Yes, they have more money." Daniel P. Moynihan and Oscar Lewis had much the same argument about the nature of the poor in the late 1960s. I was covering the White House for *The Washington Star* when President Nixon brought in Moynihan to come up with welfare reform to replace Lyndon Johnson's old "war on poverty," not unlike what Mrs. Thatcher has tried to do.

Lewis contended it was easier to eliminate poverty itself than the "culture of poverty" which "affects participation in the larger culture." He was all for organizing neighborhood groups to take on city hall. Moynihan, who was poor himself (he got his start with a postwar scholarship at the London School of Economics), did not go along with Lewis's theory. Like Professor Kinsey, to Moynihan the poor were just like anybody else, they just had less money. His daring solution to eliminate poverty in America—a guaranteed minimum income for everybody—was never tried. But he did get across the truth that America's biggest domestic problem was the social isolation of the black in the inner cities of the North and West. And that this was the root cause of our urban decay, rising crime, and family breakdown.

What is remarkable to an American in Britain is that you can go down its supposedly meanest streets—Granby Street in Liverpool, Railton Road in Brixton, Lumb Lane in Bradford—and find there is usually still a pub or a grocer or a news agent. There are Indians or Pakistanis about, maybe punky whites or Rastas from the West Indies. You may see women pushing prams, old people, mixed races.

It is the totally empty derelictions like Glasgow's Possil that are really scary: houses barricaded or boarded up, streets half-demolished, glass and broken bricks lying about, graffiti. Locals get scared too. Going along Lumb Lane, I saw in Peel Square that the house doors were gaily painted in green with puce, peach with crimson, a sure sign the Asians had moved in. I stopped to speak in Urdu to some little Pakistani boys, delighted to ask about America; then a man shouted from one of the houses to come away, I might be a kidnapper.

You sometimes hear the claim that since Mrs. Thatcher came to power, 80 percent of the British got richer, but the bottom 20 percent got a good deal poorer. The truth is the bottom 20 percent, while a bit better off, did not share in the general income rise; the gap grew. As William Waldegrave pointed out, Mrs. Thatcher avoided any drop in real wages for the many at the cost of extremely high unemployment for the few.

In the United States the recession of the 1980s was handled the other way. Average real wages have declined since 1973, in 1985–90 by 5 percent, against a rise of 14 percent in Britain—for those with jobs. As Frank Levy, a University of Maryland economist, analyzes it, in the twenty-eight years from the end of World War II until the 1973–74 OPEC oil-price rise, American workers' real wages went up by 2.5–3.5 percent a year. Productivity went up an average 3.5 percent a year. The oil-price rise led to both recession and inflation and by 1975 real wages in America had fallen by 5 percent. Productivity gains in 1973–79 slowed down to less than 0.9 percent a year. Real wages did not return to their 1973 levels until the late 1970s when the revolution in Iran and the second big oil-price increase started the cycle all over again.

Washington demographer Calvin Beale ties the fall of real wages in America to competition with Japan and East Asia's cheap-labor industries. "If you cannot produce cheaply enough to compete," Beale told me, "you've got to reduce your costs and your standard of living or go out of business." So we saw company after company in the United States—airlines, railroads, meat packers, steel—renegotiate wages downward to hold on to their markets. Americans in high tech, Wall Street and finance, Washington itself, show business, and the media and other well-paid areas have not had to take pay cuts. But across the country, ordinary people were forced to take lower wages or defer home buying or do work that paid more in real terms a decade earlier. Family incomes of the poorest 20 percent actually dropped 10 percent in real terms in 1973–87. Beale says Americans do not like to admit they are poorer. They will have smaller families, go into debt, have both husband and wife work, or work longer hours to keep up consumer spending. So Americans have a North-South divide too, though it's geographically scattered and dispersed.

In Britain during the 1980s real wages for those with jobs kept going up. But companies lost their competitiveness and closed; it also meant high unemployment, though it dropped from 11 percent to 7 percent in 1986–89. But America's rate has drifted down to 5.2 percent. Long-term unemployment in Britain is stuck at about a million. Who gets left out? Half of Britain's poorest 20 percent used to be old people; now only a fourth of them are elderly. Younger working people, if you count unmarried girls with children, make up nearly two thirds of the poor. Others are unskilled young men who in the old days would have got jobs as manual laborers.

Nobody should go hungry or without a doctor. If you go on the dole tomorrow, under Mrs. Thatcher's 1988 Social Security Act, and you are out of work, single, and over twenty-five, you'd get £33.40 a week ($56.78). Couples get £51.45 ($87.46). This is not a lot in a country where most prices are higher than they are in America. (Americans keep saying, "This costs as much in pounds as it does in dollars back home.") You would get more with children (usually £6.15 or $10.45 per child), if you are disabled (£13.05 or $22.18), or elderly (£10.65 or $18.10).

This is after the most far-reaching reform of Britain's welfare since the system proposed by Lord Beveridge was started forty years ago. Mrs. Thatcher's stated aim is to push welfare in a new direction —away from handouts and toward self-help, tying benefits to training schemes or, in Thatcherite rhetoric, away from a "dependency culture" to an "enterprise culture" (and certainly not to a "poverty culture").

The big losers of the reform were young people under twenty-five. Their weekly benefit was cut from £30.40 ($51.68) to £26.05 ($44.28). Those aged sixteen to eighteen get even less, being cut to £19.40 ($33). The whole idea of a single, childless teenager getting weekly payments from the government is novel to Americans. Many young British take it for granted, though Mrs. Thatcher's government found it easier than expected to remove the right to benefit from jobless school-leavers. Some were unhappy about it. Said one eighteen-year-old, miffed at the cuts, "People are going to get so narked off I reckon the crime figures will go up."

Unemployment's worse side may be its loss of self-confidence. Middle-aged Arthur Fowler, a character on BBC's "EastEnders," practically went to pieces staring at old cartoons on television when he couldn't find work; most people tend to blame themselves for what is really society's failure.

Arthur:

> When I was a kid you knew what to expect. If they'd told me that I'd be a cabbage, I'd be prepared for it now.

Idleness takes its toll. A picture of what unemployment did to five workingmen, *Boys from the Blackstuff,* became a British television landmark in the early 1980s. A series of five plays, set in Liverpool, it was about a gang of Liverpudlian jobless ex-tarmac-layers. Their author, Alan Bleasdale, a Liverpool schoolteacher when he began to write, first became known for his Scully stories, Scully being a streetwise Liverpool teenager about to leave school. Bleasdale, who is marvelous to hear when he reads his own work, has an ear for the distinctive Merseyside, or Scouse, dialect of Liverpool. "I have to tell you that I love many things American," he told me, "which probably comes from my mother, who was an avid reader of American mystery and murder fictions. When other kids were reading *My Friend Flicka* I was galloping through *Farewell, My Lovely.*" Like so many of Liverpool's sixteen-year-olds, his Scully dreams of becoming a professional footballer. Here he sits in class:

> There's nothin' down for y'. Not for our class anyway. Some of us in here give up tryin' at playschool. But it's all right, 'cos most of the teachers gave up before we were born . . . No thanks, y' not goin' to catch me stayin' on—y' may as well go on the dole straight away around here than after you've been to university.

His father no longer lives at home:

> He couldn't keep off the ale . . . He was a good skin, me dad, when he was sober, but he wasn't sober much and he was always out of work.

Bleasdale can be very funny, but ultimately his work is grim and tragic. He has described *Scully* as a "morality tale." Menace is embodied in Isaiah, a malevolent Liverpool policeman, who threatens to get Scully:

> I'll have you. Good an' proper. Make no mistake . . . I just have to look into your eyes, it's all there, that's where it is—y' eyes—trickery, lyin', deceit, plain thuggery an' violence . . . An' I know as sure as night follows day what lies ahead of you lot . . . petty crimes, a little muggin', a few burglaries, Borstal, gaol, in an' out of courtrooms an' prison yards all y' empty slimy little lives. . . .

Remember what Jimmy Boyle said? "How dumb we were. We wasted all those lives." Prince Charles mentioned "wasted" lives too. After *Boys from the Blackstuff* was first shown in late 1982, the Anglican Bishop of Liverpool, David Sheppard, said, "It's about people with great gifts and abilities being robbed of a chance to use them."

Again Bleasdale, even as he has them laughing, doesn't spare his audience. The great hit of *Boys from the Blackstuff* was a character, Yosser Hughes, whose regular utterances "I can do that" and "Gizza job" passed into Liverpool folklore. Yosser, unemployed, loses home, wife, children, everything he's got, even losing, at last, an attempt to escape two policemen and drown himself. Much of Bleasdale's dialogue in the series is searing. Here Chrissie, the most important character and the one who fights back, has a row with his wife, Angie. He says:

> I had a job, Angie. It wasn't a bad job, and I was good at it. I laid the roads, girl. *I laid the roads.* Motorways, lay-bys, country lanes . . . No, no. Let me finish. I could tamper and grit like nobody you ever saw. Nobody put the black stuff down quite like me. *(He shrugs)* But I lost that job, it was all right, I deserved to lose it, I was a dickhead—but haven't we all been at one time or another—haven't we all woken up the next mornin' an gone "oh Jesus, did I do that?" Yeah, well, once you could get away with it. But not now. That's the problem.

They argue and Angie grabs one of her shoes; it has a hole in it filled with cardboard. She says:

> It's not funny. It's not friggin' funny. I've had enough of that—if you don't laugh, you'll cry—I've heard it for years—this stupid soddin' city's full of it—well, why don't you cry—why don't you scream—why don't you fight back, you bastard. . . .
>
> CHRISSIE: . . . And what do you think it's like for me? Hey? A second-class citizen. A second-rate man. With no money and no job . . . and no . . . no place!
>
> ANGIE: *(Turning away, speaking flatly)* Tell it to the kids, Chrissie, tell it to the cupboards and the fridge. See how full y' words can make them. . . .

Like Glasgow, Liverpool was a big seaport and industrial center. It milled flour, refined sugar, made soap and margarine and chemicals, and imported and exported along nearly ten miles of docks. ("Ah, there'd be hundreds of us coming along here," one of Bleasdale's older characters says, "the ship repair men, scalers, dockers, the Mary Ellens who used to swab the big liners, and behind us the great big Shire cart horses.")

Another native of Liverpool who has tried to come to grips with what industrial decline does to people is novelist Beryl Bainbridge. In her 1987 book, *Forever England: North and South,* she asks:

> What do you think in the head, I wonder, when you keep being told that the North is in decline and that there'll be nothing for your children to do when they're grown? Do you look into those shop windows and dream, or do you see in those perfectly featured mannequins a reflection of those remote and alien beings who rule from the South, who posture behind the glass of the television screen talking of economic factors and budgets and global considerations?

One way out is to go to the booming South, take the "Tebbit Express." Liverpool, like Glasgow, is steadily losing population. Jeff Collinson, twenty-seven, told me in 1988 London migrants are mainly men in their thirties and forties who already are skilled in a trade:

> Plasterers, painters, decorators, bricklayers, it's easy to get work like that in London. Good pay, seventy to eighty quid a week. Maybe a pile of 'em go down. Stay three weeks and come back for a week. It splits up families as nobody can afford to buy or rent at London prices.

Roy Glover, a car dealer, says the same thing: "There's a lot of work in London if you've got a skill. Bricklayers. Joiners. Welders. They're earning good money. Living rough. Four or five people sleeping on the floor. But the work is there."

Of all Britain's cities, Liverpool, with its great "twin" Catholic and Anglican cathedrals and grandiose pier buildings and its cocky, irreverent people of mainly Irish and Welsh stock, seems at once the most funny and angry, touching and tragic. Grimly, a big heroin problem came with high unemployment in the 1980s. As late as 1970, there were only about three thousand known addicts in all Britain, most of them in London. About 1979 and 1980, word of "chasing the drag," "skag," and "having a toot" started to be heard in the worst of the country's slums. Heroin, mostly smoked by heating it on aluminum foil and inhaling the fumes, was coming in from Iran and Pakistan. Relatively few, outside Edinburgh, were injecting ("fixing," "hitting it up," or "cranking").

By the mid-1980s addicts of all drugs in Britain were officially estimated to be no more than twelve thousand, double the amount a

decade earlier but still not alarming. Since then their numbers have
jumped to between fifty thousand and eighty thousand. This may
seem small compared to at least half a million addicts in America,
with perhaps as many as seven thousand in Harlem alone. In Hong
Kong, where thirty-seven thousand heroin addicts are registered,
there may be over 100,000 in all. In Britain it is not the scale but the
speed at which heroin addiction is growing that has shocked people.
Olivia Channon, the daughter of one of Mrs. Thatcher's Cabinet
members and a bright young student at Oxford, was found dead of a
drug overdose the summer I was there. Boy George and other pop
singers have been in the headlines for drug abuse. But Britain's new
heroin epidemic is mainly tied to working-class unemployment,
both at their worst in Liverpool.

In his 1987 book *The New Heroin Users,* Professor Geoffrey
Pearson of London's Middlesex Polytechnic quoted a large number
of young addicts, such as Eddie, twenty-one, of Liverpool:

> I was curious so I tried it and I liked it . . . There was a few of us, we
> were all good mates and that like, we all tried it and eventually every-
> one just got hooked . . . It's no one's to blame. It's you. You're the one
> that's saying, "Yeh!" . . .

Professor Pearson makes the point that even at the street level,
heroin is "surrounded by a constant flurry of economic exchanges,
whether in the form of small-scale drug-dealing, robbing and thieving, prostitution, or a myriad of other forms of daily hustle." He
said the daily routines of a heroin user involved "getting up, hustling
for money, buying heroin, smoking it, and then hustling for the next
bag."

Eddie again:

> When I . . . when you're hooked on it like, you don't want to go rob-
> bin' until you had a toot like, cos you can't run or nothin' if you got
> grabbed by the busies [police]. You won't be able to leg away, and that
> like. So you'd have a toot to get your head together and then go out
> mooching . . .

John, a nineteen-year-old from Liverpool, asked what kind of crime
he got up to, said mainly petty theft and shoplifting, adding:

> But everything that you can do, like petty things to snatches. Like rob-
> bing car radios—that's petty—but the next minute I'd do a till-snatch
> and that's not right, that's a bad thing to do. You get some gaol for that.
> But I didn't care. I didn't care.

Take a look at a Liverpool paper:

HEARTLESS! Rats Prey on People Too Ill to Hit Back.
Cruel thieves have swooped again for easy pickings at Merseyside hospital's disabled unit.

DESPICABLE THIEVES STOLE FROM ELDERLY
Two young thieves robbed a charity worker as she collected pensions for elderly victims of violence, Liverpool Crown Court heard yesterday.

SAVAGE MUGGER HUNTED
. . . Mrs. Grovers said, "Before I could do anything he grabbed me by the collar and slammed my face against a tree. Then he grabbed my bag and ran off. I was in pain but my only concern was with my baby who was crying . . ."

Welcome to Liverpool. The first time I went there I set out for Toxteth, scene of the 1981 conflagration. Outside a car dealer's, I stopped to ask the way from a man who was sweeping the sidewalk. This was Roy Glover, who turned out to own the store, which both sold and rented cars. He kindly offered to drive me through Toxteth —perhaps thinking I wouldn't make it on foot. When I went back a couple of years later, Roy was as hospitable as before; we went to a pub by his store and had a pint or two with the locals. "We've reached the bones," Roy said when I asked how things were going. "Not much picking on the bones."

Since my earlier visit, he'd had fifty to sixty car radios stolen. The thieves, youngsters wanting to buy heroin, smash the windows; the radio comes out easily. "It has good value for kids getting cash quick for drugs, ten, fifteen pounds. Of course the radio is worth maybe a hundred pounds and it costs twenty, twenty-five pounds to replace the window." One of his rental cars had been stolen three days earlier.

"When I see a new car coming out," Roy said, "my heart sinks if I see it has a fancy radio. When somebody's on drugs, they're totally reckless. I mean, they'll rob their own family. It's all unemployment. There's no doubt about it."

Roy had solved his problem by putting in cheap car radios and leaving the interior lights on in his cars. "So they can see the radio's not worth taking. It's not vandalism in the sense that some kid is mad that I've got a car and he hasn't. They just want money for drugs. One or two stolen car radios a day supports a habit. The cars are broken into in broad daylight. You wouldn't believe it."

The next day I did. At about eleven o'clock in the morning I was interviewing Allan Parry, who runs Liverpool's Regional Drugs

Training and Information Centre. He told me Maryland Street outside, just a few blocks long, had more car break-ins than any place in Liverpool. His own office and a drug clinic next door brought a lot of addicts into it. "Chances are," Parry told me, "that while we're sitting here you'll hear a car alarm going off outside."

Sure enough, in about ten minutes, a siren went off. "There you go!" cried Parry, and we climbed up on chairs to look down into the street. We could see a young man reaching into a broken car window. In seconds he was running down the street with its radio.

"These drug people are crazy," I said. "Here you are helping them and they rob your cars." Parry, a tall, rugged-looking blond in his early thirties, took it with Liverpudlian panache. "I bet we hear twenty car alarms a day going off here. You can see all the glass in the road where they've pushed in the windows." His own car had been broken into eleven times. Car break-ins were going up as fast as heroin addiction, now up to nearly fifteen thousand in the Merseyside area alone. "That's heroin," Parry said. "You could probably triple that with people who smoke cannabis or try an amphetamine now and then."

When I interviewed him, Parry had been running for two years a controversial program to supply addicts with syringes and clean needles to curb AIDS. Unlike Edinburgh, very few of Liverpool's addicts carried the AIDS virus in 1988. But New York's experience, where 60 percent of two hundred thousand addicts did carry the virus, scared everybody. Parry's center also worked with prostitutes, female and male ("rent boys"), to get them to use condoms and clean needles.

Parry told me he himself took drugs from the age of thirteen until he was twenty-one. When I said he could have fooled me, he held out his hands, palms down. You couldn't see any veins; they were a mess. "I lost a finger and some toes, bits and pieces," he said. "See, look at all the veins you've got. When you inject dirty heroin mixed up with brick dust, talcum powder, maybe cement, it blocks up the veins with rubbish. So they collapse." Once he broke the habit, he started working in antidrug programs. He felt employment would solve the whole thing.

> The drugs aren't all that important. What's important is the lifestyle that revolves around the drugs. You wake up in the morning and you've got an occupation. You do what your mates do. And what they're interested in is playing cowboy. It's the illegal side of it they find exciting. The conspiracy. Going out and scoring. Avoiding the cops. Stealing.

Shoplifting. Ripping radios off cars. It's almost like an exciting full-time job. You have to go out and find where to buy and get the money for it. It's something illegal, something forbidden. And because of that, young people want to try it. When you consider the conditions of life in Liverpool anyway, there's really no competition to the heroin lifestyle.

Is Liverpool getting any better? Derek Worlock, its Catholic Archbishop, says no, Thatcherism's trickle-down economics are still failing to reach its underclass. He has told church leaders, "If you walk around the perimeter estates of Liverpool, you will see the poor, their lack of job opportunities, the desperation of their families." Britain's clergymen, whether Anglicans, Roman Catholics, Methodists, Baptists, or the Church of Scotland, have several times joined forces to attack what the Archbishop of Canterbury, Dr. Robert Runcie, an outspoken liberal, calls the "Pharisee" society of self-interest that has emerged in Britain under Mrs. Thatcher.

Maria's Story

IN BRADFORD, just an hour's drive from Liverpool, you can find the same hopelessness among displaced English mill workers. Maria Glot, a pretty, dark-haired woman of Polish descent who runs Bradford's tourism, told me, "People keep being told the place is depressed. That there's no jobs, all the jobs have gone." Maria says it starts in the home.

> Maybe the father's worked twenty years in the mill and is made redundant. Parents pass it on to their children. They get to feel they're doomed to live on the dole. You hear them ask, "What's the point of going to school? What's the point of learning?" Some youngsters, after two, three years of doing nothing, they get where they say, "I'm not putting up with this any longer." And they get out and do things. But there are people who never, never elevate themselves.

I told Maria it was like a refugee camp. I'd worked with Hungarian refugees in Austria in 1958. Some of them had been in the camp so long they had fallen into a kind of doomed mentality: fatalism and despair.

"That's exactly what happens," Maria said. Paradoxically it happened among the English themselves, not people who were in fact refugees. What sets Bradford apart from great port cities like Glasgow and Liverpool is that it is ethnic England. It has a history of minorities brought in as cheap labor for the mills—Irish first, as in Glasgow and Liverpool, but then, starting in World War II, German Jews, Poles and Ukrainians, and now Pakistanis; Bradford has Britain's biggest concentration of Asians, over sixty thousand of them. Bradford's Muslims were the first to attack Salman Rushdie's *Satanic Verses* for blasphemy, and, as we saw, burn it.

Over lunch at Dick Hudson's, a famous pub up on the Yorkshire moors overlooking the chimney-filled city, Maria told how it was to be a second-generation immigrant in Bradford. Her mother's family had been uprooted from their home in Poland and sent to Siberia by the Russians. Maria's grandmother, young enough to be still giving birth and still conceiving, had five small children. Two starved to death and a third was scalded by accident and got no medical attention. The grandmother died of starvation too. Her body was just thrown in a ditch. Just Maria's mother and one other child survived; they came to England with their father, then fifty-five, who worked in Dunlops and then on the railway.

Maria's mother had come to Bradford when she was seventeen. After what she had survived, it seemed like heaven. Maria's father, who met her there, had an equally terrible history. In Maria's words:

He was born in 1917 in German-occupied Poland. So when the war broke out he was conscripted into the German army. He escaped and joined the Polish army. Well, the Nazis didn't take to that too kindly when they caught him. They tortured him, smashed his body, and hung him from a tree, a traitor. They left him to die. A German woman found him and cut him down. She nursed him back to health. Somehow he got to England and rejoined the Polish army.

He was tall and handsome, Maria remembers, with dark hair and light eyes. Her parents had five children and lived in a cottage, her grandfather with them. They couldn't get over being safe in a country where all the children could go to school, even university, and there were doctors to go to if you got sick. Her father never recovered fully from the wounds the Nazis inflicted; he died of rheumatoid arthritis when Maria was eight.

My mother had seen so much despair. And here, she thought, you know, "We'll make it good. And the only way we can make it good is to do it ourselves." We did it as Polish refugees. Now the Asians are doing it. And when that happens people resent it. They resent people getting up and doing things. And that's sad. Instead of emulating them and thinking: "If they can do it, I can do it."

Maria says you get the feeling from some of the English that they fought a hundred years for their trade union rights and now they can take it easy.

It's a crazy attitude. It really is. You know, this nine o'clock to five o'clock idea; that's when I work and no more. This mentality is wrong. And there's no way you can go into shops on a Sunday in England. Sunday dies. I'm sure you've noticed. Originally a lot of it was to protect workers from exploitation. But it's no good to anybody really. The problem of a place like Bradford is they're very traditional, the people. For years and years they've been in the wool trade. It's been their way of life. For years and years, parents would tell their children, "Your future is in the wool trade." And because it's gone they can't see an alternative. Therefore they're doomed. But we have to get on with it.

Maria used to live in Liverpool and she liked the Liverpudlian vitality and humor. But after her car got broken into ten or twelve times, she felt enough was enough and came home.

Bradford is one of the cities where Britain sustained its postwar prosperity for nearly a quarter century by importing cheap labor from overseas. It had made its fortune from its tropical empire. When it began to lose it, this seemed one way out. It proved very temporary. Industrial growth and immigration slowed down together by the 1980s. British-born Indians and Pakistanis, West Indians and Africans, now outnumber their immigrant parents. Large-scale immigration is over.

This means Britain's population of just over 57 million people in 1990 has more than 2 million whose skins are other than white—about 4 percent. Higher birthrates could bring this to 6 or 7 percent by the end of the century. This is hardly the black and brown flood, setting off a white backlash, that Enoch Powell warned about in 1968: "As I look ahead, I am filled with foreboding that, like the Romans, I seem to see the river Tiber foaming with much blood." It compares with 23 percent nonwhites in America—12 percent black, 8 percent Latin, and 3 percent Asian in a population that was 248 million in January 1990. Because Britain is an island, control of its ports is relatively easy. There is not much the United States can do to stem the flow of Hispanics across a two thousand-mile southern border; cheap labor from a growing Latin minority helps to sustain American prosperity and hold down inflation anyway.

Well over half of Britain's nonwhites are of Indian or Pakistani origin. Most of the rest are at least partly African, mainly from the West Indies. A few are Chinese or Vietnamese. Until recently there was a tendency by politicians to lump everybody as "black," startling to me since as *kala* it's an insult in color-conscious India. The Asians came last, mainly brought in, as I said, to keep dying industries going—in metalworking (Coventry, Sheffield, the Black Country) and textiles (Manchester, Leeds, Bradford, Nottingham). Indians and Pakistanis, who came with more entrepreneurial skills, have concentrated on retailing, keeping their small grocery stores, restaurants, and news agents open longer hours than do the English. They also sacrifice to invest heavily in education.

For the blacks it has been a different story. Until the early 1950s, Britain had very few of them, outside long-established black settlements in the ports of Cardiff and, as mentioned, Liverpool. The first group from the West Indies came in 1948, five hundred Jamaicans who had served with British forces during the war; they stepped off the ship in double-breasted suits and trilby hats, proud military veterans, full of hope. Immigration from the West Indies soared to a peak in the early 1960s, as London's Underground and bus system recruited staff there. So did hospitals looking for nurses. But most West Indians ended up in low-paid manual jobs or on the dole; immigration fell rapidly as controls were imposed.

Today West Indians are twice as likely to be without a job as white Britons. Less than half are likely to finish high school. More commit crime and go to prison than any other ethnic group. They are more dependent on public housing; nearly half of them rent council houses and flats, compared to a third of whites. Caribbean-born women have the highest illegitimacy rate in Britain; nearly half their babies are born out of wedlock, compared to a fourth for babies of British-born mothers. As in America, a great many black children are being brought up by a lone mother, either on welfare or in a low-paying job, living in an inner-city tower block or an Easterhouse-type housing estate. With no family pressure, as with the highly motivated Asians, to stay in school, they leave with poor qualifications and find it that much harder to find a job. More sink into crime and drugs.

What immigrants from Asia and the West Indies find in common in Britain is racism, even if most of the native-born speak with Cockney, Liverpudlian, or other regional accents and have adopted many British ways. In 1948 only half of Britain's whites had ever met a black person (nor, growing up among the Norwegians, Swedes, and Germans of North Dakota and being seventeen that year, had I). The image brought back by the British Tommy from empire was Fuzzy Wuzzy, Gunga Din, the "pore benighted 'eathen" (like the "gooks," "slant-eyes," and "ragheads" of American GIs). One hears a lot of casual racial slurs in Britain; most educated Americans would shrink from saying "nigger" in the offhand way some British do. Yet racism in Britain, if more overt, lacks the deep-seated hate and fear it has at its worst in America, say, in parts of the Deep South; at least 12 percent of the 244 million Americans are descended from African slaves.

In Birmingham, which has Britain's biggest concentration of

Asian and black immigrants (113,000 or 15 percent), I got a glimpse of racism from its victims' viewpoint when I was invited to join an after-school talk by teachers at the city's Park View School. Over 80 percent of Park View's pupils are Pakistani. That day in the school auditorium they were rehearsing a celebration of the Prophet Muhammad's birthday. Racial harassment in the form of verbal abuse from skinheads and such was bad enough that the teachers had taken to walking the children home in groups. Some sample remarks from a white teacher:

> We treat the children as equals. What happens when they leave this place? We've got to prepare them for racism if they're going to survive.

From a Pakistani teacher:

> Education is to equip them to cope. I told a girl, "You're black. You'll make nine applications and get one interview. A white child might get one with three."

Both of these teachers were young women. An older, white-haired man, a Jamaican, told them:

> I've taught here for sixteen years and I'd be quite happy if England wasn't so cold. What I say is, don't try to increase "racial awareness" like that. Celebrate the differences. Observe Divali, Christmas, Muhammad's birthday.

Birmingham's Asians, like London's, seem relatively sophisticated. What is striking about Bradford's is how many of them seem to have come straight from their villages, the Kashmiris from the countryside around Mirpur, the Pathans from settlements in the North-West Frontier; almost everybody wears traditional dress. On streets with shops like Pakistan Airlines, the Muslim Commercial Bank, Mirza Electronics, Saddique Hosiery and Footwear, you might as well be in Rawalpindi.

As I mentioned, Bradford even has its Asian supermarket (the one selling framed prayers to Allah). Again, amidst the pungent spices, girls in *shalwar kameez,* saris, or even a few hooded women in purdah, and with all the grain, rice, lentils, and beans heaped about, you don't get much feeling of being in Britain. The only non-Asian in sight, a middle-aged Englishwoman, was introduced to me by Maria as Joyce Thirkill, the Panorama Stores' manageress. When her boss, a Pakistani businessman, was made general manager of the Asian supermarket, a co-op, he asked Miss Thirkill, who was running his office, to look after it for him. She seemed terribly English in the Asian setting. "Now people come up to me and say, 'Hello, Joyce,' as though I belonged," she explained. "They used to accept me but feel I was different, I think. Now I'm just part of the store."

The supermarket is known to Bradford's Muslims as *Al Halal,* which roughly translates as "It's kosher." It imports most of its food directly from Karachi and Bombay. Very un-British, it stays open every single day of the year. Maria includes it on a "Flavors of Asia" tour she dreamed up. A tourist to Bradford, who tires of the moors and the Brontës, can visit a Hindu temple or a Muslim mosque, buy a sari, or even learn to make curry.

I noticed how few women were shopping. It was mostly men, brown-faced under woolly hats or white Gandhi caps. Miss Thirkill said many Pakistani women let their husbands shop for them.

> A few that do come are in purdah. If they're veiled, they'll almost always come with a man. What you find is that those from the villages are much more orthodox. The villagers keep their customs. Some will let their girls go to mixed-sex schools, but a lot of them won't. I think in the next generation there are going to be a lot more cultural clashes.

She said some of the Pakistani parents took their daughters out of school at thirteen. Marriages were arranged. If a girl took a job at the supermarket, a male member of her family had to walk her to and from. "I know it sounds daft," said Miss Thirkill, "but it's true."

It was the same with movies. Bradford used to have eleven Asian cinemas; they just showed Hindu or Urdu films made in Bombay or Karachi. Once home videos came on the market, all the cinemas had to close. Parents want to see and censor everything first.

Miss Thirkill leaned forward and spoke in a hushed undertone. "If an unmarried girl gets pregnant, she's never seen again." She threw Maria a dark look. "I could never be a Muslim myself."

Some of its English inhabitants lament Bradford's past, when everybody was busy spinning and the remote and mysterious East stayed that way. Not everybody. Maria and I stopped for coffee at a restaurant up on the moorland near the Pennine Way; the building it was in had once been a spinning mill. It turned out our waitress, a woman in her forties, worked in the mill as a girl.

"Twenty-seven years ago, it was," she said. "Oh, much harder work, mind you. And just seven pound a week, if you can imagine. I enjoy this now. Oh, absolutely."

Maria gave a squeal of delight. "It's just so often," she told us, "I get screamed at by quite old-fashioned city council members who say, 'Stop giving people Mickey Mouse jobs. They want to go back to the mills.' A lot of people say that. They say, 'We shouldn't be spending money to promote tourism. We should put the people back in the mills where they belong. Where they were happy and want to be!' "

"No, no!" cried the waitress. "I'm so glad about it. I'd *never* want my children to work in the mills." Her grim tone left no room for doubt.

We all get spoiled, taking the gains won by an older generation as the starting point for our own expectations. Maybe that is why so many of Britain's older immigrants seem content. They are like Maria's mother. She knows that if she is suddenly seized by pain she'll get medical help, that Maria's children will be able to go to school, and that unlike her own mother, she is in no danger of starving and being thrown in a ditch.

Irish Ways and Irish Laws

NORTHERN IRELAND is where all the North's contradictions meet, clash, ignite, and explode.

It has all the things we've been talking about: a depressed economy; unemployment (16 percent in 1989, Britain's highest, massively higher still in West Belfast); a woefully old, government-propped-up industry as the main employer (Belfast's Harland and Wolff shipyards, which built the Titanic); a lot of Catholics (40 percent); an egalitarian Celtic culture (like Scotland, Wales, and much of Liverpool); separatist feelings against Britain's rich and class-ridden Anglo-Saxon South; and senseless violence, in the unending round of Catholic-Protestant killing and revenge.

Elsewhere these might make it simmer. In Northern Ireland the difference is that in the IRA you've got bloody-minded armed terrorists bringing it all to a boil.

I felt uneasy to go. You can tell, right away at Heathrow, you are headed into a high-tension zone. When you go to board your British Airways Super Shuttle to Belfast, you get herded to a separate gate, 49, and a little terminal just for Northern Ireland (in case it gets bombed?). The first surprise is how well-dressed, in pinstripe and gray flannel, your fellow passengers are; in most of the North, jeans, an anorak, and jogging shoes are the virtual uniform.

The flight is under an hour, like Washington to New York. I was met, a second surprise, by a strapping young Australian, Richard Robinson. At twenty-seven he came to work for the tourist board for a couple of months, fell in love with Northern Ireland, and just stayed on; he had been there a year. Richard, six-two, curly black hair, a big grin, and the build of a rugby player, was wearing the loudest sweater I ever saw—red, yellow, purple, green; he said his Irish girlfriend knitted it for him. We popped into his low-slung, bright-green MG convertible and zoomed into Belfast, Richard breezily pointing out the sights. Somehow it wasn't at all the war zone I expected. Even the city, a onetime river fort transformed by textiles and shipbuilding into a great red-brick Victorian port, had the same friendly look of Glasgow or Liverpool, if smaller.

My fear stemmed from nearly four years of covering the Vietnam war; my hair went from brown to gray and I'd only just escaped three or four big terrorist explosions. The Vietcong aimed to kill as many, mainly Vietnamese, as they could; the message was always: keep away from the Americans. I expected Belfast to look like Saigon did—sandbagged bunkers and concertina wire everywhere, war-torn. Instead it resembled any other bustling British city. Richard parked the MG in a multistory garage near his office and we headed for lunch.

He suggested we go to the famous Crown Liquor Saloon, used as a set in such films as *The Thirty-Nine Steps* and *The Third Man*. Richard said it was "just around the corner," and we set out, going down Ann Street and Castle Lane to the city's Donegal Square. Belfast's Edwardian City Hall was a splendor of turrets and gingerbread. Then we went by Howard and Victoria streets past the restored opera house and the Hotel Europa ("the most bombed hotel in Europe," Richard boasted cheerily). At the Crown we drank Irish Guinness. After lunch we took another route back; it was about a mile each way.

I mention this because afterward Richard drew a map to show we in fact had just made a tour of the biggest IRA explosions. He hadn't said anything for fear I wouldn't go (he was right). Just days before my trip to Belfast, a two hundred-pound Semtex bomb hidden in a hijacked mail van had rocked Donegal Square; the blast echoed as far as Belfast's outer suburbs. I'd seen the wreckage on television. It looked terrible, windows shattered for blocks around. A woman had been killed. Now the same streets were full of shoppers. There was no sign of damage. Again I noticed how well-dressed everybody was.

"The IRA has never stopped bombing the city center," a city senior official said. "People who have invested here have done so against a background of violence. They see an opportunity to make money." As we drove around, Belfast seemed particularly attractive. The large leafy suburbs in the south of the city have fine old brick Edwardian houses on big lawns. There is a wooded university area and botanic gardens. Only slogan-daubed West Belfast, which you usually see in pictures, looks blighted, especially along the "Peace Line" between the warring communities of Shankill and Ardoyne.

The worst of the city's slums went in a £2 billion urban renewal program in the 1980s. To come is a restoration of the old wharfs and docks along the Lagan River; from here you get fine views of the Antrim mountains. Property values are soaring. A new £60 million Castle Court shopping and office center, which they told us would open in 1990, may be Belfast's biggest commercial draw, which is why the IRA has repeatedly tried to stop it in its tracks. I asked Richard why, when the big Donegal Square car bomb went off, no buildings were blown down.

"Because they tape the explosives underneath. So you cause disintegration of a vehicle. And that's about it."

"You could get hit by a piece of flying car."

"Yeah. Often they'll show what's left from a bomb. And all you'll see is the gear box or the differential or whatever is left of the car."

"Why are so few people killed?"

"A warning is put through to, say, Grosvenor Road. That's one of the main police stations. Grosvenor Road receives a phone call saying, 'This is the IRA. We've got a bomb planted on the corner of West and Smith streets. It's due to go off in ten minutes.' They'll have units there within two and a half minutes. They'll clear the area. Get people out of the buildings. Divert all the traffic. Everything before that ten minutes is up."

"So the IRA wants to show its power and scare everybody, not necessarily inflict deaths?"

"If it's not a direct military attack, it's more to disrupt life."

The Vietcong never gave warning. After one of their bombs, a hotel, a street, an embassy, once a children's playground beside a floating restaurant, would be full of dead and dying. I used to love thunder and lightning; no more. "But," I said, "say their wives or mothers are downtown buying something at British Home Stores or Sainsbury's and get hit by flying debris?"

"That's the chance they take. That's the whole point of why there's more targeting at security forces, whether they're police, army, or undercover fellows. The IRA works very hard on their surveillance to make sure they target the right people. If they get them wrong they lose supporters."

The IRA bombers had great impact in Britain itself. Just among people I had interviewed, Barbara Cartland had lost her friend Lord Mountbatten in an IRA explosion aboard his boat off the coast of Ireland. Mrs. Thatcher lost a close adviser, Airey Neave, when terrorists put a bomb under his car just outside Parliament in central

London in 1979. Norman Tebbit was left injured and his wife Margaret crippled in the IRA blast of the Grand Hotel in Brighton in 1984. In his book *Upwardly Mobile*, Tebbit described the Brighton bombing:

> There was just time for Margaret to call out in alarm and for me to reply: "It's a bomb" before the ceiling came crashing down on us and then, in a hail of debris, the floor collapsed, catapulting us down under an avalanche of bricks, timber and plaster.
> The force of the impact was indescribable—blow after blow . . . then I stopped falling . . . I called for Margaret, I found I could move my left arm and, reaching out, our fingers touched and we grasped each other . . .

Polls show that when British voters think of Northern Ireland at all, far more want British troops to withdraw than to stay. Only 27 percent favor the province remaining part of the United Kingdom. There is a relentless cycle of murder, funerals, and revenge played out on the evening TV news. So why doesn't Britain get out? It would mean either handing Northern Ireland over to the Republic of Ireland—which doesn't necessarily want it—or allowing it to become an independent state. Just 1.5 million people are involved, 40 percent of them Catholic. With a higher birthrate, the Catholics might one day be a majority. But today's Protestant majority of 60 percent wants to stay British. Many families came to Ulster three hundred years ago in triumphs over the Catholics still celebrated in Protestant rallies and parades. Their six counties separated from the rest of the island of Ireland when it became independent from Britain in 1920.

Ultimately most people expect Northern Ireland to join the Republic. Culturally, they are all Irish; in things like rugby there is virtually no distinction. But in the Catholic Republic, where divorce is forbidden, it would mean a fifth of its people being Protestant. In a united Ireland, the IRA terrorists might not stop fighting and look for jobs. Sinn Fein, the IRA's political front, aims not just to unite Ireland but to bring socialism to it.

If British withdrawal led to the formation of a separate Protestant state, it would leave many Catholics to be uprooted, seventy-six thousand in West Belfast alone. *The Economist:*

> Either way, a British withdrawal that was against the wishes of the northern majority would risk creating widespread, lasting turmoil and bloodshed on Europe's western shore. Stop and think, and it cannot be contemplated. But if not that, then what? Most political problems have

solutions. A few do not. Northern Ireland is one of them, certainly now and perhaps for decades.

The Anglo-Irish agreement, which led to cross-border security cooperation, has survived since 1986. Ireland's Prime Minister Charles Haughey has worked hard to keep it afloat. Economic recovery is badly needed; the Catholic rate of unemployment is twice as high as that of Protestants. Richard said he heard there is less anti-Catholic discrimination than there was some years ago. Catholics and Protestants study side by side at the university; many of the brightest graduates leave for Britain.

Northern Ireland, despite a misleadingly prosperous air, is Britain's poorest province; since 1979 manufacturing jobs fell 40 percent. Nearly 90 percent of about a hundred thousand manufacturing jobs left are supported by the state. Even to persuade a private firm to build the Castle Court Center, the Northern Ireland office had to underwrite the project to the tune of £10 million and promise to help fill up the office space with its own civil agencies. Just under half of all Northern Ireland's employment and three quarters of its GDP are in the public sector. After government, the second biggest employer is Harland and Wolff, Belfast's enormous shipyard. With four thousand workers, after a decade's shipbuilding slump, it has eaten up over £1 billion ($1.7 billion) in government subsidies. But if the shipyard closed, one of Northern Ireland's last few remaining basic industries would be gone. As in the rest of Britain, the new food processors, textiles, electronics, and software that come in do not fill the employment gap.

"The IRA should be wiped off the civilized world," says Mrs. Thatcher. I found in Belfast people tend to talk about the "provos," or Provisional Irish Republican Army, perhaps to avoid confusing the present, purely terrorist IRA with its pre-1920 parent which won Ireland's independence from Britain and formed the Republic's government. There are other Irish terror groups, some Catholic ones and some Protestant "loyalist" ones. The "provos" are said to number two hundred, of whom a hard core of sixty are specialists in shootings, bombings, or mortar attacks, backed up by a third tier of supporters, sons of Catholic farm families, urban youths active in street demonstrations, and ex-IRA men out of prison. It is hard to see any way out of the mad, despairing cycle of murder and revenge. Most Catholics and Protestants alike in Belfast just want the senseless killing to stop. People are sick of meaningless atrocities.

A problem for the British, Douglas Hurd told me when he was still Home Secretary, is that very few Americans seem aware that Northern Ireland has had totally free elections; as Hurd says, in the last election Sinn Fein got just 11 percent of the vote. An Irish politician told us, "We're all prisoners of history here."

After Belfast, Richard Robinson and I hiked in the Antrim glens, a misty green Irish world of ferns and forest and peat-brown mountain streams dropping into the Glenariff waterfalls. The sun kept breaking through rain clouds; I never saw so many rainbows nor such bright ones. Northern Ireland struck me as the most beautiful place I had seen in the British Isles. On a fine September day, my last there, Richard and I hiked along the grassy cliff tops of the Causeway coast. North was the Atlantic and the Hebrides. Our cliff path took us to Port na Spaniagh, a small bay where the *Gerona*, a ship of the Spanish Armada, crashed on the rocks in 1588. All aboard perished. A diving team found the wreck twenty years ago. Just half the Armada reached home; many Spaniards who got ashore in Ireland, sick, starving, and burdened with armor and gold, were killed by Irish peasants or English troops. You could look inland and see a patchwork of small fields, the greenest green I had ever seen, fields of barley and pasture, white sheep, herds of beef cattle and cows, everything sparkling in the autumn sun. Few villages, just scattered farmhouses, all white-washed and looking new and one now and then with barns and machinery used collectively in the peculiar Irish way. An empty landscape; for the first time in months I felt no sense of overcrowding.

Once Richard said, "Stop. Say nothing. Listen. What do you hear?"

The sea, birds, wind. It was like those lines of Auden:

> Stand stable here
> And silent be,
> That through the channels of the ear
> May wander like a river
> The swaying sound of the sea.
> Here at the small field's ending pause
> Where the chalk wall falls to the foam . . .

"Why is Ireland so empty, so spacious?"

"History. Cromwell had a hard time here, so much so he simply started on one side of Ireland and burnt it. He burnt Ireland bare. You find most of the glens are very naked of trees. When the redcoats were putting down the Scots, they were putting down the Irish too. They'd come in and raid villages."

I told Richard my grandmother's parents fled County Cork during the potato famine; my father was half-Irish. "The English owned so much of the land and the Irish were only tenant farmers on it," he said. "The potato crop was their staple diet and the grain was used to pay the land taxes. When the Irish were starving, thousands of tons of grain were shipped off to England. When it should have been staying in Ireland to feed its people."

The romantic, irrational mythology of the Irish is caught in a pop song by a now-disbanded group, Moving Hearts. A young Irishman sings:

> Once upon a time there was
> Irish ways and Irish laws
> Villages of Irish blood
> Waking to the morning,
> Waking to the morning.
>
> Then the Vikings came around
> Turned us up and turned us down
> Started building bogs and towns
> They tried to change our living,
> Tried to change our living.
>
> Cromwell and his soldiers came
> Started centuries of shame
> But they could not make us turn
> We are a river flowing,
> We're a river flowing.
>
> Again, again the soldiers came
> Burnt our houses, stole our grain
> Shot the farmers in their fields
> Working for a living . . .

The first time I heard it, as we drove along in a driving rain, I told Richard, "It's very sad."

"Very sad, but it's also accurate, though they've taken an awful lot of lyrical license in there. It covers roughly what has happened over eight hundred years. First the Vikings came. Then Cromwell and his soldiers . . ." Richard said he had heard it was banned from being played on Belfast radio.

We both had British ancestors, Richard an Irish gold prospector and an English sea captain. But it was crazy for an American and an Australian to get worked up over something that happened three hundred and forty years ago; our countries had barely been discovered yet. It was like Auden's eulogy to Yeats, how mad Ireland had hurt him into poetry ("Now Ireland has her madness and her weather still"). It was Yeats who said of the Irish armed rebellion in 1916 "a terrible beauty is born." The hatreds of Ulster's IRA thugs and Protestant fanatics now go beyond all reason.

In the spring of 1988, two young English soldiers were lynched by a Catholic mob. They had encountered a funeral cortege for a man killed by a crazed Protestant who had made a grenade attack on another Catholic burial three days before of three IRA members killed by British soldiers in Gibraltar. Aghast at the savagery, killings, and counterkillings, Cahal Daly, Catholic Bishop of Down and Connor, appealed to the conscience of IRA supporters. "For God's sake rid our hearts of this poison," the bishop said.

> The evil of IRA violence is often disguised with a mask of romantic rhetoric and militaristic mock ritual. For a ghastly half hour on Saturday, the mask slipped. The real face of IRA violence was shown and it was horrible to see . . . Protestants and Catholics, unionists and nationalists, will always have to live together and share this land together. Either we live together in peace, or we destroy one another and ourselves in conflict.

The bishop took the Thatcher government to task as well.

> . . . It is an urgent necessity that the government tackle the social, economic, industrial, and environmental neglect which West and North Belfast have for so long suffered . . . We must show that there is a peaceful and constitutional way to justice and that it works.

And not just Belfast. It is true of all of the North. Take a map of Britain and draw a line, left to right, up from Bristol to Cheltenham and on over to Northampton and Peterborough as far as the Wash. If you don't find people north of this line—in Cardiff, Birmingham, Liverpool, Manchester, Bradford, Leeds, Sheffield, Newcastle, Glasgow, and Edinburgh—poorer, their clothes shabbier, their cities seedier, even if they themselves are cheerier, I would be amazed. It is also true that Ireland is peculiarly tribal, less individualistic.

In J. G. Farrell's novel, *Troubles,* an English army major says to the Irish girl he comes to love: "Surely there is no reason to abandon one's reason simply because one is in Ireland." "In Ireland," the girl replies, "you must choose your tribe. Reason has nothing to do with it." Irish myth, Irish history, perhaps Irish poverty too, have made one of the world's most beautiful settings a prison. The Catholic conviction of inequitable treatment is just reinforced by all the romantic mythology.

Christopher Patten, Mrs. Thatcher's Environment Secretary, who served in Northern Ireland, quotes poet Louis MacNeice, who came from Belfast, saying, "Forget the unhappy past. Forget the story of the old feuds, the old animosities, the old triumphs, the old humiliations."

MacNeice once wrote:

> I can say Ireland is hooey, Ireland is
> A gallery of fake tapestries,
> But I cannot deny my past to which my self is wed,
> The woven figure cannot undo its thread.

Patten points out that over 5 million British, himself included, have some Irish blood, and that there are maybe a million Ireland-born Irish living in Britain. Even the Scots and their Gaelic language have Irish origins if you go back far enough. "This is the reality of Anglo-Irish relations," Patten told me. "It is why they are so intense. The people of these islands are inextricably intertwined."

The irony of this can be seen in the Irish literary renaissance at the turn of the century. The greatest effect of Ireland's awakening to its Gaelic culture, going back to the tribal bard and storyteller, was to enrich English literature. Many of its most towering figures were Irish—Oscar Wilde, George Bernard Shaw, William Butler Yeats, James Joyce, Sean O'Casey, Samuel Beckett. (Just as Dylan Thomas was Welsh, T. S. Eliot American, and Joseph Conrad Polish.)

Somehow, however bitingly Shaw satirized all aspects of British society, the exuberant Irish escaped the bleakness that has come to characterize so much of English writing since the old literary dynamism went the way of the Victorian era. This is also true of Seamus Heaney, often said to be the best Irish poet since Yeats. A Catholic who grew up on a farm near Belfast, Heaney draws on mythology and a feeling for the land. He sees the religious violence as part of Ireland's old, old predicament, a "tribal, intimate revenge" going back centuries. Ireland is a curious place, well fitting G. K. Chesterton's:

> For the great Gaels of Ireland
> Are the men that God made mad,
> For all their wars are merry,
> And all their songs are sad.

Heaney's Irishness sets him apart, even if he has been co-opted to be Oxford's professor of poetry (good for Oxford, bad for his poetry). The true voice for the mood of the times in Britain would be the late Philip Larkin's—stoic, satirical, chilly, witty, sad. While the postimperial years have not been a great time for English literature, I would argue, and will, that British mastery of words is still, in the main, supreme. Certainly in articulacy in speech, criticism and some forms of popular fiction. Missing is Ireland's madness. Why is the place so haunting? Where else would a pop song be so moving it would get banned?

> Once upon a time there was
> Irish ways and Irish laws
> Villages of Irish blood
> Waking to the morning
> Waking to the morning

IV

MASTERY
OF WORDS—
LETTERS

The Chattering Class

"WONDERFUL, wonderful talkers," says Eric Sevareid of CBS, who first came to Britain to report in 1937, staying on as a radio commentator with Edward R. Murrow during the Blitz. "You stop with your microphone and a camera on the street corner anywhere in England and you go up and, by God, you'll get a strong opinion, said right out, colorful language, a beginning, a middle, and an end. Whereas Americans have to mumble a bit and it's 'Yeah, well, yeah, man, you know what I mean?'"

The British look on the world as apparent, clear. They do not expect to be surprised. Americans find it more of a puzzle; they are more tentative, need more observation. The British are so articulate —by that I mean the way they are able to think abstractly and put it into words—it gives them an acknowledged supremacy in the English language. We've taken a look at how Britain's geography, history, religion, and economy shape its society; here I will argue that its social and political culture is based on articulacy.

I asked George Steiner, as one of the best known of modern intellectuals and one at home on both sides of the Atlantic, about it. He agreed. He feels in America, for example, "to mumble or speak badly can be an asset; it is thought to be symptomatic of honesty, and of a certain untutored decency." Not so in Britain:

> This society has, since Elizabethan times, rewarded almost extravagantly the articulate, the eloquent, the witty, the masters of words and repartee. It has rewarded them politically, in its parliamentary system, and in the elite education which was an elite not of the numerate but of speakers. It has been a society whose almost miraculous political tolerance, even under great strain, has been based on a shared—I would like to call it as in physics—a shared echo chamber of verbal articulacy, fluency, elegance, and reference.

This articulacy, I think, has left out the bulk of Britain's people for much of its history. Even today the public school Oxbridge elite dominates through speech; a member of the lower classes, say, somebody with a marked Cockney or Liverpudlian accent, is unable to communicate in the same way or answer back. As Sevareid says, all the British are great talkers when it comes to sheer forcefulness and blunt, trenchant language to get their point across. But it takes a public school Oxbridge education to master the accent, elegance, and nuances that subtly shut out everybody else. In American terms, it's like a Sylvester Stallone trying to hold his own against a William F. Buckley. As Steiner says of the lower-class British: "The famous question of accent is merely a superficial symptom of this ostracism and exclusion. They are *left out.*"

I asked Kenneth Baker, who is thought to be a mite too smooth and ambitious to be properly establishment himself (one aristocrat told me of Baker, "He is not a gent"), what he thought about it. Baker argued the common Englishman does get heard from. He said:

> There has been a sort of cussedness in English political history. You know, "Some mute inglorious Milton here may rest, / Some Cromwell guiltless of his country's blood." A village-Hampden standing for the rights of the rural people against the King. Throughout our history we've had awkward people doing that. They've stood out against authority.

I said I thought Gray's point was that most of the would-be Miltons stayed mute and inglorious. I asked Baker about the "chattering class" of intellectuals itself, and all the give-and-take, the bite, the cutting edge, the it's-absolute-bosh-and-you-know-it-and-it's-absolutely-disgusting-to-say-so sort of thing. Baker said a deeply ingrained habit of controversy and argument and dispute was part of the British parliamentary system.

> I think it probably flows from our national character and our history. In America, you have to think: which is he, Democrat or Republican? It's just Senator So-and-So or Congressman Such-and-Such. Here you know a Tory or a Labourite right away.

It is true. And the reason, of course, is that each speaks, by and large, with a distinct regional and class accent. (One of my old friends in London, who has a pukka Oxbridge accent, is a native of Yorkshire. When I asked him if it wasn't tiring to speak with such elegance all the time, he confessed it sometimes was.)

A wonderful irony about English is the way it has become the world's lingua franca, it being neither Latin nor French. Latin had its chance under Catholicism and the Holy Roman Empire, French in the eighteenth century. But it is English that prevailed. About a billion people, a fifth of mankind, have it as a mother tongue. Even this is misleading, as everybody today is plugged into the same global jet-and-electronic network. As the language of science, English is the escalator to the future whether you're in Vladivostok or Beijing or Valparaíso.

"If you want to use the verb 'being' in the future tense," says Steiner, "namely, 'tomorrow things will get better,' you use it in English." He said British English and American English have built into them a subtle and powerful promise of futurity; French, for instance, has almost no promise of tomorrow.

> English does have that promise. Until very recently England could say, "Look. Not only has Shakespeare's speech and Milton's speech and Wordsworth's and Churchill's and Gladstone's and Darwin's and Newton's and everyone you want—the law and the English Bible above all —been *our* cement and *our* power relationship, but we've conquered the earth. We, a tiny island in the rotten North Sea, have in fact dominated." So the triumph of the English language is incomparable, we have no other phenomenology for it. Is there a challenger? Yes, there is. Spanish. That's very exciting. But not, I think, in the Middle East, in Africa, in Russia, in China, in the rest of Asia, where it is English of course. So that to speak of the condition of this land is to speak of its language.

Steiner, I should mention, has been the preeminent authority on English to me ever since I was a student at lectures he gave in Innsbruck in 1958 while he was writing his *Tolstoy or Dostoevsky*. He was so good I kept my notes for years; a few of his words still stick in the mind. For instance, on Faulkner's world: "Exhausted earth, scrub pine, dusty ground, red dust; old men sitting on pillared steps, chewing tobacco, spitting, and waiting for something to happen." In a *New Yorker* review not long ago, Steiner described "the sheer genius of intellectual exhilaration, the passionate electricity of the spirit" he found as a student at the University of Chicago. Not long after that I happened to tune into a Bill Moyers interview on television and there Steiner was, saying a student should be exposed to those "passionate, possessed beings who eat ideas, who live thought." He was that way in Innsbruck. After one of Steiner's lectures you wanted to rush out and read everything you could get your hands on. When my last book, the story of a Midwestern family, came out, Bill Moyers wrote that he and his wife, Judith, read parts of it aloud. Steiner taught us that the sound of words, their euphony, also mattered, particularly poems learned as a child by heart. "Some of the most haunting poetry is minor poetry," he said on the Moyers show. "And it sings to us as a child." Now, over thirty years later, we met for lunch at a country pub near Cambridge and then went back and talked in his office at Churchill College; I'll be quoting a lot of his views.

But first let me mention how curious it is that despite our great power and access to the world's people through movies and satellite television, America is not the capital of English. Britain remains its curator, its custodian. This was plain when the second edition of the Oxford English Dictionary, all twenty volumes and 21,728 pages of it, came out in 1989. (The first emerged piecemeal, 1884 to 1933.) "The ultimate authority on the tongue of Shakespeare and the King James Bible," pronounced *Time*. (Hugh Kenner did irreverently call it a "Victorian epic poem," and told how the explosive development of English outside England had shook up the OED.) Nobody questioned it was *the* authoritative work, even if the dictionary shows how English is used and is not a prescriptive work or arbiter. The OED proved once again that Britain continues to be seen as sort of the curator of a very high quality museum of Anglo-Saxon culture.

Yet British English and American English keep moving apart. I asked Paul Theroux, as an American writer who lives in London, to define the difference. He said the whole concept of eloquence, of mastery, is not the same:

> There is an English language as it's spoken and used. And it's a fixed thing which you can be very good at. Because the language is the language of Shakespeare, of Dickens, of Churchill, of all the great writers and speakers. And it is a graspable, knowable entity, something you can master. And in America we don't have a language of that kind. The American language is a much more fluid, elusive, difficult and dynamic thing. It's something that's still growing. It's something that people are always trying to enlarge, always trying to add slang to. And it's something which a good American writer will try to bend. And in a way to accommodate a concept. Or hammer into shape. A good American writer, in a way, is an innovator in language. Whereas the greatest British writer is someone who has mastered a language that already exists.

This is why it is easy to be impressed by the way any member of the British establishment speaks. They practically all went to Oxbridge and a good public school. Everybody is more or less speaking the same language. If you talk to a group of Americans, their opposite numbers, they'll be speaking a lot of different tongues, as it were. A lawyer will be from New England, a film director from the Bay Area. If he's young, he will try to shock you or use a different sentence structure.

Theroux says you do come across a writer of real brilliance in Britain who doesn't stay with the fixed language. He says it is rare and always someone writing about their own distinct region or class. Alan Bennett writes about West Yorkshire's Bradford, Alan Bleasdale or Beryl Bainbridge about Liverpool, William Trevor about Ireland.

> That's why D. H. Lawrence was such a surprise to people. He was the first writer who seemed to represent the working class, or the lower class, as well as a different region. Until then there were writers like Thomas Hardy, who was basically a middle-class writer of good pedigree, who was writing about farm laborers and a region. He wasn't doing the same as Lawrence, who was actually writing in an idiom. In the way Saul Bellow does or Jack Kerouac did. All the American buzzwords, neologisms, jargon, are hated here. They're *hated*. They're seen as the most pernicious influence.

I said they *were* a pernicious influence. "It's not a pernicious thing to want to loosen a language," Theroux countered, "to make it accommodate a world that's also changing. The thing is that we're too quick to seize on something new. We *love* new things, we Americans."

Novelist John Fowles, when I repeated Paul Theroux's remarks to him, said that while he agreed modern America is "much more dynamic and fluid—or inventive" than Britain, he would put the difference in another way:

> I should have thought the division is much more between playing games as one likes and preferring to play them by the rules; as in poetry, between set forms and free verse, say between Tennyson and Walt Whitman. Of course both sides, rule breakers with you, rule obeyers with us, sometimes hanker after each other's tenets and provide curious "mixed" or hybrid cases, like T. S. Eliot.

I told Theroux how I'd found in early nineteenth century letters that Americans in New England kept their English eloquence, but they lost it almost as soon as they went West as pioneers, taking on folksy Hoosier or Great Plains dialects. "But they became themselves," he protested, sounding like Robert Frost. "They became part of the land. They weren't evolving downward or deteriorating. They were becoming Americans."

You could say, I suppose, that in losing the old formal literary English, Americans have gained a spontaneity or a better sense of themselves. George Steiner says the fixed, rule-obeying English of Britain's better-educated people is a reflection of the deeper crisis in the country's culture. The classic novel, he says, has failed England for more than a hundred years. The great writers are Irish or American.

> We all know that. It's an open secret. They're called Joyce and they're called Bernard Shaw and they're called Oscar Wilde and Beckett and Hemingway and Faulkner and everything that's happened since. They're called Eliot from St. Louis, Missouri, and Pound from Idaho and New York.
>
> Has there been a single English English-giant? Well, hell, I'd say Hardy. That's my own conviction. That's a long time ago. And very problematic, but one name that is thrown at us is Lawrence. I don't buy it, but I may be totally wrong. But that's my own personal problem. Let's say Lawrence. But that's not yesterday. That's not even the day before.

To Steiner, as to many, the giants writing in English today are from outside England—Patrick White, Nadine Gordimer, Salman Rushdie, V. S. Naipaul. Steiner would rank Naipaul as the best of today's prose writers, "the only real descendant of Joseph Conrad whom I would put very close to Conrad; Naipaul's prose is of that distinction."

And there is no English novel like *Absalom, Absalom!* or *The Sound and the Fury*. There's no Hemingway. There's no *Great Gatsby*. Steiner finds what excites his students and young people in Britain is the "fantastic energy, the demotic power, the generosity of American English, of African English, of Indian English." Steiner:

> So something has gone very, very wrong. English English is dead. It's dead as cold mutton, one would say. What do I mean by that? I mean whereas Elizabethan English could absorb twenty, thirty outside languages pouring in on it, whereas late eighteenth century English could bounce with the new Industrial Revolution, with the French Revolution, with the coming of nationalism, of modern science, and so on, the decline of this land, the *deep* decline, has been reflected in the atrophy, the stiffening of language.

How do the British react? Steiner says in two ways. The first is to put your head in the sand, roar like a lion, and say, "I hate America. I hate the blacks. I hate the Pakis." And be more English than the English. He says this is Kingsley Amis's answer essentially:

To become a purist. To become even more English. To say, "Hurrah, Little England!" and to close inward like that great critic here, F. R. Leavis, for whom all the outside stank. And who preferred a provincial, parochial, dug-in, but very pure, very intense, very Puritan Little England. The Little England of Bunyan, of George Eliot. *The Spectator* is very much of that school.

Or, he said, you can do what Amis's son, Martin Amis, has done.

You can go to New York and San Francisco, you can bathe yourself in the Tom Wolfe culture and language, in the electronic kookery and savagery, and the black English and the drug English. And you can say: the only way to speak, to be alive at the moment, is to know where the action is. And that's out there.

Steiner gave a delighted grin. "Isn't it fun," he said, "that a father and son, both of immense gifts, have defined between them the alternatives?"

That Sun Never Sets

I F IT IS TRUE, why is the best English writing being done by writers from outside England? Names from the former colonies
sometimes mentioned, besides Trinidad's Naipaul, Australia's
White, South Africa's Gordimer, and India's Rushdie, are Nigeria's
Chinua Achebe; another South African, J. M. Coetzee; another Australian, Thomas Keneally; New Zealand's Keri Hulme; and Ruth
Prawer Jhabvala, like Rushdie shaped by India.

I'm not at all sure, if one excepts the American golden age of
Faulkner, Hemingway, and Fitzgerald, that it is true. The case was
put in some detail by Michael Gorra, a teacher at Smith College, in
"The Sun Never Sets on the English Novel," in *The New York Times
Book Review* in 1987. Gorra gave the above names.

> Some of these writers are . . . the descendants of the colonialists
> rather than the colonized. Nevertheless they share in the essential prob-
> lem . . . : the need to adapt the English language and literature to
> their own countries' experience . . .
>
> In such writers, in such questions, lies the vitality of the novel in
> English today. In England itself the novel remains as entertaining as
> ever. But the entertainment it affords seems inseparable from its con-
> ventionality, its reliance upon a serio-comic examination of the limita-
> tions of being English. Such fiction has seemed most alive when, in the
> words of novelists like Barbara Pym or Margaret Drabble, it faces up to
> its own conventionality, and accepts its modest place in what Miss
> Drabble has called "a dying tradition." And contemporary British fic-
> tion has, of course, been successful in exploring the death of the society
> upon which that tradition was based, in multi-volume works about the
> end of the British Empire, of which the most important is Paul Scott's
> *Raj Quartet.*
>
> Yet such novels have inevitably the air of footnote about them; and
> nearly all the creative energy has passed to those on the other side of
> the colonial equation.

Often the English themselves are the first to agree. Robert Mc-Crum of Faber and Faber, for instance, who coauthored *The Story of English*, told me:

> There's a tremendous argument for saying that the spirit of the English language is frozen by tradition here. And that the place to find vitality is in the newer English cultures: America, Canada, Australia, New Zealand, the Caribbean, South Africa.

The thesis of cultural decline reflected in English literature as voiced by George Steiner is popular among Americans. Hugh Kenner's testy but hugely enjoyable 1988 book, *A Sinking Island*, is one example. Another is an essay by Joseph Epstein in *Commentary* a couple of years earlier, which typifies this literary vogue. "There will always be an England," pronounces Epstein, "yet, slightly seedy and exhausted land that it now seems, there is less likelihood of there always being Anglophiles to admire it." Forty years ago, Epstein says, "if it was English it was well made." Churchill towered over the age. A public school education in classics, polished at Oxbridge, was the best there was. Britain's literary culture (the Russian nineteenth century stars excepted) ran deeper than any other.

Epstein concedes that English acting is as good as ever (he had better, at the twilight of an age that saw Olivier, Gielgud, Richardson, Redgrave, Guinness, and Ashcroft on the stage all at once). He is grateful for "Masterpiece Theatre." But he doubts that Henry James or T. S. Eliot, if alive today, would move to London (what about Paul Theroux?). He happily quotes Philip Larkin's poem "Going, Going:"

> And that will be England gone,
> The shadows, the meadows, the lanes,
> The guildhalls, the carved choirs.
> There'll be books; it will linger on
> In galleries; but all that remains
> For us will be concrete and tyres.

Perhaps so. But Mr. Epstein, much as he claims Britain's heroic age has been brought low by loss of empire, decides maybe it is not such a bad thing. For writers can now produce work that concentrates on "the small but crucial pleasures that make life bearable." On second thought he concludes that if "it can continue to produce writers of the special quality of Barbara Pym and Philip Larkin, then long live England." Which is just about what Gorra and the other Americans say.

More recently I asked Epstein if he still felt the same way. He replied:

> I chiefly think that the current English story is rather a sad one. The fall was so quick and from so high . . . I find I grew up as a great Anglophile. I've lost this as I've grown older. As I said in *Commentary,* I find the *Times Literary Supplement* is kind of awful. The *Spectator* has a lot of strongly anti-American reporters. The theater, journalism, are still strong, but feel less true to me now. Britain is the saddest country in the world.

Charles Moore, editor of the *Spectator,* who had seen the *Commentary* article, objected to Epstein's charge the *Spectator* "cannot let go of its anti-Americanism." He told me over tea in front of an old-fashioned fireplace at his Doughty Street office, "I think people confuse a sort of cultural curled lip with fundamental political hostility." (Moore made me wait twenty minutes downstairs and I got the impression the scene, tea set, roaring fire in the hearth, the delay, and all, had been carefully staged.)

> America is revolutionary. You invent a society which tries to embody certain beliefs: life, liberty, and the pursuit of happiness. We have none of that. I don't believe in universal principles of that sort. What I believe, and I think most of our writers believe, is in the idea of an English, or British, cultural and political tradition that is quite distinct from that of America. That doesn't mean we're hostile. But our culture is quite distinct. And we want to make sure it stays distinct.

This cut-and-thrust has been going on a long time. Sir Isaiah Berlin, whom I met one evening at the Athenaeum (he talked off the record about geniuses he had met—Freud, Virginia Woolf, Bertrand Russell, Auden), has written about taking critic Edmund Wilson around Oxford years ago:

> He asked me whether it was to be his fate to meet more academics at lunch or dinner . . . Would he prefer to dine in a restaurant? No, he said, he wished to plumb the depths of old, decayed, conservative English academic life in its death throes—I remember his words: "It can't be long now," he said ominously. "I think we're in at the kill."

Some of the best contemporary English fiction, it is true, deals with loss of empire as Britain finds itself just another medium-sized European power. This theme of decline, betrayal, the worm at the heart, is perhaps at its strongest in the novelist John le Carré:

> Connie's lament rang in his ears. "Poor loves. Trained to Empire, trained to rule the waves . . . You're the last, George, you and Bill." He saw with painful clarity an ambitious man born to the big canvas,

brought up to rule, divide and conquer, whose visions and vanities were all fixed, like Percy's, upon the world's fame; for whom reality was a poor island with scarcely a voice that would carry across the water.

British pop and rock also speak of loss. Not this I-feel-chilly-and-grown-old upper middle-class despair, but in the anarchic, outraged cry of a jobless under-class that feels cheated. Merseyside must produce as many rock stars as militants. A sense of something going wrong, of things not working, pervades rock music, as was true of Johnny Rotten and the Sex Pistols or as in Frankie Goes to Hollywood's cassette *Liverpool,* with songs like "Rage Hard," "Kill the Pain," "Is Anybody Out There?" See some of these youths in central London—green mohawks or skinheads, dirty jeans, tattoos—climbing out of the Underground like troglodytes to gape at Lord Nelson on his column, victor of Trafalgar and the Nile, and it is like being in a museum of culture whose language nobody understands. Britain has settled continents, launched the Industrial Revolution, ruled the greatest empire in history. The new cave dwellers are wondering who built it all.

The real success of British culture among the world's one billion English speakers does not depend on protest or decline. And even le Carré returns to hope and humanity in his *Russia House,* turning away from "the safe bastion of infinite distrust" and toward "the dangerous path of love." This more lasting success has partly to do with that other Britain where most of the British live. This is a society of civil, courteous, cozily old-fashioned values where people know their places, a society so orderly and predictable that characters emerge as stock figures to be handled with elegance and wit. It also has partly to do with King Alfred beating the Danes at Ethándune a thousand years ago and decreeing that all free men would read and write English.

Here I part company a bit from the critics and novelists I've quoted. I find as a journalist a good rule in linguistics is that the farther you get from its place of origin, the more you find a language's older, more stilted forms. This was very marked when I taught journalism in India. Innovation in language (just as in plant species, oddly enough) takes place in the core area, at least when it comes to contemporary newspaper writing. Which is why journalism of all kinds is so much livelier in London than in Singapore, Bombay, or Los Angeles, no matter how many new words Americans invent (a truth driven home if you happen to write for both

British and American papers; it is the Americans who cling to the older, more stilted forms, a few exceptions like Tom Wolfe and his imitators notwithstanding).

The sense of decline is also not uniquely British. When I quoted Steiner's remark that the world to an American was "endless possibilities" and to an Englishman "endless remembrances," Theroux responded:

> It's a Steinerism, but you could also say that Americans believe the world has endless possibilities because they don't know the world. And the British are cynical because they've tried. We didn't have an empire. What do *we* know? What do Americans know about Africa? Or South America? Or Asia? Nothing. There's a kind of weariness which is not just British. It's a European weariness about the world and its remembrances. If the British have a virtue in, say, a situation like Vietnam, it's that they don't force the issue. They don't care whether they're loved. They don't commit themselves. To the things Americans were committing themselves to in Vietnam. Huge casualties. Vast amounts of money. A big effort that might, as it did, turn into a humiliation.

"Isn't it characteristic," I said, "that whatever we do, we do with all our might? We either succeed intensely or fail intensely. Once we lost our nerve in Vietnam, we fell apart radically."

The English are so far from this, says Theroux, they will even use language to take the place of action:

> The English have a lot of phrases for delay—"I'm doing it." "We're seeing to it." "It's in the pipeline." "I'm dealing with that." "It's in my in-tray." "Yes, that's vexing us at the moment." "I'm very exercised by it." These are phrases and words for inaction which are either to delay action or not do something. It's an elegant or obscure way to avoid taking a decision or doing something. Talking can be a way of avoiding action, of being elegantly in repose.

Theroux confirms what Sir Terence Conran and others said earlier, that action and ambition, work and energy, indeed anyone who seems on the make is despised in England.

> Really despised. Because it seems vulgar. Because, mainly the only reason anyone would be busy is to make money. And people who make money are envied or hated. That is, by the English. When I talk about language taking the place of action and the way they act socially, that's all English. It's not Scottish. It's not Irish. And it's not Welsh.

Theroux recalls how V. S. Naipaul once told him, after coming from Trinidad to Oxford and staying on in Britain, "I find it very hard to write about my own society." Theroux asked him why. "Because it has never been written about," Naipaul said. Theroux says he replied, "I don't see that. Because to me it's a lot easier."

He finds, he says, England is *the* hardest society to write about because so many of the descriptions of it are so good.

> It's very hard to break free of the literary influences and the very strong impressions of other writers, brilliant writers of genius like Tennyson, Wordsworth, Dickens. What society has been written about more than this? You're always seeing England or Scotland or Wales through someone else's eyes.

And yet, for a British writer, what else is he or she to write about? Clive Bradley, who directs Britain's Publishers Association and was educated on both sides of the Atlantic, feels it is quite difficult for a writer to cope with a decline in world power:

> I think it does force you back on yourself and onto a quite small canvas. Whereas the Americans, who may be passing over the top, so to speak, of world power, do see things in terms of a broader canvass. They're interested in America's role in the world. The British writer is interested in the role of withdrawing to the British Isles. The Little Englanders.

Little England

I feel it is a great shame if ordinary sane novels about ordinary sane people doing ordinary sane things can't find a publisher these days. This is the tradition of Jane Austen and Trollope, and I refuse to believe that no one wants its successors today. Why should I have to choose between spy rubbish, science fiction rubbish, Negro-homosexual rubbish, or dope-take nervous-breakdown rubbish? I like to read about people who have done nothing spectacular, who aren't beautiful and lucky, who try to behave well in the limited field of activity they command, but who can see, in the little autumnal moments of vision, that the so called "big" experiences of life are going to miss them; and I like to read about such things presented not with self-pity or despair or romanticism, but with realistic firmness and even humor.

THESE WORDS, from a famous letter sent by Philip Larkin to a Faber and Faber editor who rejected Barbara Pym's novels, describes the fiction of Little England. Whenever one sees an elderly couple trudging in a rainy park behind a cocker spaniel, or stops for tea in a little shop where middle-aged ladies are fussing about, or sees a vicar shaking hands with churchgoing spinsters after service, you know this is where you are. It has a good deal to do with resignation, as in one of Larkin's last, uncollected verses:

> Life is first boredom, then fear
> Whether or not we use it, it goes
> And leaves what something hidden from
>   us chose
> And age, and then the only end of age.

"No one stands better for twentieth century intellectual England than Larkin," John Fowles told me. Joseph Epstein believes part of Larkin's appeal, as with Barbara Pym, is his common sense; he says he cannot say the same for "the novels of Norman Kurt Updike or Philip Marquez Doctorow, which, with their violence, sex and politics, come to seem from the perspective of a certain age, like the Hardy boys with an X-rating."

Epstein observes that Pym endlessly describes small domestic things: clothes, furniture, gardens, houses, food. The compass is kept narrow.

> Barbara Pym characters go off to their jobs, lunch carefully, sometimes have a boiled egg with their tea, take comfort from hot milky drinks, and put out of mind as best they can that life can be as "empty as the house one was coming back to." Most days are given over to doing dull undramatic things: shopping, cooking, eating, washing up, then up to bed to read a few pages of a novel by Charlotte M. Yonge or perhaps a poem or two in a sound anthology of seventeenth-century verse. The following day may provide a jumble sale or a conference on copy editing or a tour of a manor house. England has never seemed smaller.

The standard line about Philip Larkin, says Epstein, is that he is above all the poet of human limitations. Larkin himself wrote: "The essence of [the poet's] gifts is to create the familiar, and it is from the familiar that he draws his strength." Like Barbara Pym, who was an assistant editor at the International Institute of African Languages and Cultures, Larkin too had a nonliterary job, as chief librarian at the University of Hull (where he ran a staff of over a hundred). Epstein feels a characteristic Larkin passage combines "precision, prosiness and beauty." Many would add stoic wit, as in "Toads Revisited" ("Give me your arm, old toad; / Help me down Cemetery Road.") A conservative, Larkin wrote sadly about Britain's withdrawal from empire:

> It's hard to say who wanted it to happen
> But now it's been decided nobody minds

There is the bleakness so characteristic of English life (again, not Scots or Welsh or Irish):

> Man hands on misery to man
> It deepens like a coastal shelf.
> Get out as early as you can
> And don't have any kids yourself.

To Epstein, Larkin's most beautiful poem is "Aubade," in which a man awakes in the middle of the night to contemplate his own approaching death ("Being brave / Lets no one off the grave"). It ends:

> Slowly light strengthens, and the room takes
> shape,

It stands plain as a wardrobe, what we know,
Have always known, know that we can't escape,
Yet can't accept. One side will have to go.
Meanwhile telephones crouch, getting ready to
    ring
In locked-up offices, and all the uncaring
Intricate rented world begins to rouse.
The sky is white as clay, with no sun.
Work has to be done.
Postmen like doctors go from house to house.

Lord Rees-Mogg, the former editor of *The Times*, told me, "Coming out of Philip Larkin's memorial service, I felt English poetry had died with him."

"Poetry never dies that easily," was Steiner's comment on this. "What died in Larkin, if you want, was for a certain generation a voice that had absolutely refused America, that had refused London, that had refused Sylvia Plath, Ted Hughes, Thom Gunn, all the big ones. Kingsley Amis loved him above all." Epstein says that Amis claims to have got the idea for *Lucky Jim* while visiting Larkin, who was working as a librarian at University College, Leicester; they shared a taste for jazz, detective fiction, and deadpan comedy. They also shared, says Steiner, a feeling of "a plot by the outside world against the sheltered integrity of English provinciality. And they had every right to that view. There are other poets who will carry on that tradition, of course."

One poet, Craig Raine, is what Steiner calls "the Diaghilev of English poetry at the moment." He says Raine, in the marketing, selling, and presentation of high-quality verse, has shown himself to be "an impresario of enormous invention and gifts." With such publicity stunts as reciting poetry from helicopters, Raine has helped to make himself and poets like Seamus Heaney and Ted Hughes household words in Britain.

"Philip Larkin was much loved," Raine said as we met for tea one afternoon in a cafe near Russell Square; it was close to Faber and Faber, where he has T. S. Eliot's old post of poetry editor. Raine:

The best-loved poet, I should have thought, since John Betjeman. And like Betjeman, Larkin was one of those poets who was the subject of serious critical acclaim, but also had wide popularity. If you look at who's left now, there's Ted Hughes. Poet laureate. The husband of Sylvia Plath; he's married again. When we publish one of his books we print thirty thousand copies and expect to sell them. Seamus Heaney, the Belfast poet, is another. Serious critics think he's very good. I'm told he sells better than any poet here or in America.

Douglas Dunn, Wendy Cope, James Fenton, and Tony Harrison, Raine said, thinking offhand, were more poets with a popular readership. (Hugh Kenner acerbically describes Raine as presiding over a "nest of sinking bards.")

"Are any of them working-class?" I asked.

"It's an interesting question. It's not one that gets asked in England." Raine said he himself was from the working class. He'd gone to Oxford on a scholarship. Raine has written a lot about his father, who lived on a war pension, having been invalided out of the RAF with epilepsy, possibly the result of a munitions factory explosion. In his book *Rich*, Raine tells about him:

> He was a good father and, since he was unemployed, I saw a lot of him. He was and is a brilliant raconteur, with a large repertoire of brutal boxing stories, in which he is always the hero. He turned professional when he was sixteen and fought for the featherweight title of Great Britain, a bout he lost to Micky McGuire. According to him, he lost on a foul punch . . . My mother says he didn't train enough because he was going out with a girl called Ticky Hinton. This was before my parents were married, so I think my mother is guessing. Shortly after this fight, my father was reinstated amateur and, as an amateur, he fought for England against Germany in 1937 at the Albert Hall, beating Otto Kastner, the Olympic champion . . .

Raine tells how at boarding school, he learned to be ashamed of his family, the bursar at the school telling him that he was poor and that "you must cut your coat according to your cloth."

> I was sixteen before I took any of my school friends home. They adored my father. He told them dirty jokes, irrepressible as ever. And I felt rich again.

His poem "The First Lesson" ends with an old soldier dreaming of past campaigns:

> Who sleeps in a dirty vest
> remembering regiments
> and all the butterflies
>
> that settled on epaulettes,
> their catkins of gold,
> when the day reached an end.

Writers, somebody said, spend their youth living and the rest of their lives writing about it. Novelist Beryl Bainbridge *(The Dress-*

maker, The Bottle Factory Outing) writes about English life that is at once "deeply ordinary and highly eccentric," where violence and black comedy are just beneath the daily domestic routine. Born in Liverpool in 1934, she began as an actress, turning to writing when she had her first baby (a daughter, Ruby Davis, is now a successful West End actress). Says Beryl, after fourteen novels and plays (a fine film of *The Dressmaker*, with Joan Plowright, came out in 1989):

> To me, the whole process of writing changes so much. When you begin, wherever you are, you're always using your roots, your background. But there comes a point when you've done five, six, seven, or eight novels. You've learned your craft by that time. And the minute you get better at a craft, the more critical you become. You don't trust your instincts so much. And you don't go out anymore because you're too busy writing. So by the time the tenth or eleventh book comes along, you've used up your experience and you're a bit of an empty vessel. I even think that one day I shall go out and get an ordinary job in a shop or something.

V. S. Naipaul has remarked on this same thing, that he "felt it as artificial, that sitting down to write a book":

> And that is a feeling that is with me still, all these years later, at the start of a book—I am speaking of an imaginative work. There is no precise theme or story that is with me. Many things are with me; I write the artificial, self-conscious beginnings of many books; until finally some true impulse—the one I have been working toward—possesses me, and I sail away on my year's labor. And that is mysterious still—that out of artifice one should touch and stir up what is deepest in one's soul, one's heart, one's memory.

Beryl experiences much the same mysterious process, though she puts it in a more down-to-earth fashion. "Once I get going I write all day and all night," she says. "I'm scared of stopping because I'm afraid I'll lose track. You don't knock it if you're onto a good thing. You keep going." Still she finds a writer lives "a very secondhand existence":

> You move away from the original person you were who sat down writing those stories. I think writers are dissatisfied with something in the beginning. I don't mean they have a message. What I mean is their lives aren't right. So they write. If they were perfectly whole, cheerful people, they'd be getting out and having a normal life. They wouldn't be sitting and scribbling away.

(Like the Duke of Gloucester's familiar "Another damned, thick, square book! Always scribble, scribble, scribble! Eh! Mr. Gibbon?") We sat over coffee in the dining room of her house in London's Camden Town, Beryl, a relaxed, warm, funny talker, puffing away on cigarettes (in her nonfiction some formidable lady on a train is forever demanding, "Put out that cigarette immediately!"). The house was eccentricly furnished. A stuffed life-size water buffalo graced the front hallway; every room was full of Victorian bric-a-brac and old photographs. It was unpretentious, comfortable, a bit rundown, like the homes of most of the successful writers I met in London. Paul Theroux compares England to "an old sofa that you throw yourself on." His study typically was none too tidy, books on the shelves piled every which way, worn chairs, good pictures, and a big window looking out on a large, somewhat neglected garden (all those long trips to China and Patagonia). Even his neighborhood near Wandsworth Common in South London, like Beryl Bainbridge's, looked like a hundred others. Theroux agrees an Englishman's house is his castle:

> Your house is your own little patch. Whatever you have, you have. It's inviolate. And there's an almost Confucian idea of family here. Weddings are big, not for what gets spent on them, but for who comes and who's invited. And making a virtue of things is an English trait too. They say "You had to walk? It's good for you." "Is it broken? It's probably just as well." "Cold baths, bad food? They'll make a man of you."

English society, he finds, values stability:

> I was with an English person once, part of a couple. I can't remember how he put it, but it was, "We don't raise our voices. We don't shout at each other." And I thought: They've been married ten or fifteen years. Never shouted? I said, "You mean, you've never?" "No, never shouted." And I thought, well, that's very interesting. I do find the English a passionate people. That's why V. S. Pritchett is such a good writer. He writes about English passion.

Exuberance does not come as naturally to the English as it does to Americans. Theroux says, "I don't say Americans are basically happy people. But they value happiness. They're not embarrassed to be happy."

John Cleese says it too. In his screenplay for *A Fish Called Wanda,* he has Archie, the English barrister, whom he plays, telling the American girl, acted by Jamie Lee Curtis: "You make me feel so free!" He goes on:

Wanda, do you have any idea what it's like to be English? Being so correct all the time, being stifled by this dread of doing the wrong thing, of saying to someone, "Are you married?" and hearing "My wife left me this morning" or saying "Do you have children?" and being told "They all burned to death on Wednesday." You see, Wanda, we're all terrified of *embarrassment.* That's why we're all so . . . *dead.* Most of my friends are dead, you know. We have these piles of corpses to dinner. But you're alive, God bless you. And I want to be. I'm so fed up with all this . . .

I said the English in America seemed happier than Americans in England. Theroux:

You know why? Because when an English person goes to America, he has a choice of being American. He can say, "I'm here. I'm an American." And no one will say, "Ah, you're English." Because he has just as much right to be an American as anybody else. And there's something liberating in that. He can say "I'm an American" or he can say "I'm English," or he can say "We Chicagoans . . ." Here an American could never do it. No one can do it. And it's a very inhibiting thing to live in a country where you are always an alien. You won't meet any American here who has become English or who has any chance of becoming English. You can't do it. I mean, for the whole of their lives they're looked upon as foreigners. I don't mind that, actually, because I know it. But I feel sorry for people who don't know it. I mean, probably the most pathetic sight here is an Anglophile who believes that he's rubbing along with the English and being treated as an equal by the English.

Both Theroux and Mrs. Bainbridge spoke of the pitfalls of becoming a London celebrity. Says Beryl, who writes a weekly newspaper column herself:

In England you find whenever you turn on the telly, it's the same old literary crowd. They are always turning up, performing on the telly. Now the difficulty is, if you get into too much of that—reviewing, chat shows, dinners, columns, lectures—you won't actually be doing any writing any more.

She also finds publishing itself is changing, but that London's literary scene is not:

I think what we have in England is probably what we've always had. There's sort of a last bastion of so-called culture. Where there are certain literary books and they get published whether they make any money or not. And underneath all that, which is totally unlike the old days, the same publishing houses are producing this mass of trivia. Which is selling. It must be selling. All these garden books and diet books and God knows what. To keep afloat this little coterie at the top.

"Books are big business and show business and many worry they will soon become merely business," says author and broadcaster Melvyn Bragg. Bragg, whom we'll interview about TV, wrote in a series in *The Sunday Times* in December 1989 that British publishing has been transformed the past decade as authors vie for huge advances and publishing houses are bought and sold for vast sums.

Faber and Faber's Robert McCrum argues a publishing house ought to be "a small group of people living in a house working with writers" and "not big business." Bernard Levin says all the mergers and takeovers came because so many publishing houses were unbusinesslike and failing. "You've got to watch your profit margins and all the rest of it," says Levin, "even if people shrink in distaste from that." One alarm is American publishers are buying up British firms. What happens, McCrum asked Bragg, "if you have people in New York or Los Angeles saying to editors in London what kind of books they should be doing?"

American publishers are notorious in London for wanting to make a lot of changes in an author's work; the English edit much less. Beryl says there are "a few—not many—good editors in London." Brenda Maddox has a funny story about the American publisher of her biography of James Joyce's wife, *Nora:*

> Not only were they trying to copy edit me, they were trying to edit Joyce. He's got this line: "Earth knows which side her bread is buttered." And this editor came back with a query, "Surely he meant 'buttered on'?"

Writers in particular seem to take pleasure in the London life. George Steiner says they love writing about it *and* living it.

> The small pleasures of life are abundant here, far more than in America. There is the general feeling of the metropolis, which Henry James wrote about so wonderfully, a London where you can within a few hours meet whomever you want to meet. There is the density of the surface, the amount of eccentric personalities which are still tolerated, the fact that there are still domestic servants. There is still an amount of silence, of leisure, of protectedness.

Steiner agrees Thatcherism has weakened Britain's old consensus. "There's a terrible breaking up of certain coherences," he says, "but at the moment the winners are on top. Savagely on top." The South has prospered so much, he said, that his home near Cambridge, which he and his wife had to go into a deep mortgage to buy, has gone up twelve times in value. "We're deluged with offers. It's a boom society." But not in the North of Britain, I said. "Not the North, no," he agreed. "The North is a derelict society. It's the Two Nations. It's Disraeli's famous formula."

Though I didn't systematically ask anybody his favorite living English writers, Steiner's evident first choice is Graham Greene, whom he feels should have won a Nobel by now. Bernard Levin ranks Anthony Burgess as Britain's best living novelist, with Kingsley Amis as runner-up, and Muriel Spark, Iris Murdoch, and William Golding in the first rank; he excludes Greene, whom he finds "much overpraised." Robert McCrum, without ranking them, lists Greene, Naipaul, Beryl Bainbridge, Iris Murdoch, and Doris Lessing; he excludes William Golding, despite his Nobel Prize. If she were living, he says, he would also leave out Barbara Pym, whose reputation, unassailable in America, is still challenged at home. To me, Pym, with her melancholy provincial landscapes and satirical tragicomedies of middle-class life, personifies the Little Englander.

While such realistic novels of late twentieth century life do not add up to a great period for English literature, I think I can say that Britain is still producing the best critics, and when it comes to the essay or review, the British remain unexcelled.

An Impeccable Sausage

"An impeccable essay . . . like an impeccable sausage, about anything or everything or nothing."

LEONARD WOOLF

THEIR MASTERY of the essay still gives the British a peculiar kind of primacy in American literary taste-setting. Look at literary criticism (V. S. Pritchett and George Steiner in *The New Yorker,* so many British in *The New York Review of Books* its contributors get dubbed "mad dogs and Englishmen"). A last vestige of colonialism? When it comes to book reviews does, after all, Anglophilia live?

Yes, says Paul Theroux. "People who review books in the United States are very Anglophile. They're Anglomaniacs really."

Yes, indeed, says Brenda Maddox. "Americans are deeply serious about British reviews. It's all 'Masterpiece Theatre.' They have this great reverence for the Mother Country and mother culture."

Not one to complain about Anglophilia is John Fowles, who also finds Americans "more literal minded." He says, "The English are usually more sophisticated—they tend to see everything metaphorically—but colder and less human. The English are much more worried about outward form (countless letters picking up one's smallest errors in grammar or punctuation, the Americans go much more by personal 'feel')."

I asked Fowles how this was reflected in book reviews. "English reviewing," he says, "is much more like entering a snake pit or a scorpion bowl—one expects to be 'unfairly' bitten or stung. As I know only too well, being praised in America is no recommendation in Britain; it just shows how naive the Yanks are."

William McNeill goes so far as to say that when it comes to criticism in the field of history, "we remain in a kind of colonial status vis-à-vis the British." Favorable reviews by two eminent Oxford professors got two of his books off and running, he feels, one by Hugh Trevor-Roper, now Lord Dacre, for *The Rise of the West* and another by Keith Thomas for *The Pursuit of Power*.

Professor McNeill, who has spent time at Balliol, has an interesting theory why the British write such good reviews. He credits the tutorial system at Oxford and Cambridge.

> The practice of writing an essay once or twice a week for three years and defending what is written before a tutor creates what I call high literacy. It's the capacity to bring miscellaneous material together into a nice memorandum in a very short period of time. It's something the British can do better than we do.

Not any more in philosophy. Sir Alfred Ayer, long the central figure of the so-called Oxford philosophers as the foremost British exponent of logical positivism told me shortly before his death that the best thinking and writing is now coming out of America. Sir Alfred felt that world leadership in philosophy has passed in the last fifteen years from Britain to the United States, really from Oxford to Berkeley. Which means, as the San Francisco earthquake was a reminder, the epicenter of Western philosophy is now on a fault line. In a 1989 interview Ayer said:

> It is confined to a very few places: Berkeley, Harvard, Princeton, Columbia, UCLA, Ann Arbor . . . We're losing all our best philosophers to America. You have quite a constellation now. This has happened partly because philosophy has become much more technical as the twentieth century has advanced and Americans are on the whole good technically and at logic.

Bernard Levin, whose column in *The Times* makes him one of Britain's most prolific essayists (his latest book is *A Walk Up Fifth Avenue*), himself a graduate of the London School of Economics, finds the tutorial-and-essay system largely limited to Oxford and Cambridge. "Most of the other British universities, I think, either never had the system or have abandoned it," he told me, when I asked him about McNeill's theory. "But then you might well say that most people who write reviews go to Oxford or Cambridge anyway."

Does the old tutorial system work? Kingman Brewster, who greatly enjoyed his stint as Master of Oxford's University College before he died in November 1988, told me in an interview some months before that "at its best, the Oxford and Cambridge tutorial experience is great and is better than what can be done by the best lecturer."

It can be superb. Not for any informational content but for the exercise of having to defend your position, whatever it is, on a one-to-one basis. For that it's unbeatable. Of course, it's a very permissive system. No coercion. It relies on the student to make the best of it. It doesn't have much to do with what particular field you use it to exercise in. Now it's true that it invests an awful lot in the particular student-tutor relationship. You can have a completely wasted year if you don't get along with your tutor.

Sir Antony Acland, the British ambassador to Washington, told me everything depends on how one's tutor works out. He himself was not all that sold on the system.

My tutor was a very distinguished economist at Oxford called Sir Roy Harrod. And the trouble with him was he was never there. He'd be at the World Bank and the International Monetary Fund. He was a Liberal candidate for Oxford. He never gave you a tutorial so I don't know if my essays were good or bad.

A product of Eton and Christ Church, Sir Antony suggested I ask the dons at high table how they viewed their students. "If they're honest with you," he said, "I think the dons would say they viewed the students as an incidental nuisance who distracted them from their own research. An awful lot of them are negligent about imparting knowledge and inspiring the young. And some of them were desperately bad."

He recalled how he would go into a lecture and it might have no beginning or end. The lecturer might ramble on until the bell would strike and he'd say, "Oh, I must stop now. The hour's up." Sir Antony said he used to go to hear the visiting Fulbright professors.

Because they had been *taught* to lecture. We may have been taught to write essays but they had been taught to lecture with a structure and a form. And a joke. After seven and a half minutes to keep you awake and a second joke after thirteen and three quarters minutes or whatever it was. It was a little bit mannered. But it was good. And I thought the visiting American lecturers at Oxford were much better than the local ones.

One celebrated Oxford don, I was told, was famous for putting his feet up on his couch during a tutorial and going to sleep. Others were legendary for hard work; a Magdalen College ancient-history don once tutored a record sixty-two hours a week. Timothy Dickinson, one of whose tutors was the historian A. J. P. Taylor, recalls fighting with him over what he wrote.

I never once got to the end of an essay with Alan Taylor. We were too busy arguing over the first page or two. Alan'd interrupt at every line. And I'd fight back. It was great.

Looking further back, to his public school days, Dickinson defines a liberal education:

In the end it is intensive, not extensive, education. It makes you think, line by line. Not big showy things but making every brick fit into the wall. Any good English boarding school will do that for you.

I asked him about my definition of articulacy as an ability to think abstractly and put it into words. He agreed, linking it to British success in pure science and a dislike of specialization. "We're supposed to be rounded," he said. "The real achievers I know are very dull when not discussing their special topics."

Professor McNeill feels the ideal book review is short, not more than ten or twelve typed pages. Which happens to be the length of an Oxbridge tutorial essay. Is there an American equivalent? The nearest thing, he says, is the training one gets at a good law school: "You have a case study. But lawyers specialize in a very limited range of human concern and their use of language is constrained by legal usage."

William P. Bundy, former American government official and editor of *Foreign Affairs* for a dozen years, says he agrees with McNeill; an American law school probably comes closest to the tutorial-essay system.

Absolutely. No question. Law school is a tremendous binding tie in terms of frames of reference. And you learnt to argue both sides of a question. The tutorial system in the hands of a good person can be enormously effective. And it does force you to examine your premises. As practically no American liberal arts or PhD program does.

But some Rhodes scholars, Bundy says, come home disappointed.

One, a former student of mine in America, recently told me, in effect, "Oxford is one of the great myths in terms of its educational quality. It is exceedingly uneven. So are the teachers. The libraries are terribly hard to use. The idea that Oxford is the greatest, greatest, greatest, is just way exaggerated." I suspect that is true and it's going downhill.

For the perspective of somebody who had been educated both in England and America, I talked to Clive Bradley. He found an English student highly specialized by age fifteen, whereas the American system is shallower but broader.

I read one play, *Henry V,* for my school certificate in Britain. I knew *Henry V* backwards and forwards. I knew how it was structured. I could compare the way Shakespeare treats the death of Falstaff with the death of York at Agincourt. I doubt if the American who read Cole's notes on *Henry V* had a clue about it. But the American got a broad view of the whole Shakespearean canon.

Sir Alfred Ayer, who lectured at many American universities, made a similar observation. He found the first two years of an American university were like the last two years of a better English public school. "The Americans catch up," he said. "They just take longer."

At public school, Bradley went out for the rugger team—you didn't become a school prefect unless you were good at sports—and he wrote lots of essays and ended up with good writing skills. But it wasn't the done thing to talk in class. Then Bradley went to Yale Law School.

> Funnily enough, a Brit like me found himself relatively shy turning up for the case method of teaching. In England, if the teacher asked you a question, you'd provide enough information to show you weren't a duffer, but you wouldn't add to it, or argue. Whereas at Yale, you were forced to argue with the professor. I thought law school was creating an extremely articulate American generation.

What I find worrying in Britain is how much advancement in professions where articulacy matters seems to depend on going to Oxford or Cambridge. Anybody coming from a place like North Dakota is bound to wonder how he would fare (or not fare) in such a system.

I asked poet Craig Raine to name offhand the universities of some contemporary English poets. James Fenton, Wendy Cope, and Raine himself went to Oxford; Ted Hughes, the poet laureate, to Cambridge; Douglas Dunn and Tom Paulin to Hull, where Philip Larkin ran the library; Seamus Heaney to Queen's in Belfast. Raine objected: look at the great originals like playwrights Harold Pinter or Tom Stoppard who didn't go anywhere; maybe it was an advantage *not* to be created in the Oxford mold.

Raine tells a story about a valet at Claridges hotel named Trevor Hollingworth who wrote to him saying he wanted to be a writer and asking how could he get to Oxford. "How is it when I look about, all the writers are from Oxford and Cambridge?" he said. "I clearly have to go there." Raine replied he might be better off not going. I wonder.

I forgot to ask what happened to Hollingworth (maybe he is still a valet at Claridges) but Raine, whose own parents were a boxer and a chambermaid, readily agreed Oxford instills confidence. It's probably good for talent, bad for genius. Says Raine:

> Really, what Oxford gives you is the kind of chutzpah, the sense of self-belief, that will allow you to consider yourself a writer when you are unable actually to write. I mean I thought of myself as a writer when I was eighteen. And I couldn't write anything.

What he did, Raine says, was write very bad parodies of Hemingway. But he got over the notion that poetry was a sissy thing, not like performing brain surgery or launching a satellite into space. Oxford took off the curse of having to prove he was macho, that if he was a poet, he'd also have to be a bullfighter or a lumberjack.

> You don't have to wear a hard hat to prove you're an okay guy. At Oxford you're automatically in this tradition of great writers. Oxford teaches you to write essays. It teaches you to think. And it lets you read. So you learn from writers. Oxford gives you the confidence to go on writing. It's what I'd call a sense of high targets.

This "sense of high targets" has been well described by Naipaul:

> I remember my first term at Oxford in 1950, going for long walks—I remember the roads, the autumn leaves, the cars and trucks whipping the leaves up—and wondering what I was going to write about. I had worked hard for the scholarship to go to Oxford, to be a writer. But now that I was in Oxford, I didn't know what to write about. And really, I suppose, unless I had been driven by great necessity, something even like panic, I might never have written. The idea of laying aside the ambition was very restful and tempting—the way sleep was said to be tempting to Napoleon's soldiers on the retreat from Moscow . . .

As a literary giant who *did* go to Oxford, Naipaul is an interesting exception. Most of the great English writers either didn't go, or like Shelley didn't stay long. Oxford's one great towering literary genius, Lewis Carroll, was mainly known to his contemporaries as the shy, eccentric, stammering, and reputedly boring Christ Church mathematics lecturer, Charles Lutwidge Dodgson.

The problem with an elitist system is not so much the truly gifted may get passed over—one hopes and assumes they don't—but the way it pushes up so much mediocrity. The American problem is the reverse. When somebody says, "There are some people who aren't bright enough to get anything out of a rigorous university education," we don't say, "Well, then, don't bother with university." We create a lot of nonrigorous university education. We figure a man can be a first-class electrical engineer without any kind of *litterae humaniores.* And why not?

In Britain the verbal skills, the ability to write a sparkling essay or review, are so esteemed, there is a distinct feeling that it is not worthy of intelligent young men or women to soil their hands with engineering or industry. As Bernard Levin says, "Again and again you see the lists crowded with arts graduates, who can't get jobs. Of course you can't tell a university to close down its department of Greek philology and open a new engineering shop. If the demand for it grows, something like that will happen."

Asa Briggs worries that any lead Britain has in the essay or review is getting "more precarious." Lord Briggs, a prolific reviewer himself, says there are still aspects of British education that make for verbal skill. "Even now a child at school in Britain will probably write a good deal more than an American child. It's easier on the whole to get people to be articulate on paper."

George Steiner says the British are such good reviewers because a good review is like a club exchange. "It is like two men who meet in the lobby of a club. One says to the other, 'Tell me about X. Is it any good?' And the other answers sharply, wittily, succinctly, in a language they both share. And that they do superbly."

The British establishment *is* like a club. All the columns and reviews, for the chattering class at least, are the badges of current membership. I asked Steiner about the so many Oxford dons in *The New York Review of Books.* "That is out of the Kennedy world," he said, "one of the last great nostalgic bridges." He went on:

> They're quite right to feel that English historians, art historians, critics, high political gossip writers, are more verbal, more articulate and they've read much more than their American counterparts. But honestly, that isn't very important.

What matters in a language, he said, is its role in creating new social and political possibilities in a society.

> What matters is the fact that this was the society of Edmund Burke and Gladstone and Disraeli, of Tawney, of Shaw, and of Lawrence. This was a society where a certain kind of debate was conducted at the highest level of articulacy. That's what matters. And this was a society which poured out its literature from Shakespeare to the great Victorians over the whole earth. And this is simply no longer on. It is no longer true.

Granted. But go down a notch or two. Maybe the highest levels of imaginative talent are not at the moment going into political eloquence or serious fiction. If one looks at the postwar outburst in the popular arts, Britain is still supreme in the spy thriller, the detective story, the bestselling Gothic novel, and the bodice-ripper romance, in the theater, television drama, humor, design, pop, and rock. And that, for a country one-fourth the size of our own, is a lot.

I Spy

MAYBE THE FLOW of talent just had to go somewhere. Now you didn't come down from Oxford and Cambridge any more to go into the Colonial Office (the colonies had vanished). You didn't go into the navy (its great days were over). Very few could get into the Foreign Office. Where did you go? So Britain (and the world) got *Beyond the Fringe.* We got "Upstairs, Downstairs" and *Jesus Christ Superstar* and "Monty Python's Flying Circus" and Carnaby Street and all the rest. Who writes the best spy thrillers? Detective stories? Historical romances? Serious plays? Even, with *The Phantom of the Opera* and *Les Misérables,* beating us Americans at our own musical game.

One place where the British really are supreme is the spy thriller. George Steiner suggests it began with Joseph Conrad's two great novels, *Under Western Eyes* and *The Secret Agent:*

> And he of course was Polish-French, not British. But he brought it in. Why is the double agent so important? Because it has brought together two great taboo subjects: homosexuality, at a very powerful level, and the secret coven. It is the last great club, the secret service. There's a wonderful story by Henry James, "The Great Good Place." He falls asleep. He has a dream of what heaven will be like, a club in London. You go to heaven and you go to a London gentleman's club. And the secret service, which recruits in that elite, has many clubs like the Apostles in Cambridge, a legendary secret society here.

Dr. Steiner feels nobody in America finally gives a damn about clubs like Yale's Skull and Bones.

> But in this country, the secret coven which recruits with an aura of the homosexual above the law, beyond good and evil, is one of the last great dreams of glory. The spy novel as set in a land caught ambiguously between the superpowers, detesting them both for being superpowers, despising itself for living under America's day-and-night protection—we live by courtesy of the American air force here. We've

always known it. Most of Britain's nuclear bases are in the vicinity of Cambridge. But it's a big taboo secret.

"Despising itself," he goes on. "Afraid of Russia until very recently. And seeking for itself that childish dream of secret power." Steiner also links the spy novel to Baron Corvo's turn-of-the-century novels like *Hadrian the Seventh* (1904), about an Englishman who becomes Pope and secretly all-powerful. Steiner finds the spy novel today "a very, very interesting symptom of a fantasy surrogate for real power. And they do it beautifully. They do it absolutely beautifully. Moreover it so happens that Graham Greene, le Carré and two or three others were in that work while becoming writers." He says:

> But what makes it so exciting to the outsider, the majority here, who can never get into that club, who've never drunk port in a common room, is that the betrayals of these men, the self-betrayals, the corruption, confirms the hunch of the outsider that the elite has gone pretty rotten. The insider smiles. He's very flattered by the books. The outsider says, "Those are the bastards who are trying to lord it over us without any moral right." Hence exposure in this country has never meant any real disgrace. A Kim Philby's the schoolboy who's done the practical joke. He's been found out. He's going to take his beating like a man.

Christopher Andrew, a Cambridge historian generally regarded as Britain's preeminent authority on intelligence, agreed that the worldwide media appeal of the Cambridge mole is an extraordinary phenomenon.

> If you look through traitors, the one who really captures the imagination is an upper-class person, homosexual, from a good public school, at Trinity College, Cambridge, who belongs to an ancient secret society, the Apostles, and has a link with the Royal Family . . . The way spy thrillers sell, I'd almost be inclined to say the traditional British caste system and the end of Empire has even more appeal to the export market than the home market.

I asked if Kim Philby was a classic case. The professor said no:

> I don't myself regard Philby as a romantic figure. I think Philby was a really tough-minded nihilist whom Graham Greene got absolutely wrong. The extent of his misunderstanding of Philby is encapsulated in Greene's introduction to Philby's memoirs, *My Silent War*. Philby seems to Graham Greene as Catholic, which he isn't, and Greene draws a false analogy with the classic conflicts of loyalties in the Elizabethan period.

In his 1986 introduction to *My Silent War,* Greene wrote:

Like many Catholics who, in the reign of Elizabeth, worked for the victory of Spain, Philby has a chilling certainty in the correctness of his judgment, the logical fanaticism of a man who, having once found a faith, is not going to lose it because of the injustices or cruelties inflicted by erring human instruments . . . If there was a Torquemada now, he would have known in his heart that one day there would be a John XXIII.

In Professor Andrew's view, what Philby actually went through was "a demeaning and degrading series of intellectual gymnastics":

In the end, they all became Stalinists. There's nothing romantic about them. But I have considerable sympathy for how most of them got into it because I'm persuaded they didn't know what they were getting into. They were young intellectual idealists capable of reworking any evidence that got in the way. So it isn't absolutely astonishing that Philby and all the others rejected what they saw as cruelty of the establishment in the face of the mass unemployment in the 1930s with its class disdain that the whole thing was simply disgusting, or felt that Britain was extremely feeble in the face of Fascism, which it was.

That's the initial recruitment, Andrew said.

They think they're entering the service of the Communist International, Comintern, with great international solidarity. It's explained to them that German workers are engaged in a secret war against Fascism. In secret groups of five. The recruiter would ask, "How about founding a secret ring yourselves? Show solidarity. Are you too snobbish to follow the example of German workers? If you are against Fascism do what they're doing. Form groups of five, groups of five." That's what Burgess always talked about when he got drunk, describing himself as a Comintern agent.

But they have to convince themselves there isn't a terror going on in Russia, that a state beginning the largest peacetime persecution in world history is any kind of viable alternative, and that after the Nazi-Soviet Pact, which is carving up Eastern Europe, you can continue the fight against Fascism. From June 1941, it becomes a bit easier. Somehow British and American visitors to the U.S.S.R. had the ability to ignore the evidence of their own eyes without conscious dishonesty.

I told Andrew I'd seen the same thing in China. He agreed, saying, "During the Great Cultural Revolution you'd get people coming back to Cambridge and saying, 'Well, at least no physical cruelty is involved.' "

Playwright Ronald Harwood feels that the spy thriller, like the detective story, has to do with English game-playing. As one of the characters in *J. J. Farr* says: "The English turn everything into a game. Their excuse is that anything enjoyable is more salutary than anything salutary."

When we met, Harwood said:

> I love spy fiction and I love detective fiction. But they're games. They're little puzzles and you have to solve them. Now in le Carré's books they're very elaborate. But they're still the same game. Who was the traitor? Who gave the secrets away? I mean, it's a whodunit of another kind. Why we're so good at the thriller is because the English have invented the best games in the world. Tennis. Lawn tennis. Cricket, one of the most beautiful games ever invented. Football, played by three quarters of the world's people. And detective fiction and spy fiction are part of that impulse.

Dr. Steiner sees another link between the spy story and games. He said that John Buchan, author of *The Thirty-Nine Steps*, a tale of espionage with an upright hero, Richard Hannay, also wrote boys'-school stories. And an enthusiasm for crossword puzzles is characteristically English.

> But I'd also take games in the athletic sense. Le Carré was a schoolmaster. Graham Greene taught. All of these people have seen the world of *Lord of the Flies*, the boys' world which has always been dominant in the inner culture of this country.

So far, Professor Andrew said, speaking as the upheaval in the Communist world was just getting started, the spy thriller novelists and the media had missed a big new development.

> It's not been grasped that the problem has been entirely turned around. An astonishing proportion of the new moles produced by the media in the 1980s have been imaginary. *Spycatcher*'s Sir Roger Hollis never did it. Graham Mitchell never did it. Number Ten's fed up, I'm sure. But what has not been noticed over the last decade is the unprecedented stream of high-ranking defectors from the Soviet bloc to Britain and the United States. There's still a problem in the West of low-level penetration. If you can seduce a Marine with the key to a code room, you're in business. But the real successors to Philby, Blunt, Burgess, and Maclean are Russians coming out of the Soviet Union.

The restaurant in Belgravia was some distance from the Knightsbridge station. A watery sleet, carried on the wind blustering down from the North Sea, had drenched even the sidewalk under the trees. For a moment I paused there shivering and staring into the mist that shrouded Lowndes Square. I remembered that I had been told to cross it and turn right.

A man was crossing ahead of me. There was no sign of anyone else about. I followed him. Except for our muffled footsteps and the sleet, the silence in the square was complete. Then, so suddenly I very nearly jumped, the man turned around. In his dark, neat French raincoat, with his slim, erect figure and sleek gray hair, he was the picture of distinguished respectability. High cheekbones and swarthy complexion, slightly hooknosed, he might well have been the member of a Levantine or Arab delegation. It was only the expression of anxiety in his eyes and something inexpressibly savage about them that made me relieved when he looked away and hurried on. It was like an Eric Ambler thriller.

Soon afterward, over sherry, I described the scene to the man I was meeting for lunch. He smiled. He *was* Eric Ambler. The master storyteller whose very name has become a sort of generic term for the classic thriller (Jacques Barzun: "mere Amblering") turns out to be remarkably good company: anecdotal, good-humored, modest, and unassuming. ("I don't think I'm modest and unassuming. I've tried to be realistic. Being unassuming can have a good foundation. It means that your talents are modest.")

Eric Ambler was eighty when I met him; his publisher was reissuing many of his books in paperback. Together with Somerset Maugham in *Ashenden: or, The British Agent* (1928), Ambler in his novels of the 1930s practically invented what we call the spy thriller. Like George Steiner, Ambler sees the spy story as a twentieth century phenomenon, possibly prompted by the Dreyfus case (1894). He calls *The Riddle of the Sands* (1903) by Irishman Erskine Childers "the first spy novel." (Childers was later executed for helping the IRA.) To Ambler, Conrad's *The Secret Agent* (1907) was "the first attempt by a major novelist to deal realistically with the secret war, with the sub-world of conspiracy, sabotage, double dealing and betrayal." It was one of Conrad's masterpieces.

The spy story became popular entertainment with William Le Queux and E. Phillips Oppenheim, who had huge outputs and were much imitated. What Ambler describes as "the early cloak-and-dagger stereotype—the black-velveted seductress, the British secret-service numbskull hero, the omnipotent spymaster" evolved. John Buchan's Hannay stories came next *(The Thirty-Nine Steps* in 1915), as did the blood-and-thunder Bulldog Drummond books.

What exactly is an Eric Ambler thriller? If you compare him, say, with Graham Greene, they both are superb storytellers and master craftsmen; both began writing thrillers in the 1930s as Europe moved out of the Depression and toward war. Greene, who is five years older, got a head start with books like *Stamboul Train (Orient Express* in America, in 1932), *A Gun for Sale (This Gun for Hire,* 1936) and *The Confidential Agent* (1939). Between 1936 and 1940, starting when he was just twenty-seven, Ambler wrote, all in long-hand in copybooks, his first six thrillers, including *The Dark Frontier* (1936), *The Mask of Dimitrios (A Coffin for Dimitrios,* 1939), and *Journey into Fear* (1940).

Ambler has called the thriller "an extension of the fairy tale" and "a melodrama so embellished as to create the illusion that the story being told, however unlikely, could be true." I asked him what he meant by saying, as he once did, that the thriller was "a story-telling structure." He told me:

> I tried to suggest the possibility that a spy story could be used—allegorically perhaps—to say things about one's life and times. What could be said in different kinds of fiction were better said in this particular form.

Ambler has also said a spy thriller is "a story in which the central character is a secret intelligence agent," a definition which fits none of his own novels, though a few, like *The Intercom Conspiracy,* are set in a world of espionage. He disclaims any real knowledge of it.

> I know nothing about spies. Greene does. Le Carré does. They used to work in the secret service. I didn't. I wouldn't be able to say a word.

(Le Carré not only worked in the secret service for five years, but in his seven Circus novels invented a secret world of his own, with an identifiable staff of over eighty people and nearly two hundred words of made-up espionage jargon, such as "lamp-lighters" and "ju ju men.") The real distinction between their work and his own is that both Greene and le Carré have extended the thriller into tragic novels on contemporary reality. Le Carré, the premier Cold War novelist, has moved from a thriller inspired by the Berlin Wall, *The Spy Who Came in from the Cold* (described by Greene as the best spy story he has ever read), to *The Honourable Schoolboy* (East Asian intrigue), *The Little Drummer Girl* (Arab-Israeli terror) and *The Russia House (glasnost* and the thaw). His protagonists are victims, just as Greene's tend to be social outcasts such as professional gunmen, leaders of revolutionary groups, or men caught on the wrong sides of civil wars; Greene's are usually in a state of spiritual chaos in a setting of seedy tropical decay, as in *The Comedians, The Honorary Consul,* the kind of milieu Auden called "grahamgreeneish."

With the winding down of the Cold War, what happens to the spy thriller? Almost certainly it will go right on, even go back to the late 1930s mood of European intrigue of the early Ambler novels. Le Carré, whose master spy George Smiley got his Russian counterpart, Karla, to defect across the Berlin Wall in his 1980 novel, *Smiley's People,* put it this way in a 1989 essay:

> Smiley had won, as the West has won now. But the sweets of victory elude us—as they eluded Smiley, partly because he had forgotten what he was fighting for, partly because he feared that his masters preferred the comforts of permanent aggression to the hardship of new choices and alignments.

"We really invent the enemies we need," le Carré, whose real name is David Cornwell, explained. "We could be making the discovery that Russia, once the military threat is removed, is a huge, untidy third world problem that will demand time, effort and money—lots of money—to fix. It could be a terrible headache."

In Ambler's work, we are back with the British tradition that law and order are the norm, terror and violence are the aberration, and order will be brought out of chaos; almost all twenty of his thrillers have happy endings *(The Intercom Conspiracy* being an exception). They all present innocent yet vulnerable characters, whether the prim English Charles Latimer, the likeable Russian agents Valeshoff and Tamara, or the battered half-Egyptian rogue Arthur Abdel Simpson, all of whom find themselves enmeshed in a web of international intrigue. In a sinister nightmare world, suspense mounts and erupts into action. But we know Ambler will keep to the rules of the game and that order will come; his thrillers satisfy a longing for order. I suggested to Ambler that some of Greene's "entertainments," like *Our Man in Havana,* which kept to the classic formula, were among his most satisfying work. He agreed:

> Yes, of course they are . . . Greene's early entertainments were contemporary with my first books. I first took him for a serious novelist potboiling. Then he called *Brighton Rock* an entertainment; I thought it could have been written by Gogol. I used to see Graham occasionally. He came to my house when I lived in London in the fifties. A couple of times, but always with someone else. I feel strongly he ought to have had the Nobel. He ought to have had the Nobel long ago.

Ambler never used Vietnam as a setting, though he had visited Saigon in the mid-fifties while doing a piece for *Holiday* magazine, "Spy Haunts of the World."

There was no war going on, much. I mean it was just a French war. What I did was set *The Quiet American* up because in Saigon at that time everybody was in the conspiracy to pretend that it was real life; it was not fiction. They would say, "That's where Fowler was sitting when the explosion took place."

I knew it well. I told Ambler I'd lived in Saigon's Continental Hotel—where the fictional Fowler *was* sitting in the terrace bar— nearly four years while reporting the war for the *Washington Star*. Edward Lansdale, in the 1950s an advisor to Ngo Dinh Diem, and an old friend of mine from Vietnam days, supposedly was one of two Americans Greene based his main character, Pyle, upon. Phrases from *The Quiet American* still echo in my mind ("nothing nowadays is fabulous and nothing rises from its ashes," "ordinary life goes on —that has saved many a man's reason"). And there was that famous rice-paddy dialogue between Pyle and Fowler, the Greene-like English journalist who tells the story:

> "You and your like are trying to make a war with the help of a people who just aren't interested."
> "They don't want Communism."
> "They want enough rice," I said. "They don't want to be shot at. They want one day to be much the same as another. They don't want our white skins around telling them what they want."

Again, Greene used the thriller form to explore a moral dilemma. Greene himself has said, "Eric Ambler is unquestionably the best thriller writer," true in the sense that Ambler probably did the most to establish the form of the classic genre. Ambler was sixteen in 1925 when Kafka's *Trial* was published ("Someone must have been telling lies about Joseph K., for without having done anything wrong he was arrested one fine morning"). (Ambler uses the phrase "A Kafka-like scene," in *The Night-Comers* and elsewhere.) He was just twenty-four when Hitler seized power. The rise of Nazism and new horrors in Central Europe created the climate of fear that informs all of Ambler's prewar novels; he told me:

> I've written a lot about fear. A lot about irrational fear. Mainly because I have a lot of it myself. Even as a child I was a conspirator who was chased by other conspirators.

Actually, as his 1985 autobiography, *Here Lies*, shows, he had a remarkably happy childhood and youth as part of a warm, close-knit, charmingly eccentric south London family. Ambler's parents, whose "great bonds were music and the making of laughter," were vaudeville performers who first put on "living marionette" shows, billing themselves as "Reg and Amy Ambrose." Later they gave concert parties where they sang Irving Berlin 1920s Charleston hits like "Everybody's Doin' It." Reg did a Harry Lauder impersonation in kilt and tammy, Amy was Marie Lloyd in a big feathered hat singing, "A Little of What You Fancy." Then there was Uncle Frank, a battered but likeable ne'er-do-well, like some of Ambler's later fictional characters, who left the scrap metal trade to take up a remarkably long career as an embezzler, later doing time in Maidstone prison. This genial and unpretentious portrait of Ambler's early life and his jobs in engineering and advertising takes up half the book.

It ends with a phrase. He is on vacation in Marseilles and has lost all his money, except his fare home and enough to pay his hotel bill, in a game of poker dice with a barman. ("The bar was dark and cool and so was the barman.") There is nothing left for food. Sitting in his room reading Joyce's *Portrait of the Artist as a Young Man,* he tries to take his mind off hunger by plotting an "assassination."

> I was in a corner room overlooking the intersection of the Canebière and the side street where the bar was . . . Through the spaces in the grille I could see the roadway at the point where the barman would cross to the tram stop. With an imaginary rifle in my hands I lined up a space in the grille with a brass curlicue on the base of the standard lamp . . . The barman never came and I returned to James Joyce.
>
> It was quite a shock, a few weeks later, to see on the newsreels that same piece of the Canebière with the intersection tramlines. The spot I had chosen for my sniper shot at the barman had also been chosen by the Croatian assassin of King Alexander of Yugoslavia . . . I felt oddly guilty, but I was also pleased. In the Mediterranean sunshine there were strange and violent men with whom I could identify, and with whom, in a way, I was now in touch.

That *now in touch* takes him, and us, into a completely different world, sinister, enthralling. Ambler, as a famous author, was to range widely geographically, moving from Europe and the Balkans to Southeast Asia, the Middle East, and Latin America; like Greene, he is a master at capturing the sights, sounds, and smells of tawdry, exotic tropical settings. *The Night-Comers (State of Siege)* is set in Indonesia. Here is a *betjak,* or cycle-rickshaw, ride:

> Once you have learned to disregard the labored breathing of the driver pedalling behind you and have overcome the feeling that you are the sitting target for every approaching car, the *betjak* is an agreeable form of transport, especially on a hot night . . . You can sit back comfort-

ably and look up at the trees and the stars without being bitten by
insects; and, providing the driver does not insist on muttering obscene
invitations to the nearest brothel in your ear, you can think.

Jacques Barzun has called *The Night-Comers* "Indonesian current
history without tears." Every detail is splendidly on target:

> Sundanese officials are peculiarly difficult to deal with, especially if you
> are an English-speaking European . . . The shifty brown eyes peer at
> you. It is your move now. You ask what the fee for the clearance would
> be if one knew where to obtain it. A figure is named . . . The eyes
> watch sullenly as you count the money out. You agreed too quickly. He
> is wishing he had asked for more and wondering if it is too late . . .

Ambler told me he was in Indonesia in 1951 and 1953, when
civil war was raging in the interior of Java:

> If you wanted to go from Jakarta to Bandung you went in daylight and
> stayed overnight. The road just wasn't safe . . . We were looking for
> places to shoot in the area, casing studios to see where to make pic-
> tures. In Java we went to one studio, the usual thing, an earth floor,
> which is very good for sound. One film sound stage was packed with
> salt. Cases of the most advanced animation equipment. It was all from
> Zeiss. It must have been ten million dollars worth, a lot of money in
> those days. Animation equipment was logical in Indonesia since you
> could make training films for villagers. The only trouble was nobody in
> the country knew how to work it. It turned out the Minister of Infor-
> mation was also the Zeiss representative.

We laughed. "The poor Indonesians," I said. "Oddly enough,
they seem to survive."

"They survive because if you stick a seed in the ground, there's a
papaya tree six months later."

Like many British authors, Ambler has divided his professional
life between England and America.

> We obviously thought of becoming citizens. And if you didn't think
> about it, every time you went through immigration, there was a re-
> minder. "What? Not a citizen yet? What's the matter with you?" You'd
> get a black man saying it. Very touchy.

Aside from his novels, Ambler has written sixteen screenplays,
mostly in Hollywood. I asked him if he felt partly American.

> Less and less. I suspect a lot of Americans feel less American. In South-
> ern California, you'd have to feel Hispanic. More and more and more
> keep coming. People who don't speak English. We used to call them
> wetbacks. With a two-thousand-mile border you won't stop it. I had the
> most extraordinary experience. We'd sold our house in California. And

rented one from Don Taylor, the director, who'd gone to do a picture in Europe. It was a nice house on San Vicente Boulevard with a pool and pool house. And we were there with our housekeeper two months before I realized that there were fifteen Mexicans—count them, one-five— living in the pool house. All illegal immigrants. We found them by accident. Coming back late from Chasen's or some restaurant and found the kitchen was occupied with this crowd of people.

After years of living abroad, in the United States and Switzerland, Eric Ambler clearly feels comfortable to be back home in Thatcher's Britain.

Of course she's the most marvelous Aunt Sally in the world. It's that Iron Lady. Or that Terrible Woman. Or she's going to hit you with her handbag. Socialism is having to come to terms with the fact that nobody any longer believes it works. Well, we didn't have socialism. What we had was sort of half-assed welfarism.

We exchanged experiences on Java, Egypt, the predators you can meet on a book tour in America (Ambler: "local wiseacres, rogue literati, and aha-school instant analysts"), having a great time until the waiters hovered impatiently about our table in the now-empty restaurant. I told Eric Ambler I'd rather have had lunch with him than anyone in London, even the Queen. It was hard to explain, but starting in North Dakota when I was just fifteen or sixteen, his books had opened up so many possibilities in life. Later, when I was traveling about the world, in a way living Eric Ambler adventures in real life, there'd be a new novel coming out every three or four years, mostly set in countries where I'd been; they kept popping up like an old friend.

Ambler remembered a researcher at a local radio station in San Diego—"just a nice middle-aged woman"—who said, "Thank you for the books."

As you did. They enabled her to think of different values, to think about radical ideas, that it was okay to think freely, without guilt.

As we came outside, a sudden icy squall lashed about us. As we shook hands at the corner I told him that people who really succeeded in life sometimes ended up with a kind of openness, a warm-heartedness, a grace.

"It's put on. It's not true," he protested.

But it is true.

Murder, They Wrote

ONE UNSOLVED MYSTERY is why the law-abiding English write the best novels about crime. In his 1948 essay "The Decline of the English Murder," George Orwell said the average *News of the World* reader likes to spend Sunday afternoon reading about a domestic killing. But the background should be of extreme propriety: a staunch member of the middle classes gives way to a passion he can no longer control.

Agatha Christie, master of the British "cozy" (country houses, quaint villages, Oxford dons, as opposed to American "hard-boiled": wisecracking and violent gumshoes), was once asked if she used real people in her books. "For me," she said, "it is quite impossible to write about anyone I know, or have ever spoken to, or indeed heard about. For some reason, it kills them for me stone dead." This unreality in the "cozy," together with a mastery of plot, nostalgia, the dream of gracious living, and old-fashioned values, may explain why Englishwomen are so good at it.

P. D. James, Christie's successor in the traditional British form, says that in the so-called Golden Age of the English mystery "everything else became subordinate to the ingenuity of the puzzle, including character and motivation." Today, she says, "the mystery is very much the modern morality play. You have an almost ritual killing and a victim, you have a murderer who in some sense represents the forces of evil, you have your detective coming in—very likely to avenge the death—who represents justice, retribution. And in the end you restore order out of disorder." She also finds there is now far greater realism in psychology and style. She herself aims to "use the formula of the detective story in a realistic manner in order to try and say something that is true about men and women and, in particular, about society." Her 1986 novel, *A Taste for Death*, for example, is a brilliant study of class conflict, raising, at least in its first shimmering chapters, the mystery genre to new heights. Her latest, *Devices and Desires,* about a Scotland Yard man on holiday who runs up against a psychopathic stranger, is more conventional, but captures the tone of nuclear Britain.

One of the attractions of detective fiction, as with the spy thriller, is that there is a solution. At the start it's chaotic: somebody is stabbed, poisoned, garroted, thrown from a train; people die and except for clues you don't know why. It seems random. The art of the mystery novel is that there *is* a pattern. There is logic in it, no matter how ingeniously contrived the plot, thrilling the suspense, or misdirected the reader. As James says of the detective genre:

> It reaffirms the reader's hope that one lives in a rational and generally benevolent universe, that there is a law both divine and public, that there are explanations.

In a law-abiding society interrupted by violence, the social order is restored, or, as Miss Marple is likely to say, evil overcome by good. (Or as Raymond Chandler, English himself, classically put it for the American private eye: "Down these mean streets a man must go who is not himself mean; who is neither tarnished nor afraid.") As real-life violence grows in Britain, crime fiction, too, is going more deeply into the working of psychotic minds. Ruth Rendell, Mrs. James's chief rival as Britain's best current mystery writer, also writes psychological thrillers. (In *A Demon in My View* Arthur, a psychopathic sex offender, sublimates his drive to kill women by "strangling" a show window dummy. In *Live Flesh* a young rapist, Victor, describes the rape of a terrified girl who "shouted and fought" as "wonderful.") Not much hope of a rational universe there; indeed, Ruth Rendell is steadily moving away from the traditional form in favor of her psychological thrillers, such as *The Bridesmaid* in 1989, published both under her own name and, with *A Dark-Adapted Eye* in 1986, *A Fatal Inversion* in 1987, and *Gallowglass* in 1990, as Barbara Vine. Over coffee in her Kensington flat, I asked her why she was not sticking to the traditional English body-in-the-library detective story.

"I no longer find the form of the detective story very entertaining to write," she said. "I mean, the need for interrogation I find very boring and tiresome. And you can't get out of it. All the questions of time, the questions of forensics." She liked coming back to the regulars in her traditional Kingsmarkham series; she'd done fourteen novels with Chief Inspector Reginald Wexford. "But then I must have a crime that must be solved and must be solved in a very complicated, convoluted way. I don't enjoy that anymore. When I write I want to write about people's character and motivations. And why they do what they do." She suspected, however, that in a year or two another Wexford plot might come to her and she'd write it.

John Mortimer, creator of the Rumpole crime series, has said, "If it weren't for a ridiculous literary snobbery about 'crime writing' Ruth Rendell would be acclaimed as one of our most important novelists."

"Dear John Mortimer was very kind," she told me. "But of course it's very exaggerated. It isn't true. And I think the Barbara Vine books *are* serious." I asked her why she had taken up another name for some of her books.

"It's a different voice. I feel I can say anything I like. Without the restraints of the detective story or the crime novel . . . It is often a first-person narration." She doesn't feel it is quite a pseudonym as some of her friends call her Barbara, her middle name, and Vine is an old family name.

The murder mystery has a long tradition in Britain, she says:

> In America Poe is the first one. And the last one for a very long time. After that you really come into Dashiell Hammett and Raymond Chandler. Whereas for the British, there was Wilkie Collins, who started it all off really. And Conan Doyle. Two giants. And then you do get other people, in every decade you've someone. You've got Chesterton with all those Father Brown stories. You've got somebody like A. E. W. Mason. And then the so-called Golden Age with Agatha Christie and Dorothy Sayers and Margery Allingham and Ngaio Marsh, the four usually given. I'd also add Josephine Tey, who I think is superior to all of them. And there you have a tradition. I think what happens with people is they feel, well, this is the genre for me to write in because I have a precedent. People do succeed in it very well in England.

We talked about writers living abroad. She said Patricia Highsmith *(Strangers on a Train)*, whose suspense fiction makes her one of the best American crime novelists, lives in Switzerland. "She lived in France for seven years. You can live in France as an artist and pay no taxes for seven years." (Graham Greene and Anthony Burgess both live in France.) I said Eric Ambler had lived in Switzerland; he'd told me he found it rather dull ("looking out at a gray lake"). Miss Rendell gave a hoot of loud, delighted laughter. "I'd rather pay *any amount* of tax than be obliged to live in Switzerland. Dreadful, dreadful. Like going to live in Ireland."

Ruth Rendell is good at getting just the right, precise detail of character and milieu, especially in the dismal suburbs and bleak housing estates of present-day England. In *The Veiled One* a depressing English shopping mall is so convincingly described, we're quite ready to believe it when a body is found in the car park. "Why I like writing contemporary fiction," Rendell says, "is the pleasure of reflecting the mores of the times I happen to live in. This is particularly true in crime fiction and perhaps more important to me in my Wexfords than in the others."

I told her I preferred the Wexfords; when she kept to the form of the classic detective story you could count on it being a rational universe where evil didn't go unpunished. A great hoot of laughter from Miss Rendell. "I'm treading on very delicate ground now," she said teasingly. "But I must tell you that those who prefer my Wexfords are usually the *less* intellectual of my readers. Let us say the middle-aged housewife likes Wexford. It is the university teacher who likes the others."

She was amused. "It gives me great pleasure *not* to resolve things," she said. "In *A Dark-Adapted Eye* you never know who is the mother of the boy. It makes my readers very angry. I get letters saying, 'We have to know.' '*You* must know.' But I don't know. Why must I know? When I wrote *A Judgement in Stone* the first line tells you what's going to happen:

> Eunice Parchment killed the Coverdale family because she could not read or write.

"Now *that* made people very angry. Some people loved it. But others said, 'I read that line and I didn't want to read another word. You disappointed me.'" Another hearty laugh.

Ruth Rendell, the daughter of schoolteachers in South Woodford, began writing as a local newspaper reporter. Her husband, Don, an ex-*Daily Mail* journalist, to whom she has been divorced and remarried, encouraged her. She did six unpublished works before her first Inspector Wexford detective novel; she's published thirty-five books in all. She also does a lot of book reviews.

"I do it for fun. I think it's good for you to be told to do six hundred words on something." Miss Rendell, who writes in lean, spare prose, is unexpectedly highbrow. She is a regular theater- and opera-goer. Half-open books lying about in her Kensington flat, which is not far from Notting Hill Gate or the home of P. D. James, were a biography of Byron and an obscure Russian novel. The flat

("I bought it two years ago for a hundred thousand pounds and confidently expect to sell it for a hundred and fifty thousand pounds this year and buy another one") is just for in-town stays; home is now a farmhouse in a Suffolk village near Colchester ("Constable country," says Rendell).

She likes to travel. For *The Speaker of Mandarin* she went to China. "I made up my mind before I went to write a book about it. So I took a lot of notes. And read a lot of books. And then took Wexford." Most often she goes to the United States, to see her publishers, visit friends, or join her son who is in college in Denver. One Wexford, *Put On by Cunning (Death Notes* in America), is set in California:

> Wexford was driving on the wrong side of the road. Or that was how he put it to himself. It wasn't as bad as he expected, the San Diego Freeway had so many lanes and traffic moved at a slower pace than at home.

Landing in Los Angeles, he finds "everything seemed so big, a bigger sea, a bigger beach, a vaster sky . . ." Driving north, Wexford finds the area "like the Cornish coast gigantically magnified," with "the finest climate on earth." Americans were "more inclined to be helpful than English people," and "if this is because they are a nation of salesmen just as the English are a nation of shopkeepers, it does little to detract from the overall pleasant impression." The dialogue rings fairly true (she had American friends look it over to avoid gaffes), though a line like "Edie, are ya decent? Reg's here to pick your brains" smacks of caricature.

A shrewd observer, Ruth Rendell feels the English are interested in other countries but not, on the whole, in other people:

> They like to go and look at them. The English have a long-standing and ongoing love affair with Italy and the Arab countries. But it's the countries, I think, rather then the people. You will constantly hear an Englishman saying, 'I love France. How wonderful it would be if it wasn't for the French.' You seldom *hear* the English talk about Americans. America? Yes! That they were in California, they were in Florida. They all love New York, so tense and so exciting. I do. But talking about New Yorkers? No, they might as well not exist.

I said I found in England, no matter how long they stayed, Americans never quite fit in. They didn't have the accent, the class identity. Rendell agreed:

I think that's true. Here we are *absurd* about that sort of thing. *I* am British. I was born here. And my mother was a Swede. Although she lived here since she was a teenager and she was a naturalized English-woman before she met my father. At the time of the Falklands War I said to my aunt—my father's sister, the *English* side—something about thinking that it was an unfortunate waste of life, time, energy, and money. And she said to me, "Oh, well, you would feel like that. You're not really English, are you?"

Rendell also agreed with me that the English were interested in American politics but not our social fabric. Whereas Americans were the other way.

"We make a mistake in thinking that because we speak the same language—and we *do* speak the same language; it's nonsense when people say we don't—that we are basically the same people. We're not. We are far from each other."

"Are Americans foreign or not? We're not totally."

Well, not *totally*. We have a language in common. But emotionally I think we're very different. The letters I get from Americans are much more emotional and much more fervent or ardent. A lot of them, ex-cept those from old people, will address me as "Dear Ruth." The En-glish never do that. They'd probably say "Miss Rendell." They're likely to apologize for taking up one's time. Americans won't do that.

"Don't you think the English are a lot more articulate?"

"No, I don't. You've been talking to a lot of erudite, sophisticated people. If you lived where I lived, in a village in Suffolk, the people there, that is, the people, the agricultural people—you know what snobs we are—they probably have a vocabulary of about three hun-dred words."

I said an odd thing about England, particularly Southeast En-gland, was that it seemed easier, once you had the credentials, to meet Who's Who people than the common herd.

She agreed. "They're *much* harder to approach. Because there's so much suspicion."

"You must encounter the same thing when you're out gathering material."

"Ah, but nobody ever knows I am. I never actually interview anybody. I just listen. I have a good ear. And I think I'm accepted in my village. You never know. With dialogue you get yourself into the shoes of the speaker. You say it over in your head: does it sound right?"

Part of the attraction of her books, she feels, is that American fascination with English society. "Americans do think of England as the Mother Country. Even if they are in no way descended from the English." "I think we're in terrible decline," she continued. "We've become very mercenary, very dirty, we're destroying the look of the country. It's a constant fight to keep Suffolk from disappearing under concrete."

Americans, she felt, tend to think of England as little and old. "You know, this little and ancient place." Class also helped form the English character, she felt. "I think we *like* it. There can be no other explanation for its enduring so long. *I* think the English *love* their class system, on all levels. It makes you feel safe, in a way. It doesn't make *me* feel safe, but I can see how it might affect some people. It's like:

> The rich man in his castle,
>   The poor man at his gate,
> God made them, high or lowly,
>   And order'd their estate.

"It's from the hymn, 'All Things Bright and Beautiful.' And I must tell you that now, if you sing it in school"—her voice dropped to a stage whisper—*"they leave that verse out."*

A mystery writer creates a whole ambience. Ruth Rendell has Chief Inspector Wexford's fictional Sussex town of Kingsmarkham. With Simon Brett we go backstage in London's West End, in television studios, or in a provincial rep.

> Charles Paris looked out from the bar of the Pinero Theatre, Warminster . . . The warmth of the third large Bell's and the glow of being in work cocooned him and he only caught the occasional word of the director's exposition of *Macbeth.*

Or we are waiting with Charles in his seedy bed-sitter on Hereford Road, hoping, if the Amazonian Swedish girls who occupy the other bed-sitters ever get off the line, that his agent Maurice Skellern will call about a juicy new part. Or that Frances, Charles's wife, headmistress at a school, will phone from her flat in Highgate; she and Charles are not divorced, but never quite reconciled either. The phone does ring.

> "Charles, it's Maurice."
>   For his agent to ring him was sufficiently unusual for Charles to do a quick mental checklist of what the call could possibly be about . . . The National Theatre had finally seen the error of its ways and was

inviting him to give his Lear? No, no, Charles, don't be ridiculous, you're far too old and cynical even to give such fantasies mind-room (and yet he still did, he still did) . . .

Whatever it is, we know it will involve a part, probably not very big, in a play, and that in its cast sparks will fly, a murder will be done, and Charles, as he has in thirteen books now, will solve the crime.

We also know, that unlike with Rendell and James, we can expect plenty of humor. And we can safely rely on the triumph of law and order by the last page. The real appeal of Brett's Charles Paris mysteries is their witty and amusing insider's look at Britain's performing arts. Rendell may be the mistress of criminal psychology, James of forensic detail; Brett gives us gentle theatrical fun.

Charles is forever remembering old reviews:

> Charles grimaced, recalling past punctures to his own ego. The bad reviews always stayed fixed, word for word, in his mind. Like the one from the *Aberdeen Evening Express:*
>
> "With Charles Paris playing Dracula, dawn couldn't come soon enough for me."
>
> Or the *Yorkshire Post's* comment:
>
> "Charles Paris kept hitching up his Northern accent like a loose bra-strap."
>
> But perhaps the most wounding of all had been *Plays and Players'* reaction to his performance in one of the great classical roles:
>
> "Charles Paris' Henry V had me rooting for the French at Agincourt."

Simon Brett, born in Surrey in 1945 and Producer of Light Entertainment for BBC radio when just out of Oxford at twenty-three, still has a youthful, vaguely undergraduate air. It's not hard to imagine him as president of the Oxford University Dramatic Society, directing its end-of-year revue in 1967. Brett now lives with his wife and three children—aged fifteen, twelve, and eight in 1990—in a village near Arundel on England's southern seacoast ("A pure Agatha Christie village of two hundred and fifty people; there's a church and a pub and a forge and about six people who think they're the squire"). He has also written a popular television sitcom, "After Henry" (featuring Prunella Scales, the wife in "Fawlty Towers"). In 1986 Scribner's reissued all twelve Charles Paris books in paperback and his thirteenth, *A Series of Murders,* came out in late 1989; he has a second crime series under way, featuring a Mrs. Pargiter, and a play is in the works. Simon Brett seems to be everything Charles Paris—middle-aged, professionally a flop, alcoholic—is not. He himself wonders. "When I wrote the first one," Brett says with an engaging grin, "Charles Paris was seventeen years older than me. I had a nice secure job at the BBC, a pension, and a solid marriage. And so to actually write about someone with no security, who lived in one room and had a broken marriage and drank too much seemed safely fictional."

I looked around. I was interviewing Brett in his London flat, which, with kitchenette and two modest rooms, was not that much a cut above Charles's Hereford Road bed-sitter. I'd told him when I arrived, "When the taxi left me I looked around and thought: Gee, just like the neighborhood Charles Paris lives in." There was a warehouse across the road. Brett grinned:

> And it's interesting. I sometimes get this . . . nightmare. That Charles Paris and I are getting closer and closer together. I mean, the marriage is all right, thank goodness. And this little flat is slightly cheating. I have a large house in the country too. But . . . I've got an Equity card now. I got it through directing but I guess I would be allowed to act. So I've sort of drawn closer to him. Both, in age and, I'm afraid, consumption of Bell's whiskey. And, um, in terms of insecurity. In that I have no guaranteed income. And I sometimes get this sense that we're going to melt together.

(Ruth Rendell, too, said she was insecure: "One bad review and it throws me for days. We're all *insecure*. We're all *raging* insecure.")

I said he told his readers a lot about the English theater.

> That's where most of the energy goes. Actually making the characters I enjoy. Charles Paris leads a miserable life in some ways, but it's kind of a free life. I suppose there's an element of wish fulfillment in it . . . But you have to make sure you get the backgrounds right. I mean most of the research involves taking actors out to drunken lunches. Which is a pleasant way of research. Often things I do feed back. I once wrote some questions for a television game show and used that background. In the current one, *A Series of Murders*, Charles gets involved in a police series on television.

What got Brett started writing mysteries was an assignment during his nine years at the BBC to produce a series of adaptations of Dorothy L. Sayers's Lord Peter Wimsey books.

> I was the producer of the radio versions, but again, as on TV, with Ian Carmichael playing Lord Peter. And it was directly out of that experience that I thought: oh, well, perhaps I could have a go at a mystery. I produced three or four of the books, *Whose Body?*, *Clouds of Witness*. After that I was a television producer for a couple years. So I was kind of researching Charles Paris every time I picked the phone up.

After he resigned from London Weekend Television, where he had gone from the BBC, Brett became a full-time writer.

There was a time, after about a year, when I got very panicky because I thought I'd lost my source of material. I wasn't in daily contact with actors and agents the same way I'd been. Today it's sort of come round. I'm writing scripts for sitcoms and meeting a lot of actors and directors and producers. From a different angle, as a writer instead of a producer.

The pattern from Oxford and Cambridge into the media, especially the BBC, was so common I asked Brett about it.

They have a tradition of comedy review which they do at the end of the festival. Writing, producing, or acting. So if you're looking for really young people—twenty-one, twenty-two—it's about the only showcase. If you want somebody who has ability for comedy, where do you find them? John Cleese, the whole "Monty Python" lot, the *Beyond the Fringe* lot, they were all either Oxford or Cambridge.

After twenty years in light entertainment, as author and producer, Brett sympathizes both with the generally more highbrow entertainment that crosses the Atlantic and what might be called the Benny Hill school, that bafflingly vulgar English streak Bernard Levin, the *Times* columnist, when I met him, called the Drop Your Trousers school. "Have you seen the *Carry On* films?" Brett asked. "There *is* a strong thread of British vulgarity. Music hall comedians like Dame Edna telling risqué jokes. The American equivalent is burlesque, the vaudeville tradition."

In the Charles Paris mystery *A Comedian Dies*, Brett paid affectionate tribute to this tacky end of British show business (as Olivier did in *The Entertainer* by John Osborne). He says:

Charles can respect as a professional actor the highbrow end of English culture and also the comic stand-up from the school of hard knocks, who's done the second house at the Glasgow Pavilion and all those gentle things comics have to do. I can see the appeal of it. The Drop Your Trousers school. Ray Cooney's West End farces are like that. All the titles are puns on "life" and "wife." *The Happiest Years of Your Wife. Run for Your Wife.*

Americans love the maniacal zaniness of "Monty Python." Mainstream English humor is much more understated. Perhaps more representative is the *Punch* cartoon about a man with a machine gun, besieged by policemen. Bullets fly, armored units move in, and, crouched behind a wall, the police spokesman tells reporters, "We believe he may be able to assist us in our enquiries." Much humor is transatlantic; sitcoms like "Cheers" go down well in Britain and I have heard the British fondly recall old Peter Arno cartoons— "Come along, we're going to the TransLux to hiss Roosevelt."

Brett feels there's a certain amount of satire in his books. "It's satire against pretension. It's fairly gentle." He does a monthly review for *Punch* and agreed with me that really hard-edged English satire, like *Serious Money* with all its cynicism, can only go so far. "If you don't care about at least one of the characters, if you don't touch base with someone, you don't care what happens to any of them." Brett noted that in the crime fiction of Dick Francis, the protagonist is always physically handicapped ("He's either got a withered hand or has a relative who does"). P. D. James softens her detective, Adam Dalgliesh, by making him a widower and a poet. Rendell's Wexford is a man of late middle age, tolerant, old-fashioned, comfortably married, and the father of grown daughters.

Brett writes at home. After taking the children to school, he is at his word processor by nine, working until six with an hour off for lunch. Weekends are free ("My timetable is still dictated by the kids"). I asked Brett about Maurice Skellern, who reminds me of agents I know; he said:

> I think the idea that agents sell things is mainly an illusion. I'm very lucky because I have an agent who does sometimes come up with ideas and says "How about this" or "I'm suggesting your name to Such-and-Such." Which is jolly good. But I think I've initiated most of the work I've done. I don't want to draw up contracts. You want more money and they want to pay less. The only thing ultimately they say is: "You're not that good. You're not worth what you're asking." Well, I mean, that would shrivel me up for days. I'd go cold writing. If your agent does all that, these conversations will go on, but you don't have to be a party to them.

The American market matters a lot to Brett and not just for the money:

> Americans are so much more outgoing. I get many more letters from America. Most of them about Charles Paris say either "Can't you give him a success?" or "Can't he get back with Frances on a permanent basis?" Either would kill the series. If Charles were completely content, you know, successful . . . A successful actor wouldn't have time to solve crimes. In quite a few of the books he's really poised on the edge of success. In *Murder Unprompted* he's actually playing a lead in the West End for about a fortnight. The audience expectation is: how long is it going to last this time?

Brett wishes the British would use the word "mystery" to cover the whole genre as Americans do. Instead, in Britain there are subtle distinctions between the detective story and the crime novel, crime fiction, the thriller and the whodunit, all mysteries. Like other crime writers, he enjoys doing other forms of writing too:

> I love writing crime fiction. I hope to be doing Charles Paris books as long as I live. But it's lovely sometimes to write something where you don't have to have a body in it. There's a lot of very good crime writers around at the moment. And a lot of them, like P. D. James in *A Taste for Death*, you get carried away in a flight of character and description and then suddenly you have a grinding change of gear and you have to go into, you know, alibis and who was standing at the top of the stair and all that. Certainly with the Charles Parises I think, aw, hell, now I've got to . . . sort it out. Just when I was enjoying this a bit. It's a problem in crime fiction.

In postscript: English crime fiction contains references that can sometimes be baffling across the Atlantic. I once asked a brother of mine, a lifelong American mystery addict, if any English words or phrases ever mystified him. He wrote back at once:

> What is the story on names, especially the double names of nobility, e.g., John Clayton/Lord Greystoke? How does one get to be a lord and aren't there at least a couple of kinds? What's Debrett? How come so many school holidays? What's "long vac" and when? What's an Oxbridge Blue? "He had an undistinguished university career, a third in history from Oriel." What's a third? A first? Is there a second? What are O levels and A levels?
>
> " 'Dead, sir, in an outside toilet.' 'Lavatory,' growled Thanet, who didn't like euphemisms." In England, is toilet a euphemism for lavatory? What's KC? Is the Isis River at Oxford a part of the Thames? How come an MP doesn't have to live in the place he represents? Games: how do you play Consequences, Snab, Greevy?
>
> Where are the Home Counties? Near London? How come "Home?" "Semidetached": houses? Plimsolls, Wellingtons: are these wellies? Both rubber boots? What is a Christmas pantomime? August Bank Holiday: what's special about cricket matches then?
>
> May Day morning: "Each house had a leafy branch of 'may' secured to its front door."?? "Do you fancy a coffee and a bacon buttie?" "At a caff?" What is this English propensity for abbreviations, like "caff" for the not too cumbersome "cafe"? . . .

It was a long list.

The Top Two

WHAT PEOPLE READ most of the time should be as worth mentioning as what they read almost none of the time. Barbara Cartland, says the *Guinness Book of World Records*, is the world's bestselling author (over 500 million copies of five hundred novels sold—actually the five hundredth came out in February 1990, five months before her eighty-ninth birthday—beating out both Agatha Christie and Erle Stanley Gardner). Jeffrey Archer, as he reminded me himself, is Britain's bestselling author; left with debts of £472,000 (about $800,000) in 1974, today he is reportedly worth over £11 million ($20 million), making him richer from his books than runners-up Catherine Cookson, Frederick Forsyth, Jack Higgins, or even Cartland herself. In 1989, however, John le Carré, with his *glasnost*-era *Russia House*, outsold everybody.

What makes a super-selling author? Q. D. Leavis, wife of the famous critic F. R. Leavis, took a look in the 1930s at the great names in popular fiction and decided they all had more than "sympathetic characters" and "a stirring tale."

> Bad writing, false sentiment, sheer silliness, and a preposterous narrative all are carried along by the magnificent vitality of the author . . .

Author John Mortimer has his own theory: many super-sellers are people in mid-life who need a new career and "it's almost as if it's too late for anything but success."

> A pattern emerges in the lives of the best-selling novelists. Many are not, it seems, born writers; they achieve writing or have it thrust upon them. It happens comparatively late in life and after a successful other career, as a steeplechase jockey, or as the manageress of a workhouse laundry, or, in the case of Frederick Forsyth, as a foreign correspondent. Then comes some disaster, the loss of a job, a nervous breakdown, a horse that unaccountably sits down when in the lead thirty yards from the winning post at Aintree.

Besides Forsyth, Mortimer had Catherine Cookson and Dick Francis in mind, but the pattern fits Jeffrey Archer too. Ruth Rendell guesses that Archer combines everything people want in books nowadays:

> Adventure, money, an international scene, moving around the world, high-powered people.
>
> For some reason people want to read about power, they get a vicarious enjoyment of power. Archer gives them politics at a certain level, scandal in high places, money, money, money, and power . . . I understand Jeffrey Archer's books have very little sex. I think that makes them rather more than less popular. People *do* want sex, but I think when they have it they want *it*, they don't want all the other things going along with it. I imagine Archer writes to a formula and that he calculates every step of the way. There's some sort of vitality there as well.

Times columnist Bernard Levin attributes Barbara Cartland's phenomenal success to her "huge energy."

> She's so good-hearted. And she's such a good sport. She's enormously positive. She has this absurd, wholly romantic view of life. But, she always says, "Isn't it better to have a romantic view than a pessimistic view?" I agree with her. She's on the side of life.

Actress Dame Wendy Hiller finds Barbara Cartland "an extremely clever woman, knows what millions of women want, whether in Oshkosh or Little Rock or Warsaw. She keeps her novels extremely simple, down to basics." Both Levin and Dame Wendy seemed pleased when I told them I had liked Miss Cartland, almost a British institution in her own right, enormously: I found her warm, generous, and fun. In contrast, Jeffrey Archer seemed flat, arrogant, and unlovable at first. Enough superlatives about Mrs. Thatcher ("the most powerful head of state in Europe at the moment, if not the world"), Britain's economy ("I find tremendous prosperity in the North"), or instant praise for anybody whose name came up ("a very impressive man," "a lovely person," "he's brilliant," "one of my best friends," "a great man") can turn anyone off. Still, Archer grows on you.

What Barbara Cartland and Jeffrey Archer have in common besides vitality is that they live in worlds just as glamorous as the ones they write about. Take him first; Archer's rags-to-riches-to-rags-to-riches story is a familiar, continuing saga in Britain. Born in 1940, the son of an army officer, Archer went to public school (Wellington) and Brasenose College, Oxford. He first entered the national limelight as an athlete, representing Britain in the 100 meters in the early 1960s. In 1969 he became the youngest member of the House of Commons. For five years he had a promising political career. The first big setback came when he was forced to resign from Parliament in 1974 after he had invested heavily in a Canadian company, Aquablast, which went into liquidation—three of its directors went to jail for fraud. Archer was left with debts of £472,000 ($800,000), enough to permanently sink most people.

Undaunted, he sat right down in a friend's country house and wrote his first novel, *Not a Penny More, Not a Penny Less.* (A much-quoted remark by his witty wife, Mary, a Cambridge energy expert: "I didn't know he could even write a letter.") Archer's plot turned around four young men who are swindled out of $1 million and get every last cent of it back. The book sold more than a million copies; Archer paid back his debts and started to get rich again. More books followed.

Kane and Abel, his second big hit, says the publisher's blurb, tells of "William Lowell Kane and Abel Rosnovski, one the son of a Boston millionaire, the other a penniless Polish immigrant—two men born the same day on opposite sides of the world, their paths destined to cross in the ruthless struggle to build a fortune." Its sequel, *The Prodigal Daughter,* follows the rise of Abel's daughter, Florentyna, to become President of the United States. Its sequel is *Shall We Tell the President?* ("At 7:30 one evening the FBI learn of a plot to kill her—the 1,572nd threat of the year. An hour later five people know all the details. By 9:30 four of them are dead.") The next novel, *First Among Equals,* describes intrigue in Britain's Parliament and *A Matter of Honor,* 1986, deals with the balance of power between America and the Soviet Union. Archer's first attempt at writing a play, *Beyond a Reasonable Doubt,* has had a long run in the West End. *(The Sunday Times:* ". . . ramshackle and patchily effective . . . Why are they queuing for returns? Answer: it's by Jeffrey Archer.") A second attempt in 1989, *Exclusive,* about a tabloid newspaper, got reviews ranging from "bland" and "turgid" to "embarrassingly awful." It, too, was expected to have a long run.

It all happened in little more than a decade. Archer also made a spectacular political comeback. A Thatcher favorite, in 1985 he was made deputy chairman of the Conservative Party. Again his triumph didn't last. A year later he was forced to resign after the tabloids *The Star* and *News of the World* front-paged stories linking him with a prostitute (he later won £500,000 damages in a libel suit with one and £50,000 in an out-of-court settlement with the other). Archer is a familiar figure at Sotheby's auctions and invests in Renoir, Picasso and Pissarro. Typically English, Archer puts his money in tangible assets. He and Mary, in 1989 appointed the first woman board member of Lloyds Bank, have two children and live in a fashionably redone vicarage near Cambridge.

Archer's London apartment, where I met him, comes right out of one of his novels: high-ceilinged, glass-walled, ego-building. The tenth-floor, riverside half of a high rise on Albert Embankment, looking down on Whitehall, Parliament, and the rest of London's power center, it could pass for the lobby of the Bank of England. A secretary sits at the end of an ultralong conference table in one corner of this vast L-shaped eyrie; Archer's outsized desk is hidden away in the other, as are some good paintings. In between, grouped to look down upon the Olympian panorama of London and the Thames, are lots of Hilton Hotel-style sofas and coffee tables. Archer, short, wiry, athletic, came striding out, telling me I was too early, never mind, ordering coffee and shouting to his secretary, who had just put down a phone, "Well done! Did you get rid of them?"

From the first it was verbal combat. I'd been up North ("I find tremendous confidence up there. Some of them are pretty damn sick of this continual chatter about how they're not doing well"). I quoted critic Sheridan Morley that Mrs. Thatcher divided society ("Bunkum! That's Sheridan pulling his personal left-wing wet, wanky, pullover views. That's a load of drivel").

The ingratiating thing about Jeffrey Archer is just when you decide he's really pugnacious and awful, his face lights up with an impish grin and he says, "I'm teasing, I'm teasing. You mustn't take me so seriously." And you realize that here is Jack the Giant Killer, Jorrocks riding to the hounds, still a Hardy Boy who whooshes to the Pierre or Willard by Concorde, plots how the Americans and Russians almost blow each other up, and does it all with enormous zest. Even wet, wanky Morley was soon forgiven and being praised as "a very impressive man, a very nice man."

And what about all the sixteen-year-old school-leavers unskilled and out of work?

"No one knows better than Americans that the great secret is to travel if you can't get what you want in your area."

"English people don't like to move."

"Well, they should jolly well start."

"Why aren't the English better entrepreneurs?"

"We're a country with a thousand years' history. America's only just begun, Wild West cowboys making good."

Okay, pard, time for a shoot-up. "Compare a supermarket here to one in America. Here the checkout girls sit, there they stand. Here they just shove your groceries aside, there they put them in a bag for you. Here you may have to pay five pence for the bag, there it's free."

Archer bristled, satisfyingly provoked. "Our goods are still as well made as anything America makes. We still work as hard. So let's don't imagine Americans work any harder. Let's don't imagine they are any better. My dealings with Americans, I've found them to be no better than we are."

"In terms of?"

"Energy, determination, ability, brains, culture, history—anything you care to name, we can beat the Americans."

Smile when you say that. "That sounds like anti-Americanism."

"Of course not. I'm a great admirer of Americans. Just because I don't think they're as good as we are, doesn't mean I'm anti-them. There's no connection at all."

"I think Americans would bridle to hear you say that."

"If they do bridle, it shows what very weak intellects they have."

"What do Americans do, when you say you're better—"

"I didn't say we were better," Archer interrupted. "I said we can do as well as they do. Please don't misquote me. As well as, any time."

"That's why I need the tape recorder. So I don't misquote." Did he think Thatcherism would fade away when Mrs. Thatcher left office?

"Good heavens, no. She's the Number One party person. She's a remarkable leader. But eventually she will go. It's called Thatcherism by the press. Not by Mrs. Thatcher. One must accept the fact that she's been Prime Minister since 1979, leader of the party since 1975, still only sixty-five years old. She knows everyone in Europe, she knows everyone in the world. She's dealt with them all. She's now their senior statesman. While still being, in political terms, young."

World leaders gave her respect. "And that in itself is power." Archer expected Mrs. Thatcher to stay as Prime Minister until the mid-1990s. "I think she still feels there's a lot to be done in education, housing, health and that it must be done in her lifetime as

Prime Minister. That's her goal in life. I have no doubt she will achieve it."

The Labour Party, Archer said, didn't know where to go. Too many, he said, enjoyed being in the opposition, enjoyed being disruptive.

"You mean they like calling Mrs. Thatcher Scrooge?"

"Your words, not mine." He said the role of the left was too often merely protest:

It seems to be that of nudging and edging and kicking us because most people do not want a left-wing government running this country. The centrists are even worse. My own view is that we'll drift back to having a sort of wishy-washy jumper-wearing Liberal Party led by a wishy-washy jumper-wearing Liberal leader. When it comes to the next election, they'll get a wishy-washy vote. The only hope is to form a middle-of-the-road party led by David Owen. That would have really frightened the Conservative Party. It would have really frightened us. Owen is the only one who is a credible leader, who's credible as an alternative Prime Minister.

I asked how he felt about so many young people coming down from Oxford and Cambridge and going into the City. He said, "Well, you can't blame them if the pay is four or five times higher than they're going to get in the Civil Service or the Foreign Office or in teaching. And politics is singularly unattractive. The pay is lousy. The hours are lousy. And people are allowed to be rude to you all the time. You stand up in that building"—he gestured down at Parliament—"and they're all tearing you apart."

Archer was full of praise for Thatcherism:

Listen, the standard of living in this country is higher than it's ever been. Wages are higher. Where there's high unemployment, those in jobs are doing better than they've ever done. So maybe there is a minority, a small minority, who are worse off. You can't get everything right. We're not gods, you know.

Archer's flatly confident, upbeat, jingoistic style, like his fiction, seems to belong to a mid-Atlantic cultural no-man's-land. "I love America," he proclaimed. "I'm a great fan. I love the enthusiasm and the life and the spirit." Are Americans his real audience?

"No, no." He was emphatic. "I have sold more books in Britain than any other writer in the world. It's just that the American audience is five times bigger." How does he describe his work?

"Simple stories."

Much-researched?

"Yes. Hours of it."

"Do you enjoy it?"

"Nope." He said he doesn't do interviews as such. "I see people who can help me." He liked writing his plays and seeing them staged. "Pure fun." He also used "fun" to describe parliamentary debate. The give-and-take was "very healthy." He said, "It'd be a good thing if your President got a bit more of it."

Jack the Giant Killer is never repressed for long. "Are you Canadian or American?" he asked.

"American."

"I'd keep rather quiet if I was you. The way your country's economy is being run. In fact the United States of America would love to have Margaret Thatcher as President. You wouldn't be in the trouble you are now."

Barbara Cartland's Who's Who entry, listing all her book titles, is eleven and a half inches long. Born in July 1901, she was still going strong when I interviewed her, keeping five secretaries busy as she dictates up to seven thousand words a day while lying on the sofa in her library. Her daughter, Countess Spencer, who has just learned Japanese and shares her mother's boundless energy, is married to Princess Diana's father.

It was another rainy winter afternoon when I went out to take tea with Barbara Cartland at her country house at Hatfield in Hertfordshire, seventeen miles from London. Camfield Place a four-hundred-acre estate, once belonged to the grandfather of Beatrix Potter; she wrote *The Tale of Peter Rabbit* there. I approached the stately old manor house on foot up a curving drive, having taken a taxi from the station to the gate. A black Labrador greeted me. This was Duke, a present to Miss Cartland from Earl Mountbatten of Burma, Admiral of the Fleet, the Christmas before he was assassinated in August 1979. The IRA blew up his yacht at Mullaghmore in County Sligo, Ireland, just as he and a fourteen-year-old grandson were going out for a sail.

The house itself was ivy-covered and imposingly grand. Mrs. Hazel Clark, a secretary whom I'd talked to on the phone, showed me into the library. There was shelf after shelf of Barbara Cartland's books: *The Hidden Heart, Again This Rapture, The Fire of Love, Lost Enchantment, Listen to Love,* hundreds of them. And not just novels: a biography of her brother, the first member of Parliament to be killed at Dunkirk in World War II (with a foreword by Winston

Churchill). The lives of Charles II, Empress Elizabeth of Austria, Empress Josephine of France, Diane de Poitiers, Metternich, King Carol; sociology *(You in the Home, Be Vivid, Be Vital, Sex and the Teenager, Look Lovely, Be Lovely);* cookbooks *(Recipes for Lovers, The Romance of Food),* advice *(Getting Older, Growing Younger).*

When Mrs. Clark took me into the drawing room, I expected it to be all in pink. Instead there were gleams of rose and yellow and pale green, fresh and artificial flowers, chandeliers, comfortable sofas, polished antique tables, enormous windows looking out onto acres of a Capability Brown landscape with beechwoods, two lakes, and riding trails. Barbara Cartland herself, rising with hand extended, was in pink, a bundle of energy and warmth behind what Gwen Robyns in Miss Cartland's authorized biography calls the famous "golden floss" hair and "outrageously false eyelashes." Randolph Churchill called her "the prettiest girl in the twenties I'd ever seen," and one could believe it. She was glad I'd brought my tape recorder.

"It's so terribly boring while people scribble, with their heads down not looking at me, fussing with their beastly little things." She'd been writing. "I have been doing an enormous amount of research for this book I am doing, which is exhausting. *A Year of Royal Days.* Every day has to be something which happened to royalty. Nobody can do the research except me. They just give me boring items about people dying or having their heads cut off. And what I want is amusing stories."

We talked about a famous television interview she once gave Mike Wallace on CBS's "60 Minutes." I told her she had given as good as she had got from perhaps America's toughest interviewer. She laughed. "No, no. He's charming to women. So he is quite easy . . . I'll tell you one thing: the interviews in America, all the press, are not half as difficult as the British, who can be perfectly foul. What I minded very much was when I was given an important award at Kennedy Airport in 1984, for thinking of carrying the first airplane-towed glider airmail in 1931, not one single English paper carried the story. I think that is very wrong." She went on:

I've just been given the Gold Medal of Paris. It's for achievement. I've sold 25 million books in France. It was at the Hôtel de Ville. In the evening my publishers bought an hour on television for a million francs. They had Charles Aznavour to sing these love songs. And I came on with masses of pink roses. And pink rose petals fell on my head. After we went outside—bitterly cold, pouring rain—and sat in a white

Rolls-Royce and they had "B.C." in pink fireworks, within a pink heart, and big pink roses in the sky. Marvelous.

Her fondness for pink, as well as turquoise, she says, comes from a visit to Tutankhamen's tomb soon after it was discovered in 1922; she has worn pink ever since. A great traveler, Miss Cartland had been to Hong Kong, Penang, Bangkok, Budapest, Scotland, India, and France just that year. I asked about eating and drinking.

Food in the East is perfectly all right, as long as you eat things that are cooked. What you mustn't have is one drop of water, don't you see? You can't have ice. They never do that properly. And you have to clean your teeth with bottled water. Years ago in India I was having lunch with Prime Minister Nehru. I had Indira Gandhi on one side of me and Pandit Nehru on the other. And I said, "Can I drink this water?" Indira said, "I'll go fetch you some." I said, "Look, I want to see your Minister of Health." And so I had the medical help sent up. I said to him, "For goodness sake, do have bottled water! You know your water upsets Westerners. And if you have one upset tummy, the Americans run for home." Tourism was then their fifth biggest foreign exchange earner. I said, "You need the tourists." A month ago I gave a luncheon party for the Maharajah of Kashmir. He had been Minister of Health at the time and he said, "It is entirely due to Barbara Cartland that we have bottled water in India."

Barbara Cartland met Nehru and Indira Gandhi through Lord Mountbatten, when he was Britain's last Viceroy, and his wife. "They introduced me to everybody. So I always have a wonderful time in India. I had known Edwina Mountbatten since 1910. It's a long time to know anybody." Later, President Anwar Sadat became a Cartland reader when Mountbatten gave Mrs. Sadat some of the novels. Once when the Egyptian president visited America and was asked, "How do you relax?" he told reporters he read Barbara Cartland novels. (He also, he told me one time in an interview, liked cowboy movies.)

There was a large portrait of Lord Mountbatten ("Uncle Dickie" to the Queen) in the drawing room. I said I gathered he had been a close friend. "I knew him for fifty years," Miss Cartland answered. I said that when I was in India, I did hear rumors about Nehru and Lady Mountbatten, adding, "It could of course have been platonic."

"I do know," Barbara Cartland replied, "that Nehru was very much in love with Edwina. He wrote me a wonderful letter about her after she died in 1960. A beautiful letter."

I remembered seeing Nehru, then himself dying, at his last Republic Day Parade in 1964 with Lord Mountbatten and his daughter and that afternoon at a garden party at Sir Edwin Lutyen's Rashtrapati Bhavan, what was during the British Raj the Viceroy's palace. (In *Barbara Cartland,* published in 1984, Gwen Robyns calls the friendship between Lord Mountbatten and Miss Cartland an *"amitie amoureuse."* She quotes Miss Cartland: "Of course I was in love with Dickie like a million other women. I loved him very much, and he loved me too, but we were both far too old to be anything but very close, and if you like, romantic friends.")

I asked Barbara Cartland why she kept on working so hard.

"That is a frightfully rude question," she answered, flaring up with indignation. "In other words you're saying: when are you going to die?" As I protested, aghast, "No, no, no . . . You could travel, enjoy . . ." she went on, "What else would I do? What else would old people do? Except do nothing. Wait for death." She went on:

> Old people should keep on working. In Russia they've got women of ninety who do a full day's work. And I'm sure a full day's work in Russia is a full day's work. It's typical of the English to think, you know, if you're old, you should sit and do nothing. Why? Why should you sit and do nothing? You have got your brains, unless you are taking tranquilizers. You have got your expertise. Older people all agree with me. But they still push Granny into the nursing home. And they *insist,* in the homes and the hospitals, that the inmates take a sleeping pill every night. Sleeping pills rot your brain. They rotted Winston Churchill's, rotted everybody's. If I took one aspirin, I couldn't dictate.

As it is, she is up early to spend the morning answering letters and writing newspaper and magazine articles; that day she had done two, one of eight hundred words and another of five hundred, and answered over fifty letters. Before lunch she walks around the garden with Duke, the Labrador, and Mai Mai, a Pekingese from Chiang Mai in Thailand (its predecessor, Twi-Twi, was the only living dog to be sculptured in Madame Tussaud's).

> Then I work from a quarter past one to a quarter past three. I do a chapter, of six to seven thousand words, every day when I'm home. I would have done today but we are two secretaries short today, home ill, which is terribly annoying. When I dictate, I just lie on the sofa and shut my eyes and tell a story. I do very little alteration. Novels I dictate and other things I write in my own hand. I like doing my own research. It is terribly hard work, I may tell you, because I am getting rather blind. Most of the pages have to be enlarged for me.

The same secretary, Audrey Elliot, has taken down most of the books in shorthand the past seventeen years. The five hundredth novel, *The Spirit of Love*, like most of the rest, took seven days to write. Barbara Cartland thinks her huge book sales are because her books bring people "beauty and love."

> In France an old woman came up to me in the Hôtel de Ville and she said, "You make me so happy." You see, that is the point. My books are happy books. Evil is overcome by good. People really fall in love. I'm still writing about *true* love, which is both physical and spiritual. Like Romeo and Juliet, Dante and Beatrice. Everybody else just writes about sex.

At the peak of the romantic novel's popularity, she said, she sold almost a million copies of every book she wrote. Then came the "permissive era" when writers were told by their publishers, she said, to write like Barbara Cartland with pornography. "You can see where they've slotted it in. Not very cleverly." Today, she went on, everyone is back to virgins. "What has happened, and it's been an awful shock, is that we've got AIDS. The girls must go back to being a virgin before marriage. I've always been very moral. My heroine may *not* go to bed until she has the ring on her finger." (*A Hazard of Hearts* ends: "His kiss, demanding, possessive, passionate, seemed to draw her very soul between her lips, and then she felt herself lifted high against his heart and heard him say in a tone of supreme triumph: 'Mine—my darling, my *wife*—my perfect love.'" (Italics mine.)

Miss Cartland's first novel to be filmed, *A Hazard of Hearts* was shown on American television by CBS in 1988, the first of a series. (Christopher Plummer loses fortune, stately home, and daughter to villainous Edward Fox on the roll of the dice but Helena Bonham Carter falls into the hands of the handsome, heartless Marquis of Vulcan, played by newcomer Marcus Gilbert, until love—and a marriage proposal—triumphs.) Aside from writing, Miss Cartland has also made *Album of Love Songs* with the Royal Philharmonic Orchestra. Since 1979 there has been an all-pink "Barbara Cartland Suite" at Bangkok's Oriental Hotel (there are Somerset Maugham and Noël Coward suites too).

Among causes Barbara Cartland has championed is one for gypsies so their children can go to school.

> Nothing had been done since the reign of Henry VIII. So I said, "Well, you may not like gypsies"—most people don't like gypsies—"but you cannot discriminate and have education for everybody except them. If they are moved every twenty-four hours the children cannot go to school." I had a bitter three-year fight but eventually won. And Keith

Joseph, who was then Home Secretary, said that every local authority had to provide camps for their gypsies.

In 1986 she campaigned to bring prayers back to state-run schools:

> That appalling Archbishop of Canterbury allowed prayers to go out of state schools. Without *one* word of opposition. You have to send your son to Eton to have him taught about God. I think it's appalling.

Her own two sons went to Harrow, a third generation there. Miss Cartland herself taught Sunday School as a girl so her mother would let her go to tea dances Sunday afternoons.

> Guidelines have always come through religion. Now the only guidelines some children get is: "Don't get caught by the police; they are your enemy." I was a County Counselor in Hertfordshire for nine years, a very noisy one.

Despite her present wealth, Barbara Cartland looks back fondly on her early days, when she admits there were hard times. "We were very poor after my father was killed in Flanders in 1918," she said. A son looks after her finances now. "I never have anything to do with money. I don't understand it. I can't be bothered." Gwen Robyns tells in her biography about Miss Cartland buying secondhand dresses to go dancing in London. I asked her about it.

> They were cheap. And then we went on doing it during the war. My daughter Raine was presented at Buckingham Palace in a dress I bought at a secondhand shop. We had no coupons, you see. It cost three and a half guineas. A Molyneux. It was very beautiful. Lots of girls today go to the Oxfam shops and get very nice clothes.

She was a reader from an early age.

> As a child I loved "The Princess and the Goblin." Remember that one? And we always had lovely religious books with pictures in them . . . When I was grown up my brother, Ronald, who was a great influence in my life, said, "You are terribly uneducated." So I read the whole of Jane Austen, the whole of Anthony Trollope, in one sitting. I was about twenty-one.

Ronald and her other brother were killed in World War II. Barbara Cartland also lost her father, an uncle, and several cousins in the trench warfare of 1914–18, and her second husband, Hugh McCorquodale, died in his sixties of wounds at Passchendaele. I said she had suffered a lot of loss in her life.

"I think everybody of my age has." Again it brought home how profoundly Britain has been affected by two world wars. She said:

> If you realize, when I was growing up, that every house in this country had a casualty. People have forgotten that now. You know, they forget. We lost a whole generation in the First World War. We just put them in France to be killed. Appalling slaughter. Appalling. My husband eventually died of his wounds. He received the military cross for gallantry. But it was a complete slaughter. Those stupid old generals.

During the interview, Mai Mai, the Pekingese, slept curled up, a warm bundle in my lap, with Duke, jealous, shoving his nose up all the time, wanting to be petted. When we went into the baronial dining room for tea—the table must have sat twenty—the two of them came with us and Miss Cartland, who ate nothing herself (she lives on health food and vitamins), fed them homemade biscuits. We talked about her books. "The period I like to write about is between 1790 and 1900," she said, "because the hero doesn't have to wear a wig. I don't think the Duke taking off his wig in bed is very romantic."

During tea a telephone rang off somewhere and Mrs. Clark came in. "Sorry to bother you," she told Miss Cartland. "It's Harriet Riley from Radio Bedfordshire. This Friday is called 'Comic Relief Day.' They're trying to raise a lot of money for starving Africans. And Radio Bedfordshire is doing a program on jokes. From unlikely people. She thought you were an unlikely person. They would ring up and record it over the telephone. Would you be prepared to take part?"

"Yes, of course," said Miss Cartland without hesitation. "Can anybody think of a joke?" She commanded me: "Think of a joke." And called after Mrs. Clark, "And you jolly well think of a joke. I can't think of a joke at all."

She fed Duke another biscuit. "Think of a joke." Miss Cartland had a good sense of humor. Earlier when I said the house was very grand, she said, "It looks like a railway station, doesn't it?" She thought of one:

> I always think of this as a good joke. One day King Edward VII arrived for lunch and there were thirteen at table. So he wouldn't sit down. And one person was late. So he got more and more and more annoyed. He began to tap his fingers, which was a sure sign he was annoyed. At last a young subaltern arrived. And the king said, "Why the hell are you late?" "I'm sorry, Sir," the young man replied. "I didn't start soon enough." It was Winston Churchill.

I laughed politely. Miss Cartland said, "I never think women are very good with jokes. Men tell them better. A Scotsman, an Irishman, and a pig, you know what I mean? They could tell it. Not women. Well, think of a joke. Think of a joke."

For a while we talked of starving Ethiopians. Miss Cartland wondered if they ever got the money or whether we were really sending machine guns to their enemies. The conversation drifted to the theater and dining out in London. She said:

> It is an awful effort to go to London and if I go out late I can't work the next day. I would much rather come back to my dogs, my hot water bottles, my room all ready for me. If I had a glorious young man to go out to dinner and to go dancing with . . . Now I'm too old for that. So I stay at home . . . I have amusing luncheon parties at weekends and last week I had my grandson, Lord Lewisham, staying here.

We talked on in the empty splendor of the enormous dining hall, just us and Duke and Mai Mai, huddled at one end of the table, having a pleasant time. At last a joke came to mind, fittingly told to me by an English grande dame, so maybe it would be all right.

> Two old spinsters lived together. One died and the other went to a clairvoyant to try to get in touch with her. The spirit was summoned and her friend said, "Oh, Edith, are you all right?" "Oh, yes, I'm having a wonderful time. It's sex in the morning, sex in the afternoon, sex in the evening." "Oh, Edith, surely not in Heaven!" "Who said anything about Heaven? I'm a rabbit in the warren behind the wood."

This time we really laughed. I urged her to tell that one.

"I can't tell that," she protested. "Don't you see? No, no, they would be shocked to death. I think it is a very good funny story. I think it is terribly funny. But they would be shocked to death to hear it from Barbara Cartland."

V

MASTERY
OF WORDS–
PERFORMING ARTS

Twilight of a Golden Age

"THE PLAY'S THE THING," William Shakespeare wrote, and he left behind him the English theatrical tradition and the most widely known drama and poetry in all literature. "We invented the business," says drama critic Sheridan Morley. "Apart from the Greeks we were the first ones with a really coherent theater." The origins of English stagecraft go back to the Norman Conquest and French and Latin dominance of the English court, universities, and monasteries, says Robert McCrum, coauthor of *The Story of English*. McCrum told me:

> You had a society occupied by a foreign power for three hundred years. So that people's art found oral expression. The theater grew out of religion and ritual. The first plays were performed with torches inside great cathedrals. And from there it was quite a short step to William Shakespeare. And all that follows. It is a combination of the history of the country and the accident of Shakespeare that has made theater the most English literary form. The novel is European, not quintessentially English, as drama is. If one wants to look at our supposed mastery of words it is in the performing arts where one has to look most carefully.

In a society famous for its pageantry—Trooping the Color, State Opening of Parliament, Changing of the Guard—where royalty still rides in gilded horse-drawn carriages and maypole dancing lives on in villages, the flair for theater obviously runs deep. Hence, even before Shakespeare the English were more sympathetic to the idea of acting than most of Europe, where it tended to be a trade for vagabonds and gypsies. London's first playhouse, known simply as The Theatre, was opened by actor James Burbage in 1576 when Shakespeare was a boy of twelve. Burbage and his more famous son Richard helped to start the Blackfriars in an old Dominican friary. Even in England, as Christopher Hibbert tells us in *London,* the city's authorities attacked the theaters as

. . . hotbeds of the vice and plague, as rendezvous for the idle and li-
centious, for evil men excited by boys dressed up as women, and for all
those who would rather answer the call of the trumpet to a play than
the tolling of a bell to a sermon.

It remains a marvel how a man of humble origins wrote our greatest dramatic masterpieces. Eighteenth-century scholar George
Steevens wrote:

All that is known with any degree of certainty is that he was born in
Stratford-upon-Avon, married and had children there, went to London
where he commenced being an actor and wrote poems and plays, returned to Stratford, made his will, died and was buried.

Today little more is known of his life from 1582, when at age eighteen he married Anne Hathaway, until 1592, when he was established in the London theatrical world. From 1594 on he was a member of the Lord Chamberlain's Company, supported by the court of
Queen Elizabeth, which later, under James I, became the King's
Men. By 1597, in the brilliant last years of the Elizabethan age (Elizabeth died in 1603), Shakespeare was rich enough to buy New Place,
the second-best house in Stratford. By 1613 he apparently retired
permanently to it. He died three years later when just fifty-two.

The prestige of the acting profession continued to rise with
David Garrick's triumph as Richard III a century later in 1741, followed by mounting applause for his Lear, Hamlet, and Macbeth,
and Edmund Kean's success as Shylock in 1814 and his great performances as Richard III, Macbeth, Iago, and Barabas in *The Jew of
Malta.* Henry Irving, whose Hamlet ran for two hundred nights in
1874, made the Lyceum the first theater in England, with Ellen
Terry as his leading lady (she was Sir John Gielgud's great-aunt).
When Irving got the first theatrical knighthood in 1895, the profession became respectable. (Today, on Bradford's Manningham Lane,
you can see the derelict Theatre Royal where Irving gave his last
performance; the hotel just down the hill, where he died, is still running.) With Laurence Olivier, in 1970 the first theatrical peer, Shakespeare was brought on movie and television screens for millions. Sir
Peter Hall gave a fitting epitaph when Olivier died in July 1989: "He
was perhaps the greatest man of the theater ever."

"We had the background, what we never really had was the
money," is the way Sheridan Morley puts it. Elizabeth, who numbered lyric poet Sir Philip Sidney among her courtiers (Edmund
Spenser honored her as *The Faerie Queene),* was fond of plays and

pageants; she extended the European system of royal patronage for painters and sculptors to the theater, including the Globe. Stratford was just a four-day ride away and it was in late Tudor London, when the old Queen was ailing on her throne, that the young actor-playwright was a London sensation; she saw many of Shakespeare's plays. James I's reign and the early Stuart years saw the full flowering of Shakespeare's genius when in 1601–05 he produced the four great tragedies of *Hamlet, Othello, King Lear,* and *Macbeth.*

Sheridan Morley says it is now quite natural to look to Britain's Arts Council in much the way Shakespeare did to the court. "We have always had a tradition of patronage," he told me. "At least up until the Thatcher government there has always been the theory that arts somehow are to be funded by the government."

Government patronage of the performing arts has become a burning issue under Mrs. Thatcher, just as the theater itself is in the twilight of its Golden Age. Bernard Levin remembers it well at its peak:

> I cut my teeth on the Old Vic Company, as it was called, just before and after the end of the Second World War. The company included, at one and the same time, Laurence Olivier, Ralph Richardson, Alec Guinness, Sybil Thorndike, Pamela Brown, Margaret Leighton, Harry Andrews, Lewis Casson . . . And Gielgud had his own company with Peggy Ashcroft, Michael Redgrave, almost as star-studded. I mean it was the greatest constellation possibly ever gathered together. Both repertory companies offered a feast of classical acting for a good many years.

Levin told me he feels English acting has changed sharply since then.

> There's a very different breed of actors now. Take Simon Callow, a good example. A good actor but not in the old classical tradition. And if asked would say he didn't want to be. The style of speaking Shakespeare has changed utterly. Meaning is all. Poetry comes a poor second. Interpretation is much, much more to the fore. Production itself looms larger.

Sir John Gielgud, who like Dame Peggy Ashcroft (whom we shall talk to later) is in his eighties, is one of the few survivors of the Golden Age still performing as we enter the 1990s. Outside the Apollo Theatre on Shaftesbury Avenue one night near curtain time of his *Best of Friends* in 1988, when Gielgud at eighty-three returned to the West End stage after ten years in television and films, I heard a plump blond woman with a Texas accent tell her teenage son: "You *must* remember him! He was the butler in *Arthur. You* know." Oh, yeah," the boy muttered. *"Him."*

I went to *The Best of Friends,* Hugh Whitemore's gentle celebration of friendship, three times, sitting in the front row just a few feet away from Gielgud. Dame Wendy Hiller told me after seeing it, "It's a charming evening. But it's not a play. We are so lucky to have Sir John back performing in the West End. He was riveting and moving." I asked Dame Wendy, interviewed before Olivier's death, if she felt a Golden Age was ending:

> We've lost Richardson, Thorndike, Evans, Redgrave . . . So many my age. It's true. There were a bunch of them all right. But I don't hold with ideas of theatrical decline. All you need is four boards, three walls, two actors, and a passion.

Gielgud himself sees great changes in the English stage. He told Sheridan Morley over lunch during rehearsals for *The Best of Friends:*

> In the theatre now they regard me as some terrible old Dalai Lama. They asked me to address the company at Stratford last year and I really couldn't think of anything at all useful to say. The style is so different, and I dread going backstage because I know I'll just drop another brick.

In another interview Gielgud said, "All we have left is the English language. Can it be salvaged, is my question." He'd moved in the late 1970s from London to a country home near Thame. He told Morley he had begun to "hate a lot of what was happening in the modern theatre":

> I can't bear the belief directors now have that they must impose their own academic ideas onto classic texts. In my time we knew that the audience had enough trouble dealing with the Shakespearean verse, let alone a lot of modern-dress relevance as well. I think that's partly why I turned to the cinema . . . And now I'm really very happy on a foreign location where they all call you Jack and have never heard of the Old Vic.

In the 1980s, amid terrorist scares, dollar slumps and the '87 crash, the London theater boomed as never before. When I talked to Sheridan Morley (who is the son of actor Robert Morley) at his office at *Punch* near Fleet Street, fifteen hit musicals were playing in the West End and five British musicals were on Broadway: *Les Misérables, Starlight Express, The Phantom of the Opera, Me and My Girl,* and *Cats.*

"Money is pouring in. The theater is booming," said Morley. But this was not all to the good.

Look a little bit closer. What is the money pouring toward? New and old musicals. Look around the West End. You're not getting exciting new plays. You're not getting dangerous plays. And why? Because this government believes the box office must be the final source of profitability. You pay for what you get. So you pay for a good night out. You pay for *South Pacific.* You pay for *Cats.*

We are in danger of becoming Broadway. A kind of waxwork museum for safe old shows, a Madame Tussaud's. It means big old shows in big old theaters for big old audiences. It does not mean experiment, danger, novelty, courage.

What's wrong with that? say the Thatcherites. Norman Tebbit, when I asked him about subsidized theater, said, "Look at the theater which is making the biggest impact in the United States."

It's not Peter Hall and the Royal Shakespeare. It's *The Phantom of the Opera.* That might not be great art. But those musicals, in my view, are just as great art as Gilbert and Sullivan. Now these days Gilbert and Sullivan is art. But they were a product of commercialism. Gilbert and Sullivan, they weren't banging on about art, they were banging on about the box office.

Luke Rittner, the Arts Council's executive director, caught in the middle, told me a lot of people say the British theater is in crisis:

Mrs. Thatcher has come in. She doesn't go to plays. She doesn't like plays. So the intellectual world feels very beleaguered at the moment. They feel this country is moving into a free-for-all, me-first sort of society that is totally alien. Sir Peter Hall says Mrs. Thatcher is destroying the artistic life of the nation. He believes passionately that the state has a duty to support the arts and that it's not living up to its duty.

Lord Rees-Mogg, a Tory and former chairman of the Arts Council, told me that annual arts subsidies were running close to £380 million ($650 million), £150 million coming from the government-funded Arts Council itself, £25–£30 million from private sponsorship and the rest from local authorities. He argues:

That is a very substantial amount of public support, much more than in the United States, less than in Europe. But the European system has meant gross overmanning of most cultural institutions and low productivity in the arts. The Vienna Opera House employs five times as many people as the Royal Opera House at Covent Garden. It's very difficult to see that it produces better operas or more performances. The Arts Council employs about a hundred and fifty people; France's Ministry of

Culture employs fifteen hundred. This kind of bureaucratization is positively harmful to the arts.

Lord Rees-Mogg claims subsidized theater in modern Britain goes back just to 1939:

> It is true that the English regional repertory theater has produced a remarkable number of fine character actors. But all the great figures of the British theatre—Olivier, Richardson, Gielgud, Peggy Ashcroft, that generation—were all presubsidization.

A subsidized theater means a government often ends up funding satires of itself. In 1985 the National Theatre's hit play *Pravda* lampooned Rees-Mogg himself. In it, a press baron resembling Rupert Murdoch takes over Fleet Street's finest newspaper, the *Victory (The Times* thinly disguised) and fires its editor, Elliot Fruit-Norton (as Murdoch fired Rees-Mogg). Out of a job, the ex-editor meets the press:

> FRUIT-NORTON: Viewed in the evening light of history, my tenure at the *Victory* may seem only a passing shadow. But the unique qualities of civilization which I have sought to advance are sempiternal. Addison, Steele, Johnson. These have been my constant companions, and as I retire now to spend my time with my wife Gilda, my animals and my two strapping lads, I know that friendly ghosts of the great journalists will join us for dinner at our Suffolk home in Much Blakely.

Rees-Mogg himself was appointed to head the Arts Council and then to head Mrs. Thatcher's new British Standards Council to monitor sex and violence on television (and some fear, engage in censorship). (Fruit-Norton is merely appointed "Chairman of the National Greyhound Racetrack Inspection Board.") Rees-Mogg was also given a peerage. When his name came up in a talk with Simon Callow, the actor groaned and said:

> William Rees-Mogg is the kind of person that just his existence depresses one. And this is the real England where a Rees-Mogg gets recycled from one eminence to another without any distinction having been exercised in any of his capacities. I mean his chairmanship of the Arts Council was an utter pompous disaster.

In the thick of the debate is Sir Peter Hall, Britain's best-known stage director, who ran the National Theatre in 1973–88, taking over from Laurence Olivier. The son of a railwayman and a scholarship student at Cambridge, Hall directed what became the Royal Shakespeare Company at Stratford when just twenty-nine and moved it to London before supervising the move of the National Theatre to the South Bank of the Thames. He brought to Shakespeare new ideas for ensemble playing and ways of speaking the text. Hall is in continual hot water. In 1986, along with Trevor Nunn, who took over from him at the Royal Shakespeare Company, Hall was accused of making huge American royalties from subsidized theater, most notably from *Amadeus*. His startlingly frank *Diaries*, published in 1983, tell of clashes (even with Olivier), delays, press attacks, firings, and strikes that still leave scars. Lord Rees-Mogg, when I asked him about Sir Peter Hall, said, "He's rather like Cardinal Wolsey, a useful thug."

He is also, Lord Rees-Mogg went on to say, a very gifted director. Simon Callow, who was the original Mozart in Hall's staging of Peter Shaffer's *Amadeus*, said Sir Peter is able to call from his audiences "a hunger . . . a feeling that they are at last getting what they have done without for too long." Hall himself, interviewed in his modest, cluttered office when he was still at the National, did look rather thuglike, unshaven and in a black leather jacket. He argued that English culture itself was threatened by Thatcherite economic zeal. Sir Peter:

> Subsidized theater has had a wonderful record since the Second World War. It has bred new playwrights, new actors, new directors, new designers. All these talents fed into television and went around the world. They dominate serious drama on American public television. The reason we have not been able to convince the Thatcher government of the value of this is their religious dogma that subsidy distorts market forces. It's religious zeal. And like any religious zeal, it's not susceptible to rational argument. What I fear is that by reducing subsidy to the performing arts and by opening the airwaves to universal satellite television, we're going to attack our language and our culture.

I said critics called Mrs. Thatcher and her Cabinet Philistines. "That's true," Hall said. "But I've never found a government yet that wasn't Philistine. They don't have time for anything else." Actually Nigel Lawson, the former Chancellor of Exchequer, was editor of the *Spectator*; Trade and Industry Secretary Nicholas Ridley does watercolors; Kenneth Baker edited *The Faber Book of English History in Verse* in 1988. Most surprisingly, Douglas Hurd has coauthored seven crime novels and two political thrillers; from *The Palace of Enchantments*, 1985:

This was the beginning of Edward's London, the London of state visits and royalty, of resplendent parks, clubs and government departments, Parliament and Privy Council meetings within the palace he had just passed. Of course it was not the only London, perhaps not the real London, but there was good in its pretences and pageantries, and he did not regret his part in them.

Radical as he sounds, Sir Peter Hall called himself "a militant classicist" when it came to performing Shakespeare. When I quoted the views of Bernard Levin and Sir John Gielgud, he said, "I'm on their side." Hall said, "I hate conceptual theater"; he also saw a decline in the way younger actors speak.

> Over the last ten years with the reduction of grants, almost none of our regional theaters can afford to do Shakespeare. So young actors don't get the experience. It takes at least twenty. Most regional theaters can't afford casts of more than six or eight. So very little Shakespeare is done any more outside the Royal Shakespeare Company and the National Theatre. That's the economic factor. I also think we're living in a society which is increasingly unverbal. It's more and more pictorial. Words are sloppier and less valued. We're almost at the point now that if somebody talks well, you distrust them.

Geraldine James, who played Portia to Dustin Hoffman's Shylock in Hall's *Merchant of Venice* this past Broadway season, found the way the Hollywood film star focused on character rather than language helped her "play a lot more physical a Portia than I might have."

> Because British actors hold Shakespeare in such reverence, we tend to go for the word, which tends to make things very intellectual.

Geraldine, whom we'll hear more from later, says Hoffman also came up with an interesting idea about transatlantic acting differences.

> He said that American actors tend to stress the little words—it's what we English love about American actors, because it's so natural. They tend to go for the pronouns, whereas the British tend to go for the verbs, the nouns. Dustin tended to say things like "what *you* believe," whereas Shakespeare does "what you *believe.*" Stressing the big words in Shakespeare tends to make it clear—go for the words that move, the words that are about a verb. That's Peter Hall's way.

Sheridan Morley agrees with Hall there is less Shakespeare done all the time.

Shakespeare will never pay for itself. A cast of forty carrying spears is never going to be economic in the theater. A dangerous new play is never going to get sponsorship.

(Even John Ford's classic seventeenth-century play, *'Tis Pity She's a Whore*, when the National staged it, could not get private support, corporation executives being leery of the title.) Says Morley: "The whole theory of sponsorship, what they call incentive funding, only really applies to the tried and tested, the safe and cheerful." Morley sees a danger in both Britain and America that the most innovative theater will desert the West End and Broadway and move out to the regions, in Britain to "isolated outposts like the Bush, the Royal Court, the Manchester Royal Exchange, the Glasgow Citizens'," in America to "Joe Papp at the Public, Playwrights Horizons in New York, Steppenwolf in Chicago."

Others see Britain's regional repertory theater in sharp decline. Wendy Hiller told me:

We're losing it. And you can only learn acting by acting. The idea of getting businesses to sponsor plays is moving toward American-style commercialism. He who pays the piper calls the tune. You can't expect big corporations to want to pay for *Hedda Gabler*.

She agreed with Peter Hall that there was some decline in the use of English itself, saying, "It wasn't helped by the Church abandoning the King James Bible, one of the vandalisms of the twentieth century." Appearing in the American play *Driving Miss Daisy* while I was in London, Dame Wendy, now in her late seventies, was still working. Just before I talked to her she had been filming a television adaptation of P. D. James's *A Taste for Death* ("I'd much rather have been the tramp who gets killed but I was boring old Lady Ursula").

To me she'll always be Eliza Doolittle. ("I've had fifty-odd years of hard work in other roles, but it's *Pygmalion* people want to talk about.") I can still remember, as a boy of seven or eight, going to the 1938 film and seeing an image of elegance that fifty years later is still fixed in my mind. Higgins, a professor of phonetics, has taken a bet he can turn the Cockney flower seller in six months into a lady who can pass as a duchess. It is Leslie Howard and he is saying, "Yes, you squashed cabbage leaf, you disgrace to the noble architecture of these columns, you incarnate insult to the English language, I can pass you off as the Queen of Sheba." And then it is an ambassador's residence in London, awning and carpet across the sidewalk; a grand reception is on. A crowd of onlookers presses forward as a

Rolls-Royce drives up. A man in evening dress hands out a young Wendy Hiller in opera cloak, glittery dress, diamonds, flowers. The camera follows the party up a grand staircase as one liveried man-servant after another calls out Eliza's name. The camera focuses on her dazzled, proud face as she moves into the ballroom; I can see her now, every bit the duchess. George Bernard Shaw after seeing Wendy Hiller in *Saint Joan* on the stage insisted she do the films of *Pygmalion* and *Major Barbara*. Who can forget her Eliza?

MRS. HIGGINS: Will it rain, do you think?

ELIZA: The shallow depression in the west of these islands is likely to move slowly in an easterly direction . . . What is wrong with that, young man? I bet I got it right.

Simon Callow, one of the most thoughtful actors in the English theater, agreed we are in the twilight of a Golden Age of acting.

A lot of things came together to create it. There were more theaters by the Second World War. The war had something to do with it too. You can't really think about modern English life without going back to the war. And I think the famous seasons of Olivier and Richardson and Gielgud very much grew out of this tremendous sense of mission and excitement. People wanted to see extraordinary performances that would affirm their heritage.

Though Callow himself wasn't born until four years after the war ended, he senses it was a grander time:

There's a big question whether great acting, as it's been understood in the age of Olivier, Richardson, Gielgud, and so on, can exist in a world which has no reference points for the qualities generally embodied in great acting, namely heroism, nobility, leadership, all that. Our acting has shrunk to mirror the world as it exists.

Also the actual structure of the theater no longer conspires, in its hierarchical way, to groom people to become great actors. The theater is so much more democratic now. Everybody is on equal terms with everybody else. Except for a few, few people.

I met Callow during the run of Goethe's *Faust*, Parts One and Two, which was shown in Britain for the first time, all eight hours of it, Callow playing the title role himself. He'd also just directed a West End comedy about a Liverpool housewife who runs off to Greece, Willy Russell's *Shirley Valentine*, later a successful film in America, and was rehearsing the role of Guy Burgess for the National Theatre's production of Alan Bennett's *Single Spies*. Callow may be London's busiest, smartest, and least pretentious actor-director. He popped up the other night on American television as Mr. Micawber in *David Copperfield*. That evening he invited me to join him for dinner, which turned out to be baked potatoes and chili in a hole-in-the-wall called the Spud U Like Club just down the street from Hammersmith's Lyric Theatre, where *Faust* was playing. He was doing Part Two that night. Once I got the Pakistani waiter to turn down the rock music, Callow talked about the theater.

I'd read his 1984 book, *Being an Actor*, part autobiography, part manifesto:

> The important thing is to restore the writer—whether dead or alive—and the actor to each other, without the self-elected intervention of the director, claiming a unique position interpreting the one to the other. We don't need an interpreter—we speak the same language; or at least we used to.

A native Londoner, born in 1949, Callow spent three childhood years in Africa, chose to study at Queen's University, Belfast, and is also the author of a biography of Charles Laughton. Americans know him best for roles in the films *A Room with a View*, *Maurice*, and Amadeus. In Britain he is most widely recognized as the zany star of a popular sitcom, "Chance of a Lifetime." He is currently directing Vanessa Redgrave in a film adaptation of Carson McCullers's novel *The Ballad of the Sad Café*. European audiences, especially German, swarmed to *Faust;* I saw both parts from early afternoon to nearly midnight the same day. The staging resembled an assault course with an arched metal climbing frame toward the back of the stage; Mephistopheles suspended himself from it in scene after scene. Everybody had to be acrobatic; sometimes a whole gymnasium descended—ladders, lassos, and a vast wall of rope netting they all climbed. The young, athletic cast appeared nude in a pagan Greek sequence, dreamily moving through dimly lit fountains, swimming in glass tanks, some of them draped in fishnet. Callow himself emerged completely naked and dripping from a translucent witch's cauldron as the rejuvenated Faust returned to youth (I believe we were supposed to be shocked; I just thought unkindly: more sit-ups and fewer baked potatoes, Simon).

I asked Callow if he agreed that the British still had supremacy in the English language. He gave it some thought.

> I think it's probably true. To be an actor in England—even with the decline of things—is to be concerned with language. We have tremendously acute antennae about a person's class, social standing, and regional origin. We play that. We always as actors ask of our characters:

How much does he earn? What is his standing in the class system? Where is he from? English actors are virtuosos at playing someone who comes from Leeds but also spent two years in Halifax.

What about regional repertory theater? "It's gone," he said. The Arts Council was partly to blame; it cut government funding. But there was more to it than that.

> When I started acting, every young actor's dream and intention was to go into a repertory company where he would work through a season or two. Learning his craft. But now the repertory companies only go from play to play. They haven't got the money for Shakespeare. Nor do they do new plays. When I started there were huge flourishing companies at Nottingham, Exeter, Manchester, Birmingham, Glasgow. Now even Glasgow doesn't have a company. It's all happened in the last decade. The regional repertory theater is gone now really. And that's why the supremacy of English acting will collapse in five more years. It will *all* be over.

Beryl Bainbridge recalls her days at the Playhouse, Liverpool's repertory theatre, starting when she was just fourteen:

> I joined the company as an assistant stage manager and character juvenile. My duties were to sit in the prompt-corner with the book, to understudy, to fetch sandwiches from Brown's Cafe in Williamson Square, and to help with props. I was expected to be present at costume fittings and be handy with the tape measure. The noting of distance between shoulder and elbow was uneventful, but knee to crotch was a nightmare . . .

She remembers *Richard II* bringing her to tears ("I have been studying how I may compare / This prison where I live unto the world"); Shaw's *Caesar and Cleopatra* ("Cleopatra's barge wouldn't slide off the stage properly"); in *Little Women* playing Beth ("a character now known as Keep Beth Off the Road because she dies pitifully in the second act"); and, at last, the leading role in *Johnny Belinda* ("I remained deaf and dumb until the final curtain, when, after starvation, rape, childbirth in a cotton field and the dawning of love, I found my tongue and stuttered the name of my child").

American actress Julie Harris, whom I met after my stay in London in California when she was touring with *Driving Miss Daisy* (she and Dame Wendy are old friends), feels America, too, suffers from too little repertory theater, especially when it comes to performing Shakespeare and classic plays. She says:

> It has never been easy for a young actor or actress to get the kind of classic training they should have here. Whenever I see any English

company doing Shakespeare it's always wonderful. They seem to just absorb it naturally, like osmosis. I think American actors come to it fighting the verse.

Harris feels repertory training is "absolutely essential" for the stage.

You see, you can't speak Shakespeare or the other classic roles if you haven't had experience on stage. You have no breath control. You have no voice projection. You have to have that kind of training. If you're a movie actor or a television actor or a beginning actor, you can't just stand up and say, "I'll do Hamlet." You don't have the physical strength to support it for three hours.

I asked her if she found a difference between English and American actors.

I think English actors are more finely tuned as instruments because they are so thoroughly trained. They begin in regional repertory and do all the great parts. And even the small parts in Shakespeare are great parts. At the Birmingham Rep or whatever, the young actor is trained from the ground up in the very finest drama. They learn how to be economical and work fast and work truthfully.

In a Broadway career that goes back to 1945, Harris is an example of an actor who has played English and American roles almost interchangeably. She was a twenty-one-year-old "walk-on" for the 1946 productions of *Oedipus Rex* and *Henry IV* when the Old Vic was at its height and came to New York, so she saw Richardson's Falstaff and Olivier's Hotspur from right onstage. Like Geraldine Page and Maureen Stapleton, Julie Harris has been one of the most durable leading figures in the American theater. She has been my favorite actress ever since the haunting Ferris wheel scene with James Dean in *East of Eden* in 1955. Director Elia Kazan has said that once Dean sensed her affection and patience "he got awfully good." In his autobiography, Kazan says Julie was goodness herself with Dean, "kind and patient and everlastingly sympathetic" and that this helped Dean more than "I did with any direction I gave him." She is most famous as Frankie in Carson McCullers' *Member of the Wedding* and Sally Bowles in Christopher Isherwood's *I Am a Camera,* which she did both on stage and in film. But Julie has gone from playing, in her early days, the White Rabbit in *Alice* ("Oh my fur and whiskers!") and one of the witches in Sir Michael Redgrave's 1948 *Macbeth* ("When shall we three meet again, / In thunder, lightning, or in rain?"), to a whole series of English and American historical figures—Queen Victoria, Florence Nightingale, Charlotte

Brontë, Emily Dickinson, Mrs. Lincoln, and others. She is also known to British TV viewers from a seven-year stint on "Knots Landing."

Julie Harris has just done one play in London, the Emily Dickinson role in *The Belle of Amherst*. When I met her she was reading up on Isak Dinesen for a new play by William Luce, who also did the Dickinson and Brontë plays. Harris agrees "an age *is* passing," and on both sides of the Atlantic. "It's the truth," she says. "In our theater you don't have people like the Lunts anymore. They were ladies and gentlemen. That's gone." She can't see why any British government would want to cut subsidies to the arts:

> Theater to London is like gorillas to Rwanda—a great tourist attraction. They must know they have to support it. It brings in all those millions of dollars. When I get to London I feel like I'm in heaven. I go to the theater two or three times a day.

Simon Callow really blames television for the decline of regional repertory in Britain:

> There just isn't the old demand for live local theater. It became elitist, you see. Instead of being a popular town institution, for everybody, it became a sort of odd little bywater. So the English theater is without branches. When Americans talk about how good British television drama is, you're talking about the fruits of a tree whose roots have died.

Television has affected acting in another way, Callow says:

> The ideal of young actors is to present a real, credible, recognizable personage on stage. That kind of limited intention is new. The old intention of actors of previous generations was to present extraordinary images, to present a kind of poetic amplification of character. And that sense has been lost. It's all dismissed and cast out.

So the end of the Golden Age isn't just the departure of a few great actors. For a while, Callow said, it looked as if Olivier, Richardson, and Gielgud were leaving the stage and the next generation of actors like Albert Finney and Alan Bates would fill their shoes. "They all," he went on, "for some reason or other, dodged the succession." A still younger generation led by Anthony Sher, Kenneth Branagh, Daniel Day-Lewis, Tim Pigott-Smith, Jeremy Irons, and Callow himself, are possible heirs, though Olivier will probably never be succeeded. Hamlet, Henry V, Romeo, Richard III, Oedipus, The Critic, Max de Winter, Heathcliff, Uncle Vanya, Othello, Archie Rice, the button moulder in *Peer Gynt*, Lord Marchmain dying in his huge bed at Brideshead, making the sign of the cross. He's become every character he ever played (though Branagh daringly created his own distinctive, if less memorably exultant, Henry V). Once, when somebody asked how he would like to be known, Britain's first theatrical peer said, "A diligent expert workman." I talked to Simon Callow before Olivier died and observed they had the same secretary; Olivier had not appeared in public in a very long time, though I'd had a note from him.

"He never will again," said Callow, who was then seeing him. "He can't go out. He's just very frail. He's all right. He's quite happy too." But he agreed, as Anthony Quayle was to say, that the loss of Olivier marked "the closing of a very great book."

I said the audience at Gielgud's *The Best of Friends* itself had a gently valedictorian air, so many distinguished older people, all the Wendy Hillers coming back. Callow knew just what I meant:

> It's the audience which feels very frustrated. Which knows everybody will speak impeccably and nobody will say the word "fuck" on the stage. They'll all come out of the theater with the illusion of having heard great thoughts and watched exquisite manners. That's an audience, a whole constituency of theatergoers, that nobody cares about at all anymore.

More Angry Young Men

"IN A CONFUSED WAY," reported *The Economist*, "Britain is having a cultural debate. At last." It said that different perceptions of changes brought to Britain by Mrs. Thatcher "now represent the single most important divide in the country's intellectual and artistic life."

The debate, *The Economist* went on, was brought into the open in *The Sunday Times* by Norman Stone, professor of modern history at Oxford, who attacked six films for their nasty portrayals of British life. Also joining the fray was Bernard Levin, who, in his column in *The Times*, criticized an exhibition at the Hayward Gallery featuring images of various artists of "contemporary Britain." Some of them—police torture, bloody tattoos of Union Jacks—looked like stills from the films attacked by Professor Stone. What Levin objected to specifically was a painting showing Mrs. Thatcher in a halo of nuclear missiles. Groaned Levin, "Ooh, the originality of it, the wit, the courage, the trenchancy!"

The audience that Simon Callow said nobody cares about was fighting back. What happened, Professor Stone explained to me over a couple of pints at the King's Arms in Oxford, was that *The Sunday Times* asked him, as a regular contributor, to look at the six films. "They asked me if I'd do a piece on how the media represents this country," he said. "They arranged for me to see them, four on videos and I went to seedy studios in Soho to see the other two. Oddly enough, there was a Pakistani projectionist in one of them. When my stomach was really turning I said, "How can you bear this job?" He said, "I often wonder."

Stone reported back in *The Sunday Times:*

They are all depressing, and are no doubt meant to be. The rain pours down; skinheads beat people up; there are race riots; there are drug fixes on squalid corners; there is much explicit sex, a surprising amount of it homosexual and sadistic; greed and violence abound;

there is grim concrete and much footage of "urban decay"; on and off there are voice-overs by Mrs. Thatcher, Hitler, etc. . . .

Somehow their visual world has been dominated by left-wing orthodoxy; the done thing is to run down Mrs. Thatcher, to assume that capitalism is parasitism, that the established order in this country is imperialist, racist, profiteering, oppressive to women and other minorities.

Professor Stone loathed all six films: Derek Jarman's *The Last of England* ("Noises of bombs and a Hitler speech . . . much declamation of *The Waste Land* . . . a naked young man either buggers, or is buggered by, an SAS soldier in black balaclava upon a Union Jack"); *My Beautiful Laundrette* (". . . a conflict within and between Asian immigrants and thugs of the National Front, resolved in a sort of homosexual *Romeo and Juliet*"); *Sammy and Rosie Get Laid* (". . . a race riot . . . a great deal of sex . . . three couples are shown simultaneously in sort of a layer cake, grunting and fumbling"); *Eat the Rich* ("a transvestite mulatto waiter . . . gets his own back by serving up the guests on the menu"); *Empire State* (". . . ends with a homosexual wrestling match of revolting sadism"); *Business as Usual* (". . . sexual harassment in Liverpool").

He lamented that the makers of the films were Britain's "promising young directors." Professor Stone's conclusion: "If this is the best they can produce, we might as well close the cinemas now." He told me he felt his argument was fairly straightforward:

They're rotten films. You get bored after five minutes. You don't care what happens to the characters. The acting is bad. The scripts are appalling. They're full of set-up, wooden, cardboard scenes. With disgustingness just thrown in as a way of relieving the tedium. And there's an extraordinary amount of homosexual propaganda, surprising in the post-AIDS period.

Hanif Kureishi, who wrote the much-acclaimed *Laundrette* and *Sammy and Rosie*, shot back in *The Guardian* that Britain had become "an intolerant, racist, homophobic, narrow-minded, authoritarian rathole." Professor Stone, relishing the hullabaloo, told me a friend of his met the writer at a party. "He said if I'd been there Kureishi would have hit me." Derek Jarman, who directed one of the films, in *his* counterattack accused Stone of a "terrible creative impotence and snobbishness." Jarman said Stone was contradictory since he supported "a government that professes freedom in the economic marketplace yet seems unable to accommodate freedom of ideas."

Kureishi, Britain-born with a Pakistani father, told an interviewer he wanted to write about defiant people who stand up for their rights.

> I've known violence. I know that many black people don't feel they belong. I think some white people are responsible. I feel I do belong—though I get abused in the street occasionally. There's a lot of anger in Britain, quite rightly.

He gives credit to London's commercial television Channel Four, under former director Jeremy Isaacs, for funding such daring films as his own and *Letter to Brezhnev, Wish You Were Here,* and the Joe Orton story, *Prick Up Your Ears.* Kureishi sees his role in Chekhovian terms as a reporter, a witness, making a kind of "filmic newspaper" of British life. He admits being out to shock people: "Introducing two gay characters in *My Beautiful Laundrette,* and having them snogging is shocking." Or *was* shocking. These earlier films are likely to pale beside two independently produced 1990 entries, the earlier mentioned story of the East End psychopathic gangsters, *The Krays,* and a film of Hubert J. Selby's 1964 novel, *Last Exit to Brooklyn,* once the object of a British obscenity trial for its relentless realistic treatment of American thugs, homosexuals, hookers, and savage violence. Professor Stone may have something.

There is an interesting similarity between the views of the left and those of more conservative writers, such as *Spectator* columnists who lament the passing of old churches, tube stations, and 1930s red telephone boxes. "Increasingly," *The Economist* said in its article, "the tone of this conservative movement seems to have been set by the poet Philip Larkin, who died in 1986, in his 1974 poem 'Going, Going.'" It's been quoted already in exemplifying the Little Englanders; another verse fits the cultural debate:

> For the first time I feel somehow
> That it isn't going to last,
> That before I snuff it, the whole
> Boiling will be bricked in,
> Except for the tourists parts—
> First slum of Europe: a role
> It won't be so hard to win,
> With a cast of crooks and tarts.
> And that will be England gone . . .

In his attack on the films, Professor Stone thought things began to go wrong with "sleazy, sick hedonism, such as the vacuous Beatles films." Jarman countered that Stone was "dreaming nostalgically of the time before the Beatles." In Larkin's words:

> So life was never better than
> In nineteen sixty-three
> (Though just too late for me)
> Between the end of the *Chatterley* ban
> And the Beatles' first LP

Sheridan Morley argues many current plays and films reflect this new anger:

> Whether or not you believe in Mrs. Thatcher, she has divided this country as no Prime Minister ever. We are no longer a smugly middle-of-the road, middle-class nation. We are now two nations, haves and have-nots, rich and poor, South and North. And the theater and cinema reflect this kind of anger, a kind of rage, a kind of cynicism. This is much more apparent now than it was ten years ago. The final irony is you're getting exactly the audience you're attacking going to see it.

I found *Pravda, Serious Money, Les Liaisons Dangereuses* and some of Alan Ayckbourn's black comedies like *A Small Family Business* (drug peddling) so cynical it got so I didn't care what happened to the characters. Howard Brenton, David Hare's coauthor of *Pravda*, claims such shows are "militantly opposed to Tory and capitalist values." My impression was they rather nastily *celebrated* greed and corruption. Simon Callow told me he himself was amazed at the success of *Les Liaisons Dangereuses* on the stage and as the Glenn Close film, and as Miloš Forman's *Valmont*. "I think Christopher Hampton, who wrote the play, perfectly distills the qualities of Laclos's novel. It's a cold, terrible story. Why it should be so popular is interesting." The novel, published in 1782, is the only notable work French writer Choderlos de Laclos ever wrote. It tells the story of a cynical and unscrupulous libertine, the Vicomte de Valmont, encouraged by his former lover, the Marquise de Merteuil, to seduce and destroy two innocent women; Valmont himself gets killed in a duel. I loathed the play when I first saw it in London. "We live in cynical times," Callow said. "There's no question about that. The loss of idealism in England is rampant."

"You're confusing, as all Americans do, irony and cynicism," George Steiner told me, when I asked him about the plays. "This is an ironical society, not a cynical one." Bernard Levin reminded me, "The British never fight their critics; we diffuse them":

So when a *Pravda* or a *Serious Money* appears, instead of the targets getting enraged and picketing the theater and booing the author, they gleefully pay money at the box office. It is of course the best way to make your opponents spit blood, to say not "How dare you!" but "I say, what fun!" Someone writes a terrible excoriating satire and the people who are being excoriated and satirized are loving every minute of it. And this has been a British habit for centuries.

The younger generation of British writers, directors, and actors, now in their thirties and forties, grew up during Vietnam. Some were much affected by it. I talked about this with playwright-director David Hare when we met for lunch at Twickenham Studios just outside London. Hare, like Callow, is extremely active, doing everything from writing the Meryl Streep film *Plenty* to an adaptation of *Fanshen,* the village classic by William Hinton, the American technician who helped Mao Tse-tung's land reform of the 1940s. I wanted to talk to Hare concerning his 1983 television play, *Saigon: Year of the Cat,* about the fall of Vietnam in April 1975. It was never shown in the United States. Hare's politics are far from my own, but I was struck by how true his film was. I told him so.

Saigon tells about a brief affair between Barbara Dean, a middle-aged Englishwoman who works at the British Embassy, and a much younger American, Bob Chesneau, a rather liberal and sympathetic CIA operative. Saigon is just about to fall. When it does, Dean and Chesneau are separately evacuated by their governments, probably not to meet again. Hare is less interested in the romance between the English spinster (Judi Dench) and the American (Frederic Forrest), than in using it as a way of looking at Vietnam and at Britain itself.

Early on Barbara voices the view:

> I would have thought the problem you have here is the money will go to a particular regime. A regime whose reputation is for corruption. And there are political prisoners as well . . .

It is the familiar, true, charge that the United States had got itself into a position of defending a corrupt, vicious military regime. What makes *Saigon* so interesting is that Hare, himself left-wing, suggests this has come about through Hanoi's subversive manipulation. I told Hare: "Barbara is expressing the conventional wisdom. It's why the world turned against us. But it's what the Communists intended the world to feel about Vietnam." I'd been in Saigon in 1964–65 when Thieu and Ky came to power in a series of nine coups d'états and was still there in 1966–67 when the United States seemed to condone it in a series of rigged elections. Like the horror shows of fiery suicides and flaming villages, so many stage-managed riots and rebellions, even the bloody battles of the cities in Tet, much of it was planned and orchestrated by Communist Party leader Le Duan. I asked Hare if he knew Le Duan.

"Yes. Absolutely. I know exactly what you're talking about."

"You do?" I was startled. Few Americans had heard of Le Duan.

"Theater was part of the Vietnam war, wasn't it?" Hare said. "There was an incident when I was in Saigon at the end of 1973":

> The kerosene dumps were apparently the subject of a rocket attack. So that one night the sky was full of clouds of smoke and fire. And, you know, it said in the paper the next morning it'd been subject to a rocket attack. And yet it hadn't been subject to a rocket attack at all. Two employees who were Vietcong who worked inside the petrol dump simply set fire to it. It was arson. The theatricals were to pretend that it was a military attack. In fact, like everything else in Vietnam, it was by subversion.

"You understood that. How interesting." I was amazed. Hanoi's agents, informers, and terrorists riddled Saigon. In 1967 I wrote my editors at the *Washington Star* that Pham Xuan An, probably the smartest and most influential Vietnamese journalist and a close acquaintance of mine, was almost certainly secretly working for Hanoi; others suspected him too but nothing happened. It was not until journalist Stanley Karnow was back in Saigon in the 1980s making a Vietnam postwar documentary for public television that he found out An had been a secret agent for the Communists the whole time. He held the rank of colonel and got Hanoi's equivalent of the Medal of Honor for it. I was distressed to have it confirmed, but not surprised. What disinformation or military intelligence An passed around doesn't bear thinking about. I told Hare you knew Hanoi had a Trojan horse in the South Vietnamese government and army; you lived with it day and night, week after week, in my case for nearly four years. It was a nightmare. I said, "You're the first person that I've met for a long time who really understands."

"To an outsider," he said, "one of the things that is absolutely clear is that there is no way the Americans will ever understand what happened to them in Vietnam." He said films like *Apocalypse Now, The Deer Hunter,* and *Platoon* failed to come to grips with reality. "The only way Americans can understand Vietnam is in terms of an American tragedy. They are *incapable* of understanding subversion or what it did to the Vietnamese. Now there's a tremendous wave of 'let's reexamine Vietnam.' "

> But this is exclusively in terms of "let's reexamine the damage it did to this country." And us. And to the men who returned. There's absolutely no sense of what happened to the Vietnamese. How many were killed? How many were tortured? How many Vietnamese lives were ruined? You know, you may have lost sixty thousand people. How many did the Vietnamese lose? A million? Half a million? The Americans can't grasp it. They can't grasp it to this day. Show me a piece of American fiction that represents it. There isn't one.

In one scene in *Saigon*, Chesneau, the American, asks Barbara, "Can you give me an idea of England?"

> BARBARA: Well . . . *[She smiles.]* The place is very wet. Which makes its greenness almost iridescent. It is almost indecently green.
>
> *(They smile.)*
>
> The people are—odd. They're cruel to each other. Mostly in silent . . . in unexpected ways. It's an emotional cruelty. You feel watched, disapproved of all the time.
>
> CHESNEAU: That's why you got away.
>
> BARBARA: There's a terrible pressure, all these little hedgerows squeezing you in, tight little lines of upright houses. Everyone spying on everyone else.
>
> *(She looks over at him and smiles.)*
>
> I'm not even . . . an unconventional woman. I need only that amount of air. But I can't get it in England.
>
> *(There is a pause. CHESNEAU is looking at her.)*
>
> I know what you're thinking. Will I ever go back?

The Vietcong decide that for her. At the American embassy, as wind from the choppers buffets the evacuees (a scene David Puttnam almost identically repeated in *The Killing Fields*, says Hare), Chesneau rushes her to a helicopter and Barbara's last words are: "God, have I really got to get on this thing?" As the helicopter rises, Hare, in his stage directions, cruelly describes her as looking like "an old English spinster." *Saigon*'s final line, voiced by a young helicopter pilot as somebody opens "a can of Heineken" for him, is: "Hey, you guys. We're all going home!"

I asked Hare what he meant by Barbara's line about not getting enough air in England.

It's a feeling in lower-middle-class life, in semidetached houses with all their snobberies, that all the time you ought to behave in a certain way. If you don't your friends and neighbors silently disapprove. There is an English way to behave. In the suburbs it involves a great deal of emotional repression.

Hare remembers that in Bexhill-on-Sea, on Britain's southern coast where he grew up, if you hung your washing out on Sunday, the neighbors' disapproval would be palpable.

If you let your garden go, the neighbors would come and say, "Please, can we do your garden for you?" And they wouldn't do it out of generosity or because they loved gardens. They were doing it because they weren't prepared to have somebody on their street who didn't keep their garden neat and tidy. English suburban life has a terrible, repressive side.

It is repression, John Fowles goes so far as to say, that helps explain the British flair for theater:

We prefer to keep most personal feelings hidden; but if they must be shown, we prefer to do it behind a mask, that is, on stage, in the "safe unreality" (as we see it) of the theater. This pushing away of intense private feeling into art is a kind of defanging of a rattlesnake . . . Art suits the British psyche, as it did the Greek.

One can accept this when applied to theater. But what about the sheer exuberance, the breaking out, that you get in so much of English pop music? I suppose you could even join with Fowles that this, too, comes from repression, since it is such a riotous eruption and bursting free.

Sgt. Pepper to Pugin

S O MUCH goes back to them.

As Henry Pleasants, the American music critic who has lived long in London, wrote in *Serious Music—And All That Jazz:*

> The ultimate congregation of these diverse strains—country and urban blues, gospel song, rock 'n' roll, country-and-western, bluegrass, folk and even the close-harmony vocal techniques of such earlier popular groups as the Four Freshmen, the Hi Los, the Weavers—was accomplished in the 1960s by the most improbable and unpredictable of all conceivable agents: a ragtag quartet from Liverpool, England, called the Beatles.

American critic Frederic V. Grunfeld hailed the Beatles in 1967 as "the great syncretists and mixmasters of our day." He called their finest record, *Sgt. Pepper's Lonely Hearts Club Band,* "a great eclectic circus of Indian raga, Salivation Army, Benjamin British, tailgate, gutbucket and aleatoric chance-music, all handled without hang-ups or uptightness." John Gabree wrote in *Down Beat:*

> They sounded raw and vital . . . But they were also safe, being white and having none of the aggressive sexuality that had been so upsetting in the likes of Elvis—all they wanted to do, remember, was hold your hand.

Sir George Martin, the Beatles's old music director, once told Pleasants how the Beatles hadn't yet learned to read music when he first met them in 1962. Nor could he, as he soon learned, play one of their acoustic guitars.

> It was a two-way street. They learned a lot from me, and I learned a lot from them. They were marvelous musicians, not in an academic sense, of course, but in terms of musicality, sensitivity, perception, invention, ideas, curiosity, and so on.

Their songs came to them in fragments; in the early days Martin showed them how to make bridges. One time Paul McCartney, in a hotel room, was playing a three-note figure. He told Martin he needed a three-syllable word for it, something like "yes-ter-day."

It was the Beatles and the Rolling Stones, inspired as they were by B. B. King, Chuck Berry, and other black American musicians, who helped popularize black music with Americans, another of those transatlantic cross-fertilizations. The Beatles spoke Merseyside and sang Motown, they spoke Liverpudlian and sang black. From that famous final chord in "A Day in the Life," played by a London symphony orchestra, in the last band of *Sgt. Pepper,* the emergence of such rock opera derivatives as *Jesus Christ Superstar* was just a matter of time. *Superstar,* by composer Andrew Lloyd Webber and lyricist Tim Rice, was a record-industry album before the show itself existed. Rock turned out to be hugely marketable. All of a sudden there were the Apostles asking Jesus, "What's the Buzz?" Or a teenage Mary Magdalene consoling him that "Everything's Alright," but telling herself, "I Don't Know How to Love Him." To a rock tempo we hear Caiaphas and the high priests decide, "This Jesus Must Die." And Jesus himself, in Gethsemane as the Roman soldiers come to arrest him, praying, "I Only Want to Say." Lloyd Webber makes his debt to black music explicit in his composer's direction for the big "Superstar" number: "Freely—'Soul' style."

It was electrifying theater. I saw it in London and New York and liked the movie, which I went to see six times in Bangkok, even better. I agree with American composer Ned Rorem, who praised *Jesus Christ Superstar* but is less pleased with Webber's later work:

> *Superstar* was a show-biz pastiche of everything from Palestrina to Penderecki. What it lacked in originality, it made up for in the infectious chutzpah of youth, all laid out with skillful clarity. The times were corny, and corn itself is not unhealthy. Well, seventeen years have passed and the chutzpah's turned into commerce, and the corn into smarm. The charming vulgarity of *Superstar* has become merely vulgarity.

"How the Brits Keep Broadway in Business" crowed the headline in London's *Daily Express* after *The Phantom of the Opera* opened in New York. Good reason for self-congratulation; five of eleven big musicals on Broadway were from the land of Gilbert and Sullivan, Noël Coward, and P. G. Wodehouse. In 1989 there were seventeen productions of *Cats* and thirty of *Starlight Express* worldwide and *Aspects of Love* opened in London. A year before *Phantom* came to town, *New York Times* critic Frank Rich warned:

> For the New York theater, the rise of London as a musical theater capital is as sobering a specter as the awakening of the Japanese automobile industry was for Detroit.

Was it, Rich asked, a true cultural phenomenon or just a passing series of coincidences? He noted most of the British musical hits relied on Andrew Lloyd Webber, director Trevor Nunn, or both:

> Successful as Mr. Lloyd Webber is, his work can't yet be compared seriously with Broadway's best of any period. He's primarily a canny, melodic pastiche artist . . .

American sour grapes? Sheridan Morley, too, feels that no other living composer of musicals can hold a candle to Stephen Sondheim, though he regards *Les Misérables* as the greatest single musical (and, he says, for playwrights, "not even in Harold Pinter or Tom Stoppard or John Osborne or Simon Gray do we have a playwright to touch Arthur Miller, nor young playwrights with that savage sense of poetry of David Mamet or Sam Shepard"). The lights aren't going out all over Broadway just yet. Nor are the British giving up. In the 1989–90 season, while *Starlight Express* had finally chugged off, *Cats* (a take of $834 million worldwide), *Phantom* ($144 million) and *Les Misérables* (over $300 million) were still around as long-running long runs, as was *Me and My Girl*. Andrew Lloyd Webber's *Aspects of Love* joined them in March. Two more British musicals were *Up Against It*, based on a screenplay that Joe Orton wrote for the Beatles in 1967, and another by Liverpool's Willy Russell (*Educating Rita, Shirley Valentine*). Rock star Sting was Mack the Knife in *3 Penny Opera*. Coming next season was the London smash hit *Miss Saigon*, by the creators of *Les Misérables*. This year's past season also saw American premieres of plays by Stoppard and Pinter, a one-man show on the works of Dylan Thomas, Sir Peter Hall's *Merchant of Venice*, Peter Shaffer's *Lettice and Lovage* with Maggie Smith, and performances by Vanessa Redgrave, Rex Harrison, and plenty of other English actors. You wondered who was left in London.

The English musical's new success, argues Rich, owes something to spectacular staging:

> Unable to compete with Broadway's high-powered choreography, the English musical had to turn elsewhere for kinetic energy. The option

chosen was spectacle: if the performers can't dance, why not let the scenery do it instead?

Its pioneer, he says, was the late English set designer Sean Kenny, who re-created the London of Dickens in *Oliver!* with mobile scaffolding, crowned with a bridge which dropped from above. Variations have appeared in *Nicholas Nickleby* and *Les Misérables.* Rich traces the Disneyland extravagance of *Cats* and *Starlight Express* to another Kenny design, done for *Blitz,* a 1962 London show that attempted to re-create the Nazi blitzkrieg of London. Only in *Les Misérables,* concludes Rich, by fusing all the musical's elements from orchestration to lighting cues, "the English have for once beaten the Americans at their own game." Lloyd Webber himself expects them to go right on beating us. He said at *Phantom*'s first night opening in New York, "I think the day of musicals like *Carousel* and *South Pacific* is probably past."

Having the chandelier drop in *Phantom* or trains zoom around in *Starlight,* and all the other new emphasis on sound, lighting, staging, and production values, has affected opera too. At London's English National Opera, Jonathan Miller put *The Mikado* in Brighton in 1920 and gave *Rigoletto* a Mafia gangland setting, with everybody smoking cigarettes. In America, Peter Sellars has set *Così fan tutte* in a diner, *Don Giovanni* in an urban slum, and Handel's *Julius Caesar* around the swimming pool of the Beirut Hilton. The ENO's *Hansel and Gretel* was Freudian (mother was the witch), *Faust* made a tart of Marguerite, and old Cadillacs and aging English pom-pom girls in swimsuits ludicrously parade outside the bullring in *Carmen.* When Sellars came to Britain in 1987 to stage Nigel Osborne's *Electrification of the Soviet Union* (Craig Raine's libretto was based on a Boris Pasternak novel), constant, sudden time and locality shifts between 1914 and 1920 and Siberia and Moscow left the audience so baffled, Sellars told it to "relax and not worry about understanding it."

Staging can steal the show from the show itself. I worried when Anthony Hopkins, as the mortally wounded general, was hoisted up in a net to the top of an Egyptian funerary temple to join Judi Dench in the National Theatre's *Antony and Cleopatra.* Bernard Levin told me he worried too:

> It never worked. I heard the pulley stuck the first night and there was hysteria in the house. The night I went, as they uncoupled the thing, they slipped the cable and he just fell on the platform. I heard Anthony Hopkins objected nightly. Once that pulley started, they lost the audience. You just wondered: oh, God, are they going to drop him?

Alison Chitty, who designed the sets and costumes of *Antony and Cleopatra* and three other Shakespeare plays directed by Sir Peter Hall while I was in London, was a bit indignant when I complained about the pulley, which she said hoisted up Hopkins fourteen feet ("It was a hell of a long way").

Lifting the mortally wounded Antony up in the net was Shakespeare's idea anyhow, Miss Chitty said,

> Shakespeare wanted that. If you listen to the words: "How heavy weighs my lord . . . Gosh, this is really hard work. How are we going to get him up here, girls?" On and on. I mean, it's famous as one of the most difficult scenes to stage in Shakespeare.

It goes:

ANTONY: O, quick, or I am gone.

CLEOPATRA: Here's sport indeed! How heavy weighs my lord!

Our strength is all gone into heaviness;

That makes the weight. Had I great Juno's power,

The strong-wing'd Mercury should fetch thee up

And set thee by Jove's side. Yet come a little—

Wishers were ever fools—O, come, come, come;

(They heave Antony aloft to Cleopatra)

And welcome, welcome! die where thou hast liv'd;

Quicken with kissing: had my lips that power,

Thus would I wear them out.

ALL: A heavy sight!

ANTONY: I am dying, Egypt, dying. . . .

Miss Chitty, one of London's top stage designers though still young, argues why it is deliberate by Shakespeare:

> I mean obviously it's a tremendous indignity for the man who's been a third of the triumverate to be dying and lifted up to his Queen . . . And he has this ignominious death. It's not a great gracious death in bed surrounded by all the servants.

Her staging of *Antony and Cleopatra* is sumptuous, with a classic Roman image superimposed on the Elizabethan-Jacobean age, in the manner of Veronese (unlike the early pharaonic look of the old Laurence Olivier-Vivien Leigh production). The National's Olivier theater expands from a small chamber to an epic stage, and a large cast of soldiers with spears and shields and banners runs up and down the aisles shouting, blowing trumpets, and beating drums. "It's exciting, isn't it?" said Miss Chitty. On an aisle seat I was a little worried about getting speared.

Bernard Levin recalls Orson Welles performing *Othello* in London years ago:

> In the killing scene he wrapped Desdemona's head in a sheet from the bed as if to suffocate her. Normally they put a pillow down. The whole audience lost the thread of the play. They were all thinking: if she doesn't get her head out, she'll really suffocate! Welles was just too clever.

Staging aside, when it comes to the music itself, Henry Pleasants told me he put British opera on a par with American, comparing Covent Garden to the Met, the ENO to the New York City Opera. Everybody suffers, he says, from a worldwide shortage of good operas—there are only about fifty—and good singers. Sutherland, Domingo, or Pavarotti command huge sums; if they sing, Covent Garden jacks up already sky-high prices. Opera is big in America now; over two hundred companies are performing.

When it comes to orchestras, London has too many: the London Symphony Orchestra, London Philharmonic Orchestra, Royal Philharmonic Orchestra, BBC Symphony Orchestra, and Philharmonia; plus, Covent Garden and the ENO each have their own. Among many regional ones, the Halle Orchestra in Manchester and the Birmingham Symphony Orchestra with its gifted director, Simon Rattle, are the best. Pleasants ranks them all below the Philadelphia, New York, Boston, Cleveland, Chicago, and Los Angeles symphonies. His reason: an English symphony orchestra has eighty-five players while an American has a hundred and five, mainly in strings and basses, which gives it a more sumptuous sound. If a few of the London orchestras merged, each could afford to be bigger.

In music, as in art, the English have never matched the Germans or Italians. Benjamin Britten, Ralph Vaughan Williams, and Sir Edward William Elgar all wrote in the German style. The popularity of baroque—everybody plays Bach and Handel in Oxford—reflects the absence of contemporary music. New music, argues Pleasants, is Afro-American, which young Britons have made their own in pop and rock. Pleasants:

> It is so offensive to those of traditional European cultural orientation—and they dominate the cultural establishment everywhere—that it is dismissed as "uncultured," "commercial," and "popular."

Pleasants finds Addison's point in a *Spectator* of April 3, 1711, still pertinent:

> Music, architecture and painting, as well as poetry and oratory, are to deduce their laws and rules from the general sense and taste of mankind, and not from the principles of those arts themselves.

Giving popular taste its lead works well in British advertising. Cultural historian Christopher Frayling told me:

> I believe that our advertising is the best in the world. It's witty and indirect. When I go to the States and look at the billboards and TV commercials I fear I'm being shouted at: "This one's cheaper!" "This one's better!" Whereas you come to England and an advertisement can be a little story with a witty punch line.

The rise of Britain's Saatchi brothers (who happen to be of Iraqi origin) is legendary; Saatchi and Saatchi is now the world's biggest advertising group. After they masterminded her 1987 election, Mrs. Thatcher was so impressed that her government has used television ads to warn against AIDS, sell off British Petroleum, and urge jobless youth into training. Jon Sommerill, another top British advertising man, is known for an antifurs slogan: "It takes up to forty dumb animals to make a fur coat but only one to wear one." But he went too far in an ad that showed Margaret Thatcher, David Owen, and Neil Kinnock swinging from nooses over the words: "Would Britain be better off with a hung parliament?"

My own favorite series of ads, seen on billboards in the underground, was for Tetley Bitter. One was headlined: "FOR A YORKSHIRE WOMAN THE JOURNEY TO THE MATERNITY WARD CAN OFTEN BE A LONG ONE." It began:

> Fate has not been kind to the Yorkshire woman.
>
> It is as though upon entering life's theatre she is immediately shown to a seat behind a pillar, allowed only a restricted view of what life has on offer.
>
> This situation has come about not as a result of any inherent defects but simply because being a Yorkshire woman automatically precludes her from being a Yorkshireman.
>
> Which, as the whole world knows, is still the only officially-recognized and accepted gender in that county.
>
> Thus it is that the unfortunate female finds herself some way down the pecking order in established Yorkshire society.
>
> Or seventh, to be absolutely accurate.
>
> Coming after, in no particular order: fishing, rugby league, insult-

ing Lancashire, football, household pets, cricket and, of course, Tetley bitter.

It is to escape this somewhat relegated status that many a woman has fled her homeland in search of a community that values her at least above rugby league. (This has often proved difficult.)

The ad then goes on to tell the story of one Nora Pilkington who went as a missionary in 1893 to Papua New Guinea where she married the chief of the tribe. But finding she was with child, she returned to Yorkshire so that her son might qualify to play cricket for the county. There are zany tales of other women who had made sacrifices for Yorkshire. Another ad in the same series goes on, in the same vein: IS NOUVELLE CUISINE FRENCH? SURELY IT WAS INVENTED IN YORKSHIRE AS LONG AGO AS 1883.

Popular taste is also much championed in architecture in Britain, says Professor Frayling:

Richard Rodgers designed the Pompidou Center in Paris; James Stirling the Stuttgart Art Gallery, the classic modern museum; Norman Foster the Hong Kong and Shanghai Bank, the most expensive building ever built. And they're all prophets without honor in their own country. Because you can't get a planning commission to agree to buildings like these in England. When Prince Charles complained that you couldn't see St. Paul's because there were so many high new buildings around it, everyone in the country said, "God, I've believed that for years. Now the Prince has said it so it must be true."

A story is told that when Queen Elizabeth was on her first world tour in the 1950s and the royal yacht Britannia came into view of the Manhattan skyline, Her Majesty turned to Prince Philip and said, "Oh, it's just like a row of hollyhocks." The same quintessentially English reaction came in the Great Exhibition of 1851. The Crystal Palace, with its nine hundred thousand square feet of glass, the brainchild of Prince Albert, was one of the wonders of the age. Six million people came to London to see its nineteen thousand exhibits set beneath the glittering glass and elm trees of the park (left during construction, after protests from tree lovers). Queen Victoria herself, Lady Longford tells us, systematically worked her way through it all, getting up early to arrive before 10 A.M. and coming back day after day. All the wonders of the mid-Victorian industrial age were on display. And what was the most popular exhibit among the British themselves?

In the middle of the Crystal Palace, at its very heart, was something called the Medieval Court. It was designed by Augustus Pugin, who led a Victorian revival of Gothic architecture; with Charles Barry he redid the House of Commons to give it the medieval look it has today. Pugin designed the court to show the eternal values of design, not industrial design but the work of the old wood turner, the weaver, the humble craftsman. It is where the British heart really lies.

> "Glorious, stirring sight!" murmured Toad, never offering to move. "The poetry! of motion! the real way to travel! The only way to travel! Here today—in next week tomorrow! Villages skipped, towns and cities jumped—always somebody else's horizon! O bliss! O poop-poop! O my! O my!"
> "O stop being an ass, Toad!" cried the Mole despairingly.

"For every Toad responding to a new invention like the car," says Christopher Frayling, "there's a Mole and a Ratty and a Badger trying to hold things back. Every person who flirts with new technology, who wants to do the latest thing, who wants to buy a word processor, there's an army of people, dressed in tweeds, teacups in hand, who, like Ratty, are trying to hold it back. And saying, 'Look, it will never catch on, it's a craze. Stop being an ass, Toad!' "

> "Hooray!" he cried, jumping up on seeing them, "this is splendid! . . . I was just going to send a boat down the river for you, Ratty, with strict orders that you were to be fetched up at once . . . You don't know how lucky it is, your turning up just now!"
> "Let's sit quiet a bit, Toady!" said the Rat, throwing himself into an easy chair, while the Mole took another by the side of him . . .

To Make a Modern World

IF POPULAR TASTE can triumph in something so visual as ads and architecture, Oxbridge is again the arbiter when it comes to serious television drama. With its lush period series and many original plays, we are back in the literary, verbal world where, except in the serious novel, Britain still rules supreme. We may excel at sitcoms, action films, and news programming, but literate Americans who would not be caught dead watching glitzy fantasies like "Dallas" or "Dynasty" provide big public television audiences for "Masterpiece Theatre." It is hard to imagine anything like Peter Brook's *Mahabharata* being produced for television in this country. Jeremy Isaacs, director of the Royal Opera House, used to run television's innovative Channel Four, which spawned the independent film productions Professor Stone lamented. He feels too many exportable series pander to nostalgia for the imagined purity of a vanished world. Isaacs:

> However safe and cozy and crinoline is the world of *Upstairs, Downstairs* or *Sherlock Holmes Meets Miss Marple*, or the remarkably effective adaptations of Trollope, Dickens, and Jane Austen, or the genteel decadence of *Brideshead Revisited* or even the imperial air of *The Jewel in the Crown*, none of this, in my view, is the best British drama. That is far more abrasive.

The best drama being made for British television, Isaacs believes, deals with the tensions that beset ordinary lives, such as Alan Bleasdale's previously quoted *Boys from the Blackstuff* (evidently its heavy Liverpudlian accents were deemed unexportable) or something like Dennis Potter's *Singing Detective*, with its daring mixture of hallucination, dream, memory, and stream of consciousness, which *was* shown in America, and Potter's contentiously explicit and equally controversial *Blackeyes*. Isaacs criticizes American television for not portraying the richness and complexity of actual life in the United States.

It's all shot in downtown Burbank in overlit bland Technicolor instead of being shot in the ghettos of Detroit or Boston or Washington, D.C. If your mother is dying of cancer or your son of AIDS, American television will tell you what she or he is going through emotionally. But if you're just poor or unhappy at work or not well enough taught or failing in your ambition, you cannot look to American television.

This was not always true, Isaacs says.

When I went into television nearly thirty years ago, the greatest dramas, the things everybody was trying to imitate, were American broadcast fiction. The dramas of Rod Serling, Paddy Chayevsky. "Marty," a butcher, out for a Saturday night. It used to be there. When American television moved from New York to Los Angeles, it all went. On the Coast everyone is happy. Tell me, when did you last see what it was like to be an underdog in American society? You display agony in soap opera as if there was no tomorrow, but you cannot be actually poor or crushed or miserable.

Isaacs, who is responsible for most of the films that drew Professor Stone's ire, feels American television won't take risks:

It doesn't say: let's cater to the highbrow viewer. Or the viewer who wants a genuinely frank and honest and explicit account of a sexual relationship or a viewer who wants a formalistically invented piece of fiction. It's saying: we need so many hours of that product and at so many hundreds of thousands of dollars and we need them six weeks from tomorrow. When I used to go to Los Angeles every year to see what American television had to offer, one was constantly in shock at the measured and calculated brutality of the selection potential. Only very rarely does something difficult, that isn't quite right, that isn't quite working, get nurtured through that very difficult first period of being on the air. It's either chopped or it's there for ten years.

David Puttnam, who spent a tumultuous year as head of Columbia Pictures in 1986–87, still dreams of making the British film industry, which has nearly collapsed from financial pressures, more powerful—in the process reinventing a romantic image of England through film, as he did in his 1981 Oscar winner, *Chariots of Fire*. But Puttnam seeks to depict English life more in the idealized manner of "Masterpiece Theatre" than in the gritty inner-city realism Isaacs favors. Even this can't be done, Puttnam feels, in Hollywood. He told Bill Moyers in a PBS interview: "It's a mistake to try to translate an essentially European view of cinema in an American milieu."

When he first went to Columbia, Puttnam told its executives that movies had been his biggest cultural influence, more even than school and family:

> My attitudes, dreams, preconceptions, and preconditions for life had been irreversibly shaped five and a half thousand miles away in a place called Hollywood . . . The medium is too powerful and too important an influence on the way we live, the way we see ourselves, to be left solely to the tyranny of the box office or reduced to the sum of the lowest common denominator.

Brenda Maddox, I think, grasps a point both Isaacs and Puttnam miss. She told me:

> Why Hollywood movies are great is that Russian Jews figured out what immigrant Americans wanted to know about the American way of life and they served up Andy Hardy. I think it's people who have never been to Iowa and never seen a judge, telling the rest of us how to eat dinner in the evening and how to talk right. That's the genius of America and also Jewish culture because they figured out what was universal.

Moyers, speaking very much as an American, told Puttnam, "The American dream is really that you can change your life. You can make it better."

"Only by belonging," retorted Puttnam, giving a very English answer. "Only by being part of the system will you survive. It's sad." Puttnam described Hollywood as a place where "the best thing that can happen is three pages in *People* magazine and a million dollars in the bank." Coca-Cola gave him a three-year contract at $3 million a year, free rein to make a picture up to a cost of $30 million, and complete control over production and distribution. Puttnam says it "declared war on prevailing attitudes but was not ready for the fallout and venom." Coca-Cola was run by businessmen who had to come up with "the short-term results required of all American businessmen." Puttnam made fine films *(The Last Emperor, Hope and Glory)* but box office profits dropped.

Puttnam admits he showed "arrogance and ignorance" in the stormy year he lasted. He talks of America now as "the lost land of my dreams." But Mrs. Maddox is right: the moviegoer's America has never been very close to reality. Remember Sinclair Lewis's description of The Rosebud Movie Palace in *Main Street* as the only place to escape into fantasy? Somehow this has helped America keep its place as the leading film-producing country right from the start, acquiring an ascendancy that has defeated challenges from Japan, Italy, France, and Britain itself. This visual supremacy has not been

matched in American literature; it is in what might be called literary
television drama that Britain can still very much hold its own.

Mrs. Maddox, who writes a media column in the *Daily Telegraph,* also says trying to compare British and American television
is like trying to grow an English garden in California, "the whole
climate is different." She told me:

> The BBC has to produce quality programs in exchange for the yearly
> hundred-pound license fee, the tax everybody who has a TV set pays.
> Independent companies like Granada, based in Manchester, enjoy a re-
> gional monopoly of commercial television advertising that comes with
> their franchise. In exchange for that monopoly, they've got certain obli-
> gations to produce good programs.

The system works well, though many British, as Granada's
chairman Sir Denis Forman told me, fear that the coming of satellite
television, with its mushrooming of channels and the future "auc-
tioning" of franchises and more government control, could be the
death of quality drama in Britain; it could get too expensive to produce. One reason why PBS imports so many British television dramas is it gets them cheaply.

British television also draws on the great English literary tradition. To Isaacs this is not a clear advantage:

> British society is so verbal, while communication on a film screen,
> even a television screen, is done with an expression of face, more than
> speech. I think British television is often wordier than it needs to be.

Others say all British culture is getting more visual. London is becoming a center of design. And it is design—the way past periods are
so ingeniously re-created in costume, setting, every detail—that
makes British television drama so distinctive. How do they do it?

The three greatest novels of this century, George Steiner told us
in Innsbruck thirty-two years ago, were Joyce's *Ulysses,* Mann's
Magic Mountain, and Proust's *Remembrance of Things Past.* "We
need new art forms," says Chekhov's Trepilov in *The Seagull.* An
imaginative series to introduce these and other great works called
The Modern World: Ten Great Writers, produced in 1988 by London
Weekend Television, a commercial channel, did just that.

The idea came from Melvyn Bragg, a writer (novels, a recent
biography of Richard Burton), but chiefly known in Britain as the
editor and host of LWT's "South Bank Show," a weekly arts program
with a twelve-year track record of innovation. Its shows are sold

individually to PBS and cable networks in the United States. Von Karajan, Horowitz, Satyajit Ray, Ingmar Bergman have been interviewed, and such writers as Arthur Miller, Marguerite Duras, Norman Mailer, Alberto Moravia, Saul Bellow, Philip Larkin, and dozens more. Bragg's profile of Laurence Olivier, seen in America, is an invaluable historical record; it showed the great actor visibly moved by a visit to his old choir school. Samuel Beckett and Graham Greene ("I would rather not be a household portrait") refused to be on the show; Bragg got John le Carré and Paul Theroux to talk about Greene's work on page and screen instead. Bragg keeps exploring what can be done with television:

> You can have Pavarotti talk about an aria, the film cut to stills of Verdi, hear from letters of Verdi and his librettist, listen to Pavarotti rehearsing and mix through to the final conclusive performance . . . This undercutting of time, place, history, and the usual accepted chronology of events is only part of what television arts programs can bring.

For the *Ten Great Writers* series, Bragg was given a £1 million ($1.8 million) budget for eleven hour-long shows (one to sum up). Besides Joyce, Mann, and Proust it was decided to do Dostoevsky, Ibsen, Conrad, T. S. Eliot, Pirandello, Kafka, and Virginia Woolf. (D. H. Lawrence had just been done in a film and Pound, Faulkner, and Henry James, Americans all, were the three runners-up.) Two young members of Bragg's "South Bank Show" team, David Thomas (Cambridge) and Nigel Wattis ("a sixties dropout"), were assigned to write, produce, and direct most of the shows and Gillian Greenwood (Oxford) did the literary research for them all.

This team came up with a three-part format: each show would combine dramatic excerpts from the author's work, explanatory material from his or her life, and expert critical comment (from some of Britain's flashiest literary commentators: Sir V. S. Pritchett, Anthony Burgess, John Mortimer, Sir Stephen Spender, George Steiner, Craig Raine). Each show would focus on a single book and take no liberties whatsoever with the author's text.

Bragg let them go to it. David Suchet, familiar as Hercule Poirot, was found for Joyce's Bloom; a relative unknown, John Shrapnel, for Mann's Hans Castorp; a Yorkshire sitcom star, Roger Rees, for Proust's Marcel. Thomas, a mountaineer, scouted out Alpine settings near Davos for *The Magic Mountain*. Vic Symonds, LWT's head of design, scrambled to find some blossom-laden hawthorne hedges for the Méséglise Way, which leads past Swann's bourgeois home, and the Guermantes Way, leading toward a royally titled estate.

Brenda Maddox, as the biographer of Nora Joyce, described the first show in her media column in the *Sunday Telegraph;* it was on *Ulysses:*

> The opening of the Joyce film veers perilously near the trap of explicitness. We are shown the green bile—bright green on colour television—that Stephen Dedalus's dying mother vomits into a bowl after he refuses to kneel at her bedside. Does it help anyone who has not braved *Ulysses* to see the bile-green dissolve into the waters of Dublin Bay? Or to have Buck Mulligan intone, with almost schoolmasterly emphasis: "A great sweet mother. The snotgreen sea . . . She is our great sweet mother." The uninitiated will miss the connection. The Joycean will miss Mulligan's extra jibe at the colour green: "A new art color for our Irish poets: snotgreen."

À la recherche du temps perdu, Proust's own French title, set his novel's subject and theme: the narrator is literally "in search of lost time," and he finds in involuntary memories stimulated by some object or circumstance the true meaning of past experience. Nigel Wattis, who did Proust, had the inspired idea of having Marcel shown entering a *belle époque* drawing room (found in Tunbridge Wells), which is empty but adjoins another one where a concert is in progress. Instead of joining the others, he stops to dunk his famous madeline in a cup of tea, triggering off memories of when, as a child, he spent some time in the country:

> As a rule I did not attempt to go to sleep at once, but used to spend the greater part of the night recalling our life in the old days at Combray with my great-aunt, at Balbec, Paris, Doncières, Venice, and the rest; remembering again all the places and people I had come to know, what I had actually seen of them, and what others had told me.

Brenda Maddox, who praised the show, again worried about its explicitness, finding it was

> . . . dangerously over-real on the screen: an actual madeline drops real crumbs into hot tea. Swann's Way becomes a kind of Rambler's Association footpath into the countryside.

"You are creating, realistically," Wattis told me, "something designed only to be imagined. You're bound to conflict with those who've read the book and see it in their imagination how it is." Designer Symonds said, "What I felt was: that drawing room has got to have a strong kind of look. We'll get clues from Proust. We decorated it. And then used its inside and cobbled together the exterior."

It was amazing how close they came to one's own imagination. *The Magic Mountain* is one of my favorite novels, first read in the tower of a Tyrolian castle in Igls when I was laid up with a ski injury (I used to say I fell "from Obergurgl to Untergurgl"); I was thrilled to see the Davos sanatorium, the snowy Swiss Alps, and not just Castorp but Clavdia Chauchat, Naphta, and Mynheer Peeperkorn looking just as I'd always pictured them. (Wattis is right about conflicting with a viewer's preconceptions; I badly missed *The Magic Mountain*'s séance scene, with its terrifying phantasm of Castorp's dead soldier cousin, Joachim, which to me was Mann's most effective metaphor for spiritual decadence.)

I asked Bragg, could Americans produce something like this?

> It isn't so much subsidies, it's systems. My company, London Weekend Television, is a commercial system. We make a lot of money, profits for our stockholders. But we get a franchise from the government giving us a right to broadcast for eight to ten years. In return we have to promise the Independent Broadcasting Authority to produce so many art shows, drama, quality television. And we have to keep our promise or they give the franchise to somebody else. This has happened enough to make it a real threat.

Bragg feels the system works well in terms of audience ratings, sales abroad, and earning profits. By turning out two hundred to three hundred dramas alone each year, the British system of television production leads to a steady crossover with the West End theater and British film industry that doesn't happen in the same way in America, where everything is so spread out. Harold Pinter, Tom Stoppard, Dennis Potter and David Hare, for example, all write for films, stage, and television. It is the same for directors, actors, and designers. Bragg finds the two countries' systems very different:

> America is full of immense talent, God knows . . . In arts and drama, American television cannot and will not set up the same kind of system. If it did, all those wonderful directors, writers, and actors would flock to it.

When Bragg's "South Bank Show" has advertised for researchers—his team numbers less than twenty—they've had nearly a thousand applicants per opening, including many honors graduates from Oxford and Cambridge.

Mrs. Maddox, summing up the themes raised by the series, said:

> One is that nobody is certain how life should be lived, or what the connection is between political and social passion. Another is that the line has become obscure between good and evil and, for that matter,

between the conscious and the unconscious. A third is that words are mere patterns on a page and come out of fragments of memory and desire, subject to infinite reworking.

"In or about December 1910, human character changed," suggested Virginia Woolf. D. H. Lawrence proposed that "it was in 1915 the old world ended." It was in the 1930s Ezra Pound declared, "Make it new." The modern spirit, at least in Britain, *Ten Great Writers* seemed to suggest, is best exemplified by T. S. Eliot's *Waste Land,* with its vision of sterility, bleakness, and cultural collapse. David Thomas, who did the Eliot episode, slightly departed from the single-work format to open with "The Love Song of J. Alfred Prufrock," with its one-night cheap hotels, singing mermaids, and rooms where women come and go, talking of Michelangelo.

> Let us go then, you and I,
> When the evening is spread out against the sky
> Like a patient etherised upon a table

Following Ezra Pound's editing, of course, Eliot cut *The Waste Land* to about half its original length. Published in 1922, it created what Professor Malcolm Bradbury, the consultant to *Ten Great Writers,* called "a dark and agonized vision of spiritual loss which belonged not to a single individual but to contemporary culture, the modern city, the postwar world." To Pound the poem was "the justification of the 'movement' of our modern experiment since 1900." To American poet William Carlos Williams, it was "the great catastrophe in our letters." Williams wanted the modern to be American, hopeful and optimistic. To Eliot, the modern was implicitly English: cosmopolitan, ironic, despairing. *The Waste Land* represents a major break in Anglo-American literary tradition. Eliot himself, a native of St. Louis, sided totally with the English; he stayed in London, took British nationality, and joined the Anglican church; his ironic vision still has great influence. In some of the most familiar words in the English language:

> April is the cruelest month, breeding
> Lilacs out of the dead land, mixing
> Memory and desire . . .

The Eliot hour had actors reading excerpts from *The Waste Land.* This worked well; when Eileen Atkins was the barmaid, you realized you'd never quite *heard* the words before, as when she talked about abortion ("It's them pills I took, to bring it off, she said") while calling shrilly for everybody in the pub to drink up, it's almost closing time:

You *are* a proper fool, I said.
Well, if Albert won't leave you alone, there it is, I said,
What you get married for if you don't want children?
HURRY UP PLEASE IT'S TIME

(Actors aren't always the best ones to read poetry. Craig Raine, who was also on the Eliot show, argues in favor of poets: "Poets know the thing depends on setting up a slightly monotonous rhythm: ta-rum, ta-rum, ta-rum, tar-rum . . . Actors are interested in expression; it's a dramatic performance for them.")

Raine, Sir Stephen Spender, Eliot biographer Peter Ackroyd and literary critic Frank Kermode met for a two-hour discussion; twenty minutes were aired. (Raine: "You try to mount a complicated argument. They take snippets. It's like showing people a car by letting them see a headlight and a spark plug.")

The Waste Land itself is made up of disconnected fragments: bits of poems, scenes, phrases, captured speech, and references that have little meaning in themselves but echo and explain each other; understanding it depends on the reader's knowledge of literature, myths, comparative religion, history, and, above all, contemporary London life. For example, as I write this I can look down from my balcony on Richmond Hill and glimpse through the treetops—it is a summer afternoon—canoes on the Thames with young couples rowing toward Kew Gardens. *The Waste Land:*

> "Trams and dusty trees.
> Highbury bore me. Richmond and Kew
> Undid me. By Richmond I raised my knees
> Supine on the floor of a narrow canoe."

Eliot's dominant imagery comes from Jessie L. Weston's *From Ritual to Romance,* a study of medieval legends such as the Grail. Eliot was writing for a specific, rather narrow Oxbridge-educated English intellectual audience. In his pastiche of past literature—Dante, Goldsmith, Pope, Webster, Browning—he draws, as in this example from Shakespeare, lyrical echoes for scenes of modern despair. The great speech of Enobarbus in *Antony and Cleopatra:*

> The barge she sat in, like a burnish'd throne,
> Burn'd on the water

becomes

> The Chair she sat in, like a burnished throne,
> Glowed on the marble

This sumptuous exoticism soon leads to modern-day anxiety (" 'My nerves are bad to-night. Yes, bad' "). The poetic dignity of the past is mocked by the vulgarities of the present:

> And still she cried, and still the world pursues,
> "Jug Jug" to dirty ears.

And pop parodies:

> O O O O that Shakespeherian Rag—
> It's so elegant
> So intelligent

Valerie, Eliot's much younger, second wife, an Englishwoman, was quoted on the Eliot episode: "He felt he had paid too high a price to be a poet, that he had suffered much."

The final show in the series was a panel discussion led by Bragg with Professor Bradbury, Hermione Lee (another academic), novelist Anthony Burgess and George Steiner. The talk ranged over the ten great writers. Where, one began to wonder, did the Americans come in? It looked, except for Eliot, that they didn't. Then Bragg asked the panel, observing the hour was coming to an end, where modernism was sustaining itself.

STEINER: We've been talking as if America wasn't. And this isn't on . . .

BURGESS: I think Americans, if I may say this, they've always been anti-modernist. I mean, it begins with William Carlos Williams, who was dead set against it . . . There's never been a modernist movement in America. Possibly the whole commercial system of book production is against it . . . I think it's essentially a European phenomenon. But it never really went beyond Europe.

LEE: You'd have to say, Anthony, that Carlos Williams's objection to Eliot was that he was reactionary, that he was traditionalist, that he . . .

BRADBURY: . . . was not modernist enough. I totally disagree with what Anthony said. I *do* think modernism started in Europe. That is true. I think it was *totally* appropriated by the Americans . . . I would argue that if it had *not* been for the Americans, modernism would simply be a hole-and-corner affair and would have remained an elite secret. And that we would still be spending all our time reading Arnold Bennett,

John Galsworthy, E. M. Forster and H. G. Wells. And maybe we should.

BRAGG: Are you saying anything more than that America marketed modernism?

BRADBURY: I'm saying that the Americans' acceptance of modernism has a great deal to do with the realization that we ourselves as human beings, as individuals, live in a modern world.

True. But then Americans never suffered the shock of watching their old world fall apart.

VI

LOSS
OF EMPIRE

Shattered Illusions

THE BRITISH EMPIRE casts a long shadow. For anybody old enough to have been personally involved in something that mostly ended over forty years ago (Hong Kong has a few years left), it was a splendor like no other. Young Englishmen went "home" to be educated at boarding school and university. They came back as soldiers and administrators, exiles from their tiny island in the North Sea to a more spacious geography. What began as trade and the need to protect it became over three hundred years for these Englishmen a whole way of life dependent on empire. It defined themselves, their professions, their duties, their behavior, their beliefs.

They held to the idea that they had a God-given right to be there. As Sir Peter Ramsbotham confirms in the next chapter, they felt they had this right because they were incorruptible, Christian, and classically educated rationalists. They were bringing law and order, schools, hospitals, roads, civilization.

The Empire is gone. But something of this mentality lives on, the idea of a rational and superior establishment that knows best (Mrs. Thatcher is not persuaded). One finds it, as I've said before, in its civil service stronghold, the Guards, the House of Commons (both sides of the aisle), Eton and the other public schools, Oxford and Cambridge, the BBC, even in the Anglican bishops' palaces. Honest and intelligent, civilized and nice, this establishment has not lost the old imperial habit of telling people what to do, only now they are just telling their own countrymen. Remember what Eton's Head Master said? He talked about the "role Eton played in the service of empire by creating inquiring minds and a willingness to take responsibility." Just like Davies, the Oxford don, saying Oxford's old role was to "train Victorian civil servants and colonial administrators." Even today, the headmaster said, Eton takes the "top people" and helps train them to "run the church and the state."

How much of this high-mindedness and sense of duty was (and is) based on illusion? How many of those "silent, sullen" colonial peoples were perfectly happy to exchange civilizing British rule for independence and backwardness and internal strife of their own making? (And some haven't done too badly in the schools, hospitals, and roads department on their own.) The end of empire was not just a colossal shock in itself. It also meant the collapse of so many illusions. It threatened the British establishment's sense of self-identity. And still does. I think the establishment is still trying to adjust, if greatly encumbered by the many institutional relics of empire. The worst shock of all came in 1947 with the loss of India and a Hindu-Muslim bloodbath that claimed at least a million lives and which the British were shown to be powerless to stop. For India was the greatest nation in the empire in every way, vast, immensely populous—India, the Raj, the jewel in the crown.

Traffic died in London's streets, I am told, on evenings during the fourteen weeks in 1984 that *The Jewel in the Crown*, the adaptation of Paul Scott's Raj Quartet, was televised on Channel Three, ITV, repeated on Channel Four a few days later. Emotions ran high. Critical acclaim was matched by fury and anger. All Britain was enthralled. The end of the British Empire had been documented before. What Scott's long saga with its enormous cast of characters did was to fully dramatize its British rulers' psychic collapse.

The television series, even more than Scott's novels, succeeded in making Britain's retreat from India, and empire, more directly intelligible to millions of British people. To almost anyone born in the last quarter century or so it was the first really electrifying representation of what the Empire meant—both to India and to themselves. As Max Beloff wrote in *Encounter* in 1976 when the last of the Quartet came out:

> Paul Scott does convey the full tragic significance of the combination between a sense of duty and a sense of permanent alienation from those to whom the duty is owed that is at the heart of the matter.

The television series also did justice to Scott's grasp of period detail: the Anglo-Indian social round, regimental traditions, class distinctions, the clothes, songs, settings of the times; for old India hands it was tremendously nostalgic.

To me, having lived in India myself five years, taking a look at how *The Jewel in the Crown* was made gives us not just a more focused view of British drama, but also gives us more of a sense, which the cast and crew felt too, of what the loss of empire was like. Nothing has played a bigger role in Britain's diminution of the last fifty years.

In his 1979 book, *Paul Scott: Images of India,* Patrick Swinden says Scott's fiction "needs to be sustained by events in the Indian sub-continent between 1942 and 1947." All his best novels are about it. Swinden feels Scott's triumph was that "he has fully understood, almost one might say shared, the illusion of India, the Englishman's India" and the "intangible idea of the rightness of [the English's] presence—more than that, their *superior* presence." Swinden divides *Jewel*'s characters into those who cling to the illusion that the British Raj will last, and those who are coming to see this illusion for what it is.

Paul Scott, a Londoner who was going to be an accountant, instead got sent to India in World War II. He held a commission in the Indian Army from 1943 to 1946. Back home he worked in publishing and as a literary agent. He turned to full-time writing in 1960—he wrote thirteen novels in all—and in 1964 made the first of several trips to India to collect material. To me his last novel, *Staying On,* is his masterpiece. The story of two minor characters from the Raj Quartet, Colonel "Tusker" Smalley and his wife Lucy, it came out in 1977 and won the Booker Prize (over Barbara Pym's *Quartet in Autumn,* though Philip Larkin was one of the judges). At the award ceremony, Scott said, "I have finished with India forever. It just needed some little valedictory thing." He died, just fifty-eight, less than six months later. The Raj Quartet begins with *The Jewel in the Crown* (1966), followed by *The Day of the Scorpion* (1967), *The Towers of Silence* (1971), and *A Division of the Spoils* (1975). It has won an increasingly high posthumous critical reputation and, after the television series, a huge worldwide popular readership. For our purposes, it gets close to the heart, in historical terms, of what ails Britain today.

It begins:

> This is the story of a rape, of the events that led up to it and followed it and the place in which it happened . . .

The time spans five years, from the "Quit India" motion of the All India Congress Committee in August 1942 to the Hindu-Muslim partition riots at the time of the British retreat in August 1947. In the first of two episodes during "Quit India" unrest, a missionary,

Edwina Crane, and an Indian teacher are attacked by bandits on the road to Dibrapur; the teacher dies and Edwina then takes her own life by putting on a sari and setting herself on fire in the manner of a traditional Indian widow's suttee.

In the other episode, in the Bibighar Gardens of Mayapore, a gang of Indian youths rape a young Englishwoman, Daphne Manners, the niece of Lady Manners, widow of an ex-governor of Ranpur, and beat up Hari Kumar, an English-reared and public-school-educated Indian whom Daphne loves. Kumar is jailed and accused of taking part in the rape by Ronald Merrick, a handsome and aspiring English lower-middle-class district superintendent of police.

Daphne dies in childbirth after refusing to implicate Kumar, who made love to her just before the gang rape. Unable to pin the crime on Kumar, Merrick detains him in prison as being "suspected" of anti-British acts during the riots. Among an enormous cast of characters—forty-eight with distinct identities—are Barbie Batchelor, a retired missionary who loses her faith and goes to pieces; Mildred Layton, gin-swigging wife of Colonel Layton of the Pancot Rifles and their two daughters, sensible Sarah and neurotic Susan (who marries Merrick after he loses an arm and is badly burned and disfigured trying to save her first husband, Teddie Bingham, from a burning ambushed jeep in Burma); Mabel Layton, the girls' step-grandmother and friend of Barbie; Guy Perron, a public-school-Oxbridge-educated sergeant in Field Security who forms an attachment to Sarah Layton; Count Bronowsky, Russian émigré adviser to the Nawab of Mirat, a princely state; Muslim Congress leader Mohammed Ali Kasim, jailed by the British, and his handsome son Ahmed.

In the *Quartet's* horrific climax, Ahmed is pulled off a train and massacred by a Hindu mob. The story ends where it began, with an Indian killed by crazed rioters on the road while members of the English ruling class stand by, powerless to save him. The full horror of what has happened on the train is revealed in the next station: Muslim men, women, and children have been butchered in their carriages. Sarah, streaked with blood and overwhelmed by guilt and futility as she tries to do what she can, tells Perron, "Ahmed and I weren't in love, but we loved one another. I'm sure he smiled just before he went . . . Nothing that we could do. Like Daphne Manners. Like Hari Kumar. After three hundred years of India, we've made this whole damned bloody mess." In a final scene, Perron tries and fails to find Kumar in a crowded Indian slum.

Each character defines some aspect of the British rule. As Lord Beloff pointed out in his piece, the fundamental barrier between English and Indian was color. Take away his brown skin and Hari Kumar is a pukka English gentleman, with the accent and manners of a good public school. But in British India to cross the color bar in either sex or platonic love is the ultimate taboo. What Daphne does in fact, Sarah does with heart and mind (and Adela Quested does in fevered fantasy in the Marabar Caves in E. M. Forster's *A Passage to India)*. Scott also uses the metaphor of sexual union to describe Britain and India as "locked in an imperial embrace."

The dark side of British colonialism comes out when we learn well into the story—the fifth episode in the series—that the apparently upright police officer Merrick has all along been a repressed homosexual and psychopathic deviant who gambles exposure against the sadistic pleasure he gets destroying his victims' characters, driving one to suicide. We finally learn from Kumar, after three years in jail, that back in Mayapore, after being falsely accused of the rape of Daphne Manners, he was stripped naked, tied to a trestle, and brutally flogged by Merrick, who tried to get him to ejaculate by sexually abusing him, the whole time talking about Daphne's rape. Kumar weeps when at last he is told of Daphne's death. Lady Manners, who has watched in secret as he gives his testimony, sees he will be released but suspects the evidence against Merrick will be suppressed. It is.

Merrick is truly evil. He dies, it is first said, in a riding accident. Later we learn the truth: he has been strangled and hacked to pieces with an axe in a ritual killing in a blood-soaked room, probably at the hands of what Count Bronowsky calls his "dark young men." With his strange mixture of perversity and bravery, part hero, part psychopath, Merrick, a man of humble origins, is not part of the ruling elite. But as long as he keeps the natives quiet, they look the other way. He personifies the sadism and arrogance Scott also saw as part of the Anglo-Indian relationship.

I first went to India in 1959, just twelve years after the British Raj ended. I stayed five years, as mentioned, first teaching at the university in Nagpur, then as a journalist in Delhi. I might have met Paul Scott. There were many British around. They had left so much behind—the army, electricity, railways, roads, irrigation, the plantation, the jute industry, the Hill Station, cricket, the Guest House, the

Anglican church, the military cantonment, Civil Lines, above all, the Club. Their life is revealed in words that entered English like memsahib, dhobi, pukka, bungalow, chit, chintz, chutney, pyjama, sandal, shawl, tonga, veranda.

James Cameron quotes from a widely used Hindustani phrasebook, "Specially Composed for Visiting Persons and Allied Officers" by one H. Achmed Ismail. It advises memsahibs how to deal with lesser breeds. From a chapter, "The Engagement of Body-Servants":

> Look sharp. Shut the door. What is your Pay? I Shall Pay You Far Less. Put on the Fan. Put off the Fan. You feign illness. Make clean yourself . . . You are too old/too young. I shall engage another bearer.

In Nagpur two English couples who managed several big manganese mines in the area still lived on an imperial scale; one had been there nearly forty years. Servants in their huge thatched-roofed and open-porched bungalows still went barefoot and wore long white coats with red cummerbunds and turbans. After I arrived for my first dinner-jacketed party on bicycle, further invitations came with instructions to wait for the driver to come with the Bentley. Most afternoons, after tea with watercress sandwiches, they all played golf. Dinner was buffet, standing up, served very late; tiny demitasses of coffee were the signal to go home. The huge lawns were not mown but handpicked by groups of squatting untouchable women. "Never mix it up with the natives," one of the English memsahibs told me. She always carried a knife and fork in her purse in case at some Indian function she wasn't given silverware ("It's so disgusting when they eat with their fingers").

Jawaharlal Nehru, the first time I took my students up to Delhi to meet him, was quite surprised to find an American teaching reporting. "Indian journalism should follow its own genius," he said. The last time I saw Nehru, four years later, was in March 1964, two months before he died. As its Delhi-based Asia correspondent, I interviewed him for the *Washington Star*. India's relations with America were strained. The United States had refused to build a steel plant and Nehru, for the first time since independence, had turned to the Russians for help. But that day, already gravely ill, he had just come from watching a rehearsal of the *Ramayana* ballet and was relaxed. He offered me an English cigarette—Nehru smoked but so discreetly few Indians knew it—and when I took it I noticed his hands were paler than mine.

I asked him what he felt was his greatest achievement. The political liberation of India's women, he said without hesitation. His greatest fear for the future?

> Fascism. By this I mean revolutionary forces trying to achieve their ends by violent or subversive means. By creating an atmosphere of violence and conflict, such forces may arise from any side. They can be communist, social fascism led by big industrialists, or Hindu fascism.

Much of this interview was about the conflict with Pakistan over Kashmir, which Nehru, "facing God," as our ambassador Chester Bowles put it, was trying in his dying days to settle. A snowstorm, isolating Kashmir for ten days from the outside world the previous January, had left me the sole reporter to witness an Islamic uprising to Indian rule (an account quoted in Gunnar Myrdal's *Asian Drama*). When I got back to Delhi I might have been expelled had not Neville Maxwell of *The Times* not gone up to confirm my story. India, in those days, didn't argue with *The Times*.

Nehru was all too human. But despite a patrician vanity, a stormy temper, and, unlike Gandhi, little real feeling for Indian village life, he had a deep and authentic belief in democracy. This parliamentary vision and rule of law, as is often said, were, I too feel, the most important legacy of the British Raj. Today certainly, the British are most remembered for all the good things they left behind. Nehru's own feelings owed a lot to Harrow and Cambridge. Was he "an Englishman in jodhpurs"? The night he died Nehru scribbled some familiar lines of Robert Frost on a notepad by his bed:

> The woods are lovely, dark and deep
> But I have promises to keep,
> And miles to go before I sleep,
> And miles to go before I sleep.

Sir Denis Forman, chairman of Granada Television, happened to be the last English commandant of Dehra Dun military academy in 1945. *Staying On*, when it won the Booker Prize in 1977, led him to the Raj Quartet. He read it and reread it, realizing Scott had gone a long way in showing how events fell out as they did. Could it be done for television? The novel jumped back and forth in time; there were shifting viewpoints and many flashbacks and retrospects. Scott made references to a now-distant political era. It would take at least four or five months' shooting in India with a cast and crew of sixty, seventy people. Nobody had attempted anything that big. (Sir Richard Attenborough's *Gandhi* wasn't shot until 1981.)

Sir Denis bought the rights. In a kind of trial run, he made *Staying On* in India in 1981. As Tusker and Lucy it reunited Trevor Howard and Celia Johnson for the first time since *Brief Encounter* in 1945. The film, a success, disappointed Scott fans. It failed to start with Tusker's death, which informs the whole thing. The book begins:

> When Tusker Smalley died of a massive coronary at approximately 9:30 A.M. on the last Monday of April 1972, his wife Lucy was out having her white hair blue-rinsed and set in the Seraglio Room on the ground floor of Pankot's new five-storey glass and concrete hotel, The Shiraz.

Scott had held his lively sense of humor in check in the Quartet. Now he let it go. *Staying On* is a terribly funny novel. Because we know how it is going to end, it is also profoundly sad.

Sir Denis knew that turning the Quartet into a screenplay would be a daunting task. The story went from 1942 to 1947. It had to be recast in chronological order if a television audience was going to follow weekly episodes for three months. There were seven main settings and so many characters. The job went to Ken Taylor, an award-winning writer who had done original screenplays and adaptations of Jane Austen and Thomas Hardy; at first he was just to do half, eventually the whole thing.

Forman was also able to get Christopher Morahan, then Sir Peter Hall's deputy at the National Theatre and in 1972–76 head of plays at the BBC, to agree to spend three years turning the Raj Quartet into a television series. "Morahan was the mastermind," Sir Denis told me. "He did it all." What was needed, he said, was a producer-director who would be true to Paul Scott's intentions. He explained:

> What you actually transfer from a novel to television is physically very little. It's dialogue. It's the only thing you transfer unaltered from the book to the screen. So you have to keep going back to the original work, the novel.

Granada had earlier done *Brideshead Revisited*. What matters, Sir Denis said, is not whether a book is really fashioned for television, whether it's easily adapted or can be split straight up and put on the screen—he said with some writers, like Dickens, you can do that pretty well. What mattered in both *Jewel* and *Brideshead* was the effect of the book on the screenplay writer, the director, the producer, the actors, the designers, the whole team; in each series it came to about a hundred and fifty people. Sir Denis explained:

> It was the ability of these people to respond to the intention of Paul Scott and Evelyn Waugh that made these series what they were. You start work on a big thing like that—and *Jewel* is the biggest thing *I've* ever done—and you absorb the interest of all the creative people. For a time you form your own world, a *Jewel in the Crown* world or a *Brideshead* world which takes aboard everybody from the designer and cameraman to the people who paint the props. So that they become imbued with the idea of what the author wrote. And *that* is what you get in a good series. Not a literal or skillful adaptation, which is then photographed. What you get is the novel which has flowed through the bloodstream of a lot of sensitive, perceptive people. And in all their different trades and professions. And who can then feed back onto the screen an accurate, refined, and dramatic version of what the author wanted.

I met Sir Denis Forman at Granada's Golden Square offices, near Piccadilly Circus. Ken Taylor, who did the screenplay, invited me out to his suburban London home for tea. East Finchley, with street after street of drab, detached redbrick houses (the Taylors have a home in Cornwall too) was a far cry from imperial India. While his wife served tea and cakes, Taylor talked enthusiastically about his work on *Jewel*. He said Scott exposed his characters to the collapse of their illusions about the British Empire and this threatened their senses of identity, even reality:

> Ronald Merrick's illusion was that the Raj can stay forever, that British power can be made permanent in India. Because power corrupts and he's a self-created man, as the story unfolds Merrick becomes both physically and spiritually corrupted. He becomes almost a satanic presence. Barbie Batchelor feels that. She says there's almost a whiff of sulphur when she meets him at Rose Cottage. The way Merrick ends, the awful butchery of his death, I think, was the only way Scott felt he could deal with that character.

Taylor said most of the main characters in *Jewel* come to see their illusions shattered:

> Hari Kumar is born of the illusion that an Indian can become an English gentleman. That India can become England. And it can't. Then there is the illusion of perpetual Edwardian sunlight that Sarah talks about, the whole idea of the British as natural rulers who will go on and on, being gentlemanly, and never having to resort to nasty, unpleasant things like torture and suppression of evidence. Which be-

comes necessary as power becomes harder and harder to impose and the subject people become more mutinous.

Taylor, like Sir Denis Forman and Scott himself, spent World War II in India, posted in Bombay as a wireless operator. His assignment to adapt *Jewel* came just months after Paul Scott died. He never met him. He did get to know Scott's daughter Carol who read his scripts at an early stage and was, he said, "a great reassurance."

Christopher Morahan himself had not been to India but his wife, actress Anna Carteret, was from an old Anglo-Indian military family like the Laytons. This personal tie to the imperial past, like his experience in the theater and with the BBC, left Morahan determined to stick closely to Scott's novels. He made a precondition to taking on the job of producer-director that Taylor write the entire series.

Taylor's screenplay tells the story in a highly literary English way through character and relationship with much less pictorial action than Hollywood-produced television drama. Morahan says the historical link between the written word and television is much stronger in Britain:

> BBC, actually the main flag-bearer of public broadcasting in this country, goes back to an amazing amount of very original radio writing in the 1950s and 1960s. People like Pinter and Stoppard, for instance, had a lot of their early work done as radio plays.

Once Taylor's screenplay, a feat of story engineering, was done, it was final. "We felt it was accurate and true," Morahan told me. "So I said, 'That's it.' And we stuck with it." He did make a few changes, mainly visual, adding such recurring motifs as Miss Crane's burning hut or Hari Kumar playing cricket. Next Morahan made three trips to India. He chose Udaipur for princely Mirat, Mysore for Mayapore where the story begins, Kashmir for itself, and Simla for Pankot, the Himalayan hill station where the Laytons and Barbie Batchelor live. Morahan also picked much of the cast and production crew, bringing in a young codirector, Jim O'Brien, to direct half the fourteen episodes.

Good drama, as every actor knows, comes from fidelity to its author. At least three of *Jewel*'s cast found their way to the character they wanted to play on their own. Peggy Ashcroft told me she "simply devoured" the novels on a trip to Canada in 1977 to play Winnie in Samuel Beckett's *Happy Days* (Beckett himself helped direct the

London opening). From the first she wanted to be Barbie. A friend urged Tim Pigott-Smith to read the Quartet, saying, "There's a part you're absolutely right for." (When I told this to Dame Peggy she was amused, saying, "I can't think why a friend would say, 'You ought to play Merrick.' When you think what a sweet person Tim is. Was it a *good* friend?") In India already to play Mira Behn in Sir Richard Attenborough's *Gandhi*, Geraldine James read the Quartet and discovered Sarah Layton. She told me: "I thought: I'm much too old. I was thirty and she was meant to be twenty-two. It took eight months to convince them that I could play the part. Nobody else was cast except Tim and Peggy. And I just hung around. I've never wanted a part so much in all my life."

This left Daphne Manners. Susan Wooldridge wrote a letter, asking to be considered. Nothing happened.

> God knows where it went. And then I was cast in the part of the assistant stage manager Flick Harold in this comedy series "Rep," which was also at Granada. They'd been looking, so I believe, for Daphne for six months. I was in rehearsal one day and I got a message: would I see Christopher Morahan and Jim O'Brien? I was in my rehearsal clothes—extremely tight jeans, a Minnie Mouse bow in my hair—I didn't look like Daphne at all. Exhausted and delighted to be working, I must say, in a great fit of energy I bounced into the meeting with them.

They gave her two scripts to take home and read.

> Well, I mean I was so delighted to be taking home some scripts. Equally I practiced disappointment on the Tube home in that I was used to "Doris enters page eighty-one" and "Doris exits page eighty-four." And so when I opened this I saw that Daphne seemed to talk an awful lot. I mean, it was the most . . . Well, I sat down with a bottle of wine and started to read. Such was my excitement I actually couldn't read the second script. I just met someone on the page I knew so well. You recognize something. And you just go: "Hello. How are you? So glad you waited for me . . ." So I went back and read for them. It wasn't a *fait accompli* at all. I then had to go back and read with Art, Art Malik who plays Hari.

Susan Wooldridge is strikingly pretty. She doesn't look at all like the gauche but sensitive Daphne Manners. Sitting across from her at her kitchen table over coffee, I told Susan it was hard to believe she was the same person. She laughed.

> It's very *easy*. I tell you, you get that hair and your sausage curls on. You take your makeup off and put a little pink on your nose. Get the specs and have the bicycle. And you're away.

Actually, it was Daphne's vulnerability that was so moving. The more she talked, the more Susan was like her after all. (Julie Harris told me Susan's performance was superb.)

Once he finished casting, Morahan called everybody to a mammoth initial reading of the complete screenplay at a rehearsal studio in Brixton in the fall of 1981. It took three days. Everybody was there but Peggy Ashcroft, who was appearing in *All's Well That Ends Well* in Stratford. The cast now included such distinguished stage veterans as Rachel Kempson (Lady Manners), widow of Sir Michael Redgrave and mother of Lynn and Vanessa; Fabia Drake (Mabel Layton); and Eric Porter (Count Bronowsky); Morahan had filled all the English and Indian roles with great skill. Susan recalls the reading:

> It was a snowy winter morning. In the rehearsal room was a long table, as long as most rooms, and I suppose nearly a hundred people around it. And you sat down at the table. And you're sitting down with some of the great figures of the English stage. And Tim, Art, and I really do the talking for the first three hours. I mean, it was the most *terrifying* . . . It was a great act of faith by Christopher, Jim and Sir Denis in that I was totally unknown. I think Christopher said to Jim, "I think we've found our Daphne and I'm taking a flier on it." Then of course having died or gone our separate ways in the story, Art and I had the delight of sitting back and listening to these masters of their craft.

The cast read the whole series of scripts. Morahan felt it was the only time they would get a sense of the overall story. It would be filmed in a fragmented way, shot on four locations in India and doing mainly interiors afterward in Manchester with many scenes out of sequence. Susan says the reading gave everyone a sense of the whole thing:

> Out of it—Daphne dying so early—came the realization for both Art and myself that Daphne and Hari are the spirits that draw the rest of it together. We are, after our demise, mentioned in every single episode. Paul Scott was very clear to make Daphne, as we say here, proper clogs. You know the adage: keep the audience wanting. Because, you know, you've grown to identify with her and maybe become fond of her. The secret of the Bibighar Gardens is why people keep reading the story.

Here Susan burst into laughter.

> And the Bibighar Gardens were . . . a gravel pit in Manchester. With the worst midges. Far worse than India. There were a couple of people

who were literally eaten alive during the filming of the rape. It was just very funny.

At first that day, Susan recalls, the veteran actors around the table tended to pick up their scripts, mark them and say their lines quietly, a typical television first read-through.

> Then Wendy Morgan, who plays Susan Layton, in her wonderful, shining, talented innocence, came to the bit where she hears her husband Teddie's been killed. On the page there were something like nine "no's." And, God love her, she absolutely went for it. What was charming and exciting was that everybody stopped muttering in their beards after that. It brought them up very short and they thought, "My God, if *that* is the level of reading . . .

Geraldine James recalls sitting across from Eric Porter.

> Susie was down at one end of this great long table, Christopher somewhere in the middle. I'd be sort of distracted, and come in late on my lines, I was so overwhelmed by sitting opposite Eric Porter. And afterwards he came up to me and he said, "That was an extremely good reading. I couldn't see how Sarah Layton was going to work out and now I see it." I was in seventh heaven. It didn't matter what Christopher or anybody said; Eric Porter had said it was all right.

One December afternoon Morahan, O'Brien, Pigott-Smith, and Geraldine went to Peggy Ashcroft's house in Hampstead for a reading of some of her scenes. As she served them tea beforehand Peggy gave them a tour of London accents, trying to find the right "shabbygenteel" one for Barbie. Geraldine recalls:

> We started off just sitting around chatting. And when Peggy was pouring tea, she asked me, "Milk?" And I went: "Yes, thank you," and laughed. I sort of thought: golly, she's a bit batty. What she was actually doing when she said, "Milk?" or "Do sit down," was testing out her accent, trying to find an accent for Barbie. And I suddenly realized she wasn't completely off her rocker.
>
> Later we really got on. But that day when we started reading the scenes, I got very nervous. Peggy Ashcroft is the greatest person for me ever. And here she was sitting on a chair near me reading all those lines I'd read a year before in the book, *being* Barbie. I couldn't put one foot in front of the other. I spluttered. I couldn't read. I was completely hopeless. And there was this sort of flicker across Peggy's face, as if she thought, "Oh, God, what have they got here?" After we left Jim said, "I don't understand. You've changed everything. Why did you read like that? It wasn't nearly as good as before." And I said, "Listen. It was Peggy Ashcroft. I was terrified. Don't, please, judge me on that. I'll never be like that again." And I don't think I ever was.

When I read this out to her, Peggy laughed and said, "They get over that very quickly." She went on: "I adored Geraldine. You see, I had a *lot* to do with Geraldine—Barbie and Sarah had so many scenes together."

I interviewed Peggy one wintry London day over coffee and cakes in the enormous, light and airy drawing room of her two-story penthouse flat south of Hampstead, taken when she gave up the old family house where she raised her two children. Happily, she had just got home from the trip to Canada where she read Scott's work when Melvyn Bragg offered her a role in a comedy film, *Hullabaloo over Georgie and Bonnie's Pictures,* which would be a two-part special on his "South Bank Show." It had a modest hundred-thousand pound budget and was to be shot in India in four weeks by James Ivory, Ismail Merchant, and Ruth Prawer Jhabvala. Peggy agreed to play Lady G, an old Anglo-Indian hand and eccentric art collector who is in pursuit of a maharajah's collection of rare miniatures on behalf of the British Museum. The trip, made in 1978 when she was seventy-one, was Peggy's first trip to India. "I fell in love with Rajasthan," she told me. The film was shot at Jodhpur's Amaid Bhawan Palace which its maharajah, still living there, has turned into a hotel. Michael Billington in his 1988 biography of Dame Peggy credits director Ivory with bringing out her best on film; she says he taught her how to "use the soft pedal," paring down her work for the screen.

Peggy Ashcroft is, I think it is safe to say, *the* greatest stage actress of our time, certainly since Dame Edith Evans and Dame Sybil Thorndike, a generation ahead, left the scene, and at least in Britain, with Vanessa Redgrave, Maggie Smith, and Dame Judi Dench a generation or so behind. Few Americans saw Peggy as Desdemona to Paul Robeson's Othello in 1930, Juliet to the Romeos of Olivier and Gielgud in 1935, Cleopatra to Michael Redgrave's Antony in 1953, or Katherina to Peter O'Toole's Petruchio in 1960. She is famous for her Chekhov: Irina in *The Three Sisters,* Madame Ranevskaya in *The Cherry Orchard,* Nina in *The Seagull.* Her 1936 performance in *The Seagull* was directed by Theodore Komisarjevsky, the second of Peggy's three husbands; his sister played Nina in Stanislavsky's original Art Theatre production. Peggy has had a continuing succession of theatrical triumphs ever since she made her stage debut opposite Ralph Richardson in J. M. Barrie's *Dear Brutus* in 1926.

Yet she has done so few films that to most Americans, indeed, to most British outside theatergoers, Peggy will always be poor old

Barbie Batchelor, lonely spinster and retired missionary, who dies insane. It is a great role; such is the power of television that it is Barbie's kindness, charity, and intelligence that act as a touchstone against which many of the world's people measure the behavior of the British in India.

To Make a Jewel

I N JANUARY 1982, Sir Denis Forman saw *Jewel*'s cast and crew, about seventy of them, off from Heathrow on their flight to India for about four months' shooting. Even without all the horror stories of India's ghastly illnesses, harsh climate, and bureaucratic red tape, the logistics were appalling. Three hundred containers carried everything from a three-ton generator to a suitcase full of aerosol sprays. Nine trucks were needed to take it all to the first location in Udaipur. A portable kitchen left over from *Gandhi*, equipped with six portable toilets, was hired; it was run by three Londoners.

In Delhi, Geraldine, the old India hand after *Gandhi*, dragooned some of the jet-lagged cast to the noisy teeming bazaar of Chandi Chowk in the old city; the heat, dust, deafeningly amplified Hindi film songs, beggars, lepers, and shouting, screeching, gaping humanity sent them all rushing back to their hotel with culture shock. Udaipur was less shattering. Susan:

> We started out up the hill in Lakshmi Villas, a wonderfully dilapidated Empire hotel. Halfway through there was a swap-around and we found ourselves in the unbelievably romantic and gorgeous Lake Palace Hotel out on the water. I found it so exotic and erotic, I couldn't work there at all, learning lines and such, and I asked if I could go back to the Lakshmi.

Soon bicycles were hired to explore Udaipur. Tim Pigott-Smith kept a diary of the trip and in 1986 published excerpts from it, along with quoted material from other books on the subcontinent, called *Out of India*. He tells how he was adopted by a young Indian street urchin called Dinesh.

> I could not get rid of him, but he turned out to be so companionable a child, that in the end I didn't want to . . . He had enough English for us to communicate. He rode alongside me, through the bazaar, telling me which shops were good, which bad . . .

"You filming star. Yes. I know. You come. This make them very happy."

Once shooting began, curious spectators became a problem, huge mobs crowding in on every scene. Police were the answer, but then *they* crowded in. Untouchable beggars were needed for a temple scene; an Indian driver refused to allow them in his vehicle. The beggars complained that the actors, entering the temple in take after take, never gave them any money. Then Eric Porter's hair, bleached white for his role, turned green from chlorine used in his hotel pool. Two rats scurried across the dining room one night; Judy Parfitt (Mildred Layton) cracked, "You'd think the management would give them a dining room of their own." Everybody soon discovered that India's weather is either too hot and dry, or too steamy and wet, or too cold and damp. In Mysore, after several of the cast and crew passed out from heat exhaustion, black umbrellas were handed around, giving the unit an *Our Town* look. In Simla shooting got delayed by unseasonal snow; old friends Peggy Ashcroft and Rachel Kempson huddled together in blankets with hot water bottles between takes. Peggy:

> Rachel and I were fortunate in that Brigadier Gurbash Singh and his wife Cuckoo said they could put up two of us. They'd lent their house for some scene in *Staying On* and enjoyed the filming. So their summer residence became Rose Cottage. They were the most delightful couple. It was an absolutely unnatural spring and they were worried about it and tried to keep us warm. I just loved them. It was April and shouldn't have been so cold. When we shot the scene with Barbie and Merrick on the terrace, that was *freezing* cold. I know I had to be taken to a fire and given brandy to warm me up. (Laughter.) It was that bitterly cold.

The crew's cost clerk carried about a suitcase with thousands of hundred-rupee notes to hand out to workmen and extras ("Never felt safer in my life"). When designer Vic Symonds wanted some housefronts built and asked for plywood, his Indian craftsmen said, "Why plywood?" and ran up the set in mud and brick as quickly. A village eagerly exchanged its old string cots, or *charpoys*, for brand-new ones.

India affected them all. In one scene Hari and Daphne go to the crowded Indian street where he lives to visit his Aunt Shalini. Susan remembers:

> It was a dark little street. As usually happened if we were shooting in a town, a couple of thousand people pressed in to watch. They were hanging off roofs and everything. And we were standing there, among

them as it were, watching. Suddenly Art looked quite shaken. I said to him, "What's the matter, old boy? Is something wrong?" And he said, "Let's walk up the road a little bit." We did and he said: "I suddenly realized if somebody from the crew wanted to say something to me or to see me, they wouldn't find me." He'd suddenly seen what Hari Kumar went through, of being, not an individual at a good public school in England, but one of an anonymous Indian mass. It was a most important discovery for both of us that day. I saw India very much through Daphne's eyes.

Since logistics, weather, and the budget dictated *Jewel* be shot out of sequence, the first scenes filmed were in the sixth episode. Cast and crew went to Udaipur and shot everything set there. This created a challenge to the actors, especially Tim Pigott-Smith, who spent the most time of any of the cast on *Jewel*—eighteen months. He was in over a hundred scenes. And Merrick's character itself keeps changing, from the original picture of an efficient police officer just doing his job to a truly evil, sadistic psychopath. Pigott-Smith:

> I started with my last scene but one. The decision that one had to make to shoot it was: is Merrick mad or is he sane? Which is a fairly monumental decision. And one got to the location and thought: "I'll have to play him mad. He's gone mad by this time. He's flipped." But then having pitched at his mind having flipped, you have to make sure in the next seventeen, eighteen months that you get the buildup right.

He found Taylor's screenplay very verbal:

> One of the difficulties we had as actors was making large chunks of script live. I don't know how else Ken could have done it. His adaptation was brilliant. But it did mean you had a lot to say. It goes, I suppose, with our literary heritage. All the great English plays are plays of language. Shakespeare, Wilde, Sheridan, Coward. If you can't speak them, you can't do them.

Ken Taylor told me Merrick was so dislikable, he thought Pigott-Smith, like Scott himself, probably had to be sustained by an intellectual concept of the role. Pigott-Smith disagreed: "I don't think Scott grew to dislike Merrick. I think he consciously doesn't tell you anything of his inside. I think Merrick was probably *him.*"

"You do? Taylor said he couldn't even write Merrick from the inside."

"It's something an actor has to do. You simply *have* to do it."

Susan feels that as Daphne, in her scenes with Tim, she was privy to Merrick's vulnerable side.

When he says, "I'm just a grammar school boy," that's an enormous thing for a boy from the lower middle class to admit. Of course it doesn't bother Daphne in the slightest because she's above all that.

When I said Tim himself was from the same background, Susan said, "He used that. And Tim's luckier than Merrick. He's in an age where it's ceasing to matter socially, or as invidiously as it did in the 1940s."

The hardest thing in directing *The Jewel in the Crown,* Christopher Morahan told me, was to be able to keep control of the storytelling of the performances and the playing of the scenes. He had to be able to judge their pace and how they should be played. He also had to keep up enough suspense to carry a television audience through fourteen weekly episodes. "It goes right back to the old two-reelers, *The Perils of Pauline,*" he explained. "You want to make sure they're going to listen the next day because something appalling will happen."

It was really Morahan's stubborn loyalty to Scott's work that made the series seem so real.

> We kept being told all the time that our pictures were not showing India. That was quite deliberate. We weren't making a travelogue. What I refused to do was start on a shot of a beautiful mountain and do a lot of lap-over, lapping dissolves. And play funny music. That's rubbish. What matters is the scene in the story.

Sir Peter Hall, when I mentioned this to him, said he thought *Jewel* was "visually specific" and that Morahan won his battle:

> It didn't seem that the relationships, the actual story, were swamped in a huge environment, in inessentials. What you saw and felt of India had meaning for the story.

Hall also felt *Jewel* was so well acted because practically the whole cast were veteran classical actors, mainly in Shakespeare, either in repertory or the West End: Susan Wooldridge, for instance, for thirteen years (Lady Macbeth, Lady Teazle), Pigott-Smith for fourteen.

The cast praised Morahan's often demanding direction. Geraldine:

> He was unyielding. If *we* couldn't see what he was reaching for, he'd get very impatient with us. But there's no point in doing something if you're not stretched a bit and told, "That's not good enough." He wouldn't budge from Ken Taylor's script. If you suggested something,

he could say, "No, I think you're wrong." He sometimes did. But you could always *talk* to him. And that was great.

Susan found Morahan ready to listen too. Once one of the sparks suggested that Daphne, fleeing into MacGregor House after Merrick has asked her to marry him, turn out the lights, so that his face bathed in light goes black. Morahan agreed. Pigott-Smith wanted Merrick to find a snake in his bath and Morahan agreed to that too. Even Peggy Ashcroft had a suggestion:

> In the book Barbie dies in her old heliotrope skirt which is all filthy. She's completely gone. She won't do anything they say. I said to Christopher, "It would be wonderful to restore that because it's so important to the image of Barbie. She doesn't die comfortably in bed." He and Jim looked at it and immediately agreed. And it was wonderful that they did it.

The last scene shot in India was done May 5, 1982, in Kashmir, Lady Manners putting flowers on Daphne's grave. Tim Pigott-Smith says he felt relief mixed with a peculiar sense of loss. Susan too felt it:

> Not only was the work extraordinarily good. There was also the privilege of going to India. We all made the journey together. We shared so many experiences. Going to the same temples, seeing the same sights. It was like a stone in a pond whose outward circles continue, for years and years and years.

Once location shooting was over in India, the filming of *Jewel* lasted another nine months, shifting to a group of Manchester warehouses converted by Granada into a massive studio. A disused Lancashire quarry, as Susan said, became the Bibighar Gardens. An old-fashioned, narrow-gauge railway station at Quainton in Buckinghamshire became the set of the massacre of Muslims on the train from Mirat; one hundred thirty extras of Indian descent were hired at local employment agencies to be the passengers and their attackers.

Most exteriors were shot in India and most interiors in Manchester. You would get a ball bounced by a child in India caught by Charles Dance (playing Guy Perron) in England. The best example of this is when Barbie moves her trunk out of the garden shed at Rose Cottage and sets off in a rickshaw pulled by two Indians. It is too heavy, they lose control, it overturns and spills her into the road in a driving rain. Viewers were unaware what a long trip it was. I asked Peggy Ashcroft about it. She said:

I know I was terribly worried about that scene. I played the first movement of it, getting into the rickshaw and going down the hill, in the Himalayas, in Simla. And the end, when she falls out, was in *Wales*. [Laughter.] I think they were afraid they wouldn't get the rain in Simla. In fact we did get rain. But we might not have. And of course it does have to be in the rain and they could be pretty sure in North Wales that we'd get rain. And they not only had the rain that was raining, they had firemen with hoses trained on me as I went down the hill. Wearing that lace shawl with the butterflies . . . [Singing:] "Champagne Charlie is my name . . ." [Laughter.] And it was marvelous because they did it in one take. I was so relieved. 'Cause I thought: "I can't go back and have to do that again." And I didn't have to. It came off.

Peggy says that when she sees the film now she is not quite sure whether it is the replica of Rose Cottage on the set in Manchester or the real thing, the copy was so exact, with a cyclorama of the Himalayas beyond. Alan Pickford, who helped Vic Symonds, *Jewel*'s main designer (Pickford did the famous set for Alan Ayckbourn's *Norman Conquests)* credits Christopher Morahan, ever a stickler for detail, for the series' realistic look. Pickford:

Chris Morahan was keen on doing India as it really is. Not glamorizing it. So I think all the time that's what everybody was working for. They had this wonderful old warehouse in Manchester. If you do the usual telly in a studio, it's small and confined. We could build huge big sets and you could have backings to a window thirty or forty feet back from the window. You could get lights at just the right angle. You could have a painted gauze. Then another gauze. And a row of trees. So that you got the visual distance.

Pickford said Morahan was extremely painstaking:

He might come in and say, "I don't think that's right." He always wanted a hand in it. He'd sometimes alter the props. And he wouldn't let any of the actors see the rushes as they usually do because they might want to change their performance. He didn't want to see pretty pictures on the screen either. He didn't think that was what it was about. He could be an awfully difficult person. So military. We used to call him the Colonel.

Then there was the battle of the ceilings. Vic Symonds said it got "quite prickly." One of the amazing things about *The Jewel in the Crown* is the way it catches the look of India, somehow capturing its light. Which Morahan told me is exactly what they tried to do:

Vic Symonds, O'Brien, and I decided if you are going to similate what it is like in India, the best way is to look at the sources of light. It's very bright outside and very dark inside because windows are small to keep the heat out and frequently are in shadow. That means there is continual contrast between light and shade. So what we did to impose that on the cameraman was to cover the set with ceilings.

I asked, didn't Ray Goode, the lighting cameraman, object? He was much praised for his work in *Brideshead Revisited.*

> Not seriously. In fact I think *Jewel* was very, very well photographed. But it was a direct imposition by Vic Symonds and myself on the style of the production. Often as not against the cameraman's wishes. As you say, it worked.

In January 1983, an hour after shooting ended one evening—it was the scene of the maharanee's tawdry, dissolute drinking party in Bombay—a fire broke out. Nobody was hurt. Nobody knew how it started. It destroyed three big sets and all the props and costumes, even Merrick's artificial arm. The next morning Morahan called cast and crew together. "Ladies and gentlemen," he said, "I give you my word that we will be back shooting on Monday. I will make it my business to see the quality is not impaired in any way." Shooting resumed that Monday.

Ken Taylor wrote two original scenes that are not in Scott's work. It was decided to extend the series by an hour to fourteen episodes (fifteen hours, as the opening sequence runs two). The India footage ran longer than planned, and Peggy Ashcroft was giving such a fine performance Morahan decided to play up Barbie's story a little more. He asked Taylor to write about thirty more minutes.

One of the scenes is between Merrick and a medical orderly, Corporal "Sophie" Dixon in the Pankot Hospital's military wing. Morahan felt a transition was needed between Merrick dragging the dying Teddie Bingham from a burning jeep in the Burmese jungle and Merrick's ability to use an artificial arm. So we watch him, lying in a hospital bed, his face partly swathed in bandages, struggle to hold a lit cigarette in his metal arm. The exercise and pressure on his stump cause him acute pain. He drops the cigarette. Corporal Dixon knocks and Merrick in frustration hurls an ashtray at the closed door.

> DIXON: Oh, did you ring, sir?
>
> MERRICK: This damn thing doesn't fit. I *told* those idiots in Poona. (*He grips his stump with his good hand as he stares at Dixon.*) What the hell do you want?
>
> DIXON: Well, I was hoping for a bit of peace and quiet, sir—but if

this goes on *(he starts to clear up the broken ashtray)* I shall ask to be put back on active service. Better to be raped by little yellow ones in Burma than picking bits of glass out of me perm.

MERRICK: Get out, Dixon. I'm not amused by your song and dance act.

In Taylor's other new scene Barbie goes to the Pankot churchyard to put flowers on her friend Mabel's grave and meets Ashok, a Hindu beggar boy. She recognizes in him a fellow outcast. I told Peggy Ashcroft it is hard to understand Britain today without some sense of how its Empire ended and the cultural divisions it left behind. "I suppose in a way it's our terrible class system," she said.

> I mean, you see, that absolutely invests the whole of *The Jewel in the Crown*. The accuracy of Paul Scott in his delineation of the class system. I mean, those terrible memsahibs who are really jumped-up suburban people in England, going out and being the British Raj.

Lord Beloff in his *Encounter* analysis, like many historians of the post-Mutiny phase of British rule, blames the breakdown of trust between the English and Indians on such memsahibs. Barbie, whose humanity transcends their racism and narrow-mindedness, is constantly made to feel the outcast by the Pankot memsahibs. When she goes with Mabel Layton, her protector, to Susan's wedding, Barbie finds her silver spoons are meanly not among the presents displayed. When Mabel dies and Barbie tries to get her buried beside her husband as she wanted, Mildred Layton, half-tight on gin, tells her, "You were born with the soul of a parlor maid. India's been very bad for you and Rose Cottage a disaster. I'd be glad if you'd be out of there by the end of the month." Dislodged from one bolt-hole after another, ill, abandoned, Barbie ends, dying, in Ranpur mission hospital, staring out in dumb despair at vultures as they circle the towers of silence where the Parsis expose their dead.

Earlier, in the churchyard scene with the little untouchable boy, he tells her he is going away, and Barbie sits and chats with him.

ASHOK: I go to Maharajah.

BARBIE: You serve a Maharajah? Where? *(He shrugs.)*

ASHOK: Many, many Maharajahs, many mahouts. I go ride elephant for Maharajah.

BARBIE: Well, there are certainly no elephants in Pankot—so you will have to go if you want to be a mahout. If you were an English boy, you'd want to be an engine driver. *(She stops again.)*

Tum rail garry chalanan passand Keroge. (He shrugs his indifference.)

ASHOK: If no elephants, *Memsahib. (Barbie smiles.)*

BARBIE: Do you know what these flowers here are for?

ASHOK: For *puja.*

BARBIE: No, I bring them for my friend.

ASHOK: I am your friend, *Memsahib.*

BARBIE: Yes. I mean my other friend.

ASHOK: He comes from Pankot?

BARBIE: From Pankot, yes. *(He looks around apprehensively.)*

ASHOK: He is my friend, too?

BARBIE: She is, yes. But you won't see her. *(She smiles at his fear.)* Like the Friend who loves us both. You remember the song I tried to teach you about our Friend? There's a Friend for little children . . . *(He nods and they both sing:)*

BARBIE/ASHOK: There's a friend for little children

ASHOK: Above the bright blue sky . . . Whose love will never die. *(She laughs as they finish together and gives him a little hug.)*

BARBIE: You are my little untouchable . . . my Harijan, one of the Children of God. *(He does not answer.)* Now tell me, Ashok . . . What am I . . . *Huma kai hai?*

ASHOK: A *burra memsahib. (She shakes her head.)*

BARBIE: No. I am a servant of the Lord Jesus. He is our mother and our father. *Man-bap.* You don't understand . . . it's too long ago and far away. The world we live in is corrupt. I offer you my love and you take it as fortune smiling. But your heart is beating in expectation of rupees. Mine hardly beats at all. I am very tired and old and far from home, Ashok. *(She looks at him.) Chalo!* You take my case and find a rickshaw-wallah. *Jaldi!. . . .*

In Nagpur there was a tale of an elderly Englishwoman who had stayed on in the old city. At night from my bungalow near the university I could hear the old city's Hindu drums and chanting. I told Dame Peggy, "I could never find her. And that always filled me with a kind of horror. I desperately wanted Barbie to get safely back to some nice little boarding house in Croydon."

"I don't think Barbie could ever have gone back to England. No."

Barbie's one meeting with Ronald Merrick, on the terrace of Rose Cottage as thunder rumbles and a monsoon downpour threatens, is heavy with symbolism—her good to his evil, even if Barbie has come to fear her idea of good may be hollow. She has just had a letter informing her of a vacancy at Dibrapur Infants School, which is just about her last hope. She asks Merrick about her dead friend, Edwina Crane, who, as mentioned, early in the story took her own life, setting herself on fire. I asked Peggy about this scene with Merrick; she said:

> The demon, the devil . . . Barbie is faced with this man whom she's come to look on as suspicious. She sees his face. She has pity for him. She is appalled by what he tells her, that Barbie's dear friend left a suicide note: "There is no God, not even on the road to Dibrapur." And Barbie says with horror, "It's where I'm going." This is the first time—isn't it?—that she expresses her religious doubts.

Vic Symonds, the designer, told me he watched the filming of this scene from just a few feet away:

> It was where she brings out the picture at Rose Cottage. She stepped onto the terrace and I got caught. I couldn't get out without wrecking the shot. So I was standing right by her, just out of sight. And she was nervous as a kitten. I've never seen anybody shake and quake so much. And then when she stepped out and told Merrick, "The jewel was not the crown, the jewel was India," it was the most magic acting I'd ever seen. Obviously there's a huge concentration and expenditure of nerves getting that kind of acting. I mean what I'll never forget was how she did it like Barbie was saying it for the first time.

Christopher Morahan told me stage fright, even after Peggy Ashcroft's more than sixty years of acting, was common to all the really great actors; he found them all nervous and extremely shy. I asked Sir Peter Hall about it; he said:

> All the great ones have a deep anxiety to be as good as they think they ought to be. To be as good as they think they *can* be. The public naturally thinks that if you're Ashcroft or Olivier or Gielgud, you just go on and do it. I've directed Peggy Ashcroft since 1957, about twenty times. And it's not easy for her to create a role. Every time the effort, the professionalism, the anxiety to be as good as she ought to be or can be is huge. It's not enough to have talent. You have to have a talent to *use* that talent.

It took seven years from the time he read it for Sir Denis Forman to put *The Jewel in the Crown* on British television screens. (A year into production he went to Mobil's Herb Schmertz, the American gray eminence behind "Masterpiece Theatre," who agreed to put up "a very large sum of money" in advance for *Jewel.*) At a goodbye party in Manchester, just about the only time all the cast and crew got together, Sir Denis asked, "Is our way of telling history good enough? Will we succeed in conveying Scott's uncanny insight into the psychology of the two principals in this great confrontation, the British and India?"

Sir Denis expected a critical success but felt *Jewel* might not go down with a mass audience. No one was prepared for the fervor of the response, good and bad, strongly favorable or unfavorable. India hands came up to say, "It's wonderful. It's all true." Attacks from Enoch Powell, James Cameron, and Salman Rushdie, Ken Taylor told me, convinced him, seeing that they came from both right and left, that the film must have got it right. Taylor described the two reactions:

> The right said, "Oh, this is another attempt to knock the British image. We did a wonderful job in India. We brought the natives civilization and all the rest of it. And now all these nasty left-wing TV people come along and they say, 'Gosh, you were very cruel to these people, you know. You beat them up in prison and you despised them for being black.' Well, we don't want to know about it."
>
> The left said, "This is a piece of imperial nostalgia. It's the British again wallowing in their glorious past. And what they should be looking at is their dreadful present."

The character of Merrick came in for the bitterest criticism. It made Pigott-Smith indignant.

> They had police inspectors on television, superintendents who had been in India, saying, "It's absolutely impossible. Tying a naked prisoner to a trestle and flogging him, subjecting those youths to long interrogations and prolonged arrests without proper charges. It could not have gone on."
>
> Why, that's rubbish. It's going on now. In Ireland. South Africa. Everywhere. *It goes on.*

Jewel was wildly acclaimed in America. Sir Denis, who flew over twice during the three months it played on PBS, says, "The Americans went overboard. We seemed to get adulation. In Britain we just got critical acclaim." He sent Geraldine, Susan, Tim Pigott-Smith, Art Malik, and Charles Dance on a cross-country tour of

American talk shows. I asked Susan if the American reaction was different.

> Oh, completely. Art and I arrived out in Los Angeles two days after Daphne had died on the screen. And I walked into the Beverly Hills Hotel, having been dropped by a stretch limo—an infinitely repeatable experience, I hope—to be greeted as though I was the Queen Mother. I mean, it was the most astonishing experience. Because here I'm not recognized at all. What was so fabulous to me was that Americans just don't look, they *see*, if you know what I mean. We tend not to interact in the same way. I was absolutely delighted to the nth degree. And because of Daphne, people would greet me with tears in their eyes. Happy to see I was alive, that I hadn't died in childbirth.

Tim was flooded with Hollywood offers to play disfigured sadomasochistic villains.

Peggy Ashcroft missed all the excitement. By the time *Jewel* was being shown on British television, she was back in India playing Mrs. Moore in David Lean's movie of *A Passage to India*. Pauline Kael praised her "transcendent acting" and Peggy won a Hollywood Oscar as Best Supporting Actress for it. But after Barbie, it was anticlimatic.

I told Peggy I felt Lean's film failed to capture E. M. Forster's novel; it was so self-consciously epic. "I quite agree," she said. "David Lean is a brilliant filmmaker. But he quite definitely said, 'This is *my* version of *A Passage to India*. It's not Forster.' There's nothing to be said after that. It was a grandiose view, too epic. Chandrapore is a scruffy little town in the novel. And in the film it was so grand. It was the British Raj in excelsis." Forster's Chandrapore:

> The very wood seems made of mud, the inhabitants of mud moving . . . Houses do fall, people are drowned and left rotting, but the general outline of the town persists, swelling here, shrinking there, like some low but indestructible form of life.

Jewel's strength, Peggy said, lay in its "complete fidelity to the author."

> I don't think Denis Forman would have wanted to do it if it wasn't going to be faithful to Paul Scott. And Christopher Morahan is a man of the theater who has that respect for the writer. And he sustained that fidelity. He made it happen. What I thought was extraordinary was that he decided on a young man, Jim O'Brien, to be his partner and they halved it, split it down the middle. And when I look at it I find it difficult sometimes to remember which scenes were shot by Christopher

and which by Jim. Because they were both so faithful to the intention of Scott.

Peggy said the emotional public response took them all by surprise.

> I don't think any of us ever thought it was going to be the success it was. We wanted to play these characters in Scott's novels and somehow it came off. And that was what we were all after. I mean we knew that what we'd been taking part in was awfully good. But we had no idea it would catch the popular imagination as it did. And I think it proves that if you are faithful to a great work the public will respond. I have such great respect for Forster's novel. But there wasn't the same attitude to the writer. To me the great disappointment was the end of the book not being there. Those two men, the Englishman and the Indian, on horseback as everything came between them.

Peggy also felt Scott could depict women in a way Forster never could.

> Scott must have known a Barbie. I never believed Forster's women quite. Forster was deeply disillusioned, wasn't he? In his knowledge of India. *Passage* is a book rather of despair. I feel that Scott writes objectively and delineates each character. Forster writes very subjectively. Somehow they're all an expression of his emotions. And in one of his notebooks he says the boum-boums in the cave were just his way out of a very tricky situation. Isn't it in his notebooks?

Peggy says Barbie is one of her favorite roles (the Viennese Frau Messner in Stephen Poliakoff's *Caught on a Train* is the other screen role; on the stage it would be Winnie in *Happy Days*, Cleopatra, Hedda Gabler, Juliet, and any Chekhov). She said she found no similarity between Mrs. Moore and Barbie "except they were both women of Christian faith who, in India, come to doubt that faith."

I later asked Julie Harris, a fellow *Jewel* fan ("I have it. I own it. I watch it whenever I can"), "Why can't Americans do a *Jewel in the Crown?*" She said:

> We aren't as good at writing. We aren't as good at adapting. We haven't the subtlety. We can't tell a complicated story simply. I mean, what happens here in America, they say: "There are too many characters in this story." And they cut out all the characters. Now the English don't do that. They keep everybody in it the way the author wrote it. But they are so skillful at it. It's astonishing.

Comparisons are also drawn with *Brideshead Revisited,* Granada Television's other big triumph. *Brideshead* had a lot going for it: Evelyn Waugh's best-loved novel; another superb cast, including Gielgud, with Olivier giving one of his last memorable film performances as Lord Marchmain; nostalgic scenes of prewar Oxford; Vanbrugh's Castle Howard, one of Britain's grandest stately homes (the Howards still live there); an emotive theme song played over and over.

One similarity is that Charles Ryder, played by Jeremy Irons, is a witness, like Sarah in *The Jewel in the Crown*, except that in *Brideshead*, Irons tells the story, using Waugh's lines from the book in a narrative voice-over. I asked Christopher Morahan about it.

> They felt it was the best way to dramatize a witness, Charles Ryder. We decided against that in *The Jewel in the Crown* because it's done from so many points of view. It was impossible to do that without confusing the audience. Now witnesses are passive. They're not heroes or heroines. That's actually how life itself goes. I mean Barbie is alone in the hospital and terrified of dying and Sarah goes away. But that happens. That happens.
>
> One of the great joys of *The Jewel in the Crown* is that Sarah emerges as a real person. As a person you care about. You can identify with her because she is like you, full of frailties. Rather than seeing her as an escapist heroine, risking things you wouldn't do.

I interviewed Jeremy Irons between takes of a film he was shooting at Twickenham Studios and asked him if the *Brideshead* cast, too, kept going back to Waugh's novel. Irons:

> I think in any work I as an actor will try to find out why an author wrote a scene. If you know why he wrote it, you'll know what he wants to show by it, in that way it gives you a good clue how to play it. Any piece of writing. You ask: Why did he write that phrase like that? What was he trying to say?

Irons is an intense actor, more the international film star than anyone I'd interviewed. He sometimes joined me at a pair of canvas chairs behind the set or, if dissatisfied with a take, strode about, chain-smoking. I asked him if he always worked under such stress.

> I think one has to. It's such an ephemeral thing, acting. I'm a great believer that if you're going to do anything, you have to do it as well as you possibly can. When I'm pacing around smoking I'm just thinking: Am I doing it right? Have I forgotten anything? Is there any slant, any angle I can put on it that I haven't? Have I done enough?

In the darkened sound stage people milled about and talked in hushed voices as an assistant director kept calling, "Quiet please! Sh-h-h-h! Quiet please! Red light on, please!" It was Irons who kept insisting shots be redone. Once the director told him, "Jeremy, I like it but you've got a strand of hair down your forehead. If you don't like it, I suggest you take a look." Unlike *Jewel*, the actor was in command.

By the time I talked to them, the cast and crew of *The Jewel in the Crown* were scattered all over. Christopher Morahan was making a film in Ireland. Susan, who won the British Academy Award for Best Supporting Actress in John Boorman's *Hope and Glory*, went to Italy to film a sitcom. Art Malik was in Hollywood. Charles Dance had been in Kenya to play Josslyn Hay, twenty-second Earl of Erroll, in *White Mischief*, based on the English peer's actual 1941 murder. Dance also did *Coriolanus* for the Royal Shakespeare Company and was seen this year on American television in the title role of *The Phantom of the Opera* miniseries. I met Geraldine, who'd had her first child, a little girl (Peggy Ashcroft had read a Shakespearean sonnet at Geraldine's wedding), and Tim Pigott-Smith in their dressing rooms at the National Theatre—she was playing Imogen in Peter Hall's *Cymbeline* (replacing, at the last minute, Sarah Miles); he was doing three Shakespearean roles, Iachimo in *Cymbeline*, Leontes in *The Winter's Tale*, and Trinculo in *The Tempest*, an acting tour de force for Hall's farewell productions at the National Theatre. Susan, Geraldine, Dance, Malik, and Pigott-Smith had all stayed good friends.

I asked Tim if he would ever be free of Merrick? "I don't think I ever will," he said. He wants to stay with serious drama. "I want to do good work. If I have to do rubbish to pay the bills, I will." He quoted Sir Michael Redgrave's "Well, I must go and do another film so I can afford to play a season at Stratford." (Not everybody has such dedication to Shakespeare. Anthony Hopkins, after three years at the National, cheerfully left for Hollywood, saying: "My idea of happiness is to wake up in the morning and think: 'I'll never have to play King Lear again.'") Geraldine stuck to Shakespeare too. Her stunning Portia in Hall's *Merchant of Venice* took Broadway by storm, winning high critical praise for her performance as the "lady richly left" who must judge the demand of Shylock, played by Dustin Hoffman, for a pound of his debtor's flesh. When it comes to her famous "quality of mercy" speech, Geraldine says of Portia, "It's as if every fiber in her being is humming."

They've all left *Jewel* behind. Or have they? Tim Pigott-Smith will have Merrick's driven quality wherever he goes. Susan, Daphne's vulnerability. Geraldine, Sarah's quiet common sense. Peggy Ashcroft, Barbie's feeling intelligence. Christopher Morahan, his dogged pursuit of reality and truth. The critic that mattered most to him was his own father-in-law, who seemed to speak for the whole vanished Anglo-Indian imperial world when he called *Jewel* "absolutely disgraceful."

Morahan told me:

> He was with the Indian Lancers and had also been on attachment to the Indian police in Bengal. In the kind of job Merrick did. He said there weren't police officers in India like that at all. He was very dismissive of Scott's ability to interpret what happened in India. He said Scott had only been there for three or four years.
>
> You see, my father-in-law was the commander of a squadron of cavalry in 1947 at the time of partition. And he saw half of his men left in Pakistan as he went with the Hindus in closed lorries to the border. He saw that regiment broken up. His friends, his colleagues, fought on opposing sides in the war between Pakistan and India that followed. He was heartbroken over it. His father had been in the diplomatic service in India. He'd been married in Calcutta. His daughter was born in Bangalore. His in-laws had been in India for generations. Like the Laytons he saw the collapse of that society that he had created. And he thought *The Jewel in the Crown* was unkind and untrue.

We take the belief in the dignity of all peoples so much for granted today, it is easy to forget how new this is or how much India's independence figured in its wide acceptance. It is a radical change in the way we look at the poorest of the world's people.

The day I met her, when our interview was over and she took me to the door to say goodbye, I told Peggy Ashcroft, if she didn't mind my saying so, how much she seemed like Barbie, kindly, good-natured, charitable. Peggy paused, as if there was something more she wanted to say. She spoke slowly, choosing her words:

> I loved India. Of course, it horrifies you up to a point. *That* you have to get over. And once you've assimilated that, the beauty of the landscape, of the antiquities and of the people . . . What serenity they seem to have, in spite of all they have to suffer. When you see people in the streets . . . And what astonishes me always when one hears about horrendous happenings in India, the violence, is how they appear on the surface to be so gentle, so philosophical, so accepting . . . I think India changes you. You can't quite say what it does to you. But it does change you in a way. I can go back in my mind and experience it again and I can smell it and hear it once more . . .

Let us do that, too, and give Paul Scott the last word, or rather his Lucy Smalley in *Staying On:*

I remember the ceremony we had here in Pankot on Independence eve very clearly still.

At sundown they beat the retreat. After that we dined at Flagstaff House. Then we went back to the parade ground, and there was a band —a pretty scratch affair. They played all the traditional martial British music. Then there were some Indian pipers, and a Scottish pipe-major. One by one all the floodlights were put out, leaving just the flagpole lit with the Union Jack flying from it. Colonel Layton and the new Indian colonel stood at attention side by side. Then the band played "Abide with me."

It was so moving that I began to cry. Tusker put his hand on mine and kept it there all through the hymn and when we were standing all through "God Save the King," and all through that terrible lovely moment when the Jack was hauled down inch by inch in utter, utter silence. The only sounds you could hear were the jackals hunting in the hills and the strange little rustles when a gust of wind sent papers and programmes scattering . . .

VII

YOUR GREECE
TO OUR ROME

Going Home

THE LOSS OF EMPIRE, like the human loss in two world wars, left Britain reduced from a Great Power to a medium-sized European nation haunted by its past.

It is easy to forget how far and fast it fell. The British Empire, which reached its peak in World War I, grew over three centuries from trade, emigration, and politics; it endured so long because of British command of the seas and the wisdom of British rule. At its height Britain ruled over a hundredfold more land than in its isles; British Red claimed a fourth of the world's people and area. In London I came across a 1900 almanac. That year, it said, Britain's 42 million people had 281,000 soldiers worldwide; the United States with 76 million people had but 71,000. Britain's annual foreign trade was twice as much as ours, so was its merchant fleet. The British navy had forty-nine battleships to our seventeen.

But in 1900 iron and steel output in America was moving way ahead, already 24 million tons annually to Britain's 14 million tons. British-born Yale professor Paul Kennedy argues in *The Rise and Fall of the Great Powers* that nations rise to greatness when their manufacturing base becomes superior to their rivals', but they eventually cannot support the military commitments this entails. His book's phenomenal success shows how much Americans fear decline too. Professor Kennedy says dozens of studies of Britain's eclipse as "the workshop of the world" blame the same causes:

> . . . the low esteem held for manufacturing and commerce (as opposed to law, or merchant banking) by the educated classes; to the inability to sell in foreign markets; to the limited technical training of the work force; and, in particular, to the comparatively low rates of investment in new manufacturing plants and in civilian research and development.

All true from the 1870s, we heard from Asa Briggs early on; all still true today, we heard from Britain's scientists and industrialists. We even had Tony Benn blaming empire for creating an economy where the "redcoats kept the market and colonials obligingly bought our goods and sold us cheap raw materials." True as well.

How did loss of empire affect the ruling class? I asked David Owen if it had led to a failure of the nerve among Britain's old establishment. "A *deep* failure of the nerve," he said. Of those I interviewed, Sir Peter Ramsbotham caught it best: "It's really a decline of self-confidence, isn't it?"

> I think we felt we had a right. You see, now we're so undermined by people saying colonialism is terrible and you shouldn't do that and no one should be so bossy and the underdog is always right. You know, all those things.

But this was not the attitude, Sir Peter said, that his generation inherited:

> Certainly not the people who went out to India and Africa. They believed that they were incorruptible, that they were teaching these people not to be corrupt. They believed they were giving them order, law, good roads, health, education, civilization. They represented the best there was. They were all brought up in classical educations, all Christians and so on. They believed, they certainly believed in self-government, that they were going to bring these people, almost as children, to the point where they could govern themselves and then through dominion status into the Commonwealth. That was the underlying concept, you see.

"And to an amazing degree, they did it."

"To a *certain* degree, they did it."

Harold Macmillan's famous remark about Britain's Greece to America's Rome was made when he was British political adviser in Algiers during the war. It was a different world. Britain had yet to get out of being a Great Power, pulling back in the next twenty years from South Asia, Africa, and the Gulf. Macmillan himself was to say, "The will at the center is gone. The legions are coming home."

Yet somehow the Greece-Rome idea held on. Some British hate it. (So do some Americans; William Bundy calls it "at best dated, at worst patronizing.") Sir Nicholas Henderson, a former ambassador to Washington, told me, "It gives me the willies, that phrase."

> It's so patronizing. So ghastly. I think it's wrong. Implying all the brains are in London. That the Americans are a mass of semieducated people. The idea that we somehow have some intellectual superiority over the Americans is insulting nonsense.

After a quarter century writing about the ex-colonial Third World, I find a certain truth in it, especially in the 1950s and 1960s: their wisdom, our power, Britain's Greece to our Rome. Former Prime Minister James Callaghan, when I told him I sometimes found British diplomats overseas possessed an ex-imperial expertise Americans lacked, said, "I think it *was* true."

> It was true of the Far East. It was true of India. It is still true of the Middle East. For some reason the people of the United States sometimes don't seem quite able to feel a situation. We only feel it because we've had long experience there. If you take the case of India that old experience is getting less. The generations are passing on.

Lord Callaghan, born in 1912, said people his age grew up with the first postcolonial rulers:

> I am one of the last of the generation, you see, who knew the African leaders like Julius Nyerere and Kenneth Kaunda when they were over here as students. I knew Indira Gandhi when she was a girl of eighteen at Somerville. It makes a tremendous difference. You have a feel for these people and their countries.

What is left of Britain's old "dominion over palm and pine"? Field Marshal Lord Carver, who used to head the British Army, told me there are still forces in Germany, Cyprus, Hong Kong, Belize, Diego Garcia, and of course Northern Ireland. (But nothing like the days when Lord Mountbatten could joke about the American navy in the Indian Ocean: "How green was my ally.") Lord Carver:

> The old imperial role has got smaller and smaller and smaller. The Gurkhas are out in Hong Kong but that finishes when Hong Kong finishes. There's always the Falklands. We're stuck there. None of it's big. The total number of Gurkhas in Hong Kong is only six thousand, the size of a training team in Oman. We've still got a battalion in Belize. We don't seem to be able to get out of that one. There's a garrison in Gibraltar. Cyprus is the most important in military terms. It's a very good air base but no air force combat units are stationed there. The intelligence-gathering facilities on Cyprus, on top of the mountain, matter a good bit.

Britain's worldwide intelligence network is one of its most lasting legacies of empire. It is particularly strong in former colonies. Sir Antony Acland, who became ambassador to Washington in 1986, says it means Britain is able to give a second opinion.

> We exchange assessments. I think our judgment on world affairs is listened to, respected, and valued. With assets like Cyprus and Hong

Kong we can, up to a point, cover some of the intelligence burden which the United States, even with its resources, can't cover.

I asked Sir Peter Ramsbotham about Macmillan's Greece-Rome idea.

"We might be the Greeks. I'm not sure you're the Romans."

"You mean we're not in decline yet?"

"No, not that. Methods. The Romans would plant their colonies of soldiers and settle down. In Dacia, which became Romania, Libya, everywhere. They made little Romans everywhere. You don't try to do that." Bundy agrees: "Vide only our performances in Iran and Vietnam; in neither case did we train people as local experts or even able to speak the language save in minute numbers, and we paid dearly for it. We just don't think in terms of empire or lasting control."

I think we wanted to, but culturally, just after the war. CBS's Eric Sevareid had suggested meeting Sir Peter Ramsbotham. In Sevareid's 1946 autobiography, *Not So Wild a Dream,* he tells of growing up in the little North Dakota town of Velva and going off to World War II, as did so many rural youths, carrying "America's bright tools and great muscles, her giant voice and will." His confidence was characteristic of America at the start of its postwar imperial era. Sevareid felt it was America's destiny to "create a world in its own image." He saw that image in terms of his hometown:

> All that America truly meant, all that Americans perished for, would be devoid of consequence or portent unless the image of society that America showed the world was that of the little Velvas as I had known, remembered and cherished them.

"It sounds naive now," I told Sir Peter. "But it's like Henry Luce's American Century. Americans believed it. Now they're disenchanted."

"I think disenchanted is a good word. You know there's no concept in England of what you call the American dream. We did have a concept of 'the white man's burden' from Kipling of course." The French, he felt, had much more the Roman concept of empire, Britain the Greek.

> The French felt everyone should be a Roman citizen. And not only that. Léopold Senghor, for instance, who invented the phrase *negritude,* and Houphouët-Boigny of the Ivory Coast, they were respected members of the French National Assembly. We never dreamt of having a Nigerian or whoever he was sitting in the House of Commons. I think the Greeks had a much looser concept of their colonialism.

The British Empire depended, he said, on values like "a sense of decency, a sense of humility, a sense of responsibility"; all, Sir Peter felt, less than they used to be.

From the first, America was uncomfortable at stepping into Britain's Great Power shoes, as it did in 1947. A Pax Britannica had ruled the seas since the Napoleonic wars. But, as Henry Brandon, chief American correspondent of *The Sunday Times* for four decades, relates in his 1988 memoirs, *Special Relationships,* people like Walter Lippmann and Averell Harriman came to hate the idea of a Pax Americana. Sir Oliver Wright, Mrs. Thatcher's ambassador to Washington in 1982–86, was a junior consular officer in New York in 1946. He remembers the mood was: "Bring the boys home. Let them all go hang." America was about to repeat the mistakes of 1918. By 1947, he said, Britain couldn't hold out any longer against Communist insurrections in Greece and Turkey. Sir Oliver:

> And Harry Truman, the greatest of modern presidents, asked Congress for aid to Greece and Turkey. I remember waiting on a March day, nail biting: what would Congress decide? And they agreed to Truman's request. That was the turning point. America decided to involve itself in world affairs. And we have the superpower adversary, the Soviet Union, to thank for that. The rest followed: the Marshall Plan, the Berlin airlift, the foundation of NATO, GATT, the IMF, everything.

"How far have we come?" I asked. Communism was having its last slow gasp, not just in Russia, but from Berlin to Beijing.
"That's the whole point, isn't it? How far have we come?"

Among those "present at the creation," to use Dean Acheson's phrase, was Oliver Franks, Britain's ambassador to Washington in 1948–52. He'd been in Churchill's wartime government; he was chairman of the Paris conference which drafted Europe's reply to Marshall's speech at Harvard; he helped negotiate the Atlantic Pact. Retired after years as provost, Worcester College, Oxford, he was eighty-four when I spent a morning with him at his home in north Oxford; no one living can probably match his historical perspective on Anglo-American ties. It was almost a decade since Deng Xiaoping's first overtures to market prosperity of 1979 and a shipyard electrician named Lech Walesa led Solidarity's revolt in Poland of 1980. The whole postwar order Lord Franks helped to build, now that the one-party state and state-run economy had been such failures everywhere, was coming to an end. We were going to have to build a new order, with the same old principle of giving democracy a chance to succeed. It meant, of course, seeing how much Eastern Europe today was like all of Europe was in the aftermath of World War II. But we needed to overcome old fears, to perceive the new realities and shed illusions.

"Illusions," Lord Franks said, "last longer than fact." In those years just after the war, Britain seemed to itself and to others to be a Great Power like Russia and the United States. "It thought it was," he said. "It was treated as if it was. It wasn't. But the illusion lasted until Suez in 1956."

> If you go back to those years, '47, '48, '49, '50, whether you were talking to Labour people, Prime Minister Attlee or Bevin, or to Tories, Winston Churchill or Anthony Eden, they all shared the view that Britain would come back to the sort of place where it had been in the world before. I mean, it was an illusion. They all shared the illusion. They worked to make it real. It couldn't be done.

"You still had the English language," I said. "You still had the Commonwealth."

"What we hadn't got was the economic power." This wasn't recognized at the time:

> When I was in Washington, Britain considered itself still to be a world power and was considered by the United States to be one. Neither knew how weakened Britain had been by the war. We were expected by the United States, and expected ourselves, to carry out all sorts of jobs all over the world. In 1949 we had as many men serving overseas, in the Far East and elsewhere, as the United States did.
>   It was an unequal partnership. There was no question that after the end of the war, the Great Powers were the U.S.S.R. and the U.S. But we British were at the table, we were at all the conferences. When the Russians and Americans met, we were there too. Bevin, Marshall, Acheson, as the case might be, Molotov on the other side of the table, sometimes Stalin. America decided to take on responsibilities in the world. Britain shed some and continued to hold some. A whole range of policies—Truman's Point Four, the Marshall Plan, the Atlantic Pact, the alliances across the Pacific with Japan, with the Philippines, the Anzus Pact with Australia and New Zealand—molded the shape of the world in which we still live today.

The early postwar years were "a time of probing, a show of strength," like the Berlin airlift. Even so, the United States alone had the nuclear bomb; its economy was half the whole world economy; it had enormous power. "This changed in 1949 when the Russians produced the bomb," Lord Franks said. "It changed slightly when we, the British, produced the bomb, and then the French."

In 1945 the Americans took the surrender of the Japanese in South Korea and the Russians in North Korea for administrative purposes. But when the Communists crossed the 38th Parallel in 1950 it became the political dividing line for Asia like the one down the center of Europe. Lord Franks:

> Don't forget, America's response was very important. Not merely in terms of the Pacific, but in terms of Europe too. It was decided that the policy of containment was real. That things had to be stopped. And they were.

Then came Suez. By then Lord Franks was back in London, chairman of Lloyds Bank. He described the crisis:

> What essentially happened was that the British, the French, and the Israelis decided to destabilize the Egyptian government and sent forces. And they were stopped. They were stopped, first by the United States and, secondly, by the U.S.S.R. It wasn't in their interests that this should happen. And this was the point at which the hollowness of our being a world power was exposed. For the first time. Naked. Everybody could see it.

Eric Sevareid told me an inside story on Suez:

> Anthony Eden was desperate. Fighting in Suez and getting the whole goddamn world down on him. Dulles wasn't speaking to him. The Alliance was really broken. Ike had lost control. The French, Israelis, and British didn't talk to us, did it without our knowledge, badly upset Dulles. Dulles was in the hospital. It was a couple days before the election in '56. Eisenhower called Eden and said, "Listen, Anthony, we can't go on like this. We must pull together. And I want you to get the Frenchman"—it was Guy Mollet, the French Prime Minister, a Socialist—"to fly over here tonight. Tomorrow on the White House steps we'll stand together and we'll announce an armistice in Suez and talk about this unshakeable alliance." Well, to Eden it was a last-minute reprieve from death. He'd almost had a nervous breakdown. He called Guy Mollet and said, "I have some *grand nouvelle.*" And Mollet said, "There can't be any good news now." "Yes, the President just called me and told me to collect you and fly over tomorrow." It was all set. Well, an hour later Eden called Mollet back. Absolutely broken. He said, "I'm sorry. The President changed his mind." Dulles had got wind of this and called Ike from his sickbed and talked him out of it somehow. And Ike caved in on it. But Ike was right. He should have followed his instincts. I got the story from a French banker who was very close to Mollet, but I was under wraps on it at the time.

Four or five years later, Lord Franks said, Harold Macmillan was trying to get into the European Community.

And being turned down by de Gaulle. That was the effect of Suez. It was a sea change. It wasn't a turning away from the United States. It was both/and, not an either/or. The whole policy of Britain since then has been to avoid either/or and insist on both/and. Well, I suppose the European limb of policy strengthened and eventually in 1974 Britain went into the Community. And has been trying to learn to live happily in it ever since.

What will happen, I asked him, in 1992?

Almost certainly less will happen than some people hope and more will happen than some people fear. There will be some movement towards a common market with all sorts of restrictions down. But they won't all fall down at the sound of a trumpet.

"So Britain is, willy-nilly, getting closer to Europe?"

Yes. And I think that people in this country now know that they are part of a Western European destiny. That goes for Mrs. Thatcher and it goes for the Labour leaders too. And it goes for the British people. They've accepted this destiny. It has taken them a long while to do it. But they've done it now.

America's role was changed, he feels, even more than by nuclear proliferation, by the experience of Vietnam.

When the policies of the United States were frustrated and it was not able to impose its will in a dispute as it wished. And since then, I think, the United States has been conscious that powerful as it is, there are limitations on its power.

I told him the illusion of American power, too, outlasted its reality. I recalled how in India in the early 1960s one felt and Nehru felt and the Indian people felt that the United States could work economic miracles for them. "Our reputation for omnipotence lasted longer than the reality," I told Lord Franks. "That America could really do something for the world's poorest people."

"This is perfectly true. And the Americans believed it. They believed it right up to Lyndon Johnson. But not beyond."

"And then the world began losing faith in us."

"Because, you see, illusions last longer than fact. We come back to that." Now, he said, it is Russia's turn to see the limitations of its power. He expected—this was before the Berlin Wall came down—a divided Germany to stay its prime foreign policy objective:

If you go back in history, the thing that has always influenced the Russians has been their vulnerability on the northern European plain. First, the king of Sweden. Then Napoleon. Then Hitler. In the years after the war, the thing that preoccupied the Russians, the ghost present at their feast, was a resurgent Germany: "Would they do it to us again?"

The weight of the Soviet military machine, the comparative prosperity of the Eastern European satellites, Islamic resurgence and problems with the Greek Orthodox Russians themselves, together with Russia's stagnating economy, combined to produce a more accommodating Gorbachev at a time America was more accommodating too. I asked Lord Franks if he thought America might pull away from the Eurasian continent in the event of global hard times and a swing to neutralist governments in Europe. Or would a Soviet decline or even breakup, Chinese growth or repression, Communism's probably prolonged death throes, and increased European unity make the Anglo-American tie all the more important?

"I think all these wonderful scenarios delude," he said. "It doesn't mean that there is no truth to them."

History doesn't turn out either as fast or as simply as they suggest. I think it's true that there will be, for a long time, a natural affinity and relationship between Britain and the United States. And sometimes it will be weaker and sometimes it will be stronger. It will always be there . . . Nobody knows what the configuration of world politics and world power will be twenty years from now.

But it is certain to continue what Henry Brandon calls the postwar "triumphs and tragedies of the Pax Americana." As an Englishman writing about America since 1949, Brandon says, "No doubt, the idea of a Pax Americana goes against the American grain." Nonetheless, he himself finds American influence has spread rapidly because "it promoted the idea of freedom of the individual and improved living standards through economic growth." Brandon:

The Pax Americana to me does not imply, as did the Pax Britannica, formal control over a great number of countries around the globe or easy access to raw materials or great international advantages—not even the satisfaction of being able to exert a civilizing influence.

Even so, Brandon finds, "an American order—some will say disorder—does exist as an almost all-pervasive presence."

Blood Is Thicker

VENICE SPENT what Venice earned. In Constantine FitzGibbon's 1960 novel, *When the Kissing Had to Stop*, Britain elects an antinuclear Labour government. The American bases go. Militants take over, impose censorship, set up a detention camp in Hyde Park. The Royal Family escapes to Canada. Russia occupies Britain with parachute divisions and renames it the British People's Republic. A fantasy, yes. Still it is George Shultz and not the fictional Secretary of State in the novel who said: "Why in the world would we put ourselves in a position where the Soviet Union can look down our throats and tell us where to go because we threw our arms away?"

The crucial fact for the twentieth century, Bismarck said, would be that Britain and America spoke the same language. This may be the last time of that little truth. As World War II and the postwar order fade into the past, and, in Henry Brandon's terms, a Pax Americana has taken over from a Pax Britannica, our two nations are moving away from the folk memory of shared experience. The Labour Party, after a change of heart by its leader Neil Kinnock, dropped its vote-losing policy commitment to pulling Britain out of the nuclear club and forbidding Americans to keep arms at any of their bases. This goes against popular opinion in Britain and helped lose Labour the 1987 election. Ask the man in the street in London; he'll say: "Nuclear weapons keep the peace."

But the policy is less unpopular than it was. A 1983 Gallup Poll showed 23 percent for unilateral nuclear disarmament, 67 percent against. Six years later it was closer to one third and two thirds. The gap is probably narrower now. If a British government ever put it into effect, it could be "goodbye NATO." A nonnuclear Britain, whatever happens on the Continent, could break the back of the American commitment that has kept the peace for forty years.

This shift is partly generational. Neil Kinnock was three when

World War II ended, five at the time of the Marshall Plan, six at the Berlin blockade and airlift, seven at the foundation of NATO, eleven when the Russians put down the East German uprising, and fourteen when they invaded Hungary. About the time someone Kinnock's age entered politics, America was being castigated by the Labour left as the villain in Vietnam, trying to bomb peasant guerrillas off the map with B-52s. David Owen, the same age, told me he discovered when he was Foreign Secretary during the Carter Administration "there are a hell of a lot of people in the United States, in the South and West, who haven't got any sentimental relationships with Britain at all. And who just get pissed off because the product they've ordered hasn't come in time."

Look how two films, one made in Hollywood in the 1940s and the second in London in the 1980s, reflect the generational change. *Mrs. Miniver,* with Greer Garson, Walter Pidgeon, Dame Mae Whitty, and others in MGM's stable of English actors, was set in wartime England at the time of Dunkirk. In its last scene the local vicar asks his flock in their bomb-ruined church why children, old people, young girls should be the ones to be killed. He declares:

> I shall tell you why. Because this is not only a war for soldiers in uniform . . . It must be fought not only on the battlefield but in the cities and in the villages, in the factories and on the farms. In the home and in the heart of every man, woman, and child who loves freedom . . . This is our war! Fight it then with all that is in us. And may God defend the right!

As the camera pans up into the sky where formations of Germany-bound RAF fighters zoom overhead, "Land of Hope and Glory" swells on the sound track. The movie was aimed at American audiences.

In John Cleese's *A Fish Called Wanda,* released in 1988, the denouement comes when Kevin Kline, as a sleazy American clown-villain, is about to shoot Cleese, the arch-Englishman.

> KLINE: You're the filth of the planet! A bunch of . . . pompous . . . badly dressed . . . poverty stricken . . . sexually repressed . . . football hooligans! Goodbye, Archie!
>
> CLEESE: Well, at least we're not irretrievably vulgar.
>
> KLINE: You know your problem? You don't like winners.
>
> CLEESE: Winners?
>
> KLINE: Yeah, winners!

CLEESE: Winners like . . . North Vietnam?

KLINE: SHUT UP! We did not lose Vietnam. It was a tie.

CLEESE: *(Slipping into a black street-wise accent)* I'm telling you, baby, they kicked an ass there. Boy, they whipped your hide real good.

KLINE: Oh, no, they didn't!

CLEESE: Oh, yes, they did!

KLINE: Oh, no, they didn't!

CLEESE: Oh, yes, they did!

KLINE: OH, NO, THEY . . . SHUT UP! *(aims his gun)* Goodbye, Archie. You hear me?

Which is much more in the spirit of the wartime British male complaint about American GIs: "They're overpaid, oversexed and over here."

Professor Christopher Andrew, young himself, says Ronald Reagan was enormously unpopular with the younger population in Europe:

> I don't believe there has ever been a President who has divided views on the two sides of the Atlantic as much. In the aftermath of the Libyan bombings, Reagan's popularity rose to some fabulously high figure like the high seventies in the United States and dropped below 20 percent in Europe. He was the first American leader in my lifetime who was widely regarded over here as a figure of fun. You can talk about Anglo-American ties and a degree of common purpose as much as you like, but you wouldn't have found 1 percent of Cambridge students willing to vote for Reagan.

After the Intermediate-Range Nuclear Forces treaty of Reagan and Gorbachev in 1988, and Gorbachev's clear willingness to cut his conventional forces, unilateralism may stage a comeback. As Lord Prior, a Tory, said to me, "Labour is being unbelievably stupid about defense because if they just sit tight and wait, everything is going their way anyhow on nuclear policy." (Kinnock himself evidently will settle for whatever wins votes; his wife Glenys is a determined ban-the-bomber.)

In spite of Mrs. Thatcher's steadfast loyalty to Washington, is there a weakening of Anglo-American ties? Old hands were divided about it when I talked to them even before the rapid changes in the last weeks of 1989. Some, like Sir John Thomson, who spent five years in New York in the 1980s as Britain's ambassador to the

United Nations, says there is; he told me over lunch at the Athenaeum:

> Without it being settled policy by anybody, there is an insidious and worrying decline in sympathy and knowledge across the Atlantic. It is just happening. And it goes up and down. You've just had the passage from center stage of the generation that collaborated so closely together during and just after the war. And Vietnam released all the latent anti-Americanism. We need more links between ordinary people across the Atlantic. However much you dislike a government, if you know two or three people from that country who you really respect and enjoy, it affects your thinking.

Sir Nicholas Henderson thinks growing Hispanic influence in the United States will paradoxically strengthen Anglo-American ties:

> They're coming fast. The more that happens, in my view, the more America will have to cling to its basic English roots. Its language, its law, its culture, its background which links it with this country. It must do it, otherwise it becomes an amorphous mass. I don't say that means we have political influence. We don't always have and we don't want to have. And you don't want us to have. But it is a very profound thing.

Two curious myths, I find, have a hold on a good many English minds. One is that America is about to be swamped by Spanish-speaking Latins. Norman Tebbit half-joked to me: "I do think Anglo-American understanding is less than it was because America is less of an Anglo-Saxon society. If you're not careful you'll have Spanish as your national language [laughter]." Another is that Americans like Germans better, at least when it comes to foreign relations. Americans *do* like the Germans' can-do efficiency, that's true. When it comes to the immediate fate of Eastern Europe, American ties to Germany do, for the time being, eclipse the old special tie to Britain. But German culture is invisible to us; who reads Goethe?

Lord Callaghan feels the Anglo-American cultural tie is strong, the political tie getting less so:

> Look, you and I can sit down immediately with a common background and talk in nuances and we don't have to explain what we're saying to each other and we understand instinctively. That relationship between Britain and America will always persist. We have a common law system. We have a common culture in so many things.

But politics are another matter:

> It doesn't exist now very much. Mrs. Thatcher may have liked Mr. Reagan and gets along well with Mr. Bush, but that is not the substance of it. The real long-term relationship ahead is going to be between Europe

and the United States and between Europe and the Soviet Union. And China and Japan. The United States is clearly not going to exercise its old dominance.

Callaghan and Denis Healey are just about the only two still fairly active important British political figures left who have been around since World War II, Callaghan rising from a Labour back-bencher under Attlee's postwar government to become Prime Minister in 1976–79, Healey as Defense Secretary, 1964–70, and Chancellor of the Exchequer, 1974–79; both careers span the whole postwar history of the Labour Party. Healey speaks of Americans in the 1940s and 1950s with a warm affection missing when he turns to them today. Healey, the Labour Party's deputy leader and seventy-three in 1990, says he will leave Parliament in the next election. He is widely held by both his Labour colleagues and Tories as one of the ablest men to have served in a British Cabinet since 1945. He landed with an American unit in North Africa during the war and, as a young major, was beachmaster for the British, fighting beside the Americans, in Anzio. As international secretary of the Labour Party under Ernest Bevin, he was on hand, like Lord Franks, when GATT, Bretton Woods, the IMF, the World Bank, and later NATO were formed.

> The first and most obvious difference from now was that Britain, the only European country unoccupied by German troops, when the war ended was one of the three important countries in the world, along with the United States and Soviet Union. Members of the Labour Party, like Attlee and Bevin, had been members of Churchill's coalition government. So the habit of working with the United States was deeply ingrained. Now at that time America was largely run by the East Coast WASP establishment who essentially looked at the world through European spectacles. So it was very much an Anglo-American partnership, farsighted people trying to organize the postwar world. Dean Acheson was an outstanding example. So was John Maynard Keynes.
>
> The postwar institutions were all inspired by this Anglo-American vision of world order. It was a very forward-looking, interventionist approach to world affairs. If I jump the forty years to now the changes are colossal. America now has little natural knowledge or understanding of European problems. Dean Acheson's rather cruel remark, "Britain has lost an empire but not yet found a role," at least showed he did. Our experience of the Third World due to our imperial past is hardly acknowledged or known by the present American leadership.

Senior knowledgeable Americans differ on this. Some argue British expertise in the Middle East is unequaled in the West. Not all agree. Said one veteran diplomat: "I differ that the great imperial past has left any present residue of wisdom about the Third World among the British, official or unofficial."

The most serious falling-out was over Suez—the sight of the United States pulling the rug from under Britain was a painful shock. But America's defeat in Vietnam was a failure of knowledge, not power—what Greece did best, not Rome. The British advisory mission there—Sir Robert Thompson, Dennis Duncanson—had an intuitive wisdom of Asian Leninism born of hard-won experience. We Americans could not match it.

Sir Robert taught me that it was never a Maoist-style "people's war"; the Communist aim was not really to win the war by winning battles, but to collapse a social structure, to fatally weaken and divide South Vietnam. Duncanson said the key phrase upon which Hanoi based its strategy to do this was Lenin's "exploiting internal contradictions in the enemy camp." They both argued that the Viet Cong's strength did not feed primarily on ideas or peasant grievances but relied upon terror, deceit, intimidation, and appeals to personal ambition. We Americans failed to see how this strategy of subversion worked; it cost us the war. I don't know why. It is as if Americans have a strong psychic interest in the world being as it seems.

Even today, when you ask the Americans who led the war effort about Vietnam, they agree that the British advisors like Duncanson saw clearly how implacable a foe we faced, as well as the nature of Communist strategy. But ask them about "exploiting internal contradictions" and they will say, in the words of one, "a fancy phrase for winning by home front turning away, what happened in the French experience." They are seeing it in terms of Americans, not Vietnamese. Whereas the British grasped that sowing division was how Hanoi worked to undermine and collapse South Vietnam's *own* social structure. We were playing checkers; the Communists—both Ho Chi Minh and Le Duan were longtime secret agents—were playing chess.

I told Denis Healey—under Harold Wilson he ran Britain's defense establishment for six years at the height of the war—that whatever understanding of the Vietnamese Communists I got came from Thompson and Duncanson. (Healey himself, in his anti-Nazi days at Oxford in the 1930s, belonged to the Communist Party for two years; he knows his Leninism.) He told me, "I remember going to Vietnam in 1963 when I was Defense Secretary and visiting two or three of

Thompson's strategic hamlets. The sullen hostility to the Americans was visible. You felt it, didn't you?"

I told him no, I did not. In nearly four years in Vietnam, 1964–67, I found little hostility among villagers, once you got to know them. In my experience the Vietnamese peasant just wanted to be left alone to till a little rice land and raise his family in peace. As the war dragged on, he got to know what Communism meant for that. The boat people should have put the lie to the idea that ordinary Vietnamese ever wanted the Vietcong to win.

Healey was undaunted. "I think you Americans totally misunderstood Vietnam as you've misunderstood most Third World issues," he said. I said I did agree with him that it was a mistake to use American ground troops, though Vietnam would have been lost in 1965 and not 1975 if we hadn't. It bought a decade's time so the rest of Southeast Asia could grow rich and stable enough to stave off Communist takeovers themselves. Healey argued that ground troops were how the British won in Malaya and, when he was Defense Secretary, in Borneo against Indonesia. He said Americans kept thinking they could win wars with "technological gimmicks." Healey:

> You know in the whole of the Confrontation we never once dropped a bomb from an aircraft. I was nagged by the commander in chief of the RAF in the Far East to allow him to bomb the Indonesian ports of entry in Borneo. I told him to bugger off.

But you can't really compare Vietnam to the Confrontation, when Indonesia opposed the British-sponsored Federation of Malaysia in 1965; it was mostly a holding action for Britain and its Commonwealth allies with few casualties and it was brought to an end not by any agreement or truce but by the ousting of Indonesia's Sukarno by General Suharto in 1965–66. The commitment of ground troops in Malaya was also extremely limited. Sir Robert Thompson in his 1963 attempt to apply Malaya's successful strategic hamlet program in Vietnam was severely handicapped: in Malaya the British called the shots and ran the government and forces without dissent or difficulty; in Vietnam the Americans had to go through the Vietnamese at every point. And you never knew whose side a Vietnamese was really on. It made all the difference.

When it comes to the bigger picture, the business about subversion and "internal contradictions" is not arcane or trivial, since the collapse of South Vietnam's confidence and culture decided the bigger picture. It turned the war into such a hopeless nightmare that much of the Labour Party from the mid-1960s, and eventually almost all of the British public and both parties, came to see Vietnam as a disaster of American "stupidity" and "brutality," at best extremely unwise and tragic, at worst bestial and savage. Healey told me, "What fed me up to the teeth was the Johnson Administration trying to persuade me to put troops in Vietnam when America was fighting a war it should never have been involved in and fighting it with none of the skill shown by our own forces fighting in Borneo at the same time. Vietnam had a traumatic effect on British respect for the United States."

I think Britain let us down. I asked William Bundy, who is Dean Acheson's son-in-law, about it. He recalled, "Actually, we never really pressed them, since we could see quite clearly they would not play. Dean Rusk always resented their attitude, while I thought it was inevitable. American resentment over the British position was certainly limited and unimportant alongside the British reaction. It was the end of an extraordinarily favorable image of America that had, mostly, survived even Suez."

So we are still coming to terms with the damage Vietnam inflicted on America's ability to lead; it destroyed the post-1945 Anglo-American consensus. Dennis Duncanson, of everybody involved, always seemed to be closest to the truth about Vietnam, which, I think in their different ways, neither the British nor the Americans have ever understood. When I met Duncanson for lunch at the Royal Commonwealth Society in London he put it starkly and simply: "I did my best. What more could I do? It was a failure. We failed, we failed."

What Britain and America have with each other and with no one else is a naval nuclear tie, Polaris, scheduled to continue with Trident, and an intelligence tie—electronic listening posts, reconnaissance satellites, submarine tracking, and early-warning radar. An end to one, or both, would break the relationship in a practical way. Denis Healey claims the value of shared intelligence is "almost zero" except for nuclear targeting. I took this as just blowing off steam, as there seems to be a broad consensus that American-British evaluations of Soviet military strength are much better for being in effect joint. Cambridge's Andrew, perhaps Britain's top authority on the subject, disagrees with Healey:

Any nuclear strategy needs two kinds of intelligence. One is offensive: nuclear targeting. Second is a defense policy against the other side's nuclear weapons. But there's also signals and other kinds of intelligence. I myself certainly don't see the intelligence alliance as a mere by-product of the nuclear alliance. It goes back a lot longer.

William Casey was the end of an era. To the best of my knowledge, he was the last intelligence officer on either side of the Atlantic who went back to World War II. He himself exemplified the special relationship; he was stationed in London. The intimacy of the special relationship during the war was all the more striking because it was so novel in history and so successful. Intelligence probably made its biggest contribution to any war in history.

If Britain went nonnuclear, and Germany neutralist, would the Americans just pack up and go home? Opinion in Congress now might well say, "Well, they don't want us. Bring the boys home."

"Congress keeps saying that," says Healey. "The risk of a big withdrawal has been hanging over us the whole time." (Of course, the way things are going in Russia and Eastern Europe, that may happen anyway.) Since 1945 the United States has stood guard over Western Europe and East Asia. Some ask: what good is it? They watch television news and see a world spinning into anarchy—people set off bombs, use poison gas, let children starve. The Third World has been disappointing: shooting its presidents, stealing aid, failing to curb births. The average president of Mexico routinely retires millions of dollars richer and Mexicans keep pouring across the border. Worn down, Americans take such setbacks as Vietnam or Japan muscling into our markets to heart. Long before the upheaval in Eastern Europe, *Washington Post* columnist Jim Hoagland commented about the late 1980s, "A renewed distrust of foreign entanglements that George Washington warned about seems to surface in a new sense of jingoism, and in talk of 'the widening Atlantic.'"

No one still active in public life did as much as Healey to maintain Britain's defense capability. The original agreement on Polaris was formalized by the British Prime Minister in 1963, Macmillan, and President Kennedy, but Healey oversaw the deployment of four Polaris submarines, each carrying sixteen missiles. This is still Britain's main nuclear deterrent, now being replaced by new, larger submarines carrying Trident missiles, costing at least £8 billion ($13.6 billion). In the 1960s Healey also played an important role in developing NATO's nuclear strategy. In 1983 he and Callaghan publicly opposed Labour's pledge unilaterally to get rid of Polaris. Looking back to 1964, Healey told me:

> We went ahead and brought Polaris in. I think now, personally, it was a mistake. We had a chance to opt out then. I think in some ways to be

dependent on a foreign country for a nuclear system gives you the worst of both worlds. You have continuously to make concessions to that foreign country for the sake of continuing the system. And renewing it, in the case of Trident. I think there was a real value, and I used to say so at the time, in having a second center of decision in NATO, although in those days McNamara was dead against third countries having their own nuclear weapons. He said third power deterrents were costly, inefficient, and prone to obsolescence. Kissinger was fairly neutral. Some, I think, rather like us to have it because maybe they could slide out of their nuclear commitment if we have nuclear weapons.

The idea that one can stand for both unilateral disarmament and NATO is "nonsensical," says Lord Jenkins, like Healey a postwar Labour Chancellor of the Exchequer and now chancellor of Oxford. "You can be for unilateralism and you can be for NATO. But you cannot be for a nonnuclear NATO." Jenkins told me:

I would always hope the Western alliance, having lasted forty years, would survive one period of foolishness. Having said that, I do not think that in the longer term, the alliance could survive either Germany or Britain moving into a unilateralist, and therefore a noncooperative, position. Defection on the part of either, and by defection I mean making American bases unwelcome, would, in my view, be fatal. I think the American government has inflicted some fairly strong strains on the alliance. Reagan's leadership was not an easy captaincy. And we're getting a very considerable reorientation of trade towards the European Economic Community. But whether there's a natural psychological movement towards Europe and away from the United States, I would be doubtful.

Healey himself sees the British turning inward, obsessed with their own internal affairs:

One thing you'll have noticed here is that interest in world affairs, which was very high in Britain in the postwar years, is now very low. When I first came into Parliament in 1952 we used to have about six widely reported debates on foreign affairs a year, each lasting two days. I used to speak in every one of them and the House was always crowded the whole time. Now we're lucky if we get two debates on foreign affairs a year, usually one day and on the fag end of the week, Friday, when nobody comes.

Maybe so. But Healey was speaking before Mikhail Gorbachev decided that Russia's postwar policies had utterly failed and it was time to start again. Quite suddenly the world—and Britain's role in it—looks like a new and unfamiliar place, ominous, unexplored, promising.

Into the Twenty-first Century

O brave new world
That has such people in't!

WILLIAM SHAKESPEARE

C AN IT BE? The triumph of Thatcherism over Marxism? The victory of the free market over state intervention?

The breathtaking turn of events this past year surely heralds even greater changes to come: the continued death crisis of Soviet Communism and its empire, a probably unstoppable renewed Chinese dash to freedom, a united and powerful Germany, the *shokku* of a militarily mighty Japan, and India and China, at last, after two hundred years, catching up with the West in science and dragging their poor billions behind them. Exciting times.

Everybody says Russia can't save its failing economy and keep Communism too. But, as Lord Callaghan says, "The Communist Party is the glue that holds the Soviet Union together." Andrei Sakharov, the day he died, said Mikhail Gorbachev was "mysterious," either "a cautious man" or "guided by the tactical and unprincipled considerations" of the Kremlin's old, ceaseless power struggle. "That," Sakharov said in what became his last testament, "could not be forgiven."

No mystery, said Gorbachev himself. "I am a Communist, a convinced Communist." But even more a realist. Hours before his fatal heart attack, Sakharov pleaded for an end to the seventy-two-year monopoly power of the Communist Party and for going to private property and free markets. Gorbachev shut him up. In February, pushed by unrest, Gorbachev reversed himself and got the Communist Party leadership to surrender its monopoly of power in the Soviet Union and accept a Western-style presidency. "If you can't beat them, join them," said an aide. "We must move with the tide." The world was agog, rather as if the Pope had said there was no God. It repudiates Leninism. But we should keep Sakharov's warning in mind. Democracy means the right to choose your leaders or to vote them out.

"Half measures can kill when on the brink of a precipice," goes a new poem by Yevgeny Yevtushenko. As winter turned to spring, amid fears of continued upheaval, forces beyond anybody's control propelled Russia toward restoring private property and giving land back to its peasants. Gorbachev's biggest worry, after the disintegration of the Soviet Union itself, was Germany emerging as an all-powerful nation and Russia's vulnerability to the south (all those uncontrolled weapons in Iran, Iraq, Pakistan, India, Israel). He still may feel a friendly Germany, with Poland as a buffer, in a prospering "common European home" can give Russia more security than the Cold War did. Mrs. Thatcher's biggest worry was a neutral Germany and all the American soldiers going home (including those in Britain, Italy, Greece, and Turkey, set to go down to 225,000, while Russia's troops drop to 195,000). The ghosts of Munich and 1939 haunt everybody.

Bring-the-boys-home is always a popular tune in America. It raises questions. What happens if some furious general throws Gorbachev out? If land armies and tactical warplanes are cut way down, what happens to NATO strategy? If you take away the trip wire of a strong, nuclear-armed, forward-deployed American force in Germany, what happens to the strategic deterrent? And beyond Europe, if NATO unravels, who will protect the oil-rich Middle East or the interests of oil-poor Pacific powers like Japan?

And a question closer to home: how will Europe resolve the contradiction between economic unity—the European Community of 1992—and the sovereign nation-state? A real United States of Europe, as Churchill envisaged it, would mean a common currency, a common passport (coming), a common parliament (evolving but slowly), and a common defense. David Owen, though he feels Mrs. Thatcher "goes on too much," favors some of her independence on Europe. He told me: "A certain amount of standing in your corner and holding your crown and fighting for British interests is a necessary part of diplomacy. You can't split the difference on everything."

The starting point in Europe is the continuation of conventional disarmament. I asked Lord Franks about Soviet superiority in ground forces. His reply:

Unless and until *they* are removed, so that the ground forces are more nearly equivalent, Mrs. Thatcher is unlikely to give way on other things. I think this is her preoccupation. But it would be a mistake to think that this is all she thinks about. She is a very intelligent woman. And has a will of her own.

Nor is she about to relinquish Britain's own nuclear deterrent. Field Marshal Lord Carver says, "Mrs. Thatcher loves Trident. She likes having it in her hand, brandishing it like Neptune." Carver, who argues Britain doesn't need its own nuclear weapons, told me he expects it to keep playing its key role in NATO.

Somebody the Americans can turn to and say, "Please help us with the Europeans." Somebody the Europeans can turn to and say, "Please help us with the Americans." But that position is very carefully watched by the Germans, who have tended at certain times in the past to say to the Americans: "You don't want to pay any attention to the British. They don't make much effort. We are the really important people."

An example of Britain's NATO role came during the 1986 Persian Gulf crisis when the Americans expanded their fleet, and the Europeans followed suit one by one (with the Russian navy tacitly cooperating to protect Gulf shipping to Kuwait). As Sir Antony Acland, British ambassador to Washington since 1986, describes it:

Mrs. Thatcher said to Europe's leaders: "This is what we're doing. France has backed us as well. Now can you? Can you, Italy? Can you, Netherlands? Can you, Belgium? Can you provide something to show we are sharing the burden with the Americans to keep the Gulf's sea-lanes open?"

David Owen, who holds the middle ground on so many issues, supports Mrs. Thatcher when it comes to nuclear weapons:

I am deeply in favor of the Atlantic relationship. But there's absolutely no way I'm going to trust the defense of Europe to any American President, thank you very much. I've watched what has happened in the past. I'm fiercely of the view that we should have our own nuclear weapons. And I'm thankful that France does as well.

To which Americans might be tempted to reply, "There's absolutely no way we're going to trust the defense of Europe to the Europeans. We've watched what happened in the past." As President Bush told NATO, "The U.S. will remain a European power." The British are forever asking: How much do their interests lie with Europe and how much with America? And is America likely to turn its back to fend off overpopulous Latins and to embrace ever-richer Asians, leaving Europe on its own, as it was in 1939?

A simple answer to the first is: Britain's economic interests lie with Europe; its security interests with America. The second has no simple answer. In 1990 we are deeply engaged in Europe, even if, since the Berlin Wall fell, when it comes to Eastern Europe, Germany, by dint of its geography and economic power, is the key player.

I asked historian Sir Michael Howard if its economic and security interests weren't pulling Britain two ways. He sees this split within the Thatcher government itself:

> The Foreign Office and old Tory wets are Eurocentric. And really would like to see Britain going into Europe and achieving a leadership in Europe. Even at the risk of frictions with the United States. They feel this is really the only way Britain can go forward and the best thing she can do for the West. Mrs. Thatcher, the Ministry of Defense, chiefs of staff, the whole defense establishment, say, "No, at all costs we must keep in with the United States." As long as she is there, the special relationship will be all right. If she were not, we'd be much more active in Europe. My own feeling is that we should be. We missed and are missing a lot of very important buses in Europe.

For example, Mrs. Thatcher has stood against a single European currency. *The Economist* has warned that while her hostility to monetary union is in tune with many British voters, history offers an unhappy parallel:

> In the 1950s Britain declined to join the EEC; its politicians and people were suspicious of foreigners' grand designs. It thereby missed out on the surge of growth that every EEC member enjoyed as the Community slashed its internal tariffs during its first 15 years. The 1992 project is Europe's next big push, with potentially the same rewards for those who join in with a will. Those who stay on the edge, muttering yesterday's slogans, risk losing out.

Michael Heseltine, Mrs. Thatcher's former Defense Secretary, who resigned over the Euro-linkup issue—he wanted Britain's insolvent helicopter-maker, Westland, to be bailed out by a European consortium, Mrs. Thatcher wanted to buy American choppers—told me Britain had too long been the "reluctant bride" to the EEC:

> We were hesitant to join. Having joined, we were hesitant about the terms on which we joined . . . We've put that behind us now. It is in Europe that Britain's potential in the twenty-first century will have to be realized. The more effective Europe is in its own interests, the stronger the link across the Atlantic will be. The more the Europeans contribute to their own defense, the more sympathetic the Americans

are likely to be about their commitment to NATO. The more Britain is at the front in NATO, the more Atlanticist Europe will remain.

NATO adapts to circumstances, of course. When Russia didn't have the bomb, its policy was massive retaliation; once it did, it switched to flexible response. As America's biggest institutional tie in Europe, NATO can now take on a more political role. Heseltine's pro-Europe views partly explain why he is consistently Mrs. Thatcher's most popular rival in the polls; in one poll last winter a third of Britain's voters felt he would do the best job of leading the Tories in a post-Thatcher election. Trailing behind Heseltine were Sir Geoffrey Howe, also strongly pro-Europe (11 percent), Norman Tebbit, more of a Little Englander (7 percent), Kenneth Baker (4 percent), Douglas Hurd (3 percent), and Christopher Patten (1 percent).

Europe, it has long been said, could be the rock on which Mrs. Thatcher's rule founders. The events of late 1989 showed up the weaknesses of a premiership long on populist rectitude and short on historical imagination. It started, you might say, when she went over to Paris for the bicentennial celebrations of Bastille Day last July. "It took us a long time to get rid of the effects of the French Revolution two hundred years ago," she told the astonished French. "We don't want another one." (American journalist Michael Kinsley observed: "Mrs. Thatcher's relish in giving gratuitous offense—her preening love of controversy—is irksome . . . But imagine Mr. Bush having any opinion at all about the French Revolution, let alone expressing one (apart from best wishes to our valued ally on the 200th anniversary of her blah blah blah).")

Maybe she didn't like the idea of anybody plotting revolt. (Dickens: "Darkness closed around, and then came the ringing of church bells, and the distant beating of drums of the Royal Guard, as the women sat knitting, knitting.") *Observer* columnist Richard Ingrams has asked if Eastern Europe's uprising might not have struck too close to home:

> How many of those who have watched the thrilling scenes on TV of huge, flag-waving crowds massing in Wenceslas Square and elsewhere have not entertained a fantasy of a vast throng massing in Trafalgar Square and moving up towards Downing Street, then tearing down the hated iron gates which the despotic ruler has erected to protect herself from her enemies.

(Ingrams is also the anonymous author of the sometimes wickedly funny "Dear Bill" letters in the humor weekly *Private Eye*. Supposedly written on the Prime Minister's stationery by Mrs. Thatcher's husband Denis to a golfing crony, the letters have comments such as, on her retirement, "The only snag, and it's a big one, is whether the Boss can be persuaded to see sense and get out before they blow her out." Actually Ingrams shows remarkable prescience in his column on Eastern Europe. In March 1990 thousands of anti–poll tax demonstrators did riot in Trafalgar Square and moved toward Downing Street, where they were fought back by the police.)

Mrs. Thatcher's biggest problem with Europe is a plan, put forward by Jacques Delors, the French head of the European Community's executive commission, who is said to be as stubborn and autocratic as she is, that goes way beyond the creation of a single European free market in 1992. Delors wants to establish a single central bank and monetary union, a strong European Parliament, and a "social charter" for the Community that would standardize labor union rights, wages and welfare.

Mrs. Thatcher is not about to transfer power to EEC bureaucrats in Brussels. A surprise ally is the greatly respected ex-deputy editor of *The Economist*, Norman Macrae, who now writes an outspoken column in *The Sunday Times*. Macrae argues "the last thing East Europe's newly liberated nations need is Brussels rules telling them what exchange rates they must have and what unemployment-creating social charters they must enforce." He urged his readers, "All who care for a true Europe should be wholly on her side."

But in the main Mrs. Thatcher's Little Englander sentiments have put her at odds with some of her Cabinet, the Tory Party's old guard, and arguably do damage to Britain's relations with France and Germany, even Russia and the United States. Those in favor of the European Community argue, as they did in the 1950s, that nobody will take Britain seriously if it is just a small island off the Continent.

Real trouble came in October 1989 when Nigel Lawson, her Chancellor of the Exchequer and the one Thatcherite as willful as herself, walked out of her Cabinet. In a damaging Halloween speech in the House of Commons, Lawson told of a long and bitter feud over European monetary union. He criticized Mrs. Thatcher's autocratic style and proclaimed, "Britain's destiny lies in Europe."

The rather arcane immediate issue was the European exchange-rate mechanism, or ERM. This is an arrangement between banks, in practice dominated by Germany's Bundesbank, to coordinate the exchange rates of European Community currencies. It is a step toward a common currency. Among the EEC, everybody but Britain, Greece, and Portugal belongs. Members of the ERM had an average inflation rate of just 3.5 percent in the year May 1988 to May 1989, while Britain's rose above 8 percent at peak, the highest of any Western country. Lawson quit over the issue and Sir Geoffrey Howe, Mrs. Thatcher's deputy, who increasingly stakes out independent positions, cautioned her not to try shelving full membership in the European monetary system indefinitely.

At home she can count on plenty of young rank-and-file Tories, Thatcherites brought into the party under her banner in three successful elections, to share her very lower-middle-class English suspicions of foreigners' grand designs. Plenty of Labourites have them too.

The rest of the European Community has simply ignored Mrs. Thatcher's objections. They are going right ahead to closely coordinate their economic policies from July 1990. They plan to create a central bank and a common currency after a special conference next December. Mrs. Thatcher, after fussing about wanting "an evolutionary approach," and voting against the workers' charter, grudgingly agreed to take part.

Sometimes the collapse of Communism seemed to be going too fast for her. "Don't disarm too fast," she told the Americans. "Turmoil can be very disturbing," she said at a NATO meeting. "And we don't know what may happen. Times of great change are times when you have even greater need for secure and stable alliances."

She showed she was just as good as her word when Bush sent troops into Panama. While the Russians and Latins condemned it and the rest of the world squirmed, the minute Bush phoned her about it, Mrs. Thatcher declared it was "a courageous decision" and that she backed him up. Suddenly the special relationship was alive and well in a shows-who-your-real-friends-are sort of way ordinary Americans, mindful of the Falklands, appreciate.

The fighting in Panama came just days after Britain forcibly repatriated fifty-one Vietnamese boat people from Hong Kong to Hanoi. Suddenly, to Americans already guilt-ridden about Vietnam, there were women and children screaming and weeping on their TV screens as helmeted riot police herded them onto a plane in the pre-dawn hours. A Bush spokesman called it "odious" and said "involuntary repatriation is unacceptable until conditions improve in Vietnam." Governments, relief agencies, the European Parliament, and the Pope joined in denouncing what they saw as an inhumane act.

Mrs. Thatcher said protesting countries would do better to provide homes for the 50,000 refugees left in Hong Kong.

If sending American troops to Panama set a bad precedent for Soviet military action in Europe, a British colony forcing innocent children back to repressive Hanoi didn't sit well with cheers for the free flow of East Europeans to the West. Hong Kong's nearly 6 million people, facing rule by China in 1997, didn't stop to think they want the West to give them the same sanctuary they would deny the Vietnamese. Mrs. Thatcher agreed to take 50,000 households from Hong Kong (about 225,000 people), a drop in the bucket. It was still too many for Norman Tebbit and the Tory Party's right wing. Their chauvinism is self-defeating; Britain's soon-to-be-shrinking population could use new blood. They would do better to think about Central Europe. Chancellor Kohl may say, "It's absurd to talk about a Fourth Reich." But one big Germany, even without another Bismarck or Kaiser Wilhelm or Hitler, still fans the embers of fears over "the German problem" and how it set off wars in 1870 and 1914 and 1939.

As somebody who spent two years studying in the German language at Austrian universities in the 1950s, I felt a shiver, as the Berlin Wall was breached, to see on television the aging members of West Germany's Parliament spontaneously rise and sing *"Deutschland, Deutschland über Alles."* The last time I'd heard the German national anthem was thirty-two years ago in Innsbruck when my roommate, a medical student from Bonn, came home from his duelling fraternity drunk one night and went out on our balcony and bellowed it defiantly at the top of his lungs. It was still banned in those days because of its association in everybody's mind with Hitler and the Nazis. At about this time, George Steiner came back from a trip to Poland traumatized by a visit to Auschwitz. Instead of his next lecture on literature, Steiner gave his mainly German and Austrian students the most courageous and moving and electrifying description of a concentration camp I ever heard. If memory serves, somebody wrote *"Juden"* on his car and slashed its tires the next day. The Tyrol has beautiful landscapes with the snow bright on its ski slopes and alpine meadows, its onion-shaped towers and post-card castles. It never looked quite as good again. Elie Wiesel, the Nobel-winning concentration camp survivor, has asked, "Is my fear unfounded? . . . What should one feel when hearing old-new Germany's anthem—'*Deutschland, Deutschland über Alles*'"?

Paul Theroux, whose views, like Dr. Steiner's, we have heard here, seems to be wary too. In late 1989 he happened to be in West Germany on an author's circuit for his latest book. He was also reading Freud's *Jokes and Their Relation to the Unconscious*. Theroux found, he wrote in a *New York Times* op-ed piece, that most Kohl jokes depicted the Chancellor as a blunderer:

> Just the mention of his nickname, "Der Birne"—the Pear, for his supposedly pear-shaped face—is enough to have most Germans laughing uncontrollably. One joke has Chancellor Kohl and Prime Minister Margaret Thatcher toasting each other with a beer. "Here's to your health," Mrs. Thatcher says. And thinking she said, "Here's to your *hell* (light beer)," he replies, "Here's to your *dunkel* (dark beer)."

Then Theroux starts telling of hearing about so many German jokes concerning Turks, being foreign, Muslim, poor, and "dark, hairy and sinister," they seem to be "the perfect victims." Theroux found it hard, though, to get Germans to give him examples of Turkish jokes.

> "They are anti-Jewish jokes with the names changed," I was told. "They are horrible. They are even about gas chambers."

So one is just as glad when it comes to allies that someone as staunch as Mrs. Thatcher is there. Or as American columnist William Pfaff wittily put it, "One is, on the whole, glad she is there and we are here."

Sir Michael Palliser, a former head of the Foreign Office, now vice chairman of the Midland Bank, and a Europeanist, told me Britain needs to work to avoid a protectionist Fortress Europe in 1992.

> I think we can work within the European Community to try to insure that it does not turn itself into an inter-Europe club which tries to keep Americans out.

But Palliser says, "There is an illusion amongst a lot of British people and a certain amount of Americans that the special relationship which developed during the war continues to affect our ties with the United States. I believe that it only does to the extent that we identify with our fellow Europeans in relating to Americans."

Norman Tebbit, who is perhaps still fairly close to Mrs. Thatcher, argues the reverse: the old "special relationship" is alive and well:

> There's no doubt at all that if the United States wants a satisfactory relationship with the European Community, then it's got to get its rela-

tionship right with the United Kingdom. And vice versa. The two leaders during the Reagan years had a good understanding of each other and, on the whole, were very willing to play ball with each other. I know there were times when one felt there was a bit of discord over who was supposed to be at the back of the court and who was supposed to be up at the net. But it worked pretty well and, with President Bush, there's a great deal of opportunity to continue it.

Like Heseltine, David Owen feels the more Britain becomes European, the more important it will be to America as a bridge:

Britain remains influential in Washington if Britain is influential in Europe. If Britain allows itself to be sidelined, Washington will look to the Bonn-Paris axis. Britain has to make up its mind to be a major player in the European Community.

Lord Callaghan, one of those who sees the world's center of gravity moving to the Pacific Basin, says it is time to go back to the old concept, never practiced, of Europe being one pillar of NATO and America the other. He told me:

It is time for Europe to create its own future, take more responsibility for its own defense, in friendship with the United States. I'm a very strong Atlanticist. But we can't just look back to 1945 and the hegemony the United States exercised. It is going to be in the lead for many years to come. Its economy will grow. It will be one of the most powerful forces in the world. But it is clearly not going to exercise its old dominance. The dollar is being displaced. This should not give you Americans a feeling of inferiority. You should not worry yourselves sick about it. It's one of the things that happens to great countries. History moving on.

Lord Callaghan is one of those who favor holding a peace conference to end World War II. He says it would be a way to get East and West Germany "to accept the existing borders of Germany" before reunifying. American experts on Germany warn this could open a Pandora's box of old wounds. The eastern third of prewar Poland went to Russia during the war. Stalin at Potsdam in 1945 bought off the Poles by handing them roughly an equal slice of Eastern Germany, up to the Oder-Neisse line. Best, they say, to let de facto integration come through economic and technical cooperation, without raising dicey "German reunification" politics.

Peter Jay, ambassador to Washington in 1977–79, argues that aside from Britain's dependence on America for its security, cultural affinity is the main tie now:

> When you talk about Anglo-American relations you have to make a fundamental and profound distinction between the relations between the two governments and the relations between the two peoples. The tie in banking, in finance, in the sciences, in the arts, in all areas where the English language is vital, is of *enormous* importance to the British. It's of far lesser importance to the Americans.

The only thing that could weaken this tie, Jay says, is militant Europeanism.

> I see a lot of it among British bureaucrats and businessmen. I see no sign of it amongst ordinary people. Some of the more militantly selfish protectionist things Europe does provoke Congress. If Europe ever alienates American public opinion, it will be a fundamental mistake. Because European integration is no substitute, in security terms, for the relationship with the United States.

Jay finds the idea of a militarily self-sufficient Fortress Europe "crazy."

> Europe has used its strength and power for the last thousand years to wreak destruction and havoc in Europe. It's only safe when it is run by non-Europeans. As it has been for the last forty years, thank God.

Britain's role should be to help the American-European relationship work better. Jay said, "By and large British governments, though they *say* they want to be honest brokers, have not delivered."

"Mrs. Thatcher has."

"Mrs. Thatcher least of all." Jay said she had low credibility.

> Mrs. Thatcher has been in the business, until recently anyway, of simply declaring herself to be shoulder to shoulder with the American President on a number of issues. Which she's perfectly entitled to do. But if you do that, in a high-profile sort of way, you can't also play the role of honest broker. I don't think Mitterrand or Kohl see her in that role. I think they talk to each other. Or direct to the Americans.

Sir Oliver Wright makes the interesting point that the British tend to see Communism as just another dimension of historic Russia. Enoch Powell, who goes back in Tory politics to Macmillan's Cabinet and was one of Mrs. Thatcher's early mentors, feels the same. He also said Macmillan's "addiction" to the Greece-Rome metaphor had "a special significance":

> After 1956 a new axiom began to prevail in this country's perception of itself: that British statecraft and policy cannot safely be out of line with those of the United States. We've lived with it for thirty years. It's breaking down now.

Since the INF treaty, more and more British perceive their safety does not depend on the United States, he argues. Powell:

> After all, those who said that to retain the supposedly indispensable American protection it was necessary that American intermediate-range weapons be sited in Great Britain are now standing by politely applauding while those are removed. The coupling is uncoupled. It goes very far and very deep.

Powell believes there will now be a reassessment of Russia, not as the Soviet Union, but as Russia.

> As the cold war diminishes, so the natural common interest of Britain and Russia in the balance of power in Europe revives. In three wars in two hundred years it has been Russia which, in our perception, saved Britain. The British may no longer feel it necessary to humor the Americans by sharing their mythology.

Powell said Mrs. Thatcher, "an unphilosophical lady," was not fully conscious of this shift nor were the Americans. "It would be bad manners to tell them. I'm only telling you because I'm out of the game. Out of the game."

The only Englishman I met who says "we Europeans" was Sir Antony Acland, who succeeded Palliser to run the Foreign Office until he went to Washington. Sir Antony says Britain has moved East, accepting it is part of Europe and its common market, just as America has moved west, with its economy shifting toward the Pacific rim (37 percent of American trade is now with East Asia, just 20 percent with the twelve EEC countries), its ethnic change (Hispanic, black, and Asian Californians will outnumber whites by 2010), and the dimming of wartime memories.

But, Sir Antony emphasizes, it is all true just up to a point. California opened a London office in 1987 to match one in Tokyo. Britain, to many Americans, is still seen as the jumping-off point to Europe. At £70 billion, Britain is the largest direct foreign investor in America (twice as much as Japan). Sir Antony:

> The truth is America has different relationships, each one special in its own way—with Britain, with Japan, with Germany, with Israel, with Saudi Arabia, with Mexico, with Canada. I think with us—what has struck me in Washington—is the intensity of the relationship. Both ways. Ministers, politicians, scientists, academics, actors, astrologers, all come pouring across the Atlantic or go the other way. We had six Cabinet ministers and three ministers of state in just the last sixty days. One's looking at the privatization of prisons, another public broadcasting, a third the electrical industry. So you've got this two-way street

whatever you call it. I'm amazed and grateful at the kindness and tolerance that the American bureaucracy and the administration and people on the Hill show in letting the British Embassy set up program after program. And they seem to enjoy it.

Russia and Germany and their neighbors, in spite of all that has happened in Europe, cannot afford to ignore the Pacific rim. This is where the Japanese and Americans come together and the new single world economy's frontier of scientific and high-tech innovation lies. As the Cold War winds down, the hope is East and West can pool their ideas and energy and money to rebuild their own societies, help the Third World, and save the planet's environment. We may be dogged by the deficit, drugs, failing schools, homelessness, and the rest, but one doesn't have to buy theories of American decline like Paul Kennedy's, the intellectual fad of the late 1980s. I'm with Jim Rohwer, a globe-hopping Californian and *The Economist*'s Asia editor, when he says that countries like Japan may be getting stronger, but nobody "has America's ability to draw together in its own hands all the threads of great-power influence: military, political, economic and ideological."

Another thing nobody can afford to ignore is nuclear weapons. As Rohwer says:

> President Reagan thought that some way out of nuclear deterrence had to be found because ordinary people would not put up much longer with a security balance based on nuclear weapons.

When I first read this I thought Cold-War weariness was purely European. Russia's economy might be failing, but it still rivals America in space, ballistic and cruise missiles, aviation, and naval power. So I was surprised in 1989 visits to Washington to find ex-cold-warriors ready to pursue, if things go well, all kinds of geopolitical pragmatism with Russia. There's an assumption both NATO and the Warsaw Pact are starting to crumble. That the exchange of Russian oil and gas for European hard currency will grow, and one big energy grid, tying Russia and Europe together, will depend more and more on the Middle East. Terrorism, drugs, and the environment are already on the U.S.–Soviet agenda.

Europe's war-weariness and Russia's nuclear arsenal will both figure in the severe tests ahead. World War II showed people can get used to bombing, people can get used to war. What they can't get used to is nuclear bombs. But the deep level of anxiety that persists year after year is much stronger in Europe. Alistair Cooke stood on the California coast one time in 1943 and tried to imagine Japanese troops coming ashore; he doubted that one American in a thousand ever thought of the possibility. On that October day in 1957 when Sputnik zoomed overhead, it looked quite different to a European and an American. Timothy Dickinson, as an Englishman long in America, puts the European feeling this way:

> People have been waiting to outsit the Soviet system for forty years. But the *damn thing is still there.* The attitude that they'll get prosperous and friendly is an attitude of a remote nation like the United States. Europeans don't believe it. They believe from history that a great power on your border is going to be a fundamental menace. The view of a people dwelling on a great plain as opposed to the view of people dwelling on oceans. It is no accident that the two great liberal people of history—the British and the Americans—have both been offshore powers.

Dickinson feels "Europe is through, politically and emotionally through. I think people feel Europe is an aging whore who will do her tricks for the Soviets next." When I protested, Dickinson went on:

> Good lord, stick around. People say Europe is afraid, that Europe sees itself as the battlefield. And that Europe will do almost anything to avoid being the battlefield. I know lots of Europeans are afraid the Americans would find an excuse for fighting nuclear war if the Soviets were taking over Europe.

In Britain's case, I suppose you could say it nerved itself to get out of the burdens of a Great Power, pulled back everywhere, refused to pay the price of maintaining itself as a world arbiter, and now discovers itself with more risks than ever. Now the risk isn't losing an empire, it's getting a hydrogen bomb in one's lap. And it has to be galling for Britain to find itself in a fiercely competitive single world economy where the main challenges are coming from the two defeated enemies of World War II—Germany and Japan.

A blurring of the lines in Europe, as the East European countries come out from under Soviet control, could in time go against Mrs. Thatcher or her successor at Number Ten if the British cannot get the defense spending they need. Or a Labour government that wishfully disarmed itself was voted in. Inevitably, if things go according to Gorbachev's plan and the Russians can undo the Iron Curtain, the Cold War, and the massive buildup of NATO and Warsaw Pact forces, the Americans will leave Europe. It could even be a gracious exit with everybody agreeing to it. Or the Russians might want some American troops to stay (agreeing with Peter Jay that Europe is safer with non-Europeans on hand). Or some Americans could be left in Britain. In the new situation, anything is possible. An American departure, if it put Europe on a long, slow slide downward, could also take us back to 1939.

Much depends on oil. Britain's North Sea oil may have peaked. As mentioned, few expect it to go back to pre-1988 levels of 2.5 million barrels per day, but present production of about 2 million barrels can be held past 1995 or longer; if prices fall the decline would be faster. But experts predict a good run for another ten years at least, especially if oil prices rise in the late 1990s.

Estimates of the world's proven reserves went up from 700 billion barrels in 1985 to nearly 900 billion in 1989. Roughly speaking, North America has 35 billion barrels, Latin America 122 billion, Western Europe 18 billion (4.3 billion in Britain, the rest in Norway), the old Soviet bloc, mainly Russia, 65 billion, Africa 56 billion, China 19 billion, and the rest of oil-poor Asia 22 billion. But the Middle East has a whopping 571 billion. Saudi Arabia, Kuwait, Iraq, and the United Arab Emirates alone, some experts say, probably have enough oil, known and still to be found, to guarantee a hundred years of production at present consumption rates. Geologists reckon nearly as much as present world reserves is left to be discovered. Yet in 2000–2025, as the Western Hemisphere and Atlantic Basin get depleted, reliance on Middle Eastern oil could go up dramatically, with a third oil shock probably coming before 2000. The acute shortage will come in Japan and the Pacific Basin.

Russia currently produces about 12.5 million barrels of oil per day. It exports about 4 million of this. Half of it goes to Western Europe for hard currency, the rest to Eastern Europe, plus Cuba and Vietnam. Russia's output of natural gas, if not disrupted, could top 800 billion cubic meters in 1990. Its great pipelines across Europe already provide West Germany and France with about a third and Italy over a fourth of their gas imports. Russian oil and gas figure significantly in the European Community's future energy calculations.

One of my brothers, James Critchfield, has argued in *The Christian Science Monitor*'s new monthly, *World Monitor*, that investment in new enhanced oil recovery techniques could more than double known reserves by extracting 940 billion barrels from heavy oils and bitumens, mainly in Venezuela and Canada. (Russia has about

100 billion barrels of potentially recoverable heavies and bitumens.) He argues:

> Mikhail Gorbachev should have a keen interest in the West's developing technology for their extraction. One conclusion seems certain, though. The world will be less likely to come to conflict over oil if the great concentrations of heavy oils and bitumens in the Western Hemisphere are developed in a time frame that reduces reliance on Middle Eastern exports before the balance tips too far in that direction.

Mrs. Thatcher has been quick to see that a role as trader and teacher in the Arab world could pay off when oil prices start to soar again in the mid-1990s. (Look what happened just after the Alaskan oil spill.) Britain is modernizing the Saudi Arabian air force with Tornado jet fighters (the European F-16) and has military advisers in Oman. Arab leaders express a preference for dealing with the British (not as blatantly self-interested as the French). And American influence in the Middle East, except for what can be exerted through Israeli guns, is hamstrung. As one American, an old Middle Eastern hand, put it, "The British haven't always been very good allies, but they have been allies."

As oil gives out, Britain, like everybody else, will have to use less, bridge over with gas, go back to coal (but spend money to clean up the air pollution from coal), swallow hard and build more (but safer) nuclear plants, or learn how to develop hydrocarbons and fossil fuels that don't warm up the atmosphere. This is going to be a great transformation as overpopulation and overpollution pose ever-greater threats to man.

So much is riding on how America handles its own problems, above all its budget deficit, and Russia the Gorbachev reforms. Looking down the road twenty years, we can imagine Europe a lot closer to union, China and India beginning to be big economic powers, Japan a Great Power, and Russia maybe coaxed into being a rather more market-minded half-democracy. But, as Lord Franks says, nobody can know what will happen in twenty years.

Either way America will doubtless still be holding up the West's side in a stable balance of power. In this, it will need its friends. "What kind of a people do they think we are?" asked Churchill at a fateful moment in history. Mrs. Thatcher is not the only reliable ally. The stability, permanence, and stubborn tenacity of the British have been proved again and again. Come hell or high water, you can count on them.

This stability and permanence is exemplified by the Royal Family. The more Britain worries about its future, the better the continuity of its oldest social institution looks. We find it reassuring too. Anthony Holden, Prince Charles's biographer and one of the shrewdest observers of royalty, was only half joking when he said, asked why Americans are so fascinated by the monarchy, "You haven't got one and you're jealous and you occasionally regret 1776."

To Look at the Queen

A SURPRISE IN Britain is how easy it is to see the Queen. Her daily round of ceremonial ribbon-cutting and orphanage-going is posted in the "Court Appointments" column in *The Times*. All you have to do is show up at the right time and join the onlookers. Just going about central London a lot for interviews, I found, one sometimes happened on to twenty or thirty people waiting outside an entrance gate; a policeman might say, "Her Majesty is inside."

The first time this happened was outside a small church near Covent Garden. Sure enough, the Queen soon came out, the familiar face smiling at everybody, a short, plump, gracious-looking woman in her early sixties, in a bright yellow hat and coat, looking a good deal friendlier and less intimidating than in pictures or on a TV screen. Her party, which included a lady-in-waiting and a tall naval officer I took to be an equerry, climbed into two Rolls-Royces and drove off just like everybody else, no sirens; they stopped for the red light. Well, well, I thought, amazed and as awed as if she'd driven off, all diamond crown and glitter, in a splendid horse-drawn stately coach escorted by troops of the Household Cavalry, plumes flying and shouts from the crowd, "God save the Queen!" It was like the old nursery rhyme: "Pussy cat, pussy cat, where have you been?" "I've been to London to look at the queen." (Indeed, maybe that is why we're so taken with royalty; it is like the nursery rhymes and fairy tales of childhood come to life.)

What struck me was how comfortable and good-humored everybody seemed: the other waiting people, the London bobbies, the Queen and her retinue. The British *are* comfortable with their monarchy. Its strength, particularly at a time of division and stress like the Thatcher years, is the way it gracefully symbolizes stability and common British values. It may sometimes seem like the world's longest-running soap opera (Is Charles happy with Di? Is Andy a dodgy dad? Fergie a fab mum?), what has been called "a continuing psychodrama starring the royal family." But in Britain itself the Queen pretty well succeeds in presenting her glamorous clan as a close-knit family with solid middle-class values dedicated to public service.

Years ago, as a young reporter just out of graduate school, I covered the Queen and Prince Philip on their 1957 royal visit to Washington. I luckily got sent to the British Embassy when the Queen awarded a handful of Americans the OBE. Afterward sherry was served. It was such a small gathering we all got to meet the Royal Couple. I can't remember what was said, just the feeling that they were sort of our Royal Couple too, the Revolutionary War and two centuries of going it alone notwithstanding. It is still true. If the *Daily Express* crows, "Americans eat up royalty like pizza"; the *Los Angeles Times* sighs, "Here we go again—genuflecting, curtsying and shamelessly salivating."

Another surprise in Britain, when you go round some miserable slum, is how often Prince Charles has been there ahead of you. The Prince's distant, melancholy image is contradicted by the enthusiasm of public housing dwellers about the real interest he takes in their problems. He has rightly accused Britain's architects, whose prisonlike housing estates and tower blocks, inspired by Le Corbusier and Mies van der Rohe, blight most British cities, of consistently ignoring "the feelings and wishes of the mass of ordinary people." (I am with Prince Charles 100 percent on this; a marvelous Palladian restoration by Quinlan Terry of the riverside in Richmond, just down the hill from my door, shows how spirit-lifting classical revivalism can be; Britain's modern architecture is uniformly drab and depressing.)

When Prince Charles speaks out there are complaints that he should stay out of politics, as if saying nothing doesn't carry just as heavy a moral responsibility. What gives his views authority is that, like a good reporter, he goes out, mingles as much as he can, and asks, asks, asks. What better experience for a future king? Britain has peculiar need of somebody like this. Mrs. Thatcher and her ministers, after more than a decade in power, are getting to that stage of isolation where messages from the grass roots don't always get through, the hazard of any long rule. The Prince has said:

> If you go round the country in my position—I've learned a lot, I've listened, I've looked a lot—you can't just sit and do nothing about it.

The Prince of Wales has many images. He is the risk-taking adventurer (parachute jumping, skin diving and frogman training, flying jets and helicopters, leading a skiing party into a Swiss avalanche that claimed one of his best friends and narrowly missed himself). Ex-military man (Royal Navy commander, Royal Air Force wing commander). Something of an intellectual (the first member of the British Royal Family ever to earn a university degree—a Cambridge B.A. in history; dabbles in Jungian psychology and homeopathic medicine, paints, plays the cello). Sportsman (steeplechasing, hunting, polo). Family man (his marriage to Princess Diana, thirteen years younger, has produced two sons, Prince William, seven in 1990, and Prince Harry, five—"the heir and spare"). Reformer and architectural critic (after he called a planned extension to the National Gallery on Trafalgar Square "a monstrous carbuncle" it was stopped, and his epithet of "glass stump" finished off Mies van der Rohe's proposed City of London tower). Globe-trotting goodwill ambassador, after-dinner speaker, television producer, author *(A Vision of Britain* in 1989). The list goes on.

Prince Charles keeps busy ("I work bloody hard right now and will continue to") and appears to find several of these roles fulfilling. But the press likes best to portray him as broodingly self-absorbed and frustrated. Howell Raines in a *New York Times Magazine* profile quoted the Prince:

> I've had to fight every inch of my life to escape royal protocol . . . I've had to fight to go to university. I've had to fight to have any sort of role as Prince of Wales. You're suggesting that I go back and play polo. I wasn't trained to do that. I've been brought up to have an active role. I am determined not to be confined to cutting ribbons.

Charles Jencks in his 1988 book, *The Prince, The Architects and New Wave Monarchy,* reports Raines attributes "this outburst to a meeting with three editors, none of whom would substantiate the quotes." But the idea that Prince Charles seeks a more active role is self-evident (supported by the Queen; sometimes, as when he described the North Sea as "a rubbish dump," she repeats his remarks like any proud mother).

When Norman Tebbit warned on BBC that too much concern for the inner-city poor could get the Prince in trouble, he blamed the Prince's outspokenness on frustration. Tebbit warned that if the Prince "advocated a socialist solution, a Labour Party solution, that would begin to get dangerous." He said:

I suppose the Prince naturally feels extra sympathy towards those who've got no job because in a way he's got no job and he's prohibited from having a job until he inherits the throne . . . He's almost forty and yet he's not been able to take responsibility for anything, and I would think that's really his problem.

Michael Heseltine told me he'd prudently refused to get into it. Enoch Powell, however, when I asked him about Prince Charles, was happy to voice what seems to be the generally held view:

If the heir apparent is to take a part in public life, it must be the part of a real man, of a human being, and not the part of a dummy. We have to accept that from time to time he will voice opinions and take up attitudes which everybody may not like. This seems to be an inevitable consequence of what is desirable, namely, that the heir should take part in public life and understand public life before he comes to the throne. I think I am speaking for most people in saying that.

Tebbit, when I met him, had already backed down, protesting he was misunderstood.

In his biography, Jencks argues that the Prince, far from having found no useful role, has mastered the media when it comes to promoting causes like classical architecture, rejuvenating dead industrial towns, or helping small businesses and the poor.

It can be argued that the Royal Family's real power lies in this very ability to influence the press. Royal correspondent Judy Wade says, "Without the media, the monarchy could have trouble staying in business." Buckingham Palace with all its heraldry and chivalry, some of it going back to the days of William the Conquerer, has to strike a balance between serving the public, satisfying the appetite of its subjects for fairy-tale romance, and resisting a wholesale invasion of its privacy and the kind of attention that conflicts with its mystique. Says Jencks: "The Prince, like the rest of the Royal Family, must keep on the good side of the press. It is their single, real organ of power."

The British monarchy has always walked this tightrope. Queen Victoria's long seclusion to mourn the death of Prince Albert led to a serious questioning of the monarchy's future. Yet most of today's royal trappings, like so much at Oxford and Cambridge and the public schools, were inventions of her age.

Walter Bagehot, *The Economist*'s great Victorian editor, wrote in *The English Constitution:*

The mystic reverence, the religious allegiance, which are essential to a true monarchy, are imaginative elements that no legislature can manufacture in any people.

He said the British regard the crown as "the head of our morality" and believe it "natural to have a virtuous sovereign." Author Anthony Holden calls this role "a quasi-religious one, a moral example, they are there to show us how Christian family life is lived." I've mentioned how Queen Elizabeth's annual Christmas messages sound like sermons, appropriate for the titular head of the Church of England. She is said to be a firmly believing Christian. But who really knows what Elizabeth II thinks about anything except horseflesh? (When James Callaghan, as Prime Minister, once asked her advice on what to do, she told him, "That's what *you're* paid for.") What the Queen really seems to represent is less religious faith than the pieties of old-fashioned English morality, someone who seldom mentions God, but says, "God bless you." You might call it worthiness, sheer worthiness. She reflects the standards of decent people in a not very religious country. Holden, an acute observer, says, "Royalty's main function has come to be as a source of good news in our lives."

Bagehot, in defining the monarchy, set down principles which are still followed:

The Sovereign has, under a constitutional monarchy such as ours, three rights—the right to be consulted, the right to encourage, the right to warn.

Royalty's strength, he felt, was its appeal to emotion, not just reason:

The best reason why Monarchy is a strong government is that it is an intelligible government. The mass of mankind understand it, and they hardly anywhere in the world understand any other.

Bagehot did see a danger in too much publicity:

Above all things our royalty is to be reverenced, and if you begin to poke about it you cannot reverence it. Its mystery is its life. We must not let in daylight upon magic.

In these tabloid days of Di and Fergie ("Naughty, Naughty" said a headline above their pictures on the cover of *People* magazine), the daylight can get pretty blinding. Prince Charles loudly complains about the "unutterable rubbish . . . written about my wife from time to time." And it would be hard to find anybody in Britain who didn't hear about the night she played bridge until one o'clock at the flat of an old flame. Princess Diana is of course a romantic heroine if there ever was one, as winsome and glamorous as any film star.

But what is one to make of *News of the World* photos of Princess Margaret snapped with three nude middle-aged male bathers cavorting on the beach of Mustique Island in the Caribbean (she herself was amply enveloped in an old-fashioned skirted swimsuit)? Not much mystique on Mustique, though Margaret is said to be the wittiest and best-read of the royals.

The British are ambivalent about it. Some say royalty always needs a black sheep (like the "Was the Duke of Clarence Jack the Ripper?" saga). Once it was Margaret, with her blighted romance and later unhappy marriage, then "randy Andy" with his parachute jumps and soft-porn film-actress friend Kim Stark. Now Prince Andrew has settled down; but when he and the Duchess of York came out of the hospital carrying their first baby in 1988, they were besieged by over two hundred photographers; using motor drives and 1200mm lenses they shot more than a thousand pictures of the baby and its bewildered parents in just a couple of minutes.

People ask: why should the monarchy not be treated like everybody else? It can be very painful to see some poor devil's private life exposed to the gaze of millions. No wonder the Queen so often seems to wear a worried frown. When Princess Anne was interrupted by a photographer while trying to work on some papers on the 7:38 from Cheltenham to Paddington and told him to "F—— off!" a tabloid screamed delightedly, "POSH TRAVELLERS LEFT SPEECHLESS AS RUDE ROYAL BLOWS HER TOP." (Auberon Waugh once described the plainspoken Princess Royal as one "whose poisonous spittle could stop a camel in its tracks at twenty paces and blind a press photographer for life at twice the distance.")

Is it too much? Some British worry about "Dynasty Di" and the royals sinking to the glitzy depths of Joan Collins. ("Too much 'Dallas' at the palace?") Not Americans, who can't get enough of the Princess of Wales; her 1989 trip to New York set off a binge of Dimania ("BIG APPLE GOES BANANAS FOR DI"). Traditionalists may wince at the pop-star antics of the Royal Family's younger set but there is genuine interest in Prince Edward's decision to quit the Marines and work on the stage, or the Duchess of York's earnest efforts to learn to fly or write her Budgie the Helicopter children's books. Insiders say the Queen, like the shrewd television producer of a series that has run an awfully long time, is not adverse to an occasional boost in the ratings. The younger generation also takes the heat off the older, more serious royals.

Except when it comes to divorce. Bagehot wrote:

> A *family* on the throne is an interesting idea. The women—one half the human race at least—care fifty times more for a marriage than a ministry. A princely marriage rivets mankind.

So does a princely divorce. Princess Anne, a horsewoman long dubbed Anne the Sourpuss and rated by opinion polls as the least popular royal, after ten years of hard work for the Save the Children Fund and treks to unglamorous villages in unlikely places like Swaziland and Malawi, was emerging with a new persona, Anne the Caring. One newspaper called her "a kind of Mother Teresa with wellies." Then the tabloid *Sun* got hold of letters written to the Princess Royal by Commander Timothy Laurence, a thirty-four-year-old royal equerry. The *Sun* virtuously turned the letters over to the police, but the episode gave rise to intense speculation over the nature of Princess Anne's friendship with Laurence and the state of her marriage to Captain Mark Phillips. Buckingham Palace soon announced that Princess Anne and Captain Phillips were to live separately, as they in effect had been doing for some time. The marriages of the Queen's only sister and only daughter have now broken up.

Why the Royal Family has always made such a fuss about divorce baffles me, since Henry VIII set the precedent. When the Pope refused to grant him a divorce from Catherine of Aragon so that he could remarry and have a male heir, Henry broke with Roman Catholicism and set up the Church of England with himself as its head. Edward VIII abdicated the throne in 1936 to marry "the woman I love," the previously twice divorced Wallis Warfield Simpson (the first abdication since Richard II's in 1399). In 1953, the first year of her reign, Elizabeth II stopped Margaret, who also risked losing her royal status and income, from marrying divorced Group Captain Peter Townsend, a World War II flying ace and royal equerry. Later Margaret married jet-set photographer Anthony Armstrong-Jones, Lord Snowdon. After two children and growing incompatibility and public squabbles, she was allowed to divorce him.

Both Di and Fergie come from broken homes. (Diana's father, Earl Spencer, who lives on fifteen-thousand-acre Althorp estate in Northamptonshire and is said to be worth £42 million—over $70 million—divorced Diana's mother and married Raine, Barbara Cartland's daughter.) Every time the marriage of Prince Charles and

Princess Diana shows any sign of cooling, there is a tidal wave of speculation over the possibility of a divorce ("CHARLES LEAVES DI AGAIN" scream the tabloids, "MY MARRIAGE OKAY SAYS DIANA.")

When Barbara Howar did a show on the Royal Family for American televiewers in 1989, "Unauthorized Biography: The Royals," a Lord St. John shrugged with weary upper-class elegance, "This is a country where humbug is a great virtue. You denounce something is being done and rush to read about it." Harold Brooks-Baker, editor of *Burke's Peerage*, used the same tone after Princess Alexandra's daughter Marina got pregnant and refused to marry her live-in boyfriend or have an abortion, saying the Royal Family "has never flinched at illegitimacy." (The couple's marriage was recently announced.)

Some of the royals keep a certain *gravitas*. The Duke of Edinburgh, after years of controversy and his now-famous "Pull your finger out" speech, today is mostly in the news as a dignified promoter of British design, and a defender of endangered species and rain forests. He and the Queen seem to have had a very happy marriage. Elizabeth II speaks in her calm, unruffled dignity for the well-being of the mostly poor and nonwhite forty-nine nations and 900 million members of the Commonwealth, regardless of the anti-Western policies of so many of her former subjects or the irrelevance of many of their concerns to Britain.

Harold Macmillan once called Mrs. Thatcher "a brilliant tyrant surrounded by mediocrities," and it is the tyrannical Prime Minister, not the housewifely Queen, who invites comparison with Elizabeth I, also a tyrant, gutsy ("if I were turned out of the realm in my petticoat, I were able to live in any place"), parsimonious, and with a penchant for surrounding herself with handsome courtiers, though hers were not mediocrities. Yet everybody says if there were ever a vote between them the Queen would beat the Prime Minister hands down. The Royal Family is the one British institution Mrs. Thatcher, a devout monarchist from girlhood, never attacks. Nobody curtsies lower.

Should she? Britain's biggest problem, to me, is its class divisions, rooted, first and foremost, in Eton and the top public schools and Oxford and Cambridge. But the tone of the public school Oxbridge establishment is also set at the very top of British society, in the Royal Family and the social pyramid of which it is the apex. Some of the elegantly-turned cynicism and world-weariness of the elite, which disguises a good deal of doubt and fear, has to be laid at royalty's door. Unwittingly perhaps, the Royal Family sets a paternalist tone that remains an obstacle to truly broadening the best education and giving science and industry their due. Any monarchy, no matter how decent, by its very existence, ratifies and helps perpetuate a hereditary class system. The Queen is unlikely to change. Maybe Prince Charles, in his role as champion of Britain's underdogs, will.

In 1992 Elizabeth II will have had forty years on the throne. (On a visit to Kenya's Treetops Hotel to see the forest wildlife a few years ago, I saw how Elizabeth "became Queen perched in a tree in Africa." You spend a night watching elephants, lions, warthogs, baboons, and other wildlife from a small hotel built in the branches of a giant old fig tree, though since 1952 it has been moved across the watering hole to a different fig tree.) Aside from Tony Benn mischievously proposing some sacrilege like taking the Queen's head off postage stamps, there is no serious talk of abolishing the monarchy. The cost to British taxpayers is great. As mentioned, nobody knows how much the Queen is really worth; estimates go from £5 billion to £50 billion.

Under an arrangement set by George III (reigned, 1760–1820), she pays the revenues of Crown Estates (worth £33 million in 1988) to the Treasury in return for an annual payment from the Civil List (£4.5 million to her, £12 million for all the royals). She also has three royal palaces (Buckingham Palace, Windsor Castle, and Holyroodhouse in Edinburgh) and two of her own (Balmoral in Scotland and Sandringham in Norfolk). Plus vast collections of antiques, old masters, jewels, the royal yacht, a fleet of Rolls-Royces, planes, helicopters, property in Europe and America, huge stockholdings, and heaven knows what all.

Some begrudge the £12 million (about $20 million) paid the Royal Family, others the fact they pay no inheritance or income taxes. But the cost to British taxpayers is vastly more than offset by tourism, in 1988 £14 billion a year and Britain's biggest growth industry and its third highest source of foreign currency. In a country with such a propensity to import, the Queen more than pays her way.

A Thatcherite proposal to "privatize" the royal palaces and parks (Hyde Park, Hampton Court Palace, and so on) did not go down well. I think the British feel that the ancient oaks and herds of deer in Richmond Park, for example (hundreds of deer run free and unfenced and have done so since the reign of Charles II), where I walked most days, exemplify what Edmund Burke called "the un-bought grace of life."

When the tabloids go too far, the Queen blows her top. She took legal action against Rupert Murdoch's *Sun* for breach of copyright after it printed a private family photograph of herself and the Queen Mother admiring the Duchess of York's baby. It is a running battle. The *Sun* earlier paid damages to charity for printing a leaked letter from Prince Philip to the Royal Marines. When Robert Maxwell's London-published *People* published pictures of a backview of Prince William peeing in a bush, his parents complained and Maxwell sacked his editor.

There is talk of "modernizing" the monarchy. Since 1969, when a historic documentary was made of the royal family at home, television has brought them a wider and wider world audience; over 750 million watched the 1981 wedding of Charles and Diana. There have been television specials on both the Queen and Prince Charles the past year. They are said to joke about the "family firm" and "living above the shop," but the Royal Family has become a huge industry. Some of its older traditions, like the law of male succession or the shadowy role given the husband of a ruling queen (Prince Philip has to walk a few paces behind) are anachronistic. Yet as Bagehot wrote:

> The existence of the crown serves to disguise change and therefore to deprive it of the evil consequences of revolution.

Certainly it is a great help to Britain's unity and cohesion. And inevitably the Queen has power, just as Prince Charles, as the heir to the throne, has influence. Nothing in British history suggests that taking no action on public issues is to be neutral. Silence, too, sets the tone.

When I asked Barbara Cartland, as Princess Diana's step-grand-mother, what she thought of royalty, she said, "We are so lucky in this country." She told me Lord Mountbatten felt Prince Charles was ideally equipped to ascend to the throne. "Prince Charles always looked on Lord Mountbatten as a sort of godfather. And he adored Prince Charles. He always said that he would make a great king."

Housewife Superstar

BRITAIN'S VAGUE, diffuse feeling of losing ground, of something being wrong that has got to be set right, explains why Mrs. Thatcher has been at Number Ten Downing Street for nearly eleven years and could be there quite a few years more. She herself, on the night of her last victory, spoke of going "on and on and on." *The Economist,* in a witty cover in late 1989, showed a disbelieving Mrs. Thatcher holding up her earphones at the annual Conservative Party Conference. "Go?" she is saying. "Did someone say go?"

As it is, despite growing challenges to her leadership, rank-and-file Tories, waving their Union Jacks and cheering to the strains of Elgar, will probably keep bringing Mrs. Thatcher back as long as she wants to stay. Yet chances are some readers will come to these pages after Margaret Thatcher has gone off to Dulwich for a happy and richly deserved retirement. She will not be sixty-five until October 1990. But it could happen. It is unlikely the Conservatives, no matter how alarmed about Europe as in 1989, would ever vote her out. But the British economy could worsen. Her husband, Denis, a decade older, could talk her into going. Driven people risk high blood pressure.

Going or staying, the unambiguous legacy of Thatcher's Britain —and why I write about her and it in the present tense—is a set of principles certain to shape both the Tory and Labour parties for a political generation. As *The Economist,* in an important essay in late 1989, described them:

> Mrs. Thatcher's achievement—and it is a great one—has been to articulate a few simple but necessary rules for British politics, when all around her were speaking in the conditional. The rules include a commitment to an open, market economy; a recognition that wealth creation is more important than redistribution, because without it there is precious little to distribute; a clear-eyed understanding that the world is a risky place, where military defences remain necessary; a determi-

nation to challenge the corruption of vested interests; perhaps above all, the incessant repetition that people must bear the consequences of their actions.

Britain is trying to accommodate itself to postindustrial technology and a smaller place in a radically changed world. Following Mrs. Thatcher's rules has brought it some success, not much, but enough to believe keeping to them will be good for the country. *The Economist* ended its article: "The Conservatives still need to be bullied by the relentless hammering of those few Thatcher rules. She should not go yet." At a time of wavering confidence, Mrs. Thatcher has plenty.

Is there no stopping her? It is Mrs. Thatcher's personal style that is the single most vivid impression you get in Britain. She is like "a mistress in a boys' school" trying to get her refractory pupils to pull themselves together. At the start she told an interviewer:

> We are doing the right things. They will work. I came in, not to have short-term expedience but to get the country on the right road to a prosperous future. It is the way I shall go.

That voice, people say. Quiet down, boys, and pay attention to the lesson. Many find single-mindedness her secret; as C. P. Snow said, "tenacity" is what matters most in the "corridors of power." I asked James Prior, who served in Mrs. Thatcher's first Cabinet, why all the vehemence of her defenders and detractors? Lord Prior, who was sharply slapped down when he criticized her policies, says, "The trouble about Mrs. Thatcher is you can't hold a general view about her. You either like her or you hate her." He went on:

> The impression she always gives is that she's hard-nosed, uncaring. And there are a lot of very nasty people around her on the right wing of the Conservative Party who lend credibility to this view. I think it's more Mrs. Thatcher's rhetoric than her actions. I don't think any government could have spent much more on the Health Service or social security. I think the public recognizes that on the whole it's not bad government. I found her very difficult to work for, partly because I had to spend my time arguing with her. In other respects I found her not unreasonable and not unsympathetic. I think she's been good for Britain.

You find the most fervent Thatcherites among the "taxi-driving classes," the real antis among the chattering classes, i.e., intellectuals. Actor Simon Callow is that rare breed in between. "Even at her most rampant," he told me, "the Antichrist to socialists, Mrs. Thatcher has never been able to galvanize the opposition to get rid of her." Callow says:

The Labour Party's got nothing left to say about Margaret Thatcher really. They just fume in impotence. I think Mrs. Thatcher is the first person in a long, long time in England to know what she wants. That in itself is sort of awe-inspiring. But more than that, she's a very English person. Part of all of us in England responds to what she's doing. All of us would like to balance our books, be sensible, and tidy up. It's the part of me I hate. She's a housewife. She's Housewife Superstar.

The image fits. Or used to. Having first seen her role as tidying up Britain and saving it from the Labour Party and socialism, and the Western world from Communism, she now looks to be taking the environmental problems of the planet in hand. After cohosting a United Nations conference in London in 1989 at which a hundred and twenty-three countries worried about threats to the ozone layer, Mrs. Thatcher spoke live over ABC to American viewers. She warned that unless steps are taken, "life won't go on existing as we know it." The Iron Lady become Green Goddess.

Just in time. Britain's people, like everybody else, are worried about the greenhouse effect, the ozone layer, toxic waste, and the rest. If reports are anywhere near true that the government-owned plant at Sellafield in the Lake District, which reprocesses so much nuclear waste from Europe and Japan, is dumping the rest in the Irish Sea, they should be. (Britain's Green Party got an astonishing 15 percent of the vote in 1989's European Parliamentary elections, though few voters presumably know it stands for scrapping all nuclear weapons, quitting NATO, and halting industrial growth.) Stung by the charge she has neglected science funding (true), Mrs. Thatcher has rehung Number Ten with portraits of British scientists. With a chemistry degree from Oxford in the early 1950s, she is proud to be a fellow of Britain's Royal Society, even as it loudly complains her government has starved research for support.

"Thatcherism is to get away from the welfare mentality, to make people self-reliant," says Sir Oliver Wright. "She's the British equivalent of the sheriff with his six guns, taming the Wild West." Sir Nicholas Henderson, like Wright a Thatcher ambassador to Washington, says, "You see, she doesn't really believe there's any such thing as useful negotiation." Tory MP Julian Critchley has famously observed: "She cannot see an institution without hitting it with her handbag." Another Tory MP, David Howell, said on a BBC radio interview: "Mrs. Thatcher does regard a great many men as 'old women,' sitting around the Athenaeum or somewhere, fudging and nudging and compromising while the ship of state sinks." (Norman

Tebbit: "It would be the Carlton Club, not the Athenaeum; that's all bishops and civil servants.")

I asked David Owen if he felt she brought divisiveness to Britain. "To hell with divisiveness," he replied. "Every now and then a Cabinet and a government have to make some decisions which people will not like." Her former Lord Chancellor, Lord Havers, asked on BBC if she were ruthless, replied, "To use a neutral word, yes." When I asked him about it, Dr. Owen told me:

> She's much more unscrupulous than people think. She has used the government office and the government machine and she has invested in taxpayers' money to promote Tory Party policies in a more flagrant manner than anyone. She uses the patronage system. She doesn't like the establishment. She just buys them off by popping them into the House of Lords and giving them this and giving them that. She hands out baubles like Lloyd George.

But Owen says he is on Mrs. Thatcher's side "inasmuch as she is trying to shake Britain out of its economic decline, inasmuch as she is not having much to do with the old establishment and its corporate consensus that got us into this bloody mess." (Mrs. Thatcher has praise for Dr. Owen too. She told Brian Walden in a 1988 *Sunday Times* interview when Owen's name came up: "I do have respect for him. He has a feel for what concerns ordinary people, and that I recognize. He has a feel for crime. He has a feel for defense. He has a feel for these fundamental things . . .")

One person who knows Mrs. Thatcher well told me, "She only understands achievers."

> She can't really cope with somebody who is inadequate. If they're frankly disabled, she'll be kind and generous. But she has no time for failures. They lack moral fiber, she says. When you hold a conversation with her, you find she's insensitive. Deeply insensitive. She's a woman of considerable instincts and considerable prejudices.

Peregrine Worsthorne, former editor of the conservative *Sunday Telegraph*, whom I interviewed, says Mrs. Thatcher made a "major blunder" looking anti-European when Europe is Britain's main hope for the future. "Perhaps what is most worrying," he wrote in 1989, "is the impression she increasingly gives of believing herself to be infallible, as much at home as abroad."

Max Hastings, the young editor of the *Daily Telegraph*, who like Dr. Owen praises Mrs. Thatcher for turning Britain's economy around, also criticized her personal style:

The gentlemanly tradition is that if your enemy wishes to put up his hands and surrender, you will give him quarter. Mrs. Thatcher gives no quarter. She and Tebbit both. They don't believe in showing mercy to the vanquished. I wrote a profile of Mrs. Thatcher to coincide with the 1987 election in which I said she is a not especially clever woman. A friend of mine who's a minister in her Cabinet corrected that. He said, "Max, you're quite wrong to say 'a not especially clever woman.' She's 'a not especially cultured woman.' It's an important distinction because the upper middle classes in Britain have traditionally respected certain tastes about reading novels and going to the theaters and picture galleries. Mrs. Thatcher is not remotely interested in them. She is a product of her background. As is Norman Tebbit. As are many of those around them.

Hastings told me this creates a cultural gap between Mrs. Thatcher and traditional Tories, who otherwise pay her great respect for what she's done politically.

On crime and punishment Mrs. Thatcher really does believe that until the breakdown of Victorian values English life ever since Good Queen Bess had been terribly well behaved. In reality, if you read the novels of Trollope, say, you know that politicians felt compelled to carry life preservers on the streets of St. James's at night. She's the supreme master of a brief, but the lack of breeding, of culture, is very strongly there.

Everybody confirms the headmistress image. Nanny, matron, governess, the anecdotes on the Thatcher style are endless. John Newhouse wrote in a 1986 *New Yorker* profile:

She is a considerable bully. "That's absolute rubbish! Stop being so wet!" she will shout at someone—almost anyone.

Sir Oliver Wright, who served her as ambassador to Washington, told me, "She knows what's good for us. Tells us what to do." Journalist Ludovic Kennedy tells a story about one time when he was filming a television series with Harold Macmillan. Noon came and Macmillan said, "And now we will go out to lunch. We will go in Mrs. Thatcher." When Kennedy looked baffled, Macmillan explained, "You see if you don't fasten your seat belts all these lights flash. And if you don't close the door, it buzzes. It's a very bossy car so we call it Mrs. Thatcher."

A glimpse backstage came at the 1988 Conservative Party Conference in Brighton. As she was being given a ten-minute ovation after her speech, television monitors picked up Mrs. Thatcher's voice shouting commands to stand up and sit down to her smiling and clapping Cabinet members, husband Denis, and the chairwoman. "Go down!" "Get up!" "Go down once more and we will all get up!" "One more time!" "This is the last time; go down and stay down!" To viewers at home she just seemed to be graciously smiling and greeting people.

Another glimpse of Mrs. Thatcher in action came when she met the press after hosting the 1989 conference on protecting the ozone layer. After she announced Britain would double its annual contribution to the U.N. Environment Program, somebody asked what it now was. She said £1.5 million. When Environment Secretary Nicholas Ridley whispered to her, "Actually, Prime Minister, it's one and a quarter million," she replied, "Well, then, you'd better make it one and a half million immediately. That will teach these people to give me the wrong briefing, won't it?" Ridley reportedly had to scare up the money from his existing budget.

One hears complaints that Mrs. Thatcher's Press Secretary Bernard Ingham, a Yorkshireman, tries to manipulate news coverage through an off-the-record daily briefing for British parliamentary reporters and a weekly briefing for the foreign press. Standard American practice, except that he has used it to attack Cabinet ministers who fall from grace. I covered Nixon's White House in 1968–69 and while Ron Ziegler often went off the record I can't remember such personal attacks. Andreas Whittam Smith, editor of *The Independent*, told me his paper, as a matter of policy, refuses to take part:

> We have not once turned up at a Bernard Ingham private briefing. We think that an unattributable briefing by the Prime Minister's office, as it has been used by this Prime Minister, often to rubbish other ministers in a nonattributable way, is not acceptable. So that the reader only learns in the paper next morning that "it was being said in Whitehall last night that Mr. Biffen is semidetached" or whatever Ingham's last killing phrase was. We won't go along with that. So we don't attend. It's had a very bad effect on the political press.

Others said the same thing. Former Trade Secretary John Biffen, former Foreign Secretaries Francis Pym and Lord Carrington, the list of Bernard Ingham's targets seems long and well known. Why does Mrs. Thatcher allow it? Whittam Smith replied:

> It's Henry II and Thomas Becket. You know, "Rid me of this unruly knight . . ." *Murder in the Cathedral.* She doesn't mind. She's got fed up with them. And Ingham takes the hint. And she's delighted if they roll off the end.

Denis Healey complains about it too: "Mrs. Thatcher ignores her Cabinet. Mr. Charles Powell, her Second Private Secretary, and Mr. Bernard Ingham, her Press Secretary, have more power over government policy than any of her ministers." But Whittam Smith agrees the power of a Powell or Ingham is essentially no different than the power of a Baker or Sununu in the White House.

> The people who run the great man's or great woman's office have tremendous power. They see them all the time. They keep the diary. And in all countries that can become sinister.

David Owen says the Cabinet is so weak because Mrs. Thatcher is so strong. He told me:

> She weeds them out. All of the people of independent mind have been dismissed or sidelined. She uses her press officer to rubbish ministers who disagree. Bernard Ingham is part of the power of the state. If it had been possible to temper Mrs. Thatcher, it would have been a far, far more effective government.

Ingham—a "Yorkshire Rasputin," says Biffen—seems shadowy because he rarely speaks on the record. One of the few times he did was in May 1988 in the wake of the SAS's shooting of three IRA members in Gibraltar. Ingham accused the media of "institutionalized hysteria." He said:

> There is nothing wrong with the British media that a renewed respect for facts, objectivity and fairness, rather than the false gods of invention and malice, would not cure.

Editors accuse the Thatcher government of suppressing, not just shaping, news. Donald Trelford, editor of *The Observer:*

> Bernard Ingham now controls the information officers in all the government departments. So one word goes out from Downing Street and that is the government's perceived view. So while we have a freedom to comment, we have no right to know what the government is doing. It's very much a question of *pas devant les enfants.* Government is adults. The public are children. And they must only be told so much.
>
> This culture of secrecy inhibits British democracy. It's always been there. It's been a kind of clubmanship before. But what this government has tried to do is formalize it, tried to put it into law. That's why the House of Lords' judgment in the *Spycatcher* case was important. Because the law lords said to the government, "Now look here, you said this book must be banned as a question of national security. And mustn't be published as a book or in a newspaper because you say so. Well, we're sorry. You fail to show national security was harmed. So we're not going to inhibit the press."

In *Spycatcher,* a retired officer, now in Australia, paid off some old debts in a book that claimed to reveal a good deal of abuse of power by M15. Mrs. Thatcher has tried to silence everyone who ever worked for M15 or M16, the domestic and external intelligence agencies. The editors expect Mrs. Thatcher's new Official Secrets Act and other legal reforms will get her into conflict with Britain's judiciary. Trelford:

> Mrs. Thatcher is a very determined lady. And she's never been part of the club. We've had Labour Prime Ministers who were more part of the club and operated more within the system than she does. Once or twice her position has looked shaky and I think since then she's determined to have an absolutely firm grip on information. We find her authoritarianism rather frightening.

I asked Lord Callaghan about this and Mrs. Thatcher's sometimes strident tone. In one *Sunday Times* interview she told Brian Walden:

> Success is not an attractive thing to many people. They do not like it. They do not like my success. And, of course, some of them are snobs. They can never forgive me from coming from a very ordinary background. It does not bother me at all. I cannot stand snobbery of any kind.

"I think she's been in office so long she feels she can afford to talk in this way," Lord Callaghan said. "It always happens when you've been in office for a long time." Lord Prior felt it could be her undoing:

> She's done a good job for the country. But I think she'll probably go on a bit too long and it will all end, as these things mostly do, in personal disaster.

David Owen felt it could go either way, saying, "Thatcherism could still end up in tears."

Ask any taxi driver (or shopkeeper or stockbroker) and Mrs. Thatcher is his champion. Ask almost anybody from the chattering class and you'll get a sour face. Academics feel Mrs. Thatcher is extremely unsympathetic to intellectuals, anybody who doesn't make money, and that she let higher education be cut in a very savage way. (Kenneth Baker told me: "The universities felt very wounded and like Hector sulk in their tent.") She has trampled on academic egos, a bit like Kipling, her favorite author, who said of England's intellectuals: "arid, aloof, incurious, unthinking, unthanking, gelt."

Though she is a long way from George I's famous opinion of intellect and the arts, voiced in his guttural German accent, "I hate all boets and bainters."

When I asked old Tory Enoch Powell, who translated Herodotus in his younger days, about the job-oriented ideas on education held by Mrs. Thatcher and Tebbit, he said, "They're barbarians." Philosopher Mary Warnock, mistress of Girton College, Cambridge, told the *Sunday Telegraph* she felt "a kind of rage" just thinking of the Prime Minister. Baroness Warnock said Mrs. Thatcher wouldn't lose a wink of sleep if Oxford and Cambridge were sold off to a private bidder, "as long as the price was right." Noël Annan, vice chancellor of London University, offered one explanation for such venom: he said his own postwar generation had dreamed of greater equality, an end to class war, a nation "pulling together"; they got Mrs. Thatcher's ideal of a highly competitive Britain.

I asked Baroness Blackstone, as a woman, an academic, and a member of the Labour Party, how she felt. She replied, with visible relish, that Mrs. Thatcher was "dictatorial," "a very bad listener," "contrived and artificial," and had "a hectoring style."

> She talks to people as if they were six-year-olds. They feel diminished by her. She finds it hard to brook opposition. Those people who stand up to her often get the push. There's been a big fallout from her Cabinets of people who have taken slightly centrist or leftist views.

What amazed me, watching Conservative Party conferences, was the demand by so many younger Tories for the return of capital and corporal punishment. I asked Baroness Blackstone about it. "Hangers *and* floggers in this day and age?" She said:

> Frightening, isn't it? They're the grocers and builders and estate agents who make up the modern Tory Party's base, the kind of Poujadist, petit bourgeois people who have no real understanding of how you cope with deviants and crime in a civilized society.

Some intellectual attacks backfire. Lady Antonia Fraser, the biographer of Mary Queen of Scots and crime novelist *(Quiet as a Nun)*, in mid-1988 formed a "June 20th Group," described in the press as "an anti-Thatcher think tank," in her Kensington drawing room (Margaret Drabble, Michael Holroyd, John Mortimer, David Hare, Germaine Greer, Salman Rushdie). The press poked fun at it, since most of those involved had got rich under Thatcherism. Both Fraser and her husband, playwright Harold Pinter, voted Tory in 1979 (he in a fit of pique when unions struck a play he was directing). I've mentioned Rushdie's "Mrs. Torture" and Hare's anti-Thatcher themes. Mortimer has mentioned Mrs. Thatcher as a terrifying nanny in one book and Pinter has tended to lump Mrs. Thatcher with such evils as El Salvador and nuclear weapons. After Mrs. Thatcher showed more backbone than many British intellectuals in defending Rushdie, I asked Lady Antonia, when she was out in California promoting her book *The Warrior Queens,* what the "June 20th Group" was up to. "Everybody still meets and talks," she said, visibly embarrassed. "It's a discussion group."

Fraser herself has mixed views. She says she admires Mrs. Thatcher, in spite of her attitudes to feminism ("What's it ever done for me?" is Mrs. Thatcher's celebrated remark about it some years ago). Certainly Lady Antonia was very muted in her critical remarks before American audiences. She compared Mrs. Thatcher's 1982 declaration to her Cabinet on the Falklands, "Gentlemen, we shall have to fight," to Elizabeth I's rallying speech at Tilbury as England faced the Spanish Armada:

> I know I have the body of a weak and feeble woman, but I have the heart and stomach of a king, and of a king of England too . . .

From Boadicea, who led a revolt against the Romans in Britain in A.D. 60, to Mrs. Thatcher, Lady Antonia sees the Warrior Queen as likely to be regarded by her contemporaries as monster, angel, or honorary male, shaming men into bravery, and being looked back upon—like Elizabeth I or Victoria—as centers of a golden age. (Mrs. Thatcher has been caricatured in Boadicean breastplates and driving a chariot with knives on its wheels.) Since Mrs. Thatcher has been compared to English queens, Americans wanted to know how she got on with Elizabeth II.

"There are all kinds of rumors," Lady Antonia told one audience. "The tabloid press loves to write about how the Queen hates her. They're the same age; the Queen is just six months younger." She went on:

> I heard a story, I have no idea if it's true, that once Mrs. Thatcher had an aide call up Buckingham Palace to ask if she should wear blue or cherry red to some occasion. A palace aide said, "Please tell Mrs. Thatcher not to worry. The Queen never notices what other people wear."

Mrs. Thatcher has her intellectual defenders. Oxford's Norman Stone, perhaps her most vociferous champion, told me about a playwright who compared the Thatcher years to living under Fascism:

And I remember thinking: the nearest thing this man came to having a toad forced down his throat by a blackshirt—which is what the early Fascists did—is eating frog legs in some upmarket restaurant. Good God! I don't know why anybody ever takes the political views of an actor or writer seriously. When you think of the long list of complete goofs and buffoons in politics who have come from literary circles or the stage.

The highest praise for Mrs. Thatcher comes from those who work directly for her. (Sir John Harvey-Jones even sees a downside to this: "It's because she'll only work with people she can dominate.") John Redwood, a young MP who headed Mrs. Thatcher's policy unit at Number Ten in 1983–85 and was one of the architects of her program to sell off the old state-owned industries, says she is a "smashing" boss.

I *loved* working for her. She's a person who thrives on debate. She is very versed in the parliamentary style of procedure because she has to answer questions twice weekly. And she'll test out new ideas. They have to work technically and administratively and politically. She has to know the snags and problems of what comes from the dispatch box. So she probes and tests. And I loved that. It was a very exciting, heady atmosphere. If you offered good advice and you'd done your homework, you had a good discussion. If you'd done your work sloppily, you knew what was coming to you. And quite rightly so.

(Not everybody felt like this. Another man who held Redwood's post for three years says: "She was deliberately unreasonable, emotional, excitable. She used the fact she was a woman very powerfully to get her way.")

Many Tory backbenchers are deeply devoted to Mrs. Thatcher. David Jenkins, the Bishop of Durham and a Thatcher critic, told me:

I have seen a real shine in the eyes of middle-aged Tory peers in the House of Lords. The old-fashioned Tory may be alienated, but a good many think she is the most remarkable and sensitive woman who has really got them somewhere. There's still a great deal of devotion to her.

In 1989 *The Economist* asked prominent figures, in Britain and outside, about Mrs. Thatcher's place in history, based on her record in ten years as Prime Minister. Many of the people I've interviewed gave replies. Mrs. Thatcher lends herself to caricature; to cartoonists she is forever the formidable governess or the helmeted bobby waving a billy club. Or a Wild West sheriff, six guns at the ready. Some of those asked see her this way too, as "the witch in the European fairy tale" or "Lady John Bull personified."

To Tony Benn, the 1980s were the worst of times when "the rich and powerful put profits before the people." To Norman Tebbit, they were the best of times as Mrs. Thatcher had the brains, energy, and skill to change the party and the country and compel "the others to adjust to her agenda." To David Owen, still in the middle, the judgment is just what he told us: "unproven."

On the left, David Blunkett, the Labour MP from Sheffield, called Mrs. Thatcher "a conviction politician whose narrowness of outlook precluded an understanding of the wider well-being." Neil Kinnock, as Labour Party leader, said she "blew the oil bonus" and "the environment became dirtier, the economy more unbalanced, the society more divided, the people more indebted." Generally the right holds she is Britain's outstanding peacetime leader this century. One Tory recalled what Napoleon asked about his generals, "Has he luck?" saying Mrs. Thatcher certainly did. Another remembered three hundred sixty-four economists in a famous letter to *The Times* in 1981 warning her budget of that year would bring recession and possibly civil disorder. He felt she had got the last word in on that.

The sourest comments came from the chattering class. "A middle-class lady with an affected accent who chills the heart and stultifies the imagination," was Anthony Burgess's grumpy response. British university scholarship and research, said Harvard's John Kenneth Galbraith, has been "scrimped, bashed and diminished" in the Thatcher years. In a milder response, Jeremy Isaacs called Mrs. Thatcher "a radical leader, bent on shake-up and reform," but he wished she did more for broadcasting and the arts.

"I have changed everything," Mrs. Thatcher said soon after being elected leader of the Conservative Party in 1975. She had not. And she has not. I'm with David Owen that Mrs. Thatcher's determination is "praiseworthy," but her record of achievement is "patchy." Her inability to break the public school Oxbridge establishment's hold on Britain is to me the fundamental failure. Before coming back to that, let us look at how she applied her economic doctrine— in favor of the market and against state intervention or regulation. The way she cut taxes, cut union power, and deregulated Britain's economy look very good for its short-term future. Just as with Britain's shrinking industrial base, Mrs. Thatcher's antipathy toward European unity and her failure to invest more in schools, science, and industry are very worrying in the long run.

One of Us

ODERN BRITAIN came out of the 1940s saddled with a hide-bound old industrial economy (coal, iron, steel, cotton, wool, shipping, railways), colonial markets in a shrinking empire, and a ruling Oxbridge establishment with ex-imperial attitudes it still can't quite shake off. Today Britain finds itself in a computer-age economy where electronic impulses get automated machines to do practically anything, and cheaper and faster than men. It trades in a jet-and-fax-paced single world economy where everybody has to scramble to compete with the Japanese and Americans.

The Labour Party, with displaced workers for a base, has been slow to adjust. So the British have kept voting back a more consciously radical government than any that has held power since Clement Attlee brought in the welfare state in the late 1940s. Its opposition is split four ways—Labour, Liberals, Greens, and Dr. Owen's Social Democrats. In 1983 and 1987, Mrs. Thatcher's Conservatives won just 42.5 percent of the popular vote. Against this divided opposition, under the British first-past-the-post, winner-take-all electoral system, it has given the Tories parliamentary majorities of a hundred plus.

This means that Mrs. Thatcher can push through almost any reform she wants, even if a policy is irredeemably unpopular. For example, 65 percent of Britons opposed cutting the top tax rate to 40 percent, which Mrs. Thatcher got through Parliament in 1988. Some 72 percent oppose removing electricity and water from state control, 70 percent oppose replacing property taxes with poll taxes. Unfazed, Mrs. Thatcher goes right ahead. You might call her a radical inegalitarian.

She does stick to a few basic principles in tune with the instincts and interests of that 42.5 percent of the British voters, her hard-core lower-middle-class supporters in London and Southeast England. It has won her three elections, making her the longest-serving British

Prime Minister this century. She saw Britain had too powerful unions, too high taxes, and too much red tape. And she did something about it.

John Redwood, as a fervent Thatcherite, described to me how a young right-wing Tory like himself saw Margaret Thatcher's coming to power in 1979. Britain then, he says, was "bankrupt, moribund, dying." Most people say the economy's long relative decline was accelerating. Even the liberal Bishop of Durham, David Jenkins, told me Britain was then "drifting into a morass." Redwood:

> Those of us who supported Mrs. Thatcher saw her as the last hope. Britain was in such a bad way. Socialism was throttling it. The cities were derelict and dying. Unemployment was rising. Inflation was too high. The unions were out of control. It was getting to be like a banana republic. Turning that around was a colossal job. It needed someone of her stature. And she's not halfway there.

Halfway where? Redwood told me reforms in health, education, and welfare had only just begun, that there were inner cities to tackle, the environment, the spread of Tory control to local governments, Whitehall's "continued disengagement from commerce and industry." With water and electricity being sold off, just Britain's coal, rail, and postal systems are still state-owned.

Under Mrs. Thatcher in 1979–89 fifty-four state–owned companies in all moved into the private sector, increasing the number of British shareowners from 2 million to 12 million.

How far can she go? Mrs. Thatcher came in on a wave of violent public reaction against the left. People were fed up with the whole concept of an inefficient welfare state running deeper and deeper into the red. The power of the unions had become insufferable. The lower middle classes were in revolt. Economists were rejecting the old full-employment policy in favor of a return to monetarism not in fashion since the 1930s. Mrs. Thatcher was able to pull all that together, beating Edward Heath in 1975 when likelier successors loyally refused to stand against him. Four years later, after James Callaghan's strike-plagued "winter of discontent," she got elected Prime Minister, the first woman in a major Western country ever to do so.

As Peter Jay said, an election is like two blades on a pair of scissors. Victory depends as much on the losers as the winners. The left ran out of steam, it floundered, impotent. The Labour Party was in an unholy mess. The moderate Social Democratic-Liberal Alliance went to pieces after the last election (what was left confusingly renamed itself the Liberal Democrats). There was a sense of not knowing what to want.

With just a minority of the popular vote, but no serious opposition, Mrs. Thatcher cut the unions down to size, notably with legislation that unions had to ballot their members before going on strike. She said, "We don't want to stop proper trade unionism from operating. We need it to operate in the interests of its members. Therefore we've got to get it reasonable."

Some workers are doing well. Ron Todd, general secretary of Britain's biggest union, the Transport and General Workers, asks:

> What do you say to a docker who earns four hundred pounds a week, owns his own house, a new car, microwave, and video, as well as a small place near Marbella in Spain? "Let me take you out of your misery, brother?"

I asked John Edmonds, general secretary of the General, Municipal, Boilermakers and Allied Trades Union, Britain's second biggest, if the decline in trade unions wasn't inevitable. If smokestack industry goes, can unions be far behind? Edmonds, who looks like a beefy labor organizer but has a Ph.D. from Oxford, says this hasn't happened in Germany or Scandinavia:

> It's true in America because the American labor unions made the same mistakes as we did. Even to a greater degree and with less foresight. American trade unions allowed themselves to be trapped in parts of the public sector on the East Coast and in the old smokestack industries. But a majority of the British trade union members are white-collar, if still in the public sector. If Thatcher can reduce the public sector, she's reducing trade union power. We have to make unions popular again.

Mrs. Thatcher's other original objective, besides trimming down the unions, was to defeat inflation. For a long time she succeeded. It fell and stayed in low single figures until 1986, when it rose from 3 percent to 8 percent in three years, before dropping some. The cost, with 3.5 million unemployed at peak and a loss of at least a fifth of British industry, was enormous. The economy started to grow again in 1982, by the late 1980s faster than the OECD average. But it was fed by a consumer and credit boom and the balance of payments worsened.

The idea of selling council houses, what Americans call public housing units, to the people who live in them goes back to Disraeli. It came up again in the 1960s but the Tories were slow to act on it. Not so Mrs. Thatcher. Under her, Britain's owner-occupancy has gone up from half to over two thirds, about 3 million more than in 1979, though high mortgages and tumbling prices at the end of the 1980s disillusioned some of the new owners. After that, it was just a logical next step, Norman Tebbit told me, to sell off Britain's eighteen nationalized industries. With all but two left ("You can be an H2Owner" goes a government slogan flogging shares in the water system), once British Coal is privatized in the early 1990s, Britain has raised its number of shareholders sixfold. Tebbit:

> The Tory voter is now someone who works in the private sector, who owns his own home or is buying it, and who may well not be a member of a trades union. The Labour voter is someone in the public sector, working for a local authority or the state in some way, living in a council house, and who's a member of a big trade union. Now the number of Tory voters is growing, the number of Labour voters is falling.

I asked Redwood how Mrs. Thatcher's policy unit worked. He said it did three things:

> First, if there was a conflict. For instance, Treasury says you shouldn't spend this money. The Home Office says we do. The Prime Minister has to chair a Cabinet committee to settle the dispute. We might write advice from the policy unit saying, "Give them the money," or "Don't give them the money," or "Split the difference," or "Spend it on something else." Sometimes she took our advice. Sometimes she didn't. At least someone was thinking about the problem from her standpoint.
>
> Second, if a department proposed a policy we thought was hazardous or shortsighted or likely to rebound to the discredit of the government, we'd put in warnings. Or we'd ask, "Do you think this is going to work?" "Have you thought about these aspects?"
>
> Lastly, there was creative advice. We'd be a voice for the future. We would write her notes like: "Your government is meant to believe in X. Nothing's happened on X for a long time. Don't you think it's time you talked to your colleagues about X and worked out a strategy to live up to the Party's expectations?" I saw Mrs. Thatcher for about half an hour every week and went through with her what she wanted, what I thought we ought to be doing, and giving her advance warning of what was coming up. Her style is firm leadership. That's what this country wants.

Lord Prior, when I met him, described Mrs. Thatcher as "the beech tree under which nothing grows." (They used to say the same thing about Nehru in India, only it was a banyan tree.) She still probably wants someone like Tebbit as her eventual successor, a younger radical populist of the same mold to arise and carry the banner. Polls, as mentioned, show Michael Heseltine as, after her, Britain's most popular politician. Little love is lost between them.

Edward Heath, who has never forgiven Mrs. Thatcher for taking the Tory leadership from him, is a sour parliamentary critic. Heseltine, a tall, ambitious tycoon-landowner with blond, unruly hair—the press has sometimes called him Tarzan ever since he once seized the ceremonial rod of the House of Commons and angrily swung it over his head at some Labour members—has a different tactic: he acts as if Margaret Thatcher doesn't exist. In an hour-long interview, he never once mentioned her name, quite a feat in today's Britain. Finally I asked point-blank about the "Thatcher Revolution." Heseltine:

> I don't accept these simplistic divisions between Tory governments and Tory parties. I've worked for all sorts of Tory leaders and I see much more evolution than revolution in politics. And that's a very good thing.

Heseltine credits the shift from state ownership to private capitalism to Harold Macmillan.

> Macmillan built the council houses. The Tories and local governments started to sell them on an individual basis. The Tories in 1979 gave occupants a statutory right to buy them. And people bought them on a large scale. The cash from these sales became a very important part of government revenue. The privatization of industry was added on the grounds that if you could sell council houses, you could sell industries too.

And what about the ideas of Thatcherism, the whole cultural shift of emphasis? Her former Defense Secretary agreed that what he calls "a climate of entrepreneurial innovation" has sprung up in Britain. He said, "It's now easier to make money, to save money, to invest money, to get returns on money." (But not always to spend it; he had a big hole in the right elbow of his navy blue sweater, even if he is worth £60 million.)

Some of Mrs. Thatcher's tax reforms, opposed by a good many Conservatives as well as Labourites, struck me as unwise and unjust (the Bishop of Durham called them "wicked" for helping the rich, not the poor). She replaced the old local rates tax, a property tax, with a poll tax equal in amount for rich and poor alike. And while she reduced the basic tax a little to 25 percent for most people, she radically cut the top rates, as mentioned, from 98 percent to 40 percent. This, she said, would stimulate wealth creation. She told Brian Walden:

They're rare people, these people who can create new businesses. We need them here. They need incentives. They need to know that they can do well, they can make profits, they can plow them back. These people are wonderful. We can all rely on them to create the industries of tomorrow.

Can we? To me it is solid investment in science and high-tech plant and training, not just high-flying entrepreneurs—the Cambridge Science Park, not Richard Branson's Virgin Group, Anita Roddick's Body Shop, and Alan Sugar's Amstrad, to name Mrs. Thatcher's favorites—that will create the industries of tomorrow. And what about all the industries of yesterday? At least a fifth, some claim a fourth, are gone for good. And they keep going. Machines still get sold off at cut-rate prices to overseas competitors. There is little investment in new capacity in what is left. In many big high-tech growth areas, Britain is doing little or no training.

Labour Party leader Neil Kinnock recognizes Britain will remain a market, capitalist economy. A decent man and persuasive speaker, Kinnock is often described as a vote loser. After supporting unilateral nuclear disarmament and opposing a bigger British role in the European Community, he has turned full circle on both issues; it doesn't carry conviction. Then too many of his party activists yearn to go back to state-owned industry; as Denis Healey says, "People don't entirely trust Labour." To Kinnock the future looks bleak unless Labour accepts something like a market economy, rejects the worst excesses of protectionism, recognizes the need for strong defenses, and sees the party is doomed if it caves in to the unions. It has to be more of a social democratic party like Dr. Owen's or those in West Germany, France, or Sweden. Kinnock has warned party members:

> Those who are afraid of developing the alternatives that will gain the support of the British people, those who say they don't want victory at such a price had better ask themselves this: If they won't pay any price for winning, what price are they prepared to pay for losing?

("I think Kinnock is desperately anxious to be sitting in a large black limousine driven by a government driver," Norman Tebbit cracked to me.)

Labour has a strong case when it comes to the Thatcher government's steady neglect of British industry. I asked Denis Healey about it. As Chancellor of the Exchequer in the five years before Mrs. Thatcher came to power (it was he who brought back monetary policies), he tried, he said, to understand the "British disease," or why Britain's industry has slipped behind so much over the past century.

> The key reason is that we started in the 1870s to live on rent from overseas investments. And we'd exhausted a lot of those investments by the end of the Second World War and had to stand on our own two feet. And it was a hellish, painful experience, earning our keep. And Thatcher, by God, has allowed all the revenue we got from oil to be invested abroad, not in Britain. The increase in our overseas investment is almost equal to the increase in oil revenue since she came to power.

Under Mrs. Thatcher, Britain—not Japan, as you might think— has become the largest foreign property owner in the United States. British investments come to about £70 billion (close to $120 billion), Japanese just half of that. This arouses little concern. Nobody batted an eyelash when the Holiday Inn chain, with fourteen hundred hotels and motels, 10 percent of the country's total, was sold in 1989 for $2.2 billion to Bass PLC, the British brewer and Britain's—and now the world's—biggest hotel operator. But when the Mitsubishi Estate Company bought Rockefeller Center for half the price, there was a terrible outcry. Somehow the idea of Radio City Music Hall, the Rockettes, and America's most famous skating rink going to aggressive bankers from the Land of the Rising Sun awoke all our latent jingoism. Maybe people were remembering Ogden Nash's old poem about the courteously encroaching Japanese, so sorry, it is my garden now.

Bryan Gould, as one of the Labour Party's top economic policymakers, feels the British still have "the habit of living on the income from overseas assets rather than running the economy as if Britain were a trading concern which has to make things and go out and sell them competitively in the growing international markets."

> Under the imperial economy we didn't have to compete. We had no need to be efficient manufacturers. We had access to cheap raw materials. We had captive markets around the world. And also we could make good our deficiencies by the immense income we were getting from our assets.

The economy is still run that way, Gould says, without people even realizing it.

> Labour, Conservative, it's not a party point. We still run Britain's economy in the interests of the financial establishment, the City of London. The people who hold the assets. Short-term variance and movements in

the value of assets are what concern us enormously. All the arguments about interest rates are about that. Ranged on one side, and they always win, are the banks. Those concerned with orthodoxy, those worried about inflation, those concerned about the value of assets. They've got the ear of government. They win. On the other side, the voice of industry is a very muted voice, a very uncertain voice. We've gone through a century of this. We've got very little industry left.

It is still too early to say whether Mrs. Thatcher, despite the recovery of the late 1980s, has reversed Britain's long economic decline, or just interrupted it. Britain's inflation rate is higher than its competitors'. Tight-money policies used to dampen demand are squeezing family budgets. Unemployment, steadily falling since 1987, is still way too high and may rise again. The 1989 current-account deficit of around £20 billion ($32 billion) was almost 4 percent of gross domestic product and proportionately much the largest of any of the big industrial economies. It looks like the balance of payments may drift back into sizable deficits even before the oil heritage runs out in the mid-1990s, or possibly not until 2000 or so. One does not need to take just the analysis of Labour Party leaders like Healey or Gould for this reasoned skepticism. Travel about Britain and most of the Confederation of British Industry officials, practically all of them Tories, will tell you the same thing. John Banham, the CBI's director-general, is cautious. He has said of Mrs. Thatcher:

> Her main contribution has been to instill, into a nation that had created almost an industry out of rationalizing its own economic failure, the belief that the future can and must be better than the past.

On and off over three years, going about Britain, I never stopped hearing of people losing their jobs; every time you went into a pub you heard the same thing. Something was shutting down. Somebody was out of work. Shoemakers in Norwich, dockers in Plymouth and Newcastle, railway men in Swindon, textile workers in Bradford.

In the short term, a drop in the number of young people seeking jobs in the 1990s will soak up unemployment. Recovery is spreading to the North even if there is a century's industrial decline to offset. In the long run, Britain will have to spend more on research and education, train workers better, and raise capital expenditure in industry if the stage is to be set for a Japanese-type renaissance. The sense of technological humiliation in the land of Newton and Darwin is real.

Almost certainly, if and when a Labour government gets back

in, it will try to restore some of the welfare state and Britain's manufacturing base. Some Conservatives, too, think Thatcherism has
gone too far. Sir Geoffrey Howe has said too many Britons have
"fallen through the safety net." The sight of teenagers and destitute
cripples in London's streets, he said, can "leave no one unmoved."
Howe would also "conquer the tendency of regarding manufacturing industry as almost a residual element, a leftover."

Such criticism, coming from her own deputy prime minister,
seems to have hit home with Mrs. Thatcher. In her New Year's message to the Tory Party last winter, she set out "six great tasks" for the
1990s: getting inflation and mortgage rates down, extending home
and share ownership, cleaning up Britain's environment, improving
public services, and, abroad, building a wider Europe and working
through NATO for arms cuts and a defense policy to keep the peace.
She said she intends to build "a Britain that is free, prosperous, generous, and secure" in which "help will always be at hand for those
who cannot help themselves." A chastened Margaret Thatcher
pledged to make the 1990s "a caring decade." The way to get a caring image is of course to care. Can she and Britain do it?

In the end it may come down to confidence and a sense of purpose, particularly among the public school Oxbridge establishment.

The Celestial City

THE GAP IS STRIKING. Mrs. Thatcher, her confidence and conviction. Britain's elite, its loss of faith, its bleakness and despair. Like Alice, British intellectuals risk being drowned in their own tears. And here comes Mrs. Thatcher, steaming right by, splashing everybody, as unflinching and formidable as the carved wooden lady on a ship's prow. Rule, Britannia.

First impressions last. I ended up my 1987 *Economist* survey, after a six-week look, saying "many of Britain's elite, caught up in the past," missed who the British voter that could swing elections now was:

> Somebody who works hard, wants to learn the new techniques, has saved up, is buying a home and is fed up with paying through the nose to support people who do none of these things. You do not hear much about them, but they vote. This has not struck a majority of the elite, anyway not everybody this correspondent interviewed.

These voters, the ones I met, were former working-class men and women who had made it into the lower middle class, something Norman Tebbit confirmed.

Why this gap in comprehension? Now a couple of hundred interviews later, it seems to matter even more. The big political questions about Mrs. Thatcher are: Has she changed Britain? The Conservative Party? The left? Socialism? I go along with the Labour Party line that a few of her policies—some tax cuts, consumer imports, easy credit, overseas investment, real estate and stock speculation, and the way North Sea oil money is spent—do smack of "short-termism driven by greed." I deplore the lack of investment in science and industry. Cuts in funding for the arts and anything to do with Britain's mastery of the English language, where it is supreme, are unwise and shortsighted. But Mrs. Thatcher's achievements in reducing trade union power, controlling inflation with monetarism, selling off state-owned industry and housing to small shareholders and tenants, are here to stay. She has reshaped British society and exploded the agenda of the left. James Callaghan speaks for many when he says, as he did to me, "Labour must find its own future. I mean its attitudes to public ownership, to the trade unions, and to defense."

Thatcherism is about "something more than material advancement," says Peter Jenkins, one of Britain's most astute political columnists, at the end of his *Mrs. Thatcher's Revolution*. But Jenkins is dead wrong when he says:

> She, more powerfully than anyone else, has articulated the moral doubts and yearnings of her age.

I think Jenkins misapprehends Mrs. Thatcher's appeal here. She doesn't go in for moral doubts and yearnings. It is part of her attraction. She has tried to give people, as Jenkins says, what they want in "an end to decline, release from the corrosive sense of failure, a government which governed, and a country to begin to be proud of once again." And, like he says, she has set the future agenda.

But moral doubts and yearnings are not in Margaret Thatcher's lexicon. This matters, I think, because what she has really done is to advance a system of moral certainties firmly rooted in Britain's past. This goes against contemporary cultural trends. It leaves her with few intellectual allies. This is why Britain's intellectuals, who *are* articulating the moral doubts and yearnings, so bitterly resent her. While they are thrashing around in the Slough of Despond, Mrs. Thatcher is sure she's found the way to the Celestial City. She herself explains it: "My policies are not based on some economic theory but on things I and millions like me were brought up with: an honest day's work for an honest day's pay; live within your means; put a nest egg by for a rainy day; pay your bills on time; support the police." She acknowledges her debt to her small-town grocer father and his creed:

> You have honest money, so you don't make reckless promises. You recognize human nature is such it needs incentives to work harder . . . It is about being worthwhile and honorable. And about family. And about what is really unique and enterprising in the British character—how we built an empire, how we gave sound administration to large areas of the world. All these things are still there in the British people.

Columnist Brian Walden, her favorite interviewer, has helped Mrs. Thatcher articulate her ideas. (Tebbit told me of Walden: "He comes from the same sort of background I do. We both have a complete contempt for left-wing intellectuals. And I think they have particularly great hatred of me." Walden on Tebbit: "He is one of the most important figures British politics has produced this century, yet rarely has a man been so maligned and underrated.")

It was Walden who first suggested to Mrs. Thatcher that she had "Victorian values." "Now is that right?" he asked her during a TV interview. "Well, exactly," she said, delighted. "Very much so." Her values were the same as Britain's at the peak of its empire when "colossal advance" was also made at home, she said. People made fortunes but voluntarily gave as charity hospitals, schools, town halls, even prisons. Mrs. Thatcher: "As people prospered, they used their initiative to help others prosper. *Not* compulsion by the state." And when it comes to powerful moral influences like television, there are limits to even Mrs. Thatcher's market-driven free-for-all philosophy. For instance, she will not have porn on British screens.

I myself think "Victorian values" an unfortunate phrase as it makes you think of Dickens: warm hearts and high intentions at home beside the blazing Wickfield hearth, while outside among the ragged street mobs the Uriah Heeps work their financial deceits, the Dorrits and Micawbers go to prison for debt, and the road from the workhouse to Fagin's thieving gang is brutal and short. When Mrs. Thatcher cries, "Gain all you can! Save all you can! Give all you can!" there is a whiff of Dotheboys Hall about it, and we hear Mr. Squeers telling his hungry charges, "Subdue your appetites my dears, and you've conquered human natur." Tebbit especially can seem Dickensian, as when he told me in his best we-are-so-very-'umble style: "Some of the Tories don't approve of people like *me* having been chairman of the Conservative Party." And a prime Victorian value was dislike of foreigners, Europeans too.

Thatcherites do use the phrase "one of us." ("Is he one of us?") Most of their us-and-them mentality is aimed at intellectuals (though, as mentioned, she strongly defended Rushdie when the protection of a British subject and basic Western morality and the freedom of ideas were at stake; indeed her forthright stand was in marked contrast to the weak-kneed American reaction). Mrs. Thatcher will accuse, however, nameless academics of "putting out what I call poison." She told Walden in one interview: "Some young people, who are thrilled to bits to get to university, had every decent value pounded out of them." She is against anybody who thinks he "has a talent and ability nobody else in the human race has."

This is the ultimate snobbery. Only put them in charge, they say, and the poor will have everything. So the poor put them in power and discover the rulers have everything and they nothing.

Some, she says, would just as soon Britain not prosper:

There are some people who would rather the bottom were lower down, provided the top were a lot lower down. They hate the top going up and pulling up the bottom. It is a policy of envy and hatred and despair.

So the divide is profound. As I mentioned early on, the great continuing theme of English letters going back to Matthew Arnold's "Dover Beach" has been the loss of spiritual faith. We find its despair echoed in Mrs. Moore's horror at life's emptiness in the Marabar Caves, in Barbie Batchelor's descent into madness as she watches vultures circle the Parsi towers of silence, in the darkness of *The Waste Land,* in Greene's novels, Pinter's plays, Larkin's poetry, Kureishi's films. It is a leading novelist, John Fowles, who tells us he has lived all his life with the strong supposition that "England is in grave decline and is done for." It is a leading literary critic, George Steiner, who sees what has happened to the English-authored novel as proof that "something has gone very, very wrong." It can be drab, humdrum, everyday. Like the alcoholic vicar's wife in Alan Bennett's *Talking Heads* who isn't sure if she believes in God. Or even if her husband does. Maybe "God's just a job like any other." We know this is not just in the realm of abstract ideas. Any society's loss of faith—in life, in the world, in the spiritual, in itself—can affect everything: how hard people work, how inventive they are, how much initiative they take, in short, their enterprise.

I think Mrs. Thatcher is right, for this reason, if she is going to move Britain from a "dependency culture" to an "enterprise culture," as she puts it, to tackle religion. It's the underpinning of any culture. She has a bit of the prophet in her in that, to Mrs. Thatcher, life has a coherent meaning and she knows exactly how everybody should behave to fit in with it. The Bishop of Durham, when I talked to him, in a way put his finger on it:

Mrs. Thatcher says: "I am against consensus. I am for conviction." But she interprets that as meaning her convictions are right and have to be carried out no matter what. The Thatcherites act as if it's a weakness to negotiate, to compromise, to bring other people in. They excuse themselves by saying, "If we do this, it will come out best for everybody." They're so hell-bent on the idea of market forces, there's a worrying lack of imagination on what happens next.

Again, the Bishop is right except that in her very lack of imagination lies Mrs. Thatcher's strength. She is the banner-carrying Valkyrie fearlessly riding into battle against the miners or Argentines without a doubt in her head. As Alan Moorehead said of the great and also fearless explorer Stanley, who had no imagination either, if you went on his African expeditions it was like being in the *corps d'élite* of a successful general—"you triumphed and you died." When Mrs. Thatcher sets down her articles of faith and voices her ideas on the relevance of Christian morality to politics, she is, in effect, admonishing the British, "Go back to church and believe again." She wants to go back to the last coherent value system Britain had. It happens to be before the two world wars and loss of empire.

Hugo Young, a *Guardian* columnist who knows Mrs. Thatcher well, put it best, I think, in his penetrating 1989 biography of her, *One of Us* (*The Iron Lady* in America). He said her two main qualities were "a sense of moral rectitude" and "pragmatism," which made her "a consummate populist." They keep her going enthusiastically year after year while "the grey men who preceded her surrendered to despair after less than half the span of her time in office."

Her religion is expectably plain, straight, materialistic, nonintellectual. Unlike the bishops of the Church of England, themselves members of the intellectual elite with its tradition of preservation, Mrs. Thatcher wants to radically renew an old faith. She sees herself speaking "personally as a Christian"; she had a Methodist upbringing over her father's store in Grantham. From the Old Testament she says she draws "a strict code of law," the Ten Commandments, and from the New Testament the teaching of Jesus to "love our neighbors as ourselves." Mrs. Thatcher:

> I believe that by taking these key elements from the Old and New Testaments, we gain a view of the universe and a proper attitude to work and principles to shape economic and social life. We are told we must work and use our talents to create wealth.

She quotes St. Paul's advice to the Thessalonians: "If a man shall not work he shall not eat."

> It is not the creation of wealth that is wrong but the love of money for its own sake. The spiritual dimension comes in deciding what one does with wealth.

Personal responsibility is central: "We are all responsible for our own actions."

In our generation, the only way we can ensure that nobody is left without sustenance, help or opportunity, is to have laws to provide for health and education, pensions for the elderly, succour for the sick and disabled. But intervention by the state must never become so great that it effectively removes personal responsibility.

She has not resisted mention of the alabaster jar of ointment, a reference to Jesus saying: "For the poor are always with you."

This moral code, handed down from her grocer father, Alfred Roberts, grew out of provincial Protestant churchgoing and reading the Bible, at a time when Britain's philosophers, theologians, and literary men, and ordinary people like the Thatchers, shared a consensus on values. Everyone agreed what was good and bad and what constituted decent and acceptable social conduct: a good home of one's own, cash savings, a decent school, children brought up to know right from wrong. She has said again and again such teachings from her father are her lodestar (mother Beatrice is rarely mentioned and is even missing from Mrs. Thatcher's Who's Who entry). As we heard from the Anglican bishops earlier, this consensus on values has today broken down in Britain at large, but not among Mrs. Thatcher's aspiring lower-middle-class constituency.

British intellectuals, except for the clergy, fail to see why Mrs. Thatcher's religious stand is so relevant to her politics. Auberon Waugh has warned the moral high ground is "precarious"; *The Observer* has complained she lacks "compassion"; even Brian Walden is left uneasy. He once chided Mrs. Thatcher, saying capitalism would not be sold by "lectures on morality." Rather, he said, "The ever wider diffusion of property ownership is the only sure way to preserve the system." As *The Economist* wittily chimed in, the Bible has little to say about the danger that caring for the poor will destroy their incentive for work, dependency not being much of an issue in Palestine's agricultural economy of two thousand years ago. Tebbit, always spoiling for a good fight, told me church leaders spend "too much time on politics and too little on moral issues." (Both Tony Benn and Norman Stone have demanded from time to time that the Church of England be disestablished, Stone once intemperately saying, "Let it join Rome, and let the Pope discipline his left-wing chaplains . . .") Tebbit:

When the Prime Minister comes out of her role as a politician and expresses views on moral issues, the clergy cries "Foul!" They are getting a taste of their own medicine.

But is Mrs. Thatcher coming out of her role? Protestant reform-
ers ever since the sixteenth century have set out to sanctify, in her
words, "a view of the universe and proper attitude to work," and set
off a furious application to the business of making money. The future in Thatcher's Britain belongs to those who not only go back to
church but work harder, use their elbows, and make more money.
Yet a surprising number of British resist this "enterprise culture,"
which is after all just the old Protestant work ethic all over again. A
self-made microchip maker in Norwich told me, "In America they
applaud success. In Britain they don't. They even stack things up
against you." Merchant banker John Forsyth says, "The City's popularity has always suffered from its success." A good many British say
they would rather have less money and more time for the garden
and the pub. They want a quiet life and, as one man told me, "don't
really like being trodden on by these aggressive Flash Harry types."

Polls show more British want a society where caring for others
is well rewarded, creating wealth less so; they favor collective welfare over individual enterprise. Even so, less government involvement in the economy and rewarding success are likely to be lasting
Thatcher legacies. A meritocracy comes with high tech. She is a mer-
itocrat herself. The grocer's girl from Grantham who goes out and
becomes Prime Minister, doing the impossible. She speaks for tens
of thousands like her. Maybe tens of millions.

Mrs. Thatcher has deliberately divided Britain, not into two nations, North-South, poor-rich, divisions which she naturally opposes,
but into believers and nonbelievers, a division which she welcomes.
In the words of David Owen and Max Hastings, who applaud her for
it, she has "broken the consensus." Not, says James Callaghan, permanently. Lord Callaghan, while protesting he was not a prophet,
told me he doubted Mrs. Thatcher had changed British politics in a
lasting way:

> I would doubt it. I think there is in both the Conservative and Labour
> parties a desire, whilst always being different, to at least have some sort
> of common understanding about where Britain is going. Even if we
> differ about the methods of getting there. I think the Norman Tebbits of
> this world are the opposite numbers of the Tony Benns. Neither of
> them, in my view, represent the mean in Britain, which I think will
> eventually reestablish itself.

Interestingly, Tebbit and Benn were the only two I interviewed
who voiced fears of social breakdown. Tebbit:

Britain's disciplined rule of law in the 1920s, 1930s and early postwar years created an exceptionally well-ordered society. When that was relaxed, at first nothing happened. Now it's a hell of a battle to put it right again. That's the downside of a richer society that has got less moral restraints and is less deferential. So there's some choppy waters there.

Benn's was the view of a Christian-Marxist ideologue:

Financial services are booming. So are retail sales, a lot of it on credit. We're importing a lot of goods from abroad. Pay levels are rising. But it's on a very ill-founded and insecure basis. So domestic tension grows. All the old historical factors, such as insularity and remnants of feudalism, and a strong sense of conflict between rich and poor, which were previously just seen as being vaguely interesting, are coming back into play. Underneath the thing is stirring, stirring. Nobody talks about it much, but people are frightened.

But let's go back to Lord Callaghan, who struck me, despite his Irish ancestry and his old constituency in Cardiff, as having the best feel for the English character (David Owen thinks so too). He says Mrs. Thatcher has destroyed the old consensus, but not forever.

I think this country on the whole operates on a consensus. That is waiting to be done. That will come *after* her.

Mrs. Thatcher says the younger generation of Tory leaders "must not be people who constantly compromise." She has said she views politicians who favor consensus "as Quislings, as traitors . . . I mean it." Lord Callaghan says compromise is the heart of British politics.

Once the Labour Party modifies its attitudes to defense, to public ownership, to the trade unions, it will enable a new consensus to be established. What we really need in Britain is a new consensus. And that will take time.

Lord Callaghan told me a story about how Lloyd George once told a group of Liberals who complained about some compromise he'd made, "Look, which would you rather do, go to Westminster or go to heaven?" Callaghan: "Now Tony Benn would sooner go to heaven." But you could say the same for Callaghan himself; his refusal to go against the unions put Mrs. Thatcher in Number Ten.

She can stay in power and keep getting reelected in the 1990s, says Tony Benn, as long as the economy grows and Labour stays divided. If she ever goes, he thinks it will be on the "moral" issue, not doing enough for the poor. The night of her last victory she

vowed, "There's plenty for us to do now. There'll be no slacking!"
She has since told Brian Walden:

> I do not hang on for the sake of hanging on. I hang on until I believe
> there are people who can take the banner forward with the same com-
> mitment, belief, vision, strength, and singleness of purpose.

A tall order. Enoch Powell told me that all Britain's postwar
Tory Prime Ministers, except for Anthony Eden, were "produced by
accident."

> Nobody sees them coming. That was true of Thatcher. And that was
> true of Heath. And that was true of Home. And that was true of Mac-
> millan. So take no notice of anybody who tells you who's likely to be
> the next Prime Minister. They'll be wrong.

Still, everybody likes to speculate. An interesting late 1989 poll
of a hundred top British executives had Kenneth Baker emerging as
the preferred candidate (23 percent), followed by Michael Heseltine
(21 percent). Other contenders interviewed for this book were Christopher Patten (fifth place), Douglas Hurd (seventh) and Norman
Tebbit (ninth). In other polls, as we have seen, the names stay pretty
much the same, but the lineup keeps changing. To me Tebbit, the
likeliest choice from this lot of Mrs. Thatcher herself, would be most
certain to carry on her populist crusade. The executives felt top priority should be given to sorting out the health service, just ahead of
promoting better education and taking a more positive stand toward
Europe.

When will she go? Or should we be asking: Will she ever go? For
a while there in 1989, after Labour won the European Parliament
election in June, there was a botched reshuffle of ministers in July,
and the Tory Party dropped in the polls to trail Labour by 14 percent, it looked like the time had come. On top of it all, at the height
of the upheaval in Europe, Mrs. Thatcher saw her chancellor resign
and faced the first Tory challenge to her leadership.

Nobody expected Sir Anthony Meyer, her challenger and a
stalking horse, to unseat her. An elderly MP and baronet who went
to Eton and Oxford, he personified the public school Oxbridge elite.
What mattered was how many anti-Thatcher votes he would get.

He got sixty (including twenty-four abstentions and three
nonvoters) to her safe majority of three hundred and fourteen.
Many viewed it as the Tory old guard's last stand. Yet anything over
forty-five votes was supposed to be damaging. "YOU'RE IN TROUBLE,
MRS T" thundered the anti-Thatcher *Daily Mirror*. "THATCHER SANITY

CRISIS" chortled *Private Eye*. Her opponents were "Euro-extremists," sniffed the pro-Thatcher *Times*. So was it "an emphatic triumph" (*The Sun*)? Or "a shattering blow" (*Daily Mirror*)?

A blow, decided the authors of perhaps the two best biographies of Mrs. Thatcher, Peter Jenkins and Hugo Young. "There is a smell of decay in the air," wrote Jenkins in *The Independent*. "There is no one strong around her anymore, no one with stature to stop her from doing what she chooses," wrote Young in *The Guardian*. Even Peregrine Worsthorne, former editor of the *Sunday Telegraph*, who struck me in an interview as being about as pro-Thatcher as you could be, felt she was giving a worrying impression of "believing herself to be infallible."

Were the vultures starting to hover? You might have thought so in another of Mrs. Thatcher's TV interviews with Brian Walden. After she shrugged off the row with Lawson, her chancellor, as "tittle tattle," and the European Community's ERM as "a higgledy-piggledy set of rules," Walden rudely asked if it was true that she couldn't "get on with anybody but yes-men." That, she replied, was "a great insult to my Cabinet." But Walden was out for blood. He asked her, "You come over as being someone who one of your backbenchers said is slightly off her trolley, authoritarian, domineering, refusing to listen to anyone else—why?" She gave him an off-with-his-head glare, looked ready to handbag him, thought better of it, and snapped, "Nonsense, Brian. I'm staying my own sweet reasonable self."

Friends said it all knocked her old sense of confidence sideways. She told the *Sunday Correspondent* that after the next election— 1991? 1992?—it would be "time for someone else to carry the torch." When the press said this made her sound like a lame duck ("I am *not* a lame duck!"), she hinted to *The Times* that "by popular acclaim" she might even go beyond a *fifth* election. Fed up with all the speculation she might retire, she even said she is not averse to being Britain's longest-serving Prime Minister. To beat Sir Robert Walpole, she would have to carry on until March 2000. Soon, more modestly, she told the BBC she would stay on as long as the voters and the party want her to. And there, at this writing, it lies. In any case, Thatcherism, with or without Thatcher, might well survive.

How does one sum up the intellectuals' counterview? I asked John Fowles, who said he had "no faith at all in Thatcher's attempt to turn us into a sort of America, with time as an arrow."

Trying to galvanize us back into what we were is fundamentally absurd, I think; what role we play in the future must be based on what we are now—and has not yet been found. In my view a return to great economic and political power is unthinkable—totally ludicrous. The lady reminds me of that stock figure in ancient Roman comedy, the *miles gloriosus*, eternally boasting of victory in a war where history has defeated, and will continue to defeat, her.

Yet one cannot but have a sneaking respect for Mrs. Thatcher. As its intellectuals should know, Britain was bound to pay the price for its cultural and class divisions.

Conclusion

N OW ANOTHER YEAR HAS GONE BY and as I end this book Mrs. Thatcher, amazingly, is gone and John Major is Britain's Prime Minister. Looking back, it is the words of the literary man, the thinkers with ideas, that ring loudest in my ears. And yet, if Mrs. Thatcher was the Queen of Hearts, saying "Hold your tongue!" and turning purple, so the chattering class, as their words come so thick and so fast, at times have seemed like Alice's pack of cards that rose into the air, and came flying down upon her, as she tried to beat them off.

Alice awoke, and found it had all been a curious dream. I feel a little that way, particularly now that the Thatcher era is over. For years, first influenced by English novels and films, and later by living years on end in former British colonies like India and Egypt, an impression formed in my mind that much of the world, if not exactly the Lobster Quadrille or Mad Tea Party, was still a strange enough adventure, far from home, vaguely threatening, the alien corn. And if someday you could just wake up someplace like that safe, cozy English village you imagined with its misty green fields and thatched cottages and Anglican church, you would live happily ever after.

This England was, I now can see, a nostalgic myth. Reality for most British people is a grim and gray urban setting of drab office blocks, long trips on the Underground, endless, unbroken rows of council flats or brick Victorian houses, mile after mile of them, so dreary and look-alike they make your heart sink.

Green and idyllic villages, like sunny summer days, do of course exist in Britain. But somehow farmers are outnumbered by stockbrokers or accountants who commute to the City of London or clever Oxbridge media types. The true villagers, who may come in to tidy things up, tend to live in low-rent housing out of sight. Their children, if not jobless, are probably too poorly educated to do much in this computer-microchip age. All over Britain this younger generation simmers in endemic revolt, restive, unruly, fed up with a class system that no longer fits the times, if ever it fit any times. This is the great hope of John Major. He, too, grew up left out, he, too, has known hard times. Education, the lack of which can stunt the lives of so many, also let him down and is at the top of his list of what Britain needs. He shares with Mrs. Thatcher a self-made man's contempt for the Britain of the old boy network and stuffy class distinctions. Major's promise to build a "classless society" is reinforced by the empathy of somebody who sees all the grafitti and hooliganism reflect frustration, and a vague, baffled sense of being taken.

If one single thing ails Britain today it is that its old social institutions, some feudal, some Victorian, are getting so creaky and musty and out of date. As Walter Bagehot, the great *Economist* editor who got so much about Britain right, had to say in 1873: "The whole history of civilization is strewn with creeds and institutions which were invaluable at first, and deadly afterwards."

This is the story in Britain. The old Britain of Eton, Oxbridge, the land, and the Guards, allied with a chattering class of literary intellectuals, so invaluable when it came to running an empire, is deadly when it comes to bringing the country into the 1990s. Winston Churchill was confident "science and democracy" would take care of it. But the old Britain persists, intent on its self-preservation. It puts its money into banks or London houses or American real estate, not into schools and science and factories. In the old smokestack industry of coal and oil, human muscle mattered; a socially stratified superior-inferior, upstairs-downstairs society of brains and brawn was easier to justify. Now, when computer-run machines can do practically everything, what matters is skill.

Britain's ruling class knows this. It has invested very heavily in expensive new science labs at Eton, Westminster, and the other top public schools so its own children won't fall behind. But it has not been prepared—the other half of Churchill's equation—to radically improve Britain's schools so that other children can compete on equal terms with its own. It has tried to be meritocratic. But never enough. Too often, the establishment's ranks get closed to those not bred into them; it accepts the scholarship boy, but only on sufferance. Britain badly needs, at last, a system of education where ability counts, not just family or money. Mrs. Thatcher's tinkering with choice and competition was not enough. But she was instinctively unhappy with the idea of spending a lot more on education. There needs to be a big investment in teachers' pay and scientific equipment to put the rest of Britain's schools on something closer to a par with Eton. Where would the money come from? There's a lot of it just sitting around. The two hundred richest Britons alone, for example, own $65 *billion* (£38.2 billion) worth of land, antiques, and a lot of Rembrandts and Vandykes.

This is not just an American's zeal for Jeffersonian equality. The British have been saying the same for years. But they don't act. Unless they do, and invest a lot more in science, schools, and industry, Britain will just limp along as a second-class power, getting seedier and shabbier and falling more and more behind.

To an American, surely to any American, a whole social mentality is missing. America is not perfect, but wherever you go in the world nowadays it's a symbol of oomph and vitality and freedom and fun; that's because it stands for opportunity, it is open and free and questioning, anybody can be anything. Or try. A British blue-collar worker who is good at his job ought to feel as well with the world as a yuppie banker in the City. More, because he's not just buying and selling, he's making things. I mean the kind of self-confidence and pride you find in a tractor mechanic in Iowa or somebody in computer software in Boston or a lab technician in St. Paul.

This means, if Britain is going to become a healthier, happier place to live, it has got to go after the class system root and branch. More science, more democracy. I keep harping on that. So simple. So undone. Mrs. Thatcher and especially Norman Tebbit talked about it ("One by one the bastions of class privilege, intellectual snobbery . . . are falling"). In fact by cutting top taxes from 98 percent to 40 percent just as the value of houses, land, antiques, and art went sky-high, they were shoring up those bastions, not tearing them down.

Mrs. Thatcher, in her free market fervor, talked about her fear that socialism has destroyed the British people's initiative. To me the fight that matters in Britain is not the fight between socialism and free market economics, important as that is, nor even the fight between "a dependency culture" and "an enterprise culture." It is the old, old fight over class and power: who is in control? Mrs. Thatcher claimed, "I have given power to the people." She did not. Money is power. Mrs. Thatcher saw herself as leading a revolt against control of the country and the Tory party by Britain's upper crust. But it is a revolt that Major's younger generation, with its greater sympathy to social needs, will have to carry on. What she did do, I think, was to postpone the day of reckoning.

The old Britain, to me, the peers and knights, the lords and ladies I met—and readers can judge what they say for themselves—itself sees the handwriting on the wall. Surely any outsider would. Whether you measure it by the increase in violent commotions as in 1981 and 1985; horrifying accidents like the King's Cross fire or the Clapham Junction collision; the football stand disasters at Sheffield, Bradford, Brussels, and Glasgow; the rising crime; the unevenness of North-South prosperity; the signs of trouble in letters and the arts; the shabbiness of dress; the backwardness of home appliances; the flimsy scaffolding and piles of debris left about; the overcrowded roads and trains and airports; the dirty streets and parks; the drugs; the homelessness; the sheer worn-outness of so much in Britain—anybody can see things are not right. Even Mrs. Thatcher's favorite British symbol—an oil rig standing alone in a stormy North Sea—let her down: one blew up. Travel the world and you feel a difference in mood between a country that has had a social revolution (Egypt) and one that has not (Morocco). Britain feels like a Morocco.

Uncle Vanya was one of the last plays I saw in London. So much in Britain has a bleak Chekhovian tone. Sonya sounds contemporary at the end when Uncle Vanya tells her how depressed he is and she replies:

> We'll live, Uncle Vanya. We shall live through a long, long succession of days and long, endless evenings; we will endure whatever fate has in store for us . . .

Luigi Barzini wrote that the British, in a word, are stoics. He said, "Kipling's 'If,' a sacred text a few generations ago, and still imbedded in many British hearts, could have been written by Marcus Aurelius." Sonya's stoicism mirrors the mood of Britain's ruling establishment today.

It seems ungracious to turn against those who have shown you kindness and hospitality, especially all the wonderfully articulate talkers in what I've called the chattering class. But when things went too far at the Knave of Hearts's trial, Alice also forgot her manners and cried, "Who cares for you? You're nothing but a pack of cards!" For it needs must be said that Britain's continued failure in schooling, science, and industry has got to call the values, even the existence, of the public school Oxbridge elite into question. Mrs.

Thatcher, when she attacked "academics and intellectuals" for putting out what she called "pure poison," was sending thunderbolts into their midst. But her lace-curtain lower-middle-class constituency longs for respectability; she led a very genteel revolt. The disinherited of North England, Scotland, and Wales had looked to Labour, with all its out-of-date socialist hang-ups, class hostilities, militant hardboys, and old-time union bosses. There was nobody else. Now they've got Major. While he shares Mrs. Thatcher's economic principles of free markets and sound money, he is more liberal on social issues; he clearly opposes, for instance, capital punishment and racism. Mrs. Thatcher also was temperamentally opposed to doing some of the things Britain must do to revive its industry and inner cities; she convinced herself that most local government was bad government.

Major is also far more worried about the rundown state of British industry and its inadequate human capital. It wastes lives. Britain lacks the scientifically skilled work force it needs to compete. Major's biggest challenge is going to be to educate Britain's youth better and reeducate so many adults who got left out.

As we have seen, Mrs. Thatcher tirelessly did battle with what she called "intellectual snobs." She worked hard to stay an outsider, steering clear of the Old Tory grandees and the Oxbridge elite. ("The adrenalin flows when they really come out fighting at me and I fight back and I stand there and I know: 'Now come on, Maggie, you are wholly on your own. No one can help you.' And I love it.") She was forever the good Christian soldier, leading her beleaguered band, repudiating all established orthodoxies, holding high the banners of progress, thrift and free markets, telling Britain what is good for it. She wanted to change Britain, she said, from "a give-it-to-me to a do-it-yourself nation; to a get-up-and-go, instead of a sit-back-and-wait-for-it Britain." Was she too inflexible? ("I don't believe they want a government to be so flexible it becomes invertebrate. You don't want a government of flexi-toys.") Too domineering? ("I go for agreement, agreement for the things I want to do.")

She won three elections largely because enough Britons thought she would hold back inflation and unleash growth better than her opponents. When she failed after 1988, the polls turned against her —so did the Tories. Now Major must unite the badly split party and restore the economy, hopefully helped by his own success in taking sterling into the European monetary system. He is enthusiastic about Europe.

Mrs. Thatcher tried to shape not just a decade, but a whole generation of British public life. In bringing ever-younger politicians into her Cabinet, as she did in successive reshuffles, she worked to keep Thatcherism going long after she left the scene. But she was not prepared to spend on schools, science, and industry in a way that would effectively break the Oxbridge elite's hold on British society. *The Economist:*

> Even now, after ten years, she still sees herself as beleaguered, her mission under threat. She cannot quit while she is ahead; with a large part of herself she does not believe she is ahead.

I think she was right. She was somehow not radical enough in the truest, most compassionate way. Her greatest triumph and legacy to Britain is that John Major probably will be.

So should we look to Britain as a model? It lost an empire. We may be on the verge, starting with defeat in Vietnam, of losing ours, such as it is. British scholars like Yale's Paul Kennedy ask if this has already begun.

Britain started out wanting to trade and protect its sea routes; its scramble for territory came later. America wanted to help Europe and Japan get back on their feet, contain Soviet power, and help the poor two thirds of the world to grow. Some parallels come to mind. In both British traders and American cold warriors there was a strong missionary streak. We both wanted to convert everybody to our way of doing things, whether it was Christianity, literacy, sanitation, democratic government, or, later on, scientific farming and the Pill and IUD.

We felt we were surely Britain's Great Power successor with our Marshall Plan, Point Four, Atlantic Pact, Korean War, the defense of the free world. A Pax Americana, everybody thought, would keep world order just like a Pax Britannica had done in the past. Americans were not Englishmen but in the conservative, moneyed, Protestant Anglophiles of Wall Street and the Council of Foreign Relations we came close.

It worked until Vietnam. I was on the beach at Da Nang the day the first American soldiers landed in 1965 and remember a Marine colonel telling me, quoting Caesar, "It is a new way of conquering, to use generosity and compassion as our defenses." American power was at flood tide; we believed in such pragmatic altruism. By the time the helicopters left the Saigon embassy's roof in 1975 nobody believed anything. America looked a lot less reliable. It began its long slide into living on credit. In the loss of prestige and foreign supporters, and America's own internal demoralization, we find another parallel with Britain.

As it turns out, Britain's worst problems are our worst problems too. America's manufacturing base is shrinking. Our schools are failing. High-tech electronics now doubles the amount of microcomponents on a piece of silicon every eighteen months, but the average American child, ranking seventeenth in world scientific literacy, can't pick out Florida on a map. Biological knowledge is exploding, galaxies and molecules being charted as never before, yet we, too, are good at basic scientific research, bad at getting it into products to sell. As greed-is-good ethics make fortunes in leveraged buyouts and hostile takeovers, anywhere from a few hundred thousand to 4 million Americans are homeless, another 15 million nearly so in a crime- and drug-ridden underclass. Half the people in American hospital emergency rooms are there from crime or drugs, much of it crack-cocaine. Our society, too, is polarized. A symbol of the times, says playwright August Wilson, is "somebody who steps over a body on the sidewalk to go in and buy a $2,000 watch." Do long years of Reaganism and Thatcherism have the same effect? Or is this a new general human condition of the postindustrial West? Was Toynbee, after all, right?

These parallels can't be pushed too far. Differences are great. British character was formed by being on a wet little island in the North Sea whose sailors and fishermen faced stormy and fog-bound seas and went out to explore and rule much of the world. American character was formed by exploring and settling a vast and wild continent of plains and mountains and deserts and swamps and forests with all kinds of weather; we have four times more people, nearly a quarter of them black (12 percent), Latin (8 percent) or Asian (3 percent). Homogeneous Britain, in spite of all the fuss about immigrants, is still practically all of white European descent (96 percent).

The cultural difference that matters most, I think, is that Americans went out into the world confident, not just in their technological know-how and work ethic, but with the sense of a God-given American code of ethics and behavior. So did the British a century ago. The Anglican church is just as much part of all those old outposts of empire as the military cantonment or the club.

But somehow the British lost their faith. This is only faintly mirrored in America, at least so far. I think it matters, aside from the spiritual, for practical nonreligious reasons. If the anthropologists are right, it is a common perception of right and wrong, and the presence of God, more than anything else, that holds a society together and keeps it from breaking down. Now, ominously, in Britain the old Christian consensus is gone. What is going to take its place? Queen Elizabeth, partly due to her conscientiousness and moral image, is the last symbol of common values and unity the whole of British society has got.

Americans are always in a hurry and I'll confess I sometimes get aggravated by the slower tempo on crowded British sidewalks, especially if rushing to the Underground. But the speed, anger, and aggression you can sometimes get from British drivers and the occasional viciousness in speech and body language represents a kind of lack of civility, a sheer meanness, I've seen nowhere else. It makes you wonder how much anxiety and alienation there is.

David Owen, when I met him, agreed there were good signs and bad signs. He too is a science and democracy man: "The worst sign is the inadequacy of our investment in skills and training. So it is unproven whether Thatcher has made a permanent change." He said:

> How I long to believe that. Even though it's to my detriment politically. I hope and pray that these last eleven years means we have permanently turned the economic corner. And that Britain will come back from being ninth in per capita income in Europe to being fifth or sixth. At the moment we are overrated. We carry a position way above our proper economic station. With a combination of good diplomacy and finesse and skill and the inertia of changing systems, we'll manage to soldier on. But I would like us to live up to what we could be.

Britain's failure of the nerve comes just when we are all going to need our nerve. The story in Europe has just begun. Russia's economy, in the words of Sir Geoffrey Howe, is "a busted flush." Communism, a terminal disappointment, is being shed. Was Thatcherism an influence? Probably not. Oh, it might have given history a little nudge. The fate of *perestroika* now lies in the character of the Russian people. Germany is reuniting, to its own self-doubts and neighbors' fears. Old ethnic tensions are reviving from the Baltic to the Balkans. The earth, at last seen to be the living, fragile organism that it is, will have double the numbers of people it had in the 1940s by the millennium. "The decline of the superpowers, the end of the Cold War, and the insistent problems of the Third World all point in one direction," says Denis Healey. "There must be a massive transfer of resources worldwide from defense to development."

If 1989 was, at last, history's answer to 1789, as that man who stopped the column of tanks in Beijing's Avenue of Eternal Peace seemed to think it was, there are dangerous times ahead. "Man is born free," said Rousseau, "and everywhere he is in chains." A lot of those chains are being thrown off pretty fast. But, remember, after the cry of "Liberty, Equality, Fraternity!" came the 18th of Brumaire and Napoleon. The flaw in the revolutionary ideal is that no ready-made formula for the good society exists. The British, with their deeply-ingrained tolerance of free expression, dissent and nonconformity, liberal, reformist, accommodating, suspicious of the quick-and-easy solution, and non-revolutionary, know this as well as anybody. Lord Callaghan:

> What is going to happen when the first flush of democratic freedom is past, is that governments have to make the hard economic decisions to get the economy right and people start to grumble. If the grumbles get too loud, you know what happens—the man on horseback.

If Britain can put its house in order, and that means investing enough in schools, science, and industry, then its history and temperament will make it well suited for the new role coming its way. The British did more than anybody else in Europe to explode the old agenda of the left. If it can overcome an attachment, like Mrs. Thatcher's, to an eighteenth-century concept of sovereignty and become a more wholehearted member of the European Community, this could give it the intellectual edge in politics, even the power-action edge. And the British know their former colonies in Africa and Asia, their languages, histories, peoples, customs, a lot better than we do. As Vietnam showed, we Americans are not very good at understanding people of another race and culture. In the social convulsions ahead Britain's wisdom is going to matter.

"Lo, all our pomp of yesterday / Is one with Nineveh and Tyre!" The old Britain that went with the Empire should leave the stage too. Not like the spoiled and selfish characters in *The Cherry Orchard*, leaving behind their faithful old servant, Firs, trapped and forgotten, to die. Firs might be speaking for all the educationally deprived Britons when he says, just before the final curtain falls, "Life has gone by, as if I'd never lived." There is that strange, dissonant sound, never explained, that we hear throughout the play. Then all is still, and the sound of the strokes of an ax against a tree, deep in the orchard, prefigures social upheaval.

At bottom, what is happening in Russia and Eastern Europe and almost certainly will happen in China, too, are attempts at radical social engineering to enable their societies to successfully adapt to late-twentieth-century science and high technology. "Science and democracy" are the answer for them too. (Just as their unrest could conceivably spread to Britain out of the same frustration.)

More democracy in schooling, more science, more industry, it is not much. Perhaps to ask a privileged class to give up its privileges is to ask the impossible. But there is something in the British character that makes them do the impossible. How did they have the gall to rule India (with just a dozen British to every eight hundred sepoys)? Or defeat the Armada? Scale Everest? Explore the Nile? Or assemble in short order a small flotilla to sail thousands of miles to the Falklands just to stand up for a principle and international law?

Britain no longer leads the van, coloring the map red everywhere it goes. But travel the earth and see the regimental bands marching up the parade grounds of Lahore or Delhi or Muscat, and you would think that sun had never set. The bureaucrats left behind in Singapore or Nairobi are just as fussy and inflexible as any in a post office in Ealing. Mrs. Thatcher talked of the Empire's "sound administration." I think of a trial of a cattle thief I saw in Sudan's Nuba Mountains, just about as far from Downing Street as you can go. The Nubas went naked except for beads and spears a generation ago, but the Nuba judge wore suit and spectacles. And when the thief demanded to be set free on the grounds he was from another tribe, the judge held up a copy of the British penal code, so yellowed and tattered and pathetically worn it had to be left over from the colonial days. "You have committed an offense in the eyes of the law," said the judge. "A crime is a crime no matter where it is committed." Or there was that time in Dacca, night, heat, monsoon rain, ragged Bengali crowds, that panicky get-me-out-of-here feeling. My Bengali interpreter stared at the scene fixedly, hysteria growing, until he blurted out: "My father loved Macaulay, and he wore a suit, tie and vest every day of his life."

In Britain, too, the myth still has its magic, in the garden parties and pageantry, the cozy cottages and pubs, the misty moorlands, the tolling bells. The British talk of doubt and despair. Do they really believe it? The most terrible things have been said about the English —that they were decadent, doomed, washed-up—ever since Brown's *Estimate,* and that was in the 1750s before the Seven Years War. And this has happened again and again and again.

But the British don't fail. They succeed. And make life more gracious and decent for the rest of us. Dickens called another age the best of times, the worst of times. Times are decided by men. And men have changed history before. These are times of marvelous prospects and terrible problems, times of decline but times of renaissance too.

It is true that Britain has a transcendent past and does not look forward to a transcendent future, that it used to act on the world and now the world acts on it. But it is not the Central African Republic. It is a great civilized power. And thank God for that. I, for one, believe the world is going to change yet more than people think. Everything is in the pot, everything is possible. Britain can have just as great a future as it has a past. Because the world is changing so much, nothing can be ruled out. It is the path as yet we cannot see.

NOTES

Most quoted remarks came in interviews. Secondary sources are, in the main, cited here, except for those bits hastily gleaned from the British papers and television news broadcasts.

xxvii   Charles Dickens, *A Tale of Two Cities* (1859).

xxix   Lewis Carroll, *Through the Looking-Glass* (1871), quoted from *The Annotated Alice* (London, Penguin Books, 1965), p. 251.

xxix   Carroll, *Alice's Adventures in Wonderland* (1865), from *The Annotated Alice*, p. 22.

xxix   Caryl Hargreaves, quoted from *Cornhill Magazine*, July 1932.

xxx   Mark Twain, *Following the Equator* (1897).

xxx   John Greenleaf Whittier, "To Englishmen."

xxx   Robert Frost, "The Gift Outright," *The Collected Poems of Robert Frost* (Garden City, N.Y.: Halcyon House, 1942), p. 445.

xxxiii   R. W. Apple, "Britain Adrift: Are the Old Values a Handicap, or the Saving Grace?" *The New York Times*, October 9, 1985.

xxxvii   Rudyard Kipling, "The English Flag," *Barrack-Room Ballads* (1892).

3   William Shakespeare, *Cymbeline.* An example: "Hath Britain all the sun that shines?" III. iv.

4   Hugh Kenner, *A Sinking Island* (New York: Alfred A. Knopf, 1988), p. 3.

4   Oliver Wendell Holmes, "A Good Time Going" (to Charles Mackay).

5   T. S. Eliot, quoted by Kenner, p. 189.

6   Julius Caesar, *De bello Gallico.*

7   Tacitus, *Agricola.*

7   Paul Theroux, *The Kingdom by the Sea* (London: Hamish Hamilton, 1983), p. 431.

7   Duc de Sully, *Royal Economies* (1638).

7   Sir John Betjeman, "A Subaltern's Love Song."

8   Matthew Arnold, "Dover Beach" (1867).

8   Robert Browning, "A Toccata of Galuppi's" (1855).

9   Stephen Jay Gould, *Time's Arrow, Time's Cycle: Myth and Metaphor in the Discovery of Geological Time* (Cambridge: Harvard University Press, 1987), p. 10.

12   John Osborne, *The Entertainer*, 1957, quoted from Kenneth Tynan, *A View of the English Stage* (New York: Methuen, 1984. First published by Davis-Poynter, 1975).

12   Asa Briggs, *A Social History of England* (London: Weidenfeld & Nicolson, 1983).

13   Anthony Sampson, *The Changing Anatomy of Britain* (London: Hodder & Stoughton, 1982), 1986 edition, p. 482.

13 Ibid., p. 483.

13 William H. McNeill, *The Pursuit of Power: Technology, Armed Force and Society since A.D. 1000* (Chicago: University of Chicago Press, 1982).

13 Briggs, p. 195.

17 William Caxton (1421–1491), the first English printer.

17 Sampson, p. 21.

18 "Britain's Rich; the Top 200," *The Sunday Times*, April 2, 1989.

18 Landholding figures from "Britain's Richest 200," *Money*, March 1988.

20 F. Scott Fitzgerald, *Tender Is the Night* (1934).

29 "MR. NASTY: Norman Tebbit Flogs a Dead Horse," *New Statesman*, May 6, 1988.

29 Sampson, p. 54.

30 Peter Jenkins, *Mrs. Thatcher's Revolution: The Ending of the Socialist Era* (Cambridge: Harvard University Press, 1988), p. 326.

   Mrs. Thatcher, *Newsweek*, November 28, 1988.

32 Charles Dickens, *A Tale of Two Cities*, 1859. Quoted from London: William Clowes Limited edition, 1986, p. 243.

33 "Corrupt from top to bottom," Alfred Roberts, quoted by Hugo Young, *One of Us* (London: Macmillan, 1989), quoted from U.S. edition, *The Iron Lady* (New York: Farrar, Straus & Giroux, 1989), p. 519.

33 "That sweet enemy, France" from Edmund Burke, *Reflection on the French Revolution* (1790).

34 John Dryden (1631–1700), "Annus Mirabilis," xli.

34 Philip Larkin, "Annus Mirabilis," *Collected Poems*, (New York: Farrar, Straus & Giroux and The Marvell Press, 1989), p. 167.

37 Caryl Churchill, *Serious Money* (London: Methuen, 1987), the song, "Five More Glorious Years" by Ian Dury and Chaz Jankel, p. 111.

37 Bernard Levin, "The Way We Live Now" column, "The Soul Sniggered Off," *The Times*, December 17, 1987.

37 Ronald Harwood, *J. J. Farr* (London: Amber Lane Press, 1988), p. 61.

43 Salman Rushdie, March 1987 interview at San Francisco State University, replayed on KQED, Channel 9, San Francisco, March 24, 1988.

45 George Bernard Shaw, *Saint Joan: A Chronicle Play in Six Scenes and an Epilogue* (New York: Brentano's, 1924).

46 Robert Redfield, as quoted by the author in *Villages* (New York: Doubleday, 1983). Redfield's "little" and "great" traditions theory is set down in *Peasant Society and Culture* (Chicago: University of Chicago Press, 1956).

46 William H. McNeill, *Mythistory and Other Essays* (Chicago: University of Chicago Press, 1986), p. 183. See also McNeill, "Arnold Joseph Toynbee, 1889–1975," from *The Proceedings of the British Academy*, London, volume LXIII, 1977.

49 Henry Steele Commager, *Britain Through American Eyes* (London: Bodley Head, 1974), p. xxi.

49 Nathaniel Hawthorne, *Our Old Home* (1863).

50 Family letters quoted from author's papers.

50 Commager, p. xli.

51 Ibid., p. xxxii

51 James Fenimore Cooper, *England, With Sketches of Society in the Metropolis* (1837).

51 Hawthorne, *Our Old Home.*

51 Ralph Waldo Emerson, *English Traits* (1856).

51 Rudyard Kipling, letter to Cecil Rhodes in 1901 quoted by Charles Carrington in *Rudyard Kipling: His Life and Work* (London: Macmillan, 1955), Penguin Books edition, 1986, p. 283.

51 George III quoted in Commager, p. 21, by John Adams, *The Works of John Adams,* Charles Francis Adams, ed.

51 Commager, p. 23. Abigail Adams quoted from *Letters of Mrs. Adams, the Wife of John Adams,* Charles Francis Adams, ed. (1840).

51 Ibid., p. 692, from George Santayana, *Soliloquies in England* (London, Constable & Co., 1922).

52 Ibid., p. 701, from Samuel Eliot Morison, "An American Professor's Reflections on Oxford," *Spectator,* November 7, November 14, 1925.

52 Ibid., pp. 722–723, 727, from Margaret Halsey, *With Malice Towards Some* (New York: Simon & Schuster, 1938).

52 Ibid., p. 737, from Vincent Sheean, *Not Peace But a Sword* (1939).

53 Ibid., p. 464, from *The Letters of John Fiske,* Ethel F. Fiske, ed. (1940).

53 Ibid., p. xxvi.

53 Ibid., pp. 517–518, Henry James quoted from a letter to Charles Eliot Norton.

53 J. D. Salinger, "For Esmé—With Love and Squalor," *Nine Stories* (Little, Brown & Co., 1954).

53 Theroux, *The Kingdom by the Sea,* p. 255, p. 3.

54 Commager, *Britain Through American Eyes,* pp. 749–750.

54 Emerson, *English Traits.*

54 Commager, pp. 751–752, p. 755.

56 Dickens, *The Chimes* (1845).

57 Jilly Cooper, *Class,* (London: Eyre Methuen, 1979).

59 Young, *The Iron Lady,* p. 519.

59 Voltaire, *Candide* (1758).

61 Norman Gelb, *The British: A Portrait of an Indomitable Island People* (New York: Everest House, 1982), p. 218.

63 Quotations of English versions of nursery rhymes and fairy tales in this chapter taken from *The Oxford Dictionary of Nursery Rhymes,* assembled by Iona and Peter Opie (London: Oxford University Press, 1951) and *The Classic Fairy Tales,* compiled by Iona and Peter Opie (London: Oxford University Press, 1974). Used by permission from Mrs. Opie. American versions from memory.

72 Opie and Opie, *The Classic Fairy Tales.*

74 *The Annotated Alice,* p. 70.

74 Ibid., p. 102.

74 Ibid., p. 217.

75 Ibid., p. 134.

75 Kenneth Grahame, *The Wind in the Willows* (New York: Charles Scribner's Sons, 1939), quoted from Scribner's 1960 golden anniversary edition, p. 3.

75 Ibid., p. 28.

75 Lewis Carroll, *Sylvie and Bruno* (1889).

75 Ethel quoted from *The Young Visiters,* Daisy Ashford (London: Chatto & Windus, The Hogarth Press, 1919), Folio Society 1984 edition, p. 22.

75 Ibid., p. 52.

76 R. S. Surtees, *Mr. Sponge's Sporting Tour* (1853). Oxford University Press World Classics edition, 1958, p. 273.

76 Rudyard Kipling, *Kim* (1901).

79 Bernard Levin, *Enthusiasms* (London: Jonathan Cape, 1983), used by permission of Bernard Levin, pp. 162–163.

82 Scene from "EastEnders" TV show, March 13, 1988, permission from BBC.

83 Gelb, *The British,* p. 198.

85 J. B. Priestley, *English Journey* (London: William Heinemann, 1934), quoted from 1987 Penguin edition, pp. 85–86.

85 Ibid., p. 91.

85 Ibid., p. 60.

85 Daphne du Maurier, *Rebecca,* 1938, p. 1.

86 Robert Browning, "Rabbi Ben Ezra" from *Dramatis Personae* (1864), quoted from *The Selected Poetry of Robert Browning* (New York: Modern Library, 1951), p. 479.

92–93 Oil data from Gulf Futures, Inc., 1990.

100 Sir George Porter, quoted from *The Guardian,* April 11, 1988.

111 Rudyard Kipling, "The Gods of the Copybook Headings."

125 Danny Danziger, *Eton Voices* (New York: Viking, 1988), p. 155.

126 Ibid., pp. 283–284.

127 Rudyard Kipling, "The Islanders" (1901).

128 Sampson, *The Changing Anatomy of Britain,* pp. 166–167.

138 Churchill, *Serious Money,* p. 25.

141 Browning, "A Toccata of Galuppi's," from *Men and Women* (1855), Selected Poetry, p. 245.

144 Adam Smith used the phrase "nation of shopkeepers" first in his *Wealth of Nations* (1776), B. E. O'Meara, in his *Napoleon at St. Helena* (1822), quotes Napoleon as saying: *"L'Angleterre est une nation de boutiquiers."*

149 William Blake in his preface to *Milton* (1809):
I will not cease from Mental Fight,
Nor shall my Sword sleep in my hand,

Till we have built Jerusalem,
In England's green & pleasant Land.

150 Oliver Goldsmith, "The Deserted Village," *The Poetical Works of Oliver Goldsmith* (Philadelphia: E. H. Butler & Co., 1864).

152 Margaret Drabble, *A Writer's Britain* (London: Thames & Hudson, 1979), pp. 22–23.

153 Branwell Brontë, quoted by Daphne du Maurier in *The Infernal World of Branwell Brontë* (London: Victor Gollancz, 1960), quoted from Penguin 1987 edition, p. 85.

154 Priestley, *English Journey*, p. 67.

155 Beryl Bainbridge, *English Journey; or, The Road to Milton Keynes* (London: BBC Books and Gerald Duckworth & Co., 1984), quoted from Fontana edition, 1985, p. 50.

155 Theroux, *The Kingdom by the Sea*, p. 50.

159 Priestley, *English Journey*, p. 373.

161 Alan Bleasdale, *Scully* (London: Century Hutchinson, 1984), p. 71.

161 Priestley, *English Journey*, p. 167.

173 Jimmy Boyle, *A Sense of Freedom* (Edinburgh and London: Canongate Publishing and Pan Books, 1977), pp. 4–5.

174 Ibid., pp. 5–6.

174 Ibid., p. 8.

176 Robert Burns, from "Ae Fond Kiss," "Auld Lang Syne," "The Bonnie Wee Thing," "Coming Through the Rye," "Flow gently, sweet Afton," "For a' that and a' that," "My Love is like a Red Red Rose," and "To a Louse."

178 Theroux, *The Kingdom by the Sea*, p. 261.

182 Richard Kinsey, John Lea, and Jock Young, *Losing the Fight Against Crime* (London: Basil Blackwell, 1986), p. 7.

182 Prison data, *The New York Times*, December 29, 1989, p. A19.

183 Ibid., p. 188.

183 Boyle, *A Sense of Freedom*, p. 15.

184 Ibid., p. 134.

184 Ibid., p. 144.

184 Ronnie Kray quoted from "Violence is Golden," *20/20* (London), December 1989, p. 108.

184 John Mortimer, *Character Parts* (New York: Viking, 1986), quoted from Penguin Books edition, 1986, p. 20.

185 Ibid., p. 22.

188 Boyle, *A Sense of Freedom*, p. 239.

190 Gelb, *The British*, p. 33.

191 Samuel Pepys, *The Diary of Samuel Pepys* (1633–1703), edited by Robert Lathem and William Mathews (Berkeley: University of California Press, 1983).

192 Lord Scarman, *The Scarman Report* (Her Majesty's Stationery Office, 1981).

192 Mrs. Thatcher quoted by Young, *The Iron Lady*, p. 239.

192 Anthony Burgess, *A Clockwork Orange*

196 *Evening Standard,* June 13, 1988.

197 Two fans quoted from "It's Like a War," by Malcolm Macalister Hall, *Telegraph Sunday Magazine,* June 19, 1988. Other fans quoted from interviews by author.

197 *The Sunday Times,* June 19, 1988.

197 Ibid.

198 Duke of Wellington, in dispatch to Torrens, August 29, 1810.

200 *The Underclass: A World Apart,* produced by London Weekend Television's "Weekend World," with Matthew Parris, January 1988.

202 F. Scott Fitzgerald, "The Rich Boy"

202 Ernest Hemingway, "The Snows of Kilimanjaro."

202 Oscar Lewis first set down his "culture of poverty" theory in *Five Families* (New York: Basic Books, 1959), amplifying it in such later works as *The Children of Sanchez* (1961) and *La Vida* (1966).

204 "EastEnders," BBC series, quoted from 1986 program.

205 Bleasdale, *Scully,* pp. 71–72.

205 Ibid., p. 8.

205 Ibid., p. 107.

206 Alan Bleasdale, *Boys from the Blackstuff* (London: Century Hutchinson, 1985), pp. 174–175.

206 Ibid., p. 251.

207 Beryl Bainbridge, *Forever England: North and South* (London: BBC Books and Gerald Duckworth & Co., 1987), p. 93.

208 Geoffrey Pearson, *The New Heroin Users* (London: Basil Blackwell, 1987), p. 7.

208 Ibid., p. 133.

208 Ibid., pp. 134 and 135.

211 Archbishop Derek Worlock and Robert Runcie, Archbishop of Canterbury, "Churches Launch New Attack on Thatcher," *The Sunday Times,* December 3, 1989, p. 5.

222 Norman Tebbit, *Upwardly Mobile* (London: Weidenfeld & Nicolson, 1988).

224 W. H. Auden, "On This Island" (1935).

225 "Irish Ways and Irish Laws," by John Gibbs, recorded by *Moving Hearts;* WEA (Ireland) Limited, a Warner Communications Company.

226 W. H. Auden, "In Memory of W. B. Yeats" (1940).

226 W. B. Yeats, "Easter 1916"

226 J. G. Farrell, *Troubles.*

227 Louis MacNeice, "Eclogue Between the Motherless," *Collected Poems 1925–1948* (New York: Oxford University Press, 1948), p. 40.

227 G. K. Chesterton, "Ballad of the White Horse," Book II.

232 George Steiner, "An Examined Life," *The New Yorker,* October 23, 1989, pp. 142–146.

     Steiner, quoted from *Bill Moyers: A Second Look,* Public Affairs Television, Inc., aired July 16, 1989.

238 Michael Gorra, "The Sun Never Sets on the English Novel," *The New York Times Book Review,* July 19, 1987.

239 Joseph Epstein, "Miss Pym and Mr. Larkin," *Commentary*, July 1986.

239 Philip Larkin, "Going, Going" from *High Windows* (1974), though originally commissioned by the Department of the Environment and Her Majesty's Stationery Office, 1972. Quoted in Epstein, "Miss Pym and Mr. Larkin."

240 Sir Isaiah Berlin, "Edmund Wilson among the 'Despicable English,'" *The New York Times Book Review*, April 12, 1987, excerpted from the winter 1987 issue of *The Yale Review*, copyright Yale University.

240 John le Carré, *Tinker, Tailor, Soldier, Spy* (London and New York: Hodder & Stoughton and Alfred A. Knopf, 1974), quoted from Bantam 1975 edition, p. 345.

241 John le Carré, *The Russia House* (New York: Alfred A. Knopf, 1989), p. 352.

244 Philip Larkin, Letter to Charles Monteith, Faber & Faber, 1963, quoted in Epstein.

244 Quoted by John Bayley, "On Philip Larkin" *The New York Review of Books*, January 16, 1986.

244 Epstein, "Miss Pym and Mr. Larkin."

245 Ibid.

245 Larkin quote from Epstein, "Miss Pym and Mr. Larkin."

245 Ibid.

245 Philip Larkin, "Toads Revisited" from *The Whitsun Weddings* (London: Faber & Faber, 1960).

245 Larkin, "Homage to a Government" from *High Windows* (New York: Farrar, Straus & Giroux, 1974).

245 Larkin, "This Be the Verse" from *High Windows*.

245 Larkin, "Aubade," from *The Collected Poems of Philip Larkin*, (London: Faber & Faber)

247 Craig Raine, *Rich* (London: Faber & Faber, 1984), p. 46.

247 Ibid., p. 64.

247 Ibid., pp. 108–109.

248 "deeply ordinary" from *The Oxford Companion to English Literature*, Margaret Drabble, ed., (Oxford: Oxford University Press, 5th edition 1985), p. 60.

248 V. S. Naipaul, quoted from "On Being a Writer," *The New York Review of Books*, April 23, 1987.

249 Duke of Gloucester, comment to Edward Gibbon upon publication of *The Rise and Fall of the Roman Empire*, quoted in Boswell's *Johnson*, vol. ii, p. 2n.

249 John Cleese, *A Fish Called Wanda* (Metro-Goldwyn-Mayer screenplay, 1988). From original story by Cleese and Charles Crichton.

251 Melvyn Bragg, Robert McCrum, and Bernard Levin quoted from "A Hard Sell" by Bragg, *The Sunday Times*, December 10, 1989, p. C1.

253 Leonard Woolf, quoted in Kenner, p. 111.

258 Naipaul, "On Being a Writer."

263 Graham Greene, introduction to *My Silent War* by Kim Philby (Aldershot, Hampshire: MacGibbon & Kee Ltd., 1968), quoted from Ballantine Books 1986 edition, p. 1.

263–64 Harwood, *J. J. Farr*, p. 39.

265 Jacques Barzun and Wendell Hertig Taylor, *A Catalogue of Crime* (New York: Harper & Row, 1971), item 87, p. 40.

265 Eric Ambler, interview in *The Times* (1974).

267 Le Carré quoted from "Unease Fills Western Allies over Rapid Changes in East," *The New York Times*, December 1, 1989, p. A9.

268 Graham Greene, *The Quiet American* (New York: Viking, 1956), quoted from Bantam 1957 edition, pp. 3, 114.

268 Ibid., p. 86.

268 Eric Ambler, *The Night-Comers (State of Siege)* (New York: Alfred A. Knopf, 1956).

268 Eric Ambler, *Here Lies* (London: Weidenfeld & Nicolson, 1985), quoted from Fontana 1986 edition, p. 26.

269 Ibid., pp. 114–115.

269 Ambler, *The Night-Comers*.

270 Barzun & Taylor, *A Catalogue of Crime*, item 49.

270 Ambler, *The Night-Comers*.

272 Agatha Christie, foreword to *The Body in the Library* (London: William Collins, 1942).

272 P. D. James, quoted from interview, *The New York Times Book Review*, October 10, 1982.

273 P. D. James, quoted from *Everywoman* (London), July 1988.

273 Raymond Chandler, "The Simple Art of Murder," *Atlantic Monthly*, December 1944.

273 Ruth Rendell, *Live Flesh* (London: Century Hutchinson, 1985).

274 Mortimer, *Character Parts*, p. 143.

275 Ruth Rendell, *A Judgement in Stone* (New York: Arrow Books, 1977).

276 Ruth Rendell, *Put On by Cunning (Death Notes)* (London: Hutchison & Co., 1981), quoted from Ballantine Books 1982 edition, p. 120, p. 121, p. 136, p. 148.

278 "The rich man . . . ," Cecil Frances Alexander: "All Things Bright and Beautiful" (1848).

278 Simon Brett, *What Bloody Man Is That?* (Victor Gollancz, 1987), quoted from Futura 1988 edition, p. 7.

278 Ibid., p. 9.

279 Simon Brett, *Murder in the Title* (New York: Charles Scribner's Sons, 1983), quoted from Dell 1984 edition, p. 58.

284 *Guinness Book of World Records*, 1989 edition (Bantam), p. 208.

284 Figures from "Britain's Richest 200," *Money*, March 1988.

284 Q. D. Leavis, *Fiction and the Reading Public*, 1939, pp. 62, 64.

284 John Mortimer, *In Character* (London: Allen Lane, 1983), quoted from Penguin 1987 edition, p. 179.

286 Jeffrey Archer, *Kane and Abel* (New York: Simon & Schuster, 1979), jacket copy.

286 Jeffrey Archer, *What Shall We Tell the President?* (New York: Fawcett Books, 1988), jacket copy.

291 Gwen Robyns, *Barbara Cartland: An Authorized Biography* (London: Sidgwick & Jackson, 1984) quoted from Javelin Books 1987 edition, pp. 15 and 16.

292 Fondness for pink and Tutankhamen's tomb, "Why I'm Still in the Pink at 88" by Barbara Cartland, *The Sun*, December 12, 1989, pp. 16–17.

292 Ibid., pp. 250 and 251.

294 Barbara Cartland, *A Hazard of Hearts* (London: Rich & Cowan, 1949), quoted from Pan 1988 edition, pp. 361–362.

301 Christopher Hibbert, *London: The Biography of a City* (London: Longmans, Green & Co., 1969), quoted from Penguin 1980 edition, p. 45.

302 George Steevens, ed. a complete annotated edition in ten volumes of Shakespeare's plays, 1773 (including notes by Samuel Johnson).

304 Sir John Gielgud, interview with Sheridan Morley published in program notes, *The Best of Friends*, January 1988; other remarks from BBC interviews, July 11, 1988 and August 7, 1988.

306 Howard Brenton and David Hare, *Pravda* (London: Methuen, 1985), p. 54.

307 Douglas Hurd and Stephen Lamport, *The Palace of Enchantments* (London: Hodder & Stoughton, 1985), quoted from Hodder and Stoughton Paperbacks edition), p. 318.

308 Geraldine James, "Knowing, and Ever Loving, Portia," *The New York Times*, January 2, 1990, p. B3.

309 George Bernard Shaw, *Pygmalion* screenplay, 1934; Gabriel Pascal production, 1938.

311 Simon Callow, *Being an Actor* (London: Methuen London, 1984), quoted from Penguin 1985 edition, p. 220.

312 Beryl Bainbridge, *English Journey*, pp. 88, 90.

313 Elia Kazan quoted from David Dalton, *James Dean: The Mutant King* (New York: St. Martin's Press, 1974) and *Elia, A Life* (New York: Alfred A. Knopf, 1988), pp. 538–39.

316 *The Economist,* January 23, 1988.

316 "Through a Lens Darkly: This Is the Grim and Ugly Face of Modern Britain as Portrayed by One of Our Avant Garde Film Makers. Norman Stone Asks: Why?" *The Sunday Times,* January 10, 1988.

317 Hanif Kureishi, *The Guardian,* January 1988, quoted in *The Economist* January 23, 1988. Also interview, *Man alive!* January 1988.

317 Derek Jarman, "Freedom fighter for a vision on the truth," *The Sunday Times,* January 17, 1988.

318 Philip Larkin, "Going, Going," from *High Windows.*

318 Larkin, "Annus Mirabilis," from *High Windows.*

320 David Hare, *Saigon: Year of the Cat* from *The Asian Plays by David Hare* (London: Faber & Faber 1986, *Saigon* first published 1983), p. 101.

321 Pham Xuan An, Communist military rank and medal confirmed, Robert Sam Anson, *War News: A Young Reporter in Indochina* (New York: Simon & Schuster, 1989), p. 310.

322 Ibid., p. 103.

324 Henry Pleasants, *Serious Music—And All That Jazz* (London: Victor Gollancz Ltd., 1969), p. 185.

324 Ibid., p. 188. Frederic V. Grunfeld quoted from *Horizon,* summer 1967.

324 Ibid., p. 188. John Gabree quoted from *Down Beat,* November 16, 1967.

324 Sir George Martin quoted from "The Fifth Beatle, 'A Little Help From a Friend'" by Henry Pleasants, *Stereo Review,* February 1971.

325 Ned Rorem, quoted in "Lloyd Webber's Opera Music Is Not So Phantastic," *International Herald Tribune,* January 30, 1988.

326 Frank Rich, "Broadway: The Empire Strikes Back," *The New York Times,* March 29, 1987.

327 Andrew Lloyd Webber, quoted from "How the Brits Keep Broadway in Business," *Daily Express* (London), January 27, 1988.

327 Peter Sellars quoted by Henry Pleasants, "Over-Produced Opera," *International Herald Tribune,* October 24, 1987.

327 William Shakespeare, *Antony and Cleopatra,* IV.xv.

330 Tetley Bitter advertising campaign, 1986–87. Used by permission.

331 Elizabeth Longford, *Victoria R.I.* (London: Weidenfeld & Nicolson Ltd, 1964). Quoted in *The Oxford Book of Royal Anecdotes* (Oxford: Oxford University Press, 1989), p. 378.

332 "Glorious, stirring sight!" Grahame, *The Wind in the Willows,* p. 36.

332 "Hooray! he cried" Grahame, *The Wind in the Willows,* Ibid., p. 26.

334 David Puttnam, views quoted from Tina Brown, "The End of the Affair," *The Sunday Times Magazine,* April 24, 1988.

334 Puttnam, interview with Bill Moyers, PBS, January 1989.

336 Anton Chekhov, *The Seagull* (1896), Trepilov's remark quoted from Malcolm Bradbury, *The Modern World: Ten Great Writers* (London: Secker & Warburg, 1988).

336 *The Modern World: Ten Great Writers,* broadcast over eleven weeks starting January 10, 1988, by London Weekend Television.

337 Graham Greene, quoted in "Something to Brag About," a profile of Melvin Bragg, *The Sunday Times Magazine,* 1988.

337 Ibid.

338 Brenda Maddox, "Media" column, the *Sunday Telegraph,* January 10, 1988.

338 Marcel Proust, "Swann's Way," *Remembrance of Things Past (À la recherche du temps perdu);* 16 vols., 1913–1927. Quoted from Vintage Books (Random House) 1982 edition, p. 9.

338 Maddox, "Media."

339 *The Magic Mountain* (New York: Alfred A. Knopf, 1927; originally published S. Fischer Verlag, Berlin, as *Der Zauberberg,* 1924). In 1969 Vintage Books paperback edition the seance scene takes place pp. 673–681.

339 Maddox, "Media."

340 Virginia Woolf, "Mr. Bennett and Mrs. Brown," *Collected Essays,* vol. I, 1967, 319–337; remark dates to 1924.

340 D. H. Lawrence, *Kangaroo* (1923).

340 T. S. Eliot, "The Love Song of J. Alfred Prufrock," published in *Poetry* in 1915.

340 Ezra Pound, quoted by Bradbury, *The Modern World,* p. 3.

340 Pound, quoted ibid., p. 200.

340 William Carlos Williams, quoted Ibid., p. 200.

340 Bradbury, *The Modern World,* p. 197.

340 T. S. Eliot, *The Waste Land* "I. The Burial of the Dead" (London: Faber & Faber, 1922).

340–41 "II. A Game of Chess."

341 "III. The Fire Sermon."

341 William Shakespeare, *Antony and Cleopatra,* II.ii.

341 Eliot, *The Waste Land,* "II. A Game of Chess."

341 Ibid.

342 Ibid.

342 Ibid.

342–43 From transcript, final episode, *The Modern World: Ten Great Writers,* London Weekend Television, March 20, 1988.

348 Max Beloff, review, "The End of the Raj: Paul Scott's Novels as History," *Encounter,* May 1976, quoted in Swinden, p. 65.

349 Patrick Swinden, *Paul Scott: Images of India* (London: Macmillan, 1980), pp. 2 and 5.

349 Paul Scott quoted in Swinden, p. x.

349 *The Jewel in the Crown* (London: Heinemann, 1966), p. 1.

352 H. Achmed Ismail's Hindustani phrasebook, quoted by James Cameron, "The Last Days of the Raj—A Personal View," *The Making of* The Jewel in the Crown (Granada Publishing, 1983), pp 101–103.

352 Jawaharlal Nehru, quoted from interview by the author, originally published in the *Washington Star,* February 1964, quoted in author's *Villages* (Garden City, N.Y.: Doubleday & Co., 1981), p. 364.

353 Gunnar Myrdal, *Asian Drama* (New York: Twentieth Century Fund, 1968), author's account of Nehru's last attempt to settle Kashmir, quoted in Volume I, p. 254 and p. 331.

353 Robert Frost, lines from "Stopping by Woods on a Snowy Evening" (1923) found by Nehru's bedside as reported in dispatch by author to the *Washington Star,* May 1964.

354 Paul Scott, *Staying On* (London: Heinemann, 1977), p. 1.

360 Michael Billington, *Peggy Ashcroft* (London: John Murray, 1988), p. 261.

362–63 Tim Pigott-Smith, *Out of India* (London: Constable, 1986), p. 29.

363 Judy Parfitt quoted from *The Making of* The Jewel in the Crown, account by Bamber Gascoigne, p. 17, who in turn was quoting the diary of Associate Producer Milly Preece. Trip details p. 360 drawn partly from Gascoigne and Preece.

368–69 Scene between Ronald Merrick and "Sophie" Dixon, the hospital orderly, written by Ken Taylor reprinted courtesy of Sir Denis Forman and Granada Television Limited; the author is also grateful to Gerald Hagan, Head of Script Department, Granada Television, for his assistance in locating the two original scenes Taylor wrote for Episode Eight, "The Day of the Scorpion." This was "329 INT ROOM PANKOT HOSPITAL MILITARY WING; DAY, p. 53."

369–70 From "The Day of the Scorpion" script, "321 EXT. ST. JOHN'S CHURCH, PANKOT, *The Jewel in the Crown,* p. 103918. Courtesy of Granada Television.

373 E. M. Forster, *A Passage to India* (New York: Harcourt, Brace & World, 1924) p. 7.

376 Geraldine James, "Knowing . . . Portia."

377–78 Paul Scott, *Staying On* (New York: William Morrow, 1977), quoted from Avon 1979 edition, p. 159.

381 1900 figures from Her Majesty's Stationery Office.

381 Paul Kennedy, *The Rise and Fall of the Great Powers* (London: Unwin Hyman, 1988), p. 480.

384 Eric Sevareid, *Not So Wild a Dream* (1946)

385 Henry Brandon, *Special Relationships* (New York: Atheneum, 1988), pp. 405–406.

389 Ibid., 406–407.

390 Constantine FitzGibbon, *When the Kissing Had to Stop* (1960)

391 *Mrs. Miniver* (1942), Metro-Goldwyn-Mayer screenplay adapted from Jan Struther novel (1939).

391–92 Cleese, *A Fish Called Wanda* (Metro-Goldwyn-Mayer screenplay).

395 Sir Robert Thompson, Dennis Duncanson, views presented in detail in the author's *The Long Charade: Political Subversion in the Vietnam War* (New York: Harcourt, Brace & World, 1968), see index for repeated references.

398 Jim Hoagland, "America's Century: Is It Over?" *International Herald Tribune,* September 1988.

400 William Shakespeare, *The Tempest.*

400 Lord Callaghan, interview with Robert MacNeil, *MacNeil/Lehrer News Hour,* November 29,1989.

400 Andrei Sakharov, *The New York Times,* December 15, 1989.

400 Mikhail Gorbachev, "Enough for Glasnost?" *The New York Times,* December 26, 1989, p. A11.

403–4 "Thatcher's Political Touch," *The Economist,* July 23, 1988.

404 Mrs. Thatcher quoted on French Revolution by Michael Kinsley, "An American in London," *The Economist,* December 23, 1989, p. 35.

404 *Ibid.*

404 Dickens, *A Tale of Two Cities,* p. 213.

404 Richard Ingrams, *The Observer*, December 21, 1989, p. 12.

404 *Private Eye*, November 10, 1989, p. 15.

405 Norman Macrae, "Almanac for the Naughty Nineties," *The Sunday Times*, December 31, 1989, p. A11.

405 Nigel Lawson, *The Economist*, November 4, 1989, p. 14.

406 Mrs. Thatcher at NATO, *MacNeil/Lehrer News Hour*, December 4, 1989.

406 Mrs. Thatcher on Panama, *International Herald Tribune*, December 21, 1989, p. 4.

406 Bush spokesman, quoted in *The Economist*, December 16, 1989, p. 29.

407 Chancellor Helmut Kohl, *International Herald Tribune*, December 21, 1989, p. 1.

407 Elie Wiesel, "I Fear What Lies Beyond the Wall," *The New York Times*, November 17, 1989, op-ed page.

407 Paul Theroux, "Heard the One About the East Friesians?" *The New York Times*, December 9, 1989, op-ed page.

408 William Pfaff, "She Is Real and She Is Serious," *The New York Times Book Review*, 1989.

409 Lord Callaghan, interview with MacNeil.

412 Jim Rohwer, "America, Asia and Europe," *The Economist*, December 24, 1988.

412–13 Ibid.

413 Ibid.

414–15 Oil data from Gulf Futures, Inc, 1990.

416 Anthony Holden, quoted from Barbara Howar's "Unauthorized Biography: the Royals," rebroadcast viewed June 1989.

418 Prince Charles, radio interview, 1987.

419 Prince Charles, Ibid.

419 "a monstrous carbuncle," "a glass stump," quoted by Charles Jencks in "The Prince Versus the Architects," *Observer*, June 12, 1988.

419 Howell Raines, "Defying Tradition—Prince Charles Recasts His Role," *The New York Times Magazine*, February 21, 1988.

419 Charles Jencks, "Charles the Misunderstood," *The Observer*, June 19, 1988, adapted from *The Prince, the Architects and New Wave Monarchy* (London: Academy Editions, 1988).

420 Norman Tebbit, quoted from interview on "Charles: Prince of Conscience," BBC *Panorama*, April 11, 1988.

420 Judy Wade, quoted by Jencks, "Charles the Misunderstood," p. 33.

420 Ibid.

420–21 Walter Bagehot, *The English Constitution* (1867) "The Monarchy."

421 Callaghan, quoted by Jencks, "Charles the Misunderstood."

421 Bagehot, *The English Constitution*.

421 Holden, quoted from Howar interview.

421 Prince Charles, quoted from Jencks.

422 Princess Anne episode with photographer on train described in "Last of the Old-Style Royals?" by Selena Hastings, the *Sunday Telegraph*, May 29, 1988.

423 Bagehot, "The English Constitution."

425 Edmund Burke, *Reflections on the Revolution in France* (1790).

427 "Did someone say go?," lead editorial, *The Economist*, October 7, 1989.

427 Bagehot, "The English Constitution."

429 Sellafield crisis described in Marilynne Robinson, *Mother Country* (New York: Farrar, Straus & Giroux, 1989).

429 Julian Critchley, quoted in "The Gamefish" by John Newhouse, *The New Yorker*, February 10, 1986.

430 David Howell quoted ibid.

430 Mrs. Thatcher on David Owen, quoted in Brian Walden interview, *The Sunday Times*, May 8, 1988.

431 John Newhouse, "The Gamefish."

433 John Biffen, quoted by Hugo Young, *The Iron Lady*, p. 445.

433 Bernard Ingham, *The Observer*, May 8, 1988.

434 Mrs. Thatcher, quoted in Brian Walden May 8, 1988 *Sunday Times* interview.

435 Mary Warnock quoted in the *Sunday Telegraph*, January 10, 1988.

435 Noël Annan, quoted ibid.

441 Mrs. Thatcher, 1986 interview with Brian Walden, *Weekend World*, LWT. Inflation figures from *The Economist*, about Mrs. Thatcher's first ten years as Prime Minister, April 29, 1989, pp. 58–59.

444 Neil Kinnock, to Labour Conference, October 4, 1988.

446 John Banham, *The Economist*, April 29, 1989, p. 59.

447 Mrs. Thatcher on "six great tasks" for 1990s, *The Sunday Times*, December 31, 1989, p. A1.

448 Quoted from the author's survey, "Britain: A View from the Outside," *The Economist*, February 21, 1987.

449 Jenkins, *Mrs. Thatcher's Revolution*, p. 379.

450 "Victorian values," suggested by Brian Walden during *Weekend World* interview on London Weekend Television.

450 Mrs. Thatcher on academics, interview by Brian Walden, *The Sunday Times*, May 8, 1988.

451 Alan Bennett, "Bed Among the Lentils," *Talking Heads* (London: BBC Books, 1988), p. 31. Maggie Smith appeared as Susan, the vicar's wife, in the original series of monologues.

452 Young, *The Iron Lady*, pp. 543-545.

452 Mrs. Thatcher speaking to Church of Scotland assembly in Edinburgh May 22, 1988.

452–53 Ibid.

453 Mother Beatrice from *The Iron Lady*, p. 4.

453 Norman Stone, "Clergy in a Wicked Muddle," *The Sunday Times*, April 10, 1988.

455 Mrs. Thatcher on consensus from *The Iron Lady*, p. 223.

455 Mrs. Thatcher, *Sunday Times* May 8, 1988 interview.

456 Poll commissioned by *The Economist* from QDM, an independent marketing-research company, published October 7, 1989, *The Economist*, p. 70.

457 Peter Jenkins and Hugo Young quoted from "Thatcher Style, Judgment Reevaluated," *The Washington Post*, October 27, 1989, p. A16.

457 Brian Walden interview, ITV television, October 29, 1989, full text published in *The Guardian*, October 30, 1989, p. 8.

462 Anton Chekhov, *Uncle Vanya* (1899), quoted from *Four Plays by Chekhov*, translated with notes by Alex Szogyi (New York: Washington Square Press, 1968).

465 August Wilson quoted from panel on arts, *MacNeil/Lehrer News Hour*, January 3, 1990.

466 Denis Healey, *The Observer*, December 31, 1989, p. 12.

467 Lord Callaghan, interview with MacNeil.

467 Kipling, "Recessional" (1897).

467 Anton Chekhov, *The Cherry Orchard* (1904), quoted from *Four Plays by Chekhov*.

468 Nuba judge and Bengali interpreter quoted from author's *Villages* (Garden City, N.Y.: Doubleday & Co., 1981), pp. 37–38 and 77.

INDEX

ABOUT THE AUTHOR

Richard Critchfield is the author of *Those Days, The Long Charade,* and a village trilogy: *Villages, Shahhat, An Egyptian,* and *The Golden Bowl Be Broken.* A long-standing contributor to *The Economist* and the *International Herald Tribune,* he has reported the Third World, mainly from its villages, for a quarter century. He was a MacArthur Fellow and has also received awards from the Overseas Press Club (for Vietnam reporting) and the Ford, Rockefeller, and Alicia Patterson foundations.